# International Handbooks on Information Systems

*Series Editors*
Peter Bernus · Jacek Błażewicz · Günter Schmidt · Michael Shaw

Springer

*Berlin*
*Heidelberg*
*New York*
*Hong Kong*
*London*
*Milan*
*Paris*
*Tokyo*

# Titles in the Series

P. Bernus, K. Mertins and G. Schmidt (Eds.)
**Handbook on Architectures of Information Systems**
ISBN 3-540-64453-9

M. Shaw, R. Blanning, T. Strader and A. Whinston (Eds.)
**Handbook on Electronic Commerce**
ISBN 3-540-65822-X

J. Błażewicz, K. Ecker, B. Plateau and D. Trystram (Eds.)
**Handbook on Parallel and Distributed Processing**
ISBN 3-540-66441-6

H. H. Adelsberger, B. Collis and J. M. Pawlowski (Eds.)
**Handbook on Information Technologies for Education and Training**
ISBN 3-540-67803-4

C. W. Holsapple (Ed.)
**Handbook on Knowledge Management 1**
**Knowledge Matters**
ISBN 3-540-43527-1
**Handbook on Knowledge Management 2**
**Knowledge Directions**
ISBN 3-540-43527-1

P. Bernus, L. Nemes and G. Schmidt (Eds.)
**Handbook on Enterprise Architecture**
ISBN 3-540-00343-6

J. Błażewicz, W. Kubiak, T. Morzy and M. Rusinkiewicz (Eds.)
**Handbook on Data Management in Information Systems**
ISBN 3-540-43893-9

S. Staab and R. Studer (Eds.)
**Handbook on Ontologies**
ISBN 3-540-40834-7

Steffen Staab
Rudi Studer

Editors

# Handbook
# on Ontologies

With 190 Figures
and 22 Tables

 Springer

PD Dr. Steffen Staab          staab@aifb.uni-karlsruhe.de
Professor Dr. Rudi Studer     studer@aifb.uni-karlsruhe.de

Institute AIFB
University of Karlsruhe
Kaiserstraße 12
76131 Karlsruhe, Germany

ISBN 3-540-40834-7 Springer-Verlag Berlin Heidelberg New York

Cataloging-in-Publication Data applied for

A catalog record for this book is available from the Library of Congress.

Bibliographic information published by Die Deutsche Bibliothek
Die Deutsche Bibliothek lists this publication in the Deutsche Nationalbibliografie;
detailed bibliographic data available in the internet at *http.//dnb.ddb.de*

Springer-Verlag is a part of Springer Science+Business Media
springeronline.com

© Springer-Verlag Berlin Heidelberg 2004
Printed in Germany

The use of general descriptive names, registered names, trademarks, etc. in this publication does
not imply, even in the absence of a specific statement, that such names are exempt from the relevant
protective laws and regulations and therefore free for general use.

Cover design: Erich Kirchner, Heidelberg

SPIN 11556503      42/3111 – 5 4 3 2 – Printed on acid-free paper

To Angela & Irene

# Preface

The Handbook on Ontologies in Information Systems provides a comprehensive overview of the current status and future prospectives of the field of ontologies.

In the early nineties, ontologies have been a research topic being addressed in a rather small research community, the Knowledge Acquisition Community. There, ontologies came into play by the conceptual shift from the 'knowledge transfer'-view on knowledge acquisition to the 'knowledge modeling'- view, most prominently reflected in the CommonKADS methodology for knowledge engingeering and management [10]. Being applied in the context of developing knowledge-based systems, ontologies were classified into domain ontologies, method ontologies, task ontologies, and top-level ontologies that cover the different aspects that are relevant when modeling knowledge-based systems [8, 11].

This rather limited role and impact of ontologies changed drastically in the late nineties by the insight that a conceptual, yet executable model of an application domain provides a significant added value for all kinds of application scenarios like knowledge management or eCommerce, to mention just a few of them. Obviously, the main push for ontologies was given by the vision of the Semantic Web as coined by Tim Berners-Lee [1, 3]. In the Semantic Web ontologies provide the conceptual underpinning for making the semantics of metadata machine interpretable. Being nowadays an important research and application topic in many subject areas, ontologies constitute a field of activities that evolves very fast, both in research and industry.

Being used in such diverse application contexts, it is not easy to agree on a common definition for an *ontology*. However, in the informatics community there has been gained some agreement on using the following definition, based on [6]: "An ontology is a formal explicit specification of a shared conceptualization for a domain of interest." What we can see from this definition on the one hand is the fact that an ontology has to be specified in a language that comes with a formal semantics. Only by using such a formal approach ontologies provide the machine interpretable meaning of concepts and relations that is expected when using an ontology-based approach. On the other hand, ontologies rely on a social process that heads for an agreement among a group of people with respect to the concepts and relations that are part of an ontology. As a consequence, domain ontologies will always be constrained to a limited domain and a limited group of people. Otherwise, such an agreement will not be feasible. That is clearly one lesson learned from the failure of specifying enterprise-wide data models in the Eighties.

The Handbook on Ontologies in Information Systems covers the fascinating developments in the field of ontologies and thus serves as a reference point for the fast growing community of people being involved in ontology research and applications.

In order to reflect the various aspects that are relevant when dealing with ontologies, the Handbook is organized into several parts.

*Part A:*

*Ontology Representation and Reasoning* addresses the main (paradigms of) languages that are currently used for formally specifying ontologies. Description Logics (Baader, Horrocks, and Sattler; Chapter 1) on the one hand and Frame Logic (Angele and Lausen; Chapter 2) on the other hand cover the two main knowledge representation paradigms that have been and are used for describing ontologies. The development of RDF(S) may be considered as one of the cornerstones in establishing basic languages for the Semantic Web (McBride; Chapter 3). The recent development of the Web ontology language OWL reflects the additional requirements that have to be met for deploying powerful ontologies in the (Semantic) Web (Antoniou and van Harmelen; Chapter 4). The last chapter in this first part of the Handbook develops the notion of an ontology algebra (Mitra and Wiederhold; Chapter 5) aiming at a well-defined set of ontology manipulation operators that should be comparable to the well-known relational algebra for relational databases.

*Part B:*

*Ontology Engineering* is devoted to various methodological aspects of developing ontologies. The first chapter describes a methodology for introducing ontology-based knowledge management solutions into enterprises (Sure, Staab, and Studer; Chapter 6). In spite of all the tool environments that are nowadays available, there is still a lack of large domain ontologies. A large scale case study in developing a medical ontology is described in the next chapter (Hahn and Schulz; Chapter 7). When dealing with such large resources there comes the urgent need to clean up the top level of the ontology in order to provide some first principles on which to build and extend a given ontology — such as defined by the OntoClean methodology (Guarino and Welty; Chapter 8). The overhead involved in building up an ontology, however, remains a major obstacle in applying ontologies. Therefore, an important research topic is ontology learning that aims at providing (semi-) automatic support for building up ontologies. This aspect is addressed in Chapter 9 by Mädche and Staab. Knowlede patterns as outlined in Chapter 10 cover inherent structures that may be found when investigating axioms in detail. Such patterns enable reuse as known from the field of Software Engineering (Clark, Thompson, and Porter; Chapter 10). The tight interaction between ontologies on the one hand and lexicons as handled in linguistics is discussed in Chapter 11 by Hirst. In the majority of applications one has to deal with multiple ontologies that reflect the different views people have on a subject field. Therefore, the need arises for being able to reconcile these views and thus to relate the corresponding ontologies to each other (Hameed, Preece, and Sleeman; Chapter 12). Goméz-Pérez introduces a field of research that emerged very recently: ontology evaluation (Chapter 13). Obviously, ontology evaluation gains more and more importance when considering the fast growing number of deployed ontologies. The last chapter in this part surveys state-of-the-art ontology engineering environments (Mizoguchi; Chapter 14) — touching on some of the aspects of the following part.

*Part C:*

*Ontology Infrastructure* covers various important aspects of managing and using ontologies. This part starts with a description of a flexible and extensible server environment for managing ontologies (Oberle, Volz, Staab, and Motik; Chapter 15). Ontologies and problem-solving methods are tightly related to each other with respect to providing a conceptualization of the static and dynamic aspects of knowledge-based systems. These relationships and the roles ontologies have for describing problem-solving methods are discussed in Chapter 16 by Crubézy and Musen. Multi-Agent systems heavily rely on the communication and cooperation between the involved agents. Therefore, ontologies play an important role in providing a semantic basis for these interactions (Sycara and Paolucci; Chapter 17). The next chapter provides the description of a tool environment that supports users in merging ontologies and define mappings between different ontologies (Noy; Chapter 18) . The topic of mapping ontologies to each other is further developed in the next chapter in which a learning approach is introduced for learning mappings between ontologies (Doan, Madhavan, Domingos, and Halevy; Chapter 19). An enduser point of view on handling ontologies is described in the last two chapters of this part. First, an exploring and browsing environment is described that supports the graphical browsing of ontologies, illustrated for RDF-based ontologies (Eklund, Cole, and Roberts; Chapter 20). The last chapter provides an insight into the visualization techniques that can be exploited for supporting the life-cycle of ontologies (Fluit, Sabou, and van Harmelen; Chapter 21).

*Part D:*

Finally, *Ontology Applications* provides a broad overview of the various application areas that nowadays exploit ontologies. The first chapters discuss knowledge management applications that address various information technology aspects of knowledge management. The general role that ontologies might play for knowledge management applications is discussed in the beginning (Abecker and van Elst; Chapter 22). An approach for ontology-based content management taylored to the needs of virtual organizations is outlined in Chapter 23 (Mika, Iosif, Sure, and Akkermans). Chapter 24 discusses flexible recommender systems that rely on user profiles which are based on an ontology (Middleton, de Roure, and Shadbolt). Ontologies also provide means for building up semantic portals that are able to integrate knowledge from heterogeneous sources. In Chapter 25 the OntoWeb portal is described as a concrete application based on such a semantic portal framework (Oberle and Spyns). The presentation of portal content is closely related to the question of how to create (non-linear) hypertext. The ability to model a domain of discourse with an ontology holds out the promise of computationally reasoned and reasonable linking services. Chapter 26 describes some attempts to augment hypermedia systems with ontologies in order to provide, or improve, hypertext. Chapter 27 (Domingue, Dzbor, and Motta) introduces a system environment in which Web resources are embedded into a semantic context that is based on ontologies. Thus, user-specific viewpoints may be offered in a flexible way. eLearning and knowledge management are fields that get more and more integrated. In Chapter 28 metadata- and ontology-based approaches for eLearning are discussed (Brase and Nejdl).

Besides knowledge management, issues of interoperability and integration of enterprise applications are a second major application field for ontologies. In Chapter 29 (Grüninger) a process language is defined that is based on ontologies and provides means for facilitating the exchange of information between manufacturing systems. Chapter 30 addresses issues of information integration in eCommerce scenarios (Ying, Fensel, Klein, Omelayenko, and Schulten). Semantic interoperability issues are further discussed in Chapter 31. They are illustrated by application scenarios from the domain of tourism (Missikoff and Taglino). Finally, ontologies may be used for capturing the semantics of vast amount of data that are handled e.g. in molecular biology (Stevens, Wroe, Lord, and Goble; Chapter 32 ).

As can be seen from the large collection of different application scenarios that are discussed in *Part D: Ontology Applications* ontologies become a major conceptual backbone for a broad spectrum of applications (cf. also [2, 4]). Integration of web resources, intranet documents, and databases as well as cooperation of web services and enterprise application, all these scenarios require a semantic characterization of the meaning of their contents and/or their functionalities. Therefore, ontologies gain a strongly increasing importance in these kinds of applications. Technologies for managing ontologies in the context of these applications have reached a maturity level that enables their usage in real life applications.

Nevertheless, a considerable amount of research problems have to be solved in the future in order to meet the increasing challenges. Some recent developments address the evolution of ontologies in distributed environments [9], creation of metadata conforming to ontologies [7], the integration of description logics and rules [5], and performance evaluation [12, 13]. Furthermore, there remain open research problems, like ontology mediation on-the-fly, efficient ontology querying, or a rule language that fits to the proposed ontology languages and meets the requirements of the application developers.

The Handbook on Ontologies in Information Systems provides a detailed overview of the current achievements and challenges in the ontology area. With its coverage of research and applications it provides valuable insights, both for researchers and practicioners. The lot of developments that are currently under way may result in a second volume that might appear in some years from now.

Karlsruhe,                                                                            *Steffen Staab*
July 2003                                                                               *Rudi Studer*

## Acknowledgements

We gratefully acknowledge efforts by all the authors who also acted as peer reviewers and helped to further improve the quality of the papers. We thank Juliane Willsenach and Holger Lewen for heroic efforts typesetting Word documents.

## References

1. T. Berners-Lee, J. Hendler, and O. Lassila (2001). The Semantic Web. *Scientific American*, May 2001.
2. J. Davies, D. Fensel, and F. van Harmelen, eds. *Towards the Semantic Web: Ontology-driven Knowledge Management.* John Wiley & Sons, 2003.
3. D. Fensel and M.A. Musen, eds. The Semantic Web: A Brain for Humankind. *IEEE Intelligent Systems, Special Issue Cooking up the Semantic Web*, 16, 2 (March/April 2001), pp. 24-25.
4. D. Fensel, W. Wahlster, H. Lieberman, and J. Hendler, eds. *Spinning the Semantic Web.* MIT Press, 2003.
5. B. Grosof, I. Horrocks, R. Volz, S. Decker. Description Logic Programs: Combining Logic Programs with Description Logic. *Proceedings of WWW-2003*, ACM Press, 2003.
6. T. Gruber. A Translation Approach to Portable Ontology Specifications, *Knowledge Acquisition*, Vol.5, 1993, pp.199-220.
7. S. Handschuh and S. Staab (eds.). *Annotation for the Semantic Web.* IOS Press, 2003.
8. G. van Heijst, G. Schreiber, and B.J. Wielinga. Using Explicit Ontologies in KBS Development. *Intl. Journal on Human-Computer Studies*, 46 (2/3) (1997), pp. 183-292.
9. A. Maedche, B. Motik, L. Stojanovic, R. Studer, and R. Volz. An Infrastructure for Searching, Reusing and Evolving Distributed Ontologies. *Proceedings of WWW-2003*, ACM Press, 2003.
10. G. Schreiber, H. Akkermans, A. Anjewierden, R. de Hoog, N. Shadbolt, W. van de Velde, and B. Wielinga. *Knowledge Engineering and Management — The CommonKADS Methodology.* The MIT Press, Cambridge, Massachusetts; London, England, 1999.
11. R. Studer, V.R. Benjamins, and D. Fensel. Knowledge Engineering: Principles and Methods. *Data & Knowledge Engineering*, 25 (1998), pp. 161-197.

12. Y. Sure, J. Angele, and S. Staab. OntoEdit: Guiding Ontology Development by Methodology and Inferencing. *1st International Conference on Ontologies, Databases and Applications of Semantics for Large Scale Information Systems - ODBASE 2002*. October 29 - November 1, Irvine, California. LNCS, Springer, 2002.
13. R. Volz, B. Motik, I. Horrocks and B. Grosof. Description Logics Programs: An Evaluation and Extended Translation. Technical Report, 2003.

# Contents

# Part I

Ontology Representation and Reasoning

# Description Logics

Franz Baader[1], Ian Horrocks[2], and Ulrike Sattler[1]

[1] Institut für Theoretische Informatik, TU Dresden, Germany
   {baader,sattler}@tcs.inf.tu-dresden.de
[2] Department of Computer Science, University of Manchester, UK
   horrocks@cs.man.ac.uk

**Summary.** In this chapter, we explain what description logics are and why they make good ontology languages. In particular, we introduce the description logic $\mathcal{SHIQ}$, which has formed the basis of several well-known ontology languages including OIL, DAML+OIL and OWL. We argue that, without the last decade of basic research in description logics, this family of knowledge representation languages could not have played such an important rôle in this context.

Description logic reasoning can be used both during the design phase, in order to improve the quality of ontologies, and in the deployment phase, in order to exploit the rich structure of ontologies and ontology based information. We show how tableaux algorithms can be used to provide sound and complete reasoning for description logics like $\mathcal{SHIQ}$, and how optimised implementations have made these services available to realistic applications. We also discuss some of the challenges associated with the extensions to $\mathcal{SHIQ}$ that are required for languages such as DAML+OIL and OWL. Finally, we sketch how novel reasoning services can support building DL knowledge bases.

## 1.1 Introduction

The aim of this section is to give a brief introduction to description logics, and to argue why they are well-suited as ontology languages. In the remainder of the chapter we will put some flesh on this skeleton by providing more technical details with respect to the theory of description logics, reasoning algorithms and implementation techniques. More detail on these and other matters related to description logics can be found in [9].

### Ontologies

There have been many attempts to define what constitutes an ontology, perhaps the best known (at least amongst computer scientists) being due to Gruber: "an ontology is an explicit specification of a conceptualisation" [52].[3] In this context, a conceptualisation means an abstract model of some aspect of the world, taking the form of a

---

[3] This was later elaborated to "a formal specification of a shared conceptualisation" [25].

definition of the properties of important concepts and relationships. An explicit specification means that the model should be specified in some unambiguous language, making it amenable to processing by machines as well as by humans.

Ontologies are becoming of increasing importance in fields such as knowledge management, information integration, cooperative information systems, information retrieval and electronic commerce. One application area which has recently seen an explosion of interest is the so called *Semantic Web* [22], where ontologies are set to play a key rôle in establishing a common terminology between agents, thus ensuring that different agents have a shared understanding of terms used in semantic markup.

The effective use of ontologies requires not only a well-designed and well-defined ontology language, but also support from reasoning tools. Reasoning is important both to ensure the quality of an ontology, and in order to exploit the rich structure of ontologies and ontology based information. It can be employed in different phases of the ontology life cycle. During ontology design, it can be used to test whether concepts are non-contradictory and to derive implied relations. In particular, one usually wants to compute the concept hierarchy, i.e., the partial ordering of named concepts based on the subsumption relationship. Information on which concept is a specialization of another, and which concepts are synonyms, can be used in the design phase to test whether the concept definitions in the ontology have the intended consequences or not. This information is also very useful when the ontology is deployed.

Since it is not reasonable to assume that all applications will use the same ontology, interoperability and integration of different ontologies is also an important issue. Integration can, for example, be supported as follows: after the knowledge engineer has asserted some inter-ontology relationships, the integrated concept hierarchy is computed and the concepts are checked for consistency. Inconsistent concepts as well as unintended or missing subsumption relationships are thus signs of incorrect or incomplete inter-ontology assertions, which can then be corrected or completed by the knowledge engineer.

Finally, reasoning may also be used when the ontology is deployed. As well as using the pre-computed concept hierarchy, one could, for example, use the ontology to determine the consistency of facts stated in annotations, or infer relationships between annotation instances and ontology classes. More precisely, when searching web pages annotated with terms from the ontology, it may be useful to consider not only exact matches, but also matches with respect to more general or more specific terms—where the latter choice depends on the context. However, in the deployment phase, the requirements on the efficiency of reasoning are much more stringent than in the design and integration phases.

Before arguing why description logics are good candidates for such an ontology language, we provide a brief introduction to and history of description logics.

## Description Logics

Description logics (DLs) [9, 19, 34] are a family of knowledge representation languages that can be used to represent the knowledge of an application domain in a structured and formally well-understood way. The name *description logics* is motivated by the fact that, on the one hand, the important notions of the domain are described by concept *descriptions*, i.e., expressions that are built from atomic concepts (unary predicates) and atomic roles (binary predicates) using the concept and role constructors provided by the particular DL. On the other hand, DLs differ from their predecessors, such as semantic networks and frames, in that they are equipped with a formal, *logic*-based semantics.

In this introduction, we only illustrate some typical constructors by an example. Formal definitions are given in Section 1.2. Assume that we want to define the concept of "A man that is married to a doctor and has at least five children, all of whom are professors." This concept can be described with the following concept description:

$$\text{Human} \sqcap \neg\text{Female} \sqcap \exists\text{married}.\text{Doctor} \sqcap (\geq 5 \text{ hasChild}) \sqcap \forall\text{hasChild}.\text{Professor}$$

This description employs the Boolean constructors *conjunction* ($\sqcap$), which is interpreted as set intersection, and *negation* ($\neg$), which is interpreted as set complement, as well as the *existential restriction* constructor ($\exists R.C$), the *value restriction* constructor ($\forall R.C$), and the *number restriction* constructor ($\geq n R$). An individual, say Bob, belongs to $\exists$married.Doctor if there exists an individual that is married to Bob (i.e., is related to Bob via the married role) and is a doctor (i.e., belongs to the concept Doctor). Similarly, Bob belongs to ($\geq 5$ hasChild) iff he has at least five children, and he belongs to $\forall$hasChild.Professor iff all his children (i.e., all individuals related to Bob via the hasChild role) are professors.

In addition to this description formalism, DLs are usually equipped with a terminological and an assertional formalism. In its simplest form, *terminological axioms* can be used to introduce names (abbreviations) for complex descriptions. For example, we could introduce the abbreviation HappyMan for the concept description from above. More expressive terminological formalisms allow the statement of constraints such as

$$\exists\text{hasChild}.\text{Human} \sqsubseteq \text{Human},$$

which says that only humans can have human children. The *assertional formalism* can be used to state properties of individuals. For example, the assertions

$$\text{HappyMan}(\text{BOB}), \quad \text{hasChild}(\text{BOB}, \text{MARY})$$

state that Bob belongs to the concept HappyMan and that Mary is one of his children.

Description logic systems provide their users with various inference capabilities that deduce implicit knowledge from the explicitly represented knowledge. The *subsumption* algorithm determines subconcept-superconcept relationships: $C$ is subsumed by $D$ iff all instances of $C$ are necessarily instances of $D$, i.e., the first description is always interpreted as a subset of the second description. For example, given the definition of HappyMan from above, HappyMan is subsumed by $\exists$hasChild.Professor—since instances of HappyMan have at least five children, all of whom are professors, they also have a child that is a professor. The *instance* algorithm determines instance relationships: the individual $i$ is an instance of the concept description $C$ iff $i$ is always interpreted as an element of $C$. For example, given the assertions from above and the definition of HappyMan, MARY is an instance of Professor. The *consistency* algorithm determines whether a knowledge base (consisting of a set of assertions and a set of terminological axioms) is non-contradictory. For example, if we add ¬Professor(MARY) to the two assertions from above, then the knowledge base containing these assertions together with the definition of HappyMan from above is inconsistent.

In order to ensure a reasonable and predictable behavior of a DL system, these inference problems should at least be decidable for the DL employed by the system, and preferably of low complexity. Consequently, the expressive power of the DL in question must be restricted in an appropriate way. If the imposed restrictions are too severe, however, then the important notions of the application domain can no longer be expressed. Investigating this trade-off between the expressivity of DLs and the complexity of their inference problems has been one of the most important issues in DL research. Roughly, the research related to this issue can be classified into the following four phases.

*Phase 1* (1980–1990) was mainly concerned with implementation of systems, such as KLONE, K-REP, BACK, and LOOM [28, 77, 87, 76]. These systems employed so-called *structural subsumption algorithms*, which first normalize the concept descriptions, and then recursively compare the syntactic structure of the normalized descriptions [79]. These algorithms are usually relatively efficient (polynomial), but they have the disadvantage that they are complete only for very inexpressive DLs, i.e., for more expressive DLs they cannot detect all the existing subsumption/instance relationships. At the end of this phase, early formal investigations into the complexity of reasoning in DLs showed that most DLs do not have polynomial-time inference problems [27, 80]. As a reaction, the implementors of the CLASSIC system (the first industrial-strength DL system) carefully restricted the expressive power of their DL [86, 26].

*Phase 2* (1990–1995) started with the introduction of a new algorithmic paradigm into DLs, so-called *tableau-based algorithms* [94, 42, 60]. They work on propositionally closed DLs (i.e., DLs with full Boolean operators) and are complete also for expressive DLs. To decide the consistency of a knowledge base, a tableau-based algorithm tries to construct a model of it by breaking down the concepts in the knowledge base, thus inferring new constraints on the elements of this model. The algorithm either stops because all attempts to build a model failed with obvious contradictions, or it stops with a "canonical" model. Since subsumption and satisfiability can be reduced to consistency in propositionally closed DLs, a consistency algorithm can solve all inference problems mentioned above. The first systems employing such algorithms (KRIS and CRACK) demonstrated that optimized implementations of these algorithm lead to an acceptable behavior of the system, even though the worst-case complexity of the corresponding reasoning problems is no longer in polynomial time [13, 30]. This phase also saw a thorough analysis of the complexity of reasoning in various DLs [42, 43, 41]. Another important observation was that DLs are very closely related to modal logics [92].

*Phase 3* (1995–2000) is characterized by the development of inference procedures for very expressive DLs, either based on the tableau-approach [66, 67] or on a translation into modal logics [38, 39, 37, 40]. Highly optimized systems (FaCT, RACE, and DLP [62, 53, 85]) showed that tableau-based algorithms for expressive DLs lead to a good practical behavior of the system even on (some) large knowledge bases. In this phase, the relationship to modal logics [38, 93] and to decidable fragments of first-order logic was also studied in more detail [23, 83, 50, 48, 49], and applications in databases (like schema reasoning, query optimization, and integration of databases) were investigated [31, 33, 35].

We are now at the beginning of *Phase 4*, where industrial strength DL systems employing very expressive DLs and tableau-based algorithms are being developed, with applications like the Semantic Web or knowledge representation and integration in bio-informatics in mind.

## Description Logics as Ontology Languages

As already mentioned above, high quality ontologies are crucial for many applications, and their construction, integration, and evolution greatly depends on the availability of a well-defined semantics and powerful reasoning tools. Since DLs provide for both, they should be ideal candidates for ontology languages. That much was already clear ten years ago, but at that time there was a fundamental mismatch between the expressive power and the efficiency of reasoning that DL systems provided, and the expressivity and the large knowledge bases that ontologists needed [44]. Through the basic research in DLs of the last 10–15 years that we have summarized above, this gap between the needs of ontologist and the systems that DL researchers provide has finally become narrow enough to build stable bridges.

The suitability of DLs as ontology languages has been highlighted by their role as the foundation for several web ontology languages, including OIL [46], DAML+OIL [63, 65], and OWL, a newly emerging ontology language standard being developed by the W3C Web-Ontology Working Group.[4] All of these languages have a syntax based on RDF Schema, but the basis for their design is the expressive DL $\mathcal{SHIQ}$ [68],[5] and the developers have tried to find a good compromise between expressiveness and the complexity of reasoning. Although reasoning in $\mathcal{SHIQ}$ is decidable, it has a rather high worst-case complexity (EXPTIME). Nevertheless, highly optimized $\mathcal{SHIQ}$ reasoners such as FaCT [62] and RACER [55] behave quite well in practice.

Let us point out some of the features of $\mathcal{SHIQ}$ that make this DL expressive enough to be used as an ontology language. Firstly, $\mathcal{SHIQ}$ provides number restrictions that are more expressive than the ones introduced above (and employed be earlier DL systems). With the *qualified number restrictions* available in $\mathcal{SHIQ}$, as

---

[4] http://www.w3.org/2001/sw/WebOnt/
[5] To be exact, they are based on an extension of $\mathcal{SHIQ}$.

well as being able to say that a person has at most two children (without mentioning the properties of these children):

$$(\leq 2\,\mathsf{hasChild}),$$

one can also specify that there is at most one son and at most one daughter:

$$(\leq 1\,\mathsf{hasChild}.\neg\mathsf{Female}) \sqcap (\leq 1\,\mathsf{hasChild}.\mathsf{Female}).$$

Secondly, $\mathcal{SHIQ}$ allows the formulation of complex terminological axioms like "humans have human parents":

$$\mathsf{Human} \sqsubseteq \exists\mathsf{hasParent}.\mathsf{Human}.$$

Thirdly, $\mathcal{SHIQ}$ also allows for *inverse roles*, *transitive roles*, and *subroles*. For example, in addition to hasChild one can also use its inverse hasParent, one can specify that hasAncestor is transitive, and that hasParent is a subrole of hasAncestor.

It has been argued in the DL and the ontology community that these features play a central role when describing properties of aggregated objects and when building ontologies [90, 96, 45]. The actual use of DLs providing these features as the underlying logical formalism of the web ontology languages OIL, DAML+OIL and OWL [46, 63] substantiates this claim [96].[6]

Finally, we would like to mention briefly two extensions to $\mathcal{SHIQ}$ that are often used in ontology languages (we will discuss them in more detail in Section 1.7).

*Concrete domains* [11, 74] integrate DLs with concrete sets such as the real numbers, integers, or strings, and built-in predicates such as comparisons $\leq$, comparisons with constants $\leq 17$, or isPrefixOf. This supports the modelling of concrete properties of abstract objects such as the age, the weight, or the name of a person, and the comparison of these concrete properties. Unfortunately, in their unrestricted form, concrete domains can have dramatic effects on the decidability and computational complexity of the underlying DL [74].

*Nominals* are special concept names that are to be interpreted as singleton sets. Using a nominal Turing, we can describe all those computer scientists that have met Turing by CSientist $\sqcap \exists\mathsf{hasMet}.\mathsf{Turing}$. Again, nominals can have dramatic effects on the complexity of a logic [97].

## 1.2 The Expressive Description Logic $\mathcal{SHIQ}$

In this section, we present syntax and semantics of the expressive DL $\mathcal{SHIQ}$ (although the DL underlying OWL is, in some respects, slightly more expressive — see Section 1.4). Moreover, we will concentrate on the *terminological* formalism, i.e., the part that supports the definition of the relevant concepts in an application

---

[6] OWL does not, however, support the use of the more expressive qualified number restrictions.

domain, and the statement of constraints that restrict interpretations to the intended ones. The *assertional* formalism will not be introduced here due to space limitations and since it only plays a minor role in ontology engineering. The interested reader is referred to [9, 91] for assertional DL formalisms in general, and to [54, 69] for assertional reasoning for $\mathcal{SHIQ}$.

In contrast to most of the DLs considered in the literature, which concentrate on constructors for defining concepts, the DL $\mathcal{SHIQ}$ [67] also allows for rather expressive roles. Of course, these roles can then be used in the definition of concepts. We start with the definition of $\mathcal{SHIQ}$-roles, and then continue with the definition of $\mathcal{SHIQ}$-concepts.

**Definition 1 (Syntax and semantics of $\mathcal{SHIQ}$-roles).** *Let* $\mathbf{R}$ *be a set of* role names, *which is partitioned into a set* $\mathbf{R}_+$ *of transitive roles and a set* $\mathbf{R}_\mathsf{P}$ *of normal roles. The set of all $\mathcal{SHIQ}$-roles is* $\mathbf{R} \cup \{r^- \mid r \in \mathbf{R}\}$*, where* $r^-$ *is called the* inverse of *the role* $r$*. A* role inclusion axiom *is of the form* $r \sqsubseteq s$*, where* $r, s$ *are $\mathcal{SHIQ}$-roles. A* role hierarchy *is a finite set of role inclusion axioms.*

*An* interpretation $\mathcal{I} = (\Delta^{\mathcal{I}}, \cdot^{\mathcal{I}})$ *consists of a set* $\Delta^{\mathcal{I}}$*, called the* domain of $\mathcal{I}$*, and a function* $\cdot^{\mathcal{I}}$ *that maps every role to a subset of* $\Delta^{\mathcal{I}} \times \Delta^{\mathcal{I}}$ *such that, for all* $p \in \mathbf{R}$ *and* $r \in \mathbf{R}_+$*,*

$$\langle x, y \rangle \in p^{\mathcal{I}} \quad \textit{iff} \quad \langle y, x \rangle \in (p^-)^{\mathcal{I}},$$
$$\textit{if } \langle x, y \rangle \in r^{\mathcal{I}} \textit{ and } \langle y, z \rangle \in r^{\mathcal{I}} \textit{ then } \langle x, z \rangle \in r^{\mathcal{I}}.$$

*An interpretation* $\mathcal{I}$ *satisfies a role hierarchy* $\mathcal{R}$ *iff* $r^{\mathcal{I}} \subseteq s^{\mathcal{I}}$ *for each* $r \sqsubseteq s \in \mathcal{R}$*; such an interpretation is called a* model *of* $\mathcal{R}$*.*

The unrestricted use of these roles in all of the concept constructors of $\mathcal{SHIQ}$ (to be defined below) would lead to an undecidable DL [67]. Therefore, we must first define an appropriate subset of all $\mathcal{SHIQ}$-roles. This requires some more notation.

1. The inverse relation on binary relations is symmetric, i.e., the inverse of $r^-$ is again $r$. To avoid writing role expressions such as $r^{--}$, $r^{---}$, etc., we define a function $\mathsf{Inv}$, which returns the inverse of a role:

$$\mathsf{Inv}(r) := \begin{cases} r^- & \text{if } r \text{ is a role name,} \\ s & \text{if } r = s^- \text{ for a role name } s. \end{cases}$$

2. Since set inclusion is transitive and an inclusion relation between two roles transfers to their inverses, a given role hierarchy $\mathcal{R}$ implies additional inclusion relationships. To account for this fact, we define $\sqsubseteq^*_{\mathcal{R}}$ as the reflexive-transitive closure of

$$\sqsubseteq_{\mathcal{R}} := \mathcal{R} \cup \{\mathsf{Inv}(r) \sqsubseteq \mathsf{Inv}(s) \mid r \sqsubseteq s \in \mathcal{R}\}.$$

We use $r \equiv_{\mathcal{R}} s$ as an abbreviation for $r \sqsubseteq^*_{\mathcal{R}} s$ and $s \sqsubseteq^*_{\mathcal{R}} r$. In this case, every model of $\mathcal{R}$ interprets these roles as the same binary relation.

3. Obviously, a binary relation is transitive iff its inverse is transitive. Thus, if $r \equiv_{\mathcal{R}} s$ and $r$ or $\mathsf{Inv}(r)$ is transitive, then any model of $\mathcal{R}$ interprets $s$ as a transitive binary relation. To account for such implied transitive roles, we define the following function Trans:

$$\mathsf{Trans}(s, \mathcal{R}) := \begin{cases} \text{true} & \text{if } r \in \mathbf{R}_+ \text{ or } \mathsf{Inv}(r) \in \mathbf{R}_+ \text{ for some } r \text{ with } r \equiv_{\mathcal{R}} s \\ \text{false} & \text{otherwise.} \end{cases}$$

4. A role $r$ is called *simple* w.r.t. $\mathcal{R}$ iff $\mathsf{Trans}(s, \mathcal{R}) = \text{false}$ for all $s \sqsubseteq^*_{\mathcal{R}} r$.

**Definition 2 (Syntax and semantics of $\mathcal{SHIQ}$-concepts).** *Let $N_C$ be a set of con-cept names. The set of $\mathcal{SHIQ}$-concepts is the smallest set such that*

1. *every concept name $A \in N_C$ is a $\mathcal{SHIQ}$-concept,*
2. *if $C$ and $D$ are $\mathcal{SHIQ}$-concepts and $r$ is a $\mathcal{SHIQ}$-role, then $C \sqcap D$, $C \sqcup D$, $\neg C$, $\forall r.C$, and $\exists r.C$ are $\mathcal{SHIQ}$-concepts,*
3. *if $C$ is a $\mathcal{SHIQ}$-concept, $r$ is a simple $\mathcal{SHIQ}$-role, and $n \in \mathbb{N}$, then $(\leqslant n\, r.C)$ and $(\geqslant n\, r.C)$ are $\mathcal{SHIQ}$-concepts.*

*The interpretation function $\cdot^{\mathcal{I}}$ of an interpretation $\mathcal{I} = (\Delta^{\mathcal{I}}, \cdot^{\mathcal{I}})$ maps, additionally, every concept to a subset of $\Delta^{\mathcal{I}}$ such that*

$$(C \sqcap D)^{\mathcal{I}} = C^{\mathcal{I}} \cap D^{\mathcal{I}}, \qquad (C \sqcup D)^{\mathcal{I}} = C^{\mathcal{I}} \cup D^{\mathcal{I}}, \qquad \neg C^{\mathcal{I}} = \Delta^{\mathcal{I}} \setminus C^{\mathcal{I}},$$
$$(\exists r.C)^{\mathcal{I}} = \{x \in \Delta^{\mathcal{I}} \mid \text{There is some } y \in \Delta^{\mathcal{I}} \text{ with } \langle x, y \rangle \in r^{\mathcal{I}} \text{ and } y \in C^{\mathcal{I}}\},$$
$$(\forall r.C)^{\mathcal{I}} = \{x \in \Delta^{\mathcal{I}} \mid \text{For all } y \in \Delta^{\mathcal{I}}, \text{ if } \langle x, y \rangle \in r^{\mathcal{I}}, \text{then } y \in C^{\mathcal{I}}\},$$
$$(\leqslant n\, r.C)^{\mathcal{I}} = \{x \in \Delta^{\mathcal{I}} \mid \sharp r^{\mathcal{I}}(x, C) \leqslant n\},$$
$$(\geqslant n\, r.C)^{\mathcal{I}} = \{x \in \Delta^{\mathcal{I}} \mid \sharp r^{\mathcal{I}}(x, C) \geqslant n\},$$

*where $\sharp M$ denotes the cardinality of the set $M$, and $r^{\mathcal{I}}(x, C) := \{y \mid \langle x, y \rangle \in r^{\mathcal{I}} \text{ and } y \in C^{\mathcal{I}}\}$. If $x \in C^{\mathcal{I}}$, then we say that $x$ is an* instance *of $C$ in $\mathcal{I}$, and if $\langle x, y \rangle \in r^{\mathcal{I}}$, then $y$ is called an $r$-successor of $x$ in $\mathcal{I}$.*

Concepts can be used to describe the relevant notions of an application domain. The terminology (TBox) introduces abbreviations (names) for complex concepts. In $\mathcal{SHIQ}$, the TBox allows one to state also more complex constraints.

**Definition 3.** *A general concept inclusion (GCI) is of the form $C \sqsubseteq D$, where $C, D$ are $\mathcal{SHIQ}$-concepts. A finite set of GCIs is called a TBox. An interpretation $\mathcal{I}$ is a model of a TBox $\mathcal{T}$ iff it satisfies all GCIs in $\mathcal{T}$, i.e., $C^{\mathcal{I}} \subseteq D^{\mathcal{I}}$ holds for each $C \sqsubseteq D \in \mathcal{T}$.*

A concept definition is of the form $A \equiv C$, where $A$ is a concept name. It can be seen as an abbreviation for the two GCIs $A \sqsubseteq C$ and $C \sqsubseteq A$.

Inference problems are defined w.r.t. a TBox and a role hierarchy.

**Definition 4.** *The concept $C$ is called* satisfiable with respect to the role hierarchy $\mathcal{R}$ *and the TBox $\mathcal{T}$ iff there is a model $\mathcal{I}$ of $\mathcal{R}$ and $\mathcal{T}$ with $C^{\mathcal{I}} \neq \emptyset$. Such an interpretation is called a* model *of $C$ w.r.t. $\mathcal{R}$ and $\mathcal{T}$. The concept $D$ subsumes the concept $C$ w.r.t. $\langle \mathcal{R}, \mathcal{T} \rangle$ (written $C \sqsubseteq_{\langle \mathcal{R}, \mathcal{T} \rangle} D$) iff $C^{\mathcal{I}} \subseteq D^{\mathcal{I}}$ holds for all models $\mathcal{I}$ of $\mathcal{R}$ and $\mathcal{T}$. Two concepts $C, D$ are* equivalent *w.r.t. $\mathcal{R}$ (written $C \equiv_{\langle \mathcal{R}, \mathcal{T} \rangle} D$) iff they subsume each other.*

By definition, equivalence can be reduced to subsumption. In addition, subsumption can be reduced to satisfiability since $C \sqsubseteq_{\langle \mathcal{R}, \mathcal{T} \rangle} D$ iff $C \sqcap \neg D$ is unsatisfiable w.r.t. $\mathcal{R}$ and $\mathcal{T}$.

As mentioned above, most DLs are (decidable) fragments of (first-order) predicate logic [23, 1]. Viewing role names as binary relations and concept names as unary relations, for example, the role inclusion axiom $r \sqsubseteq s^-$ translates into $\forall x \forall y.r(x, y) \Rightarrow s(y, x)$, and the GCI $A \sqcap \exists r.C \sqsubseteq D \sqcup \forall s^-.E$ translates into

$$\forall x.(A(x) \wedge \exists y.r(x, y) \wedge C(y)) \Rightarrow (D(x) \vee \forall y.s(y, x) \Rightarrow E(x)).$$

This translation preserves the semantics: we can easily view DL interpretations as predicate logic interpretations, and then prove, e.g., that each model of a concept $C$ w.r.t. a TBox $\mathcal{T}$ and a role hierarchy $\mathcal{R}$ is a model of the translation of $C$ conjoined with the (universally quantified) translations of $\mathcal{T}$ and $\mathcal{R}$.

Before sketching how to solve the satisfiability problem in $\mathcal{SHIQ}$, we try to give an intuition on how $\mathcal{SHIQ}$ can be used to define ontologies.

## 1.3 Describing Ontologies in $\mathcal{SHIQ}$

In general, an ontology can be formalised in a TBox as follows. Firstly, we restrict the possible worlds by introducing restrictions on the allowed interpretations. For example, to express that, in our world, we want to consider humans, which are either muggles or sorcerers, we can use the GCIs

Human $\sqsubseteq$ Muggle $\sqcup$ Sorcerer and Muggle $\sqsubseteq$ ¬Sorcerer.

Next, to express that humans have exactly two parents and that all parents and children of humans are human, we can use the following GCI:

Human $\sqsubseteq$ ∀hasParent.Human $\sqcap$ ($\leqslant 2$ hasParent.$\top$) $\sqcap$ ($\geqslant 2$ hasParent.$\top$) $\sqcap$
    ∀hasParent$^-$.Human,

where $\top$ is an abbreviation for the top concept $A \sqcup \neg A$.[7]
  In addition, we consider the *transitive* role hasAncestor, and the role inclusion

hasParent $\sqsubseteq$ hasAncestor.

---

[7] When the qualifying concept is $\top$, this is equivalent to an unqualified restriction, and it will often be written as such, e.g., ($\leqslant 2$ hasParent).

The next GCI expresses that humans having an ancestor that is a sorcerer are themselves sorcerers:

$$\text{Human} \sqcap \exists \text{hasAncestor.Sorcerer} \sqsubseteq \text{Sorcerer}.$$

Secondly, we can define the relevant notions of our application domain using concept definitions. Recall that the concept definition $A \equiv C$ stands for the two GCIs $A \sqsubseteq C$ and $C \sqsubseteq A$. A concept name is called *defined* if it occurs on the left-hand side of a definition, and *primitive* otherwise.

We want our concept definitions to have definitional impact, i.e., the interpretation of the primitive concept and role names should uniquely determine the interpretation of the defined concept names. For this, the set of concept definitions together with the additional GCIs must satisfy three conditions:

1. There are no multiple definitions, i.e., each defined concept name must occur at most once as a left-hand side of a concept definition.
2. There are no cyclic definitions, i.e., no cyclic dependencies between the defined names in the set of concept definitions.[8]
3. The defined names do not occur in any of the additional GCIs.

In contrast to concept definitions, the GCIs in $\mathcal{SHIQ}$ may well have cyclic dependencies between concept names. An example are the above GCIs describing humans.

As a simple example of a set of concept definitions satisfying the restrictions from above, we define the concepts grandparent and parent:[9]

$$\text{Parent} \equiv \text{Human} \sqcap \exists \text{hasParent}^-.\top,$$
$$\text{Grandparent} \equiv \exists \text{hasParent}^-.\text{Parent}.$$

The TBox consisting of the above concept definitions and GCIs, together with the fact that hasAncestor is a transitive superrole of hasParent, implies the following subsumption relationship:

$$\text{Grandparent} \sqcap \text{Sorcerer} \sqsubseteq \exists \text{hasParent}^-.\exists \text{hasParent}^-.\text{Sorcerer},$$

i.e., grandparents that are sorcerers have a grandchild that is a sorcerer. Though this conclusion may sound reasonable given the assumptions, it requires quite some reasoning to obtain it. In particular, one must use the fact that hasAncestor (and thus also hasAncestor$^-$) is transitive, that hasParent$^-$ is the inverse of hasParent, and that we have a GCI that says that children of humans are again humans.

To sum up, a $\mathcal{SHIQ}$-TBox can, on the one hand, axiomatize the basic notions of an application domain (the primitive concepts) by GCIs, transitivity statements, and role inclusions, in the sense that these statements restrict the possible interpretations of the basic notions. On the other hand, more complex notions (the defined concepts)

---

[8] In order to give cyclic definitions definitional impact, one would need to use fixpoint semantics for them [81, 4].

[9] In addition to the role hasParent, which relates children to their parents, we use the concept Parent, which describes all humans having children.

can be introduced by concept definitions. Given an interpretation of the basic notions, the concept definitions uniquely determine the interpretation of the defined notions.

The *taxonomy* of such a TBox is then given by the subsumption hierarchy of the defined concepts. It can be computed using a subsumption algorithm for $\mathcal{SHIQ}$ (see Section 1.5 below). The knowledge engineer can test whether the TBox captures her intuition by checking the satisfiability of the defined concepts (since it does not make sense to give a complex definition for the empty concept), and by checking whether their place in the taxonomy corresponds to their intuitive place. The expressive power of $\mathcal{SHIQ}$ together with the fact that one can "verify" the TBox in the sense mentioned above is the main reason for $\mathcal{SHIQ}$ being well-suited as an ontology language [90, 45, 96].

## 1.4 $\mathcal{SHIQ}$ and OWL

As already discussed, OWL is a semantic web ontology language (based on DAML+ OIL, and developed by the W3C Web-Ontology working group) whose the semantics can be defined via a translation into an expressive DL.[10] This is not a coincidence— it was a design goal. The mapping allows OWL to exploit formal results from DL research (e.g., regarding the decidability and complexity of key inference problems) and use implemented DL reasoners (e.g., FaCT [61] and RACER [55]) in order to provide reasoning services for OWL applications.

An OWL (Lite or DL) ontology can be seen to correspond to a DL TBox together with a role hierarchy, describing the domain in terms of *classes* (corresponding to concepts) and *properties* (corresponding to roles). An ontology consists of a set of *axioms* that assert, e.g., subsumption relationships between classes or properties.

As in a standard DL, OWL classes may be names or expressions built up from simpler classes and properties using a variety of constructors. The set of constructors supported by OWL, along with the equivalent DL abstract syntax, is summarised in Figure 1.1.[11] The full XML serialisation of the RDF syntax is not shown as it is rather verbose, e.g., Human ⊓ Male would be written as

```
<owl:Class>
  <owl:intersectionOf rdf:parseType="Collection">
    <owl:Class rdf:about="#Human"/>
    <owl:Class rdf:about="#Male"/>
  </owl:intersectionOf>
</owl:Class>
```

while ($\geqslant$ 2 hasChild.Thing) would be written as

---

[10] In fact there are 3 "species" of OWL: OWL Lite, OWL DL and OWL full, only the first two of which have DL based semantics. The semantics of OWL full is given by an extension to RDF model theory [57].

[11] In fact, there are a few additional constructors provided as "syntactic sugar", but all are trivially reducible to the ones described in Figure 1.1.

```
<owl:Restriction>
  <owl:onProperty rdf:resource="#hasChild"/>
    <owl:minCardinality
       rdf:datatype="&xsd;NonNegativeInteger">2
    </owl:minCardinality>
</owl:Restriction>
```

Prefixes such as `owl:` and `&xsd;` specify XML namespaces for resources, while `rdf:parseType="Collection"` is an extension to RDF that provides a "shorthand" notation for lisp style lists defined using triples with the properties first and rest (it can be eliminated, but with a consequent increase in verbosity). E.g., the first example above consists of the triples $\langle r_1, \text{owl} : \text{intersectionOf}, r_2 \rangle$, $\langle r_2, \text{owl} : \text{first}, \text{Human} \rangle$, $\langle r_2, \text{rdfs} : \text{type}, \text{Class} \rangle$, $\langle r_2, \text{owl} : \text{rest}, r_3 \rangle$, etc., where $r_i$ is an anonymous resource, Human stands for a URI naming the resource "Human", and owl : intersectionOf, owl : first, owl : rest and rdfs : type stand for URIs naming the properties in question.

| Constructor | DL Syntax | Example |
|---|---|---|
| intersectionOf | $C_1 \sqcap \ldots \sqcap C_n$ | Human $\sqcap$ Male |
| unionOf | $C_1 \sqcup \ldots \sqcup C_n$ | Doctor $\sqcup$ Lawyer |
| complementOf | $\neg C$ | $\neg$Male |
| oneOf | $\{x_1 \ldots x_n\}$ | $\{\text{john}, \text{mary}\}$ |
| allValuesFrom | $\forall P.C$ | $\forall$hasChild.Doctor |
| someValuesFrom | $\exists r.C$ | $\exists$hasChild.Lawyer |
| hasValue | $\exists r.\{x\}$ | $\exists$citizenOf.$\{\text{USA}\}$ |
| minCardinality | $(\geqslant n \, r)$ | $(\geqslant 2 \text{ hasChild})$ |
| maxCardinality | $(\leqslant n \, r)$ | $(\leqslant 1 \text{ hasChild})$ |
| inverseOf | $r^-$ | hasChild$^-$ |

**Fig. 1.1.** OWL constructors

An important feature of OWL is that, besides "abstract" classes defined by the ontology, one can also use XML Schema *datatypes* (e.g., string, decimal and float) in `someValuesFrom`, `allValuesFrom`, and `hasValue` restrictions. E.g., the class Adult could be asserted to be equivalent to Person$\sqcap\exists$age.over17, where over17 is an XML Schema datatype based on decimal, but with the added restriction that values must be at least 18.[12] Using a combination of XML Schema and RDF this could be written as:

```
<xsd:simpleType name="over17">
  <xsd:restriction base="xsd:positiveInteger">
  <xsd:minInclusive value="18"/>
  </xsd:restriction>
```

---

[12] This construction would be valid in DAML+OIL, but the range of datatypes supported by OWL has yet to be determined.

```
</xsd:simpleType>

<owl:Class rdf:ID="Adult">
  <owl:intersectionOf rdf:parseType="Collection">
    <owl:Class rdf:about="#Person"/>
    <owl:Restriction>
      <owl:onProperty rdf:resource="#age"/>
      <owl:someValuesFrom rdf:resource="#over17"/>
    </owl:Restriction>
  </owl:intersectionOf>
</owl:Class>
```

As already mentioned, an OWL ontology consists of a set of axioms. Figure 1.2 summarises the axioms supported by OWL. These axioms make it possible to assert subsumption or equivalence with respect to classes or properties, the disjointness of classes, and the equivalence or non-equivalence of individuals (resources). Moreover, OWL also allows properties of properties (i.e., DL roles) to be asserted. In particular, it is possible to assert that a property is transitive, functional, inverse functional or symmetric.

| Axiom | DL Syntax | Example |
|---|---|---|
| subClassOf | $C_1 \sqsubseteq C_2$ | Human $\sqsubseteq$ Animal $\sqcap$ Biped |
| equivalentClass | $C_1 \equiv C_2$ | Man $\equiv$ Human $\sqcap$ Male |
| subPropertyOf | $P_1 \sqsubseteq P_2$ | hasDaughter $\sqsubseteq$ hasChild |
| equivalentProperty | $P_1 \equiv P_2$ | cost $\equiv$ price |
| disjointWith | $C_1 \sqsubseteq \neg C_2$ | Male $\sqsubseteq \neg$Female |
| sameAs | $\{x_1\} \equiv \{x_2\}$ | $\{\text{President\_Bush}\} \equiv \{\text{G\_W\_Bush}\}$ |
| differentFrom | $\{x_1\} \sqsubseteq \neg\{x_2\}$ | $\{\text{john}\} \sqsubseteq \neg\{\text{peter}\}$ |
| TransitiveProperty | $P \in \mathbf{R}_+$ | hasAncestor$^+ \in \mathbf{R}_+$ |
| FunctionalProperty | $\top \sqsubseteq (\leqslant 1\, P)$ | $\top \sqsubseteq (\leqslant 1\,\text{hasMother})$ |
| InverseFunctionalProperty | $\top \sqsubseteq (\leqslant 1\, P^-)$ | $\top \sqsubseteq (\leqslant 1\,\text{isMotherOf}^-)$ |
| SymmetricProperty | $P \equiv P^-$ | isSiblingOf $\equiv$ isSiblingOf$^-$ |

**Fig. 1.2.** OWL axioms

This shows that, except for individuals and datatypes, the constructors and axioms of OWL can be translated into $\mathcal{SHIQ}$. In fact, OWL is equivalent to the extension of $\mathcal{SHIN}$ ($\mathcal{SHIQ}$ with only the $\top$ concept being allowed in qualified number restrictions) with nominals and a simple form of concrete domains (this extension will be discussed in more detail in Section 1.7).

## 1.5 Reasoning in $\mathcal{SHIQ}$

As in Section 1.2, we concentrate on *terminological* reasoning, that is, satisfiability and subsumption w.r.t. TBoxes (i.e., sets of general concept inclusions) and role hierarchies. Assertional reasoning problems such as deciding consistency of ABoxes w.r.t. a TBox can be decided using quite similar techniques [91, 9, 54, 69]. As shown in Section 1.2, subsumption can be reduced (in linear time) to satisfiability. In addition, since $\mathcal{SHIQ}$ allows for both subroles and transitive roles, TBoxes can be internalized, i.e., satisfiability w.r.t. a TBox and a role hierarchy can be reduced to satisfiability w.r.t. the empty TBox and a role hierarchy. In principle, this is achieved by introducing a (new) transitive superrole $u$ of all roles occurring in the TBox $\mathcal{T}$ and the concept $C_0$ to be tested for satisfiability. Then we extend $C_0$ to the concept

$$\widehat{C}_0 := C_0 \sqcap \prod_{C \sqsubseteq D \in \mathcal{T}} (\neg C \sqcup D) \sqcap \forall u.(\neg C \sqcup D).$$

We can then show that $\widehat{C}_0$ is satisfiable w.r.t. the extended role hierarchy iff the original concept $C_0$ is satisfiable w.r.t. the TBox $\mathcal{T}$ and the original role hierarchy [2, 92, 8, 67].

Consequently, it is sufficient to design an algorithm that can decide satisfiability of $\mathcal{SHIQ}$-concepts w.r.t. role hierarchies and transitive roles. This problem is known to be EXPTIME-complete [97]. In fact, EXPTIME-hardness can be shown by an easy adaptation of the EXPTIME-hardness proof for satisfiability in propositional dynamic logic [47]. Using automata-based techniques, Tobies [97] shows that satisfiability of $\mathcal{SHIQ}$-concepts w.r.t. role hierarchies is indeed decidable within exponential time.

In the remainder of this section, we sketch a tableau-based decision procedure for this problem. This procedure, which is described in more detail in [67], runs in worst-case *nondeterministic* double exponential time.[13] However, according to the current state of the art, this procedures is more practical than the EXPTIME automata-based procedure in [97]. In fact, it is the basis for the highly optimised implementation of the DL system FaCT [62].

When started with a $\mathcal{SHIQ}$-concept $C_0$, a role hierarchy $\mathcal{R}$, and information on which roles are transitive, this algorithm tries to construct a model of $C_0$ w.r.t. $\mathcal{R}$. Since $\mathcal{SHIQ}$ has a so-called tree model property, we can assume that this model has the form of an infinite tree. If we want to obtain a decision procedure, we can only construct a finite tree representing the infinite one (if a (tree) model exists at all). This can be done such that the finite representation can be *unravelled* into an infinite tree model $\mathcal{I}$ of $C_0$ w.r.t. $\mathcal{R}$. In the finite tree representing this model, a node $x$ corresponds to an individual $\pi(x) \in \Delta^{\mathcal{I}}$, and we label each node with the set of concepts $\mathcal{L}(x)$ that $\pi(x)$ is supposed to be an instance of. Similary, edges represent role-successor relationships, and an edge between $x$ and $y$ is labelled with the roles supposed to connect $x$ and $y$. The algorithm either stops with a finite representation of a tree model, or with a *clash*, i.e., an obvious inconsistency, such as $\{C, \neg C\} \subseteq \mathcal{L}(x)$. It answers "$C_0$ is satisfiable w.r.t. $\mathcal{R}$" in the former case, and "$C_0$ is unsatisfiable w.r.t. $\mathcal{R}$" in the latter.

---

[13] This is due to the algorithm searching a tree of worst-case exponential depth. Re-using previously computed search results, cashing, this algorithm can run in nondeterministic exponential time. However, cashing introduces a considerable overhead which turns out to be not always useful in practice.

The algorithm is initialised with the tree consisting of a single node $x$ labelled with $\mathcal{L}(x) = \{C_0\}$. Then it applies so-called *completion rules*, which break down the concepts in the node labels syntactically, thus inferring new constraints for the given node, and then extend the tree according to these constraints. For example, if $C_1 \sqcap C_2 \in \mathcal{L}(x)$, then the $\sqcap$-rule adds both $C_1$ and $C_2$ to $\mathcal{L}(x)$. The $\geq$-rule generates $n$ new $r$-successor nodes $y_1, \ldots, y_n$ of $x$ with $\mathcal{L}(y_i) = \{C\}$ if $(\geq n\ r.C) \in \mathcal{L}(x)$ and $x$ does not yet have $n$ distinct $r$-successors with $C$ in their label. In addition, it asserts that these new successors must remain distinct (i.e., cannot be identified in later steps of the algorithm). Other rules are more complicated, and a complete description of this algorithm goes beyond the scope of this chapter. However, we would like to point out two issues that make reasoning in $\mathcal{SHIQ}$ considerably harder than in less expressive DLs.

First, *qualified number restrictions* are harder to handle than the unqualified ones used in most early DL systems.[14] Let us illustrate this by an example. Assume that the algorithm has generated a node $x$ with $(\leqslant 1\ \mathsf{hasChild}.\top) \in \mathcal{L}(x)$, and that this node has two hasChild-successors $y_1, y_2$ (i.e., two edges labeled with hasChild leading to the nodes $y_1, y_2$). In order to satisfy the number restriction $(\leqslant 1\ \mathsf{hasChild}.\top)$ for $x$, the algorithm identifies node $y_1$ with node $y_2$ (unless these nodes were asserted to be distinct, in which case we have a clash). Now assume that we still have a node $x$ with two hasChild-successors $y_1, y_2$, but the label of $x$ contains a qualified number restriction like $(\leqslant 2\ \mathsf{hasChild}.\mathsf{Parent})$. The naive idea [98] would be to check the labels of $y_1$ and $y_2$ whether they contain Parent, and identify $y_1$ and $y_2$ only if both contain this concept. However, this is not correct since, in the model $\mathcal{I}$ constructed from the tree, $\pi(y_i)$ may well belong to $\mathsf{Parent}^{\mathcal{I}}$ even if this concept does not belong to the label of $x$. The first correct algorithm that can handle qualified number restrictions was proposed in [59]. The main idea is to introduce a so-called *choose-rule*. In our example, this rule would (nondeterministically) choose whether $y_i$ is supposed to belong to Parent or $\neg$Parent, and correspondingly extend its label. Together with the choose rule, the above naive identification rule is in fact correct.

Second, in the presence of *transitive roles*, guaranteeing termination of the algorithm is a non-trivial task [56, 88]. If $\forall r.C \in \mathcal{L}(x)$ for a transitive role $r$, then not only must we add $C$ to the label of any $r$-successor $y$ of $x$, but also $\forall r.C$. This ensures that, even over an "$r$-chain"

$$x \xrightarrow{r} y \xrightarrow{r} y_1 \xrightarrow{r} y_2 \xrightarrow{r} \ldots \xrightarrow{r} y_n$$

we get indeed $C \in \mathcal{L}(y_n)$. This is necessary since, in the model constructed from the tree generated by the algorithm, have

$$(\pi(x), \pi(y)),\ (\pi(y), \pi(y_1)),\ \ldots,\ (\pi(y_{n-1}), \pi(y_n)) \in r^{\mathcal{I}},$$

and thus the transitivity of $r^{\mathcal{I}}$ requires that also $(\pi(x), \pi(y_n)) \in r^{\mathcal{I}}$. Consequently, the value restriction on $x$ applies to $y_n$ as well. Propagating $\forall r.C$ over $r$-edges makes sure that this is taken care of. However, it also may lead to nontermination. For

---

[14] Note that, unlike DAML+OIL, OWL supports only unqualified number restrictions.

example, consider the concept $\exists r.A \sqcap \forall r.\exists r.A$ where $r$ is a transitive role. It is easy to see that the algorithm then generates an infinite chain of nodes with label $\{A, \forall r.\exists r.A, \exists r.A\}$. To prevent this looping and ensure termination, we use a cycle-detection mechanism called *blocking*: if the labels of a node $x$ and one of its ancestors coincide, we "block" the application of rules to $x$. The blocking condition must be formulated such that, whenever blocking occurs, we can "unravel" the blocked (finite) path into an infinite path in the model to be constructed. In description logics, blocking was first employed in [3] in the context of an algorithm that can handle the transitive closure of roles, and was improved on in [7, 32, 6]. In $\mathcal{SHIQ}$, the blocking condition is quite complicated since the combination of transitive and inverse roles with number restrictions requires a rather advanced form of unravelling [67]. In fact, this combination of constructors is responsible for the fact that, unlike most DLs considered in the literature, $\mathcal{SHIQ}$ does not have the finite model property, i.e., there are satisfiable $\mathcal{SHIQ}$-concepts that are only satisfiable in infinite interpretations [67].

## 1.6 Practical Reasoning Services for $\mathcal{SHIQ}$

As mentioned in Section 1.5, reasoning in $\mathcal{SHIQ}$ is of high complexity (ExpTime). The pathological cases that lead to such high *worst case* complexity are rather artificial, and rarely occur in practice [80, 58, 95, 62]. Even in realistic applications, however, problems can occur that are much too hard to be solved by naive implementations of theoretical algorithms such as the one sketched in Section 1.5. Modern DL systems, therefore, include a wide range of optimisation techniques, the use of which has been shown to improve *typical case* performance by several orders of magnitude [64]. These systems exhibit good typical case performance, and work well in realistic applications [10, 30, 62, 55, 85].

A detailed description of optimisation techniques is beyond the scope of this chapter, and the interested reader is referred to [9] for further information. It will, however, be interesting to sketch a few of the key techniques such as lazy unfolding, absorption and dependency directed backtracking.

### Lazy Unfolding

In an ontology, or DL TBox, large and complex concepts are seldom described monolithically, but are built up from a hierarchy of named concepts whose descriptions are less complex. The tableau-based algorithm can take advantage of this structure by trying to find contradictions between concept names before adding expressions derived from TBox axioms. This strategy is known as *lazy unfolding* [10, 62].

The benefits of lazy unfolding can be maximised by lexically *normalising* and *naming* all concept expressions and, recursively, their sub-expressions. An expression $C$ is normalised by rewriting it in a standard form (e.g., disjunctions are rewritten as negated conjunctions); it is named by substituting it with a new concept name $A$, and adding an axiom $A \equiv C$ to the TBox. The normalisation step allows lexically equivalent expressions to be recognised and identically named, and can even detect syntactically "obvious" satisfiability and unsatisfiability.

**Absorption**

Not all axioms are amenable to lazy unfolding. In particular, so called *general concept inclusions* (GCIs), axioms of the form $C \sqsubseteq D$ where C is non-atomic, must be dealt with by explicitly making every individual in the model an instance of $D \sqcup \neg C$. Large numbers of GCIs result in a very high degree of non-determinism and catastrophic performance degradation [62].

Absorption is another rewriting technique that tries to reduce the number of GCIs in the TBox by absorbing them into axioms of the form $A \sqsubseteq C$, where $A$ is a concept name. The basic idea is that an axiom of the form $A \sqcap D \sqsubseteq D'$ can be rewritten as $A \sqsubseteq D' \sqcup \neg D$ and absorbed into an existing $A \sqsubseteq C$ axiom to give $A \sqsubseteq C \sqcap (D' \sqcup \neg D)$ [70]. Although the disjunction is still present, lazy unfolding ensures that it is only applied to individuals that are already known to be instances of $A$.

**Dependency Directed Backtracking**

Inherent unsatisfiability concealed in sub-expressions can lead to large amounts of unproductive backtracking search known as thrashing. For example, expanding the expression $(C_1 \sqcup D_1) \sqcap \ldots \sqcap (C_n \sqcup D_n) \sqcap \exists R.(A \sqcap B) \sqcap \forall R.\neg A$ could lead to the fruitless exploration of $2^n$ possible expansions of $(C_1 \sqcup D_1) \sqcap \ldots \sqcap (C_n \sqcup D_n)$ before the inherent unsatisfiability of $\exists R.(A \sqcap B) \sqcap \forall R.\neg A$ is discovered. This problem is addressed by adapting a form of dependency directed backtracking called *backjumping*, which has been used in solving constraint satisfiability problems [20].

Backjumping works by labeling concepts with a dependency set indicating the non-deterministic expansion choices on which they depend. When a clash is discovered, the dependency sets of the clashing concepts can be used to identify the most recent non-deterministic expansion where an alternative choice might alleviate the cause of the clash. The algorithm can then jump back over intervening non-deterministic expansions *without* exploring any alternative choices. Similar techniques have been used in first order theorem provers, e.g., the "proof condensation" technique employed in the HARP theorem prover [82].

## 1.7 Extensions and Variants of $\mathcal{SHIQ}$

As mentioned above, the ontology languages DAML+OIL and OWL extend $\mathcal{SHIQ}$ with nominals and concrete datatypes. In this section, we discuss the consequences of these extensions on the reasoning problems in $\mathcal{SHIQ}$.

Concrete datatypes, as available in both DAML+OIL and OWL, are a very restricted form of concrete domains [11]. For example, using the concrete domain of all nonnegative integers equipped with the $<$ predicate, a (functional) role age relating (abstract) individuals to their (concrete) age, and a (functional) subrole father of hasParent, the following axiom states that children are younger than their fathers:

$$\text{Animal} \sqsubseteq (\text{age} < (\text{father} \circ \text{age})).$$

Extending expressive DLs with concrete domains may easily lead to undecidability [12, 75]. However, DAML+OIL and OWL provide only a very limited form of concrete domains. In particular, the concrete domain must not allow for predicates of arity greater than 1 (like < in our example), and the predicate restrictions must not contain role chains (like father ∘ age in our example). In [84], decidability of $\mathcal{SHIQ}$ extended with a slightly more general type of concrete domains is shown.

Concerning nominals, things become a bit more complicated. Firstly, we believe that we can use the same (relativised axiomatization) technique as used for $\mathcal{SHIQ}$ in [97] to translate $\mathcal{SHIQ}$ extended with nominals into a fragment of C2, the two-variable fragment of first order logic with counting quantifiers [51, 83]. Since this translation is polynomial, satisfiability and subsumption are decidable in NEXP-TIME. This is optimal since the problem is also NEXPTIME-hard [97]. Roughly speaking, the combination of GCIs (or transitive roles and role hierarchies), inverse roles, and number restrictions with nominals is responsible for this leap in complexity (from EXPTIME for $\mathcal{SHIQ}$ to NEXPTIME). To the best of our knowledge, no "practicable" decision procedure for $\mathcal{SHIQ}$ with nominals has so far been described. By "practicable" we mean a decision procedure that works in some "goal-directed" way, in contrast to "blindly" guessing a model $\mathcal{I}$ of at most exponential size and then checking whether $\mathcal{I}$ is indeed a model of the input.

## 1.8 Novel Reasoning Services

As argued in the introduction, standard DL reasoning services (such as satisfiability and subsumption algorithms) can be used in different phases of the ontology life cycle. In the design phase, they can test whether concepts are non-contradictory and can derive implied relations between concepts. However, for these services to be applied, one already needs a sufficiently developed TBox. The result of reasoning can then be used to develop the TBox further. Until now, however, DL systems provide no reasoning support for writing this initial TBox. The development of so-called non-standard inferences in DLs (like computing least common subsumers [36, 17, 71, 73], most specific concepts [14, 72], rewriting [18], approximation [29], and matching [24, 16, 15, 5]) tries to overcome this deficit. In the following, we will sketch how these novel inferences can support building a DL knowledge base.

Assume that the knowledge engineer wants to introduce the definition of a new concept into the TBox. In many cases, she will not develop this new definition from scratch, but rather try to re-use things that are already present in some knowledge base (either the one she is currently building or a previous one). In a chemical process engineering application [89, 78], we have observed two ways in which this is realized in practise:

1. The knowledge engineer decides on the basic structure of the newly defined concept, and then tries to find already defined concepts that have a similar structure. These concepts can then be modified to obtain the new concept.

2. Instead of directly defining the new concept, the knowledge engineer first gives examples of objects that belong to the concept to be defined, and then tries to generalize these examples into a concept definition.

Both approaches can be supported by the non-standard inferences mentioned above, though this kind of support is not yet provided by any of the existing DL systems.

The first approach can be supported by matching concept patterns against concept descriptions. A *concept pattern* is a concept description that may contain variables that stand for descriptions. A *matcher* $\sigma$ of a pattern $D$ onto the description $C$ replaces the variables by concept descriptions such that the resulting concept $\sigma(D)$ is equivalent to $C$. For example, assume that the knowledge engineer is looking for concepts concerned with individuals having a son and a daughter sharing some characteristic. This can be expressed by the pattern

$$\exists\mathsf{hasChild}.(\mathsf{Male} \sqcap X) \sqcap \exists\mathsf{hasChild}.(\mathsf{Female} \sqcap X).$$

The substitution $\sigma = \{X \mapsto \mathsf{Tall}\}$ shows that this pattern matches the description $\exists\mathsf{hasChild}.(\mathsf{Male} \sqcap \mathsf{Tall}) \sqcap \exists\mathsf{hasChild}.(\mathsf{Female} \sqcap \mathsf{Tall})$. Note, however, that in some cases the existence of a matcher is not so obvious.

The second approach can be supported by algorithms that compute most specific concepts and least common subsumers. Assume that the examples are given as ABox individuals $i_1, \ldots, i_k$. In a first step, these individuals are generalized into concepts by respectively computing the most specific (w.r.t. subsumption) concepts $C_1, \ldots, C_k$ in the available DL that have these individuals as instances. In a second step, these concepts are generalized into one concept by computing the least common subsumer of $C_1, \ldots, C_k$, i.e., the least concept description (in the available DL) that subsumes $C_1, \ldots, C_k$. In this context, rewriting of concepts comes into play since the concept descriptions produced by the algorithms for computing least common subsumers may be rather large (and thus not easy to comprehend and modify for the knowledge engineer). Rewriting minimizes the size of these description without changing their meaning by introducing names defined in the TBox.

Until now, the results on such non-standard inferences are restricted to DLs that are considerably less expressive than $\mathcal{SHIQ}$. For some of them, they only make sense if used for inexpressive DLs. For example, in DLs that contain the disjunction constructor, the least common subsumer of $C_1, \ldots, C_k$ is simply their disjunction, and computing this is of no help to the knowledge engineer. What one would like to obtain as a result of the least common subsumer computation are the structural similarities between the input concepts.

Thus, support by non-standard inferences can only be given if one uses DLs of restricted expressive power. However, this also makes sense in the context of ontology engineering. In fact, the users that will require the most support are the naive ones, and it is reasonable to assume that they will not use (or even be offered) the full expressive power of the underlying DL. This two-level approach is already present in tools like OilEd [21], which offer a frame-like user interface. Using this simple interface, one gets only a fragment of the expressive power of OIL. To use the full expressive power, one must type in DL expressions.

Another way to overcome the gap between DLs of different expressive power is to use the approximation inference [29]. Here, one tries to approximate a given concept description $C$ in an expressive DL $\mathcal{L}_1$ by a description $D$ in a less expressive DL $\mathcal{L}_2$. When approximating from above, $D$ should be the least description in $\mathcal{L}_2$ subsuming $C$, and when approximating from below, $D$ should be the greatest description $\mathcal{L}_2$ subsumed by $C$.

## 1.9 Conclusion

The emphasis in DL research on a formal, logic-based semantics and a thorough investigation of the basic reasoning problems, together with the availability of highly optimized systems for very expressive DLs, makes this family of knowledge representation formalisms an ideal starting point for defining ontology languages. The reasoning services required to support the construction, integration, and evolution of high quality ontologies are provided by state-of-the-art DL systems for very expressive languages.

To be used in practice, these languages will, however, also need DL-based tools that further support knowledge acquisition (i.e., building ontologies), maintenance (i.e., evolution of ontologies), and integration and inter-operation of ontologies. First steps in this direction have already been taken. For example, OilEd is a tool that supports the development of OIL, DAML+OIL and OWL ontologies. On a more fundamental level, non-standard inferences that support building and maintaining DL knowledge bases are now an important topic of DL research. All these efforts aim at supporting users that are not DL-experts in building and maintaining DL knowledge bases.

## References

1. Franz Baader, Diego Calvanese, Deborah McGuinness, Daniele Nardi, and Peter Patel-Schneider, editors. *The Description Logic Handbook*. Cambridge University Press, 2003.
2. Franz Baader. Terminological cycles in KL-ONE-based knowledge representation languages. In *Proc. of the 8th Nat. Conf. on Artificial Intelligence (AAAI'90)*, pages 621–626, Boston (Ma, USA), 1990.
3. Franz Baader. Augmenting concept languages by transitive closure of roles: An alternative to terminological cycles. In *Proc. of the 12th Int. Joint Conf. on Artificial Intelligence (IJCAI'91)*, 1991.
4. Franz Baader. Using automata theory for characterizing the semantics of terminological cycles. *Ann. of Mathematics and Artificial Intelligence*, 18(2–4):175–219, 1996.
5. Franz Baader, Sebastian Brandt, and Ralf Küsters. Matching under side conditions in description logics. In Bernhard Nebel, editor, *Proc. of the 17th Int. Joint Conf. on Artificial Intelligence (IJCAI 2001)*, pages 213–218, Seattle, Washington, 2001. Morgan Kaufmann.

6. Franz Baader, Martin Buchheit, and Bernhard Hollunder. Cardinality restrictions on concepts. *Artificial Intelligence*, 88(1–2):195–213, 1996.

7. Franz Baader, Hans-Jürgen Bürckert, Bernhard Hollunder, Werner Nutt, and Jörg H. Siekmann. Concept logics. In John W. Lloyd, editor, *Computational Logics, Symposium Proceedings*, pages 177–201. Springer-Verlag, 1990.

8. Franz Baader, Hans-Jürgen Bürckert, Bernhard Nebel, Werner Nutt, and Gert Smolka. On the expressivity of feature logics with negation, functional uncertainty, and sort equations. *J. of Logic, Language and Information*, 2:1–18, 1993.

9. Franz Baader, Diego Calvanese, Deborah McGuinness, Daniele Nardi, and Peter F. Patel-Schneider, editors. *The Description Logic Handbook: Theory, Implementation and Applications*. Cambridge University Press, 2002. To appear.

10. Franz Baader, Enrico Franconi, Bernhard Hollunder, Bernhard Nebel, and Hans-Jürgen Profitlich. An empirical analysis of optimization techniques for terminological representation systems or: Making KRIS get a move on. *Applied Artificial Intelligence. Special Issue on Knowledge Base Management*, 4:109–132, 1994.

11. Franz Baader and Philipp Hanschke. A schema for integrating concrete domains into concept languages. In *Proc. of the 12th Int. Joint Conf. on Artificial Intelligence (IJCAI'91)*, pages 452–457, 1991.

12. Franz Baader and Philipp Hanschke. Extensions of concept languages for a mechanical engineering application. In *Proc. of the 16th German Workshop on Artificial Intelligence (GWAI'92)*, volume 671 of *LNCS*, pages 132–143. Springer-Verlag, 1992.

13. Franz Baader and Bernhard Hollunder. A terminological knowledge representation system with complete inference algorithm. In *Proc. of the Workshop on Processing Declarative Knowledge (PDK'91)*, volume 567 of *LNAI*, pages 67–86. Springer-Verlag, 1991.

14. Franz Baader and Ralf Küsters. Computing the least common subsumer and the most specific concept in the presence of cyclic $\mathcal{ALN}$-concept descriptions. In *Proc. of the 22nd German Annual Conf. on Artificial Intelligence (KI'98)*, volume 1504 of *LNCS*, pages 129–140. Springer-Verlag, 1998.

15. Franz Baader and Ralf Küsters. Matching in description logics with existential restrictions. In *Proc. of the 7th Int. Conf. on Principles of Knowledge Representation and Reasoning (KR'2000)*, pages 261–272, 2000.

16. Franz Baader, Ralf Küsters, Alex Borgida, and Deborah L. McGuinness. Matching in description logics. *J. of Logic and Computation*, 9(3):411–447, 1999.

17. Franz Baader, Ralf Küsters, and Ralf Molitor. Computing least common subsumers in description logics with existential restrictions. In *Proc. of the 16th Int. Joint Conf. on Artificial Intelligence (IJCAI'99)*, pages 96–101, 1999.

18. Franz Baader, Ralf Küsters, and Ralf Molitor. Rewriting concepts using terminologies. In *Proc. of the 7th Int. Conf. on Principles of Knowledge Representation and Reasoning (KR'2000)*, pages 297–308, 2000.

19. Franz Baader and Ulrike Sattler. An overview of tableau algorithms for description logics. *Studia Logica*, 69(1):5–40, October 2001.

20. Andrew Baker. *Intelligent Backtracking on Constraint Satisfaction Problems: Experimental and Theoretical Results*. PhD thesis, University of Oregon, 1995.

21. Sean Bechhofer, Ian Horrocks, Carole Goble, and Robert Stevens. OilEd: a reason-able ontology editor for the semantic web. In *Proc. of the 2001 Description Logic Workshop (DL 2001)*, pages 1–9. CEUR (http://ceur-ws.org/), 2001.

22. Tim Berners-Lee. *Weaving the Web*. Harpur, San Francisco, 1999.
23. Alexander Borgida. On the relative expressiveness of description logics and predicate logics. *Artificial Intelligence*, 82(1–2):353–367, 1996.
24. Alexander Borgida and Deborah L. McGuinness. Asking queries about frames. In *Proc. of the 5th Int. Conf. on the Principles of Knowledge Representation and Reasoning (KR'96)*, pages 340–349, 1996.
25. Pim Borst, Hans Akkermans, and Jan Top. Engineering ontologies. *International Journal of Human-Computer Studies*, 46:365–406, 1997.
26. Ronald J. Brachman. "Reducing" CLASSIC to practice: Knowledge representation meets reality. In *Proc. of the 3rd Int. Conf. on the Principles of Knowledge Representation and Reasoning (KR'92)*, pages 247–258. Morgan Kaufmann, Los Altos, 1992.
27. Ronald J. Brachman and Hector J. Levesque. The tractability of subsumption in frame-based description languages. In *Proc. of the 4th Nat. Conf. on Artificial Intelligence (AAAI'84)*, pages 34–37, 1984.
28. Ronald J. Brachman and James G. Schmolze. An overview of the KL-ONE knowledge representation system. *Cognitive Science*, 9(2):171–216, 1985.
29. Sebastian Brandt, Ralf Küsters, and Anni-Yasmin Turhan. Approximation and difference in description logics. In D. Fensel, F. Giunchiglia, D. McGuiness, and M.-A. Williams, editors, *Proc. of the 8th Int. Conf. on Principles of Knowledge Representation and Reasoning (KR'2002)*, pages 203–214. Morgan Kaufmann, Los Altos, 2002.
30. Paolo Bresciani, Enrico Franconi, and Sergio Tessaris. Implementing and testing expressive description logics: Preliminary report. In *Proc. of the 1995 Description Logic Workshop (DL'95)*, pages 131–139, 1995.
31. Martin Buchheit, Francesco M. Donini, Werner Nutt, and Andrea Schaerf. A refined architecture for terminological systems: Terminology = schema + views. *Artificial Intelligence*, 99(2):209–260, 1998.
32. Martin Buchheit, Francesco M. Donini, and Andrea Schaerf. Decidable reasoning in terminological knowledge representation systems. *J. of Artificial Intelligence Research*, 1:109–138, 1993.
33. Diego Calvanese, Giuseppe De Giacomo, and Maurizio Lenzerini. On the decidability of query containment under constraints. In *Proc. of the 17th ACM SIGACT SIGMOD SIGART Symp. on Principles of Database Systems (PODS'98)*, pages 149–158, 1998.
34. Diego Calvanese, Giuseppe De Giacomo, Maurizio Lenzerini, and Daniele Nardi. Reasoning in expressive description logics. In Alan Robinson and Andrei Voronkov, editors, *Handbook of Automated Reasoning*, chapter 23, pages 1581–1634. Elsevier Science Publishers (North-Holland), Amsterdam, 2001.
35. Diego Calvanese, Giuseppe De Giacomo, Maurizio Lenzerini, Daniele Nardi, and Riccardo Rosati. Description logic framework for information integration. In *Proc. of the 6th Int. Conf. on Principles of Knowledge Representation and Reasoning (KR'98)*, pages 2–13, 1998.
36. William W. Cohen, Alex Borgida, and Haym Hirsh. Computing least common subsumers in description logics. In William Swartout, editor, *Proc. of the 10th Nat. Conf. on Artificial Intelligence (AAAI'92)*, pages 754–760. AAAI Press/The MIT Press, 1992.
37. Giuseppe De Giacomo. *Decidability of Class-Based Knowledge Representation Formalisms*. PhD thesis, Dipartimento di Informatica e Sistemistica, Università di Roma "La Sapienza", 1995.

38. Giuseppe De Giacomo and Maurizio Lenzerini. Boosting the correspondence between description logics and propositional dynamic logics. In *Proc. of the 12th Nat. Conf. on Artificial Intelligence (AAAI'94)*, pages 205–212, 1994.

39. Giuseppe De Giacomo and Maurizio Lenzerini. Concept language with number restrictions and fixpoints, and its relationship with $\mu$-calculus. In *Proc. of the 11th Eur. Conf. on Artificial Intelligence (ECAI'94)*, pages 411–415, 1994.

40. Giuseppe De Giacomo and Maurizio Lenzerini. TBox and ABox reasoning in expressive description logics. In *Proc. of the 5th Int. Conf. on the Principles of Knowledge Representation and Reasoning (KR'96)*, pages 316–327, 1996.

41. Francesco M. Donini, Bernhard Hollunder, Maurizio Lenzerini, Alberto Marchetti Spaccamela, Daniele Nardi, and Werner Nutt. The complexity of existential quantification in concept languages. *Artificial Intelligence*, 2–3:309–327, 1992.

42. Francesco M. Donini, Maurizio Lenzerini, Daniele Nardi, and Werner Nutt. The complexity of concept languages. In *Proc. of the 2nd Int. Conf. on the Principles of Knowledge Representation and Reasoning (KR'91)*, pages 151–162, 1991.

43. Francesco M. Donini, Maurizio Lenzerini, Daniele Nardi, and Werner Nutt. Tractable concept languages. In *Proc. of the 12th Int. Joint Conf. on Artificial Intelligence (IJCAI'91)*, pages 458–463, 1991.

44. Jon Doyle and Ramesh S. Patil. Two theses of knowledge representation: Language restrictions, taxonomic classification, and the utility of representation services. *Artificial Intelligence*, 48:261–297, 1991.

45. D. Fensel, F. van Harmelen, M. Klein, H. Akkermans, J. Broekstra, C. Fluit, J. van der Meer, H.-P. Schnurr, R. Studer, J. Hughes, U. Krohn, J. Davies, R. Engels, B. Bremdal, F. Ygge, T. Lau, B. Novotny, U. Reimer, and I. Horrocks. On-To-Knowledge: Ontology-based tools for knowledge management. In *Proceedings of the eBusiness and eWork 2000 (eBeW'00 Conference*, October 2000.

46. Dieter Fensel, Frank van Harmelen, Ian Horrocks, Deborah L. McGuinness, and Peter F. Patel-Schneider. OIL: An ontology infrastructure for the semantic web. *IEEE Intelligent Systems*, 16(2):38–45, 2001.

47. Michael J. Fischer and Richard E. Ladner. Propositional dynamic logic of regular programs. *J. of Computer and System Sciences*, 18:194–211, 1979.

48. Erich Grädel. Guarded fragments of first-order logic: A perspective for new description logics? In *Proc. of the 1998 Description Logic Workshop (DL'98)*. CEUR Electronic Workshop Proceedings, http://ceur-ws.org/Vol-11/, 1998.

49. Erich Grädel. On the restraining power of guards. *J. of Symbolic Logic*, 64:1719–1742, 1999.

50. Erich Grädel, Phokion G. Kolaitis, and Moshe Y. Vardi. On the decision problem for two-variable first-order logic. *Bulletin of Symbolic Logic*, 3(1):53–69, 1997.

51. Erich Grädel, Martin Otto, and Eric Rosen. Two-variable logic with counting is decidable. In *Proc. of the 12th IEEE Symp. on Logic in Computer Science (LICS'97)*, 1997.

52. Thomas Gruber. A translation approach to portable ontology specifications. *Knowledge Acquisition*, 5(2):199–220, 1993.

53. Volker Haarslev and Ralf Möller. RACE system description. In *Proc. of the 1999 Description Logic Workshop (DL'99)*, pages 130–132. CEUR Electronic Workshop Proceedings, http://ceur-ws.org/Vol-22/, 1999.

54. Volker Haarslev and Ralf Möller. Expressive ABox reasoning with number restrictions, role hierarchies, and transitively closed roles. In *Proc. of the 7th Int. Conf. on Principles of Knowledge Representation and Reasoning (KR'2000)*, pages 273–284, 2000.
55. Volker Haarslev and Ralf Möller. RACER system description. In *Proc. of the Int. Joint Conf. on Automated Reasoning (IJCAR 2001)*, volume 2083 of *LNAI*, pages 701–705. Springer-Verlag, 2001.
56. Joseph Y. Halpern and Yoram Moses. A guide to completeness and complexity for modal logics of knowledge and belief. *Artificial Intelligence*, 54:319–379, 1992.
57. Patrick Hayes. RDF model theory. W3C Working Draft, April 2002. `http://www.w3.org/TR/rdf-mt/`.
58. Jochen Heinsohn, Daniel Kudenko, Bernhard Nebel, and Hans-Jürgen Profitlich. An empirical analysis of terminological representation systems. *Artificial Intelligence*, 68:367–397, 1994.
59. Bernhard Hollunder and Franz Baader. Qualifying number restrictions in concept languages. In *Proc. of the 2nd Int. Conf. on the Principles of Knowledge Representation and Reasoning (KR'91)*, pages 335–346, 1991.
60. Bernhard Hollunder, Werner Nutt, and Manfred Schmidt-Schauß. Subsumption algorithms for concept description languages. In *Proc. of the 9th Eur. Conf. on Artificial Intelligence (ECAI'90)*, pages 348–353, London (United Kingdom), 1990. Pitman.
61. Ian Horrocks. The FaCT system. In Harrie de Swart, editor, *Proc. of the 2nd Int. Conf. on Analytic Tableaux and Related Methods (TABLEAUX'98)*, volume 1397 of *LNAI*, pages 307–312. Springer-Verlag, 1998.
62. Ian Horrocks. Using an expressive description logic: FaCT or fiction? In *Proc. of the 6th Int. Conf. on Principles of Knowledge Representation and Reasoning (KR'98)*, pages 636–647, 1998.
63. Ian Horrocks and Peter Patel-Schneider. The generation of DAML+OIL. In *Proc. of the 2001 Description Logic Workshop (DL 2001)*, pages 30–35. CEUR (`http://ceur-ws.org/`), 2001.
64. Ian Horrocks and Peter F. Patel-Schneider. Optimizing description logic subsumption. *J. of Logic and Computation*, 9(3):267–293, 1999.
65. Ian Horrocks, Peter F. Patel-Schneider, and Frank van Harmelen. Reviewing the design of DAML+OIL: An ontology language for the semantic web. In *Proc. of the 19th Nat. Conf. on Artificial Intelligence (AAAI 2002)*, 2002.
66. Ian Horrocks and Ulrike Sattler. A description logic with transitive and inverse roles and role hierarchies. *J. of Logic and Computation*, 9(3):385–410, 1999.
67. Ian Horrocks, Ulrike Sattler, and Stephan Tobies. Practical reasoning for expressive description logics. In Harald Ganzinger, David McAllester, and Andrei Voronkov, editors, *Proc. of the 6th Int. Conf. on Logic for Programming and Automated Reasoning (LPAR'99)*, volume 1705 in *LNAI*, pages 161–180. Springer-Verlag, 1999.
68. Ian Horrocks, Ulrike Sattler, and Stephan Tobies. Practical reasoning for very expressive description logics. *J. of the Interest Group in Pure and Applied Logic*, 8(3):239–264, 2000.
69. Ian Horrocks, Ulrike Sattler, and Stephan Tobies. Reasoning with individuals for the description logic $\mathcal{SHIQ}$. In David McAllester, editor, *Proc. of the 17th Int. Conf. on Automated Deduction (CADE 2000)*, volume 1831 of *LNCS*, pages 482–496. Springer-Verlag, 2000.

70. Ian Horrocks and Stephan Tobies. Reasoning with axioms: Theory and practice. In *Proc. of the 7th Int. Conf. on Principles of Knowledge Representation and Reasoning (KR'2000)*, pages 285–296, 2000.

71. Ralf Küsters and Alex Borgida. What's in an Attribute? Consequences for the Least Common Subsumer. *J. of Artificial Intelligence Research*, 14:167–203, 2001.

72. Ralf Küsters and Ralf Molitor. Approximating Most Specific Concepts in Description Logics with Existential Restrictions. In F. Baader, editor, *Proc. of the Joint German/Austrian Conference on Artificial Intelligence, 24th German / 9th Austrian Conference on Artificial Intelligence (KI 2001)*, volume 2174 of *LNAI*. Springer-Verlag, 2001.

73. Ralf Küsters and Ralf Molitor. Computing Least Common Subsumers in ALEN. In Bernard Nebel, editor, *Proc. of the 17th Int. Joint Conf. on Artificial Intelligence (IJCAI 2001)*, pages 219–224. Morgan Kaufmann, Los Altos, 2001.

74. Carsten Lutz. Description logics with concrete domains—a survey. In *Advances in Modal Logics Volume 4*. World Scientific Publishing Co. Pte. Ltd., 2003.

75. Carsten Lutz. NEXPTIME-complete description logics with concrete domains. In *Proc. of the Int. Joint Conf. on Automated Reasoning (IJCAR 2001)*, volume 2083 of *LNAI*, pages 45–60. Springer-Verlag, 2001.

76. Robert MacGregor. The evolving technology of classification-based knowledge representation systems. In John F. Sowa, editor, *Principles of Semantic Networks*, pages 385–400. Morgan Kaufmann, Los Altos, 1991.

77. Eric Mays, Robert Dionne, and Robert Weida. K-Rep system overview. *SIGART Bull.*, 2(3):93–97, 1991.

78. Ralf Molitor. *Unterstützung der Modellierung verfahrenstechnischer Prozesse durch Nicht-Standardinferenzen in Beschreibungslogiken*. PhD thesis, LuFG Theoretical Computer Science, RWTH-Aachen, Germany, 2000. In German.

79. Bernhard Nebel. *Reasoning and Revision in Hybrid Representation Systems*, volume 422 of *LNAI*. Springer-Verlag, 1990.

80. Bernhard Nebel. Terminological reasoning is inherently intractable. *Artificial Intelligence*, 43:235–249, 1990.

81. Bernhard Nebel. Terminological cycles: Semantics and computational properties. In John F. Sowa, editor, *Principles of Semantic Networks*, pages 331–361. Morgan Kaufmann, Los Altos, 1991.

82. Franz Oppacher and E. Suen. HARP: A tableau-based theorem prover. *J. of Automated Reasoning*, 4:69–100, 1988.

83. Leszek Pacholski, Wieslaw Szwast, and Lidia Tendera. Complexity of two-variable logic with counting. In *Proc. of the 12th IEEE Symp. on Logic in Computer Science (LICS'97)*, pages 318–327. IEEE Computer Society Press, 1997.

84. Jeff Z. Pan and Ian Horrocks. Semantic web ontology reasoning in the $\mathcal{SHOQ}(\mathbf{D_n})$ description logic. In *Proc. of the 2002 Description Logic Workshop (DL 2002)*, 2002.

85. Peter F. Patel-Schneider. DLP. In *Proc. of the 1999 Description Logic Workshop (DL'99)*, pages 9–13. CEUR Electronic Workshop Proceedings, `http://ceur-ws.org/Vol-22/`, 1999.

86. Peter F. Patel-Schneider, Deborah L. McGuiness, Ronald J. Brachman, Lori Alperin Resnick, and Alexander Borgida. The CLASSIC knowledge representation system: Guiding principles and implementation rational. *SIGART Bull.*, 2(3):108–113, 1991.

87. Christof Peltason. The BACK system — an overview. *SIGART Bull.*, 2(3):114–119, 1991.
88. Ulrike Sattler. A concept language extended with different kinds of transitive roles. In Günter Görz and Steffen Hölldobler, editors, *Proc. of the 20th German Annual Conf. on Artificial Intelligence (KI'96)*, volume 1137 in *LNAI*, pages 333–345. Springer-Verlag, 1996.
89. Ulrike Sattler. *Terminological knowledge representation systems in a process engineering application.* PhD thesis, RWTH Aachen, 1998.
90. Ulrike Sattler. Description logics for the representation of aggregated objects. In *Proc. of the 14th Eur. Conf. on Artificial Intelligence (ECAI 2000)*, 2000.
91. Andrea Schaerf. Reasoning with individuals in concept languages. *Data and Knowledge Engineering*, 13(2):141–176, 1994.
92. Klaus Schild. A correspondence theory for terminological logics: Preliminary report. In *Proc. of the 12th Int. Joint Conf. on Artificial Intelligence (IJCAI'91)*, pages 466–471, 1991.
93. Klaus Schild. *Querying Knowledge and Data Bases by a Universal Description Logic with Recursion.* PhD thesis, Universität des Saarlandes, Germany, 1995.
94. Manfred Schmidt-Schauß and Gert Smolka. Attributive concept descriptions with complements. *Artificial Intelligence*, 48(1):1–26, 1991.
95. Piet-Hein Speel, Frank van Raalte, Paul van der Vet, and Nicolas Mars. Runtime and memory usage performance of description logics. In G. Ellis, R. A. Levinson, A. Fall, and V. Dahl, editors, *Knowledge Retrieval, Use and Storage for Efficiency: Proc. of the 1st Int. KRUSE Symposium*, pages 13–27, 1995.
96. Robert Stevens, Ian Horrocks, Carole Goble, and Sean Bechhofer. Building a reason-able bioinformatics ontology using OIL. In *Proceedings of the IJCAI-2001 Workshop on Ontologies and Information Sharing*, pages 81–90. CEUR (http://ceur-ws.org/), 2001.
97. Stephan Tobies. *Complexity Results and Practical Algorithms for Logics in Knowledge Representation.* PhD thesis, RWTH Aachen, 2001.
98. Wiebe Van der Hoek and Maarten de Rijke. Counting objects. *J. of Logic and Computation*, 5(3):325–345, 1995.

# 2

# Ontologies in F-logic

Jürgen Angele[1] and Georg Lausen[2]

[1]Ontoprise GmbH
Amalienbadstraße 36
D-76227 Karlsruhe
angele@ontoprise.de

[2]Universität Freiburg
D-79098 Freiburg
lausen@informatik.uni-freiburg.de

**Summary.** F-logic ("F" stands for "Frames") combines the advantages of conceptual high-level approaches typical for frame-based languages and the expressiveness, the compact syntax, and the well defined semantics from logics. The salient features of F-logic include signatures, object identity, complex objects, methods, classes, inheritance and rules. We give an overview of the syntax and the intuitive semantics of F-logic. We discuss the semantics behind and the different ways how F-logic has been implemented. The language primitives are further demonstrated by discussing a real world application resulting in the ontology based configuration tool *OnKo* developed for the German Telecom.

## 2.1 Introduction

Conceptual (or Ontology) modelling deals with the question of how to describe in a declarative and abstract way the domain information of an application, its relevant vocabulary, and how to constrain the use of the data, by understanding what can be drawn from it. Corresponding abstract representation languages support the understanding of such descriptions, their rapid development, their maintenance and their reuse.

Conceptual modelling has a long history in the area of database systems, starting with the Entity/Relationship(ER) model [Che76]. Entitytypes represent sets of homogeneous entities by specifying attributes and their range. Entitytypes are instantiated by concrete entities with individual values for the attributes.

Relationshiptypes specify the domain and range of relations between entities. Relationshiptypes are instantiated by concrete relations between entities. By this way a simple schema (or ontology) for a relational databases may be given. Later on, this restricted set of concepts has been extended to the EER model (Extended Entity Relationship) [RES94] by adding modelling primitives like specialisation, grouping etc. in a similar way to modelling languages like UML and ODMG which have been developed for object-oriented models in the context of software engineering.

From the beginning, for database systems languages have been developed which allow to express complex relationships (constraints) between entities/objects and to query the database. For efficiency reasons traditional database query languages (relational algebra and calculus, SQL) have a rather limited expressiveness. However, when database systems approached knowledge-based applications, rule-base languages became attractive. Datalog [AHV95] is the most famous language paradigm in this context. Datalog has a model-theoretic semantics and introduced general recursion while still allowing powerful optimization techniques. However, Datalog is a logical rule language without function symbols and restricted negation and thus still has a limited expressive power. In particular, when object-oriented database systems became popular, function symbols became mandatory because of their ability to give object identities a logical semantics. From a logical point of view, these languages are variants of Horn-Logics with function symbols and negation in the rule bodies. In this paper we will elaborate on F-logic [KLW95], which accounts in a clean and declarative fashion for most of the structural aspects of frame-based and object-oriented languages. A general overview of languages in this context is given in [L99]. Similar languages have also been introduced for semi-structured, respective XML-databases (e.g. [GPQ97], [M01]).

F-logic ("F" stands for "Frames") combines the advantages of the conceptual high-level approach typical for frame-based languages and the expressiveness, the compact syntax, and the well defined semantics from logics. The original features of F-logic [KLW95] include signatures, object identity, complex objects, methods, classes and inheritance. Implementations of F-logic (Florid [LHL98], Ontobroker [DEFS99], Flora [YK00]) introduced extensions and restrictions of the original features to make F-logic a powerful and efficient language for the respective intended application domain.

In this paper we will look on F-logic as a language for ontology applications. In the following we first give an overview of the syntax and the intuitive semantics of F-logic by concentrating on examples which allow the presentation of the various concepts in a concise way. It follows a discussion of the semantics and the different ways how F-logic has been implemented. Finally we present an example of an ontology application based on F-logic. This example is based on OntoBroker™, an implementation of F-logic specific for the ontology domain.

## 2.2 F-logic by Examples

Now we are going to give an introduction into F-logic by examples, which will introduce the various syntax elements and their intuitive semantics. F-logic's syntax in its original form has been extended to comply to the specific needs of its practical applications.

### 2.2.1 A Simple Ontology-based Application

F-logic allows to describe ontologies, i.e. classes of objects, hierarchies of classes, their attributes and relationships between classes in an object-oriented style (cf. [FHK97]).

```
/* ontology */

woman::person.
man::person.
person[father=>man].
person[mother=>woman].
person[daughter=>>woman].
person[son=>>man].

/* rules consisting of a rule head and a rule body */
FORALL X,Y X[son->>Y] <- Y:man[father->X].
FORALL X,Y X[son->>Y] <- Y:man[mother->X].
FORALL X,Y X[daughter->>Y] <- Y:woman[father->X].
FORALL X,Y X[daughter->>Y] <- Y:woman[mother->X].

/* facts */
abraham:man.
sarah:woman.
isaac:man[father->abraham; mother->sarah].
ishmael:man[father->abraham; mother->hagar:woman].
jacob:man[father->isaac; mother->rebekah:woman].
esau:man[father->isaac; mother->rebekah].


/* query */
FORALL X,Y <- X:woman[son->>Y[father->abraham]].
```
(1)

The first part of this example consists of a very simple and small ontology. It is stated that every woman is a person, every man is a person. For a person the attributes father, mother, daughter together with their respective ranges are given. The following set of rules states what else can be derived from the ontology.

The first rule describes that if X is the father of Y and Y is a man, then Y is the son of X. A similar relationship holds for sons and mothers, for daughters and fathers and daughters and mothers. The given set of facts instantiates the concepts introduced so far. They indicate that some people belong to the classes man and woman, respectively, and give information about the father and mother relationships among them. According to the object-oriented paradigm, relationships between objects are modelled by method applications, e.g., applying the method father to the object isaac yields the result object abraham. All these facts may be considered as the extensional database of the F-logic program. Hence, they form the basis of an object base which still has to be completed by some closure properties, e.g. inheritance. The rules derive new information from the given object base. By evaluating the set of rules, new relationships between the objects, denoted by the methods son and daughter, are added to the object base as intensional information.

The final part of Example 1 contains a query to the object base. The query shows the ability of F-logic to nest method applications. It asks for all women and their sons, whose father is Abraham. The same query could be written as a conjunction of atomic expressions:

FORALL X,Y <- X:woman AND X[son->>Y] AND Y[father->abraham].

Methods may either be single-valued (->), i.e. can have one value only or they may be multi-valued (->>), i.e. can have more values. If more values are given for multi-valued attributes the values must be enclosed in curly brackets:

## 2.2.2 Objects and Their Properties

As we have already seen in Example 1 objects are the basic constructs of F-logic. Objects model real world entities and are internally represented by object identifiers which are independent of their properties. According to the principles of object-oriented systems these object identifiers are invisible to the user. To access an object directly the user has to know its object name. Every object name refers to exactly one object. Following the object-oriented paradigm, objects may be organized in classes. Furthermore, methods represent relationships between objects. Such information about objects is expressed by *F-atoms*.

### 2.2.2.1 Object Names and Variable Names

Object names and variable names are also called *id-terms* and are the basic syntactical elements of F-logic. To distinguish object names from variable names, the later are always declared using logical quantifiers FORALL and EXISTS.

Object names start with a lower case letter while, as usual, variables are indicated by a capital first letter. Examples of object names are abraham, man, daughter, of variable names X, or Method. There are two special types of object names that carry additional information: integers and strings. Every positive or negative integer may be used as an object name, e.g., +3, 3, -3, as well as every string enclosed by quotation marks "". *Complex id-terms* may be created from function symbols and other id-terms, e.g., couple(abraham, sarah), f(X). An id-term that contains no variable is called a *ground id-term*.

### 2.2.2.2 Methods

In F-logic, the application of a method to an object is expressed by *data-F-atoms* which consist of a host object, a method and a result object, all denoted by id-terms. Any object may appear in any of these locations: host object, result position, or method position. Thus, in our Example 1 the method names father and son are object names just like isaac and abraham. Variables may also be used be used at all positions of a data-F-atom, which allows queries about method names like

> FORALL X,Y <- isaac[X->>Y].
> jacob[son->>{reuben, simeon, levi, judah, issachar, zebulun}].

Sometimes the result of the invocation of a method on a host object depends on other objects, too. For example, Jacob's sons are born by different women. To express this, the method son is extended by a parameter denoting the corresponding mother of each of Jacob's sons. Like methods, parameters are objects as well, denoted by id-terms. Syntactically a parameter list is always included in parentheses and separated by "@" from the method object.

> jacob[son@(leah)->>
>         {reuben, simeon, levi, judah, issachar, zebulun};
> son@(rachel)->>{joseph, benjamin};
> son@(zilpah)->>{gad, asher};
> son@(bilhah)->>{dan, naphtali}].           (2)

The syntax extends straightforwardly to methods with more than one parameter. If we additionally want to specify the order in which the sons of Jacob were born, we need two parameters which are separated by commata:

> jacob[son@(leah,1)->>reuben; son@(leah,2)->>simeon;
> son@(leah,3)->>levi; son@(leah,4)->>judah;
> son@(bilhah,5)->>dan; son@(bilhah,6)->>naphtali;
> son@(zilpah,7)->>gad; son@(zilpah,8)->>asher;
> son@(leah,9)->>issachar; son@(leah,10)->>zebulun;
> son@(rachel,11)->>joseph; son@(rachel,12)->>benjamin].    (3)

In Examples 2 and 3 the method son is used with a different number of parameters. This so-called overloading is supported by F-logic. Given the object base described in Example 1, asking for the sons of Isaac

> FORALL X <- isaac[son->>X].

yields all his known sons:

> X = jacob
> X = esau

Note that variables in a query may only be bound to individual objects, never to sets of objects, i.e., the above query does not return X = {jacob,esau}. As a consequence, with respect to the object base above, all the following queries yield the answer true.

> <-isaac[son->>{jacob, esau}].
> <-isaac[son->>jacob].
> <-isaac[son->>esau].

If we want to know if a set of objects is the exact result of a multi-valued method applied to a certain object, we have to use negation (see Example 21).

### 2.2.2.3 Class Membership and Subclass Relationship

*Isa-F-atoms* state that an object belongs to a class, *subclass-F-atoms* express the subclass relationship between two classes. Class membership and the subclass relation are denoted by a single colon and a double colon, respectively. In the following example the first three isa-F-atoms express that Abraham and Isaac are members of the class man, whereas Sarah is a member of the class woman. Furthermore, two subclass-F-atoms state that both classes man and woman are subclasses of the class person:

> abraham:man.
> isaac:man.
> sarah:woman.
> woman::person.
> man::person.                                                    (4)

In isa-F-atoms and subclass-F-atoms, the objects and the classes are also denoted by id- terms because, in F-logic, classes are objects as well as methods are objects. Hence, classes may have methods defined on them and may be instances of other classes which serve as a kind of metaclass. Furthermore, variables are permitted at all positions in an isa- or subclass-F-atom. In contrast to other object-oriented languages where every object is an instance of exactly one most specific class (e.g., ROL [L99]), F-logic permits that an object is an instance of several classes that are incomparable by the subclass relationship. Analogously, a class may have several incomparable direct superclasses. Thus, the subclass relationship specifies a partial order on the set of classes, so that the class hierarchy may be considered as a directed acyclic (but not reflexive) graph with the classes as its nodes.

## 2.2.2.4 Expressing Information about an Object: F-Molecules

Instead of giving several individual atoms, information about an object can be collected in *F-molecules*. For example, the following F-molecule denotes that Isaac is a man whose father is Abraham and Jacob and Esau are amongst his sons.

isaac:man[father->abraham; son->>{jacob,esau}].                    (5)

This F-molecule may be split into an equivalent set of several F-atoms:

isaac:man.
isaac[father->abraham].
isaac[son->>jacob].
isaac[son->>esau].

For F-molecules containing a multi-valued method, the set of result objects can be split into singleton sets (recall that our semantics is multivalued, not set-valued). For singleton sets, it is allowed to omit the curly braces enclosing the result set, so that the three subsequent sets are equivalent, which means that they represent the same object base:

isaac[son->>{jacob,esau}].                                         (6)

isaac[son->>{jacob}].
isaac[son->>{esau}].                                               (7)

isaac[son->>jacob].
isaac[son->>esau].                                                 (8)

## 2.2.2.5 Signatures

*Signature-F-atoms* define which methods are applicable for the instances of certain classes. In particular, a signature-F-atom declares a method on a class and gives type restrictions for parameters and results. These restrictions may be viewed as typing constraints. Signature-F-atoms together with the class hierarchy form the schema of an F-logic database. To distinguish signature-F-atoms from data-F-atoms, the arrow body consists of a double line instead of a single line. Here are some examples for signature-F-atoms:

person[father=>man].
person[daughter=>>woman].
man[son@(woman)=>>man].

The first one states that the single-valued method father is defined for members of the class person and the corresponding result object has to belong to the class man. The second one defines the multi-valued method daughter for members of the class person restricting the result objects to the class woman. Finally, the third signature-F-atom allows the application of the multi-valued method son to objects belonging to the class man with parameter objects that are members of the class woman. The result objects of such method applications have to be instances of the class man. By using a list of result classes enclosed by parentheses, several signature-F-atoms may be combined in an F-molecule. This is equivalent to the conjunction of the atoms: the result of the method is required to be in all of those classes:

$$person[father=>\{man, person\}]. \qquad (9)$$

$$person[father=>man].$$
$$person[father=>person]. \qquad (10)$$

Both expressions in the Examples 9 and 10 are equivalent and express that the result objects of the method father if applied to an instance of the class person have to belong to both classes man and person.

F-logic supports method overloading. This means that methods denoted by the same object name may be applied to instances of different classes. Methods may even be overloaded according to their arity, i.e., number of parameters. For example, the method son applicable to instances of the class man is used as a method with one parameter in Example 11 and as a method with two parameters in Example 12. The corresponding signature-F-atoms look like this:

$$man[son@(woman)=>>man]. \qquad (11)$$

$$man[son@(woman,integer)=>>man]. \qquad (12)$$

Of course, the result of a signature needs not to be enclosed in parentheses, if it consists of just one object.

As already shown in Example 5, properties of an object may be collected into a single, complex F-molecule instead of several F-atoms. For that purpose, a class membership or subclass relationship may follow after the host object. Then, a list of method applications (with or without parameters) separated by semicolons, may be given. If a method yields more than one result, those can be collected in curly braces, separated by commas; if a signature contains more than one class, those can be collected in parentheses, also separated by commas:

$$isaac[father->abraham; mother->sarah].$$
$$jacob:man[father->isaac; son@(rachel)->>\{joseph, benjamin\}].$$
$$man::person[son@(woman)=>>\{man, person\}]. \qquad (13)$$

This means that the range of the son method is the conjunction of man and person, i.e. values of this method must belong to class man and class person.

The following set of F-atoms is equivalent to the F-molecules above:

$$isaac[father->abraham].$$
$$isaac[mother->sarah].$$

```
jacob:man.
jacob[father->isaac].
jacob[son@(rachel)->>joseph].
jacob[son@(rachel)->>benjamin].
man::person.
man[son@(woman)=>> man].
man[son@(woman)=>>person].
```
                                                                    (14)

Besides collecting the properties of the host object, the properties of other objects appearing in an F-molecule, e.g., method applications, may be inserted, too. Thus, a molecule may not only represent the properties of one single object but can also include nested information about different objects, even recursively:

```
isaac[father->abraham:man[son@(hagar:woman)->>ishmael];
        mother->sarah:woman].
jacob:(man::person).
jacob[(father:method)->isaac].
```
                                                                    (15)

The equivalent set of F-atoms is:

```
isaac[father->abraham].
abraham:man.
abraham[son@(hagar)->>ishmael].
hagar:woman.
isaac[mother->>sarah].
sarah:woman.
man::person.
jacob:man.
jacob[father->isaac].
father:method.
```

F-logic molecules are evaluated from left to right. Thus, nested properties have to be included in parentheses if those properties belong to a method object (cf. Section 7), class object or superclass object. Note the difference between the following two F-molecules. The first one states that Isaac is a man and Isaac believes in god, whereas the second one says that Isaac is a man and that the object man believes in god (which is probably not the intended meaning).

```
isaac:man[believesin->>god].
isaac:(man[believesin->>god]).
```

### 2.2.2.6 F-molecules Without any Properties

If we want to represent an object without giving any properties, we have to attach an empty method-specification list to the object name, e.g.

```
thing[].
```

If we use an expression like this that consists solely of an object name as a molecule, it is treated as a 0-ary predicate symbol (see next section).

### 2.2.2.7 Predicate Symbols

In F-logic, predicate symbols are used in the same way as in predicate logic, e.g., in Datalog, thus preserving upward-compatibility from Datalog to F-logic. A predicate symbol followed by one or more id-terms separated by commas and included in parentheses is called a *P-atom* to distinguish it from F-atoms. Example 16 shows some P-atoms. The last P-atom consists solely of a 0-ary predicate symbol, where parentheses are ommitted.

>     married(isaac,rebekah).
>     male(jacob).
>     sonof(isaac,rebekah,jacob).
>     true.                                                      (16)

Information expressed by P-atoms can usually also be represented by F-atoms, thus obtaining a more natural style of modelling. For example, the information given in the first three P- atoms can also be expressed as follows:

>     isaac[marriedto->>rebekah].
>     jacob:man.
>     isaac[son@(rebekah)->>jacob].                              (17)

Similar to F-molecules, *P-molecules* may be built by nesting F-atoms or F-molecules into P-atoms. The P-molecule

>     married(isaac[father->abraham], rebekah:woman).

is equivalent to the following set of P-atoms and F-atoms:

>     married(isaac,rebekah).
>     isaac[father->abraham].
>     rebekah:woman.

Note, that only F-atoms and F-molecules may be nested into P-atoms, but not vice versa.

### 2.2.3 Built-in Features

#### 2.2.3.1 Built-in Operations

As an extension to the original F-logic, Florid[LHL98] and OntoBroker™ provide a large amount of built-ins. These include built-ins to compare strings and numbers, arithmetic built-ins and String built-ins. More complex built-ins in Ontobroker provide solving linear equations, vector arithmetics, matrix operations or regular expressions. Example 18 shows some examples.

> FORALL X,A,B,C,Z1,Z2,Z3 <-
> jacob[son@(X,A)->>Z1; son@(X,B)->>Z2; son@(X,C)->>Z3] AND
> (B is A+1) AND
> (C is A+2).
>
> FORALL X,Y,Z <- jacob[son@(X,Y)->>Z] AND less(Y,4).
> FORALL X <- married(X) and regexp("[pt]",X,Y).                  (18)

#### 2.2.3.2 Access to External Information Sources

Built-ins are also used to access external information sources. These include text indexers, data bases, web search engines and other various applications.

E.g. Microsofts index server may be used to search for documents. The following rule

> FORALL X,Y <-
> msindex("contains(\"car\"") and contains(\"motor\"")",X,Y)

delivers the paths of all files containing "car" and "motor".

In a similar way OntoBroker™ supports the access to the usual commercial JDBC databases.

### 2.2.4 Path Expressions

Objects may be accessed directly by their object names. On the other hand it is also possible to navigate to them by applying a method to another object using path expressions. For example, the object described by the object name abraham may also be accessed by calling the method father on the object isaac. The corresponding constructs are called *path expressions* and have been introduced by the Florid-implementation of F-logic. A simple example of a path expression is: isaac.father. Example 19 shows that path expressions may also contain multi-valued methods and methods with parameters and that it is possible to chain up path expressions by successively applying methods to the result object of the preceding method call. With respect to the underlying object base in Examples 1 and 2 we get:

| | | |
|---|---|---|
| isaac..son | | {jacob, esau} |
| jacob..son@(rachel,11) | joseph | |
| benjamin.father.father.mother | sarah | (19) |

### 2.2.4.1 Path Expressions in Queries

Path expressions in a rule body or query help the user to describe the information in question more concisely, avoiding auxiliary variables for intermediate results. If for example the grandfather of Isaac is requested, this query can be written as

> FORALL X <- isaac.father[father->X].

instead of

> FORALL X,Y <- isaac[father->Y] AND Y[father->X].

Path expressions may be eliminated from F-molecules in rule bodies or queries by decomposing the molecules into a set of F-atoms using new variables for the result values.

### 2.2.5 Rules and Queries

### 2.2.5.1 Rules

Based upon a given object base (which, in fact, can be considered as a set a facts), rules offer the possibility to derive new information, i.e., to extend the object base by intensional information. Rules encode generic information of the form: Whenever the precondition is satisfied, the conclusion also is. The precondition is called *rule body* and is formed by a conjunction of molecules. In addition to original F-logic a rule-body in OntoBroker™ allows an arbitrary logical formula consisting of P- or F-molecules, which are combined by OR, NOT, AND, <-, -> and <->. A -> B in the body is an abbreviation for NOT A OR B, A <- B is an abbreviation for NOT B OR A and <-> is an abbreviation for (A->B) AND (B<-A). Variables in the rule body may be quantified either existentially or universally. The conclusion, the *rule head*, is a conjunction of P- and F-molecules. Syntactically the rule head is separated from the rule body by the symbol <- and every rule ends with a dot. Non-ground rules use variables for passing information between subgoals and the head. Every variable in the head of the rule must also occur in a positive F-atom in the body of the rule. Assume an object base defining the methods father and mother for some persons, e.g., the set of facts given in Example 1. The rules in Example 20   define the transitive closure of these methods as the result of a new method ancestor:

> FORALL X,Y X[ancestor->>Y] <- X[father->Y].
> FORALL X,Y X[ancestor->>Y] <- X[mother->Y].
> FORALL X,Y,Z X[ancestor->>Y] <- X[father->Z] AND Z[ancestor->>Y].
> FORALL X,Y,Z X[ancestor->>Y] <- X[mother->Z] AND Z[ancestor->>Y].

$$(20)$$

Logical formulae in the rule body may be negated. E.g. the following rule computes for every person X all persons Y not related to X :

> FORALL X,Y
> X[notrelated->>Y] <-
>     X:person AND
>     Y:person AND
>     NOT X[ancestor->>Y] AND
>     NOT Y[ancestor->>X].

$$(21)$$

In this example stratified semantics of negation is sufficient; however in general, F-logic programs require more expressive forms of negation as, for example, the well-founded semantics   [GRS91. A discussion of these various forms of negation is beyond the scope of this paper. The interested reader is referred to [AHV95]. In well-founded semantics not all possible models are considered but one "most obvious" model is selected as the semantics of a set of rules and facts. It is a three valued logic, i.e. the model consists of a set of true facts and a set of unknown facts and a set of facts known to be false. In contrast to the stratified semantics the well-founded semantics is also applicable for rules which depend on each other in a cyclic way, where the cycle may be implied  through negative rule bodies.

### 2.2.5.2 Queries

A query can be considered as a special kind of rule with empty head. The following query asks about all female ancestors of Jacob:

> FORALL Y <- jacob[ancestor->>Y:woman].                (22)

The answer to a query consists of all variable bindings such that the corresponding ground instance of the rule body is true in the object base. Considering the object base described by the facts of Example 1 and the rules in Example 20, the query  yields the following variable bindings:

> Y = rebekah
> Y = sarah

The following query computes the maximum value X for which p(X) holds. The rule body expresses that all Y for which p(Y) holds must be less or equal to the searched X.

    p(1).
    p(2).
    p(3).
    FORALL X <- p(X) AND FORALL Y (p(Y) -> lessorequal(Y,X)).

## 2.2.6 Name Spaces

Without namespaces in F-logic the names in different ontologies could not be distinguished from each other. For instance, a concept named "person" in ontology "car" is the same concept as the concept "person" in ontology "finance". Handling more than one ontology thus needs a mechanism to distinguish these concepts. This is the reason why Ontobroker has extended F-logic by namespaces.

### 2.2.6.1 Declaring Namespaces

The namespace mechanism of F-logic is similar to that of XML. Similar to XML-namespaces, namespaces and their associate aliases may appear anywhere where a rule or query is allowed. The namespace declaration contains the XML-Element <ns> with a number of XML-attributes with the prefix "ontons". The scope of declared namespaces ends when the corresponding end-element </ns> is reached in the program, e.g.

    <ns     ontons:cars="www.cars-r-us.tv"
            ontons:finance="www.financeWorld.tv"
            ontons="www.myDomain.tv/private">

    //Here the aliases "cars" and "finance" can be used.
    <ns     . . .>
            // Here inner aliases can be used.
            // Outer aliases are also visible if not redefined.
    </ns>

    </ns>                                                              (23)

In the example three namespaces are declared. Each namespace must represent a valid URI according to RFC 2396 and can optionally be associated with an alias. The namespaces *www.cars-r-us.tv* and *www.financeWorld.tv* are associated with the aliases "cars" and "finance", respectively. The third namespace is not associated with an alias and thus, represents the default namespace.

As in XML these namespace declarations can be arbitrarily nested and aliases may be temporarily associated with other URIs by inner namespace declarations.

### 2.2.6.2 Using Namespaces in F-logic Expressions

In F-logic expressions every concept, method, object, function, and predicate may be qualified by a namespace. To separate the namespace from the name the "#"-sign is used (as conventionally used in the RDF world and in HTML to locate local links inside a web page). The following examples use the name space declaration of Example 23:

```
cars#Car[      cars#driver => cars#Person;
               cars#passenger =>> cars#Person;
               cars#seats => NUMBER].
cars#Person[cars#name => STRING;
               cars#age => NUMBER;
               cars#drivingLicenseId => STRING].

finance#Bank[finance#customer => finance#Person;
               finance#location =>> finance#City].
finance#Person[cars#name => STRING;
               finance#monthlyIncome => NUMBER].

FORALL X,Y Y[finance#hasBank ->> X] <-
        Y:finance#Person AND
        X:finance#Bank[finance#customer ->> Y].

#me:cars#Person[cars#age -> 32].
#myBank:finance#Bank[finance#location ->> karlsruhe].           (24)
```

The semantics of a namespace-qualified object  is always a pair of strings, i.e. each object is represented by a URI (its namespace) and a local name. Thus finance#Person and cars#Person become clearly distinguishable. During parsing of the F-logic program the aliases are resolved, such that the following pairs are constructed.

- finance#Person stands for ("www.financeWorld.tv", Person)
- cars#Person stands for ("www.cars-r-us.tv", Person)

In case no declared namespace URI is found for a used alias, the alias itself is assumed to represent the namespace of  an F-logic object. Because pure URIs conflict with the F-logic grammar, literal namespaces, i.e. URIs, must be quoted, e.g.

- "www.cars-r-us.tv"#Person is equivalent to cars#Person

Note, that declared namespace URIs are taken literally, i.e. two URIs are equivalent only if they syntactically do not differ, e.g. *www.cars-r-us.tv* is ***not*** equivalent to *http://www.cars-r-us.tv*.

### 2.2.6.3 Querying for Namespaces

This mechanism enables users even to query for namespaces (URIs not aliases) and to provide variables in namespaces. For instance, the following query asks for all namespaces X that contain a concept "Person".

FORALL X <- X#Person[].                                            (25)

### 2.2.7 Non-Monotonic Inheritance

Class-hierarchies in F-logic are partial orders. Moreover, a class hierarchy may be defined by rules as part of the F-logic program. This general scenario makes inheritance an ambitious non-trivial concept. A general discussion of inheritance is far beyond the scope of this paper. Interested readers are refered to [KLW95, ALUW93, MK01, YK02]. The following example demonstrates how the intended effects of inheritance of methods with overwriting can be achieved for F-logic programs using a rewriting. For simplicity, let us add the following (not very intelligent) rules to the program in Example 1:

```
/* additional rules stating that persons are sons and daughers at the same time*/
FORALL X,Y X[son->>Y] <- Y:person[father->X].
FORALL X,Y X[daughter->>Y] <- Y:person[father->X].
FORALL X,Y X[son->>Y] <- Y:person[mother->X].
FORALL X,Y X[daughter->>Y] <- Y:person[mother->X].
```

Now remember that, according to our ontology, every man and woman is also a person. Thus, whenever an object is a woman or a man, the new program defines incorrect information. Therefore, adequate handling of inheritance makes a rewriting of the original set rules necessary:

```
/* rules stating that persons, which are neither man nor woman, are sons and daughers at the same time*/
FORALL X,Y X[son->>Y] <- Y:person[father->X] AND NOT Y:man AND NOT Y:woman.
FORALL X,Y X[daughter->>Y] <- Y:person[father->X] AND NOT Y:man AND NOT Y:woman.
FORALL X,Y X[son->>Y] <- Y:person[mother->X] AND NOT Y:man AND NOT Y:woman.
FORALL X,Y X[daughter->>Y] <- Y:person[mother->X] AND NOT Y:man AND NOT Y:woman.
```

In general, such rewritings are not as obvious as in the preceeding example, however, as demonstrated in e.g. [ALUW93], they can be algorithmically derived.

## 2.3 Implementation of F-logic Semantics

F-logic's semantics of its higher-order syntax can be equivalently represented using first-order predicate expressions. For example, the reader may have noticed, that the higher-order concepts of methods and classes in F-logic are represented by id-terms, which are used as names of the concepts. In addition, sets are not manipulated as a whole, however element by element. In the sequel we will give some insight into the different implementations of F-logic: Ontobroker, Florid and Flora. All implementations have in common the way to represent the higher-order constructs in Horn-Logic rules:

- First, molecular expressions are represented by an equivalent set of atomic expressions. We have given several examples of this process in the preceding paragraphs.
- Then these atomic expressions are represented by first-order predicates.
- The resulting set of rules finally is extended by specific closure rules to capture those semantic aspects of F-logic which do not follow from the transformation so far.

For example, Ontobroker uses a transformation of F-atoms as stated table 1.

**Table 1.** Transformation of F-logic atoms into predicates in Ontobroker

| F-atom | predicate |
|--------|-----------|
| $C[A => R]$ | $atttype\_(C,A,R)$ |
| $C[A =>> R]$ | $setatttype\_(C,A,R)$ |
| $C[A@(B_1,..,B_n) => R]$ | $atttype\_(C,A(B_1,..,B_n),R)$ |
| $A::B$ | $sub\_(A,B)$ |
| $o:C$ | $isa\_(o,C)$ |
| $o[A -> b]$ | $att\_(o,A,b)$ |
| $o[A ->> b]$ | $setatt\_(o,A,b)$ |
| $p(b_1,..,b_n)$ | $p(b_1,..,b_n)$ |

Ontobroker adds a set of axioms which describe *monotonic* attribute inheritance, class-hierarchy, etc.:

```
// closure rules for X :: Y
FORALL X,Y,Z sub_(X,Z) <-  sub_(X,Y) and sub_(Y,Z).

// attributes are inherited
FORALL C1,C2,A,T atttype_(C1,A,T) <- sub_(C1,C2) and atttype_(C2,A,T).
FORALL C1,C2,A,T setattype_(C1,A,T) <- sub_(C1,C2) and setattype_(C2,A,T).

// closure rules for X : C
FORALL O,C,C1 isa_(O,C) <-  sub_(C1,C) and isa_(O,C1).
```

The result of this transformation process of F-logic is a logic program in normal logic (Horn logic with negation), which is evaluated according to the well-founded semantics [GRS91]. Remember that in contrast to the stratified semantics the well-founded semantics is also applicable for rules which depend on each other in a cyclic way, where the cycle may be implied through negative rule bodies. Because of the syntactic higher-orderness, during the translation to normal programs such negative cycles may quite often arise.

While all implementations of F-logic are similar with respect to the described transformation, there are many differences in the way the resulting set of rules is evaluated. Ontobroker evaluates the rules directly in a deductive database style. The characteristic feature of the Florid-implementation is its dedicated object-manager which allows to implement features in a natural way which on the higher level of logic programs turned out to be difficult. One example is F-logics equality theory. In contrast the Flora-implementation is based on the XSB-Prolog system and thus can directly profit from XSB-Prologs tabelling concepts which can be used to implement the well-founded semantics. Finally, while Florid is a mere research prototype, Ontobroker and Flora are in addition commercial products.

## 2.4 A Case Study

The following is an extract of the ontology based configuration tool *OnKo* developed for the German Telecom [SSA02]. It represents a set of IT components together with their complex interrelationships. It supports an interactive configuration process of such components to IT systems and IT landscapes. It contains intelligent search and retrieval of already existing IT systems with similar functionality and thus integrates already existing experience of the company.

The components are arranged in an isa-hierarchy:

```
Hardware::ITComponent.
Software::ITComponent.
SystemSoftware::Software.
OperatingSystem::SystemSoftware.
WebServer::SystemSoftware.
OmniWebServer:WebServer.
WindowsOS::OperatingSystem.
Linux::OperatingSystem.
```

Properties of these components and relations between these components are represented by methods:

```
WebServer[
usesUtility  =>> WebServerUtility;
```

supportsServerSideLanguage =>> ProgrammingLanguage;
runsOnOS =>> OperatingSystem].

The current configuration is given by a set of facts:

omni[runsOnOS->>linux]
omni: OmniWebServer.
Linux:OperatingSystem.

Constraints are represented by rules. E.g. the following rule expresses that the webserver *omni* does not run on an operating system other than a windows system:

FORALL X,Y,S
check(S) <-
X:OmniWebServer[runsOnOS->>Y] and not Y:WindowsOS and
S is "webserver "+X+" does not run on operating system "+Y.

The ontology is exploited for navigation purposes. The user can switch between different views, i.e. *specialization view*, *part-of view* etc. to the available components and thus the user is able to choose the best presentation for the current configuration task. These views are represented as hierarchical trees and additional links between the nodes enabling a simple interactive search within the available IT components. By this way the user subsequently searches for components. For selected components a form for the properties is presented.

The forms are directly based on the ontologies. Queries where variables quantify over the concepts and their attribute names are sent to the ontology server. For instance the following query:

FORALL C,A,R <- C[A=>>R].

provides all concepts with their attribute names and the ranges of the attributes.

After a component has been selected and the attribute values have been filled in, the component is added to the current configuration. In each step the interrelationships of the components of the current configuration are checked for consistency. For this purpose again queries are sent to the ontology server and the answers are presented to the user. For instance the following query:

FORALL S <- check(S).

yields to the answer:

S = "webserver omni does not run on operating system linux"

Thus upcoming dead ends of configurations which would not work are recognized early. The system automatically derives new knowledge and makes further suggestions about possible extensions of the current configuration which therefore must not be specified by the user. This "mixed initiative intelligence" strategy enables the development of a configuration in close cooperation with the user and thus supports the user without telling him what to do.

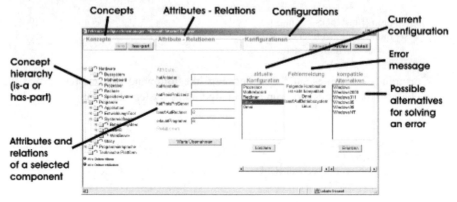

**Fig. 1.** Screenshot of the application

In Figure 1 a screenshot of OnKo is shown. In the left frame the user navigates within an is-a hierarchy of the components. This view may be switched to a part-of hierarchy. The attribute values of a selected component are editable in a form in the middle frame. The selected component together with its attribute values are used to derive attribute values of dependent components, i.e. the frequency of the processor is propagated upwards in the part-of hierarchy to the frequency of the entire computer. The current configuration with all its components is shown in the right frame. If a configuration contains inconsistent components which is checked by applying consistency rules, appropriate error and warning messages are immediately given and alternatives for a selected component are presented to the user which make the configuration consistent.

In each step the current configuration may be compared to similar existing configurations in the company. This makes existing experience transparent to the user compiling a new configuration. In our screenshot the current configuration contains two incompatible components: "Omni" does not work on "Linux". To solve this incompatibility, the system suggests to use "Windows" or "Windows2000" or ... etc. instead of "Linux". A user may now replace incompatible components to get a valid configuration for a computer system.

## 2.5 Conclusion

We have presented F-logic as a language to represent ontologies and their instances. F-logic is a frame based language which allows to describe application domains in an OO-style manner. F-logic enables reasoning about instances and also about concepts and their relations. Various practical applications of F-logic [ASS00] [StM01] have not only shown, that F-logic is very well suited for representing the respective domains, but also that the inference engine for F-logic is such efficient, that it can be used as a run time system for ontology based applications.

Currently a www committee[http://www.daml.org/committee/] works on a definition of a  rule language for OWL and RDF(S). SiLRI, a predecessor of Ontobroker, is the first implementation of an inference and query service for RDF(S) [DBS98]. Therefore it became evident, that RDF(S) can be represented in F-logic[SEM01] (see also [YK02a]). In future also OWL lite [http://www.w3.org/2001/sw/WebOnt/] will entirely be represented in F-logic. Description logics [BCM03], which are another inference paradigm well known in the ontology community, provide subsumption for classes and thus are very useful during the modelling of ontologies. However, in contrast to F-logic, description logics are not applicable for reasoning in large sets of instances and thus can not be used as a run time system for ontology-based applications.

# References

[AHV95] Serge Abiteboul, Richard Hull, Victor Vianu: Foundations of Databases. Addison-Wesley 1995.

[ALUW93] Serge Abiteboul, Georg Lausen, Heinz Uphoff, Emmanuel Waller: Methods and Rules. *Proceedings SIGMOD Conference 1993*. pages 32-41

[ASS00] Jürgen Angele, Hans-Peter Schnurr, Steffen Staab, Rudi Studer. The Times They Are A-Changin' - The Corporate History Analyzer. In: *D. Mahling & U. Reimer.Proceedings of the Third International Conference on Practical Aspects of Knowledge Management*. Basel, Switzerland, October 30-31, 2000.

[Che76] P.P. Chen: The entity relationship model. Toward a unified view of data. In *ACM Transactions on Database Systems*, Vol. 1, 1976, 9-36.

[BCM03] Franz Baader, Diego Calvanese, Deborah McGuinness, Daniele Nardi, Peter Patel-Schneider (eds.). The Description Logic Handbook, Cambridge, 2003

[DBS98] S. Decker, D. Brickley, J. Saarela und J. Angele: A Query and Inference Service for RDF.
In *Proceedings of the W3C Query Language Workshop (QL-98)*, Boston, MA, 3.-4. Dezember, 1998.

[DEFS99] S. Decker, M. Erdmann, D. Fensel, and R. Studer. OntoBroker™: Ontology based access to distributed and semi-structured information. In R. Meersman et al., editor, *Database Semantics: Semantic Issues in Multimedia Systems*. Kluwer Academic, 1999.

[FHK97] J. Frohn, R. Himmer, P.-Th. Kandzia, C. Schlepphorst: How to Write F-Logic Programs in FLORID. Available from
fpt://ftp.informatik.uni-freiburg.de/pub/florid/tutorial.ps.gz, 1997.

50     Jürgen Angele and Georg Lausen

[GPQ97] Hector Garcia-Molina, Yannis Papakonstantinou, Dallan Quass, Anand Rajaraman, Yehoshua Sagiv, Jeffrey D. Ullman, Vasilis Vassalos, Jennifer Widom: The TSIMMIS Approach to Mediation: Data Models and Languages. JIIS 8(2): 117-132 (1997)

[GRS91] A. Van Gelder, K. A. Ross, and J. S. Schlipf. The well-founded semantics for general logic programs. *Journal of the ACM*, 38(3):620–650, July 1991.

[KLW95] M. Kifer, G. Lausen, and J.Wu. Logical foundations of object-oriented and framebased languages. *Journal of the ACM*, 42:741–843, 1995.

[L99] Mengchi Liu: Deductive Database Languages: Problems and Solutions. ACM Computing Surveys 31(1): 27-62 (1999)

[LHL98] Bertram Ludäscher, Rainer Himmeröder, Georg Lausen, Wolfgang May, Christian Schlepphorst. Managing Semistructured Data with FLORID: A Deductive Object-Oriented Perspective. Information Systems 23(8): 589-613 (1998)

[M01] Wolfgang May: A Rule-Based Querying and Updating Language for XML. In *Proceedings of DBPL 2001*, LNCS 2397, pages 165-181

[MK01] Wolfgang May, Paul-Thomas Kandzia. Nonmonotonic Inheritance in Object-Oriented Deductive Database Languages, *Journal of Logic and Computation 11(4)*, 2001.

[RES94]Ramez Elmasri, Shamkant B. Navathe: Fundamentals of Database Systems, 2[]nd Edition. Benjamin/Cummings 1994, ISBN 0-8053-1748-1

[SEM01] Steffen Staab, Michael Erdmann, Alexander Mädche, Stefan Decker. An extensible approach for Modeling Ontologies in RDF(S). In *Knowledge Media in Healthcare: Opportunities and Challenges*. Rolf Grütter (ed.). Idea Group Publishing, Hershey USA / London, UK. December 2001.

[SSA02] Y. Sure, S. Staab, J. Angele. OntoEdit: Guiding Ontology Development by Methodology and Inferencing. In: R. Meersman, Z. Tari et al. (eds.). *Proceedings of the Confederated International Conferences CoopIS, DOA and ODBASE 2002*, October 28th - November 1st, 2002, University of California, Irvine, USA, Springer, LNCS 2519 , pages 1205-1222.

[StM01] Staab, S. and Maedche, A.: Knowledge Portals - Ontologies at Work. In: AI Magazine, 21(2), Summer 2001.

[YK00] Guizhen Yang, Michael Kifer. FLORA: Implementing an Efficient DOOD System Using a Tabling Logic Engine. *Proceedings Computational Logic 2000*, Springer LNAI 1861, pages 1078-1093.

[YK02] Guizhen Yang, Michael Kifer: Well-Founded Optimism: Inheritance in Frame-Based Knowledge Bases. *Proceedings CoopIS/DOA/ODBASE 2002*. pages 1013-1032.

[YK02a] Guizhen Yang, Michael Kifer: On the Semantics of Anonymous Identity and Reification. *Proceedings CoopIS/DOA/ODBASE 2002*. pages 1047-1066.

# 3

# The Resource Description Framework (RDF) and its Vocabulary Description Language RDFS

Brian McBride

Hewlett Packard Laboratories, Bristol, UK.

**Summary.** An informal introduction to the W3C's updated Resource Description Framework (RDF) and its vocabulary description language is given. RDF's role in the semantic web and its relationship to other semantic web languages is described. The basic concepts of RDF and RDF Schema are explained and an example RDF schema is given. Limitations of RDF are described.

## 3.1 Introduction

The Resource Description Framework (RDF) [1,2] is a W3C recommendation that defines a language for describing resources. It was designed for describing Web resources such as Web pages. However, RDF does not require that resources be retrievable on the Web. RDF resources may be physical objects, abstract concepts, in fact anything that has identity. Thus, RDF defines a language for describing just about anything.

RDF describes resources in terms of named properties and their values. The RDF Vocabulary Description language, RDF Schema (RDFS) [3] describes vocabularies used in RDF descriptions. RDF vocabularies describe properties, classes of resources and relationships between them.

RDF is the foundation of the Semantic Web [4]. Just as the Web is a global infrastructure representing information in documents, the Semantic Web is a global infrastructure representing information in a form that can be processed by computer. Like the Web, the semantic Web is decentralized, which imposes a severe constraint on the mechanism it uses to represent information.

Traditional frame based and object oriented systems are resource-centric. They define classes and the properties instances of those classes must or may have. This is a centralized approach. Whoever defines a class defines what properties its instances have. To add more properties requires either the cooperation of the owner of the class or the definition of a new subclass.

Both RDF and RDFS[1] are Web languages. They are designed to allow information and vocabularies to be developed in a decentralized fashion. Just as the Web permits anyone with access to a server to create a Web page and link it to any other Web page, RDF(S) was designed following the principle that anyone should be able to say anything about anything[2]. To be able to say anything about anything, anyone must be able to define new properties for a class. Further, they should be able to use the same property to describe any class they choose. To support this need, RDF(S) is property centric. It enables properties to be defined and then used to describe resources.

RDF(S) has a formal semantics [5]. A formal semantics is needed for two reasons. Firstly, it brings precision to the specification of RDF. Without a formal semantics, there is too much scope for implementations to differ. Secondly, languages such as Owl [6] that extend RDF(S) have a formal semantics. Such languages require RDF(S) to have a formal semantics that they can extend, otherwise, they must define their own semantics for RDF, creating the possibility that different extension languages define different semantics.

RDF(S) are members of a family of Semantic Web languages. They builds on URI's [7] the Web's language for naming things, and on XML [8], the standard syntax for representing information in the Web. The DAML+OIL ontology language and its standardized form, the Owl [6] family of ontology languages, are extensions of RDF(S). Research on languages for querying the semantic Web [9, 10] and for expressing rules is likely to inform future efforts to standardize such languages.

The remainder of this chapter is organized as follows. Section 2 describes RDF, its abstract syntax, the use of blank nodes, support for datatypes and how it may written as XML. Section 3 describes RDFS, the notions of class and subclass, property and subproperty, domain and range constraints and the built in vocabularies for containers, collections and reification. Section 4 summarizes the key features of RDF(S), describes some of its limitations and refers to later chapters that describe more powerful languages that overcome these limitations.

The reader should note that at the time of writing (March 2003), the W3C's RDFCore Working Group are revising the original specification of RDF [11] and completing work on the RDF Schema specification [3]. Whilst this work is thought to be nearly complete, late changes made by the working group may not be represented in here.

---

[1] For the remainder of this chapter, the term RDF(S) will be used instead of "both RDF and RDFS".

[2] There are things that RDF is too weak to express; for example, it lacks negation and universal quantification. It is not possible to say everything about everything using RDF.

## 3.2 The Resource Description Framework

RDF's abstract syntax can be represented as a directed graph with labels on both nodes and edges:

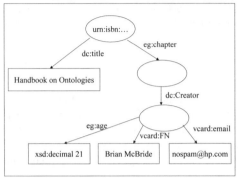

**Fig. 1.** An example RDF graph

RDF graphs are interpreted as follows:

☐ An elliptical node with a label represents a resource. If present, the label on the node is a URI[3] [7] that identifies the resource. In fig 1 the URI of the top node is not given in full, but is intended to identify this book. URI's often come in groups, called a vocabulary. Since URI's are often long and clumsy, rather than write them in full, in this chapter they are written in the form prefix:name, where the prefix identifies a vocabulary, and name is a name in that vocabulary. This is convenient shorthand for representing the full URI. The prefix "rdf" identifies names from the RDF vocabulary, "rdfs" names from the RDFS vocabulary, "dc" names from the Dublin Core [12] vocabulary, "vcard" names from the Vcard [13] vocabulary, "xsd" names from the XML Schema datatypes [14] vocabulary and "eg" names from an example vocabulary.

☐ An elliptical node with no label is called a blank node, or sometimes a b-node. It represents a resource for which no URI is given.

☐ An arc in the graph represents a property of the resource at the blunt end of the arc. The label on the arc, also a URI, identifies the property. The node at the sharp end of the arc represents the value of the property.

☐ Rectangular nodes represent literal values. Literals may be untyped or they may have a datatype.

Each arc in an RDF graph represents a *statement* that the resource at the blunt end of the arc, called the *subject* of the statement, has a property, called the *predicate* of the statement with a value, called the *object* of the statement. The notion

---

[3] Strictly, they are absolute URI's, but allowing international characters, with an optional fragment identifier. For convenience, the term 'URI' will be used throughout this chapter.

of statement corresponds to the English language notion of a simple sentence making a statement:

Sky hasColour Blue

The sky is the subject of the statement, hasColour is the predicate of the statement and Blue is the object of the statement

### 3.2.1 Blank Nodes

Blank nodes have a number of uses. A blank node may be used to represent a resource which either has no URI or for which no URI is known. In figure 1 for example, the top blank node represents this chapter of this book. The lower blank node represents a person. That person is uniquely identified, since, for the sake of this description, we assume that there is only one person with the email address given by the vcard:email property.

Blank nodes may be used to represent structured values. For example, the weight of a person may be represented by a blank node with two properties, one stating the value of the weight and the other stating the units of measurement.

Blank nodes may also be used to represent n-ary relationships. A single RDF statement can only represent a relationship between two nodes; so called binary relationships. N-ary relationships can be represented by introducing a blank node as in figure 2.

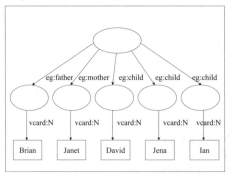

**Fig. 2.** Using a blank node to represent the n-ary relationship 'family'

Formally, blank nodes do not necessarily denote a specific resource. Instead, they are similar to existentially qualified variables in first order logic. Blank nodes can be read as "There is at least one resource with the given properties".

### 3.2.2 Datatypes and Datatype Values

RDF has adopted the XML Schema [14] model of datatypes. A datatype consists of a lexical space, a value space and a mapping from each member of the lexical space to one member of the value space.

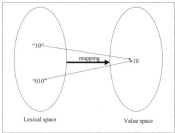

**Fig. 3.** The structure of a datatype

As with everything else in RDF, a datatype is identified by a URI. A datatype value is represented in RDF graphs by a rectangle containing the URI for the datatype and a string from the lexical space of the datatype. An example of this can be seen in the *eg:age* property in figure 1. Anyone can define a new datatype. Provided a URI is defined to identify it, it can be used in RDF graphs. However, for the full benefits of using datatypes to be realized, for example to process the integer 010 the same as the integer 10, software processing a graph must have specific knowledge of the datatypes referred to in the graph. The built-in datatypes defined by XML Schema have a "first amongst equals" status in RDF. They are the most likely to be interoperable amongst different software implementations.

### 3.2.3 RDF/XML

A graph is a convenient representation of small RDF information models for humans. For machine communication, or for large graphs, a way of representing an RDF graph as a sequence of symbols is needed. RDF/XML [15] is an XML language for representing RDF. Only a brief introduction to the syntax is possible here. For a fuller treatment the reader is referred to the language specification [15] and the RDF primer [1].

The graph in figure 1 can be written in RDF/XML as:
<rdf:Description rdf:about="urn:isbn:...">[4]
 <dc:Title>Handbook on Ontologies</dc:Title>

---

[4] For clarity and brevity, XML examples omit the XML header element and namespace declarations.

```
<eg:chapter>
  <rdf:Description>
    <dc:Creator>
      <rdf:Description>
        <vcard:FN>Brian McBride</vcard:FN>
        <vcard:email>nospam@hp.com</vcard:email>
        <eg:age rdf:datatype="&xsd;decimal"⁵>21</eg:age>
      </rdf:Description>
    </dc:Creator>
  </rdf:Description>
</eg:chapter>
</rdf:Description>
```

The first *rdf:Description* element represents a resource with the URI "urn:isbn:...". It has a title property represented by the *dc:Title* element. It also has a chapter property whose value is a blank node. The blank node is represented by an *rdf:Description* element without an *rdf:about* attribute. This node in turn has a single *dc:Creator* property whose value is another blank node which in its turn has two vcard properties and an *eg:age* property. The *rdf:datatype* attribute specifies the datatype of the value of the *eg:age* property.

Two other syntaxes for representing RDF, though non-standard, are in common use. Notation 3 [16], otherwise known as N3 is a more convenient notation than XML for humans to read and write. N-triples [17] is a subset of N3 used for defining test cases and for testing implementations. N-triples simply lists the subject, predicate and object of each arc in a graph, one per line.

## 3.3 RDF Schema

RDF enables assertion of simple statements consisting of a subject, a predicate and an object. It has no means to describe what these subjects, predicates and objects mean, nor to describe relationships between them.

RDF Schema introduces some simple ontological concepts. It defines a type system by introducing the concept of class and defines how resources may be described as belonging to one or more classes. It defines the concepts of subclass and subproperty, enabling description of hierarchies of classes and properties. It also defines the properties domain and range of a property. These are used to assert that the subject and object of a property respectively, belong to one or more classes.

---

⁵ XML entities, which are assumed to be defined, are used as abbreviations in XML examples

### 3.3.1 Classes and Subclasses

A class represents a collection of resources, for example, the class of Web pages. Classes are themselves resources and are usually identified by URI's. A resource may be stated to be a member of a class using the *rdf:type* property as illustrated in Figure 4.

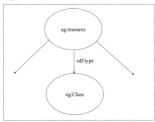

**Fig. 4.** eg:resource is a member of eg:Class

This graph can be written in RDF/XML as:

```
<rdf:Description rdf:about="http://example.org/resource">
  <rdf:type rdf:resource="http://example.org/Class"/>
  .... other properties
</rdf:Description>
```
The RDF/XML syntax provides a short hand notation for the rdf:type property. This graph may be written as:

```
<eg:Class rdf:about="http://example.org/resource">
  .... other properties
</eg:Class>
```
Those who expect that a class is the set of its members may be surprised to learn that in RDF Schema, the collection of all classes is itself a class.

Many modeling languages, such as UML [18] are layered. On the bottom layer is the instance data, akin to RDF statements. On the next layer there is metadata about the instance data, e.g. information about classes of data. On the layer above there is metadata about the first layer of metadata, and so on. Mixing data from the different layers is forbidden as is one layer being used for metadata about itself. RDF Schema is not layered in this sense. It allows self-reference, as in *rdfs:Class* being a member of itself.

At first sight, the class of all classes being a member of itself appears to conflict with the axiom of foundation of standard (Zermelo-Fraenkel) set theory. RDF avoids this difficulty by distinguishing between a class, which is a resource, and the *class extension* of the class, that is the set of members of the class. A class may be a member of its own class extension without violating the axiom of foundation.

The *rdfs:subClassOf* property is used to state that one class is a subclass of another, i.e. that the class extension of a class is a subset of the class extension of another.   Stating that one class is a subclass of another may be written in RDF/XML as:

```
<rdf:RDF xml:base="http://example.org/example">
  <rdfs:Class rdf:ID="Person"/>
  <rdfs:Class rdf:ID="Man">
    <rdfs:subClassOf rdf:resource="#Person"/>
  </rdfs:Class>
</rdf:RDF>
```

Not just hierarchies, but arbitrary graphs of subClassOf relationships between classes can be defined.  Where two or more classes are arranged in a loop of *rdfs:subClassOf* properties, their class extensions must all have the same members.  This does not mean they are the same classes.  One of the classes may have a property that is not true of the others.  For example, the Inland Revenue may define the class of people living in the author's house.  The Post Office may define the class of people whose postcode is the same as the author's.  Both these classes have the same members, but one has the property that it was defined by the post office and the other does not.

### 3.3.2 Properties and SubProperties

RDF properties are resources.  They too form a class.  RDF Schema defines *rdf:Property* to be the class of all RDF properties.

The reader familiar with other modeling languages might expect that an RDF property would be represented mathematically as a set of pairs, each pair representing two objects related by the property.  This however, can lead to difficulties with standard set theory similar to those described above with the formal definition of classes.

A similar technique as used in the formal treatment of classes is used to avoid this difficulty and to maintain consistency.  Formally, a property is a resource that has a *property extension* that is the set of pairs of objects related by the property.

One property may be a subproperty of another, which means that any two objects related by the subproperty are also related by the superproperty, i.e. the property extension of the subproperty is a subset of the property extension of the super property.  Stating that one property is a subproperty of another may be written in RDF/XML as:

```
<rdf:RDF xml:base="http://example.org/example">
  <rdf:Property rdf:ID="partnerOf"/>
  <rdf:Property rdf:ID="husbandOf">
    <rdfs:subPropertyOf rdf:resource="#partnerOf"/>
  </rdf:Property>
</rdf:RDF>
```

As with subclass relationships arbitrary graphs of properties may be related with the subproperty relationship.  Where two or more properties form a loop of subproperty relationships, then they must all have the same property extensions, though again, this does not mean that they are the same property.

RDF does not require that classes and properties are disjoint. The technique of using class and property extensions means that it is possible for a resource to be both a property and a class. However, where a concept may be used both as a property and a class, it is usually beneficial to have a different resource for each. By distinguishing between the class and the property, more accurate representation of information is possible. It is clear whether some statement applies to the property or the class. At least one style checker for RDF assumes that classes and properties are disjoint and will issue warnings where the same term is used for both.

### 3.3.3 Domain and Range

RDF Schema can state that all the subjects of a property belong to a given class. Similarly it can state that all the objects of a property belong to a given class.

The rdfs:domain property is used to state that all the subjects of a property belong to a class:

```
<rdf:RDF xml:base="http://example.org/example">
    <rdf:Property rdf:ID="husbandOf">
    <rdfs:domain rdf:resource="#Woman"/>6
    <rdfs:domain rdf:resource="#MarriedPerson"/>
    </rdf:Property>
</rdf:RDF>
```

This states that all subjects of the *eg:husbandOf* property are members of *eg:Woman* class and of the *eg:MarriedPerson* class. If more than one domain property is given, then subjects are members of all the classes.

Similarly, the *rdfs:range* property is used to state that all the objects of a property are members of a class.

```
<rdf:RDF xml:base="http://example.org/example">
    <rdf:Property rdf:ID="wifeOf">
    <rdfs:range rdf:resource="#Woman"/>
    <rdfs:range rdf:resource="#MarriedPerson"/>
    </rdf:Property>
</rdf:RDF>
```

As in the case of domain, where there is more than one range property, the object of the property is a member of all the classes.

### 3.3.4 Datatypes

The basic RDF model for datatypes was described in a previous section. RDF Schema defines the class *rdfs:Datatype*, the class of all datatypes. *rdfs:Datatype* is a subclass of *rdfs:Class*, i.e. all datatypes have class extensions. The class extension of a datatype is the set of values in the value space of the datatype.

---

6 The property eg:husbandOf is used to represent heterosexual relationships.

### 3.3.5 Other Properties

The full name of a resource such as a class or property is a URI. URI's are often long and complex rendering them unsuitable for presentation in a user interface. *rdfs:label* may be used to provide a human readable name for a resource that can be used in a user interface.

*rdfs:comment* is a property that may be used to provide further information about a resource. This information is usually represented in natural language and is not amenable to machine processing.

*rdfs:seeAlso* may be used to link one resource to another that may provide further information about that resource. No constraints are placed on the linked resource; it may be a schema in a formal language or a description in natural language or anything else.

*rdfs:isDefinedBy* is a subproperty of *rdfs:seeAlso*. Whilst it still does not require that the linked resource be in any particular form, it is commonly used to indicate an RDF Schema that describes the resource.

### 3.3.6 Built in Vocabulary

RDF(S) defines vocabulary for representing containers, collections and occurrences of RDF statements.

### 3.3.6.1 Containers

An *rdfs:Container* is a resource that contains literals or resources. Three subclasses of *rdfs:Container* are defined; *rdf:Seq*, *rdf:Bag* and *rdf:Alt*. Formally, all three subclasses are ordered. However, an *rdf:Seq* is typically used where the order is significant. *rdf:Bag* is used where the order is not significant. *rdf:Alt* is used where typical processing will be to select one member of the container. These distinctions however, are not captured in the formal semantics.

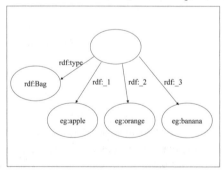

**Fig. 5.** A bag of fruit

Membership of a container is represented using container membership properties. The first member of the container is the value of its rdf:_1 property, the second the value of its rdf:_2 property and so on, as illustrated in figure 5. This can be written in RDF/XML as:

```
<rdf:RDF xml:base="http://example.org/">
  <rdf:Seq>
    <rdf:li rdf:resource="apple"/>
    <rdf:li rdf:resource="banana"/>
    <rdf:li rdf:resource="orange"/>
  </rdf:Seq>
</rdf:RDF>
```

where the rdf:li elements represent rdf:_1, rdf:_2 etc in sequence.

### 3.3.6.2 Collections

Collections were introduced into RDF(S) to overcome two disadvantages of containers. The first is that there is no way to close a container; to express the fact that there are no more members. The second is that programmers are used to using lists to represent collections. Figure 6 shows how a list structure is used to represent a collection in RDF.

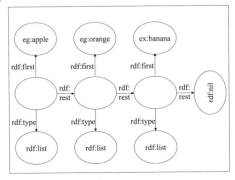

**Fig. 6.** An RDF Collection

Special syntax has been introduced into RDF/XML to represent collections. The collection in figure 6 can be written as

```
<rdf:RDF xml:base="http://example.org/">
  <rdf:Description rdf:parseType="Collection">
    <rdf:Description rdf:about="apple"/>
    <rdf:Description rdf:about="banana"/>
    <rdf:Description rdf:about="orange"/>
  </rdf:Description>
</rdf:RDF>
```

Note the *rdf:parseType* attribute.

### 3.3.6.3 Reification

RDF(S) is designed for representing information on the Web. Not all information on the Web is correct or even consistent. Consider, for example, the *eg:age* property in figure 1. It can therefore be important to track the provenance of information so that an application may decide whether to trust it, or trace back to the source of incorrect information. Reification is the tool that RDF provides to support this.

A reified statement is a resource that represents an occurrence of an RDF statement. Such a resource is a member of the class *rdf:Statement* and has three natural properties. *rdf:subject* is the subject of the statement, *rdf:predicate* is the predicate of the statement and *rdf:object* is the object of the statement. Other properties, such as where the statement occurred, when, who was responsible for it may then be attached to it. Figure 7 illustrates a reified statement.

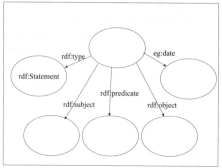

**Fig. 7.** A reified statement with *eg:date* property

### 3.3.7 Example RDF Schemas

A fuller version of the schema used in the examples above is given in table 1. Other examples of RDF schemas include:

~  Platform for Privacy Preferences (P3P) [19] [20]
~  Topic Maps [21] [22]
~  Oil Ontology Language [23]

## 3.4 Conclusion

This chapter has described how RDF and RDFS were developed following the Web principle of decentralization to enable distributed integration and evolution of information models and vocabularies. The goal of decentralization led to their property centric design, which contrasts with the resource centric approach of frame and object oriented systems.

Whilst it is useful on its own, RDFS does not support many ontological concepts such as equivalence, inverse relations and cardinality constraints found in other ontology languages. RDFS's role is to be extended by more powerful languages such as OWL [5] that are described later in this book. This ensures some level of interoperability between these languages by ensuring that each such extended language shares a common definition of the basic ontological notions, such as class and property, defined in RDFS.

RDF(S) has no notion of negation and hence no notion of contradiction. If an RDF schema states that the range of a property is both a plant and a metal, an RDF(S) processor will assume that all values of that property are members of the class of plants and the class of metals. RDF(S) cannot represent the fact that plants and metals are disjoint classes and that there can be no values for such a property.

RDF Schema can be used in one of two ways. It can be used to avoid the redundant specification of the same information. For example, by defining a range for a property, there is no need to specify for every value of that property, that it is of the type specified by the range property. That knowledge is implied by the range property.

Alternatively, it can be used to check that domain and range constraints are adhered to by checking redundant specification of the types of property values. A validator can issue an error or a warning if it cannot confirm that the subjects and objects of properties conform to range and domain constraints from other information, such as explicit type properties on the subjects and objects.


## Acknowledgements

RDF and RDFS are the product of three W3C working groups, the Model and Syntax working group, the RDF Schema working group and the RDFCore working group. The members of those working groups are too numerous to acknowledge individually here. Their names are listed in the various specifications to which they contributed.

**Table 1** A simple RDF schema

```
<rdf:RDF xmlns:rdf="http://www.w3.org/1999/02/22-rdf-syntax-ns#"
         xmlns:rdfs="http://www.w3.org/2000/01/rdf-schema#"
         xml:base="http://example.org/schema">
 <rdfs:Class rdf:ID="Person">
  <rdfs:label>person</rdfs:label>
  <rdfs:comment>The class of all people</rdfs:comment>
 </rdfs:Class>
 <rdfs:Class rdf:ID="MarriedPerson">
  <rdfs:label>married person</rdfs:label>
  <rdfs:comment>The class of all married people</rdfs:comment>
  <rdfs:subClassOf rdf:resource="#Person"/>
 </rdfs:Class>
 <rdfs:Class rdf:ID="Man">
  <rdfs:label>man</rdfs:label>
  <rdfs:comment>The class of all men</rdfs:comment>
  <rdfs:subClassOf rdf:resource="#Person"/>
 </rdfs:Class>
 <rdfs:Class rdf:ID="Woman">
  <rdfs:label>woman</rdfs:label>
  <rdfs:comment>The class of all women</rdfs:comment>
  <rdfs:subClassOf rdf:resource="#Person"/>
 </rdfs:Class>
 <rdf:Property rdf:ID="partnerOf">
  <rdfs:label>partner</rdfs:label>
  <rdfs:comment>Relates a person to their partner</rdfs:comment>
  <rdfs:domain rdf:resource="#Person"/>
  <rdfs:range   rdf:resource="#Person"/>
 </rdf:Property>
 <rdf:Property rdf:ID="wifeOf">
  <rdfs:label>wife of</rdfs:label>
  <rdfs:comment>Relates a wife to her husband</rdfs:comment>
  <rdfs:subPropertyOf rdf:resource="#partnerOf"/>
  <rdfs:domain rdf:resource="#Woman"/>
  <rdfs:domain rdf:resource="#MarriedPerson"/>
  <rdfs:range   rdf:resource="#Man"/>
  <rdfs:range   rdf:resource="#MarriedPerson"/>
 </rdf:Property>
 <rdf:Property rdf:ID="husbandOf">
  <rdfs:label>husband of</rdfs:label>
  <rdfs:comment>Relates a husband to his wife</rdfs:comment>
  <rdfs:subPropertyOf rdf:resource="#partnerOf"/>
  <rdfs:domain rdf:resource="#Man"/>
  <rdfs:domain rdf:resource="#MarriedPerson"/>
  <rdfs:range   rdf:resource="#Woman"/>
  <rdfs:range   rdf:resource="#MarriedPerson"/>
 </rdf:Property>
</rdf:RDF>
```

# References

1. Manola, F., Miller, E. (eds) (2002): RDF Primer. http://www.w3.org/TR/rdf-schema/
2. Klyne, G., Carroll, J. (eds) (2002):Resource Description Framework (RDF) Concepts and Abstract Syntax. http://www.w3.org/TR/rdf-concepts/
3. Brickley, D., Guha, R.V. (eds) (2002): RDF Vocabulary Description Language 1.0: RDF Schema http://www.w3.org/TR/rdf-schema/
4. Berners-Lee, T., Hendler, J., Lassila, O. (2001): The Semantic Web. Scientific American, May 2001.
5. Hayes, P. (ed) (2002): RDF Semantics. http://www.w3.org/TR/rdf-mt/
6. Dean, M. et al (eds) (2002): OWL Web Ontology Language 1.0 Reference. http://www.w3.org/TR/owl-ref/ http://www.w3.org/TR/owl-features/
7. Berners-Lee, T. et al (1998): RFC 2396: Uniform Resource Identifiers (URI): Generic Syntax. http://www.ietf.org/rfc/rfc2396.txt
8. Bray, T., Paoli, J., C. M. Sperberg-McQueen, C. M., Maler, E. (2000): Extensible Markup Language (XML) 1.0 (Second Edition) http://www.w3.org/TR/REC-xml
9. Miller, L., Seaborne, A., Reggiori, A. (2002): Three Implementations of SquishQL, a Simple RDF Query Language. First International Semantic Web Conference (ISWC2002) 2002
10. Karvounarakis' K., Alexaki, S., Christophides, V., Plexousakis, D., Scholl, M. (2002): World Wide Web Conference 2002, http://www2002.org/CDROM/refereed/329/
11. Lassila, O., Swick, R. (eds) (1999):Resource Description Framework (RDF) Model and Syntax Specification. http://www.w3.org/TR/1999/REC-rdf-syntax-19990222/
12. Beckett, D., Miller, E., Brickley, D. (2002): Expressing Simple Dublin Core in RDF/XML. http://dublincore.org/documents/2002/07/31/dcmes-xml/
13. Iannella, R. (2001): Representing vCard Objects in RDF/XML. http://www.w3.org/TR/vcard-rdf
14. Biron, P.V., Malhotra, A. (2001): XML Schema Part 2: Datatypes. http://www.w3.org/TR/xmlschema-2/
15. Beckett, D. (ed) (2002): RDF/XML Syntax Specification (Revised). http://www.w3.org/TR/rdf-syntax-grammar/
16. Berners-Lee, T. (2002): Primer: Getting into RDF and the Semantic Web using N3. http://www.w3.org/2000/10/swap/Primer
17. Grant, J., Beckett, D. (eds) (2002): RDF Test Cases. http://www.w3.org/TR/rdf-testcases/
18. Booch, G., Jacobson, I., Rumbaugh, J. (2001): OMG Unified Modelling Language Specification. http://www.omg.org/technology/documents/formal/uml.htm
19. Crannor, L. et al (2002): The Platform for Privacy Preferences 1.0 (P3P1.0) Specification. http://www.w3.org/TR/P3P/
20. McBride, B., Wenning, R., Crannor, L. (2002): An RDF Schema for P3P. http://www.w3.org/TR/p3p-rdfschema/
21. Pepper, S., Moore, G. (eds) (2001): XML Topic Maps (XTM) 1.0. http://www.topicmaps.org/xtm/index.html
22. Garshol, L.M. (2002): An RDF Schema for topic maps. http://psi.ontopia.net/rdf/
23. Horrocks, I., Fensel, D. et al (2000) The Ontology Inference Layer OIL. http://www.cs.vu.nl/~dieter/oil/Tr/oil.pdf

# 4

# Web Ontology Language: OWL

Grigoris Antoniou[1] and Frank van Harmelen[2]

[1] Department of Computer Science, University of Crete, ga@csd.uoc.gr
[2] Department of AI, Vrije Universiteit Amsterdam, Frank.van.Harmelen@cs.vu.nl

**Summary.** In order to extend the limited expressiveness of RDF Schema, a more expressive Web Ontology Language (OWL) has been defined by the World Wide Web Consortium (W3C). In this chapter we analyse the limitations of RDF Schema and derive requirements for a richer Web Ontology Language. We then describe the three-layered architecture of the OWL language, and we describe all of the language constructs of OWL in some detail. The chapter concludes with two extensive examples of OWL ontologies.

## 4.1 Motivation and Overview

The expressivity of RDF and RDF Schema that was described in [12] is deliberately very limited: RDF is (roughly) limited to binary ground predicates, and RDF Schema is (again roughly) limited to a subclass hierarchy and a property hierarchy, with domain and range definitions of these properties.

However, the Web Ontology Working Group of W3C[3] identified a number of characteristic use-cases for Ontologies on the Web which would require much more expressiveness than RDF and RDF Schema.

A number of research groups in both America and Europe had already identified the need for a more powerful ontology modelling language. This lead to a joint initiative to define a richer language, called DAML+OIL[4] (the name is the join of the names of the American proposal DAML-ONT[5], and the European language OIL[6]).

DAML+OIL in turn was taken as the starting point for the W3C Web Ontology Working Group in defining OWL, the language that is aimed to be the standardised and broadly accepted ontology language of the Semantic Web.

In this chapter, we first describe the motivation for OWL in terms of its requirements, and the resulting non-trivial relation with RDF Schema. We then describe the various language elements of OWL in some detail.

---

[3] http://www.w3.org/2001/sw/WebOnt/
[4] http://www.daml.org/2001/03/daml+oil-index.html
[5] http://www.daml.org/2000/10/daml-ont.html
[6] http://www.ontoknowledge.org/oil/

## Requirements for ontology languages

Ontology languages allow users to write explicit, formal conceptualizations of domains models. The main requirements are:

1. a well-defined syntax
2. a well-defined semantics
3. efficient reasoning support
4. sufficient expressive power
5. convenience of expression.

The importance of a *well-defined syntax* is clear, and known from the area of programming languages; it is a necessary condition for *machine-processing* of information. All the languages we have presented so far have a well-defined syntax. DAML+OIL and OWL build upon RDF and RDFS and have the same kind of syntax.

Of course it is questionable whether the XML-based RDF syntax is very user-friendly, there are alternatives better suitable for humans (for example, see the OIL syntax). However this drawback is not very significant, because ultimately users will be developing their ontologies using authoring tools, or more generally *ontology development tools*, instead of writing them directly in DAML+OIL or OWL.

*Formal semantics* describes precisely the meaning of knowledge. "Precisely" here means that the semantics does not refer to subjective intuitions, nor is it open to different interpretations by different persons (or machines). The importance of formal semantics is well-established in the domain of mathematical logic, among others.

One use of formal semantics is to allow humans to reason about the knowledge. For ontological knowledge we may reason about:

- *Class membership:* If $x$ is an instance of a class $C$, and $C$ is a subclass of $D$, then we can infer that $x$ is an instance of $D$.
- *Equivalence of classes:* If class $A$ is equivalent to class $B$, and class $B$ equivalent to class $C$, then $A$ is equivalent to $C$, too.
- *Consistency:* Suppose we have declared $x$ to be an instance of the class $A$. Further suppose that
  - $A$ is a subclass of $B \cap C$
  - $A$ is a subclass of $D$
  - $B$ and $D$ are disjoint

  Then we have an inconsistency because $A$ should be empty, but has the instance $x$. This is an indication of an error in the ontology.
- *Classification:* If we have declared that certain property-value pairs are sufficient condition for membership of a class $A$, then if an individual $x$ satisfies such conditions, we can conclude that $x$ must be an instance of $A$.

Semantics is a prerequisite for *reasoning support*: Derivations such as the above can be made mechanically, instead of being made by hand. Reasoning support is important because it allows one to

- check the consistency of the ontology and the knowledge;
- check for unintended relationships between classes.
- automatically classify instances in classes

Automated reasoning support allows one to check many more cases than what can be done manually. Checks like the above are valuable for

- *designing* large ontologies, where multiple authors are involved;
- *integrating and sharing* ontologies from various sources.

Formal semantics and reasoning support is usually provided by mapping an ontology language to a known logical formalism, and by using automated reasoners that already exist for those formalisms. We will see that OWL is (partially) mapped on a description logic, and makes use of existing reasoners such as FaCT and RACER.

Description logics are a subset of predicate logic for which efficient reasoning support is possible. See [13] for more detail.

**Limitations of the expressive power of RDF Schema**

RDF and RDFS allow the representation of *some* ontological knowledge. The main modelling primitives of RDF/RDFS concern the organization of vocabularies in typed hierarchies: subclass and subproperty relationships, domain and range restrictions, and instances of classes. However a number of other features are missing. Here we list a few:

- *Local scope of properties:* `rdfs:range` defines the range of a property, say `eats`, for all classes. Thus in RDF Schema we cannot declare range restrictions that apply to some classes only. For example, we cannot say that cows eat only plants, while other animals may eat meat, too.
- *Disjointness of classes:* Sometimes we wish to say that classes are disjoint. For example, `male` and `female` are disjoint. But in RDF Schema we can only state subclass relationships, e.g. `female` is a subclass of `person`.
- *Boolean combinations of classes:* Sometimes we wish to build new classes by combining other classes using union, intersection and complement. For example, we may wish to define the class `person` to be the disjoint union of the classes `male` and `female`. RDF Schema does not allow such definitions.
- *Cardinality restrictions:* Sometimes we wish to place restrictions on how many distinct values a property may or must take. For example, we would like to say that a person has exactly two parents, and that a course is taught by at least one lecturer. Again such restrictions are impossible to express in RDF Schema.
- *Special characteristics of properties:* Sometimes it is useful to say that a property is *transitive* (like "greater than"), *unique* (like "is mother of"), or the *inverse* of another property (like "eats" and "is eaten by").

So we need an ontology language that is richer than RDF Schema, a language that offers these features and more. In designing such a language one should be aware of the *tradeoff between expressive power and efficient reasoning support*. Generally speaking, the richer the language is, the more inefficient the reasoning support becomes, often crossing the border of non-computability. Thus we need a compromise, a language that can be supported by reasonably efficient reasoners, while being sufficiently expressive to express large classes of ontologies and knowledge.

## Compatibility of OWL with RDF/RDFS

Ideally, OWL would be an extension of RDF Schema, in the sense that OWL would use the RDF meaning of classes and properties ( rdfs:Class, rdfs:subClassOf, etc), and would add language primitives to support the richer expressiveness identified above.

Unfortunately, the desire to simply extend RDF Schema clashes with the tradeoff between expressive power and efficient reasoning mentioned before. RDF Schema has some very powerful modelling primitives, such as the rdfs:Class (the class of all classes) and rdf:Property (the class of all properties). These primitives are very expressive, and will lead to uncontrollable computational properties if the logic is extended with the expressive primitives identified above.

## Three species of OWL

All this as lead to a set of requirements that may seem incompatible: efficient reasoning support and convenience of expression for a language as powerful as a combination of RDF Schema with a full logic.

Indeed, these requirements have prompted W3C's Web Ontology Working Group to define OWL as three different sublanguages, each of which is geared towards fulfilling different aspects of these incompatible full set of requirements:

- *OWL Full:* The entire language is called OWL Full, and uses all the OWL languages primitives (which we will discuss later in this chapter). It also allows to combine these primitives in arbitrary ways with RDF and RDF Schema. This includes the possibility (also present in RDF) to change the meaning of the predefined (RDF or OWL) primitives, by applying the language primitives to each other. For example, in OWL Full we could impose a cardinality constraint on the class of all classes, essentially limiting the number of classes that can be described in any ontology.

  The advantage of OWL Full is that it is fully upward compatible with RDF, both syntactically and semantically: any legal RDF document is also a legal OWL Full document, and any valid RDF/RDF Schema conclusion is also a valid OWL Full conclusion.

  The disadvantage of OWL Full is the language has become so powerful as to be undecidable, dashing any hope of complete (let alone efficient) reasoning support.

- *OWL DL:* In order to regain computational efficiency, OWL DL (short for: Description Logic) is a sublanguage of OWL Full which restricts the way in which the constructors from OWL and RDF can be used. We will give details later, but roughly this amounts to disallowing application of OWL's constructor's to each other, and thus ensuring that the language corresponds to a well studied description logic.

The advantage of this is that it permits efficient reasoning support.

The disadvantage is that we loose full compatibility with RDF: an RDF document will in general have to be extended in some ways and restricted in others before it is a legal OWL DL document. Conversely, every legal OWL DL document is still a legal RDF document.

- *OWL Lite:* An ever further restriction limits OWL DL to a subset of the language constructors. For example, OWL Lite excludes enumerated classes, disjointness statements and arbitrary cardinality (among others).

  The advantage of this is a language that is both easier to grasp (for users) and easier to implement (for tool builders).

  The disadvantage is of course a restricted expressivity.

Ontology developers adopting OWL should consider which sublanguage best suits their needs. The choice between OWL Lite and OWL DL depends on the extent to which users require the more-expressive constructs provided by OWL DL and OWL Full. The choice between OWL DL and OWL Full mainly depends on the extent to which users require the meta-modeling facilities of RDF Schema (e.g. defining classes of classes, or attaching properties to classes). When using OWL Full as compared to OWL DL, reasoning support is less predictable since complete OWL Full implementations will be impossible.

There are strict notions of upward compatibility between these three sublanguages:

- Every legal OWL Lite ontology is a legal OWL DL ontology.
- Every legal OWL DL ontology is a legal OWL Full ontology.
- Every valid OWL Lite conclusion is a valid OWL DL conclusion.
- Every valid OWL DL conclusion is a valid OWL Full conclusion.

OWL still uses RDF and RDF Schema to a large extent:

- all varieties of OWL use RDF for their syntax
- instances are declared as in RDF, using RDF descriptions and typing information
- OWL constructors like `owl:Class`, `owl:DatatypeProperty` and `owl:ObjectProperty` are all specialisations of their RDF counterparts. Figure 4.1 shows the subclass relationships between some modelling primitives of OWL and RDF/RDFS.

The original hope in the design of OWL was that there would be a downward compatibility with corresponding re-use of software across the various layers. However, the advantage of full downward compatibility for OWL (that any OWL aware processor will also provide correct interpretations of any RDF Schema document) is only achieved for OWL Full, at the cost of computational intractability.

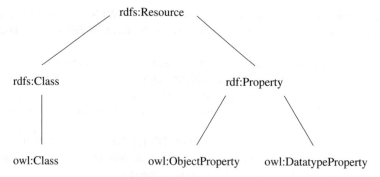

**Fig. 4.1.** Subclass relationships between OWL and RDF/RDFS

## Chapter overview

Section 4.2 presents OWL in some detail. Because OWL is such a new language, only very limited examples of its use have been published. Section 4.3 therefore illustrates the language by giving a few examples.

## 4.2 The OWL Language

### Syntax

OWL builds on RDF and RDF Schema, and uses RDF's XML syntax. Since this is the primary syntax for OWL, we will use it here, but it will soon become clear that RDF/XML does not provide a very readable syntax. Because of this, other syntactic forms for OWL have also been defined:

- an XML-based syntax which does not follow the RDF conventions. This makes this syntax already significantly easier to read by humans.
- an abstract syntax which is used in the language specification document. This syntax is much more compact and readable then either the XML syntax or the RDF/XML syntax
- a graphical syntax based on the conventions of the UML language (Universal Modelling Language). Since UML is widely used, this will be an easy way for people to get familiar with OWL.

### Header

OWL documents are usually called *OWL ontologies*, and are RDF documents. So the root element of a OWL ontology is an `rdf:RDF` element which also specifies a number of namespaces. For example:

```
<rdf:RDF
  xmlns:owl ="http://www.w3.org/2002/07/owl#"
```

```
xmlns:rdf ="http://www.w3.org/1999/02/22-rdf-syntax-ns#"
xmlns:rdfs="http://www.w3.org/2000/01/rdf-schema#"
xmlns:xsd ="http://www.w3.org/2001/XLMSchema#">
```

An OWL ontology may start with a collection of assertions for house-keeping purposes. These assertions are grouped under an `owl:Ontology` element which contains comments, version control and inclusion of other ontologies. For example:

```
<owl:Ontology rdf:about="">
 <rdfs:comment>An example OWL ontology</rdfs:comment>
 <owl:priorVersion
      rdf:resource="http://www.mydomain.org/uni-ns-old"/>
 <owl:imports
      rdf:resource="http://www.mydomain.org/persons"/>
 <rdfs:label>University Ontology</rdfs:label>
</owl:Ontology>
```

The only of these assertions which has any consequences for the logical meaning of the ontology is `owl:imports`: this lists other ontologies whose content is assumed to be part of the current document. ontology. Notice that while namespaces are used for disambiguation purposes, imported ontologies provide definitions that can be used. Usually there will be an import element for each used namespace, but it is possible to import additional ontologies, for example ontologies that provide definitions without introducing any new names.

Also note that `owl:imports` is a transitive property: if ontology $A$ imports ontology $B$, and ontology $B$ imports ontology $C$, then ontology $A$ also imports ontology $C$.

### Class elements

Classes are defined using a `owl:Class` element[7]. For example, we can define a class `associateProfessor` as follows:

```
<owl:Class rdf:ID="associateProfessor">
 <rdfs:subClassOf rdf:resource="#academicStaffMember"/>
</owl:Class>
```

We can also say that this class is disjoint from the `professor` and `assistantProfessor` classes using `owl:disjointWith` elements. These elements can be included in the definition above, or can be added by referring to the id using `rdf:about`. This mechanism is inherited from RDF.

```
<owl:Class rdf:about="#associateProfessor">
 <owl:disjointWith rdf:resource="#professor"/>
 <owl:disjointWith rdf:resource="#assistantProfessor"/>
</owl:Class>
```

---

[7] `owl:Class` is a subclass of `rdfs:Class`.

Equivalence of classes can be defined using a `owl:equivalentClass` element:

```
<owl:Class rdf:ID="faculty">
  <owl:equivalentClass rdf:resource="#academicStaffMember"/>
</owl:Class>
```

Finally, there are two predefined classes, `owl:Thing` and `owl:Nothing`. The former is the most general class which contains everything (everything is a thing), the latter is the empty class. Thus every class is a subclass of `owl:Thing` and a superclass of `owl:Nothing`.

## Property elements

In OWL there are two kinds of properties:

- *Object properties* which relate objects to other objects.
  Examples are `isTaughtBy`, `supervises` etc.
- *Datatype properties* which relate objects to datatype values.
  Examples are `phone`, `title`, age etc. OWL does not have any predefined data types, nor does it provide special definition facilities. Instead it allows one to use XML Schema data types, thus making use of the layered architecture the Semantic Web

Here is an example of a datatype property.

```
<owl:DatatypeProperty rdf:ID="age">
  <rdfs:range rdf:resource=
    "http://www.w3.org/2001/XLMSchema#nonNegativeInteger"/>
</owl:DatatypeProperty>
```

User-defined data types will usually be collected in an XML schema, and then used in an OWL ontology.

Here is an example of an object property:

```
<owl:ObjectProperty rdf:ID="isTaughtBy">
  <rdfs:domain rdf:resource="#course"/>
  <rdfs:range rdf:resource="#academicStaffMember"/>
  <rdfs:subPropertyOf rdf:resource="#involves"/>
</owl:ObjectProperty>
```

More than one domain and range may be declared. In this case the intersection of the domains, respectively ranges, is taken.

OWL allows us to relate "inverse properties". A typical example is isTaughtBy and `teaches`.

```
<owl:ObjectProperty rdf:ID="teaches">
  <rdfs:range rdf:resource="#course"/>
  <rdfs:domain rdf:resource="#academicStaffMember"/>
```

```
  <owl:inverseOf rdf:resource="#isTaughtBy"/>
 </owl:ObjectProperty>

 <owl:ObjectProperty rdf:ID="teaches">
  <rdfs:range rdf:resource="#course"/>
  <rdfs:domain rdf:resource="#academicStaffMember"/>
  <owl:inverseOf rdf:resource="#isTaughtBy"/>
 </owl:ObjectProperty>
```

Actually domain and range can be inherited from the inverse property (interchange domain with range).

Equivalence of properties can be defined using a
`owl:equivalentProperty` element.

```
 <owl:ObjectProperty rdf:ID="lecturesIn">
  <owl:equivalentProperty rdf:resource="#teaches"/>
 </owl:ObjectProperty>
```

**Property restrictions**

With `rdfs:subClassOf` we can specify a class $C$ to be subclass of another class $C'$; then every instance of $C$ is also an instance of $C'$.

Now suppose we wish to declare, instead, that the class $C$ satisfies certain conditions, that is, all instances of $C$ satisfy the conditions. Obviously it is equivalent to saying that $C$ is subclass of a class $C'$, where $C'$ collects all objects that satisfy the conditions. That is exactly how it is done in OWL, as we will show. Note that, in general, $C'$ can remain anonymous, as we will explain below.

The following element requires first year courses to be taught by professors only (according to a questionable view, older and more senior academics are better at teaching).

```
 <owl:Class rdf:about="#firstYearCourse">
  <rdfs:subClassOf>
   <owl:Restriction>
    <owl:onProperty rdf:resource="#isTaughtBy"/>
    <owl:allValuesFrom rdf:resource="#Professor"/>
   </owl:Restriction>
  </rdfs:subClassOf>
 </owl:Class>
```

`owl:allValuesFrom` is used to specify the class of possible values the property specified by `owl:onProperty` can take (in other words: all values of the property must come from this class). In our example, only professors are allowed as values of the property `isTaughtBy`.

We can declare that mathematics courses are taught by David Billington as follows:

```
<owl:Class rdf:about="#mathCourse">
 <rdfs:subClassOf>
  <owl:Restriction>
   <owl:onProperty rdf:resource="#isTaughtBy"/>
   <owl:hasValue rdf:resource="#949352"/>
  </owl:Restriction>
 </rdfs:subClassOf>
</owl:Class>
```

owl:hasValue states a specific value that the property, specified by owl:onProperty must have.

And we can declare that all academic staff members must teach at least one undergraduate course as follows:

```
<owl:Class rdf:about="#academicStaffMember">
 <rdfs:subClassOf>
  <owl:Restriction>
   <owl:onProperty rdf:resource="#teaches"/>
   <owl:someValuesFrom
        rdf:resource="#undergraduateCourse"/>
  </owl:Restriction>
 </rdfs:subClassOf>
</owl:Class>
```

Let us compare owl:allValuesFrom and owl:someValuesFrom. The example using the former requires *every* person who teaches an instance of the class, a first year subject, to be a professor. In terms of logic we have a *universal quantification*.

The example using the latter requires that *there exists* an undergraduate course that is taught by an instance of the class, an academic staff member. It is still possible that the same academic teaches postgraduate courses, in addition. In terms of logic we have an *existential quantification*.

In general, a owl:Restriction element contains a owl:onProperty element, and one or more restriction declarations. One type of restriction declarations are those that define restrictions on the kinds of values the property can take: owl:allValuesFrom, owl:hasValue and owl:someValuesFrom. Another type are *cardinality restrictions*. For example, we can require every course to be taught by at least someone.

```
<owl:Class rdf:about="#course">
 <rdfs:subClassOf>
  <owl:Restriction>
   <owl:onProperty rdf:resource="#isTaughtBy"/>
   <owl:minCardinality
       rdf:datatype="&xsd;nonNegativeInteger">
     1
   </owl:minCardinality>
  </owl:Restriction>
 </rdfs:subClassOf>
```

```
</owl:Class>
```

Notice that we had to specify that the literal "1" is to be interpreted as a nonNeg-ativeInteger (instead of, say, a string), and that we used the xsd namespace declara-tion made in the header element to refer to the XML Schema document.

Or we might specify that, for practical reasons, a department must have at least ten and at most thirty members.

```
<owl:Class rdf:about="#department">
 <rdfs:subClassOf>
  <owl:Restriction>
   <owl:onProperty rdf:resource="#hasMember"/>
   <owl:minCardinality
       rdf:datatype="&xsd;nonNegativeInteger">
    10
   </owl:minCardinality>
  </owl:Restriction>
 </rdfs:subClassOf>
 <rdfs:subClassOf>
  <owl:Restriction>
   <owl:onProperty rdf:resource="#hasMember"/>
   <owl:maxCardinality
       rdf:datatype="&xsd;nonNegativeInteger">
    30
   </owl:maxCardinality>
  </owl:Restriction>
 </rdfs:subClassOf>
</owl:Class>
```

It is possible to specify a precise number. For example, a PhD student must have exactly two supervisors. This can be achieved by using the same number in owl:minCardinality and owl:maxCardinality. For convenience, OWL offers also owl:cardinality.

We conclude by noting that owl:Restriction defines an anonymous class which has no id, is not defined by owl:Class and has only a local scope: it can only be used in the one place where the restriction appears. When we talk about classes please bare in mind the twofold meaning: classes that are defined by owl:Class with an id, and local anonymous classes as collections of objects that satisfy certain restriction conditions, or as combinations of other classes, as we will see shortly. The latter are sometimes called *class expressions*.

## Special properties

Some properties of property elements can be defined directly:

- owl:TransitiveProperty defines a transitive property, such as "has better grade than", "is taller than", "is ancestor of" etc.

- owl:SymmetricProperty defines a symmetric property, such as "has same grade as", "is sibling of", etc.
- owl:FunctionalProperty defines a property that has at most one unique value for each object, such as "age", "height", "directSupervisor" etc.
- owl:InverseFunctionalProperty defines a property for which two different objects cannot have the same value, for example the property "isThe-SocialSecurityNumberfor" (a social security number is assigned to one person only).

An example of the syntactic form of the above is:

```
<owl:ObjectProperty rdf:ID="hasSameGradeAs">
  <rdf:type rdf:resource="&owl;TransitiveProperty" />
  <rdf:type rdf:resource="&owl;SymmetricProperty" />
  <rdfs:domain rdf:resource="#student" />
  <rdfs:range rdf:resource="#student" />
</owl:ObjectProperty>
```

**Boolean combinations**

It is possible to talk about Boolean combinations (union, intersection, complement) of classes (be it defined by owl:Class or by class expressions). For example, we can say that courses and staff members are disjoint as follows:

```
<owl:Class rdf:about="#course">
 <rdfs:subClassOf>
  <owl:Restriction>
   <owl:complementOf rdf:resource="#staffMember"/>
  </owl:Restriction>
 </rdfs:subClassOf>
</owl:Class>
```

This says that every course is an instance of the complement of staff members, that is, no course is a staff member. Note that this statement could also have been expressed using owl:disjointWith.

The union of classes is built using owl:unionOf.

```
<owl:Class rdf:ID="peopleAtUni">
 <owl:unionOf rdf:parseType="Collection">
  <owl:Class rdf:about="#staffMember"/>
  <owl:Class rdf:about="#student"/>
 </owl:unionOf>
</owl:Class>
```

The rdf:parseType attribute is a shorthand for an explicit syntax for building list with <rdf:first> and <rdf:rest> tags. Such lists are required because the built-in containers of RDF have a serious limitation: there is no way to close them, i.e., to say "these are all the members of the container". This is because, while one graph may describe some of the members, there is no way to exclude the possibility that there is another graph somewhere that describes additional members. The list syntax provides exactly this facility, but is very verbose, which motivates the `rdf:parseType` shorthand notation.

Note that this does not say that the new class is a subclass of the union, but rather that the new class is *equal* to the union. In other words, we have stated an *equivalence of classes*. Also, we did not specify that the two classes must be disjoint: it is possible that a staff member is also a student.

Intersection is stated with `owl:intersectionOf`.

```
<owl:Class rdf:ID="facultyInCS">
 <owl:intersectionOf rdf:parseType="Collection">
  <owl:Class rdf:about="#faculty"/>
  <owl:Restriction>
   <owl:onProperty rdf:resource="#belongsTo"/>
   <owl:hasValue rdf:resource="#CSDepartment"/>
  </owl:Restriction>
 </owl:intersectionOf>
</owl:Class>
```

Note that we have built the intersection of two classes, one of which was defined anonymously: the class of all objects belonging to the CS department. This class is intersected with `faculty` to give us the faculty in the CS department.

Further we note that Boolean combinations can be nested arbitrarily. The following example defines administrative staff to be those staff members that are neither faculty nor technical support staff.

```
<owl:Class rdf:ID="adminStaff">
 <owl:intersectionOf rdf:parseType="Collection">
  <owl:Class rdf:about="\#staffMember"/>
   <owl:Class>
    <owl:complementOf>
     <owl:Class>
      <owl:unionOf rdf:parseType="Collection">
       <owl:Class rdf:about="\#faculty"/>
       <owl:Class rdf:about="\#techSupportStaff"/>
      </owl:unionOf>
     </owl:Class>
    </owl:complementOf>
   </owl:Class>
 </owl:intersectionOf>
</owl:Class>
```

### Enumerations

An enumeration is a `owl:oneOf` element, and is used to define a class by listing all its elements.

```
<owl:Class rdf:ID="daysOfTheWeek">
  <owl:oneOf rdf:parseType="Collection">
    <owl:Thing rdf:about="\#Monday"/>
    <owl:Thing rdf:about="\#Tuesday"/>
    <owl:Thing rdf:about="\#Wednesday"/>
    <owl:Thing rdf:about="\#Thursday"/>
    <owl:Thing rdf:about="\#Friday"/>
    <owl:Thing rdf:about="\#Saturday"/>
    <owl:Thing rdf:about="\#Sunday"/>
  </owl:oneOf>
</owl:Class>
```

### Instances

Instances of classes are declared as in RDF. For example:

```
<rdf:Description rdf:ID="949352">
  <rdf:type rdf:resource="#academicStaffMember"/>
</rdf:Description>
```

or equivalently:

```
<academicStaffMember rdf:ID="949352"/>
```

We can also provide further details, such as:

```
<academicStaffMember rdf:ID="949352">
  <uni:age rdf:datatype="&xsd;integer">
    39
  </uni:age>
</academicStaffMember>
```

Unlike typical database systems, OWL does not adopt the *unique names assumption*, thus: just because two instances have a different name (or: ID), that does not imply that they are indeed different individuals. For example, if we state that each course is taught by at most one one staff member:

```
<owl:ObjectProperty rdf:ID="isTaughtBy">
  <rdf:type rdf:resource="&owl;FunctionalProperty" />
</owl:ObjectProperty>
```

and we subsequently state that a given course is taught by two staff members:

```
<course rdf:about="CIT1111">
  <isTaughtBy rdf:resource="#949318"/>
  <isTaughtBy rdf:resource="#949352"/>
</course>
```

this does *not* cause an OWL reasoner to flag an error. After all, the system could validly infer that the resources "949318" and "949352" are apparently equal. To ensure that different individuals are indeed recognised as such, we must explicitly assert their inequality:

```
<lecturer rdf:ID="949318">
  <owl:differentFrom rdf:resource="#949352">
</lecturer>
```

Because such inequality statements occur frequently, and the required number of such statements would explode if we wanted to state the inequality of a large number of individuals, OWL provides a shorthand notation to assert the pairwise inequality of all individuals in a given list:

```
<owl:AllDifferent>
  <owl:distinctMembers rdf:parseType="Collection">
    <lecturer rdf:about="#949318"/>
    <lecturer rdf:about="#949352"/>
    <lecturer rdf:about="949111"/>
  </owl:distinctMembers>
</owl:AllDifferent>
```

Note that `owl:distinctMembers` can only be used in combination with `owl:AllDifferent`.

**Datatypes**

Although XML Schema provides a mechanism to construct user-defined datatypes (e.g. the datatype of `adultAge` as all integers greater than 18, or the datatype of all strings starting with a number), such derived datatypes cannot be used in OWL. In fact, not even all of of the many built-in XML Schema datatypes can be used in OWL. The OWL reference document lists all the XML Schema datatypes that can be used, but these include the most frequently used types such as string, integer, boolean, time and date.

**Versioning information**

We have already seen the *owl:priorVersion* statement as part of the header information to indicate earlier versions of the current ontology. This information has not formal model-theoretic semantics but can be exploited by humans readers and programs alike for the purposes of ontology management.

Besides *owl:priorVersion*, OWL has three more statements to indicate further informal versioning information. None of these carry any formal meaning.

- An `owl:versionInfo`statement generally contains a string giving information about the current version, for example RCS/CVS keywords.
- An `owl:backwardCompatibleWith` statement contains a reference to another ontology. This identifies the specified ontology as a prior version of the containing ontology, and further indicates that it is backward compatible with it. In particular, this indicates that all identifiers from the previous version have the same intended interpretations in the new version. Thus, it is a hint to document authors that they can safely change their documents to commit to the new version

(by simply updating namespace declarations and `owl:imports` statements to refer to the URL of the new version).

- An `owl:incompatibleWith` on the other hand indicates that the containing ontology is a later version of the referenced ontology, but is not backward compatible with it. Essentially, this is for use by ontology authors who want to be explicit that documents cannot upgrade to use the new version without checking whether changes are required.

## Layering of OWL

Now that we have discussed all the language constructors of OWL, we can completely specify which features of the language can be used in which sublanguage (OWL Full, DL and Lite):

*OWL Full*

In OWL Full, all the language constructors can be used in any combination as long as the result is legal RDF.

*OWL DL*

In order to exploit the formal underpinnings and computational tractability of Description Logics, the following constraints must be obeyed in an OWL DL ontology:

- *Vocabulary Partitioning:* any resource is allowed to be only either a class, a datatype, a datatype properties, an object properties, an individuals, a data value or part of the built-in vocabulary, and not more than one of these. This means that, for example, a class cannot be at the same time an individual, or that a property cannot have values some values from a datatype and some values from a class (this would make it both a datatype property and an object property).
- *Explicit typing:* not only must all resources be partitioned (as prescribed in the previous constraint), but this partitioning must be stated explicitly. For example, if an ontology contains the following:

```
<owl:Class rdf:ID="C1">
  <rdfs:subClassOf rdf:resource="#C2" />
</owl:Class>
```

this already entails that C2 is a class (by virtue of the range specification of rdfs:subClassOf). Nevertheless, an OWL DL ontology must *explicitly* state this information:

```
<owl:Class rdf:ID="C2"/>
```

- *Property Separation:* By virtue of the first constraint, the set of object properties and datatype properties are disjoint. This implies that inverse properties, and functional, inverse functional and symmetric characteristics can never be specified for datatype properties.

- *No transitive cardinality restrictions:* no cardinality restrictions may be placed on transitive properties (or their subproperties, which are of course also transitive, by implication).
- *Restricted anonymous classes:* anonymous classes are only allowed in the domain and range of `owl:equivalentClass` and `owl:disjointWith`, and in the range (not the domain) of `rdfs:subClassOf`.

*OWL Lite*

An OWL ontology must be an OWL DL ontology, and must further satisfy the following constraints:

- the constructors `owl:oneOf`, `owl:disjointWith`, `owl:unionOf`, `owl:complementOf` and `owl:hasValue` are not allowed
- cardinality statements (both minimal, maximal and exact cardinality) can only be made on the values 0 or 1, and no longer on arbitrary non-negative integers.
- `owl:equivalentClass` statements can no longer be made between anonymous classes, but only between class identifiers.

## 4.3 Examples

### 4.3.1 An African wildlife ontology

This example shows an ontology that describes part of the African wildlife. Figure 4.2 shows the basic classes and their subclass relationships.

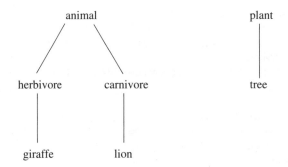

**Fig. 4.2.** Classes and subclasses of the African wildlife ontology

Note that the subclass information is only part of the information included in the ontology. The entire graph is much bigger. Figure 4.3 shows the graphical representation of the statement that branches are parts of trees.

Below we show the ontology, with comments written using `rdfs:comment`.

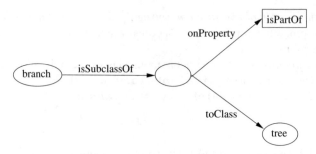

**Fig. 4.3.** Branches are parts of trees

```
<rdf:RDF
 xmlns:rdf="http://www.w3.org/1999/02/22-rdf-syntax-ns#"
 xmlns:rdfs="http://www.w3.org/2000/01/rdf-schema#"
 xmlns:owl ="http://www.w3.org/2002/07/owl#"
 xmlns="http://www.cs.vu.nl/~frankh/spool/wildlife.owl#">

<owl:Ontology rdf:about="">
 <owl:versionInfo>
  My example version 1.2, 17 October 2002
 </owl:versionInfo>
</owl:Ontology>

<owl:Class rdf:ID="animal">
 <rdfs:comment>Animals form a class</rdfs:comment>
</owl:Class>

<owl:Class rdf:ID="plant">
 <rdfs:comment>
  Plants form a class disjoint from animals
 </rdfs:comment>
 <owl:disjointWith rdf:resource="#animal"/>
</owl:Class>

<owl:Class rdf:ID="tree">
 <rdfs:comment>Trees are a type of plants</rdfs:comment>
 <rdfs:subClassOf rdf:resource="#plant"/>
</owl:Class>

<owl:Class rdf:ID="branch">
 <rdfs:comment>Branches are parts of trees </rdfs:comment>
 <rdfs:subClassOf>
  <owl:Restriction>
   <owl:onProperty rdf:resource="#is-part-of"/>
   <owl:allValuesFrom rdf:resource="#tree"/>
  </owl:Restriction>
 </rdfs:subClassOf>
```

```
</owl:Class>

<owl:Class rdf:ID="leaf">
 <rdfs:comment>Leaves are parts of branches</rdfs:comment>
 <rdfs:subClassOf>
  <owl:Restriction>
   <owl:onProperty rdf:resource="#is-part-of"/>
   <owl:allValuesFrom rdf:resource="#branch"/>
  </owl:Restriction>
 </rdfs:subClassOf>
</owl:Class>

<owl:Class rdf:ID="herbivore">
 <rdfs:comment>
  Herbivores are exactly those animals that eat only plants,
  or parts of plants
 </rdfs:comment>
 <owl:intersectionOf rdf:parseType="Collection">
  <owl:Class rdf:about="#animal"/>
  <owl:Restriction>
   <owl:onProperty rdf:resource="#eats"/>
   <owl:allValuesFrom>
    <owl:Class>
     <owl:unionOf rdf:parseType="Collection">
      <owl:Class rdf:about="#plant"/>
      <owl:Restriction>
       <owl:onProperty rdf:resource="#is-part-of"/>
       <owl:allValuesFrom rdf:resource="#plant"/>
      </owl:Restriction>
     </owl:unionOf>
    </owl:Class>
   </owl:allValuesFrom>
  </owl:Restriction>
 </owl:intersectionOf>
</owl:Class>


<owl:Class rdf:ID="carnivore">
 <rdfs:comment>Carnivores are exactly those animals
    that eat also animals</rdfs:comment>
 <owl:intersectionOf rdf:parseType="Collection">
  <owl:Class rdf:about="#animal"/>
  <owl:Restriction>
   <owl:onProperty rdf:resource="#eats"/>
   <owl:someValuesFrom rdf:resource="#animal"/>
  </owl:Restriction>
 </owl:intersectionOf>
</owl:Class>
```

```
<owl:Class rdf:ID="giraffe">
 <rdfs:comment>Giraffes are herbivores, and they
    eat only leaves</rdfs:comment>
 <rdfs:subClassOf rdf:resource="#herbivore"/>
 <rdfs:subClassOf>
  <owl:Restriction>
   <owl:onProperty rdf:resource="#eats"/>
   <owl:allValuesFrom rdf:resource="#leaf"/>
  </owl:Restriction>
 </rdfs:subClassOf>
</owl:Class>


<owl:Class rdf:ID="lion">
 <rdfs:comment>Lions are animals that eat only herbivores
 </rdfs:comment>
 <rdfs:subClassOf rdf:resource="#carnivore"/>
 <rdfs:subClassOf>
  <owl:Restriction>
   <owl:onProperty rdf:resource="#eats"/>
   <owl:allValuesFrom rdf:resource="#herbivore"/>
  </owl:Restriction>
 </rdfs:subClassOf>
</owl:Class>

<owl:Class rdf:ID="tasty-plant">
 <rdfs:comment>Tasty plants are plants that are eaten
       both by herbivores and carnivores</rdfs:comment>
 <rdfs:subClassOf rdf:resource="#plant"/>
 <rdfs:subClassOf>
  <owl:Restriction>
   <owl:onProperty rdf:resource="#eaten-by"/>
   <owl:someValuesFrom>
    <owl:Class rdf:about="#herbivore"/>
   </owl:someValuesFrom>
  </owl:Restriction>
 </rdfs:subClassOf>
 <rdfs:subClassOf>
  <owl:Restriction>
  <owl:onProperty rdf:resource="#eaten-by"/>
  <owl:someValuesFrom>
   <owl:Class rdf:about="#carnivore"/>
  </owl:someValuesFrom>
  </owl:Restriction>
 </rdfs:subClassOf>
</owl:Class>

<owl:TransitiveProperty rdf:ID="is-part-of"/>
```

```
<owl:ObjectProperty rdf:ID="eats">
 <rdfs:domain rdf:resource="#animal"/>
</owl:ObjectProperty>

<owl:ObjectProperty rdf:ID="eaten-by">
 <owl:inverseOf rdf:resource="#eats"/>
</owl:ObjectProperty>

</rdf:RDF>
```

### 4.3.2  A printer ontology

The classes and subclass relationships in this example are shown in Figure 4.4

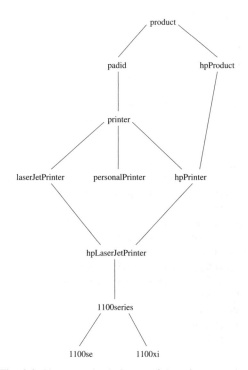

**Fig. 4.4.** Classes and subclasses of the printer ontology

```
<!DOCTYPE owl [
    <!ENTITY xsd  "http://www.w3.org/2001/XLMSchema#" >
]>

<rdf:RDF
```

```
     xmlns:rdf="http://www.w3.org/1999/02/22-rdf-syntax-ns#"
     xmlns:rdfs="http://www.w3.org/2000/01/rdf-schema#"
     xmlns:owl ="http://www.w3.org/2002/07/owl#"
     xmlns:xsd="http://www.w3.org/2001/XLMSchema#"
     xmlns="http://www.cs.vu.nl/~frankh/spool/printer.owl#">

<owl:Ontology rdf:about="">
 <owl:versionInfo>
  My.example version 1.2, 17 October 2002
 </owl:versionInfo>
</owl:Ontology>

<owl:ObjectProperty rdf:ID="manufactured-by"/>

<owl:Class rdf:ID="product">
 <rdfs:comment>Products form a class</rdfs:comment>
</owl:Class>

<owl:Class rdf:ID="padid">
 <rdfs:comment>Printing and digital imaging devices
     form a subclass of products
 </rdfs:comment>
 <rdfs:label>Device</rdfs:label>
 <rdfs:subClassOf rdf:resource="#product"/>
</owl:Class>

<owl:Class rdf:ID="hpProduct">
 <rdfs:comment>HP products are exactly those products
    that are manufactured by Hewlett Packard
 </rdfs:comment>
 <owl:intersectionOf rdf:parseType="Collection">
  <owl:Class rdf:about="#product"/>
  <owl:Restriction>
   <owl:onProperty rdf:resource="#manufactured-by"/>
   <owl:hasValue rdf:datatype="&xsd;string>
    Hewlett Packard"
   </owl:hasValue>
  </owl:Restriction>
 </owl:intersectionOf>
</owl:Class>


<owl:Class rdf:ID="printer">
 <rdfs:comment>Printers are printing and
  digital imaging devices
 </rdfs:comment>
 <rdfs:subClassOf rdf:resource="#padid"/>
</owl:Class>
```

```
<owl:Class rdf:ID="personalPrinter">
 <rdfs:comment>Printers for personal use form
     a subclass of printers
 </rdfs:comment>
 <rdfs:subClassOf rdf:resource="#printer"/>
</owl:Class>

<owl:Class rdf:ID="hpPrinter">
 <rdfs:comment>HP printers are HP products and printers
 </rdfs:comment>
 <rdfs:subClassOf rdf:resource="#printer"/>
 <rdfs:subClassOf rdf:resource="#hpProduct"/>
</owl:Class>


<owl:Class rdf:ID="laserJetPrinter">
<rdfs:comment>Laser Jet printers are exactly those printers
  that use laser jet printing technology</rdfs:comment>
 <owl:intersectionOf rdf:parseType="Collection">
  <owl:Class rdf:about="#printer"/>
  <owl:Restriction>
   <owl:onProperty rdf:resource="#printingTechnology"/>
   <owl:hasValue rdf:datatype="&xsd;string">
    laser jet
   </owl:hasValue>
  </owl:Restriction>
 </owl:intersectionOf>
</owl:Class>

<owl:Class rdf:ID="hpLaserJetPrinter">
 <rdfs:comment>HP laser jet printers are HP products
     and laser jet printers
 </rdfs:comment>
 <rdfs:subClassOf rdf:resource="#laserJetPrinter"/>
 <rdfs:subClassOf rdf:resource="#hpPrinter"/>
</owl:Class>


<owl:Class rdf:ID="1100series">
<rdfs:comment>1100series printers are HP laser jet printers
    with 8ppm printing speed and 600dpi printing resolution
 </rdfs:comment>
 <rdfs:subClassOf rdf:resource="#hpLaserJetPrinter"/>
 <rdfs:subClassOf>
  <owl:Restriction>
   <owl:onProperty rdf:resource="#printingSpeed"/>
   <owl:hasValue rdf:datatype="&xsd;string">
    8ppm
   </owl:hasValue>
```

```
    </owl:Restriction>
   </rdfs:subClassOf>
   <rdfs:subClassOf>
    <owl:Restriction>
     <owl:onProperty rdf:resource="#printingResolution"/>
     <owl:hasValue rdf:datatype="&xsd;string">
      600dpi
     </owl:hasValue>
    </owl:Restriction>
   </rdfs:subClassOf>
  </owl:Class>

  <owl:Class rdf:ID="1100se">
   <rdfs:comment>1100se printers belong to the 1100 series
        and cost $450
   </rdfs:comment>
   <rdfs:subClassOf rdf:resource="#1100series"/>
   <rdfs:subClassOf>
    <owl:Restriction>
     <owl:onProperty rdf:resource="#price"/>
     <owl:hasValue rdf:datatype="&xsd;nonNegativeInteger">
      450
     </owl:hasValue>
    </owl:Restriction>
   </rdfs:subClassOf>
  </owl:Class>

  <owl:Class rdf:ID="1100xi">
   <rdfs:comment>1100xi printers belong to the 1100 series
        and cost $350
   </rdfs:comment>
   <rdfs:subClassOf rdf:resource="#1100series"/>
   <rdfs:subClassOf>
    <owl:Restriction>
     <owl:onProperty rdf:resource="#price"/>
     <owl:hasValue rdf:datatype="&xsd;nonNegativeInteger">
      350
     </owl:hasValue>
    </owl:Restriction>
   </rdfs:subClassOf>
  </owl:Class>

  <owl:DatatypeProperty rdf:ID="manufactured-by">
   <rdfs:domain rdf:resource="#product"/>
   <rdfs:range rdf:resource="&xsd;string"/>
  </owl:DatatypeProperty>

  <owl:DatatypeProperty rdf:ID="price">
   <rdfs:domain rdf:resource="#product"/>
```

```
    <rdfs:range rdf:resource="&xsd;nonNegativeInteger"/>
  </owl:DatatypeProperty>

  <owl:DatatypeProperty rdf:ID="printingTechnology">
    <rdfs:domain rdf:resource="#printer"/>
    <rdfs:range rdf:resource="&xsd;string"/>
  </owl:DatatypeProperty>

  <owl:DatatypeProperty rdf:ID="printingResolution">
    <rdfs:domain rdf:resource="#printer"/>
    <rdfs:range rdf:resource="&xsd;string"/>
  </owl:DatatypeProperty>

  <owl:DatatypeProperty rdf:ID="printingSpeed">
    <rdfs:domain rdf:resource="#printer"/>
    <rdfs:range rdf:resource="&xsd;string"/>
  </owl:DatatypeProperty>

</rdf:RDF>
```

This ontology demonstrates that siblings in a hierarchy tree need not be disjoint. For example, a personal printer may be a HP printer or a LaserJet printer, though the three classes involved are subclasses of the class of all printers.

## 4.4  Summary

- OWL is the proposed standard for Web ontologies. It allows us to describe the semantics of knowledge in a machine-accessible way.
- OWL builds upon RDF and RDF Schema: (XML-based) RDF syntax is used; instances are defined using RDF descriptions; and most RDFS modelling primitives are used.
- Formal semantics and reasoning support is provided through the mapping of OWL on logics. Predicate logic and description logics have been used for this purpose.

While OWL is sufficiently rich to be used in practice, extensions are in the making. They will provide further logical features, including rules.

**Acknowledgement**

We are grateful to Sean Bechhofer of the University of Manchester and Raphael Volz of the University of Karlsruhe for their development of the first "OWL Ontology Validator", which we have used to great benefit while writing this chapter.

## References

The key references for OWL (at the date of writing, April 2003):

1. D. McGuinness and F van Harmelen (eds) *OWL Web Ontology Language Overview*
   `http://www.w3.org/TR/2003/WD-owl-features-20030331/`
2. M. Dean, G. Schreiber (eds), F. van Harmelen, J. Hendler, I. Horrocks, D. McGuinness, P. Patel-Schneider, L. Stein, *OWL Web Ontology Language Reference*
   `http://www.w3.org/TR/2003/WD-owl-ref-20030331/`
3. M. Smith, C. Welty, D. McGuinness, *OWL Web Ontology Language Guide*
   `http://www.w3.org/TR/2003/WD-owl-guide-20030331/`
4. P. Patel-Schneider, P. Hayes, I. Horrocks, *OWL Web Ontology Language Semantics and Abstract Syntax*
   `http://www.w3.org/TR/2003/WD-owl-semantics-20030331/`
5. J. Hefflin, *Web Ontology Language (OWL) Use Cases and Requirements*
   `http://www.w3.org/TR/2003/WD-webont-req-20030331/`

Further interesting articles related to DAML+OIL and OIL include:

6. J. Broekstra et al. Enabling knowledge representation on the Web by Extending RDF Schema. In *Proc. 10th World Wide Web Conference (WWW'10)*, 2001.
7. D. Fensel et al. OIL: An Ontology Infrastructure for the Semantic Web. *IEEE Intelligent Systems* 16,2 (2001).
8. D. McGuinness. Ontologies come of age. In D. Fensel et al. (eds): *The Semantic Web: Why, What, and How*. MIT Press 2002.
9. P. Patel-Schneider, I. Horrocks, F. van Harmelen, Reviewing the Design of DAML+OIL: An Ontology Language for the Semantic Web, *Proceedings of AAAI'02*.

There is a number of interesting Web sites. A key site is:

10. On OWL: `http://www.w3.org/2001/sw/WebOnt/`
11. On its precursor DAML+OIL: `http://www.daml.org` Interesting subpages include:
    a) `http://www.daml.org/language`
    b) `http://www.daml.org/ontologies`
    c) `http://www.daml.org/tools`

The two most relevant chapters from this Handbook are

12. B. McBride, *The Resource Description Framework (RDF) and its Vocabulary Description Language RDFS*, in: *The Handbook on Ontologies in Information Systems*, S. Staab, R. Studer (eds.), Springer Verlag, 2003.
13. F. Baader, I. Horrocks and U. Sattler, *Description Logics*, in: *The Handbook on Ontologies in Information Systems*, S. Staab, R. Studer (eds.), Springer Verlag, 2003.

# 5

# An Ontology-Composition Algebra

Prasenjit Mitra and Gio Wiederhold

Stanford University, Stanford CA, 94017, U.S.A., {mitra, gio}@db.stanford.edu

**Summary.** The need for an algebra to manipulate ontologies is motivated by the impossibility of achieving a globally consistent ontology. Our approach is to integrate information from diverse sources by focusing on the intersection of their ontologies and articulating them accordingly. These articulations typically require rules to define semantic correspondences like synonymy, homonymy, hypernymy, overlapping semantics, and abstraction among the terms of interest. The algebra, needed to compose multiple articulations, has to manipulate the ontologies based on these articulation rules.

The properties of the operators depend upon those of the articulation generation function deployed. The necessary and sufficient conditions that must be satisfied by the articulation generating function in order for the algebraic operators to satisfy properties like commutativity, associativity and distributivity have been identified in this work. Based on whether these properties are satisfied, a task of composing multiple ontologies can be expressed as multiple equivalent algebraic expressions. Using a cost model, the most optimal algebraic expression can be chosen and executed to derive the composed ontology.

## 5.1 Introduction

The semantics of an information source is captured by its ontology, the collection of terms and their relationships as used in the domain of discourse for the source. Most of the focus of *ontologists* has been on developing ever larger, static ontologies[12], without an explicit contextual constraint, even though the developmental efforts were typically initiated in a specific application domain. When new, related applications arise, existing ontologies must be broadened. For instance, to serve a set of intelligence queries hundreds of new definitions had to be added to the already very broad Cyc ontology [14].

We argue below that it is impossible, and not even desirable to achieve a comprehensive ontology that is also globally consistent. To satisfy the needs of an application no single source is adequate, and therefore, we have to exploit a universe of sources. These sources are autonomous, and hence, without a global mandate, mutually inconsistent. In the absence of global consistency it becomes necessary, when information has to be integrated from diverse sources, to compose ontologies that can serve the application domain. We refer to the process of selecting and exploiting linkages as articulation [10].

### 5.1.1 Towards Global Consistency

Global consistency is often assumed by applications that want to exploit the wealth of information that is available today. A cogent and significant example is the semantic net, intended to bring world-wide electronic commerce to the web [15]. We do not argue with the objective, but believe that the required infrastructure must be layered.

While global consistency might be wonderful for the users of information systems, it also has significant costs for the providers of information, and in many cases the costs will be greater than the benefits for specific information providers. We will cover three problems that are being encountered: the process of achieving consistency, the costs of being consistent especially when the objectives of the agents that use the information differ, and the most serious issue, the cost of maintaining consistency over time.

**The process of achieving consistency**

There have been a number of efforts to achieve consistency from multiple sources, typically by merging the terminologies with as much care as is possible. For large terminologies the efforts are large [20]. Problems arise in combining ontologies when the objectives of the sources differ, for instance while combining terms used for diagnosis and reporting of diseases (to the agencies that reimburse for their treatment) with the terms used in the research literature. If exact semantic identity is lacking, terms can be unified at a higher level, and information that is possibly related can be retrieved as well. When the application objective is to study and understand, the end-user can reject misleading records. In such an application scenario, the volume of information retrieved is larger than needed, and the searcher is assured of not missing anything. Ranking of retrieved material can help the searcher in dealing with excessive volume, although ranking based on popularity, as provided by Google is not always the best.

In certain cases a complete unification of a large number of widely disparate ontologies into one monolithic ontology is not feasible due to unresolvable inconsistencies between them that are irrelevant to the application. Even if it is feasible, to preserve their autonomies, multiple ontologies are not integrated into a single ontology. Besides, creating an unified ontology is not scalable and is costly. An integrated ontology would need to be updated frequently [13].

## The cost of being consistent

Apart from occurring due to differences in terminology, semantic mismatches also occur due to differences in abstraction and structure. A householder will use the term `nail' for pointed things to be hit with a hammer, while a carpenter talks about brads, sinkers, in addition to modifiers as 8-penny nails, etc. For the householder to acquire the carpenter's terminology will be costly, to require the carpenter to just use the term nail and then specify length, diameter, head size and material engender much inefficiency.

Simple scope differences, that can still create troublesome inconsistencies, abound. A vehicle is defined differently for the highway police, for an architect, and for government registration. Registration in California covers houseboats, excluded from the concern of the police and architects. The subsidiary structure will also differ for distinct objectives, since classifications serving processing purposes differ, and alternate application will partition their world to allow effective assignment of processing functions.

When information is to be used for an alternate application we often encounter arrogance: `I can't see why they classified x in category y', forestalling attempts at cooperation and integration. Similarly, error rates are often high when data is exploited for unintended purposes, say billing data for medical research, since differences at low levels in clinical hierarchy would not affect billing.

## The cost of maintaining consistency

As indicated initially, the most serious issue in dealing with large, integrated ontologies is their maintenance. Our knowledge continues to evolve, and ontologies capture knowledge of the world. The intellectual process of splitting and lumping concepts, essential to the progress of science requires updating of source ontologies. Derived, integrated ontologies have to be updated then as well, a substantial effort when all possibly related linkages have to be re-verified. Cyc uses microtheories to addresses that problem, but certainly has not solved the issue in a formal manner [17].

When the breadth of coverage is such that committees are needed to define terms, compromises are likely and precision suffers. Development and maintenance costs increases more rapidly than the size of the sources, due to the exponential increase in possible interactions [6]. The reintegration of changes in ICD-9 codes into UMLS [11] induced a delay of several years. A comprehensive model of maintaining medical ontologies has been proposed, but not yet assessed in a large scale [13]. Given that ontology maintenance is likely to be similar to software maintenance, we can assume that over the life-time of an ontology maintenance costs will range from 60 to 90%, with increasing values for large collections [16].

There continue to be extensive debates about establishing a single top-level on-tological taxonomy underpinning all terms in existence. The expectation is that a comprehensive ontology is reusable and will also force consistency onto the world. However, global agreement is hard to achieve, and even if it is achieved at an instant, our knowledge, and hence the meaning attached to the terms changes over time. At a given size of ontology the maintenance required to keep the ontology up-to-date will require all available resources.

### 5.1.2 Composition

If global consistency is not feasible then the alternatives are to have distinct on-tologies for every application or an ability to compose smaller domain ontologies for applications that cover more than one domain. Composition of ontologies for an application by merging has been performed for many instances [14]. It serves immediate needs effectively, but avoids the long-term maintenance problem. The maintenance problem is exacerbated when many sources must be composed.

Rapid composition for new applications has been demonstrated within the DAML and RKF projects. Participating knowledge engineers must comprehend the shape of the ontology and its relationships in order to accurately gauge how changes will affect the knowledge base's performance. At a workshop, a presen-tation [7] described preliminary efforts to align and merge two ontologies con-taining over 3000 concepts apiece. From an observers perspective it became evi-dent that the original structure of the ontology was so fragile enough that no substantial transformation or enhancement was feasible. Many current approaches envisage much larger ontologies [17].

It is also possibly to defer wholesale composition closer to the time of use. In this case, the end user must use the available tools to bring the sources together. For researchers this task is natural, they do not expect that linkages among con-cepts have been provided to them. For regular users, as envisaged for the seman-tic web, that deferred approach is clearly impractical; there is neither sufficient time nor the broad expertise at the point of need. Besides, in this case, several end-users with similar applications, e.g., in a travel-reservation application to book flight tickets and hotel rooms, have to repeat the same task of linking con-cepts across sources before they can use the sources. If the desired semantics of the applications, say as in several travel-reservation applications, is simple, well-defined and match exactly, it makes more sense to establish the linkages between the concepts correctly once and for all. The task of the end-user is then greatly simplified since she does not have to understand the semantics of the sources and bring them together, but can simply log-on to the application and have all the in-formation of the different sources available to her.

**5.1.2.1 The Need for a Composition Algebra:**

Often, creating an ontology from scratch is unnecessary and more expensive than constructing an ontology by composing selected parts of existing ontologies. Applications that reuse the same ontology can easily communicate with each other because the terms they use come from the same ontology. In this paper, we describe an algebra that is used to declaratively specify how to derive ontologies by reusing and composing existing ontologies. A declarative specification allows easy replay of the composition task when the source ontologies change and the change needs to be propagated to derived ontologies. Besides, the properties of a declarative specified composition task can be characterized more easily than those of a programatically specified one.

## 5.2 Articulation of Ontologies

We now present our alternative to integrating ontologies into ever larger bodies. Two important aspects of articulation - as we define it - are:

1. Instead of merging the sources we will create linkages to the sources. Physically the source ontologies might remain with their creators and owners, or be copied for faster access, but logically they should remain unchanged by our needs.

2. Instead of establishing all meaningful linkages between all terms in the source ontologies we only create linkages relevant to a particular application. The articulation is limited to a relevant intersection of the terms.

Since the sources are still accessible, domain specific, unlinked information can still be extracted from those sources, but such information is then not already matched with corresponding information across the sources.

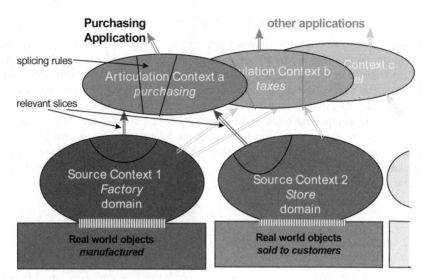

**Figure 1:** Concepts of the SKC approach

Figure 1. illustrates our approach. We consider two sources of information, a Factory and a Store, that must share information in order to enable the purchasing of the Factory's goods by the Store. An articulation serves the Purchasing agents, which can be humans or automated agents. Other articulations between the two sources are feasible, however, they are distinct from the Purchasing articulation. The initial knowledge needed to define the Purchasing articulation precisely would come from the existing purchasing agents, or on a broader level, from experts at a Society of Purchasing Agents for specific types of goods. Other articulations, say regarding taxes, would be developed and maintained by other experts.

### 5.2.1 Mismatch Between Specifications and Their Extension

Mismatches abound in today's information sources between the specification of a concept and the extension of the specification in the sources. Figure 2 below expresses such a mismatch.

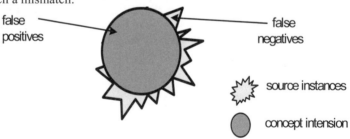

**Figure 2:** Concept specification mismatch

An agent can resolve mismatches between specifications and the actual instances of a class by extracting information about the mismatch and refining specification rules, including constructing rules to include or exclude single anomalous instances. In realistic settings, serving existing applications there are always some people that have dealt with resolving such mismatches in their daily work. Finding them may be hard. Formally describing the articulations is a useful aspect of retaining corporate knowledge, as our organizations change, shrink, and merge.

We assume that narrow, domain-specific ontologies are internally consistent. An ontology, by itself, can be reused in its narrow domain, however, if we are able to compose an adequate new context from the existing ontologies using algebraic operations, following our model, new applications can use it too. The ability to compose ontologies reduces the overall cost of building and maintaining an ontology specific to each application.

### 5.2.2 Defining the Intersection

Maintainability is made simpler by keeping the amount of material to be maintained small. Hence we will only include linkage rules in an articulation that

1. are in the semantic intersection of the domains, and
2. define or relate concepts needed in the application.

Concepts that exist in both ontologies but are irrelevant to the application should not be placed into the articulation ontology.

As we have seen, in our scenario, information resides in multiple sources. An application that answers the queries or performs other tasks posed by an end-user needs to compose information from these sources. In order to compose the information, an articulating agent needs to examine the source ontologies and establish rules that relate the concepts in the ontologies. We will refer to such an agent as the *articulation generator*.

Ideally, we would like an automatic articulation generator that would precisely understand the semantics of the information sources and the application and generate the minimum articulation between pairs of ontologies as needed by the application. However, in order to declaratively capture the semantics of the ontologies and the application that uses them, we would have to use a very expressive language. Automated reasoning with very expressive languages soon becomes intractable. Therefore, we have built a semi-automated articulation generator that uses a simple rule language and interacts with a domain expert.

The articulation generator generates articulation rules semi-automatically. It is based on the SKAT (Semantic Knowledge Articulation Tool) system [19] developed to articulate ontologies and involves the participation of an expert who can ratify the automatically generated semantic matching rules.

## 5.3 The Ontology-Composition Algebra

In this section, we will describe the algebra for the composition of ontologies that we have designed for use in our ONION (ONtology compositION) system[18]. Before we can examine the algebraic operators, we will introduce the format in which the articulation generator we designed expects ontologies to be and then introduce a few definitions that we use later on in the discussion.

### 5.3.1  The ONION Ontology Format

The term "ontology" has many definitions[9],[8]. Our approach is to use a definition and data format that is simple - a "least common format". The format captures the basic features common to most machine-represented ontologies and is simple enough to allow easy transformations from various other ontology formats to ours.

The ONION Ontology Format is based on the work done by Gyssens, et al., [20]. At its core, we represent an ontology as a graph. Formally, an ontology $O$ = $(G,R)$ is represented as a directed labeled graph $G$ and a set of rules $R$. The graph $G=(V,E)$ comprises a finite set of nodes $V$ and a finite set of edges $E$. $R$ is expressed as Horn clauses.

An edge $e$ belonging to the set of edges $E$ is written as (n1, $\alpha$, n2), where n1 and n2 are the labels of two nodes belonging to the set of nodes V and $\alpha$ is the label of the edge between them. In the context of ontologies, the label is often a noun-phrase that represents a concept. The label $\alpha$ of an edge e = (n_1, $\alpha$, n_2) is a string. The label of an edge is the name of a semantic relationship among the concepts that are depicted as nodes in the edge and it can be null. We assume that tno two nodes in the same ontology share the same label and no two ontologies are named the same. Thus, we will use the label of a node along with the ontology name as a unique identifier for the node.

Rules in an ontology are expressed in a logic-based language. The choice of the rule language, in principle, is left open to the ontology constructor. However, to keep the system simple, ONION uses the language of Horn Clauses.

The semantics of the relationships are typically specified in the document it is defined in and the namespace of the relationship is tagged along to clarify the relationship we are referring to. For example, *rdfs : subClassOf*, where *rdfs* is an alias of http://www.w3.org/2000/01/rdfschema# indicates that the relationship that is being used is the relationship *"subclassOf"* as specified in the document whose URL is aliased by *rdfs*. In the rest of the paper, we omit the namespace unless we need to differentiate between two relationships of the same name or the actual URL is relevant to the discussion.

A more detailed description of the ontology format can be found in [21].

### 5.3.2 Preliminaries

For ease of description of the algebra, we will introduce the following terminology:

For a statement *s = (Subject R Object)*, *Nodes*(s) contains *Subject(Object)* provided *Subject(Object)* is not a variable ( that is, it is a node in some ontology graph). For an ontology O1, *Nodes*(O1) represents the nodes in the ontology graph for O1. For a set of rules *R*, *Nodes(R)* represents the union of *Nodes(r)* for all rules *r ε R*, where *Nodes(r)* is the set of all nodes used in the rule *r*.

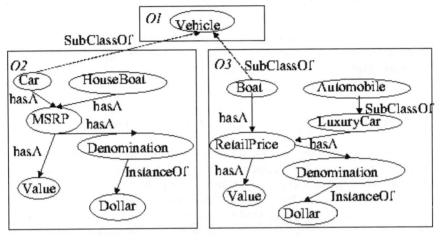

Articulation Rules:

true => (O2.Car SubClassOf O1.Vehicle)

(X InstanceOf O1.Car),(X hasA X.MSRP),(Y InstanceOf X.MSRP),
(Y hasA Y.Value), (Z InstanceOf Y.Value), (Y.Value > 40,000)
=> (X InstanceOf O2.LuxuryCar)

**Figure 3:** Articulation Rules among ontologies

**Example 1:** We introduce an example in Figure 3. O1, O2, and O3 are three ontologies. We only show selected portions of the ontology graphs corresponding to the three ontologies. In order to specify which ontology a concept is defined in, we tag the name of the ontology it belongs to the name of the node. For example, the node labeled O2.Car refers the concept Car as defined in the ontology O2. However, where the origin of the definition is not important (or is obvious) to the topic of discussion, we will simply use the concept name without mentioning the fully qualified name (that is, drop the ontology name tagged in front of it). Let the articulation rules among ontologies O1 and O2 be given by:

$R = \{(O2.Car \ SubClassOf \ O1.Vehicle), \ (O2.HouseBoat \ SubClassOf \ O1.Vehicle)\}$

then $Nodes(R) = \{O2.Car, \ O1.Vehicle, \ O2.HouseBoat\}$.

$Edges(E, \ n)$, where $E$ is a set of edges and $n$ is a node in an ontology graph, represents all edges in $E$ incident upon or incident from the node $n$. Formally, $Edges(E, \ n) = \{s \ \varepsilon E, \ \exists n_1 \mid s = (n_1 \ r \ n) \ or \ s = (n \ r \ n_1)\}$. $Edges(E, \ N)$, where $N$ and $E$ are a set of nodes and edges respectively in an ontology graph, represents a set of edges $S \subseteq E$. Both nodes (the node from which an edge is incident from and the node to which it is incident upon) of each edge in the set $S$ must belong to the set of nodes $N$. Formally, $Edges(E, \ N) = \{ s \varepsilon E, \exists n1, n2 \ \varepsilon N, \exists r \mid s = (n1 \ , \ r, \ n2 \ ) \ \varepsilon E\}$.

Similarly, $Rules(R, N)$ where $R$ is a set of rules and $N$ is a set of nodes, represents the set of rules $R' \subseteq R$, such that all nodes used in any rule in $R'$ is in $N$. Formally, $Rules(E, \ N) = \{ r \varepsilon R \mid Nodes(r) \subseteq N\}$.

### 5.3.3 Articulation Rules and Articulation Generating Functions

As we have seen before, to resolve heterogeneity among ontologies, we need a procedure to generate articulation rules. We refer to procedures that generate articulation rules between ontologies as *articulation generating functions*. An articulation generating function $f$ takes is two ontologies (domain: O x O, where O is the set of ontologies in a particular semantic domain) and outputs a subset of the set of all possible rules (range: the set of all possible rules $R$ among the domain ontologies) between them (f : $OxO \rightarrow 2^R$). We expect the articulation generation to be a complete. That is, for any two ontologies in the domain, the function always terminates and outputs a set of articulation rules that link them. An articulation rule $r$ articulating two ontologies $O1$ and $O2$ is such that $(\exists n \ \varepsilon \ O1, \ \exists n' \ \varepsilon \ O2 \mid n, n' \ \varepsilon \ Nodes(R))$.

**Example 2**: In our running example, we show a few of the articulation rules generated by an articulation generating function. For lack of space, all articulation rules are not shown in Figure 3, but we show two rules graphically, and two textually at the lower part of the figure. The two graphical rules are shown by dotted arrows spanning different ontologies in contrast to the edges in an ontology indicated by solid arrows. Specifically, we see that $O2.Car$ is related via the relationship *SubClassOf* to $O1.Vehicle$. Similarly $O3.Boat$ is related via the relationship *SubClassOf* to $O1.Vehicle$. We show the rule expressing the first relationship both graphically and textually, and the second only graphically. The second articulation rule indicated textually at the bottom of the figure gives a Horn Clause that indicates the relationship between $O2.Car$ and $O3.LuxuryCar$. Any instance of $O2.Car$ that has a $O2.MSRP$ that, in turn, has a $O2.Value$ that is greater than 40,000 is a $O3.LuxuryCar$. Of course, such a rule should also consider the $O2.Denomination$ of the $O2.MSRP$ but for the sake of simplicity we have omitted the denomination from the rule. Note that we use the notation $On.Concept$ to refer to *Concept* as defined in ontology *On*. We assume that in the names of concepts are unique within an ontology.

In this work, we do not consider articulation rules that might introduce new nodes. For example, while articulating between *PoundSterling* and *Guilders*, an articulation generating function might generate an intermediate node called *Euro* and then give the relation between *PoundSterling* and the *Euro* and that between the *Guilder* and the *Euro*.

However, the presence of such an intermediate node influences the properties of the algebraic operators. For example, if an articulation generating function generates intermediate nodes, the intersection operation between ontologies can not be guaranteed to be associative. Thus, we do not consider such articulation generating functions in this work but it is an interesting problem to handle in future.

### 5.3.3.1 Properties of Articulation Generating Functions

We now define a few properties of articulation generating functions that are necessary to describe the effects of articulation generating functions on the properties of the algebraic operators.

A desirable property of an articulation generating function is *concept-level monotonicity*:

**Definition 3.1:**  An articulation generating function f is said to be concept-level monotonic only if it satisfies the following condition:

Let $C_i$ represent a set of concepts represented as the set of nodes $N_i$ in ontology $O_i$. $\forall O_1, O_2, O_3, O_4 \varepsilon$ O:: If $(C_1 \subseteq C_3)$, and $(C_2 \subseteq C_4)$, then $f(O1,O2) \subseteq f(O3,O4)$.

Between any pair of concepts, a concept-level monotonic articulation generating function always generates the same articulation rules irrespective of the ontologies or ontology contexts (neighbourhoods) in which the nodes representing the concepts occur. To see why, construct two ontologies *O1* and *O2* each with a single concept $c_1$ and $c_2$ respectively. Let $f$ be a concept-level monotonic articulation generation function. Let $f$ generate the set of articulation rules $R$ between the ontologies *O1* and *O2*. While articulating any pair of ontologies containing the concepts $c_1$ and $c_2$, $f$ must generate $R$. Thus, whenever the concepts $c_1$ and $c_2$ occur across ontologies being matched, $f$ always generates the set of rules $R$ between $c_1$ and $c_2$.

For example, consider, an ontology matcher that implements an articulation generation function based only on the labels of nodes, say, using natural language processing systems that generate similarities of noun phrases. Such a function is concept-level monotonic since it only checks the node-labels, which remain the same in the source ontologies as well as in the intermediate ontologies.

On the other hand, an ontology matcher that articulates the ontologies based on the context in which the nodes occur, is not guaranteed to be concept-level mono-tonic. Articulation rules generated by an ontology matcher depend that looks at the structure of the ontology graphs is based upon the neighbourhood in which a node appears - that is the nodes in close proximity to it. During the process of on-tology composition selected portions of ontologies can be grafted into *intermedi-ate ontologies*. While performing operations like select, intersection, or differ-ence, (defined in the next section), all nodes in the source ontologies are not selected into the intermediate ontologies. Therefore, the context in which nodes appear in source ontologies and that in which nodes appear in intermediate on-tologies differ. Thus, when matching two intermediate ontologies, a structure-based matcher may generate different artiulation rules while articulating a pair of nodes in the source ontologies and the same pair in the intermediate ontologies. Therefore, a structural matcher is not concept-level monotonic.

A second desirable property of articulation functions is transitive connectivity as defined below:

**Definition 3.2:** An articulation generator function $f$ is said to be {\em transi-tively connective} iff it satisfies the following condition:

If $\forall O1, O2, O3 \; \varepsilon \; O$: $\exists r_1, r_2, O1.A, O2.B, O3.C \mid r_1 \; \varepsilon \; f(O1,O2), r_2 \; \varepsilon \; f(O2,O3)$, $(O1.A, O2.B \; \varepsilon \; Nodes(r_1))$, and $(O2.B, O3.C \; \varepsilon \; Nodes(r_2))$,

then $\exists r_3, r_4, O1.D, O3.E \mid r_3, r_4 \; \varepsilon \; f(O1, O3)$, $O1.A, O3.E \; \varepsilon \; Nodes(r_3)$, $O1.D$, $O3.C \; \varepsilon \; Nodes(r_4)$ holds.

In other words, if the articulation generating function discovers that $O1.A$ is re-lated to $O2.B$ and $O2.B$ is related to $O3.C$, then a transitively connective articula-tion generation function will discover that $O1.A$ is related to some node in $O3$, and $O3.C$ is related to some node in $O1$.

***Example:*** In our running example, if $f$ discovers *(O2.Car SubClassOf O1.Vehicle)* and *(O3.Boat SubClassOf O3.Vehicle)*, we expect a transitively con-nective articulation generator to find some node in *O2* that is related to *O3.Boat* (it might generate the edge *(O2.HouseBoat SubClassOf O3.Boat))* and some node in *O3* (presumably either of *O3.Automobile* and *O3.LuxuryCar*) that is re-lated to *O2.Car*.

### 5.3.4 The Ontology-Composition Algebra

We propose an algebra for the composition of ontologies. The algebra has one unary operator: *Select*, and three binary operations: *Intersection*, *Union*, and *Dif-ference*.

### 5.3.4.1 Unary Operator

**Select**: Using the Select operator, an ontology composer, can select portions of an ontology that might be of interest. For example, a car-dealer is interested about cars does not care about houseboats. The car-dealer will select only portions of ontology *O2* that contain terminology about cars and delete the portions that are not related to cars.

The Select operation has the following four forms:

*Reachability-based Select*: This form of the *Select* operator selects all nodes that can be reached from on a start node and is defined as follows:

**Definition 3.3:** Given an ontology $O = ((N, E), R)$, and a node $n \varepsilon N$, *Select(O, n)* $= (G_n ; R_n)$ where $G_n = (N_n, E_n)$ is a subgraph of $G$ such that for all nodes $n' \varepsilon$ $N_n$, there exists a path from $n$ to $n'$ in $G$. The set $E_n = \{e = (n1 \, R \, n2) \, \varepsilon \, E, n1, n2 \, \varepsilon$ $N_n\}$ is such that each edge in $E_n$ exists in $E$ and expresses a relationship $R$ between nodes *n1* and *n2* where both nodes *n1* and *n2* are in $N_n$. Similarly, $Rn = \{r \, \varepsilon \, R \, |$ $Nodes(r) \, \varepsilon \, N_n\}$ contains all rules in $O$ whose concepts that are all in $N_n$.

The next three forms of the Select operation are based on a set of nodes, a set of edges, or a set of rules:

*Node-based Select:* This form of the Select operation is based on a given set of nodes and is defined as follows:

**Definition 3.4:** Given an ontology $O = ((N, E), R)$, and a set of nodes $V$, *Select(O,V )* $= (G, R_v)$ where $G = (V, E_v)$). The set $E_v = \{e = (n1 \, R \, n2) \, \varepsilon \, E, n1, n2 \, \varepsilon$ $V\}$ and the set $R_v = \{r \, \varepsilon \, R \, | \, Nodes(R) \subseteq V\}$.

*Edge-based Select:* This form of the Select operation is based on a given set of edges and is defined as follows:

**Definition 3.5:** Given an ontology $O = ((V, E), R)$, and a set of edges $E'$, *Select(O,E')* $= (G, R_e)$ where $G = (V_e, E'))$. The set $V_e = Nodes(E')$ and the set $R_e = \{r \, \varepsilon \, R \, | \, Nodes(R) \subseteq V\}$.

*Rule-based Select:* Similarly, this form of the Select operation is based on a given set of rules and is defined as follows:

**Definition 3.6:** Given an ontology $O = ((V, E), R)$, and a set of edges $R'$, *Select(O,R' )* $= (G, R')$, where $G = (V_r, E_r))$. The set $V_r = Nodes(R')$ and the set $E_r = \{e \, \varepsilon \, E \, | \, Nodes(e) \subseteq V\}$.

**Example 3.** In our example, the ontology O3 contain the edges *(O3.LuxuryCar SubClassOf O3.Automobile)*, and *(O3.LuxuryCar hasA O3.RetailPrice)*.

*Select(O3, Automobile)* selects all nodes reachable from the node *O3.Automobile* namely *{LuxuryCar, RetailPrice, Denomination, Value, and Dollar)*, and the edges between them. *Select(O3, {Automobile, LuxuryCar})*, on the other hand, only selects the nodes *{O3.LuxuryCar, O3.Automobile}* and the edge *(O3.LuxuryCar SubClassOf O3.Automobile)*.

Note that a rule *r* in *R* that does not involve any node in *O* has *Nodes*(r) = *{}*. *r* is included in the selected ontology since the empty set is a subset of *N*. For example, a rule expressing the transitivity of the relationship *SubClassOf*:

$$(X \; SubClassOf \; Y), \; (Y \; SubClassOf \; Z) \;) \Rightarrow \; (X \; SubClassOf \; Z)$$

contains only variables *X*, *Y*, and *Z* and no concepts from any ontology. *r* is included in any selected ontology *S* since potentially, *r* can be used to reason about relationships and concepts in *S*.

There are edges (and rules) that are absent in the source ontology but can be derived using the edges and rules available in the source ontology. There is a case for including such edges and rules in the results of the select operation. For example, let us suppose that we had edges *(LuxuryCar SubClassOf Car)*, and *(Car SubClassOf Vehicle)* in an ontology *O*. *Select(O, {Vehicle, Car})* contains the last edge. On the other hand, *Select(O, {Vehicle, LuxuryCar})* selects the nodes *Vehicle*, and *LuxuryCar* but no edges since there are no edges between *Vehicle* and *LuxuryCar* in the source ontology. We could define *Select* to add an edge *(LuxuryCar SubclassOf Vehicle)* if such a relationship could be derived from the ontology *O*, for example, using a rule that said that the relationship *SubClassOf* is transitive.

Similarly, it is easy to see that we could introduce additional rules over and above the ones that the current *Select* operation includes in the selected ontology. However, in order to generate these derived edges and rules, the ontology composition engine would need to interpret the rules of the ontology. In order to allow our framework to be applicable to different ontologies with different interpretation semantics for rules and because potentially we could derive an infinite number of facts in certain scenarios (say with recursive rules), the ontology composition engine does not interpret the rules to maintain its simplicity. Moreover, interpreting rules and deducing relationships and additional rules during a select operation would result in the select operation being extremely expensive to compute especially in the presence of recursive rules where the recursion results in potentially infinite number of instances (of classes). An alternative future work is to only derive relationships from a limited, well-understood set of special relationships that results in a finite number of edges in the selected ontology graph, e.g., derive *SubClassOf* relationships between all nodes while performing the select operation.

### 5.3.4.2  Binary Operators

Each binary operator takes as operands two ontologies that we want to articulate, and generates an ontology as a result, using the articulation rules. The articulation rules have been generated by an articulation generating function.

**Intersection:** is the most important and interesting binary operation.

The intersection of two ontologies $O1 = ((V_1, E_1), R_1)$, and $O2 = ((V_2, E_2), R_2)$ with respect to the set of articulation rule generating function $f$ is:

$OI_{1,2} = O1 \cap_f O2 = ((VI, EI), RI)$, where

$\quad VI = Nodes(f(O1, O2))$,

$\quad EI = Edges(E_1, VI \cap V_1) \cup Edges(E_2, VI \cap V_2) \cup Edges(f(O1, O2))$,

and $RI = Rules(O1, VI \cap V_1) \cup Rules(O2, VI \cap V_2) \cup f(O1, O2)))$.

The nodes in the intersection ontology are those nodes that appear in the articulation rules. An edge in the intersection ontology is an edge among the nodes in the intersection ontology that were either present in the source ontologies or have been output by the articulation generating function as an articulation rule. The rules in the intersection ontology are the articulation rules that are present in the source ontology that use only concepts that occur in the intersection ontology.

Note that since we consider each node as an object instead of the subtree rooted at the node, we will get only the node in the intersection by virtue of its appearing in an articulation rule and not automatically include its attributes or subclasses. Again, a minimal linkage keeps the intersection ontologies small and avoids the inclusion of possibly irrelevant concepts.

Each node in the intersection has a label that contains the URI of the source in which it appears. If the attributes of the object that it represents are required, the application's query processor has to get that information from the original source. Defining the intersection with a minimal outlook reduces the complexity of the composition task, and the maintenance costs, which all depend upon the size of the articulation.

**Union:** The union of two ontologies $O1 = ((V_1, E_1), R_1)$ and $O2 = ((V_2, E_2), R_2)$ with respect to an articulation generating function $f$ is:

$OU_{1,2} = O1 \cup_f O2 = ((VU, EU), RU)$ where

$\quad VU = V_1 \cup V_2 \cup VI$,

$\quad EU = E_1 \cup E_2 \cup EI$,

and $RU = R_1 \cup R_2 \cup RI$,

and where $OI_{1,2} = O1 \cap_f O2 = ((VI, EI), RI)$ is the intersection of the two ontologies with respect to $f$.

The set $VI$ adds nodes that are neither in $V1$ nor $V2$ to $VU$ only if the articulation rules introduce nodes that are neither in $V1$ nor $V2$. The articulation rules indicate relationships between nodes in the two source ontologies and thus introduce new edges (the set EI) that were not there in the source ontologies.

**Difference:** The difference between two ontologies $O1 = ((V_1, E_1), R_1)$ and $O2 = ((V_2, E_2), R_2)$ with respect to an articulating function f is:

$OD = O1 -_f O2 = ((VD, ED), RD)$, where

$\quad VD = V_1 - VI$,

$\quad ED = Edges(E_1, VD)$,

and $RD = Rules(R_1, VD)$,

and where $OI_{1,2} = O1 \cap_f O2 = ((VI, EI), RI)$ is the intersection of the two ontologies with respect to $f$.

That is, the difference ontology includes portions of the first ontology that are not common to the second ontology. The nodes, edges and rules that are not in the intersection ontology but are present in the first ontology comprise the difference ontology.

### 5.3.5 The Influence of the Articulation Generation Function on the Operators

We defined the operators in the algebra on the basis of the articulation rules produced by the articulation generating function. Not surprisingly, most of the properties of the binary operations are based on the properties of the articulation generating function. For example, the intersection and union operators are commutative if and only if the articulation generating function, on which they are based, is commutative (for proofs see [22]).

#### Idempotence:

Idempotence is a very important property that should hold for operations like $Union$ and intersection.

Intuitively, we believe that the *Union* (and *Intersection*) of an ontology with itself should result in the same ontology. It is easy to see that the *Union* and *Intersection* operators are not idempotent since the articulation rules are absent in the source ontologies but included in the result ontology.

**Theorem 3.1 (Idempotence):** The Union and Intersection operators are not idempotent.

Although the strict definition of idempotence is not satisfied, we introduce the concept of *semantic idempotence*.

**Definition 3.7:** A binary operator is *semantically idempotent* if and only if the result of the operation on two copies of the same ontology results in an ontology from which if we remove all self-edges and self-rules, the resulting ontology is the same as the source ontology.

Recall that self-edges are edges between one node and itself and a self-rule is a rule that has only one node (concept) in its definition.

Now we identify the conditions that the articulation generating function must satisfy for semantic idempotence of Union and Intersection.

**Theorem 3.2:** The *Union* operator is semantically idempotent if and only if the corresponding articulation generating function generates only self-edges and self-rules.

Similar to *Union*, it is easy to see that the *Intersection* operator is semantically idempotent, if and only if, the articulation generating function that generated the articulation rules between an ontology and itself generates only self-edges and self-rules for each node in the ontology. This requirement is obvious since we are matching the same ontology to itself and would expect a set of rules to be generated that matches each node to itself.

**Theorem 3.3:** The *Intersection* operator is semantically idempotent if and only if the corresponding articulation generating function generates only self-edges and self-rules and generates at least one self-edge or self-rule for each node in a source ontology.

It is easy to see that the difference operator is not idempotent, nor is it semantically idempotent, but a difference operation using a "well-behaved" articulation generating function - one for which intersection is semantically idempotent - should return the null ontology.

**Commutativity:** Commutativity of operators is another important and desirable property. If an operator is commutative, the operands can be swapped. For certain cost models, the order of the operands influence the cost of the operation. An optimizer that is generating a plan for the composition of the ontologies can optimize the composition by swapping the operands if the operator is commutative.

By the symmetry of the definitions of *Intersection* and *Union*, it is easy to see that these operators are commutative if and only if the articulation generating function they are based on are commutative.

**Theorem 3.4 (Commutativity):** The *Intersection* (and *Union*) operator is commutative if and only if the associated articulation generating function is commutative.

Automatically proving an articulation generating function to be commutative is not always feasible or is prohibitively expensive. In the absence of an automated proof, an ontology composition system requires input from the provider of the articulation generating function or a human expert familiar with the function to indicate whether the function is commutative. In the absence of such manual input, the system conservatively assumes that the operation is not commutative if it cannot prove otherwise and eschews any optimization that results from assuming commutativity.

**Theorem 3.5 (Associativity):** The *Union* operator is associative if and only if the associated articulation generating function is concept-level monotonic and the *Intersection* operator is associative if and only if the corresponding articulation generating function is concept-level monotonic and transitive connective.

**Theorem 3.6 (Distributivity):** $\forall O1,O2,O3$, $((O1 \cup_f O2) \cap_f f\ O3) = (O1 \cap_f O3) \cup_f (O2 \cap_f O3))$ holds iff the articulation generating function $f$ is concept-level monotonic.

Furthermore, for a particular domain, it is easy to define ontologies that are the identity ontology and the null ontology with respect to the *Intersection* and *Union* operators. However, there is no single complement or inverse of ontology in the algebra. We defined an inverse with respect to intersection and another with respect to union, but the two are not the same. The last observation is the only aspect where our algebra differs from a Boolean Algebra [23].

For detailed discussions and proofs of the theorems regarding the necessary and sufficient conditions for the operators to have properties (like commutativity, associativity, and distributivity), please see [22].

### 5.3.6 The Effect of Concept-level Monotonicity

It follows from the necessary and sufficient conditions that the *Intersection* or *Union* operations are neither guaranteed to be associative nor distributive when the articulating generating function is not concept-level monotonic. Certain functions, like structural matchers , depend upon the presence of certain edges between nodes in an ontology to generate matches. Intersection is a "lossy" operation. That is, not all edges in the neighbourhood of a node may be included in an intersection ontology. Since a structural matcher can potentially generate different sets of rules while articulating a pair of nodes at least one of which is in a derived ontology (like an intersection ontology) versus while articulating the pair of nodes in the source ontologies, it is not concept-level monotonic.

Therefore, if the articulation generating function depends upon structural matchers, optimizations enabled by associativity must be disabled unless the structural matcher is guaranteed to be concept-level monotonic. Articulation generating functions that are based on linguistic matchers just look at concept-names and thus typically satisfy concept-level monotonicity conditions. Therefore, with respect to optimizing compositions of ontologies, linguistic matchers are preferred to structural matchers. However, if the structural matchers generate significant semantic matches that are necessary for the application, the composer should use the semantic matcher and not optimize the composition process.

## 5.4 Related Work

Even though a lot of work has been done on suggesting heuristics for articulating and aligning ontologies (or mapping schemas) [2], [3], [4], [5], [24],to the best of our knowledge, no prior work has studied the properties of these heuristic algorithms and shown how the task of composition of ontologies (or databases) is affected by their properties.

Camara, et al., [25], describe an algebra for composing ontologies. However, their work only focuses on obtaining an *Union* of ontologies. Unlike our approach where the ontologies and articulation rules can contain any relationships, they restrict themselves to only three relationships (equivalent, is-a, and part-of). In addition, they do not consider the effects of the articulation generating function on the properties of the composition operation.

Recently, Bernstein, et al. [26], [27] have designed an "algebra" for model management. The intentions of their work are the same as that of ours. In their work, the operands are models and mappings. Their work has identified a set of functions that can be used to manipulate models. They describe models as abstract concepts that have similar properties as ontologies. All nodes in a model must be connected to a root node. Ontologies in our work do not have such constraints. From their preliminary descriptions, their "diff" operator is analogous to "difference" in our work, "merge" is similar to a duplicate-eliminating "union" that we have defined (see [22]). Their algebra does not have an analog to "intersection" but they have a "match" operator that is analogous to an articulation generation function. However, they require the root nodes of each model to match. Their mappings must be expressed using a "mapping" structure that primarily represents binary relationships, whereas we have a rule language to express our articulation rules. Their description of the algebra is at a rudimentary stage. Unlike in our work, they have not yet studied the properties of the algebraic operators and have not shown how the semantic matching functions influence them. They implicitly assume that compositions of mappings are transitive, which our work does not assume.

## 5.5 Conclusion

In this paper, we propose an algebra for the composition of ontologies. The algebraic operators depend upon the properties of an articulation generating function that generates the rules on which the algebra is based. Optimizations can be enabled if the operations are commutative, associative and distributive. We identified the necessary and sufficient conditions that articulation generating functions must satisfy for the operators to be idempotent, commutative, associative, and distributive. As an important corollary, we find that articulating generating functions that deploy linguistic matchers allow more scope for optimizing the process of composing ontologies than structural matchers.

The algebra provides a declarative framework for specifying how ontologies are composed from source ontologies and can be readily replayed automatically when the ontologies change and the composition has to be repeated. This formal basis for the composition of ontologies allows us to perform large tasks that require composing information systematically, and scalably and thereby enables efficient interoperation. Since our model allows the sources to be autonomous, we achieve greater precision by virtue of having fresher information than other methods where information is integrated.

# References:

1. Wiederhold, G. (1994) An algebra for ontology composition. In: Monterey Workshop on Formal Methods., Naval Postgraduate School, 56--61
2. Melnik, S., Garcia-Molina, H., Rahm, E. (2002) Similarity flooding: A versatile graph matching algorithm and its application to schema matching. In: Proc. of the 12th Int. Conf. on Data Engineering, (ICDE), San Jose, California.
3. Doan, A., Domingos, P., Halevy, A.Y. (2001) Reconciling schemas of disparate data sources: A machine-learning approach. In: SIGMOD.
4. Madhavan, J., Bernstein, P.A., Rahm, E. (2001) Generic schema matching with cupid. In: 27$^{th}$ Intl. Conf. VLDB, Roma, Italy, 49—58.
5. Noy, N., Musen, M. (2000) Prompt: Algorithm and tool for automated ontology merging and alignment. In: 7$^{th}$ Natl. Conf. of AAAI-2000.
6. Brooks, F.P. (1995). The Mythical Man-Month, Addison Wesley, 1975, reprinted'95.
7. Chalupsky, H., Hove, E., and Russ, T. (1997) Presentation on Ontology Alignment at ad hoc group on ontology, NCITS.TC.T2 ANSI.
8. Gruber, T.R., (1993) A Translation Approach to Portable Ontology Specifications, Knowledge Acquisition, Vol.5 No. 2, pp.199-220.
9. Gruber, T. R. (1993) Toward principles for the design of ontologies used for knowledge sharing. Talk Padua workshop on Formal Ontology, March . Ed. Nicola Guarino.
10. Guha, R.V. (1991) Contexts: A formalization and some application, Ph.D. dissertation, Stanford University. Also {MCC}Technical Report Number {ACT-CYC}-423-91.
11. Humphreys, B. and Lindberg, D. (1993) The project : Making the conceptual connection between users and the information they need, *Bulletin of the Medical Library Association*, 1993, see also http://www.lexical.com
12. Lenat, D., and Guha R.V. (1990) Building Large Knowledge-Based Systems, Addison-Wesley.
13. Oliver D.E., Shahar, Y., Shortliffe E.H., and Musen, M.A. (1998) Representation of Change on Controlled Medical Terminologies, In Proc. AMIA Conference, October.
14. Teknowledge (1997) High-Performance Knowledge-Bases (HPKB), maintained by Teknowledge Corp. for the DARPA, http://www.teknowledge.com/HPKB.

15. Hendler J., Berners-Lee T, and Miller E. (2001) "The Semantic Web". In Scientific American. May.
    http://www.scientificamerican.com/2001/0501issue/0501berners-lee.html
16. Jones T.C. (1998) Estimating Software Costs; McGraw-Hill.
17. Lenat, D. B. (1995) Cyc: A Large-Scale Investment in Knowledge Infrastructure. Communications of the ACM 38, no. 11 (November).
18. Mitra P., Kersten M. and Wiederhold G. (2000) Graph-Oriented Model for Articulation of Ontology Interdependencies. Proc. 7th Extending Database Technology, EDBT.
19. Mitra P., Wiederhold G., and Jannink J. (1999) Semi-automatic Integration of Knowl edge Sources. In Proceedings of Fusion '99, Sunnyvale, USA, July.
20. Gysenns M., Paredaens J.,  Van den Bussche J., and van Gucht D. (1994) A graph-oriented object database model. In IEEE Trans. on KDE, Vol. 6, No. 4, pp. 572-586.
21.  Mitra P., Wiederhold G., and Decker S. (2001) A Scalable Framework for Interoperation of Information Sources. 1st Int. Semantic Web Working Symp. (SWWS `01).
22.  Mitra P., http://www-db.stanford.edu/~prasen9
23.  Boole, G. (1854) An investigation into the Laws of Thought, on Which are founded the Mathematical Theories of Logic and Probabilities.
24.  McGuiness, D.L., Fikes R., Rice, J., and Wilder, S. (2000) The Chimaera Ontology Environment.  Seventh National Conference on Artificial Intelligence (AAAI-2000).
25.  Camara, G., Fonseca, F., and Monteiro A.M. (2002) Algebraic Structures For Spatial Ontologies.  Poster at GIScience 2002, Boulder, CO, USA, Annals, AAG, September 25-28,
    http://www.dpi.inpe.br/gilberto/papers/ontologies_giscience2002.pdf
26.  Bernstein, P.A. (2003) Applying Model Management to Classical Meta Data Problems, *Proc. CIDR 2003*, pp. 209-220
27.  Bernstein, P.A., Levy, A.Y., and Pottinger, R.A., A Vision for Management of Complex Models, Microsoft Research Technical Report MSR-TR-2000-53, June.

# Part II

# Ontology Engineering

# On-To-Knowledge Methodology (OTKM)

York Sure[1], Steffen Staab[1,2,4], and Rudi Studer[1,2,3,4]

[1] Institute AIFB, University of Karlsruhe
   Postfach, 76128 Karlsruhe, Germany
   http://www.aifb.uni-karlsruhe.de
   Contact: sure@aifb.uni-karlsruhe.de
[2] Ontoprise GmbH
   Karlsruhe, Germany
   http://www.ontoprise.de
[3] FZI Research Center for Information Technologies
   Knowledge Management Department (WIM)
   Karlsruhe, Germany
   http://www.fzi.de/wim
[4] L3S Learning Lab
   Hannover/Karlsruhe, Germany
   http://www.learninglab.de

**Summary.** In this chapter we present the On-To-Knowledge Methodology (OTKM) for introducing and maintaining ontology based knowledge management applications into enterprises with a focus on Knowledge Processes and Knowledge Meta Processes. While the former process circles around the usage of ontologies, the latter process guides their initial set up. We illustrate our methodology by an example from a case study on skills management.

## 6.1 Introduction

In recent years Knowledge Management (KM) has become an important success factor for enterprises. Increasing product complexity, globalization, virtual organizations or customer orientation are developments that ask for a thorough and systematic management of knowledge – within an enterprise and between several cooperating enterprises. Obviously, KM is a major issue for human resource management, enterprise organization and enterprise culture – nevertheless, information technology (IT) plays the crucial enabler for many aspects of KM. As a consequence, KM is an inherently interdisciplinary subject.

IT-supported KM solutions are built around some kind of organizational memory [1] that integrates informal, semi-formal and formal knowledge in order to facilitate its access, sharing and reuse by members of the organization(s) for solving their individual or collective tasks [7]. In such a context, knowledge has to be modelled, appropriately structured and interlinked for supporting its flexible integration and its personalized presentation to the consumer. Ontologies have shown to be the right answer to these structuring and modeling problems by providing a formal conceptualization of a particular domain that is shared by a group of people in an organization [23, 14].

There exist various proposals for methodologies that support the systematic introduction of KM solutions into enterprises. One of the most prominent methodologies is CommonKADS that puts emphasis on an early feasibility study as well as on constructing several models that capture different kinds of knowledge needed for realizing a KM solution [26]. Typically, these methodologies conflate two processes that should be kept separate in order to achieve a clear identification of issues [28]: whereas the first process addresses aspects of introducing a new KM solution into an enterprise as well as maintaining it (the so-called "Knowledge Meta Process"), the second process addresses the handling of the already set-up KM solution (the so-called "Knowledge Process") (see Figure 6.1). *E.g.* in the approach described in [25], one can see the mixture of aspects from the different roles that, *e.g.* "knowledge identification" and "knowledge creation" play. The Knowledge Meta Process would certainly have its focus on knowledge identification and the Knowledge Process would rather stress knowledge creation. However, Knowledge Management is a process which is not only governed by IT. Hence, one needs to keep the balance between human problem solving and automated IT solutions. This balancing distinguishes KM from traditional knowledge-based systems.

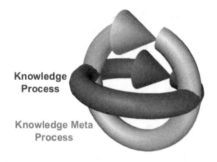

**Knowledge Process**

**Knowledge Meta Process**

**Fig. 6.1.** Two orthogonal processes with feedback loops

The here presented methodology was developed and applied in the EU project On-To-Knowledge[5] [6]. We now describe some general issues when implementing and inventing knowledge management applications. Then we focus on the knowledge meta process and the knowledge process and illustrate the instantiation of the knowledge meta process by an example from a skills management case study of the On-To-Knowledge project.

---

[5] http://www.ontoknowledge.org

## 6.2 Implementation and Invention of KM Applications

To implement and invent any KM application, one has to consider different processes (*cf.* Figure 6.2). We experienced mainly three major process that influenced our case study, *i.e.* "Knowledge Meta Process", "Human Issues" and "Software Engineering". These processes are not completely separate but also interfere. As mentioned in the introduction, KM is an inherently interdisciplinary subject which is not only governed by information technology (IT). Hence, one needs to keep the balance between human problem solving and automated IT solutions. As a rule of thumb it was carefully estimated by KM experts at a "Dagstuhl Seminar on Knowledge Management"[6] (*cf.* [24]) that in "real life" IT support cannot cover more than 10—30% of KM.

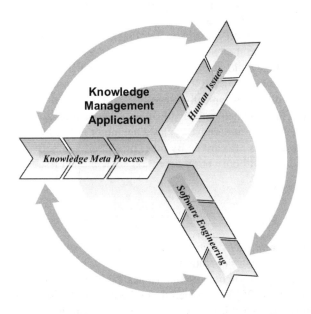

**Fig. 6.2.** Relevant processes for developing and deploying KM applications

Human issues (HI) and the related cultural environment of organizations heavily influence the acceptance of KM. It is often mentioned in discussions that the success of KM – and especially KM applications – strongly depends on the acceptance by the involved people. As a consequence, "quick wins" are recommended for the initial phase of implementing any KM strategy. The aim is to quickly convince people that KM is useful for them and adds value to their daily work.

Software engineering (SE) for knowledge management applications has to fit to the other processes. Especially the requirements coming from the knowledge processes need to be reflected.

---

[6] http://dagstuhl-km-2000.aifb.uni-karlsruhe.de/

In the following sections we will now focus on the Knowledge Meta Process as the core process and illustrate some cross-links to the other mentioned processes.

## 6.3 Knowledge Meta Process

The Knowledge Meta Process (*cf.* Figure 6.3) consists of five main steps. Each step has numerous sub-steps, requires a main decision to be taken at the end and results in a specific outcome. The main stream indicates steps (phases) that finally lead to an ontology based KM application. The phases are "Feasibility Study", "Kickoff", "Refinement", "Evaluation" and "Application & Evolution". Below every box depicting a phase the most important sub-steps are listed, *e.g.* "Refinement" consists of the sub-steps "Refine semi-formal ontology description", "Formalize into target ontology" and "Create prototype" etc. Each document-flag above a phase indicates major outcomes of the step, *e.g.* "Kickoff" results in an "Ontology Requirements Specification Document (ORSD)" and the "Semi-formal ontology description" etc. Each node above a flag represents the major decisions that have to be taken at the end to proceed to the next phase, *e.g.* whether in the Kickoff phase one has captured sufficient requirements. The major outcomes typically serve as decision support for the decisions to be taken. The phases "Refinement – Evaluation – Application & Evolution" typically need to be performed in iterative cycles. One might notice that the development of such an application is also driven by other processes, *e.g.* software engineering and human issues. We will only briefly mention some human issues in the example section.

### 6.3.1 Feasibility Study

Any knowledge management system may function properly only if it is seamlessly integrated in the organization in which it is operational. Many factors other than technology determine success or failure of such a system. To analyze these factors, we initially start with a *feasibility study* [26], *e.g.* to identify problem/opportunity areas and potential solutions. In general, a feasibility study serves as a decision support for economical, technical and project feasibility, determining the most promising focus area and target solution.

### 6.3.2 Kickoff

In the kickoff phase the actual development of the ontology begins. Similar to requirements engineering and as proposed by [10] we start with an **ontology requirements specification document** (ORSD). The ORSD describes what an ontology should support, sketching the planned area of the ontology application and listing, *e.g.* valuable knowledge sources for the gathering of the semi-formal ontology description. The ORSD should guide an ontology engineer to decide about inclusion and exclusion of concepts and relations and the hierarchical structure of the ontology.

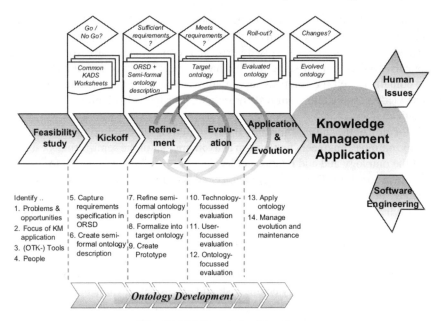

**Fig. 6.3.** The Knowledge Meta Process

In this early stage one should look for already developed and potentially reusable ontologies.

The **outcome** of this phase is (beside the ontology requirement specification document (ORSD)) a semi-formal description of the ontology, *i.e.* a graph of named nodes and (un-)named, (un-)directed edges, both of which may be linked with further descriptive text *e.g.* in form of mind maps (*cf.* [4, 30]). If the requirements are sufficiently captured, one may proceed with the next phase. The **decision** is typically taken by ontology engineers in collaboration with domain experts. "Sufficiently" in this context means, that from the current perspective there is no need to proceed with capturing or analyzing knowledge. However, it might be the case that in later stages gaps are recognized. Therefore, the ontology development process is cyclic.

### 6.3.3  Refinement

During the kick-off and refinement phase one might distinguish in general two concurrent approaches for modeling, in particular for refining the semi-formal ontology description by considering relevant knowledge sources: top-down and bottom-up. In a **top-down**-approach for modeling the domain one starts by modeling concepts and relationships on a very generic level. Subsequently these items are refined. This approach is typically done manually and leads to a high-quality engineered ontology. Available top-level ontologies may here be reused and serve as a starting point to develop new ontologies. In our example scenario we encountered a **middle-out** approach, *i.e.* to identify the most important concepts which will then be used to obtain the remainder of the hierarchy by generalization and specialization. However, with the support of an automatic document analysis, a typical **bottom-up**-approach may be applied. There, relevant concepts are extracted semi-automatically from available documents. Based on the assumption that most concepts and conceptual structures of the domain as well the company terminology are described in documents, applying knowledge acquisition from text for ontology design helps building ontologies automatically.

To **formalize** the initial semi-formal description of the ontology into the target ontology, ontology engineers firstly form a taxonomy out of the semi-formal description of the ontology and add relations other than the "is-a" relation which forms the taxonomical structure. The ontology engineer adds different types of relations as analyzed *e.g.* in the competency questions to the taxonomic hierarchy. However, this step is cyclic in itself, meaning that the ontology engineer now may start to interview domain experts again and use the already formalized ontology as a base for discussions. It might be helpful to visualize the taxonomic hierarchy and give the domain experts the task to add attributes to concepts and to draw relations between concepts (*e.g.* we presented them the taxonomy in form of a mind map as mentioned in the previous section). The ontology engineer should extensively document the additions and remarks to make ontological commitments made during the design explicit.

The **outcome** of this phase is the "target ontology", that needs to be evaluated in the next step. The major **decision** that needs to be taken to finalize this step is whether the target ontology fulfills the requirements captured in the previous kickoff phase. Typically an ontology engineer compares the initial requirements with the current status of the ontology. This decision will typically be based on the personal experience of ontology engineers. As a good rule of thumb we discovered that the first ontology should provide enough "flesh" to build a prototypical application. This application should be able to serve as a first prototype system for evaluation.

### 6.3.4 Evaluation

We distinguish between three different types of evaluation: (i) technology-focussed evaluation, (ii) user-focussed evaluation and (iii) ontology-focused evaluation.

Our evaluation framework for **technology-focussed evaluation** consists of two main aspects: (i) the evaluation of properties of ontologies generated by development tools, (ii) the evaluation of the technology properties, i.e. tools and applications which includes the evaluation of the evaluation tool properties themselves. In an overview these aspects are structured as follows:(i) Ontology properties (*e.g.* language conformity (Syntax), consistency (Semantics)) and (ii) technology properties (*e.g.* interoperability, turn around ability, scalability etc.).

The framework shown above concentrates on the technical aspects of ontologies and related ontologies. However, the aspect of **user-focussed evaluation** remains open. The most important point from our perspective is to evaluate whether users are satisfied by the KM application. More specific, whether an ontology based application is at least as good as already existing applications that solve similar tasks.

Beside the above mentioned process oriented and pragmatic evaluation methods, one also need to **formally evaluate ontologies**. One of the most prominent approaches here is the OntoClean approach (*cf. e.g.* [15]), which is based on philosophical notions. Applying this approach leads to more correct hierarchies of ontologies.

The **outcome** of this phase is an evaluated ontology, ready for the roll-out into a productive system. However, based on our own experiences we expect in most cases several iterations of "Evaluation – Refinement – Evaluation" until the outcome supports the decision to roll-out the application. The major **decision** that needs to be taken for finalizing this phase is whether the evaluated ontology fulfills all evaluation criteria relevant for the envisaged application of the ontology.

### 6.3.5 Application & Evolution

The **application** of ontologies in productive systems, or, more specifically, the usage of ontology based systems, is being described in the following Section 6.4 that illustrates the knowledge process.

The **evolution** of ontologies is primarily an organizational process. There have to be strict rules to the update, insert and delete processes of ontologies (*cf.* [29]). We recommend, that ontology engineers gather changes to the ontology and initiate the switch-over to a new version of the ontology after thoroughly testing all possible effects to the application. Most important is therefore to clarify *who* is responsible for maintenance and *how* it is performed and in *which time intervals* is the ontology maintained.

The **outcome** of an evolution cycle is an evolved ontology, *i.e.* typically another version of it. The major **decision** to be taken is when to initiate another evolution cycle for the ontology.

## 6.4 Knowledge Process

Once a KM application is fully implemented in an organization, knowledge processes essentially circle around the following steps (*cf.* Figure 6.4).

- *Knowledge creation* and/or *import* of documents and meta data, *i.e.* contents need to be created or converted such that they fit the conventions of the company, *e.g.* to the knowledge management infrastructure of the organization;
- then knowledge items have to be *captured* in order to elucidate importance or interlinkage, *e.g.* the linkage to conventionalized vocabulary of the company by the creation of relational metadata;
- *retrieval of* and *access to knowledge* satisfies the "simple" requests for knowledge by the knowledge worker;
- typically, however, the knowledge worker will not only recall knowledge items, but she will process it for further *use* in her context.

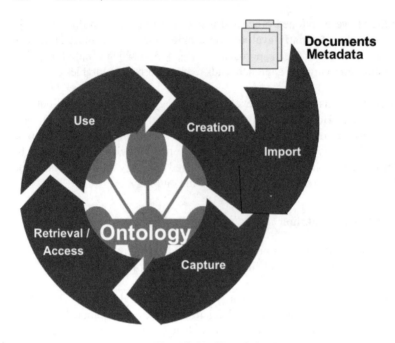

**Fig. 6.4.** The Knowledge Process

## 6.5 Example: Skills Management @ Swiss Life

We now give an example of the Knowledge Meta Process instantiation of a skills management case study at Swiss Life (*cf.* [18]). Skills management makes skills of employees explicit. Within the case study existing skill databases and documents (like *e.g.* personal homepages) are integrated and expanded. Two aspects are covered by the case study: first, explicit skills allow for an advanced expert search within the intranet. Second, one might explore his/her future career path by matching current skill profiles *vs.* job profiles. To ensure that all integrated knowledge sources are used in the same way, ontologies are used as a common mean of interchange to face two major challenges. Firstly, being an international company located in Switzerland, Swiss Life has internally four official languages, *viz.* German, English, French and Italian. Secondly, there exist several spellings of same concepts, *e.g.* "WinWord" *vs.* "MS Word". To tackle these problems, ontologies offer external representations for different languages and allow for representation of synonymity. Figure 6.5 shows a screenshot from the skills management application. The prototype enables any employee to integrate personal data from numerous distributed and heterogeneous sources into a single coherent personal homepage.

### 6.5.1 Feasibility Study

For identifying factors which can be central for the success or failure of the ontology development and usage we made a requirement analysis of the existing skills management environment and evaluated the needs for a new skills management system. We identified mainly the human resources department and the management level of all other departments as actors and stakeholders for the skills management. After finding the actors and stakeholders in the skills management area, we named the ontology experts for each department, which are preferably from the associated training group of each department.

### 6.5.2 Kickoff

The departments private insurance, human resources and IT constitute three different domains that were the starting point for an initial prototype. The task was to develop a skills ontology for the departments containing three trees, *viz.* for each department one. The three trees should be combined under one root with cross-links in between. The root node is the abstract concept "skills" (which means in German "Kenntnisse/Faehigkeiten") and is the starting point to navigate through the skills tree from the top.

During the **kickoff** phase two workshops with three domain experts[7] were held. The first one introduced the domain experts to the ideas of ontologies. Additional potential knowledge sources were identified by the domain experts, that were exhaustively used for the development of the ontologies, *e.g.* a book of the Swiss Association of Data Processing ("Schweizerischer Verband fuer Datenverarbeitung") describing professions in the computing area in a systematic way similar to an ontology. Obviously, this was an excellent basis to manually build the skills ontology for the IT domain. First experiments with extracting an ontology semi-automatically by using information extraction tools did not satisfy the needs for a clearly structured and easily understandable model of the skills. The domain experts and potential users felt very uncomfortable with the extracted structures and rather chose to build the ontology by themselves "manually". To develop the first versions of the ontologies, we used a mind mapping tool ("MindManager"). It is typically used for brainstorming sessions and provides simple facilities for modelling hierarchies very quickly. The early modelling stages for ontologies contain elements from such brainstorming sessions (*e.g.* the gathering of the semi-formal ontology description).

During this stage a lot of "concept islands" were developed, which were isolated sets of related terms. These islands are subdomains of the corresponding domain and are self-contained parts like "operating systems" as sub domain in the IT domain. After developing these concept islands it was necessary to combine them into a single tree. This was a more difficult part than assembling the islands, because the islands were interlaced and for some islands it was possible to add them to more than

---

[7] Thanks to Urs Gisler, Valentin Schoeb and Patrick Shann from Swiss Life for their efforts during the ontology modelling.

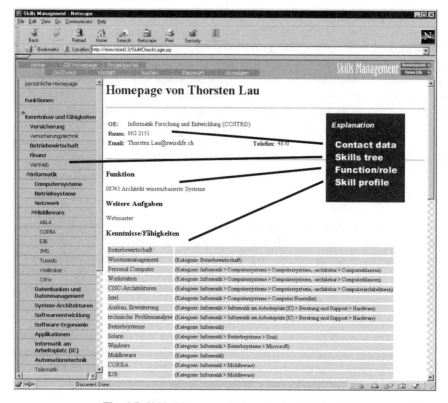

**Fig. 6.5.** Skills Management Case Study @ Swiss Life

one other island, which implies awkward skills trees that contain inconsistencies after merging. For each department one skills tree was built in separate workshops. A problem that came up very early was the question where to draw the line between concepts and instances. *E.g.* is the programming language Java instantiated by "jdk1.3" or is "jdk1.3" so generic that it still belongs to the concept-hierarchy? Another problem was the size of the ontology. What is the best depth and width of each skills tree? Our solution was, that it depends on the domain and should be determined by the domain expert.

As **result** of the kick-off phase we obtained the semi-formal ontology descriptions for the three skills trees, which were ready to be formalized and integrated into a single skills ontology. At this stage the skills trees reached a maturity that the combination of them caused no major changes for the single skills trees.

### 6.5.3 Refinement

During the **refinement** phase we formalized and integrated the semi-formal ontology descriptions into a single coherent skills ontology. An important aspect during the formalization was (i) to give the skills proper names that uniquely identify each skill and (ii) to decide on the hierarchical structure of the skills. We discussed two different approaches for the hierarchical ordering: we discovered that categorization of skills is typically not based on an is-a-taxonomy, but on a much weaker HASSUBTOPIC relationship that has implications for the inheritance of attached relations and attributes. However, for our first prototype this distinction made no difference due to missing cross-taxonomical relationships. But, according to [15], subsumption provided by is-a taxonomies is often misused and a later formal evaluation of the skills ontology according to the proposed OntoClean methodology possibly would have resulted in a change of the ontology.

In a second refinement cycle we added one more relation type, an "associative relation" between concepts. They express relations outside the hierarchic skills tree, *e.g.* a relation between "HTML" and "JSP", which occur not in the same tree, but correspond with each other, because they are based on the same content. "HTML" is in the tree "mark-up languages", while the tree "scripting languages" contains "JSP". This is based on the basic characteristics and the history of both concepts, which changed over time. But in reality they have a close relationship, which can be expressed with the associative relation.

The other task in this phase was to integrate the three skills ontologies into one skills ontology and eliminate inconsistencies in the domain ontology parts and between them. Because the domain ontologies were developed separately, the merger of them caused some overlaps, which had to be resolved. This happened for example in the computer science part of the skills trees, where the departments IT and private insurance have the same concepts like "Trofit" (which is a Swiss Life specific application). Both departments use this concept, but each uses a different view. The IT from the development and the private insurance from the users view. Additionally the personal skills of any employee are graded according to a generic scale of four levels: basic knowledge, practical experience, competency, and top specialist. The employees will grade their own skills themselves. As known from personal contacts to other companies (*e.g.* Credit Suisse, ABB and IBM), such an approach proved to produce highly reliable information.

As a **result** at the end of the refinement phase the "target skills ontology" consisted of about 700 concepts, which could be used by the employees to express their skill profile.

### 6.5.4 Application & Evolution

The **evaluation** of the prototype and the underlying ontology was unfortunately skipped due to internal restructuring at Swiss Life which led to a closing down of the whole case study.

Still, we considered the following aspects for the **evolution** of our skills management application: The competencies needed from employees are a moving target. Therefore the ontologies need to be constantly evaluated and maintained by experts from the human resource department. New skills might be suggested by the experts themselves, but mainly by employees. Suggestions include both, the new skill itself as well as the position in the skills tree where it should be placed. While employees are suggesting only new skills, the experts decide which skills should change in name and/or position in the skills tree and, additionally, decide which skill will be deleted. This was seen as necessary to keep the ontology consistent and to avoid that *e.g.* similar if not the same concept appear even in the same branch. For each ontology (and domain) there should exist a designated ontology manager who decides if and how the suggested skill is integrated.

## 6.6 Related Work on Methodologies

A first overview on methodologies for ontology engineering can be found in [8]. More recently, there have been joint efforts of OntoWeb[8] members, who produced an extensive state-of-the-art overview of methodologies for ontology engineering (*cf.* [13, 9]). There exist also deliverables on guidelines and best practices for industry (*cf.* [19, 20]) with a focus on applications for E-Commerce, Information Retrieval, Portals and Web Communities. With respect to this work, especially the following approaches are noteworthy.

**CommonKADS** [26] is not *per se* a methodology for ontology development. It covers aspects from corporate knowledge management, through knowledge analysis and engineering, to the design and implementation of knowledge-intensive information systems. CommonKADS has a focus on the initial phases for developing knowledge management applications, we therefore relied on CommonKADS for the early feasibility stage. *E.g.* a number of worksheets is proposed that guide through the process of finding potential users and scenarios for successful implementation of knowledge management.

**Cyc** [21] arose from experience of the development of the Cyc knowledge base (KB)[9], which contains a huge amount of common sense knowledge. Cyc has been used during the experimentation in the High Performance Knowledge Bases (HPKB), a research program to advance the technology of how computers acquire, represent and manipulate knowledge[10]. Until now, this methodology is only used for building the Cyc KB. However, Cyc has different micro-theories showing the knowledge of different domains from different viewpoints. In some areas, several micro-theories can be used, and each micro-theory can be seen from different perspectives and with different assumptions. The Cyc project strongly enhanced the visibility of the knowledge engineering community, but at the same time it suffered from his very high goal to model "the world". Recently this goal has been lowered and now one has divided this too complex task into smaller ones,*e.g.* the Cyc top-level ontology was separated.

Recently, the **DOGMA** modelling approach [17, 27] has been presented. The database-inspired approach relies on the explicit decomposition of ontological re-

---

[8] OntoWeb, a European thematic network, see http://www.ontoweb.org for further information.

[9] Cyc knowledge base, see http://www.cyc.com

[10] HPKB, see http://reliant.teknowledge.com/HPKB/about/about.html

sources into *ontology bases* in the form of simple binary facts called lexons and into so-called ontological commitments in the form of description rules and constraints.

The **Enterprise Ontology** [35] [36] proposed three main steps to engineer ontologies: (i) to identify the purpose, (ii) to capture the concepts and relationships between these concepts, and the terms used to refer to these concepts and relationships, and (iii) to codify the ontology. In fact, the principles behind this methodology influenced many work in the ontology community and they are also reflected in the steps kickoff and refinement of our methodology and extended them.

The **KACTUS** [3] approach requires an existing knowledge base for the ontology development. They propose to use means of abstraction, *i.e.* a bottom-up strategy, to extract on ontology out of the knowledge base as soon as an application in a similar domain is built.

**METHONTOLOGY** [11, 10] is a methodology for building ontologies either from scratch, reusing other ontologies as they are, or by a process of re-engineering them. The framework enables the construction of ontologies at the "knowledge level". The framework consists of: identification of the ontology development process where the main activities are identified (evaluation, configuration, management, conceptualization, integration implementation, *etc.*); a lifecycle based on evolving prototypes; and the methodology itself, which specifies the steps to be taken to perform each activity, the techniques used, the products to be output and how they are to be evaluated. METHONTOLOGY is partially supported by WebODE. Our combination of the On-To-Knowledge Methodology and OntoEdit (*cf.* [30, 31]) is quite similar to the combinations of METHONTOLOGY and WebODE (*cf.* [2]. In fact, they are the only duet that has reached a comparable level of integration of tool and methodology.

**SENSUS** [33] is a top-down and middle-out approach for deriving domain specific ontologies from huge ontologies. The approach does not cover the engineering of ontologies as such, therefore offers a very specialized methodology.

**TOVE** [34] proposes a formalized method for building ontologies based on competency questions. We found the approach of using competency questions, that describe the questions that an ontology should be able to answer, very helpful and integrated it in our methodology.

## 6.7 Conclusion

The described methodology was developed and applied in the On-To-Knowledge project. One of the core contributions of the methodology that could not be shown here is the linkage of available tool support with case studies by showing when and how to use tools during the process of developing and running ontology based applications in the case studies (cf. [32]).

Lessons learned during setting up and employing the methodology in the On-To-Knowledge case studies include: (i) different processes drive KM projects, but "Human Issues" might dominate other ones (as already outlined by Davenport [5]), (ii) guidelines for domain experts in industrial contexts have to be pragmatic, (iii) collaborative ontology engineering requires physical presence *and* advanced tool support and (iv) brainstorming is very helpful for early stages of ontology engineering, especially for domain experts not familiar with modelling (more details on be found *e.g.* in [30, 31]).

In this chapter we have shown a process oriented methodology for introducing and maintaining ontology based knowledge management systems. Core to the methodology are Knowledge Processes and Knowledge Meta Processes. While Knowledge Meta Processes support the setting up of an ontology based application, Knowledge Processes support its usage. Still, there are many open issues to solve, *e.g.* how to handle a distributed process of emerging and aligned ontologies that is likely to be the scenario in the semantic web.

## 6.8 Acknowledgments

The research presented in this chapter greatly benefits from contributions of our colleagues at the Institute AIFB/University of Karlsruhe, the closely related company Ontoprise GmbH and our project partner SwissLife from On-To-Knowledge. We thank especially Hans-Peter Schnurr (now Ontoprise GmbH) and Hans Akkermans (VU Amsterdam) for their seminal work while setting up the baseline version of this methodology. Part of this work has been financed by the EU in the project IST-1999-10132 On-To-Knowledge.

## References

1. A. Abecker, A. Bernardi, K. Hinkelmann, O. Kuehn, and M. Sintek. Toward a technology for organizational memories. *IEEE Intelligent Systems*, 13(3):40–48, 1998.
2. J. C. Arpírez, O. Corcho, M. Fernández-López, and A. Gómez-Pérez. WebODE: a scalable workbench for ontological engineering. In *Proceedings of the First International Conference on Knowledge Capture (K-CAP) Oct. 21-23, 2001, Victoria, B.C., Canada*, 2001.
3. A. Bernaras, I. Laresgoiti, and J. Corera. Building and reusing ontologies for electrical network applications. In *Proceedings of the European Conference on Artificial Intelligence (ECAI'96)*, 1996.
4. T. Buzan. *Use your head*. BBC Books, 1974.
5. T. H. Davenport and L. Prusak. *Working Knowledge – How organisations manage what they know*. Havard Business School Press, Boston, Massachusetts, 1998.
6. J. Davies, D. Fensel, and F. van Harmelen, editors. *On-To-Knowledge: Semantic Web enabled Knowledge Management*. J. Wiley and Sons, 2002.
7. R. Dieng, O. Corby, A. Giboin, and M. Ribiere. Methods and tools for corporate knowledge management. *Int. Journal of Human-Computer Studies*, 51(3):567–598, 1999.
8. M. Fernández-López. Overview of methodologies for building ontologies. In *Proceedings of the IJCAI-99 Workshop on Ontologies and Problem-Solving Methods: Lessons Learned and Future Trends*. CEUR Publications, 1999.

9.  M. Fernandéz-López, A. Gómez-Pérez, J. Euzenat, A. Gangemi, Y. Kalfoglou, D. M. Pisanelli, M. Schorlemmer, G. Steve, L. Stojanovic, G. Stumme, and Y. Sure. A survey on methodologies for developing, maintaining, integrating, evaluating and reengineering ontologies. OntoWeb deliverable 1.4, Universidad Politecnia de Madrid, 2002.
10. M. Fernández-López, A. Gómez-Pérez, J. P. Sierra, and A. P. Sierra. Building a chemical ontology using Methontology and the Ontology Design Environment. *Intelligent Systems*, 14(1), January/February 1999.
11. A. Gómez-Pérez. A framework to verify knowledge sharing technology. *Expert Systems with Application*, 11(4):519–529, 1996.
12. A. Gómez-Pérez and V. R. Benjamins, editors. *Proceedings of the 13th International Conference on Knowledge Engineering and Knowledge Management: Ontologies and the Semantic Web (EKAW 2002)*, volume 2473 of *Lecture Notes in Artificial Intelligence (LNAI)*, Siguenza, Spain, 2002. Springer.
13. A. Gómez-Pérez, M. Fernandéz-López, O. Corcho, T. T. Ahn, N. Aussenac-Gilles, S. Bernardos, V. Christophides, O. Corby, P. Crowther, Y. Ding, R. Engels, M. Esteban, F. Gandon, Y. Kalfoglou, G. Karvounarakis, M. Lama, A. López, A. Lozano, A. Magkanaraki, D. Manzano, E. Motta, N. Noy, D. Plexousakis, J. A. Ramos, and Y. Sure. Technical roadmap. OntoWeb deliverable 1.1.2, Universidad Politecnia de Madrid, 2002.
14. T. R. Gruber. Towards principles for the design of ontologies used for knowledge sharing. *International Journal of Human-Computer Studies*, 43(5/6):907–928, 1995.
15. N. Guarino and C. Welty. Evaluating ontological decisions with OntoClean. *Communications of the ACM*, 45(2):61–65, February 2002.
16. I. Horrocks and J. A. Hendler, editors. *Proceedings of the First International Semantic Web Conference: The Semantic Web (ISWC 2002)*, volume 2342 of *Lecture Notes in Computer Science (LNCS)*, Sardinia, Italy, 2002. Springer.
17. M. Jarrar and R. Meersman. Formal ontology engineering in the DOGMA approach. In Meersman et al. [22], pages 1238–1254.
18. T. Lau and Y. Sure. Introducing ontology-based skills management at a large insurance company. In *Proceedings of the Modellierung 2002*, pages 123–134, Tutzing, Germany, March 2002.
19. A. Léger, H. Akkermans, M. Brown, J.-M. Bouladoux, R. Dieng, Y. Ding, A. Gómez-Pérez, S. Handschuh, A. Hegarty, A. Persidis, R. Studer, Y. Sure, V. Tamma, and B. Trousse. Successful scenarios for ontology-based applications. OntoWeb deliverable 2.1, France Télécom R&D, 2002.
20. A. Léger, Y. Bouillon, M. Bryan, R. Dieng, Y. Ding, M. Fernandéz-López, A. Gómez-Pérez, P. Ecoublet, A. Persidis, and Y. Sure. Best practices and guidelines. OntoWeb deliverable 2.2, France Télécom R&D, 2002.
21. D. B. Lenat and R. V. Guha. *Building large knowledge-based systems. Representation and inference in the CYC project*. Addison-Wesley, Reading, Massachusetts, 1990.
22. R. Meersman, Z. Tari, et al., editors. *Proceedings of the Confederated International Conferences: On the Move to Meaningful Internet Systems (CoopIS, DOA, and ODBASE 2002)*, volume 2519 of *Lecture Notes in Computer Science (LNCS)*, University of California, Irvine, USA, 2002. Springer.
23. D. O'Leary. Using AI in knowledge management: Knowledge bases and ontologies. *IEEE Intelligent Systems*, 13(3):34–39, May/June 1998.
24. D. O'Leary and R. Studer. Knowledge management: An interdisciplinary approach. *IEEE Intelligent Systems, Special Issue on Knowledge Management*, 16(1), January/Febrary 2001.
25. G. Probst, K. Romhardt, and S. Raub. *Managing Knowledge*. J. Wiley and Sons, 1999.

26. G. Schreiber, H. Akkermans, A. Anjewierden, R. de Hoog, N. Shadbolt, W. van de Velde, and B. Wielinga. *Knowledge Engineering and Management — The CommonKADS Methodology.* The MIT Press, Cambridge, Massachusetts; London, England, 1999.

27. P. Spyns, R. Meersman, and M. Jarrar. Data modelling versus ontology engineering. *SIGMOD Record – Web Edition*, 31(4), December '02 2002. Special Section on Semantic Web and Data Management; R. Meersman and A. Sheth (eds.); Available at http://www.acm.org/sigmod/record/.

28. S. Staab, H.-P. Schnurr, R. Studer, and Y. Sure. Knowledge processes and ontologies. *IEEE Intelligent Systems, Special Issue on Knowledge Management*, 16(1):26–34, January/Febrary 2001.

29. L. Stojanovic, A. Maedche, B. Motik, and N. Stojanovic. User-driven ontology evolution management. In Gómez-Pérez and Benjamins [12], pages 285–300.

30. Y. Sure, M. Erdmann, J. Angele, S. Staab, R. Studer, and D. Wenke. OntoEdit: Collaborative ontology development for the semantic web. In Horrocks and Hendler [16], pages 221–235.

31. Y. Sure, S. Staab, and J. Angele. OntoEdit: Guiding ontology development by methodology and inferencing. In Meersman et al. [22], pages 1205–1222.

32. Y. Sure and R. Studer. On-To-Knowledge Methodology — final version. On-To-Knowledge deliverable 18, Institute AIFB, University of Karlsruhe, 2002.

33. B. Swartout, P. Ramesh, K. Knight, and T. Russ. Toward distributed use of largescale ontologies. In *Symposium on Ontological Engineering of AAAI*, Stanford, CA., 1997.

34. M. Uschold and M. Grueninger. Ontologies: Principles, methods and applications. *Knowledge Sharing and Review*, 11(2), June 1996.

35. M. Uschold and M. King. Towards a methodology for building ontologies. In *Workshop on Basic Ontological Issues in Knowledge Sharing, held in conjunction with IJCAI-95*, Montreal, Canada, 1995.

36. M. Uschold, M. King, S. Moralee, and Y. Zorgios. The enterprise ontology. *Knowledge Engineering Review*, 13(1):31–89, 1998.

# Building a Very Large Ontology from Medical Thesauri

Udo Hahn[1] and Stefan Schulz[2]

[1]  Text Knowledge Engineering Lab
    Universität Freiburg, Werthmannplatz 1, D-79085 Freiburg, Germany
    hahn@coling.uni-freiburg.de
[2]  Department of Medical Informatics
    Universitätsklinikum Freiburg, Stefan-Meier-Str. 26, D-79104 Freiburg, Germany
    stschulz@uni-freiburg.de

**Summary.** We report on a large-scale knowledge conversion and curation case study. Medical knowledge from a comprehensive, though semantically shallow terminological repository, the UMLS, is transformed into a formally rigorous, expressive description logics format. This way, the broad coverage of the UMLS is combined with inference mechanisms for consistency and cycle checking. They are the key not only to proper cleansing of the knowledge directly imported from the UMLS, but also to subsequent updating and refinement of large amounts of rich and complex terminological knowledge structures. The emerging biomedical ontology currently comprises more than 240,000 conceptual entities and, hence, constitutes one of the largest formal knowledge bases ever built.

## 7.1 Introduction

Tasks such as disease and medical procedure encoding, or searches for medical documents in bibliographic data bases usually require reference to shared domain knowledge. Typically, this sort of common knowledge is made available through nomenclatures (controlled vocabularies), thesauri or classification codes. They serve the need to unify the use of lexical or phrasal variants of a single concept (by reference to a preferred term), to link terms via semantic relations (e.g., X is a broader or narrower term than Y, X is synonymous to Y, X is part of (or has part) Y), or to create a hierarchical system of numerical or symbolic categories ordered by increasing specificity of the terms they stand for.

Unlike many other disciplines, medicine has a long standing tradition in assembling and structuring its knowledge, disease taxonomies, medical procedures, anatomical terms, etc., in a wide variety of medical terminologies, thesauri and classification systems. These efforts are typically restricted to the provision of broader and narrower terms, related terms or (quasi-)synonymous terms. This is most evident in the UMLS, the *Unified Medical Language System* [18], an umbrella system which covers more than 60 medical thesauri and classifications (e.g., MESH, ICD, SNOMED, DIGITAL ANATOMIST).

From a conceptual perspective, the UMLS can be divided into two major parts. The UMLS *Semantic Network (SN)*, on the one hand, forms the upper ontology and consists of 134 semantic types linked by 54 types of semantic relations, which makes a total of 7,473 vertices. The UMLS *Metathesaurus*, on the other hand, contains 875,255 concepts (2003 version), each of which is assigned to one or more UMLS SN types. These concepts are linked by the semantic relations also supplied by the UMLS SN. In total, 10,552,299 semantic links between these Metathesaurus concepts exist, most of them directly taken from the sources, some added by the UMLS developers. The vast majority of these links reflect thesaurus-style broader/narrower term relationships.

The UMLS SN and the Metathesaurus form a huge semantic network. Its semantics is shallow and entirely intuitive, which is due to the fact that their usage was primarily intended for humans in order to support health-related knowledge management. Given the size, the evolutionary diversity and inherent heterogeneity of the UMLS, there is no surprise that the lack of a formal semantic foundation leads to inconsistencies, circular definitions, etc. [6, 5]. This may not cause utterly severe problems when humans are in the loop and its use is limited to disease or procedure encoding, accountancy or document retrieval tasks. Anticipating its use for more knowledge-intensive applications such as medical decision making [23] or the understanding of medical narratives [11] those shortcomings might lead to an impasse.

As a consequence, formal models for dealing with medical knowledge have been proposed such as conceptual graphs, semantic networks or description logics [7, 17, 22, 34, 10]. Not surprisingly, there is a price to be paid for more expressiveness and formal rigor, *viz.* increasing modeling efforts and, hence, increasing maintenance costs [20]. Operational systems which make full use of such rigid approaches, especially those which employ high-end knowledge representation languages, are usually restricted to rather small subdomains. The most comprehensive of these sources we know of is the GRAIL-encoded GALEN knowledge base which covers up to 9,800 concepts [22]. The limited coverage hampers their routine usage, an aspect which is always highly rewarded in the medical informatics community.

Almost all of the knowledge bases developed on the basis of formal representation languages have been designed from scratch – without making systematic use of the large body of knowledge contained in widely spread medical terminologies. So it would be an intriguing approach to join the massive coverage offered by informal medical terminologies with the high level of expressiveness and deductive reasoning capabilities supported by state-of-the-art knowledge representation systems in order to develop formally solid medical ontologies on a larger scale. This idea has already been fostered by Pisanelli et al. [19] who extracted knowledge from the UMLS SN and from parts of the Metathesaurus, and merged them with logic-based top-level ontologies from various sources. Another example is the re-engineering of SNOMED [8] from a multi-axial coding system into a formally well-founded ontology [33, 32]. These efforts, however, are entirely focused on generalization-based reasoning along taxonomies and lack a reasonable coverage of partonomies, another crucial part of medical knowledge.

## 7.2 Reasoning Along Part-Whole Hierarchies

Medical knowledge is mainly organized around generalization hierarchies – on which taxonomic reasoning along *is-a* relations is based – and part-whole hierarchies – allowing partonomic reasoning along *part-of* or *has-part* relations. Unlike generalization-based reasoning in concept taxonomies, no fully conclusive mechanism exists up to now for reasoning along part-whole hierarchies (for a survey of different approaches, cf. Artale et al. [1]).

Within the description logics paradigm (for a survey, cf. [2]) several extensions to representation languages have been proposed which provide special constructors for part-whole reasoning [22, 14]. From a medical perspective, a major challenge comes with the propagation of properties across part-whole hierarchies, often referred to as 'inheritance across transitive roles' (e.g., *inflammation-of* ∘ *part-of* → *inflammation-of*) [4, 21]. Unfortunately, this reasoning pattern cannot be generalized, since it faces lots of exceptions. In a similar vein, the transitivity property of the part-whole relation is generally assumed to hold. For medicine [12], as well as in commonsense domains [9, 35], however, this view has also been invalidated. Both the expression of regular transitive use, as well as exception handling for nontransitive *part-of* relations then equally have to be taken into consideration within a homogeneous formal framework.

Motivated by previous approaches [26, 28], we formalized a model of partonomic reasoning [12] that accounts for the above considerations. Moreover, our solution does not exceed the expressiveness of the well-understood, parsimonious concept language $\mathcal{ALC}$ [3],[3] since we wanted our model to be as simple as possible. Our proposal is centered around a particular data structure for the encoding of concepts, so-called *SEP triplets*. They define a characteristic pattern of *is-a* hierarchies which support the emulation of inferences typical of transitive *part-of* relations. In this format, the relation *anatomical-part-of* describes the partitive relation between physical parts of an organism.

An SEP triplet (cf. Figure 7.1) consists, first of all, of a composite *Structure* concept, the so-called *S-node* (e.g., *Hand-Structure*, $H_S$). Each *Structure* concept subsumes directly an anatomical *Entity* concept, on the one hand, and a common subsumer of anything that is a *Part* of that entity concept, on the other hand. These two concepts are called *E-node* and *P-node*, e.g., *Hand-Entity* ($H_E$) and *Hand-Part* ($H_P$), respectively. While E-nodes denote the anatomical concepts proper to be modelled in our domain, S-nodes and P-nodes constitute representational artifacts required for

---

[3] $\mathcal{ALC}$ allows for the construction of concept hierarchies, where '⊑' denotes subsumption and '≐' definitional equivalence. Existential (∃) and universal (∀) quantification, negation (¬), disjunction (⊔) and conjunction (⊓) are also supported. Role filler constraints (e.g., typing by $C$) are linked to the relation name $R$ by a dot, $\exists R.C$.

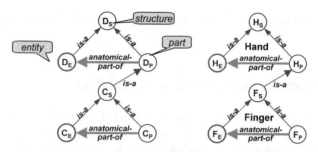

**Fig. 7.1.** SEP Triplets: Partitive Relations within Taxonomies

the formal reconstruction of the systematic patterns as well as the exceptions underlying partonomic reasoning.

More precisely, a P-node is the common subsumer of those concepts that have their role *anatomical-part-of* filled by the corresponding E-node concept, as an existential condition. For example, *Hand-Part* subsumes those concepts all instances of which have a *Hand-Entity* as a necessary whole. As an additional constraint, E-nodes and P-nodes can be modelled as being mutually disjoint. This is a reasonable assumption for most concepts denoting singleton objects, where parts and wholes cannot be of the same type (a red blood cell cannot be part of yet another red blood cell). On the contrary, masses and collections can have parts and wholes of the same type, e.g., a tissue can be part of another tissue.[30]

For the formal reconstruction of the *anatomical-part-of* relation by taxonomic reasoning, we assume $C_E$ and $D_E$ to denote E-nodes, $C_S$ and $D_S$ to denote the S-nodes that subsume $C_E$ and $D_E$, respectively, and $C_P$ and $D_P$ to denote the P-nodes related to $C_E$ and $D_E$, respectively, via the role *anatomical-part-of* (cf. Figure 7.1). These conventions can be captured by the following terminological expressions:

$$C_E \sqsubseteq C_S \sqsubseteq D_P \sqsubseteq D_S \tag{7.1}$$

$$D_E \sqsubseteq D_S \tag{7.2}$$

The P-node is defined as follows (we here introduce the disjointness constraint between $D_E$ and $D_P$, i.e., no instance of $D$ can be *anatomical-part-of* any other instance of $D$):

$$D_P \doteq D_S \sqcap \neg D_E \sqcap \exists anatomical\text{-}part\text{-}of.D_E \tag{7.3}$$

Since $C_E$ is subsumed by $D_P$ (according to (1)), we infer that the relation *anatomical-part-of* holds between $C_E$ and $D_E$, too:[4]

$$C_E \sqsubseteq \exists anatomical\text{-}part\text{-}of.D_E \tag{7.4}$$

---

[4] An extension of this encoding scheme which allows additional reasoning about *has-part* in a similar way is proposed in [30], though it has not been considered in the ontology described in this article.

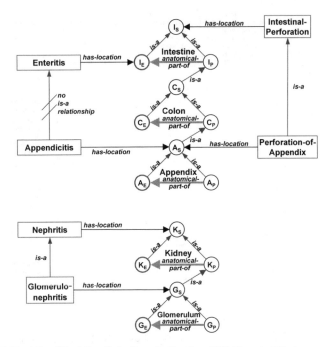

**Fig. 7.2.** Enabling/Disabling Role Propagation in a SEP-Encoded Partonomy

The encoding of concept hierarchies via SEP triplets allows the knowledge engineer to switch the role propagation property of part-whole relations off and on, dependent on whether the E-node or the S-node, respectively, is addressed as the target for a conceptual relation. In the first case, the propagation of roles across part-whole hierarchies is disabled, in the second case it is enabled. As an example (cf. Figure 7.2), *Enteritis* is defined as *has-location Intestine$_E$*, i.e., the range of the relation *has-location* is restricted to the E-node of *Intestine*. This precludes the classification of *Appendicitis* as *Enteritis* although *Appendix* is related to *Intestine* via an *anatomical-part-of* relation. In the 'on' mode, however, *Glomerulonephritis* (*has-location Glomerulum$_S$*) is classified as *Nephritis* (*has-location Kidney$_S$*), with *Glomerulum* being an *anatomical-part-of* the *Kidney*. In the same way, *Perforation-of-Appendix* is classified as *Intestinal-Perforation* (cf. [12] for an in-depth analysis).

## 7.3 Ontology Engineering Workflow: Re-engineering the UMLS

Our goal is to extract conceptual knowledge from two major subdomains of the UMLS, *viz.* anatomy and pathology, in order to construct a formally sound ontology using description logics. The knowledge conversion workflow consists of four distinct steps (cf. also the diagram depicted in Figure 7.3):

| UMLS relation | number of links | Step 1<br>Automatic generation of Loom definitions, augmented by P-Loom language elements<br>;;; = comment line | Step 2<br>Submission to Loom classifier.<br>Validation for formal consistency by Loom | Step 3<br>Manual restitution of formal consistency | Step 4<br>Manual rectification and refinement of the resulting knowledge base |
|---|---|---|---|---|---|
| **Anatomy Concepts Linked to Anatomy Concepts** | | | | | |
| sibling_of | 267.218 | ;;; SIB | | | add negations in order to express taxonomic or partitive disjointness |
| child_of | 59.808 | ;;; CHDRN | | | include related concepts into :is-primitive or :part-of clause where plausible |
| narrower_term | 24.223 | ;;; CHDRN | | | |
| isa | 9.755 | :is-primitive | check for definitional cycles | remove taxonomic parent concepts | substitute of primitive links by non-primitive ones where possible |
| location_of | 4.803 | ;;; LOCATION_OF | | | include related concepts into :has-part clause where plausible |
| has_location | 4.803 | ;;; HAS_LOCATION | | | include related concepts into :part-of clause, where plausible |
| has_part | 4.321 | | | | check whether this part is mandatory (under "real-anatomy" assumption) |
| has_conceptual_part | 126 | :has-part | | | |
| part_of | 4.321 | | 1. check for partonomic cycles<br>2. check for disjointness between E and P node | 1. remove partonomic or taxonomic parent concepts<br>2. redefine triplet as single concept | check for plausibility and completeness |
| conceptual_part_of | 126 | :part-of | | | |
| parent | 59.808 | ;;; PARRB | | | include related concepts into :has-part clause where plausible |
| broader_term | 24.223 | ;;; PARRB | | | |
| inverse_isa | 9.755 | | | | |
| associated_with | 14 | | | | |
| mapped_from | 2.643 | | | | |
| other_relation | 10.908 | <do nothing> | | | |
| qualified_by | 1.864 | | | | |
| allowed_qualifier | 1.864 | | | | |
| mapped_to | 2643 | | | | |
| <other named relations> | 11.886 | (:some x) | check for inherited constraints | remove constraints | remove or add constraints |
| **Pathology Concepts Linked to Pathology Concepts** | | | | | |
| sibling_of | 457.542 | ;;; SIB | | | add negations in order to express taxonomic disjointness |
| child_of | 72.426 | | | | substitute primitive links by non-primitive ones whenever possible |
| narrower_term | 26.972 | :is-primitive | check for definitional cycles | remove parent concepts | |
| isa | 3.635 | | | | |
| inverse_isa | 3.635 | | | | |
| associated_with | 13.902 | | | | |
| mapped_to | 15.024 | | | | |
| mapped_from | 15.024 | | | | |
| part_of | 1 | | | | |
| has_part | 1 | <do nothing> | | | |
| parent | 72.426 | | | | |
| broader_term | 28.972 | | | | |
| other_relation | 25.796 | | | | |
| qualified_by | 6.255 | | | | |
| allowed_qualifier | 6.255 | | | | |
| <other named relations> | 4.162 | (:some x) | check for inherited constraints | remove constraints | remove or add constraints |
| **Pathology Concepts Linked to Anatomy Concepts** | | | | | |
| CUlpat = CUlana | 2.247 | (:some has_anatomic_correlate) | | | plausibility check of concept "duplication" (assignment to both domains) |
| <missing> | | <do nothing> | | | add pathology-anatomy links |
| associated_with | 2.314 | (:some associated_with <anatomy_concept>_S) | | check for consistency | render links complete, link to E-node instead of S-node when role propagation has to be disabled |
| has_location | 9.230 | (:some has_location <anatomy_concept>_S) | | | |
| <other> | | <do nothing> | | | |

**Fig. 7.3.** Workflow for the construction of a LOOM Knowledge Base from the UMLS

1. Terminological axioms in the format of description logics are automatically generated from the relational table structures imported from the UMLS source. While all the domain concepts from its anatomy and pathology section were taken into account, only a carefully selected subset of relation types from the UMLS were incorporated. Among those were relations such as *part-of/has-part*, *is-a* or *has-location*, since we considered them as reliable indicators for partonomic and taxonomic hierarchies, as well as spatial knowledge, respectively. We excluded overly general ones such as *sibling-of* or *associated-with* from further consideration at this level of processing, since they are likely to introduce noise into the relational structure of the emerging knowledge base.
2. The 'raw' ontology is then immediately checked automatically by the description logics classifier (for details, cf. [16]) whether it contains definitional cycles or whether it is inconsistent.
3. If inconsistent or cyclic knowledge structures are encountered, a biomedical domain expert resolves the inconsistencies or cycles manually. After that, the classifier is re-run in order to check whether the modified ontology is consistent and non-cyclic with the changes made. A knowledge base at that level directly reflects the (still shallow) expressiveness of UMLS but is already embedded in a valid formal framework.
4. For many applications, the completeness and granularity (level of specificity) of UMLS specifications will not be sufficient. Hence, the ontology needs additional manual curation. We here incorporate those relations as a heuristic support for ontological re-modeling, which had not been taken into consideration in previous rounds (e.g., *sibling-of* or *associated-with*), while also entirely new, quite specific relations are created (e.g., *inflammation-of*, *perforation-of* or *linear-division-of*). The latter are needed for deep automatic knowledge extraction from medical narratives, our major application [11].

**Step 1: Automatic Generation of Description Logic Expressions.** Sources for concepts and relations were the 1999 release of the UMLS SN and the *mrrel, mrcon* and *mrsty* tables of the 1999 release of the UMLS Metathesaurus. The *mrrel* table provides the semantic links between two UMLS CUIs (concept unique identifier), cf. Figure 7.4.[5] These tables, available as ASCII files, were imported into a Microsoft Access relational database and manipulated using SQL embedded in the VBA programming language. For each CUI in the *mrrel* subset its alphanumeric code was substituted by the English preferred term.

After manual remodeling of the top-level concepts of the UMLS SN (in variable depth, according to the target domain) we extracted, from a total of 85,899 concepts, 38,059 anatomy and 50,087 pathology concepts from the Metathesaurus. The crite-

---

[5] As a convention in UMLS, any two CUIs must be connected by at least a shallow relation (in Figure 7.4, CHilD relations in the column REL are assumed between CUIs). Shallow relations may be refined in the column RELA, if a thesaurus is available which contains more specific information. Some CUIs are linked either by *part-of* or *is-a*. In any case, the source thesaurus for the relations and the CUIs involved is specified in the columns X and Y (e.g., MeSH 1999, SNOMED International 1998).

| CUI1 | REL | CUI2 | RELA | x | y |
|------|-----|------|------|---|---|
| C0005847 | CHD | C0014261 | part_of | MSH99 | MSH99 |
| C0005847 | CHD | C0014261 |  | CSP98 | CSP98 |
| C0005847 | CHD | C0025962 | isa | MSH99 | MSH99 |
| C0005847 | CHD | C0026844 | part_of | MSH99 | MSH99 |
| C0005847 | CHD | C0026844 |  | CSP98 | CSP98 |
| C0005847 | CHD | C0034052 |  | SNMI98 | SNMI98 |
| C0005847 | CHD | C0035330 | isa | MSH99 | MSH99 |
| C0005847 | CHD | C0042366 | part_of | MSH99 | MSH99 |
| C0005847 | CHD | C0042367 | part_of | MSH99 | MSH99 |
| C0005847 | CHD | C0042367 |  | SNM2 | SNM2 |
| C0005847 | CHD | C0042449 | isa | MSH99 | MSH99 |

**Fig. 7.4.** Semantic Relations in the UMLS Metathesaurus

rion for the inclusion into one of these sets is the assignment to predefined semantic types. Also, 2,247 concepts were found to be included in both sets, anatomy and pathology. Since we wanted to keep the two subdomains strictly disjoint, we duplicated these overlapping concepts, and prefixed all concepts by *ana-* or *pat-* according to their respective subdomain. This can be justified by the observation that, indeed, these hybrid concepts exhibit multiple meanings. For instance, *tumor* has the meaning of a malignant disease on the one hand, and of an anatomical structure on the other hand.

As target structures for the anatomy domain we chose SEP triplets, one for each anatomy concept. These are expressed in the terminological language LOOM [15] which we had previously extended by a special *deftriplet* macro (cf. Table 7.1 for an example). Only UMLS-supplied *part-of*, *has-part* and *is-a* relation attributes were considered for the construction of taxonomic and partonomic hierarchies (cf. Figure 7.3). The result is a mixed *is-a* and *part-whole* hierarchy.

For the pathology domain, we treated *CHD* (child) and *RN* (narrower relation) from the UMLS as indicating taxonomic (*is-a*) links. No part-whole relations were considered, since this category does not apply to the pathology domain. For all anatomy concepts contained in the definitional statements of pathology concepts the S-node assigned to the anatomy concept is the default concept to which they are

```
(deftriplet Heart
    :is-primitive Hollow-Viscus
    :has-part (:p-and
        Fibrous-Skeleton-Of-Heart
        Wall-Of-Heart
        Cavity-Of-Heart
        Left-Side-Of-Heart
        Right-Side-Of-Heart
        Aortic-Valve
        Pulmonary-valve ))
```

**Table 7.1.** Generated Triplets in LOOM Format

linked by the relation *has-location*, thus enabling the propagation of roles across the part-whole hierarchy (cf. Section 7.2).

As a fundamental assumption, all roles generated in this process were considered as being existentially quantified. This means that any relation $r$ (*part-of*, *has-location*, etc.) which holds between two concepts, $A$ and $B$, is mapped to a role $\exists r.B$ which is a necessary condition in the definition of the concept $A$. All conceptual constraints for a concept definition are mapped to a conjunction of constraints.

In both subdomains, shallow relations such as the extremely frequent *sibling* relation (*SIB*) were preserved (as comments in code lines) to provide heuristic guidance for the subsequent manual refinement phase (cf. Step 4).

**Step 2: Automatic Consistency Checking by the Description Classifier.** The import of UMLS anatomy concepts resulted in 38,059 *deftriplet* expressions for anatomical concepts and 50,087 *defconcept* expressions for pathological concepts. Each *deftriplet* was expanded into three *defconcept* (S-, E-, and P-nodes), and two *defrelation* (*anatomical-part-of-x*, *inv-anatomical-part-of-x*) expressions, summing up to 114,177 concepts. This yielded (together with the concepts from the UMLS SN) a total of 240,764 definitory LOOM expressions.

From 38,059 anatomy triplets, 1,219 *deftriplet* statements contained a *:has-part* clause followed by a list of a variable number of triplets, with more than one argument in 823 cases (average cardinality: 3.3). 4,043 *deftriplet* statements contained a *:part-of* clause followed by more than one argument (average cardinality: 1.1), only in 332 cases. The resulting knowledge base was then submitted to the description classifier and checked for terminological cycles and consistency. In the anatomy subdomain, one terminological cycle and 2,328 inconsistent concepts were found, in the pathology subdomain 355 terminological cycles though not a single inconsistent concept were determined (cf. Table 7.2).

| | Anatomy | Pathology |
|---|---|---|
| Triplets | 38,059 | — |
| defconcept statements | 114,177 | 50,087 |
| cycles | 1 | 355 |
| inconsistencies | 2,328 | 0 |

**Table 7.2.** Empirical Data from the Knowledge Conversion Process

**Step 3: Manual Restitution of Consistency.** The inconsistencies in the anatomy part of the ontology identified by the classifier could all be traced back to the simultaneous linkage of two triplets by both *is-a* and *part-of* links, an encoding that raises a conflict due to the disjointness required for corresponding P- and E-nodes we used as a default (cf. expression (3)). In most of these cases the affected parent nodes belonged to a class of concepts that obviously cannot be appropriately modeled as SEP triplets, e.g., *Subdivision-Of-Ascending-Aorta* or *Organ-Part*. The meaning of each of these concepts almost paraphrases that of a P-node, so that the violation of the SEP-internal disjointness condition could be accounted for by substituting the triplets involved with simple LOOM concepts, by matching them with already existing P-nodes, or by disabling *is-a* or *part-of* links.

In the pathology part of the ontology, we expected a large number of terminological cycles to occur, simply as a consequence of interpreting the semantically weak *narrower term* and *child* relations in terms of taxonomic subsumption (*is-a*). Bearing in mind the size of the ontology, we consider 355 cycles a tolerable number. Those cycles were primarily due to very similar concepts, e.g., *Arteriosclerosis vs. Atherosclerosis, Amaurosis vs. Blindness*, and residual categories ("other", "NOS" = *not otherwise specified*). These were directly inherited from the source terminologies and are notoriously difficult to interpret out of their definitional context, e.g., *Other-Malignant-Neoplasm-of-Skin vs. Malignant-Neoplasm-of-Skin-NOS*. In many cases the decision which relations could be maintained and which relations had to be eliminated was taken arbitrarily, since in biomedical terminology often no consensus can be achieved on the exact meaning of terms. From further analysis we obtained a negative list which consisted of 630 concept pairs. In a subsequent extraction cycle we incorporated this list in the automated construction of the LOOM concept definitions and, with these new constraints, a fully consistent knowledge base was generated.

**Step 4: Manual Rectification and Refinement.** Setting up this high-volume ontology based on the aforementioned working steps required three months of work for a single person. The fourth step – when performed for the whole ontology – is expected to be very time-consuming and requires broad and in-depth medical expertise. Random samples from both subdomains, 100 anatomy and 100 pathology concepts, were analyzed by the second author, a domain expert. This took one person about a single month. From the experience we gained, the following workflow can be derived:

- *Checking the correctness of the taxonomic and partonomic hierarchies.* Taxonomic and partonomic links were manually added or removed. Primitive subsumption is substituted by non-primitive one whenever possible. This is a crucial point, because the automatically generated hierarchies contain only information about the parent concepts and necessary conditions. As an example, the automatically generated definition of *Dermatitis* includes the information that it is an *Inflammation*, and that the role *has-location* must be filled by the concept *Skin*. An *Inflammation* that *has-location Skin*, however, cannot be automatically classified as *Dermatitis*.

  *Results:* In the *anatomy* sample, only 76 concepts out of 100 could be unequivocally classified as belonging to 'canonical' anatomy. (The remainder, e.g., *ana-Phalanx-of-Supernumerary-Digit-of-Hand*, referring to pathological anatomy was immediately excluded from analysis.) Besides the assignment to the UMLS semantic types, only 27 (direct) taxonomic links were found. 83 UMLS relations (mostly *child* or *narrower* relations) were manually upgraded to taxonomic links. 12 (direct) *part-of* and 19 *has-part* relations were found. Four *part-of* relations and one *has-part* relation had to be removed, since we considered them as implausible. 51 UMLS relations (mostly *child* or *narrower* relations) were manually upgraded to *part-of* relations, and 94 UMLS relations (mostly *parent* or *broader* relations) were upgraded to *has-part* relations. After this workup and upgrade of shallow UMLS relations to semantically more specific relations, the sample was checked for completeness again. As a result, 14 *is-a* and 37 *part-of* relations were still considered missing.

In the *pathology* sample, the assignment to the pathology subdomain was considered plausible for 99 of 100 concepts. A total of 15 false *is-a* relations was identified in 12 concept definitions. 24 *is-a* relations were found to be missing.

- *Check of the* :has-part *arguments assuming 'real anatomy'*. In the UMLS sources *part-of* and *has-part* relations are considered as symmetric. According to our transformation rules, the attachment of a role *has-anatomical-part* to an E-node $B_E$, with its range restricted to $A_E$, implies the existence of a concept $A$ for the definition of a concept $B$. On the other hand, the classification of $A_E$ as being subsumed by the P-node $B_P$, the latter being defined via the role *anatomical-part-of* restricted to $B_E$, implies the existence of $B_E$ given the existence of $A_E$. These constraints do not always conform to 'real' anatomy, because anatomical structures may exhibit pathological modifications. Figure 7.5 (left) sketches a concept $A$ that is necessarily *anatomical-part-of* a concept $B$, but whose existence is not required for the definition of $B$. This is typical of the results of surgical interventions, e.g., a large intestine without an appendix, or an oral cavity without teeth.

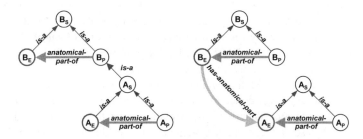

**Fig. 7.5.** Patterns for Part-whole Reasoning Using SEP triplets

*Results:* All 112 *has-part* relations obtained by the automatic import and the manual workup of our sample were checked. The analysis revealed that more than half of them (62) should be eliminated in order not to obviate a coherent classification of pathologically modified anatomical objects. For instance, maintaining *has-anatomical-part.Thumb* as an existential restriction in the definition of *Hand* would disallow to classify as *Hand* all those entities that have no thumb due to congenital or acquired abnormalities.[6] As an example, most instances of *Ileum* do not contain a *Meckel's Diverticulum*, whereas all instances of *Meckel's*

---

[6] In Table 7.1 the concepts marked by *italics*, *viz. Aortic-valve* and *Pulmonary-valve* should be eliminated from the *:has-part* list, because the anatomical entities they denote may be

*Diverticulum* are necessarily *anatomical-part-of Ileum*. Many surgical interventions that remove anatomical structures (appendix, gallbladder, etc.), produce similar patterns. In our formalism, this corresponds to a single taxonomic link between an S-node and a P-node (cf. Figure 7.5, left part). The contrary is also possible (cf. Figure 7.5, right part): the definition of $A_E$ does not imply that the role *anatomical-part-of* be filled by $B_E$, but $B_E$ does imply that the inverse role be filled by $A_E$. As an example, a *Lymph-node* necessarily contains *Lymph-follicles*, but there exist *Lymph-follicles* that are not part of a *Lymph-node*. This pattern is typical of the mereological relation between macroscopic (countable) objects, such as organs, and multiple uniform microscopic objects, cf. [30].

- *Analysis of the sibling relations and defining concepts as being disjoint.* In UMLS, the *SIB* relation links concepts that share the same parent in a taxonomic or partonomic hierarchy. Pairs of sibling concepts may have common descendants or not. If not, they constitute the root of two disjoint subtrees. In a taxonomic hierarchy, this means that one concept implies the negation of the other (e.g., a benign tumor cannot be a malignant one, *et vice versa*). In a partitive hierarchy, this can be interpreted as spatial disjointness, *viz.* one concept does not spatially overlap with another one. As an example, *Esophagus* and *Duodenum* are spatially disjoint, whereas *Stomach* and *Duodenum* are not (they share a common transition structure, called *Pylorus*), such as all neighbor structures that have a surface or region in common. Spatial disjointness can be modeled so that the definition of the S-node of the concept *A* implies the negation of the S-node of the concept *B* (for a more detailed discussion, cf. [31]).
  *Results:* We found, on the average, 6.8 siblings per concept in the anatomy domain, 8.8 in the pathology domain. So far, the analysis of sibling relations has been performed only for the anatomy domain. From a total of 521 sibling relations, 9 were identified as *is-a*, 14 as *part-of*, and 17 as *has-part*, whereas 404 referred to topologically disconnected concepts.
- *Completion and modification of anatomy–pathology relations.* Surprisingly, only very few pathology concepts contained an explicit reference to a corresponding anatomy concept. Therefore, these relations have to be added by a domain expert. In each case, a decision must be made whether the E-node or the S-node has to be addressed as the target concept for modification such that the propagation of roles across part-whole hierarchies is disabled or enabled.
  *Results:* In the sample we found 522 anatomy-pathology relations, from which 358 (i.e., 69%!) were judged as incorrect by the domain expert. In 36 cases an adequate anatomy-pathology relation was missing. All 164 *has-location* roles were analyzed as to whether they were to be filled by an S-node or an E-node of an anatomical triplet. In 153 cases, the S-node (which allows propagation across the part-whole hierarchy) was considered to be adequate, in 11 cases the E-node was preferred. The analysis of the 100 pathology concepts revealed that only 17 were to be linked with an anatomy concept. In 15 cases, the default linkage to the

---

missing in certain cases as a result of congenital malformations, inflammatory processes or surgical interventions.

S-node was considered to be correct, in one case the linkage to the E-node was preferred, in another case the linkage was judged to be false.

The high number of implausible constraints points to the lightweight semantics of *has-location* links in the UMLS sources. While we interpreted them in terms of a conjunction for the import routine, a disjunctive meaning seems to prevail implicitly in many definitions of top-level concepts such as *Tuberculosis*. In this example, we find all anatomical concepts that can be affected by this disease linked by *has-location*. All these constraints (e.g., *has-location Urinary-Tract*) are inherited to subconcepts such as *Tuberculosis-of-Bronchus*. A thorough analysis of the top-level pathology concepts is necessary, and conjunctions of constraints will have to be substituted by disjunctions where necessary.

## 7.4 Discussion and Conclusions

In medicine, domain knowledge has to be supplied on a larger scale. Instead of developing sophisticated medical ontologies from scratch, we here propose a 'conservative' approach — reuse existing large-scale resources, but refine the data from these resources so that advanced modeling requirements imposed by more expressive knowledge representation languages are met. The resulting ontologies can then be used for sophisticated applications requiring formally sound medical reasoning such as text understanding.

The benefits and problems of converting conceptual knowledge from semantically weak specifications to a rigorous knowledge representation formalism have been described by Pisanelli et al. [19]. They extracted knowledge from the UMLS Semantic Network, as well as from parts of the Metathesaurus and converted it into a description logics system. Spackman & Campbell [33] describe how the SNOMED nomenclature evolves from a multi-axial coding system into a formally founded ontology. Their general goal is to avoid ambiguous or semantically invalid representations of composite concepts. However, both approaches do not provide a special reasoning mechanism for partonomic relations.

Within the formal framework of GALEN, a fragment of the Read Thesaurus was translated into GRAIL, a knowledge representation system also based on description logics [24]. In a cross-validation study it was checked, on the one hand, whether the definitions contained in the Read Thesaurus were logically consistent and, on the other hand, whether the GRAIL domain model was rich enough to encode them. Although GRAIL comes with a special-purpose reasoning mechanism dedicated to partonomies, the adaptation was limited to simple generic hierarchies as only these structure the Read Thesaurus.

The developers of VOXEL-MAN [27], a multimedia tutoring systems for anatomy, and of the DIGITAL ANATOMIST FOUNDATIONAL MODEL (UWDA FM), an anatomical semantic network [25], have both emphasized partitive hierarchies though at an informal level. In VOXEL-MAN, a fine-grained ontology of partonomic relations is sketched that accounts for various part-whole relations found in the anatomy domain. The UWDA FM developers restrict themselves to a small set of relations leading to a precise separation between partonomic and taxonomic hierarchies. They excel with a high granularity of description and a broad coverage.

Our approach tries to combine the broad coverage and fine-grained concept descriptions of the UWDA FM with the formal rigor of description logics. Additionally, we enhance the imported knowledge with part-whole specific reasoning capabilities indispensable in the medical domain, though this has already been described as a hard problem for terminological (i.e, description logics) languages [13].

It remains to be seen whether conservative structural extensions of a stable language platform are able to carry over to the many varieties of partonomic reasoning and different part-whole relations, or whether newly designed operators or other fundamental language extensions are needed. In the medical domain, at least, where the restriction to one subrelation of *part-of*, viz. *anatomical-part-of*, is sufficient, a relatively simple "data structure" extension like the SEP triplets yields already adequate results, without the necessity to resort to profound language extensions. We have evidence that the triplet mechanism we here propose can be straightforwardly extended to cover mereotopological and (limited) spatial reasoning, as well [31, 29].

Our study shows that it is relatively straightforward to restitute consistency of the UMLS-grown ontology, but it is nearly impossible to reach a high degree of both adequacy and completeness due to the huge amount of manual work required. Restituting adequacy should, however, not be primarily taken as eliminating obvious 'errors' contained in the UMLS sources, but rather as making choices between alternative conceptualizations of medical terms whose meaning differs slightly due to the heterogeneity of the knowledge sources. Another aspect is the need of rectification of concept definitions which have become incorrect due to rigid axiomatic assumptions driving the automated export procedure (e.g., the conjunctive reading of defining attributes), which is not true in all cases, and, thus, necessarily requires individual manual specification.

A realistic workflow may consist in the manual elimination of obviously inadequate statements, followed by the completion of those concept definitions from the subdomain in focus. In these repetitive manual refinement cycles we found the implications of using the terminological classifier, the inference engine which computes subsumption relations, of utmost importance and of outstanding heuristic value. Hence, the knowledge refinement cycles are truly semi-automatic, fed by medical expertise on the side of the human knowledge engineer, but also driven by the reasoning system which makes explicit the consequences of (im)proper concept definitions.

Abstracting away from the particularities of our approach, some more general methodological problems for knowledge conversion and knowledge curation of this sort arise:

- *Knowledge Integration.* When several knowledge sources have to be combined, some knowledge portions may be overlapping, others may be far too distant so that appropriate conceptual bridges have to be defined. Even knowledge sources which complement each other nicely require suitable interfaces so that transition from one to the other is possible.

- *Granularity.* Different knowledge sources, sometimes even a single one, often exhibit subdomain descriptions which are very fined-grained as opposed to ones which are treated with much less specificity. Mediating between those different granularity levels of knowledge representation becomes an important requirement for adequate knowledge use. In addition, it might become necessary to provide intentionally different abstraction levels for the description of a single subdomain.

- *Views.* There is no single, canonical view on particular domain knowledge. A tumor, for instance, is at the same time an anatomical structure as well as a pathological phenomenon. This kind of ambiguity has immediate implications on its conceptual representation and the inferences derivable therefrom. Even more, alternative schools of thought differ in the way they organize the same subdomain. Hence, one has to provide formal devices which support different conceptual views on the same subject matter rather than enforcing consensus in a dogmatic way.

- *Top-Level Ontology.* The attempt to integrate the subdisciplines of a large science domain such as biology or medicine by a unifying ontological umbrella inevitably leads to the need to structure the abstract, 'upper' part of the underlying conceptual system. At this level, high-level concepts such as 'organism' (e.g., animal, plant, virus), 'process' (photosynthesis, digestion), 'substance' (chlorophyll, blood) or 'structure' (animal or plant anatomy, cell morphology, etc.) have to be properly organized and conceptually represented so that they link to the more specific, concrete domain descriptions in a valid way.

# References

1. Alessandro Artale, Enrico Franconi, Nicola Guarino, and Luca Pazzi. Part-whole relations in object-centered systems: An overview. *Data & Knowledge Engineering*, 20(3):347–383, 1996.
2. Franz Baader, Diego Calvanese, Deborah McGuinness, Daniele Nardi, and Peter Patel-Schneider, editors. *The Description Logic Handbook. Theory, Implementation and Applications.* Cambridge, U.K.: Cambridge University Press, 2003.
3. Franz Baader and Werner Nutt. Basic description logics. In Franz Baader, Diego Calvanese, Deborah McGuinness, Daniele Nardi, and Peter Patel-Schneider, editors, *The Description Logic Handbook. Theory, Implementation and Applications*, pages 43–95. Cambridge, U.K.: Cambridge University Press, 2003.
4. Jochen Bernauer. Analysis of part-whole relation and subsumption in the medical domain. *Data & Knowledge Engineering*, 20(3):405–415, 1996.
5. Olivier Bodenreider. Circular hierarchical relationships in the UMLS: Etiology, diagnosis, treatment, complications and prevention. In S. Bakken, editor, *AMIA 2001 – Proceedings of the Annual Symposium of the American Medical Informatics Association. A Medical Informatics Odyssey: Visions of the Future and Lessons from the Past*, pages 57–61. Washington, D.C., November 3-7, 2001. Philadelphia, PA: Hanley & Belfus, 2001.
6. James J. Cimino. Distributed cognition and knowledge-based controlled medical terminologies. *Artificial Intelligence in Medicine*, 12(1):153–168, 1998.

7. James J. Cimino, Paul D. Clayton, George Hripsack, and Stephen B. Johnson. Knowledge-based approaches to the maintenance of a large controlled medical terminology. *Journal of the American Medical Informatics Association*, 1(1):35–50, 1994.

8. Roger Côté, David J. Rothwell, Ronald S. Beckett, James L. Palotay, and Louise Brochu. *The Systemised Nomenclature of Medicine:* SNOMED *International*. Northfield, IL: College of American Pathologists, 1993.

9. D. Alan Cruse. On the transitivity of the part-whole relation. *Journal of Linguistics*, 15:29–38, 1979.

10. Aldo Gangemi, Domenico M. Pisanelli, and Geri Steve. An overview of the ONION project: Applying ontologies to the integration of medical terminologies. *Data & Knowledge Engineering*, 31(2):183–220, 1999.

11. Udo Hahn, Martin Romacker, and Stefan Schulz. MEDSYNDIKATE: A natural language system for the extraction of medical information from finding reports. *International Journal of Medical Informatics*, 67(1/3):63–74, 2002.

12. Udo Hahn, Stefan Schulz, and Martin Romacker. Part-whole reasoning: A case study in medical ontology engineering. *IEEE Intelligent Systems & Their Applications*, 14(5):59–67, 1999.

13. Ira J. Haimowitz, Ramesh S. Patil, and Peter Szolovits. Representing medical knowledge in a terminological language is difficult. In R. A. Greenes, editor, *SCAMC'88 – Proceedings of the 12th Annual Symposium on Computer Applications in Medical Care*, pages 101–105. Washington, D.C.: IEEE Computer Society Press, 1988.

14. Ian Horrocks and Ulrike Sattler. A description logic with transitive and inverse roles and role hierarchies. *Journal of Logic and Computation*, 9(3):385–410, 1999.

15. Robert MacGregor and Raymond Bates. The LOOM knowledge representation language. Technical Report RS-87-188, Information Sciences Institute, University of Southern California, 1987.

16. Robert M. MacGregor. A description classifier for the predicate calculus. In *AAAI'94 – Proceedings of the 12th National Conference on Artificial Intelligence*, volume 1, pages 213–220. Seattle, WA, USA, July 31 - August 4, 1994. Menlo Park, CA: AAAI Press & MIT Press, 1994.

17. Eric Mays, Robert Weida, Robert Dionne, Meir Laker, Brian White, Chihong Liang, and Frank J. Oles. Scalable and expressive medical terminologies. In J. J. Cimino, editor, *AMIA'96 – Proceedings of the 1996 AMIA Annual Fall Symposium (formerly SCAMC). Beyond the Superhighway: Exploiting the Internet with Medical Informatics*, pages 259–263. Washington, D.C., October 26-30, 1996. Philadelphia, PA: Hanley & Belfus, 1996.

18. Alexa T. McCray and Stuart J. Nelson. The representation of meaning in the UMLS. *Methods of Information in Medicine*, 34(1/2):193–201, 1995.

19. Domenico M. Pisanelli, Aldo Gangemi, and Geri Steve. An ontological analysis of the UMLS metathesaurus. In C. G. Chute, editor, *AMIA'98 – Proceedings of the 1998 AMIA Annual Fall Symposium. A Paradigm Shift in Health Care Information Systems: Clinical Infrastructures for the 21st Century*, pages 810–814. Orlando, FL, November 7-11, 1998. Philadelphia, PA: Hanley & Belfus, 1998.

20. Alan L. Rector. Clinical terminology: Why is it so hard? *Methods of Information in Medicine*, 38:239–252, 1999.

21. Alan L. Rector. Analysis of propagation along transitive roles: Formalisation of the GALEN experience with medical ontologies. In Ian Horrocks and Sergio Tessaris, editors, *DL 2002 – Proceedings of the 2002 International Workshop on Description Logics*. Toulouse, France, April 19-21, 2002. Published via http://CEUR-WS.org/Vol-53/.

22. Alan L. Rector, Sean Bechhofer, Carole A. Goble, Ian Horrocks, W. Anthony Nowlan, and W. Danny Solomon. The GRAIL concept modelling language for medical terminology. *Artificial Intelligence in Medicine*, 9:139–171, 1997.

23. James A. Reggia and Stanley Tuhrim. An overview of methods for computer-assisted medical decision making. In James A. Reggia and Stanley Tuhrim, editors, *Computer-Assisted Medical Decision Making. Vol. 1*, pages 3–45. New York, N.Y.: Springer, 1985.

24. Jeremy E. Rogers, Colin Price, Alan Rector, W. Daniel Solomon, and Nick Smeijko. Validating clinical terminology structures: Integration and cross-validation of READ THESAURUS and GALEN. In C. G. Chute, editor, *AMIA'98 – Proceedings of the 1998 AMIA Annual Fall Symposium. A Paradigm Shift in Health Care Information Systems: Clinical Infrastructures for the 21st Century*, pages 845–849. Orlando, FL, November 7-11, 1998. Philadelphia, PA: Hanley & Belfus, 1998.

25. Cornelius Rosse, José Leonardo V. Mejino, Bharath R. Modayur, Rex Jakobovits, Kevin P. Hinshaw, and James F. Brinkley. Motivation and organizational principles for anatomical knowledge representation: The DIGITAL ANATOMIST symbolic knowledge base. *Journal of the American Medical Informatics Association*, 5(1):17–40, 1998.

26. James G. Schmolze and William S. Mark. The NIKL experience. *Computational Intelligence*, 7(1):48–69, 1991.

27. Rainer Schubert and Karl-Heinz Höhne. Partonomies for interactive explorable 3D-models of anatomy. In C. G. Chute, editor, *AMIA'98 – Proceedings of the 1998 AMIA Annual Fall Symposium. A Paradigm Shift in Health Care Information Systems: Clinical Infrastructures for the 21st Century*, pages 433–437. Orlando, FL, November 7-11, 1998. Philadelphia, PA: Hanley & Belfus, 1998.

28. Erich B. Schulz, Colin Price, and Philip J. B. Brown. Symbolic anatomic knowledge representation in the READ CODES Version 3: Structure and application. *Journal of the American Medical Informatics Association*, 4(1):38–48, 1997.

29. Stefan Schulz and Udo Hahn. Mereotopological reasoning about parts and (w)holes in bio-ontologies. In Chris Welty and Barry Smith, editors, *Formal Ontology in Information Systems. Collected Papers from the 2nd International FOIS Conference*, pages 210–221. Ogunquit, Maine, USA, October 17-19, 2001. New York, NY: ACM Press, 2001.

30. Stefan Schulz and Udo Hahn. Necessary parts and wholes in bio-ontologies. In D. Fensel, F. Giunchiglia, D. McGuinness, and M.-A. Williams, editors, *Principles of Knowledge Representation and Reasoning. Proceedings of the 8th International Conference – KR 2002*, pages 387–394. Toulouse, France, April 22-25, 2002. San Francisco, CA: Morgan Kaufmann, 2002.

31. Stefan Schulz, Udo Hahn, and Martin Romacker. Modeling anatomical spatial relations with description logics. In J. M. Overhage, editor, *AMIA 2000 – Proceedings of the Annual Symposium of the American Medical Informatics Association. Converging Information, Technology, and Health Care*, pages 779–783. Los Angeles, CA, November 4-8, 2000. Philadelphia, PA: Hanley & Belfus, 2000.

32. Kent A. Spackman. Normal forms for description logic expression of clinical concepts in SNOMED RT. In S. Bakken, editor, *AMIA 2001 – Proceedings of the Annual Symposium of the American Medical Informatics Association. A Medical Informatics Odyssey: Visions of the Future and Lessons from the Past*, pages 627–631. Washington, D.C., November 3-7, 2001. Philadelphia, PA: Hanley & Belfus, 2001.

33. Kent A. Spackman and Keith E. Campbell. Compositional concept representation using SNOMED: Towards further convergence of clinical terminologies. In C. G. Chute, editor, *AMIA'98 – Proceedings of the 1998 AMIA Annual Fall Symposium. A Paradigm Shift in Health Care Information Systems: Clinical Infrastructures for the 21st Century*, pages 740–744. Orlando, FL, November 7-11, 1998. Philadelphia, PA: Hanley & Belfus, 1998.

34. Françoise Volot, Michel Joubert, and Marius Fieschi. Review of biomedical knowledge and data representation with Conceptual Graphs. *Methods of Information in Medicine*, 37(1):86–96, 1998.
35. Morton Winston, Roger Chaffin, and Douglas J. Herrmann. A taxonomy of part-whole relationships. *Cognitive Science*, 11:417–444, 1987.

# 8

# An Overview of OntoClean

Nicola Guarino[1] and Christopher A. Welty[2]

[1]Laboratory for Applied Ontology (ISTC-CNR)
Polo Tecnologico, Via Solteri 38, 38100 Trento, ITALY
guarino@isib.cnr.it

[2]IBM Watson Research Center
19 Skyline Dr., Hawthorne, NY 10532, USA
welty@us.ibm.com

**Summary.** OntoClean is a methodology for validating the ontological adequacy of taxonomic relationships. It is based on highly general ontological notions drawn from philosophy, like *essence*, *identity*, and *unity*, which are used to characterize relevant aspects of the intended meaning of the properties, classes, and relations that make up an ontology. These aspects are represented by formal metaproperties, which impose several constraints on the taxonomic structure of an ontology. The analysis of these constraints helps in evaluating and validating the choices made. In this chapter we present an informal overview of the philosophical notions involved and their role in OntoClean, review some common ontological pitfalls, and walk through the example that has appeared in pieces in previous papers and has been the basis of numerous tutorials and talks.

## 8.1 Introduction

The OntoClean methodology was first introduced in a series of conference-length papers in 2000 [Guarino and Welty, 2000a-c; Welty and Guarino, 2001], and received much attention and use in subsequent years. The main contribution of OntoClean was the beginning of a formal foundation for ontological analysis. Alan Rector, a seasoned veteran at ontological analysis in the medical domain, said of OntoClean, "…what you have done is reduce the amount of time I spend arguing with doctors that the way I want to model the world is right…" [Rector, 2002]. A similar comment came from the CYC people attending our AAAI-2000 tutorial, "You showed why the heuristic choices we adopted were right." Most experienced domain modelers can see the correct way to, e.g. structure a taxonomy, but are typically unable to justify themselves to others. OntoClean has provided a logical basis for arguing against the most common modeling pitfalls, and arguing for what we have called "clean ontologies".

In this chapter we present an informal overview of the basic notions *essence, identity,* and *unity,* and their role in OntoClean. We then review the basic ontology pitfalls, and walk through the example that has appeared in pieces in previous papers and has been the basis of numerous tutorials and talks beginning with AAAI-2000.

## Background

The basic notions in OntoClean were not new, but existed in philosophy for some time. Indeed, the practice of modeling the world for information systems has many parallels in philosophy, whose scholars have been trying to describe the universe in a formal, logical way since the time of Aristotle. Philosophers have struggled with deep problems of existence, such as God, life and death, or whether a statue and the marble from which it is made are the same entity. While these problems may seem irrelevant to the designer of an information system, we found that *the conceptual analysis and the techniques used to address these problems* are not, and form the basis of our methodology.

## Properties, Classes, and Subsumption

Many terms have been borrowed by computer science from mathematics and logic, but unfortunately this borrowing has often resulted in a skewed meaning. In particular, the terms *property* and *class* are used in computer science with often drastically different meanings from the original. The use of the term *property* in RDF is an example of such unfortunate deviation from the usual logical sense.

In this chapter, we shall consider properties as the *meanings* (or *intensions*) of expressions like *being an apple* or *being a table*, which correspond to unary predicates in first-order logic. Given a particular maximal state of affairs (or *possible world*), we can associate with each property a *class* (its *extension*), which is the set of entities that exhibit that property in that particular world. The members of this class will be called *instances* of the property. Classes are therefore sets of entities that share a property in common; they are the extensional counterpart of properties. In the following, we shall refer most of the time to properties rather than classes or predicates, to stress the fact that their ontological nature (characterized by means of *metaproperties*) does not depend on syntactic choices (as it would be for predicates), nor on specific states of affairs (as it would be for classes).

The independence of properties from states of affairs gives us the opportunity to make clear the meaning of the term *subsumption* we shall adopt in this paper. A property $p$ subsumes $q$ if and only if, *for every possible state of affairs*, all instances of $q$ are also instances of $p$. On the syntactic side, this corresponds to what is usually held for description logics, P subsumes Q if and only if there is no model of $Q \wedge \neg P$.

## 8.2   The Basic Notions

### Essence and Rigidity

A property of an entity is *essential* to that entity if it *must* be true of it in every possible world, i.e. if it *necessarily holds* for that entity. For example, the property of *having a brain* is essential to human beings. Every human *must* have a brain in every possible world.

A special form of essentiality is rigidity; a property is *rigid* if it is essential to all its possible instances; an instance of a rigid property cannot stop being an instance of that property in a different world. For example, while having a brain may be essential to humans, it is not essential to, say, scarecrows in the *Wizard of Oz*. If we were modeling the world of the *Wizard of Oz*, the property of *having a brain* would not be rigid, though still essential to humans. On the other hand, the property *being a human* is typically rigid, every human is necessarily so.

Note that we use the word "typically" here to stress that the point of Onto-Clean is *not* to help people decide about the ontological nature of a certain property, but rather to help them explore the logical consequences of making certain choices. Rigidity is the first ingredient of this framework: it is a *metaproperty,* deciding whether it holds or not for the relevant properties in an ontology helps to clarify its *ontological commitment.*

Obviously there are also *non-rigid* properties, which can acquire or lose (some of) their instances depending on the state of affairs at hand. Of these we distinguish between properties that are essential to *some* entities and not essential to others (*semi-rigid*), and properties that are not essential to *all* their instances (*anti-rigid*). For example, the property *being a student* is typically anti-rigid – *every* instance of student can cease to be such in a suitable state of affairs, whereas the property *having a brain* in our *Wizard of Oz* world is semi-rigid, since there are instances that must have a brain as well as others for which a brain is just a (desirable) option.

Rigidity and its variants are important metaproperties, every property in an ontology should be labeled as rigid, non-rigid, or anti-rigid. In addition to providing more information about what a property is intended to mean, these metaproperties impose constraints on the subsumption relation, which can be used to check the ontological consistency of taxonomic links. One of these constraints is that anti-rigid properties cannot subsume rigid properties. For example, the property *being a student* cannot subsume *being a human* if the former is anti-rigid and the latter is rigid. To see this, consider that, if $p$ is an anti-rigid property, all its instances can cease to be such. This is certainly the case for *student*, since any student may cease being a student. However, no instance of *human* can cease to be a human, and if all humans are necessarily students (the meaning of subsumption), then no person could cease to be a student, creating therefore an inconsistency.

## Identity and Unity

Although very subtle and difficult to explain without experience, identity and unity are perhaps the most important notions we use in our methodology. These two things are often confused with each other; in general, *identity* refers to the problem of being able to recognize individual entities in the world as being the same (or different), and *unity* refers to being able to recognize all the parts that form an individual entity.

Identity *criteria* are the criteria we use to answer questions like, "is that my dog?" In point of fact, identity criteria are conditions used to *determine* equality (sufficient conditions) and that are *entailed by* equality (necessary conditions).

It is perhaps simplest to think of identity criteria over time (*diachronic* identity criteria), e.g. how do we recognize people we know as the *same* person even though they may have changed? It is also very informative, however, to think of identity criteria at a single point in time (*synchronic* identity criteria). This may, at first glance, seem bizarre. How can you ask, "are these *two* entities the same entity?" If they are the same then there is one entity, it does not even make sense to ask the question.

The answer is not that difficult. One of the most common decisions that must be made in ontological analysis concerns identifying circumstances in which one entity is actually two (or more). Consider the following example, drawn from actual experience: somebody proposed to introduce a property called *time duration* whose instances are things like *one hour* and *two hours*, and a property *time interval* referring to specific intervals of time, such as "1:00 – 2:00 next Tuesday" or "2:00 – 3:00 next Wednesday." The proposal was to make *time duration* subsume *time interval*, since all time intervals are time durations. Seems to make intuitive sense, but how can we evaluate this decision?

In this case, an analysis based on the notion of identity can be informative. According to the identity criteria for time durations, two durations of the same length are the same duration. In other words, all one-hour time durations are identical – they are the *same* duration and therefore there is only one "one hour" time duration. On the other hand, according to the identity criteria for time intervals, two intervals of the same duration occurring at the same time are the same, but two intervals occurring at different times, even if they are the same duration, are different. Therefore the two example intervals above would be different intervals. This creates a contradiction: if all instances of *time interval* are also instances of *time duration* (as implied by the subsumption relationship), how can they be two instances of one property and a single instance of another?

This is one of the most common confusions of natural language when used for describing the world. When we say "all time intervals are time durations" we really mean "all time intervals *have* a time duration" – the duration is a component of an interval, but it is not the interval itself. In this case we cannot model the relationship as subsumption, time intervals have durations (essentially) as *qualities*. More examples of such confusions are provided at the end of this article.

One of the distinctions proposed by OntoClean is between properties that *carry an identity criterion* and properties that do not. The former are labeled with an *ad-hoc* metaproperty, **+I**. Since criteria of identity are inherited along property subsumption hierarchies, a further distinction is made to mark those properties that *supply* (rather just *carrying*) their "own" identity criteria, which are not inherited from the subsuming properties. These properties are marked with the label **+O** (where **O** stands for "own").

Unfortunately, despite their relevance, recognizing identity criteria may be extremely hard. However, in many cases identity analysis can be limited to detecting the properties that are just *necessary* for keeping the identity of a given entity, i.e. what we have called the *essential properties*. Obviously, if two things do not have the same essential properties they are not identical. Take for instance the classical example of the statue and the clay: is the statue identical to the clay it is made of? Let's consider the essential properties: having (more or less) a certain shape is essential for the statue, but not essential for the clay. Therefore, they are different: we can say they have different identity criteria, even without knowing exactly what these criteria are. In practice, we can say that "sharing the essential property P", where P is essential for all the instances of a property Q different from P, is the weakest form of an identity criterion carried by Q. Such criterion can be used to make conclusions about non-identity, if not about identity.

A second notion that is extremely useful in ontological analysis is *Unity*. Unity refers to the problem of describing the parts and boundaries of objects, such that we know in general what is part of the object, what is not, and under what conditions the object is *whole.*

Unity can tell us a lot about the intended meaning of properties in an ontology. Certain properties pertain to wholes, that is, all their instances are wholes, others do not. For example, *being (an amount of) water* does not have wholes as instances, since each amount can be arbitrarily scattered or confused with other amounts. In other words, knowing an entity is an amount of water does not tell us anything about its parts, nor how to recognize it as a single entity. On the other hand, *being an ocean* is a property that picks up whole objects, as its instances, such as "the Atlantic Ocean," are recognizable as single entities. Of course, one might observe that oceans have vague boundaries, but this is not an issue here: the important difference with respect to the previous example is that in this case we have a criterion to tell, at least, what is *not* part of the Atlantic Ocean, and still part of some other ocean. This is impossible for amounts of water.

In general, in addition to specifying whether or not properties have wholes as instances, it is also useful to analyze the specific conditions that must hold among the parts of a certain entity in order to consider it a whole. We call these conditions *unity criteria* (UC). They are usually expressed in terms of a suitable *unifying relation*, whose ontological nature determines different kinds of wholes. For example, we may distinguish *topological wholes* (a piece of coal), *morphological wholes* (a constellation), *functional wholes* (a hammer, a bikini). As these examples show, nothing prevents a whole from having parts that are themselves wholes (under different unifying relations). Indeed, a *plural whole* can be defined as a whole that is a mereological sum of wholes.

In OntoClean, we distinguish with suitable metaproperties the properties *all* whose instances *must* carry a *common* UC (such as *ocean*) from those that do not. Among the latter, we further distinguish properties all of whose instances must be wholes, although with different UCs, from properties all of whose instances are not necessarily wholes. An example of the former kind may be *legal agent*, if we include both people and companies (with different UCs) among its instances. *Amount of water* is usually an example of the latter kind, since none of its instances *must* be wholes. We say that *ocean* carries unity (+U), *legal agent* carries no unity (-U), and *amount of water* carries anti-unity (~U).

The difference between unity and anti-unity leads us again to interesting problems with subsumption. It may make sense to say that "Ocean" is a subclass of "Water", since all oceans are water. However, if we claim that instances of the latter must not be wholes, and instances of the former always are, then we have a contradiction. Problems like this again stem from the ambiguity of natural language, oceans are not "kinds of" water, they are *composed* of water.

## Constraints and Assumptions

A first observation descending immediately from our definitions regards some *subsumption constraints*. Given two properties, *p* and *q*, when *q* subsumes *p* the following constraints hold:

1.  If *q* is anti-rigid, then *p* must be anti-rigid
2.  If *q* carries an identity criterion, then *p* must carry the same criterion
3.  If *q* carries a unity criterion, then *p* must carry the same criterion
4.  If *q* has anti-unity, then *p* must also have anti-unity

Finally, we make the following assumptions regarding identity (adapted from Lowe [Lowe, 1989]):

*   *Sortal Individuation.* Every domain element must instantiate some property carrying an IC (+I). In this way we satisfy Quine's dicto "No entity without identity" [Quine, 1969].
*   *Sortal Expandability.* If something is an instance of different properties (for instance related to different times), then it must be also instance of a more general property carrying a criterion for its identity.

Together, the two assumptions imply that every entity must instantiate a *unique* most general property carrying a criterion for its identity.

## 8.3   An Extended Example

In this section we provide a walk-through of the way the OntoClean analysis can be used. This example is based on those presented at various tutorials and invited talks.

We begin with a set of classes arranged in a taxonomy, as shown in Figure 1. The taxonomy we have chosen makes intuitive sense *prima facie*, and in most cases the taxonomic pairs were taken from existing ontologies such as Wordnet[1], Pangloss[2], and the 1993 version of CYC[3].

We have chosen, following our previous papers, to use a shorthand notation for indicating metaproperty choices on classes. Rigidity is indicated by **R**, identity by **I**, unity by **U**, and dependence by **D**. Each letter is preceded by +, - or ~, to indicate the positive, negative, or *anti* metaproperty, e.g., being rigid (**+R**), carrying an identity criterion (**+I**), carrying a common unity criterion (**+U**); not rigid (**-R**), not carrying an identity criterion (**-I**), not carrying a common unity criterion (**-U**); being anti-rigid (**~R**) and having anti-unity (**~U**). We also used (**+O**) to indicate when a property carries its *own* identity criterion, as opposed to inheriting one from a more general property.

---

[1] http://www.cogsci.princeton.edu/~wn/
[2] http://www.lti.cs.cmu.edu/Research/Pangloss/
[3] The current version of Cyc no longer contains these errors: http://www.cyc.com

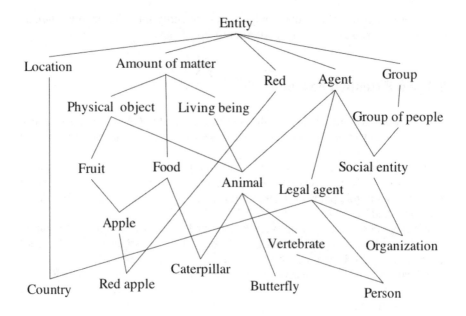

Figure 1. An uncleaned taxonomy

## Assigning Metaproperties

The next step is to assign the metaproperties discussed above to each property in the taxonomy. When designing a new ontology, this step may occur first, before arranging the properties in a taxonomy. Note that the assignments discussed here are not meant to be definitive at all: rather, these represent *prima facie* decisions reflecting our intuitions about the meaning ascribed to the terms used. The point of this exercise is not so much to discuss the ontological nature of these properties, but rather *to explore and demonstrate the logical consequences of making these choices.* As we shall see, in some cases they will be contradictory with respect to the formal semantics of our metaproperties, although intuitive at a first sight. In our opinion, this proves the utility of a formal approach to ontology analysis and evaluation.

### Entity
Everything is necessarily an entity. Our metaproperties assignment is -I-U+R. This is the most abstract property, indeed it is not necessary to have an explicit predicate for it.

## Location

A location is considered here as a generalized region of space. Our assignment is +O~U+R. We assume the property to be rigid since instances of locations cannot change being locations. Identity is given by the fact that two locations are the same if and only if they have the same parts. This kind of criterion is fairly common, and is known as *mereological extensionality*. It applies to all entities that are trivially defined to be the sum of their parts. It is important to realize that this criterion implies that a location or region cannot "expand" – if so then the identity criteria would have to be different. So, extending a location makes it a different one. So we see that identity criteria are critical in specifying precisely what a property is intended to mean.

## Amount of Matter

We conceptualize an amount of matter as a clump of unstructured or scattered "stuff" such as a liter of water or a kilogram of clay. Amounts of matter should not be confused with *substances*, such as water or clay; an amount of matter is a particular amount of the substance. Therefore, amounts of matter are mereologically extensional, so we assign +O to this property. As discussed above, they are not necessarily wholes, so our assignment is ~U. Finally, every amount of matter is necessarily so, therefore the property is +R.

## Red

What we have in mind here is the property of being a red *thing*, not the property of being a particular shade or color. We see in this case that it is useful to ask ourselves *what* the instances of a certain property are: Do we have apples and peppers in the extension of this property, or just their colors? In this case, we do include the apples and peppers, and not the colors. Red entities share no common identity criteria, so our assignment is –I. A common confusion here regarding identity criteria concerns the fact that all instances of *red* are colored red, therefore we have a clear *membership criterion*. Membership criteria are not identity criteria, as the latter gives us information about how to distinguish entities from each other. Having a color red is common to all instances of this property, and thus is not informative at all for identity.

A red amount of matter would be an instance of this property, which is not a whole, as would a red ball, which is a whole. Therefore we must choose –U, indicating that there is no common unity criterion for all instances.

Finally, we choose –R since some instances of *Red* may be necessarily so, and most will not. This weak and unspecific combination of metaproperties indicates that this property is of minimal utility in an ontology, we call them *attributions* [Welty and Guarino 2001]. We discuss this point further below.

## Agent

We intend here an entity that plays a causal part in some event. Just about anything can be an agent, a person, the wind, a bomb, etc. Thus there is no common identity nor unity criterion for all instances, and we choose **-I-U**. No instance of *agent* is necessarily an agent, thus the property is **~R**. Clearly this assignment of metaproperties selects a particular meaning of *agent* among the many possible ones. See for example [Gangemi *et al.* 2003] for a discussion on the meaning of *causal agent* in WordNet.

**Group**

We see a group as an *unstructured* finite collection of wholes. Instances of *group* are mereologically extensional as they are defined by their members, thus **+O**. Since, given a group, we have no way to isolate it from other groups, no group is *per se* a whole, thus **~U**. In any case, like many general terms, *Group* is fairly ambiguous, and once again this choice of identity criteria and anti-unity exposes the choice we have made. Finally, it seems plausible to assume that every instance of group is necessarily so, thus **+R**.

**Physical Object**

We think of physical objects as isolated material entities, i.e. something that can be "picked up and thrown" (at a suitable scale, since a planet would be considered an instance of a physical object as well). Under this vision, what characterizes physical objects is that they are *topological wholes* – so we assign **+U** to the corresponding property.

For the sake of simplicity, we assume here that no two instances of this property can exist in the same spatial location at the same time. This is an identity criterion, so we assign **+O** to this property. Note that this is a *synchronic* identity criterion (see identity and unity, above) – we do not assume a common diachronic identity criterion for all physical objects.

*Physical object* is a rigid property, so we have **+R**. To see this, consider the alternative: there must be some instance of the property that can, possibly, *stop* being a physical object, yet still exist and retain its identity. By assigning rigidity to this property, we assert that there is no such instance, and that every instance of *Physical Object* ceases to exist if it ceases to be a physical object.

**Living Being**

Instances of *living being* must be wholes according to some common biological unity criterion. We don't need to specify it to assign **+U** to this property.

For identity, it is difficult to assume a single criterion that holds for all instances of living being. The way we, e.g. distinguish people may be different from the way we distinguish dogs. However, a plausible diachronic criterion could be *having the same DNA* (although only-necessary, since it does not help in the case of clones). Moreover, we can easily think of essential properties that characterize living beings (e.g., the need for taking nutrients from the environment), and this is enough for assigning them **+O**.

We assume *living being* to be a rigid property (**+R**), so if an entity ceases to be living then it ceases to exist. Notice that this is a precise choice that goes a long way to reveal our intended meaning: nothing would exclude considering life as a *contingent* (non-rigid) property; by considering it as rigid, we are indeed *constructing* a new kind of entity, justified by the fact that this property is very relevant for us.

### Food

Nothing is necessarily food, and just about anything is possibly food. In a linguistic sense, 'food' is a role an entity may play in an eating event. Considering that anything that is food can also possibly *not* be food, we assign ~R to this property. We also assume that any quantity of food is an amount of matter and inherits its extensional identity criterion, thus +I and ~U.

### Animal

Like *living being*, the identity criteria for *animal* may be difficult to characterize precisely, but we can devise numerous essential properties that apply only to them, or only-sufficient conditions that act as heuristics especially for diachronic identity criteria. Humans, in particular, are quite good at recognizing most individual animals, typically based on clues present in their material bodies. The undeniable fact is that we do recognize "the same" animal over time, so there must be some way that is accomplished. Therefore, we assign **+O**.

The property is clearly rigid (+R); moreover, being subsumed by *living being*, it clearly carries unity (+U).

### Legal Agent

This is an agent that is recognized by law. It exists only because of a legal recognition. Legal agents are entities belonging to the so-called *social reality*, insofar as their existence is the result of social interaction. All legal systems assign well-defined identity criteria to legal agents, based on, for example, an id number. Therefore, it seems plausible to assign **+O**. Concerning unity, if we include companies (as well as persons) among legal agents, then probably there is no unity criteria shared by all of them, so we assign **-U**. Finally, since nothing is necessarily a legal agent, we assign **~R**. For instance, we may assume that a typical legal entity, such as a person, becomes such only after a certain age.

### Group of People

A special kind of *Group* all of whose members are instances of *Person*. Identity and unity criteria are the same as *Group*, and thus we have **+I~U**. Finally, we consider *Group of People* to be rigid, since any entity which is a group of people must necessarily be such. Note here that having the same identity criteria does not imply having the same *membership* criteria, nor indeed anything at all about it, as the membership criteria for this property is clearly more refined than for *Group*.

## Social Entity
A group of people together for social reasons, such as the "Bridge Club" (i.e. people who play cards together). We can't imagine a common identity criteria for this property, however we assume it is rigid and carries unity. **-I+U+R**.

## Organization
Instances of this property are intended to be things like companies, departments, governments, etc. They are made up of people who play specific roles according to some structure. Like people, organizations seem to carry their own identity criterion, and are wholes with a functional notion of unity, so we assign +O+U+R.

## Fruit
We are thinking here of individual fruits, such as oranges or bananas. We assume they have their own essential properties, and can clearly be isolated from each other. Therefore, +O+U+R seems to be an obvious assignment.

## Apple
This likely adds its own essential properties to those of fruits, so we assign it +O+U+R.

## Red-Apple
Red apples don't have essential metaproperties in addition to apples. Moreover, no red apple is necessarily red, therefore we assign +I+U~R.

## Vertebrate
This property is actually intended to be vertebrate-*animal*. This is a biological classification that adds new *membership* criteria to *Animal* (has-backbone), but apparently no new identity criteria: +I+U+R.

## Person
Like *Living Entity* and *Animal*, the *Person* property is +U+R. It seems clear that specializing from *Vertebrate* to *Person* we add some further essential properties, thus we assume that *Person* has its own identity criteria, and we assign +O.

## Butterfly and Caterpillar
Like *Animal*, *Butterfly* and *Caterpillar* have +I+U. However, every instance of *Caterpillar* can possibly become a non-caterpillar (namely a butterfly), and every instance of *Butterfly* can possibly be (indeed, must have been) a non-butterfly (namely a caterpillar), thus we assign ~R to each.

## Country
Intuitively, a country is a place recognized by convention as having a certain political status. Identity may be difficult to characterize precisely, but some essential

properties seem to be clearly there, so +O.  Countries are certainly wholes, so +U. Interestingly, it seems clear that some countries, like Prussia, still exist but are no longer countries, so we must assign ~R.

## Analyzing Rigid Properties

### The backbone Taxonomy

We now focus our analysis on what we have called the *backbone taxonomy*, that is, the rigid properties in the ontology, organized according to their subsumption relationships.  These properties are the most important to analyze first, since they represent the invariant aspects of the domain. Our sortal expandability and individuation principles guarantee that no element of the domain is "lost" due to this restriction, since *every element must instantiate at least one of the backbone properties*, that supplies an identity criterion for it.

The backbone taxonomy based on the initial ontology is shown in **Figure 2**.

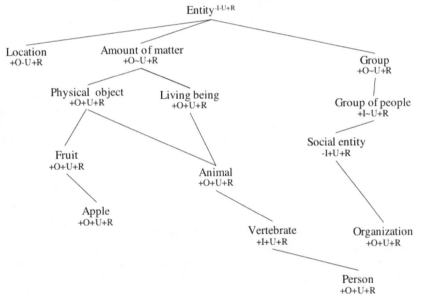

**Figure 2**. The initial backbone taxonomy with metaproperties

### Backbone Constraint Violations

After making the initial decisions regarding metaproperties and arranging the properties in a taxonomy, we are then in a position to verify whether any constraints imposed by the metaproperties are violated in the backbone.  These violations have proven to be excellent indicators of misunderstandings and improperly constructed taxonomies. When a violation is encountered, we must reconsider the assigned metaproperties and/or the taxonomic link, and take some corrective action.

**Living beings are not amounts of matter**. The first problem we encounter is between Amount of Matter and Living Being. The problem is that a ~U property can't subsume one with +U. While it certainly seems to make sense to say that all living beings are amounts of matter, based on the meaning we have assigned there is an inconsistency: every amount of matter can be arbitrarily scattered, but this is certainly not the case for living beings. A further reason against this subsumption link is in the identity criteria: amounts of matter have an extensional identity, that is, they are different if any of their parts is substituted or annihilated – if you remove some clay from a lump of clay, it is a different amount. Living beings, on the other hand, can change parts and still remain the same – when you cut your fingernails off you do not become a different person.

This is one of the most common modeling problems we have seen. Living beings are *constituted* of amounts of matter, they are not themselves the matter. Natural language convention fails to capture this subtle distinction, but it is a violation of the intended meaning to claim that all living beings are mereologically extensional.

The solution here is to remove the subsumption link between these two properties, and represent the relationship as one of constitution.

**Physical objects are not amounts of matter**. Again, we see a violation since a ~U property can't subsume one with +U. This is yet another example of constitution being confused with subsumption. Physical objects are not themselves amounts of matter, they are constituted of matter. The solution is to make *Physical Object* subsumed directly by *Entity*.

**Social entities are not groups of people**. Another ~U/+U violation, as well as a violation of identity criteria. Social entities are constituted of people, but, as with other examples here, they are not merely groups of people, they are more than that. A group of people does not require a unifying relation, as we assume these people can be however scattered in space, time, or motivations. On the contrary, a social entity *must* be somehow unified. Moreover, although both properties supply their own identity criteria, these criteria are mutally inconsistent. Take for instance two typical examples of social entities, such as a bridge club and a poker club. These are clearly two separate entities, even though precisely the same people may participate in both. Thus we would have a state of affairs where, if the social entity was the group of people, the two clubs would be the same under the identity criteria of the group, and different under the identity criteria of the social entity. Note also that if a club changes its members it is still the same club, but a different group of people. The solution to the puzzle is that this is, once again, a constitution relationship: a club is constituted of a group of people.

**Animals are not physical objects**. Although no constraints involving metaproperties are violated in this subsumption link, a closer look at the identity criteria of the two properties involved reveals that the link is inconsistent. Animals, by our account, cease to exist at death, since *being alive* is an essential property for them. However their physical bodies remain for a time after: *being alive* is not essential to them. Indeed, under our assumption *no* physical object has *being alive* as an essential property. Now, if an animal is a physical object, as implied by subsumption, how could it be that it is at the same time necessarily alive and not necessarily alive? The answer is that there must be two entities, related by a form of constitution, and the subsumption link should be removed.

In this example, it is not the metaproperties, but the methodology requiring identity criteria in terms of essential properties that reveals the error.

### Analyzing Non-Rigid Properties

Let us now turn our attention to the *non-rigid* properties, which – so to speak – "flesh out" the backbone taxonomy. In [Welty and Guarino 2001] we have discussed a taxonomy of property kinds based on an analysis of their metaproperties, which distinguishes three main cases of non-rigid properties: *phased sortals, roles,* and *attributions*. All these cases appear in our example, and are discussed below.

Among other things, the differences among these property kinds are based on a metaproperty not discussed here, the notion of *dependence*. Dependence is rather difficult to formalize, however a formalization not essential for an introductory understanding of the OntoClean methodology, so we shall rely on intuitive examples only.

### Phased Sortals

The notion of a phased sortal was originally introduced by Wiggins [Wiggins, 1980]. A phased sortal is a property whose instances are allowed to change certain of their identity criteria during their existence, while remaining the same entity. The canonical example is a caterpillar. The intuition here is that when the caterpillar changes into a butterfly, something fundamental about the way it may be recognized and distinguished has changed, even though it is still the same entity. Phased sortals are recognized in our methodology by the fact that they are independent, anti-rigid, and supply identity criteria.

In the typical case, phased sortals come in clusters of at least two properties – an instance of a phased sortal (e.g., *Caterpillar*) should be able to "phase" into another one (*e.g., Butterfly*), and these clusters should have a common subsuming property providing an identity criterion across phases, according to the sortal individuation principle.

**Caterpillars and butterflies**. Consider now our example. *Caterpillar* and *Butterfly* appear in our initial taxonomy, but there is no single property that subsumes *only* the phases of the same entity. Our formal analysis shows that there *must* be such a property. After some thinking, we find what we need: it is the property *Lepidopteran*, which is +O+U+R. This is what supplies the identity criteria needed to recognize the same entity across phases.

**Countries**. The property *Country* does not, prima facie, appear to be a phased sortal, yet it meets our definition (+O~R). This is an example where reasoning on the metaproperties assignments and their consequences helps us to push our onto-logical analysis further: what are we talking of, here? Is it a region that occasion-ally becomes a country, and in this case acquires some extra (yet temporary) iden-tity criteria? What happens when something is not a country any more? Does it *cease to exist*, or does it just undergo the change of a property, like changing from being sunny and being shady? While answering these questions, we realize we are facing a common problem in building ontologies, that of lumping together multiple meanings of a term into a single property. It seems there are two differ-ent interpretations of "country", one as a geographical region, and another as a geopolitical entity. It is the latter that ceases to exist when the property does not hold any more.

So there are two entities: the *Country* Prussia and the *Geographical Region* Prussia. These two entities are related to each other (e.g. countries occupy re-gions), but are not the same, and therefore we must break the current property into two.

We assign +O+U+R to Country, and +I-U+R to *Geographical Region*. The intui-tion is that countries have their own identity criteria, while geographical regions inherit the identity of locations. Countries clearly have unity, while this is not the case for arbitrary geographical regions. Both properties are now rigid. Interest-ingly enough, we replaced an anti-rigid property with two rigid properties.

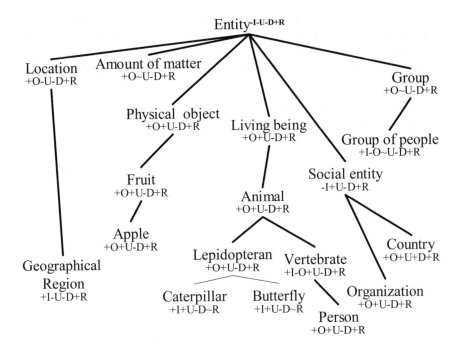

**Figure 3**. The taxonomy after backbone and phased sortals

**Roles.**
After analyzing phased sortals, we end up with the taxonomy shown in , and we
are now ready to consider adding *roles* back into
the taxonomy. Roles are properties that
characterize the way something participates in
a *contingent* event or state of affairs. It is
because of such contingency that these
properties are anti-rigid. Differently from
phase sortals, roles do not supply identity criteria.

**Agent**. The analysis of roles often
exposes subsumption violations concerning rigidity, in particular that a
property with ~R cannot subsume a property with +R. Indeed, when we add the
*Agent* property back to the backbone we see that it originally subsumed two
classes, *Animal* and *Social Entity*. These subsumption links (shown on the previous page as dotted lines) should be removed, as they are incorrect.

This is a different kind of problem in which subsumption is being used to represent a type restriction. The modeler intends to mean, not that all animals are
agents, but that animals *can be* agents. This is a very common misuse of sub-

sumption, often employed by object-oriented programmers. The correct way to represent this kind of relationship is with a covering, i.e. all agents are either animals or social entities. Clearly this is a different notion than subsumption. The solution is to remove the subsumption links and represent this information elsewhere.

**Legal Agent**. The next problem we encounter is when the role *Legal Agent* is added below *Agent*, with its subsuming links to *Person*, *Organization*, and *Country*. Again, as with the previous example, we have a contradiction, an anti-rigid property cannot subsume a rigid one, so these subsumption links (shown as dotted lines at right) must be removed.

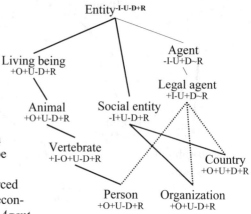

As with the *Agent* role, being forced to remove these links forces us to reconsider the meaning of the *Legal Agent* property. A legal agent is simply an entity recognized by law as an agent in some transaction or contract. Again, as with the *Agent* example, this is not a true subsumption link, but rather another type restriction. The links should be removed and replaced with a covering axiom.

**Food**. We chose to model the notion of food as a role, that is a property of things that may or can be food *in some state of affairs*. So nothing is essentially food –

even a stuffed turkey during a holiday feast or an enormous bowl of pasta with pesto sauce may avoid being eaten and end up not being food (it's *possible*, however unlikely).

While our notion of what an apple means may seem to be violated by removing the subsumption link to *food*, the point is that we have chosen to represent the property in a particular way, as a role, and this link is inconsistent

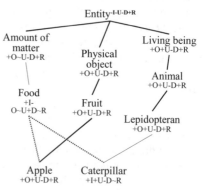

with that meaning and should be removed. In this case, the links are probably being used to represent *purpose* (see, e.g., [Fan, et al, 2001]), not subsumption.

**Attributions.**
The final category of properties we consider are *attributions*. We have one such property in our example, *Red*, whose instances are intended to be red things. We think that in general it is not useful to represent attributions explicitly in a taxonomy, and that the proper way to model attributions is with a simple attribute, like color, and a value, such as red. This quickly brings us to the notion of *qualities*, discussed in the related chapter of this handbook on Dolce, and we avoid that discussion here.

Attributions do, however, come in handy on occasions. Their practical utility is often found in cases where there are a large number of entities that need to be partitioned according to the value of some attribute. We may have apples and pears, for example, and decide we need to partition them into red and green ones. Ontologically, however, the notion of red-thing does not have much significance, since there is nothing we can necessarily say of red-things, besides their color. This seems to us a very good reason eliminate attributions from the backbone. The backbone taxonomy helps in focusing on the more important classes for understanding the invariant aspects of domain structure, whereas attributions may help in organizing the instances on an ad-hoc, temporary basis.

## 8.4   Conclusion

The final, cleaned, taxonomy is shown in Figure 4. The heavier lines indicate subsumption relationships between members of the backbone taxonomy. Although it is not always the case, the cleaned taxonomy has far fewer "multiple inheritance" links than the original. The main reason for this is that subsumption is often used to represent things other than subsumption, that can be described in language using "is a". We may quite naturally say, for example, that an animal is a physical object, however we have shown in this chapter that this kind of linguistic use of "is a" is not logically consistent with the subsumption relationship. This results in many subsumption relationships being removed after analysis.

## Acknowledgements

Many people have made useful comments on OntoClean, and have participated in its refinement. We would like to thank in particular Mariano Fernandez Lopez, Aldo Gangemi, Giancarlo Guizzardi, Claudio Masolo, Alessandro Oltramari, Bill Andersen and Mike Uschold. This work has been partially supported by the IST Project 2001-33052 WonderWeb (Ontology Infrastructure for the Semantic Web) and the National project TICCA (Cognitive Technologies for Communication and Cooperation with Artificial Agents).

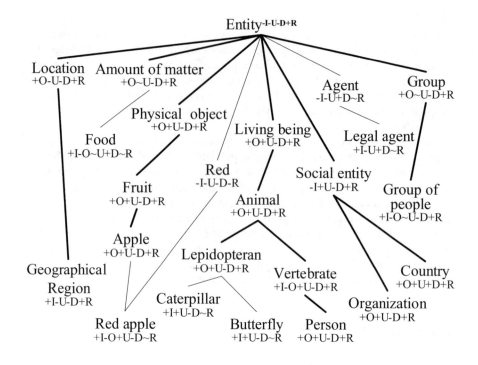

**Figure 4.** The final cleaned ontology

# References

Fan, James, Ken Barker, Bruce Porter, and Peter Clark. 2001. Representing Roles and Purpose. In *Proceedings of the 1st International Conference on Knowledge Capture (K-Cap'01)*. Vancouver: ACM Press.

Gangemi, A., Guarino, N., Masolo, C., and Oltramari, A. 2003. Restructuring Wordnet's Top-level. To appear on *AI Magazine*.

Guarino, N. 1998. Formal Ontology in Information Systems. In N. Guarino (ed.) *Formal Ontology in Information Systems. Proceedings of FOIS'98, Trento, Italy, 6-8 June 1998*. IOS Press, Amsterdam: 3-15.

Guarino, Nicola and Chris Welty. 2000a. Identity, Unity, and Individuality: Towards a formal toolkit for ontological analysis. In, Horn, W. ed., *Proceedings of ECAI-2000: The European Conference on Artificial Intelligence.* Pp. 219-223. Berlin: IOS Press. August, 2000.

Guarino, Nicola and Chris Welty. 2000b. A Formal Ontology of Properties. In, Dieng, R., and Corby, O., eds, *Proceedings of EKAW-2000: The 12th International Conference on Knowledge Engineering and Knowledge Management.* Spring-Verlag LNCS Vol. 1937:97-112. October, 2000.

Guarino, Nicola and Chris Welty. 2000c. Ontological Analysis of Taxonomic Relationships. In, Veda Storey and Alberto Laender, eds., *Proceedings of ER-2000: The 19th
International Conference on Conceptual Modeling.* Springer-Verlag LNCS Vol.
1920:210-224. October, 2000.

Guarino, Nicola and Chris Welty. 2002. Identity and Subsumption. In Rebecca Green,
Carol Bean, and Sung Hyon Myaeng, eds., *The Semantics of Relationships: An Interdisciplinary Perspective.* Pp 111-125. Dordrecht:Kluwer.

Lowe, E. Jonathan. 1989. *Kinds of Being: A Study of Individuation, Identity, and the Logic
of Sortal Terms.* Oxford:Basil Blackwell.

Quine, Willard. 1969. *Ontological Relativity and Other Essays.* New York:Columbia
University Press.

Rector, Allan. 2002. *Are top-level ontologies worth the effort?* Panel at KR-2002. Toulouse, April, 2002.

Simons, Peter. 1987. *Parts: A study in ontology.* Oxford: Clarendon Press.

Welty, C. and Guarino, N. 2001. Supporting Ontological Analysis of Taxonomic Relationships. *Data and Knowledge Engineering*, **39**(1): 51-74.

Wiggins, David. 1980. *Sameness and Substance.* Oxford: Blackwell.

# 9

# Ontology Learning

Alexander Maedche[1] and Steffen Staab[2]

[1] FZI Research Center for Information Technologies, University of Karlsruhe, Germany
   email: maedche@fzi.de
[2] Institute AIFB, University of Karlsruhe, Germany
   email: sst@aifb.uni-karlsruhe.de

**Summary.** *Ontology Learning* greatly facilitates the construction of ontologies by the ontology engineer. The notion of ontology learning that we propose here includes a number of complementary disciplines that feed on different types of unstructured and semi-structured data in order to support a semi-automatic, cooperative ontology engineering process. Our ontology learning framework proceeds through ontology import, extraction, pruning, and refinement, giving the ontology engineer a wealth of coordinated tools for ontology modelling. Besides of the general architecture, we show in this paper some exemplary techniques in the ontology learning cycle that we have implemented in our ontology learning environment, KAON Text-To-Onto.

## 9.1 Introduction

Ontologies constitute a formal conceptualization of a particular domain of interest that is shared by a group of people. When building ontologies into information systems, it is possible to modularize many software aspects mostly related to the domain (e.g., taxonomic structures) from ones mostly related to the processing (e.g., querying) and visualization (e.g., layouting) of data.

One could argue that the drawback one encounters there is that such information systems software cannot be built with an implicit understanding of the domain, but rather it is necessary to make conceptualizations of the domain explicit — which may be a difficult task, resulting in a well-known knowledge engineering bottleneck. While one answer to this argument, also found in software engineering, certainly is: you should make your structures explicit in order to be able to adapt and extend them easily, the quest for faster and cheaper ontology engineering remains. Though ontology engineering tools have matured over the last decade, the manual building of ontologies still remains a tedious, cumbersome task.

Thus, when using ontologies as a basis for information systems, one has to face questions about development time, difficulty, confidence and the maintenance of ontologies. Thus, what one ends up with is similar to what knowledge engineers have dealt with over the last two decades when elaborating methodologies for knowledge acquisition or workbenches for defining knowledge bases. A method which has proven to be extremely beneficial for the knowledge acquisition task is the integration of knowledge acquisition with machine learning techniques.

Ontology Learning [22] aims at the integration of a multitude of disciplines in order to facilitate the construction of ontologies, in particular ontology engineering [49, 11] and machine learning. Because the fully automatic acquisition of knowledge by machines remains in the distant future, the overall process is considered to be semi-automatic with human intervention. It relies on the "balanced cooperative modeling" paradigm [33], describing a coordinated interaction between human modeler and learning algorithm for the construction of ontologies. This objective in mind, an approach that combines ontology engineering with machine learning is described here.

*Organization*

This chapter is organized as following. Section 9.2 introduces a generic architecture for ontology learning and its relevant components. In Section 9.3 we introduce various complementary basic ontology learning algorithms that may serve as a basis for ontology learning. Section 9.4 describes how we have implemented our notion of ontology learning in the form of a concrete system called KAON Text-To-Onto. Section 9.5 surveys related work.

## 9.2 An Architecture and Process Model for Ontology Learning

The purpose of this section is to introduce a generic ontology learning architecture and its four major components, before we continue in detail describing the conceptual model we have developed for our KAON Text-To-Onto system.

Thereby, our process model builds on the principal idea of data mining as a process (e.g., [6]) with the phases of business and data understanding, data preparation, modeling, evaluation and deployment. This implies that our notion of ontology learning makes all process steps transparent — in contrast to some focused ontology learning application for which one may decide to configure a concrete processing pipeline. The latter would have to be configured from the general modules provided in KAON Text-To-Onto.

- **Ontology Management Component**: The ontology engineer uses the ontology management component to manually deal with ontologies. In particular, it allows for the inclusion of existing ontologies, their browsing, validation [48], modification, versioning, and evolution [29].
- **Resource Processing Component**: This component contains a wide range of techniques for *discovering, importing, analyzing and transforming* relevant input data. An important sub-component is a natural language processing system. The general task of the resource processing component is to generate a set of preprocessed data as input for the algorithm library component.

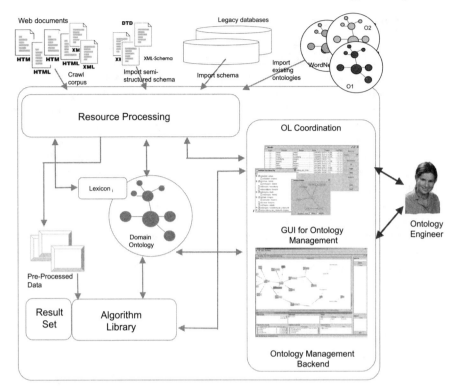

**Fig. 9.1.** Ontology Learning Conceptual Architecture

- **Algorithm Library Component**: This component acts as the algorithmic back-bone of the framework. A number of algorithms are provided for the extraction and maintenance of the ontology parts contained in the ontology model. In order to be able to combine the extraction results of different learning algorithms, it is necessary to standardize the output in a common way. Therefore a common result structure for all learning methods is provided. If several extraction algorithms obtain overlapping or complementary results, they are combined and presented to the user only once.
- **Coordination Component**: The ontology engineer uses this component to inter-act with the ontology learning components for resource processing and for the algorithm library. Comprehensive user interfaces are provided to the ontology engineer to help select relevant data, apply processing and transformation tech-niques or start a specific extraction mechanism. Data processing can also be trig-gered by the selection of an ontology learning algorithm that requires a specific representation. Results are merged using the result set structure and presented to the ontology engineer with different views of the ontology structures.

In the following we provide a detailed overview of the four components.

### 9.2.1 Ontology Management

As core to our approach we have built on our ontology management and application infrastructure called KArlsruhe ONtology and Semantic Web Infrastructure (KAON; also cf. [39]), allowing easy ontology management and application.

KAON is based on an ontology model as introduced in [37]. Briefly, the ontology language is based on RDF(S), but with clean separation of modeling primitives from the ontology itself (thus avoiding the pitfalls of self-describing RDFS primitives such as subClassOf), providing means for modelling meta-classes and incorporating several commonly used modelling primitives, such as transitive, symmetric and inverse properties, or cardinalities. All information is organized in so-called OI-models (ontology-instance models), containing both ontology entities (concepts and properties) as well as their instances. This allows the grouping of concepts with their well-known instances into self-contained units. E.g. a geographical information OI-model might contain the concept Continent along with its seven well-known instances. An OI-model may include another OI-model, thus making all definitions from the included OI-model automatically available (cf. [23]).

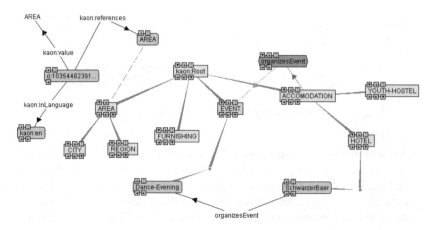

**Fig. 9.2.** OI-model example

A lexical OI-model extends an OI-model by specific entries that reflect various lexical properties of ontology entities. For instance, concepts like PLANET-VENUS (but also relations) have a label (e.g., 'Venus'), synonyms (e.g., 'evening star', 'morning star'), a lexical stem and textual documentation.

There is an n : m relationship between lexical entries and instances, established by the property REFERENCES. Thus, the same lexical entry (e.g., 'his jaguar') may be associated with several elements (e.g., an instance representing a Jaguar car or a jaguar cat). The value, i.e. its literal occurrence, of the lexical entry is given by the property VALUE, whereas the language of the value is specified through the INLANGUAGE property that refers to the set of all languages as defined by the ISO standard 639.

## 9.2.2 Coordination Component

The ontology engineer uses the coordination component to select input data, i.e. relevant resources such as HTML documents from the Web that are exploited in the further discovery process. Secondly, using the coordination component, the ontology engineer also chooses among a set of resource processing methods available at the resource processing component and among a set of algorithms available in the algorithm library.

## 9.2.3 Resource processing

As mentioned earlier this component contains a wide range of techniques for *discovering, importing, analyzing and transforming* relevant input data. An important sub-component is a natural language processing system. The general task of the resource processing component is to generate a set of pre-processed data as input for the algorithm library component.

Resource processing strategies differ depending on the type of input data made available:

- Semi-structured documents, like dictionaries, may be transformed into a predefined relational structure as described in [16]. HTML documents may be indexed and reduced to free text.
- For processing free text the system accesses language dependent natural language processing systems. E.g., for German we have used SMES (Saarbrücken Message Extraction System), a shallow text processor [35]. SMES comprises a *tokenizer* based on regular expressions, a *lexical analysis* component including various word *lexicons*, a *morphological analysis* module, a *named entity recognizer*, a *part-of-speech tagger* and a *chunk parser*. For English, one may build on many available language processing resource, e.g. the GATE system as described in [7]. In the currently supported implementation that is described in Section 9.4 we just use the well-known Porter stemming algorithm [42] as a very simple means for normalizing natural language terms.

After preprocessing according to one of these or similar strategies, the resource processing module transforms given data into an algorithm-specific relational representation.

## 9.2.4 Algorithm Library

An ontology may be described by sets of concepts, relations, lexical entries, and links between these entities. An ontology may be built following this specification using various algorithms working on the preprocessed input data. Thereby, different algorithms may generate definitions for overlapping as well as complementary ontology parts. For instance, an information extraction module specialized for processing appositions[3] may find subclass relationships similar to classification with statistical techniques by kNN (cf., e.g., [40]). Machine learning with association rules, however, may rather be used to detect general binary relationships [25]. Hence, we may reuse algorithms from the library for acquiring different parts of the ontology definition.

Subsequently, we introduce some of the algorithms available in our implementation. In general, we use a result combination approach, i.e. each algorithm that is provided by the library generates normalized results that follow the ontology structures sketched above and contributes to a coherent ontology definition. In the future, more research is needed on how overlapping results may contribute to a common result in a really multi-strategy learning fashion.

## 9.3 Ontology Learning Algorithms

Some example learning algorithms are described here. They cover different parts of the ontology definition — parts that may also be evaluated in isolation of each other [27].

### 9.3.1 Lexical Entry & Concept Extraction

A simple technique for extracting relevant lexical entries that may indicate concepts is counting frequencies of terms in a given set of (linguistically preprocessed) documents, the corpus $\mathcal{D}$. In general this approach is based on the assumption that a frequent term in a set of domain-specific texts indicates occurrence of a relevant concept. Research in information retrieval has shown that there are more effective methods of term weighting than simple counting of frequencies. A standard information retrieval approach is pursued for term weighting, based on the following measures.

- The **lexical entry frequency lef**$_{l,d}$ is the frequency of occurrence of lexical entry $l \in \mathcal{L}$ in a document $d \in \mathcal{D}$.
- The **document frequency df**$_l$ is the number of documents in the corpus $\mathcal{D}$ that $l$ occurs in.
- The **corpus frequency cf**$_l$ is total number of occurrences of $l$ in the overall corpus $\mathcal{D}$.

The reader may note that $df_l \leq cf_l$ and $\sum_d lef_{l,d} = cf_l$. The relevance of terms is measured based on the information retrieval measure **tfidf (term frequency inverted document frequency)**.

**Definition 1.** *Let lef*$_{d,l}$ *be the term frequency of the lexical entry l in a document d. Let df*$_l$ *be the overall document frequency of lexical entry l. Then tfidf*$_{l,d}$ *of the lexical entry l for the document d is given by:*

---

[3] An example for an apposition is given in the following sentence. "Ryokans, a typical Japanese accomodation, are frequented by Europeans, too". There accomodation is an apposition to and a superconcept of Ryokan.

$$tfidf_{l,d} = lef_{l,d} * \log\left(\frac{|\mathcal{D}|}{df_l}\right). \tag{9.1}$$

Tfidf weighs the frequency of a lexical entry in a document with a factor that discounts its importance when it appears in almost all documents. Therefore terms that appear too rarely or too frequently are ranked lower than terms that hold the balance. To rank the importance of a term not only for a document, but for a whole corpus, tfidf values for lexical entries $l$ are computed as follows:[4]

**Definition 2.**

$$tfidf_l := \sum_{d \in \mathcal{D}} tfidf_{l,d}, \qquad tfidf_l \in \mathbf{R}. \tag{9.2}$$

The user may define and vary a **threshold** $k \in \mathbf{R}^+$ that tfidf$_l$ has to exceed. This threshold is then used to explore terms from the corpus for inclusion into the set of lexical entries and possibly into the concept hierarchy.

### 9.3.2 Extraction of Taxonomic Relations

The extraction of taxonomic relations may be done in various ways. In our framework we mainly include the following three kinds of approaches:

- Statistics-based extraction using clustering
- Statistics-based extraction using classification
- Lexico-syntactic pattern extraction

In the following we will shortly elaborate on the three approaches.

*Clustering*

Distributional data about words may be used to build concepts and their embedding into a hierarchy "from scratch" using clustering mechanisms.

A distributional representation describes a term by the (weighted) frequency of terms that occur in a delineated context. The delineation may be defined by sequential vicinity of terms ("How many terms appear between the represented and the representing term?" — which is what we use), by a syntactic delineation ("Which terms may have a syntactic dependency to the represented term?") or by some text structural criterion ("What terms appear in the same paragraph delineated by HTML tags?").

Clustering can be defined as the process of organizing objects into groups whose members are similar in some way based on the distributional representation (see [15]). In general there are three major styles of clustering:

1. Agglomerative: In the initialization phase, each term is defined to constitute a cluster of its own. In the growing phase larger clusters are iteratively generated by merging the most similar/least dissimilar ones until some stopping criterion is reached.

---

[4] A list of stopwords being excluded.

2. Partitional: In the initialization phase, the set of all terms is a cluster. In the re-finement phase smaller clusters are (iteratively) generated by splitting the largest cluster or the least homogeneous cluster into several subclusters.

   Both, agglomerative and partitional clustering techniques, are used to produce hierarchical descriptions of terms. Both rely on notions of (dis-)similarity, for which a range of measures exist (e.g., Jacquard, Kullback-Leibler divergence, L1-norm, cosine; cf. [21]).

   In practice, partitional clustering (like the K-Means clustering technique) is faster as it can be performed in runtime of $\mathcal{O}(n)$ compared to $\mathcal{O}(n^2)$ for ag-glomerative techniques, where $n$ is the number of represented terms.
3. Conceptual: Conceptual clustering builds a lattice of terms by investigating the exact overlap of representing terms between two represented terms. In the worst case, the complexity of the resulting concept lattice is exponential in $n$. Thus, people either just compute a sublattice [47] or use a heuristics.

Either way one may construct a hierarchy of term clusters for detailed inspection by the ontology engineer.

*Classification*

When a substantial hierarchy is already given, e.g. by basic level categories from a general resource like WordNet [32], one may rather decide to refine the taxonomy by classifying new relevant terms into the given concept hierarchy. The distributional representation described above is then used to learn a classifier from a training corpus and the set of predefined concepts with their lexical entries.

Afterwards, one may construct the distributional representations of relevant, un-classified terms and let the learned classifier propose a node on which to subclass the new term (cf, e.g., [40]). k nearest neighbor (kNN) and support vector machines are typical learning algorithms exploited for this purpose.

*Lexico-Syntactic Patterns*

The idea of using lexico-syntactic patterns in the form of regular expressions for the extraction of semantic relations, in particular taxonomic relationships, has been in-troduced by [16]. Pattern-based approaches in general are heuristic methods using regular expressions that originally have been successfully applied in the area of in-formation extraction. In this lexico-syntactic ontology learning approach the text is scanned for instances of distinguished lexico-syntactic patterns that indicate a rela-tion of interest, e.g. the taxonomy. Thus, the underlying idea is very simple: Define a regular expression that captures re-occurring expressions and map the results of the matching expression to a semantic structure, such as taxonomic relations between concepts.

*Example*

In [16] the following lexico-syntactic pattern is considered

$$\ldots NP\{,NP\}*\{,\} \text{ or other } NP\ldots$$

When we apply this pattern to a sentence it can be infered that the NP's referring to concepts on the left of *or other* are sub concepts of the NP referring to a concept on the right. For example from the sentence

*Bruises, wounds, broken bones or other injuries are common.*

we extract the taxonomic relations (Bruise,Injury), (Wound,Injury) and (Broken-Bone,Injury).

Within our ontology learning system we have applied different techniques to dictionary definitions in the context of the insurance and telecommunication domains as described in [19]. An important aspect in this system and approach is that existing concepts are included in the overall process. In contrast to [16] the extraction operations have been performed on the concept level. Thus, patterns have been directly matched onto concepts. Hence, besides of extracting taxonomic relations from scratch, the system can refine existing relationships and refer to existing concepts.

### 9.3.3 Extraction of General Binary Relationships

Association rules have been established in the area of data mining, thus, finding interesting association relationships among a large set of data items. Many companies become interested in mining association rules from their databases (e.g. for helping in many business decisions such as customer relationship management, cross-marketing and loss-leader analysis. A typical example of association rule mining is market basket analysis. This process analyzes customer buying habits by finding associations between the different items that customers place in their shopping baskets. The information discovered by association rules may help to develop marketing strategies, e.g. layout optimization in supermarkets (placing milk and bread within close proximity may further encourage the sale of these items together within single visits to the store). In [1] concrete examples for extracted associations between items are given. The examples are based on supermarket products that are included in a set of transactions collected from customers' purchases. One classical anecode is that "diapers are purchased together with beer".

For the objective of ontology learning, this data mining algorithm may be applied to syntactic structures and statistical co-occurrences appearing in text. To illustrate its working, we here show an example. The example is based on actual ontology learning experiments as described in [25]. A text corpus given by a WWW provider for tourist information has been processed. The corpus describes actual objects referring to locations, accomodations, furnishings of accomodations, administrative information, or cultural events, such as given in the following example sentences.

(1)  a.  "Mecklenburg's" schönstes "Hotel" liegt in Warnemuende. ("Mecklenburg's" most beautiful "hotel" is located in Warnemuende.)
     b.  Ein besonderer Service für unsere Gäste ist der "Frisörsalon" in unserem "Hotel". (A "hairdresser" in our "hotel" is a special service for our guests.)

c. Das Hotel Mercure hat "Balkone" mit direktem "Strandzugang". (The hotel Mercure offers "balconies" with direct "access" to the beach.)

d. Alle "Zimmer" sind mit "TV", Telefon, Modem und Minibar ausgestattet. (All "rooms" have "TV", telephone, modem and minibar.)

Processing the example sentences (1a) and (1b) the dependency relations between the terms are extracted (and some more). In sentences (1c) and (1d) the heuristic for prepositional phrase-attachment (minimal attachment: attach a prepositional phrase to its nearest noun phrase) and the sentence heuristic[5] relate pairs of lexical entries, respectively. Thus, four concept pairs – among many others – are derived with knowledge from the lexicon.

**Table 9.1.** Examples for Linguistically Related Pairs of Concepts

| $L_1$ | $a_{i,1}$ | $L_2$ | $a_{i,2}$ |
|---|---|---|---|
| "Mecklenburgs" | AREA | hotel | HOTEL |
| "hairdresser" | HAIRDRESSER | hotel | HOTEL |
| "balconies" | BALCONY | access | ACCESS |
| "room" | ROOM | TV | TELEVISION |

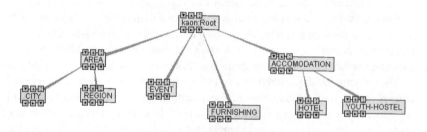

**Fig. 9.3.** An Example Concept Taxonomy as Background Knowledge for Extracting General Binary Relationships

The algorithm for learning generalized association rules uses a taxonomy. The taxonomy may be built with methods such as described in Section 9.3.2. An excerpt involving the concept pairs from above (among some more) is depicted in Figure 9.3. In our actual experiments, the algorithm discovered a large number of interesting and important general binary conceptual relationships. A few of them are listed in Table 9.2. Note that in this table we also list two conceptual pairs, viz. (AREA, HOTEL) and (ROOM, TELEVISION), that are not presented to the user, but that are pruned. The

---

[5] The sentence heuristic essentially says: if no parse tree can be built, relate concepts represented by nouns that are adjacent to each other – abstracting from terms that do not refer to concepts or relationships.

reason is that there are ancestral association rules, viz. (AREA, ACCOMODATION) and (ROOM,FURNISHING), respectively with higher confidence and support measures.

**Table 9.2.** Examples of Discovered General Binary Relationships

| Discovered relation | Confidence | Support |
|---|---|---|
| (AREA, ACCOMODATION) | 0.38 | 0.04 |
| (AREA, HOTEL) | 0.1 | 0.03 |
| (ROOM, FURNISHING) | 0.39 | 0.03 |
| (ROOM, TELEVISION) | 0.29 | 0.02 |
| (ACCOMODATION, ADDRESS) | 0.34 | 0.05 |
| (RESTAURANT, ACCOMODATION) | 0.33 | 0.02 |

Other algorithms use verbs as potential indicators for general binary relationships and acquire selectional restrictions from corpus data [5].

### 9.3.4 Ontology Pruning

Pruning is needed, if one adopts a (generic) ontology to a given domain. We assume that the occurrence of specific concepts and conceptual relations in web documents are vital for the decision whether or not a given concept or relation should remain in an ontology. We exploit a frequency-based approach determining concept frequencies in a corpus. Entities that are frequent in a given corpus are considered as a constituent of a given domain. But - in contrast to ontology extraction - the mere frequency of ontological entities is not sufficient.

To determine domain relevance, ontological entities retrieved from a domain corpus are compared to frequencies obtained from a generic corpus. The user can select several relevance measures for frequency computation. The ontology pruning algorithm uses the computed frequencies to determine the relative relevancy of each concept contained in the ontology. All existing concepts and relations, which are more frequent in the domain-specific corpus remain in the ontology. The user can also control the pruning of concepts which are neither contained in the domain-specific nor in the generic corpus.

## 9.4 KAON Text-To-Onto

This section describes the implemented ontology learning system KAON Text-To-Onto that is embedded in KAON, the Karlsruhe Ontology and Semantic web infrastructure (cf. [39]). KAON[6] is an open-source ontology management and application infrastructure targeted for semantics-driven business applications. It includes a comprehensive tool suite allowing easy ontology management and application.

---

[6] http://kaon.semanticweb.org

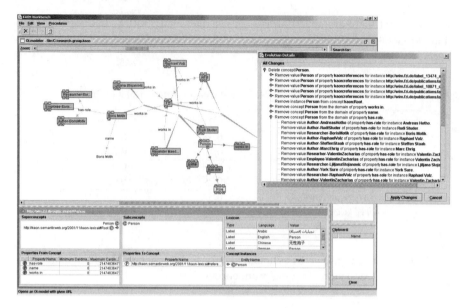

**Fig. 9.4.** KAON OI-Modeler

Within KAON we have developed KAON OI-modeler, an end-user application that realizes a graph-based user interface for OI-model creation and evolution [29]. Figure 9.4 shows the graph-based view onto an OI-model.

A specific aspect of KAON OI-modeler is that it supports ontology evolution at the user level (see right side of the screenshot). The figure shows a modelling session where the user attempted to remove the concept Person. Before applying this change to the ontology, the system computed the set of additional changes that must be applied. The tree of dependent changes is presented to the user, thus allowing the user to comprehend the effects of the change before it is actually applied. Only when the user agrees, the changed will be applied to the ontology.

KAON Text-To-Onto[7] builds on the KAON OI-modeler. KAON Text-To-Onto provides means for defining a corpus as a basis for ontology learning (see right lower part of Figure 9.5). On top of the corpus various algorithms may be applied. In the example depicts in Figure 9.5 the user has selected different parameters and executed a pattern-based extraction and an association rule extraction algorithm in parallel. KAON Text-To-Onto implements the aforementioned algorithms, though not (yet!) partitional and conceptual clustering.

Finally, the results are presented to the user (see Figure 9.5) and graphical means for adding lexical entries, concepts and conceptual relations are provided.

---

[7] KAON Text-To-Onto is open-source and available for download at the KAON Web page.

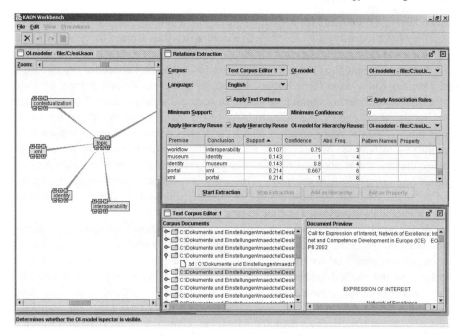

**Fig. 9.5.** KAON Text-To-Onto

## 9.5 Related Work

Until recently ontology learning *per se*, i.e. for comprehensive construction of ontologies, has not existed. We here give the reader a comprehensive overview of existing work that has actually researched and practiced techniques for solving parts of the overall problem of ontology learning.

There are only a few approaches that described the development of frameworks and workbenches for extracting ontologies from data: Faure & Nedellec [9] present a cooperative machine learning system, ASIUM, which acquires taxonomic relations and subcategorization frames of verbs based on syntactic input. The ASIUM system hierarchically clusters nouns based on the verbs that they are syntactically related with and *vice versa*. Thus, they cooperatively extend the lexicon, the set of concepts, and the concept heterarchy. A more recent approach is described by Missikoff et al. [36] who combine an ontology engineering environment with focus on consensus building with sophisticated tools for extracting concepts that have multi-word lables (e.g. 'swimming pool') and for extracting relationships other than taxonomy, e.g. pertainance.

Hahn and Schnattinger [14] introduced a methodology for the maintenance of domain-specific taxonomies. An ontology is incrementally updated as new concepts are acquired from real-world texts. The acquisition process is centered around linguistic and conceptual "quality" of various forms of evidence underlying the generation and refinement of concept hypotheses. Their ontology learning approach is embedded in a framework for natural language understanding, named Syndicate [13], and they have recently extended their framework to a dual learner for grammars and ontologies [12].

Mikheev & Finch [31] have presented their KAWB Workbench for "Acquisition of Domain Knowledge form Natural Language". The workbench comprises a set of tools for uncovering internal structure in natural language texts. The main idea behind the workbench is the independence of the text representation and text analysis phases. At the representation phase the text is converted from a sequence of characters to features of interest by means of the annotation tools. At the analysis phase those features are used by statistics gathering and inference tools for finding significant correlations in the texts. The analysis tools are independent of particular assumptions about the nature of the feature-set and work on the abstract level of feature elements represented as SGML items.

Much work in a number of disciplines — computational linguistics, information retrieval, machine learning, databases, software engineering — has actually researched and practiced techniques for solving part of the overall problem. Hence, techniques and methods relevant for ontology learning may be found under terms like the acquisition of selectional restrictions (cf. Resnik [43] and Basili et al. [4]), word sense disambiguation and learning of word senses (cf. Hastings [51]), the computation of concept lattices from formal contexts (cf. Ganter & Wille [10]) and Reverse Engineering in software engineering (cf. Mueller et al. [38]).

Ontology Learning puts a number of research activities, which focus on different types of inputs, but share their target of a common domain conceptualization, into one perspective. One may recognize that these activities are spread between very different communities. Further references may in particular be found at the three ontology learning workshops [45, 28, 3].

## 9.6 Conclusion

We have introduced ontology learning as an approach that may greatly facilitate the construction of ontologies by the ontology engineer. The notion of Ontology Learning introduced in this article aims at the integration of a multitude of disciplines in order to facilitate the construction of ontologies. The overall process is considered to be semi-automatic with human intervention. It relies on the "balanced cooperative modeling" paradigm, describing a coordinated interaction between human modeler and learning algorithm for the construction of ontologies for the Semantic Web.

## References

1. Agrawal, R. and Imielinski, T. and Swami, A.: Mining Associations between Sets of Items in Massive Databases, In Proceedings of the 1993 ACM SIGMOD International Conference on Management of Data, Washington, D.C., May 26-28, 1993.

2. H. Assadi. Construction of a regional ontology from text and its use within a documentary system. In *Proceedings of the International Conference on Formal Ontology and Information Systems - FOIS'98*, Trento, Italy, 1998.

3. N. Aussenac-Gilles, and A. Maedche (eds.). *Workshop on Machine Learning and Natural Language Processing for Ontology Engineering*, http://www-sop.inria.fr/acacia/OLT2002

4. R. Basili, M. T. Pazienza, and P. Velardi. Acquisition of selectional patterns in a sublanguage. *Machine Translation*, 8(1):175–201, 1993.

5. Paul Buitelaar. CORELEX: *Systematic Polysemy and Underspecification*. PhD thesis, Brandeis University, Department of Computer Science, 1998.

6. P. Chapman, R. Kerber, J. Clinton, T. Khabaza, T. Reinartz, and R. Wirth. The CRISP-DM Process Model. Discussion Paper, March 1999. http://www.crisp-dm.org/

7. H. Cunningham and R. Gaizauskas and K. Humphreys and Y. Wilks: Three Years of GATE, In Proceedings of the AISB'99 Workshop on Reference Architectures and Data Standards for NLP, Edinburgh, U.K. Apr, 1999.

8. F. Esposito, S. Ferilli, N. Fanizzi, and G. Semeraro. Learning from parsed sentences with inthelex. In *Proceedings of Learning Language in Logic Workshop (LLL-2000), Lisbon, Portugal, 2000*, 2000.

9. D. Faure and C. Nedellec. A corpus-based conceptual clustering method for verb frames and ontology acquisition. In *LREC workshop on adapting lexical and corpus resources to sublanguages and applications*, Granada, Spain, 1998.

10. B. Ganter and R. Wille. *Formal Concept Analysis: Mathematical Foundations*. Springer, Berlin - Heidelberg - New York, 1999.

11. A. Gomez-Perez. Ontology Engineering. Springer Verlag, 2002/2003.

12. U. Hahn and K. Marko: An integrated, dual learner for grammars and ontologies. *Data and Knowledge Engineering*, 42(3): 273-291, 2002.

13. U. Hahn and M. Romacker. Content management in the syndikate system — how technical documents are automatically transformed to text knowledge bases. *Data & Knowledge Engineering*, 35:137–159, 2000.

14. U. Hahn and K. Schnattinger. Towards text knowledge engineering. In *Proc. of AAAI '98*, pages 129–144, 1998.

15. L. Kaufman and P. Rousseeuw: Finding Groups in Data: An Introduction to Cluster Analysis, John Wiley, 1990.

16. Hearst, M.: Automatic acquisition of hyponyms from large text corpora. In Proceedings of the 14th International Conference on Computational Linguistics. Nantes, France, 1992.

17. J. Jannink and G. Wiederhold. Thesaurus entry extraction from an on-line dictionary. In *Proceedings of Fusion '99, Sunnyvale CA, July 1999*, 1999. http://www-db.stanford.edu/SKC/publications.html.

18. P. Johannesson. A method for transforming relational schemas into conceptual schemas. In M. Rusinkiewicz, editor, *10th International Conference on Data Engineering*, pages 115 – 122, Houston, 1994. IEEE Press.

19. Kietz, J.-U. and Volz, R. and Maedche, A.: Semi-automatic ontology acquisition from a corporate intranet. In International Conference on Grammar Inference (ICGI-2000), Lecture Notes in Artificial Intelligence, LNAI, 2000.

20. J.-U. Kietz and K. Morik. A polynomial approach to the constructive induction of structural knowledge. *Machine Learning*, 14(2):193–218, 1994.

21. L. Lee. Measures of distributional similarity. In *Proc. of the 37th Annual Meeting of the Association for Computational Linguistics*, 1999, pp. 25-32.

22. A. Maedche: Ontology Learning for the Semantic Web. Kluwer Academic Publishers, 2002.

23. A. Maedche, B. Motik, L. Stojanovic, R. Studer, and R. Volz. An infrastructure for searching, reusing and evolving distributed ontologies. In *Proceedings 12th International World Wide Web Conference (WWW12)*, Semantic Web Track, 2003, Budapest, Hungary, pp. 439-448.
24. A. Maedche, V. Pekar and S. Staab. Ontology Learning Part One - On Discoverying Taxonomic Relations from the Web. In: Ning Zhong et al. (eds) *Web Intelligence*, Springer, 2003, pp. 301-320.
25. A. Maedche and S. Staab. Discovering conceptual relations from text. In *Proceedings of ECAI-2000*. IOS Press, Amsterdam, 2000.
26. A. Maedche and S. Staab. Mining ontologies from text. In Proceedings of EKAW-2000, Springer Lecture Notes in Artificial Intelligence (LNAI-1937), Juan-Les-Pins, France, 2000.
27. A. Maedche and S. Staab. Measuring Similarity between Ontologies. In: *Proc. Of the European Conference on Knowledge Acquisition and Management - EKAW-2002*. Madrid, Spain, October 1-4, 2002. LNCS/LNAI 2473, Springer, 2002, pp. 251-263.
28. A. Maedche, S. Staab, E. Hovy, and C. Nedellec (eds.). *The IJCAI-2001 Workshop on Ontology Learning. Proceedings of the Second Workshop on Ontology Learning - OL'2001*, Seattle, WA, USA, August 4, 2001. CEUR Proceedings.
29. A. Maedche, B. Motik, L. Stojanovic, R. Studer, and R. Volz: Ontologies for Enterprise Knowledge Management, IEEE Intelligent Systems, December, 2002.
30. Manning, C. and Schuetze, H.: Foundations of Statistical Natural Language Processing. MIT Press, Cambridge, Massachusetts, 1999.
31. A. Mikheev and S. Finch. A workbench for finding structure in text. In *In Proceedings of the 5th Conference on Applied Natural Language Processing — ANLP'97, March 1997, Washington DC, USA*, pages 372–379, 1997.
32. G. Miller. WordNet: A Lexical Database for English. *Communications of the ACM*, 38(11), pp. 3941.
33. K. Morik and S. Wrobel and J.-U. Kietz and W. Emde *Knowledge acquisition and machine learning: Theory, methods, and applications*, London: Academic Press, 1993.
34. E. Morin. Automatic acquisition of semantic relations between terms from technical corpora. In *Proc. of the Fifth International Congress on Terminology and Knowledge Engineering - TKE'99*, 1999.
35. G. Neumann and R. Backofen and J. Baur and M. Becker and C. Braun: An Information Extraction Core System for Real World German Text Processing. In Proceedings of ANLP-97, Washington, USA, 1997.
36. M. Missikoff, R. Navigli, and P. Velardi: The Usable Ontology: An Environment for Building and Assessing a Domain Ontology. *Proceedings of the International Semantic Web Conference 2002*. Springer, 2002, pp. 39-53.
37. B. Motik and A. Maedche and R. Volz: A Conceptual Modeling Approach for building semantics-driven enterprise applications. 1st International Conference on Ontologies, Databases and Application of Semantics (ODBASE-2002), California, USA, 2002.
38. H. A. Mueller, J. H. Jahnke, D. B. Smith, M.-A. Storey, S. R. Tilley, and K. Wong. Reverse Engineering: A Roadmap. In *Proceedings of the 22nd International Conference on Software Engineering (ICSE-2000), Limerick, Ireland*. Springer, 2000.
39. D. Oberle, R. Volz, S. Staab, and B. Motik. An extensible ontology software environment. In this book.
40. V. Pekar and S. Staab. Taxonomy Learning — Factoring the structure of a taxonomy into a semantic classification decision. In: *Proceedings of the 19th Conference on Computational Linguistics, COLING-2002*, August 24 – September 1, 2002, Taipei, Taiwan, 2002.

41. Pereira, F. and Tishby, N. and Lee, L.: Distributation Clustering of English Words. In Proceedings of the ACL-93, 1993.
42. Porter, M. F.: An algorithm for suffix stripping. In *Program*, 14(3), 1980, pp. 130137.
43. P. Resnik. *Selection and Information: A Class-based Approach to Lexical Relationships.* PhD thesis, University of Pennsylania, 1993.
44. S. Schlobach.    Assertional mining in description logics.    In *Proceedings of the 2000 International Workshop on Description Logics (DL2000)*, 2000. http://SunSITE.Informatik.RWTH-Aachen.DE/Publications/CEUR-WS/Vol-33/.
45. S. Staab, A. Maedche, C. Nedellec, and P. Wiemer-Hastings (eds.). *The ECAI'2000 Workshop on Ontology Learning. Proceedings of the First Workshop on Ontology Learning - OL'2000*, Berlin, Germany, August 25, 2000. CEUR Proceedings, Vol-31.
46. L. Stojanovic, N. Stojanovic, and R. Volz. A reverse engineering approach for migrating data-intensive web sites to the semantic web. In *IIP-2002, August 25-30, 2002, Montreal, Canada (Part of the IFIP World Computer Congress WCC2002)*, 2002.
47. G. Stumme, R. Taouil, Y. Bastide, N. Pasqier, and L. Lakhal. Computing Iceberg Concept Lattices with Titanic. *Journal on Knowledge and Data Engineering*, 42(2), pp. 189222.
48. Y. Sure, J. Angele, and S. Staab. OntoEdit: Guiding Ontology Development by Methodology and Inferencing In S. Spaccapietra, S. March, and K. Aberer (eds.).  LNCS - Semantics of Data, Springer, 2003 (to appear). (Extended version from ODBase-2002).
49. Y. Sure, S. Staab, and R. Studer.  Methodology for Development and Employment of Ontology based Knowledge Management Applications In this book.
50. Z. Tari, O. Bukhres, J. Stokes, and S. Hammoudi.  The Reengineering of Relational Databases based on Key and Data Correlations. In *Proceedings of the 7th Conference on Database Semantics (DS-7), 7-10 October 1997, Leysin, Switzerland*. Chapman & Hall, 1998.
51. P. Wiemer-Hastings, A. Graesser, and K. Wiemer-Hastings.  Inferring the meaning of verbs from context. In *Proceedings of the Twentieth Annual Conference of the Cognitive Science Society*, 1998.
52. Y. Wilks, B. Slator, and L. Guthrie. *Electric Words: Dictionaries, Computers, and Meanings*. MIT Press, Cambridge, MA, 1996.

**Table 9.3.** Classification of Ontology Learning Approaches

| Domain | Method | Features used | Prime purpose | Papers |
|---|---|---|---|---|
| Free Text | Clustering | Syntax | Extract | Buitelaar [5], Assadi [2] and Faure & Nedellec [9] |
| | Inductive Logic Programming | Syntax, Logic representation | Extract | Esposito et al. [8] |
| | Association rules | Syntax, Tokens | Extract | Maedche & Staab [25] |
| | Frequency-based | Syntax | Prune | Kietz et al. [19] |
| | Pattern-Matching | Syntax | Extract | Morin [34] |
| | Classification | Syntax, Semantics | Refine | Schnattinger & Hahn [14, 4] |
| | Formal Concept Analysis | Syntax, Semantics | Refine | [14, 24] |
| Dictionary | Information extraction | Syntax | Extract | Hearst [16], Wilks [52] and Kietz et al. [19] |
| | Page rank | Tokens | | Jannink & Wiederhold [17] |
| Knowledge base | Concept Induction, A-Box mining | Concept Induction, Relations | Extract | Kietz & Morik [20] and Schlobach [44] |
| Relational schemata | Data Correlation | Relations | Reverse engineering | Johannesson [18], Tari et al. [50], Stojanovic et al. [46] |

# 10

# Knowledge Patterns

Peter Clark[1], John Thompson[1], and Bruce Porter[2]

[1] Mathematics and Computing Technology
Boeing Phantom Works
MS 7L66, PO Box 3707, Seattle, WA 98124
{peter.e.clark,john.a.thompson}@boeing.com

[2] Computer Science Dept.
University of Texas
Austin, TX 78712
porter@cs.utexas.edu

**Summary.** This Chapter describes a new technique, called "knowledge patterns", for helping construct axiom-rich, formal ontologies, based on identifying and explicitly representing recurring patterns of knowledge (theory schemata) in the ontology, and then stating how those patterns map onto domain-specific concepts in the ontology. From a modeling perspective, knowledge patterns provide an important insight into the structure of a formal ontology: rather than viewing a formal ontology simply as a list of terms and axioms, knowledge patterns views it as a collection of abstract, modular theories (the "knowledge patterns") plus a collection of modeling decisions stating how different aspects of the world can be modeled using those theories. Knowledge patterns make both those abstract theories and their mappings to the domain of interest explicit, thus making modeling decisions clear, and avoiding some of the ontological confusion that can otherwise arise. In addition, from a computational perspective, knowledge patterns provide a simple and computationally efficient mechanism for facilitating knowledge reuse. We describe the technique and an application built using them, and then critique its strengths and weaknesses. We conclude that this technique enables us to better explicate both the structure and modeling decisions made when constructing a formal, axiom-rich ontology.

## 10.1 Introduction

At its heart, ontological engineering is a modeling endeavor. In a formal ontology, in particular, the knowledge engineer attempts to identify concepts and axioms which reflect (to a certain approximation) the real-world phenomena which he/she is interested in. A common observation is that, when doing this, one often finds oneself repeating structurally similar patterns of axioms. For example, when formalizing an ontology about a space science experiment (called KB-PHaSE [1]), we found that axioms about connectivity in electrical circuits, and about connectivity in optical systems, had substantial structure in common. To make this shared structure explicit, and hence reusable, we have developed a knowledge engineering technique based on the explicit representation of these *knowledge patterns*, i.e., general templates denoting recurring theory schemata, and their transformation (through symbol renaming) to create specific theories, which we present in this Chapter.

From a knowledge engineering point of view, knowledge patterns provide considerable flexibility, as they can be transformed in multiple ways, and can be used in whole or in part. We describe how this overcomes some of the limitations of trying to use inheritance to achieve the same effect. From a philosophical point of view, knowledge patterns are also significant as they provide structure to the knowledge in an ontology, explicitly modularizing and separating the abstract theories (the knowledge patterns) from the phenomena in the world which those theories are deemed to reflect. For example, rather than encoding a theory about *electrical circuits*, we encode a knowledge pattern about *directed graphs*, and then state how an electrical circuit can be *modeled as* as a directed graph. In this way, knowledge patterns make explicit (and reusable) the "computational clockwork" of our axioms, and the modeling decisions made to apply that clockwork to the task at hand. As a result, a formal ontology can be viewed as a collection of theories mapped onto the domain of interest (perhaps in multiple ways), rather than simply as a "sea of axioms".

Consider, for example, constructing a formal ontology about banking. We might include axioms such as: if an amount X is deposited into a bank account, then the the amount in that account is increased by X. We could write many such axioms, and as a result have a useful theory about banking. However, what is not represented here is a fundamental – and perhaps subconscious – insight by the knowledge engineer, namely that *a bank account can be modeled as a kind of container*, and thus that a theory of containers can be applied, in this case, to bank accounts. The axiom above, for example, asserts a container-like behavior on bank accounts, but nowhere is the abstract container theory itself stated, nor the mapping from it to bank accounts made explicit. Without this insight, the knowledge engineer will find him/herself writing the same pattern of axioms many times for different container-like phenomena. Our goal with knowledge patterns is to avoid this by making such abstract theories explicit, distinct from their application to a particular domain, and hence reusable. We aim to separate the "computational clockwork" of an axiom set from the real-world phenomena which (according to the knowledge engineer) seems to behave in a similar way to that axiom set.

As another example, consider the various formal ontologies of time, with axioms about time points, time intervals, etc. In fact, large parts of these theories are not specifically about time; rather, they can be viewed as (in part) as theories about *lines*, along with the implicit insight that "time can be modeled as a line". Again, our goal with knowledge patterns is to make explicit the underlying model (here, of lines), and its application to some phenomenon (here, time).

It might seem that this type of reuse could also be achieved using normal inheritance mechanisms (e.g., asserting "a bank account isa container", or "time isa line"). However, this works poorly in two situations: when the abstract theory applies to a specific theory in more than one way, and when only a selected portion of the abstract theory is applicable. In the next Section, we discuss in detail an example to illustrate these problems, and subsequently describe the knowledge pattern approach, and how it overcomes these limitations. We conclude that this technique enables us to better modularize axiom-rich ontologies and reuse their general theories.

## 10.2 The Limitations of Inheritance

Consider constructing an ontology about computers, including formal axioms to define the meaning of the terms and relations used in that ontology. We might include relations in the ontology such as `ram_size` (the amount of RAM a computer has), `expansion_slots` (the number of expansion slots a computer has), `free_slots` (the number of free slots a computer has), etc., and formalize the meaning of these terms using axioms such as the following, here expressed in Prolog[3]:

```
% "Available RAM is the total RAM minus the occupied RAM."
available_ram(Computer,A)  :-
      isa(Computer,computer),
      ram_size(Computer,S),
      occupied_ram(Computer,R),
      A is S - R.
```

```
% "The number of free expansion-slots is the total number
.  %   of slots minus the number filled."
free_slots(Computer,N)  :-
      isa(Computer,computer),
      expansion_slots(Computer,X),
      occupied_slots(Computer,O),
      N is X - O.
```

The two axioms above are syntactically different, yet they both instantiate the same general axiom, which we could explicate as:

```
FREE_SPACE(X,S)  :-
      isa(X,CLASS),
      CAPACITY(X,C),
      OCCUPIED_SPACE(X,O),
      S is C - O.
```

As part of a general *container* theory, this axiom relates a container's free space, capacity, and occupied space.

   The axioms for `available_ram` and `free_slots` are instantiations of this axiom just when a computer is modeled as a container of data and expansion cards, respectively. However, unless this general theory of *containers* is represented explicitly, its application to the domain of computers is only implicit. Clearly, we would prefer to explicitly represent the theory, then to reuse its axioms as needed.

---

[3] Variables start with upper-case letters and are universally quantified; ':-' denotes reverse implication (←); ',' denotes conjunction; and `is` denotes arithmetic computation.

This is typically done with inheritance. The knowledge engineer encodes an explicit theory of *containers* at a high-level node in a taxonomy, then its axioms are automatically added to more specific theories at nodes lower in the taxonomy. One axiom in our *container* theory might be:

```
free_space(Container,F) :-
    isa(Container,container),
    capacity(Container,C),
    occupied_space(Container,O),
    F is C - O.
```

To use inheritance to import this axiom into our *computer* theory, we assert that computers are containers and that `ram_size` is a special case (a 'subslot,' in the terminology of frame systems) of the `capacity` relation:

% *"Computers are containers."*[4]
```
subclass_of(computer,container).
```

% *"RAM size is a measure of capacity."*
```
capacity(X,Y) :-
        isa(X,computer),
        ram_size(X,Y).
```

However, this becomes problematic here as there is a second notion of "computers as containers" in our original axioms, namely computers as containers of expansion cards. If we map this notion onto our *computer* theory in the same way, by adding the axiom:

% *"Number of expansion slots is a measure of capacity"*
```
capacity(X,Y) :-
        isa(X,computer),
        expansion_slots(X,Y).
```

then the resulting representation captures that a computer has two capacities (memory capacity and slot capacity), but loses the constraints among their relations. Consequently, memory capacity may be used to compute the number of free expansion slots, and slot capacity may be used to compute available RAM. This illustrates how the general container theory can be "overlaid" on a computer in multiple ways, but inheritance fails to keep these overlays distinct.

This problem might be avoided in various ways. We could insist that a general theory (e.g., *container*) is applied at most once to a more specific theory (although there is no obvious, principled justification for this restriction). We would then revise our representation so that it is not a computer, but a computer's *memory*, which contains data, and similarly that a computer's *expansion slots* contain cards. While this solves the current problem, the general problem remains. For example, we may also want to model the computer's memory as a container in other senses (e.g., of transistors, files, information, or processes), which this restriction prohibits.

---

[4] We assume a general inheritance axiom:
```
isa(I,SuperC) :- isa(I,C), subclass_of(C,SuperC).
```

Another pseudo-solution is to parameterize the container theory, by adding an argument to the *container* axioms to denote the *type* of thing contained, to distinguish different applications of the *container* theory. With the changes italicized, our axioms become:

% *"Free space for content-type T = capacity for T - occupied T."*
```
free_space(Container,ContentType,F)  :-
    isa(Container,container),
    capacity(Container,ContentType,C),
    occupied_space(Container,ContentType,O),
    F is C - O.
```

% *"ram_size denotes a computer's RAM capacity."*
```
capacity(X,ram,Y)  :-
    isa(X,computer),
    ram_size(X,Y).
```

Again, this solves the current problem (at the expense of parsimony), but is not a good general solution. Multiple parameters may be needed to distinguish different applications of a general theory to a more specific one. For example, we would need to add a second parameter about the container's Dimension (say) to distinguish physical containment (as in: "a computer contains megabytes of data") from meta-physical containment (as in: "a computer contains valuable information"). This complicates our *container* axioms further, and still other parameters may be needed.

A second limitation of inheritance is that it copies axioms (from a general theory to a more specific one) in an "all or nothing" fashion. Often only a selected part of a theory should be transferred. To continue with our example, the general *container* theory may include relations for a container wall and its porosity, plus axioms involving these relations. Because the relations have no counterpart in the *computer* theory, these relations and axioms should not be transferred.

These two problems arise because inheritance is being misused, not because it is somehow "buggy." When we say "A computer is a container," we mean "A computer (or some aspect of it, such as its memory) *can be modeled as* a container." Inheritance is designed to transfer axioms through the *isa* relation, not the *can-be-modeled-as* relation. Nevertheless, knowledge engineers often conflate these relations, probably because inheritance has been the only approach available to them. This leads to end-less (and needless) debates on the placement of abstract concepts in taxonomies. For example, where should *container* be placed in a taxonomy with respect to *object, substance, process* and so on? Almost anything can be thought of as a container in some way, and if we pursue this route, we are drawn into debating these modeling decisions as if they were issues of some objective reality. This was a recurrent problem in our earlier work on the Botany Knowledge-Base [2], where general theories used as models (such as *connector* and *interface*) sit uncomfortably high in the taxonomy. The same issue arises in other ontologies. For example, *product* is placed just below *individual* in Cyc [3] and *place* is just below *physical-object* in Mikrokosmos [4].

## 10.3 Knowledge Patterns

Our approach for handling these situations is conceptually simple but architecturally significant because it enables us to better modularize a knowledge-base. We define a *pattern* as a first-order theory whose axioms are not part of the target knowledge-base, but can be incorporated via a renaming of their non-logical symbols.

A theory acquires its status as a pattern by the way it is used, rather than by having some intrinsic property. First, the knowledge engineer implements the pattern as an explicit, self-contained theory. For example, the *container* theory would include the axiom:

```
free_space(Container,F) :-
    isa(Container,container),
    capacity(Container,C),
    occupied_space(Container,O),
    F is C - O.
```

Second, using terminology from category theory [5], the knowledge engineer defines a *morphism* for each intended application of this pattern in the target knowledge-base. A morphism is a consistent[5] mapping of the pattern's non-logical symbols, or *signature*, to terms in the knowledge-base, specifying how the pattern should be transformed. Finally, when the knowledge base is loaded, morphed copies of this pattern are imported, one for each morphism. In our example, there are two morphisms for this pattern:

```
container -> computer
capacity -> ram_size
free_space -> available_ram
occupied_space -> occupied_ram
isa -> isa
```
and
```
container -> computer
capacity -> expansion_slots
free_space -> free_slots
occupied_space -> occupied_slots
isa -> isa
```

(The reason for mapping a symbol to itself, e.g., the last line in these morphisms, is explained in the next paragraph). When these morphisms are applied, two copies of the *container* pattern are created, corresponding to the two ways, described above, in which computers are modeled as containers.

There may be symbols in the pattern that have no counterpart in the target knowledge base, such as the thickness of a *container wall* in our computer example. In this

---

[5] Two examples of inconsistent mappings are: (i) mapping a symbol twice, e.g., {A->X,A->Y}, (ii) mapping a function f to g, where g's signature as specified by the mapping conflicts with g's signature as already defined in the target KB, e.g., {f->g,A->X,B->Y}, where f : A → B in the source pattern but g is already in the target and does not have signature g : X → Y.

event, the knowledge engineer omits the symbols from the morphism, and the morphing procedure maps each one to a new, unique symbol (generated by Lisp's gensym function, for example). This restricts the scope of these symbols to the morphed copy of the pattern in the target knowledge base. Although the symbols are included in the imported theory, they are invisible (or more precisely, hidden) from other axioms in the knowledge base. Note that we cannot simply delete axioms that mention these symbols because other axioms in the imported theory may depend on them.[6]

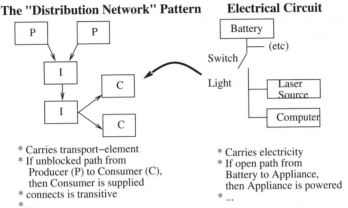

**The "Distribution Network" Pattern**

* Carries transport–element
* If unblocked path from
   Producer (P) to Consumer (C),
   then Consumer is supplied
* connects is transitive
* ...

**Electrical Circuit**

* Carries electricity
* If open path from
   Battery to Appliance,
   then Appliance is powered
* ...

**Fig. 10.1.** A knowledge pattern is created by abstracting the structure of a theory (here, about electrical circuits).

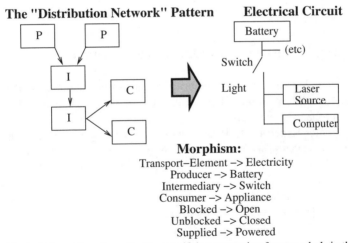

**Morphism:**
Transport–Element –> Electricity
Producer –> Battery
Intermediary –> Switch
Consumer –> Appliance
Blocked –> Open
Unblocked –> Closed
Supplied –> Powered

**Fig. 10.2.** A knowledge pattern is applied by specifying a mapping from symbols in the pattern to symbols in the target ontology of interest.

---

[6] Although specific axioms may be removed if they do not contribute to assertions about symbols that are imported. A dependency analysis algorithm could, in principle, identify and remove such "dead code".

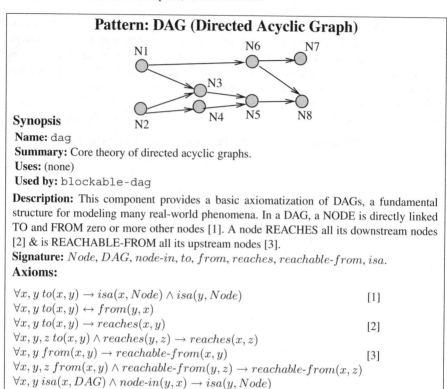

**Synopsis**
**Name:** dag
**Summary:** Core theory of directed acyclic graphs.
**Uses:** (none)
**Used by:** blockable-dag

**Description:** This component provides a basic axiomatization of DAGs, a fundamental structure for modeling many real-world phenomena. In a DAG, a NODE is directly linked TO and FROM zero or more other nodes [1]. A node REACHES all its downstream nodes [2] & is REACHABLE-FROM all its upstream nodes [3].
**Signature:** $Node, DAG, node\text{-}in, to, from, reaches, reachable\text{-}from, isa.$
**Axioms:**

$$\forall x, y \; to(x, y) \rightarrow isa(x, Node) \land isa(y, Node) \qquad [1]$$
$$\forall x, y \; to(x, y) \leftrightarrow from(y, x)$$
$$\forall x, y \; to(x, y) \rightarrow reaches(x, y) \qquad [2]$$
$$\forall x, y, z \; to(x, y) \land reaches(y, z) \rightarrow reaches(x, z)$$
$$\forall x, y \; from(x, y) \rightarrow reachable\text{-}from(x, y) \qquad [3]$$
$$\forall x, y, z \; from(x, y) \land reachable\text{-}from(y, z) \rightarrow reachable\text{-}from(x, z)$$
$$\forall x, y \; isa(x, DAG) \land node\text{-}in(y, x) \rightarrow isa(y, Node)$$

**Fig. 10.3.** A knowledge pattern used in KB-PHaSE.

## 10.4 Using Patterns for Building a Knowledge-Base

We encountered the limitations of inheritance and developed the approach of knowledge patterns while building KB-PHaSE, a prototype knowledge-based system for training astronauts to perform a space payload experiment called PHaSE (Physics of Hard Spheres Experiment). PHaSE involves projecting a laser beam through various colloidal suspensions of tiny spheres in liquids, to study the transitions among solid, liquid, and glass (not gas) states in micro-gravity. KB-PHaSE trains the astronaut in three ways. First, it provides a simple, interactive simulator in which the astronaut can step through the normal procedure of the experiment. Second, it introduces simulated faults to train the astronaut to recover from problems. Finally, it supports exploratory learning in which the astronaut can browse concepts in the knowledge-base and ask questions using a form-based interface. All three tasks use the underlying knowledge-base to infer: properties of the current experimental state, valid next actions, and answers to user's questions. The prototype was built as a small demonstrator, rather than for in-service use, to provide input to Boeing and NASA's Space Station Training Program. Details of KB-PHaSE are presented in [1] and the question-answering technology is described in [6].

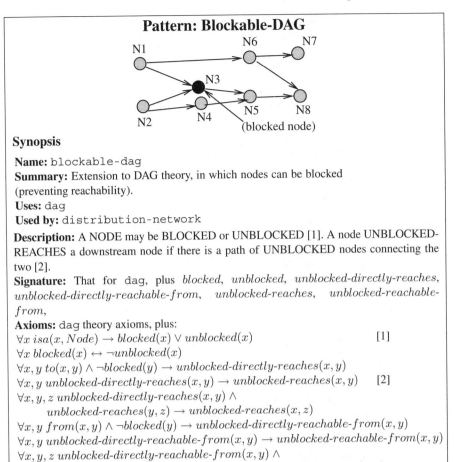

## Pattern: Blockable-DAG

### Synopsis

**Name:** blockable-dag
**Summary:** Extension to DAG theory, in which nodes can be blocked (preventing reachability).
**Uses:** dag
**Used by:** distribution-network
**Description:** A NODE may be BLOCKED or UNBLOCKED [1]. A node UNBLOCKED-REACHES a downstream node if there is a path of UNBLOCKED nodes connecting the two [2].
**Signature:** That for dag, plus *blocked, unblocked, unblocked-directly-reaches, unblocked-directly-reachable-from, unblocked-reaches, unblocked-reachable-from,*
**Axioms:** dag theory axioms, plus:

$\forall x\ isa(x, Node) \rightarrow blocked(x) \vee unblocked(x)$         [1]

$\forall x\ blocked(x) \leftrightarrow \neg unblocked(x)$

$\forall x, y\ to(x, y) \wedge \neg blocked(y) \rightarrow unblocked\text{-}directly\text{-}reaches(x, y)$

$\forall x, y\ unblocked\text{-}directly\text{-}reaches(x, y) \rightarrow unblocked\text{-}reaches(x, y)$    [2]

$\forall x, y, z\ unblocked\text{-}directly\text{-}reaches(x, y) \wedge$
$\qquad unblocked\text{-}reaches(y, z) \rightarrow unblocked\text{-}reaches(x, z)$

$\forall x, y\ from(x, y) \wedge \neg blocked(y) \rightarrow unblocked\text{-}directly\text{-}reachable\text{-}from(x, y)$

$\forall x, y\ unblocked\text{-}directly\text{-}reachable\text{-}from(x, y) \rightarrow unblocked\text{-}reachable\text{-}from(x, y)$

$\forall x, y, z\ unblocked\text{-}directly\text{-}reachable\text{-}from(x, y) \wedge$
$\qquad unblocked\text{-}reachable\text{-}from(y, z) \rightarrow unblocked\text{-}reachable\text{-}from(x, z)$

**Fig. 10.4.** Another knowledge pattern used in KB-PHaSE.

Our interest here is how the underlying knowledge-base was assembled from component theories, rather than written from scratch. KB-PHaSE includes representations of many domain-specific objects (such as electrical circuits) and processes (such as information flow) that are derived from more general theories. For example, we can think of an electrical circuit in terms of a simple model of distribution, in which producers (a battery) distribute a product (electricity) to consumers (a light), illustrated schematically in Figures 10.1 and 10.2. To capture this in a reusable way, we formulated the general model of distribution as an independent, self-contained pattern, shown in Figure 10.5. Then we defined a morphism that creates from it a model of electrical circuits, as shown Figure 10.6.

Our general theory of distribution was built, in turn, by extending a general theory of blockable directed acyclic graphs (blockable-DAGs), which in turn was built

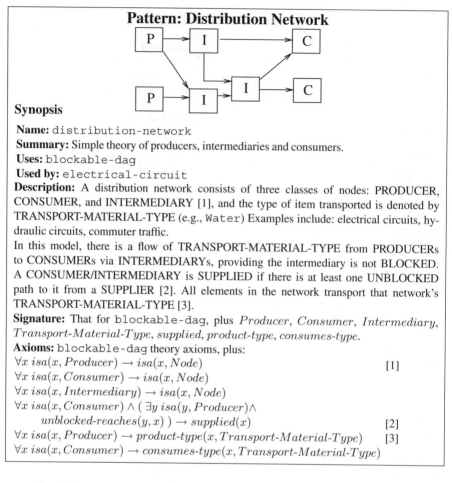

**Pattern: Distribution Network**

**Synopsis**

**Name:** distribution-network
**Summary:** Simple theory of producers, intermediaries and consumers.
**Uses:** blockable-dag
**Used by:** electrical-circuit
**Description:** A distribution network consists of three classes of nodes: PRODUCER, CONSUMER, and INTERMEDIARY [1], and the type of item transported is denoted by TRANSPORT-MATERIAL-TYPE (e.g., Water) Examples include: electrical circuits, hydraulic circuits, commuter traffic.

In this model, there is a flow of TRANSPORT-MATERIAL-TYPE from PRODUCERs to CONSUMERs via INTERMEDIARYs, providing the intermediary is not BLOCKED. A CONSUMER/INTERMEDIARY is SUPPLIED if there is at least one UNBLOCKED path to it from a SUPPLIER [2]. All elements in the network transport that network's TRANSPORT-MATERIAL-TYPE [3].

**Signature:** That for blockable-dag, plus *Producer, Consumer, Intermediary, Transport-Material-Type, supplied, product-type, consumes-type.*
**Axioms:** blockable-dag theory axioms, plus:

$\forall x \, isa(x, Producer) \rightarrow isa(x, Node)$                          [1]
$\forall x \, isa(x, Consumer) \rightarrow isa(x, Node)$
$\forall x \, isa(x, Intermediary) \rightarrow isa(x, Node)$
$\forall x \, isa(x, Consumer) \land (\exists y \, isa(y, Producer) \land$
      $unblocked\text{-}reaches(y, x)\,) \rightarrow supplied(x)$           [2]
$\forall x \, isa(x, Producer) \rightarrow product\text{-}type(x, Transport\text{-}Material\text{-}Type)$    [3]
$\forall x \, isa(x, Consumer) \rightarrow consumes\text{-}type(x, Transport\text{-}Material\text{-}Type)$

**Fig. 10.5.** The knowledge pattern for distribution networks, used by KB-PHaSE.

by extending a general theory of DAGs (Figures 10.3 and 10.4). The application, including these and other theories, is implemented in the frame-based language KM [7].

By separating these theories as modular entities, they are available for reuse. In this application, we also modeled information flow in the optical circuit (laser to camera to amplifier to disk) using a morphed pattern describing a processing network, which, in turn, was defined as an alternative extension of the basic blockable DAG theory, thus reusing this theory. Similarly, the general pattern of a "two-state object" occurs several times within KB-PHaSE (e.g., switches, lights, and open/closed covers), and this pattern was again made explicit and morphed into the knowledge base as required. These patterns and their inter-relationships are shown in Figure 10.7.

---

## Theory: Electrical Circuit

**Synopsis**

**Name:** electrical-circuit
**Summary:** Top level concepts for reasoning about electrical circuits.
**Uses:** distribution-network, with morphism:

$$
\begin{array}{llll}
DAG & \rightarrow Electrical\text{-}Circuit & consumes\text{-}type & \rightarrow consumes\text{-}type \\
Node & \rightarrow Electrical\text{-}Device & product\text{-}type & \rightarrow product\text{-}type \\
to & \rightarrow wired\text{-}to & isa & \rightarrow isa \\
from & \rightarrow wired\text{-}from & blocked & \rightarrow open \\
supplied & \rightarrow powered & unblocked & \rightarrow closed \\
\end{array}
$$

$$
\begin{array}{l}
unblocked\text{-}reachable\text{-}from \rightarrow circuit\text{-}between \\
Transport\text{-}Material\text{-}Type \rightarrow Electricity \\
Producer \rightarrow Electrical\text{-}Power\text{-}Supply \\
Consumer \rightarrow Electrical\text{-}Appliance \\
Intermediary \rightarrow Electrical\text{-}Connector
\end{array}
$$

**Description:** In this model, an ELECTRICAL-POWER-SUPPLY provides ELEC-
TRICITY to ELECTRICAL-APPLIANCES via ELECTRICAL-CONNECTORS.
ELECTRICAL-CONNECTORS (e.g., a switch) may be OPEN (off) or CLOSED (on).
An appliance is POWERED if there is an open connection from at least one power sup-
ply [1].
**Signature:** Morphed version of distribution-network, using above mapping.
**Axioms:** Morphed version of distribution-network axioms, e.g.,
$\forall x\, isa(x, Electrical\text{-}Power\text{-}Supply) \rightarrow product\text{-}type(x, Electricity)$
$\forall x\, isa(x, Electrical\text{-}Appliance) \land (\, \exists y\, isa(y, Electrical\text{-}Power\text{-}Supply)$
$\quad \land\, circuit\text{-}between(y, x)\, ) \rightarrow powered(x)$  [1]

**Fig. 10.6.** The theory for electrical circuits in KB-PHaSE, defined as a morphism of the "distribution network" knowledge pattern.

## 10.5  The Semantics of Knowledge Patterns

A knowledge pattern is incorporated into a knowledge base by a syntactic process
of symbol renaming (morphing). As the process is syntactic, it might seem difficult
to provide semantics for the morphing process itself. However, we can take some
steps towards this by considering the result of morphing to be logically equivalent
to adding the knowledge pattern directly into the knowledge base, along with some
mapping axioms relating knowledge base terms to that knowledge pattern[7]. If we
can do this, then those mapping axioms will have defined the semantics of what
the morphing operation has achieved. We provide here an outline of an approach to
doing this, although a full solution requires further work.

When morphing a knowledge pattern, we are "bringing the abstract theory to
the application", i.e., converting the vocabulary (ontology) used in the pattern to
that of the application domain in which it is to be used, via symbol renaming. An

---

[7] We are endebted to Richard Fikes for making this suggestion.

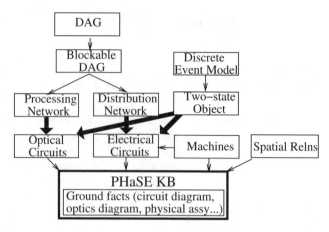

**Fig. 10.7.** The component theories used in KB-PHaSE. Each box denotes a theory (set of rules) describing a phenomenon, and arcs denote inclusion relations, the thick arcs involving morphing the source.

alternative, but functionally equivalent, approach would be to take a domain-specific problem, and convert *its* vocabulary to that used in the pattern, solve the problem using the pattern, and then convert the result back to the domain-specific vocabulary. This can be done, given a domain-specific problem, by establishing an isomorphic problem to solve using the pattern, solve it, and then translate the results back. This can be viewed as the complement to morphing, namely "bringing the application to the abstract theory." The approach is illustrated schematically in Figure 10.8.

This method is exactly that used in both object-oriented composition, and reasoning by analogy. A classic example used in object-oriented composition ([8], pp18-22) is the task of using a Rectangle concept to specify the area of a (graphics) Window. Rather than doing this through inheritance, by stating that a Window ISA Rectangle, the programmer states that a Window HAS a Rectangle instance associated with it. The Window object then delegates some queries (eg. its area) to the Rectangle, which computes the answer and passes the answer back. In this example, the Window is the application-specific object, while the Rectangle (along with its methods) is equivalent to the knowledge pattern, and a domain-specific problem (e.g., the area of the Window) is solved by creating an isomorphic problem (e.g., creating a Rectangle, and finding *its* area), and converting the result back. A similar mechanism is used in reasoning by analogy, where a problem is transferred between a base and a target theory [9].

If we can express this approach logically, we will have expressed the semantics of a process equivalent to morphing, and hence provided a semantics for morphing itself. In the earlier example of a computer, these "mapping axioms" would be:

*% For each computer, assert that there exists an isomorphic container...*
$\forall x \, isa(x, Computer) \rightarrow \exists x' \, isa(x', Container) \wedge is\text{-}modeled\text{-}by_1(x, x')$

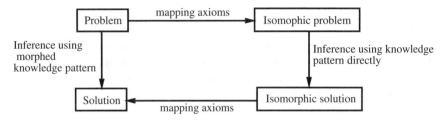

**Fig. 10.8.** To provide semantics for the syntactic process of morphing (the left down arrow), we consider its equivalence to using the knowledge pattern directly, along with mapping axioms to translate a domain-specific problem into/out of an isomorphic one expressed using the pattern's ontology (the other three arrows).

% ...whose spatial properties model the slot capacities of that computer.
$\forall x, x'$ is-modeled-by$_1(x, x') \rightarrow$
   $(\ \forall i\ capacity(x', i) \leftrightarrow expansion\text{-}slots(x, i)\ \wedge$
   $\forall j\ occupied\text{-}space(x', j) \leftrightarrow occupied\text{-}slots(x, j)\ \wedge$
   $\forall k\ free\text{-}space(x', k) \leftrightarrow free\text{-}slots(x, n)\ )$

By adding the Container knowledge pattern directly into the KB, along with these mapping axioms, the result will be the same as if we had added a morphed version of the Container knowledge pattern:

( Knowledge Pattern $\cup$ Mapping Axioms ) $\equiv$ Morph(Knowledge Pattern)

Hence, in this case, the mapping axioms provide the semantics of what the morphing operation would have achieved. In the more general case, a domain-specific problem may involve multiple objects (e.g., an electrical circuit of electrical components), requiring setting up an isomorphic problem also involving multiple, corresponding objects expressed in the knowledge pattern's ontology.

As this alternative approach is equivalent to morphing knowledge patterns, why not simply use it, rather than morphing? This is a valid, alternative approach to applying knowledge patterns, and achieves many of the same goals (namely to make the abstract theories explicit, and to make explicit the modeling decisions about how they apply to real-world phenomena). The tradeoffs are largely computational, the mapping approach being more complex to implement and computationally more expensive at run-time, but also having the advantage that the knowledge pattern itself is then an explicit part of the final KB (rather than the KB containing only morphed copies of that pattern).

## 10.6 Related Work

There are several important areas of pattern-related work, differing in the type of reusable knowledge they encode and the way they encode it.

In software engineering there has been considerable work on formal methods for software specification, based on the construction and composition of theories, and using category theory (applied to algebraic specifications) as a mathematical basis (e.g., [10, 11]). SpecWare is an example of a software development environment which is based on this approach and is capable of synthesizing software semi-automatically [12]. As described in Section 10.3, our work can be viewed as motivating, simplifying, and applying similar ideas to the task of knowledge engineering.

Work on reusable problem-solving methods (PSMs), in particular KADS [13] and generic tasks [14], addresses modularity and reuse in the context of procedural knowledge. PSMs are based on the observation that a task-specific method can be decomposed into more primitive – and more reusable – sub-methods, and that working with a library of such primitives may accelerate building a system and make it more understandable and maintainable. Work on PSMs shares the same general goal that we have — to identify and make explicit recurring generalizations — but it differs in two respects. First, while PSMs are (mostly) patterns of procedural inference, we have been targeting the basic domain knowledge (models) which those procedures may operate on. (Although, since logic has both a declarative and procedural interpretation, this distinction becomes blurred). Second, the mechanics of their usage differ: implementations of PSMs can be thought of as parameterized procedures, applied through instantiating their "role" parameters with domain concepts (e.g., the "hypotheses" role in a diagnosis PSM applied to medical diagnosis might be filled with disease types); in contrast, our patterns are closer to schemata than procedures, and applied instead through morphing.

Research on compositional methods for constructing ontologies and knowledge bases (eg [15, 16, 17]) has explored factoring domain knowledge into component theories, analogous to factoring procedural knowledge into PSMs. A component theory describes relationships among a set of objects (its participants) and is applied in an analogous way to PSMs, by instantiating these participants with domain concepts. Knowledge patterns develop this idea in two ways. First, they provide further generalization, capturing the abstract structure of such theories. Second, their method of application differs (morphing, rather than axioms linking participants with domain concepts). This permits a pattern to be applied in multiple, different ways to the same object, as discussed in Section 10.2. Compositional modeling has also explored the automated, run-time selection of appropriate components to use [15, 18], an important issue which we have not addressed here.

"Design patterns" in object-oriented programming (e.g., [8]) are descriptions of common, useful organizations of objects and classes, to help create specific object-oriented designs. They again try to capture recurring abstractions, but (in contrast to the approaches described earlier) their primary intent is as architectural guidance to the software designer, not as computational devices directly. As a result, they are (and only need be) semi-formally specified, and they do not require a method for their automatic application. ([19] gives an excellent discussion of the relationship between object-oriented patterns and problem-solving methods). Another area of related work from programming languages is the use of template programming methods, where a code template is instantiated by syntactic substitution of symbols within it (e.g., Ada generics, C++ templates), corresponding to the syntactic implementation of pattern morphing, but without the associated semantics.

In a similar way to design patterns, "semantic patterns" [20, 21] were intended as a means of describing knowledge in an "implementation neutral" way, i.e., above the level of any particular representation language, with the objective of reusing semantics across representational languages (in particular, for Web-based applications). As with design patterns, they are intended as a means for communication among human developers, but in addition they contain various implementations of that knowledge, expressed in different knowledge representation schemes. Semantic patterns share some similarities with knowledge patterns, in particular the goal of abstraction and reuse. However, they also are rather different in other respects: semantic patterns were primarily intended for knowledge sharing across a wide range of representation systems, i.e., their language neutrality was a primary goal (with the consequence that each implementation of the pattern has to be largely written by hand). In contrast, knowledge patterns are intended for use within a particular representational scheme in an automated way, with the primary goals of uncovering and making explicit the abstract theories used in the knowledge base, and capturing the modeling decisions made about how these theories apply to the domain of interest.

Work on analogical reasoning is also closely related, as it similarly seeks to use a theory (the base) to provide extra knowledge about some domain (the target), by establishing and using a mapping between the two. However, work on analogy has mainly focussed on identifying what the appropriate mappings between the base and target should be [9], a task which we have not addressed and which could be beneficial for us to explore further. In addition, an alternative way of applying our patterns would be to transform a domain-specific *problem* into the vocabulary of a pattern (and solve it there, and transform the solution back), rather than transforming the pattern into the vocabulary of the domain. In the PHaSE KB, for example, a query about the electrical circuit would be transformed to a query about a distribution network which was isomorphic to the electrical circuit, solved there, and the answer transformed back to the electrical circuit. This alternative approach is similar to (one form of) solution by analogy, in which the pattern (e.g., the distribution network) takes the role of the base, and the domain facts (e.g., the electrical circuit) the target [9]. It is also similar to the use of delegation in object-oriented programming (the target 'delegates' the problem to the base, which solves it and passes the solution back [8, p20]). This variant approach for using patterns would allow some run-time flexibility, but would be more complex to implement and computationally more expensive at run-time.

Finally, work on microtheories and contexts (e.g., [22, 23]) is also related, where a microtheory (context) can be thought of as a pattern, and lifting axioms provide the mapping between predicates in the microtheory and the target KB which is to incorporate it. However, this work has typically been used to solve a different problem, namely breaking a large KB into a set of smaller, simpler (and thus more maintainable) pieces, rather than making recurring axiom patterns explicit, and it does not account for mapping the same microtheory multiple times (and in different ways) into the same target KB. Reasoning with lifting axioms can also be computationally expensive except in the simplest cases.

Note that patterns are not an essential prerequisite for building a knowledge-based system. In the PHaSE application, for example, we could have simply defined the PHaSE electrical circuit, implemented axioms about the behavior of electrical circuits, and answered circuit questions, all within the electrical vocabulary. This would be a completely reasonable approach for a single-task system; however, to achieve reuse within a multifunctional system (such as KB-PHaSE), or between systems, it becomes preferable to extract the more general abstractions, as we have described. Patterns do not enable better reasoning, rather they are to help reuse.

## 10.7 Summary

Ontological engineering is fundamentally a modeling endeavor. In this Chapter, we have described a knowledge engineering technique aimed at helping in this endeavor, by making recurring theory schemata, or knowledge patterns, explicit, and available for manipulation. From a computational perspective, knowledge patterns provide a simple and computationally efficient mechanism for facilitating knowledge reuse. From a modeling perspective, knowledge patterns also provide an important insight into the process of ontological engineering, namely that it is not simply about "writing axioms", but also involves recognizing that the "computational clockwork" of one or more abstract theories seem to behave (to a reasonable approximation) in the same way as some system of objects in the world, and hence can be used to describe it. Knowledge patterns make both those abstract theories and their mappings to the domain of interest explicit, thus making modeling decisions clear, and avoiding some of the ontological confusion that can otherwise arise.

However, our approach also has limits. First, it does not allow a system to make run-time modeling decisions, as general theories are morphed when the knowledge base is loaded. Second, it does not address the issue of *finding* relevant knowledge patterns in the first place, or deciding the appropriate boundaries of patterns (this is left to the knowledge engineer). Finally, we do not address the issue of finding the appropriate mappings between patterns and the domain; this again is left to the knowledge engineer. As mentioned earlier, this is a primary focus of research in the related field of analogical reasoning [9].

Despite these, the significance of this approach is that it allows us to better modularize the axioms which underly formal ontologies, and isolate general theories as self-contained units for reuse. It also allows us to control and vary the way those theories are mapped onto an application domain, and it better separates the "computational clockwork" of a general theory from the domain phenomena which it is considered to reflect. In addition, the approach is technically simple and not wedded to a particular implementation language. In the long-term, we hope this will help foster the construction of reusable theory libraries, an essential requirement for the construction of large-scale, formal ontologies and knowledge-based systems.

# References

1. Clark P, Thompson J, Dittmar M (1998) KB-PHaSE: A knowledge-based training tool for a space station experiment. Technical Report SSGTECH-98-035, Boeing Applied Research and Technology, Seattle, WA
2. Porter B, Lester J, Murray K, Pittman K, Souther A, Acker L, Jones T (1988) AI research in the context of a multifunctional knowledge base: The botany knowledge base project. Tech Report AI-88-88, Dept CS, Univ Texas at Austin
3. Cycorp, Inc. (1996) The cyc public ontology. (http://www.cyc.com/public.html)
4. Mahesh K, Nirenberg S (1995) A situated ontology for practical NLP. In:Proc. IJCAI-95 Workshop on Basic Ontological Issues in Knowledge Sharing
5. Pierce B (1991) Basic Category Theory for Computer Scientists. MIT Press
6. Clark P, Thompson J, Porter B (1999)  A knowledge-based approach to question-answering. In: Fikes R, Chaudhri V (eds) Proc. AAAI'99 Fall Symposium on Question-Answering Systems. AAAI
7. Clark P, Porter B (1999). KM – the knowledge machine: Users manual. Technical report, AI Lab, Univ Texas at Austin
8. Gamma E, Helm R, Johnson R, Vlissides J (1995) Design Patterns. Addison-Wesley
9. Falkenhainer B, Forbus K, Gentner D (1986) The structure-mapping engine. In: AAAI-86, pages 272–277
10. Goguen J (1986)  Reusing and interconnecting software components.  In: Computer 19(2):16–28
11. Srinivas Y V, Jullig, R (1995) Specware: Formal support for composing software. In: Proc. Conf. on the Mathematics of Program Construction, Kloster Irsee, Germany (Also Kestrel Tech Rept KES.U.94.5, http://www.kestrel.edu/HTML/publications.html)
12. Jullig R, Srinivas Y, Blain L, Gilham L, Goldberg A, Green C, McDonald J, Waldinger R (1995) Specware language manual. Technical report, Kestrel Institute
13. Wielinga B J, Schreiber A T, Breuker J A (1992)  KADS: A modelling approach to knowledge engineering. Knowledge Acquisition 4(1)
14. Chandrasekaren B (1986) Generic tasks in knowledge-based reasoning: High-level building blocks for expert system design. IEEE Expert, pages 23–30
15. Falkenhainer B, Forbus K (1991) Compositional modelling: Finding the right model for the job. Artificial Intelligence 51:95–143
16. Clark P, Porter B (1997)  Building concept representations from reusable components. In: AAAI-97, pages 369–376, CA:AAAI
17. Noy N, Hafner, C (1998) Representing scientific experiments: Implications for ontology design and knowledge sharing. In: AAAI-98, pages 615–622
18. Rickel J, Porter B (1997) Automated modeling of complex systems to answer prediction questions. Artificial Intelligence 93(1-2):201–260
19. Menzies T (1997) Object-oriented patterns: Lessons from expert systems. Software – Practice and Experience 27(12):1457–1478
20. Staab S, Erdmann M, Maedche A (2001)  Engineering ontologies using semantic patterns. In: Preece A, O'Leary D (eds) Proc. IJCAI-01 Workshop on e-Business and the Intelligent Web
21. Staab S, Erdmann M, Maedche A (2001)  Semantic patterns. Technical report, Univ. Karlsruhe
22. Buvac S (ed) (1995) Proc AAAI-95 Fall Symposium on Formalizing Context. CA:AAAI
23. Blair P, Guha R, Pratt W (1992) Microtheories: An ontological engineer's guide. Tech Rept CYC-050-92, MCC, Austin, TX

# 11

# Ontology and the Lexicon

Graeme Hirst

Department of Computer Science, University of Toronto,
Toronto M5S 3G4, Ontario, Canada
e-mail: gh@cs.toronto.edu

**Summary.** Ontologies and lexicons enjoy a complex relationship. Although words denote concepts and concepts make up ontologies, a lexicon is at best an ersatz ontology: there is no clear mapping between the words and word relationships that it contains and the concepts and concept relationships in an ontology. The reasons for this include the following: Word senses overlap in complex ways; many concepts are not lexicalized in some or all languages; and languages make semantic distinctions that are not ontological. Nonetheless, a lexicon can sometimes be the basis for the development of a practical ontology.

## 11.1 Lexicons and lexical knowledge

### 11.1.1 Lexicons

A **lexicon** is a list of words in a language—a **vocabulary**—along with some knowledge of how each word is used. A lexicon may be general or domain-specific; we might have, for example, a lexicon of several thousand common words of English or German, or a lexicon of the technical terms of dentistry in some language. The words that are of interest are usually **open-class** or **content** words, such as nouns, verbs, and adjectives, rather than **closed-class** or **grammatical function** words, such as articles, pronouns, and prepositions, whose behaviour is more tightly bound to the grammar of the language. A lexicon may also include multi-word expressions such as fixed phrases (*by and large*), phrasal verbs (*tear apart*), and other common expressions (*merry Christmas!; teach ⟨someone⟩'s grandmother to suck eggs; Elvis has left the building*).

Each word or phrase in a lexicon is described in a **lexical entry**; exactly what is included in each entry depends on the purpose of the particular lexicon. The details that are given (to be discussed further in sections 11.2.1 and 11.3.2 below) may include any of its properties of spelling or sound, grammatical behaviour, meaning, or use, and the nature of its relationships with other words. A lexical entry is therefore a potentially large record specifying many aspects of the linguistic behaviour and meaning of a word.

Hence a lexicon can be viewed as an index that maps from the written form of a word to information about that word. This is not a one-to-one correspondence, however. Words that occur in more than one syntactic category will usually have a separate entry for each category; for example, *flap* would have one entry as a noun and another as a verb. Separate entries are usually also appropriate for each of the senses of a **homonym**—a word that has more than one unrelated sense even within a single syntactic category; for example, the noun *pen* would have distinct entries for the senses writing instrument, animal enclosure, and swan. **Polysemy**—related or overlapping senses—is a more-complex situation; sometimes the senses may be discrete enough that we can treat them as distinct: for example, *window* as both opening in wall and glass pane in opening in wall (*fall through the window; break the window*). But this is not always so; the word *open*, for example, has many overlapping senses concerning unfolding, expanding, revealing, moving to an open position, making openings in, and so on, and separating them into discrete senses, as the writers of dictionary definitions try to do, is not possible (see also sections 11.2.3 and 11.3.1 below).

On the other hand, morphological variants of a word, such as plurals of nouns and inflected forms of verbs might scarcely warrant their own complete lexical entry. Rather, the entry for such forms might be little more than a pointer to that for the base form of the word. For example, the entries for *takes, taking, took,* and *taken* might just note that they are inflected forms of the base-form verb *take*, and point to that entry for other details; and conversely, the entry for *take* will point to the inflected forms. Similarly, *flaps* will be connected both to the noun *flap* as its plural and to the verb *flap* as its third-person singular. The sharing of information between entries is discussed further in section 11.2.2 below.

A lexicon may be just a simple list of entries, or a more-complex structure may be imposed upon it. For example, a lexicon may be organized hierarchically, with default inheritance of linguistic properties (see section 11.2.2 below). However, the structures that will be of primary interest in this chapter are semantic, rather than morphological or syntactic; they will be discussed in section 11.3.2 below.

### 11.1.2  Computational lexicons

An ordinary dictionary is an example of a lexicon. However, a dictionary is intended for use by humans, and its style and format are unsuitable for computational use in a text or natural language processing system without substantial revision. A particular problem is the dictionary's explications of the senses of each word in the form of definitions that are themselves written in natural language; computational applications that use word meanings usually require a more-formal representation of the knowledge. Nonetheless, a dictionary in a machine-readable format can serve as the basis for a computational lexicon, as in the ACQUILEX project (Briscoe, de Paiva, and Copestake 1993)—and it can also serve as the basis for a semantic hierarchy (see section 11.5.2 below). (An alternative or complementary source of lexical information is inference from the usage observed in text corpora; see, e.g., Boguraev and Pustejovsky (1996).)

Perhaps the best-known and most widely used computational lexicon of English is WordNet (Fellbaum 1998). The primary emphasis of WordNet is on semantic relationships between words; it contains little syntactic and morphological data and no phonetic data. The basic lexical entry in WordNet is the **synset** (for "synonym set"), which groups together identical word senses. For example, the synonymous nouns *boarder, lodger,* and *roomer* are grouped together in a synset. WordNet includes an extensive network of relationships between synsets; this will be discussed in detail in section 11.3.2. Following the success of WordNet for English, wordnets with a similar (but not necessarily identical) structure have been (or are being) developed for a number of other languages, including several European languages (some as part of the EuroWordNet project (Vossen 1998)), Hindi, Tamil, and Basque (see *www.globalwordnet.org*).

Some other important general-purpose lexicons include CELEX (Baayen, Piepenbrock, and van Rijn 1993), which is a set of large, detailed lexicons of Dutch, German, and English, and the PAROLE project (*www.hltcentral.org/projects/PAROLE*) and its successor SIMPLE (Lenci et al. 2000), which are large, rich lexicons for 12 European languages.

Two important sources for obtaining lexicons are these:

**ELDA:** The Evaluations and Language resources Distribution Agency (*www.elda.fr*) distributes many European-language general-purpose and domain-specific lexicons, both monolingual and multilingual, including PAROLE and EuroWordNet.

**LDC:** The Linguistic Data Consortium (*www.ldc.upenn.edu*), although primarily a distributor of corpora, offers CELEX and several other lexicons.

In addition, English WordNet is available free of charge from the project's Web page (*www.cogsci.princeton.edu/~wn*).

## 11.2 Lexical entries

### 11.2.1 What's in a lexical entry?

Any detail of the linguistic behaviour or use of a word may be included in its lexical entry: its phonetics (including pronunciations, syllabification, and stress pattern), written forms (including hyphenation points), morphology (including inflections and other affixation), syntactic and combinatory behaviour, constraints on its use, its relative frequency, and, of course, all aspects of its meaning. For our purposes in this chapter, the word's semantic properties, including relationships between the meaning of the word and those of other words, are the most important, and we will look at them in detail in section 11.3.2 below.

Thus, as mentioned earlier, a lexical entry is potentially quite a large record. For example, the CELEX lexicons of English, Dutch, and German (Baayen, Piepenbrock, and van Rijn 1993) are represented as databases whose records have 950 fields. And in an **explanatory combinatorial dictionary** (ECD) (e.g., Mel'čuk 1984,

Mel'čuk and Zholkovsky 1988), which attempts to explicate literally every aspect of the knowledge that a speaker needs to have in order to use a word correctly, lexical entries can run to many pages. For example, Steele's (1990) ECD-style entry for eight senses of *hope* (noun and verb) is 28 book-sized pages long, much of which is devoted to the combinatory properties of the word, such as that the noun *hope* permits *flicker of* to denote a small amount (whereas *expectation*, in contrast, does not).

Many linguistic applications will require only a subset of the information that may be found in the lexical entries of large, broad-coverage lexicons. Because of their emphasis on detailed knowledge about the linguistic behaviour of words, these large, complex lexicons are sometimes referred to as **lexical knowledge bases**, or **LKBs**. Some researchers distinguish LKBs from lexicons by regarding LKBs as the larger and more-abstract source from which instances of lexicons for particular applications may be generated. In the present chapter, we will not need to make this distinction, and will just use the term *lexicon*.

### 11.2.2 Inheritance of linguistic properties

Generally speaking, the behaviour of words with respect to many non-semantic lexical properties in any given language tends to be regular: words that are phonetically, morphologically, or syntactically similar to one another usually exhibit similar phonetic, morphological, or syntactic behaviour. For example, in English most verbs form their past tense with either *-ed* or *-d*, and even most of those that don't do so fall into a few small categories of behaviour; and quite separately, verbs also cluster into a number of categories by their **alternation** behaviour (see section 11.4.3 below).

It is therefore possible to categorize and subcategorize words by their behaviour—that is, build an ontology of lexical behaviour—and use these categories to construct a lexicon in which each word, by default, inherits the properties of the categories and subcategories of which it is a member. Of course, idiosyncratic properties (such as many of the combinatory properties listed in an ECD) will still have to be specified in each word's entry. Inheritance of properties facilitates both economy and consistency in a large lexicon. A hierarchical representation of lexical knowledge with property inheritance is really just a special case of this style or method of knowledge representation. Accordingly, the inheritance of properties in the lexicon and the design of formal languages for the representation of lexical knowledge have been areas of considerable study (e.g., Briscoe, de Paiva, and Copestake 1992, Gazdar and Daelemans 1992; for an overview, see Daelemans, De Smedt, and Gazdar 1992; for the DATR language for lexical knowledge representation, see Evans and Gazdar 1996).

It should be clear that a hierarchical representation of similarities in lexical behaviour is quite distinct from any such representation of the **meaning** of words; knowing that *boy* and *girl* both take *-s* to make their plural form whereas *child* does not tells us nothing about the relationship between the meanings of those words. Relationships between meanings, and the hierarchies or other structures that they might form, are a separate matter entirely; they will be discussed in section 11.3.2.

### 11.2.3  Generating elements of the lexicon

Even with inheritance of properties, compiling a lexicon is a large task. But it can be eased by recognizing that because of the many regularities in the ways that natural languages generate derived words and senses, many of the entries in a lexicon can be automatically predicted.

For example, at the level of inflection and affixation, from the existence of the English word *read*, we can predict that (among others) *reading, reader, unreadable,* and *antireadability* are also words that should be in the lexicon, and in three out of these four cases we'd be right. Viegas et al. (1996) present a system of **lexical rules** that propose candidate words by inflection and affixation (an average of about 25 from each base form), automatically generating lexical entries for them; a lexicographer must winnow the proposals. In their Spanish lexicon, about 80% of the entries were created this way. But a lexicon can never anticipate all the nonce words and neologisms that are easily created from combinations of existing words in languages such as German and Dutch; additional word-recognition procedures will always be needed.

At the level of word sense, there are also regularities in the polysemy of words. For example, the senses of the word *book* include both its sense as a physical object and its sense as information-content: *The book fell on the floor; The book was exciting.* (A problem for natural language processing, which need not concern us here, is that both senses may be used at once: *The exciting book fell on the floor.*) In fact, the same polysemy can be seen with any word denoting an information-containing object, and if a new one comes along, the polysemy applies automatically: *The DVD fell on the floor; The DVD was exciting.* There are many such regularities of polysemy; they have been codified in Pustejovsky's (1995) theory of the **generative lexicon**. Thus it is possible to write rules that generate new lexical entries reflecting these regularities; if we add an entry for *DVD* to the lexicon as an information-containing object, then the other sense may be generated automatically (Buitelaar 1998). (*A fortiori*, the theory of the generative lexicon says that a purely enumerative lexicon— one that is just a list of pre-written entries—can never be complete, because the generative rules always permit new and creative uses of words.)

## 11.3  Word senses and the relationships between them

Most of the issues in the relationship between lexicons and ontologies pertain to the nature of the word senses in the lexicon and to relationships between those senses— that is, to the semantic structure of the lexicon.

### 11.3.1  Word senses

By definition, a **word sense**, or the "meaning" of a word, is a semantic object—a **concept** or **conceptual structure** of some kind, though exactly what kind is a matter of considerable debate, with a large literature on the topic. Among other possibilities, a word sense may be regarded as a purely **mental object**; or as a structure of some kind of **primitive units of meaning**; or as the **set of all the things in the world that the sense may denote**; or as a **prototype** that other objects resemble to a greater or lesser degree; or as an **intension** or **description** or **identification procedure**— possibly in terms of necessary and sufficient conditions—of all the things that the sense may denote.

Word senses tend to be fuzzy objects with indistinct boundaries, as we have seen already with the example of *open* in section 11.1.1 above. Whether or not a person may be called *slim*, for example, is, to some degree, a subjective judgement of the user of the word. To a first approximation, a word sense seems to be something like a category of objects in the world; so the word *slim* might be taken to denote exactly the category of slim objects, with its fuzziness and its subjectivity coming from the fuzziness and subjectivity of the category in the world, given all the problems that are inherent in categorization (see also Lakoff 1987). Indeed, some critics have suggested that word senses are *derived, created,* or *modulated* in each context of use, and can't just be specified in a lexicon (Ruhl 1989, Kilgarriff 1997).

Nonetheless, one position that could be taken is that a word sense *is* a category. This is particularly appealing in simple practical applications, where the deeper philosophical problems of meaning may be finessed or ignored. The problems are pushed to another level, that of the ontology; given some ontology, each word sense is represented simply as a pointer to some concept or category within the ontology. In some technical domains this may be entirely appropriate (see section 11.5.1 below). But sometimes this move may in fact make matters worse: all the problems of categorization remain, and the additional requirement is placed on the ontology of mirroring some natural language or languages, which is by no means straightforward (see section 11.4 below); nonetheless, an ontology may act as an interpretation of the word senses in a lexicon (see section 11.5.4 below).

In addition to the **denotative** elements of meaning that refer to the world, word senses also have **connotation**, which may be used to express the user's attitude: a speaker who chooses the word *sozzled* instead of *drunk* is exhibiting informality, whereas one who chooses *inebriated* is being formal; a speaker who describes a person as *slim* or *slender* is implying that the person's relative narrowness is attractive to the speaker, whereas the choice of *skinny* for the same person would imply unattractiveness.

### 11.3.2  Lexical relationships

Regardless of exactly how one conceives of word senses, because they pertain in some manner to categories in the world itself, **lexical relationships** between word senses mirror, perhaps imperfectly, certain relationships that hold between the categories themselves. The nature of lexical relationships and the degree to which they may be taken as ontological relationships are the topics of most of the rest of this chapter. In the space available, we can do no more than introduce the main ideas of lexical relationships; for detailed treatments, see Cruse (1986), Evens (1988), and Green, Bean, and Myaeng (2002).

The "classical" lexical relationships pertain to identity of meaning, inclusion of meaning, part–whole relationships, and opposite meanings. **Identity of meaning** is **synonymy**: Two or more words are synonyms (with respect to one sense of each) if one may substitute for another in a text without changing the meaning of the text. This test may be construed more or less strictly; words may be synonyms in one context but not another; often, putative synonyms will vary in connotation or linguistic style (as in the *drunk* and *slim* examples in section 11.3.1 above), and this might or might not be considered significant. More usually, "synonyms" are actually merely near-synonyms (see section 11.4.1 below).

The primary **inclusion** relations are **hyponymy** and its inverse **hypernymy** (also known as **hyperonymy**) (Cruse 1986, 2002). For example, *noise* is a hyponym of *sound* because any noise is also a sound; conversely, *sound* is a hypernym of *noise*. Sometimes names such as *is-a* and *a-kind-of* are used for hyponymy and *subsumption* for hypernymy; because these names are also used for ontological categories, we avoid using them here for lexical relationships. The inclusion relationship between verbs is sometimes known as *troponymy*, emphasizing the point that verb inclusion tends to be a matter of "manner"; *to murmur* is *to talk* in a certain manner (Fellbaum 2002). Inclusion relationships are transitive, and thus form a **semantic hierarchy**, or multiple hierarchies, among word senses; words without hyponyms are leaves and words without hypernyms are roots. (The structures are more usually networks than trees, but we shall use the word *hierarchy* to emphasize the inheritance aspect of the structures.)

The **part–whole** relationships **meronymy** and **holonymy** also form hierarchies. Although they may be glossed roughly as *has-part* and *part-of*, we again avoid these ontologically biased terms. The notion of part–whole is overloaded; for example, the relationship between *wheel* and *bicycle* is not the same as that of *professor* and *faculty* or *tree* and *forest*; the first relationship is that of functional component, the second is group membership, and the third is element of a collection. For analysis of part–whole relationships, see Cruse (1986), Iris, Litowitz, and Evens (1988), or Pribbenow (2002).

Words that are opposites, generally speaking, share most elements of their meaning, except for being positioned at the two extremes of one particular dimension. Thus *hot* and *cold* are opposites—**antonyms**, in fact—but *telephone* and *Abelian group* are not, even though they have no properties in common (that is, they are "opposite" in every feature or dimension). Cruse (1986) distinguishes several different lexical relations of oppositeness, including **antonymy** of gradable adjectives, **complementarity** of mutually exclusive alternatives (*alive–dead*), and directional opposites (*forwards–backwards*).

These "classical" lexical relationships are the ones that are included in the Word-Net lexicon. Synonymy is represented, as mentioned earlier, by means of synsets: if two words have identical senses, they are members of the same synset. Synsets are then connected to one another by pointers representing inclusion, part–whole, and opposite relations, thereby creating hierarchies.

In addition to the "classical" lexical relationships, there are many others, which may be broadly thought of as **associative** or **typicality** relations. For example, the relationship between *dog* and *bark* is that the former is a frequent and typical agent of the latter. Other examples of this kind of relationship include typical instrumentality (*nail–hammer*), cause (*leak–drip*), and location (*doctor–hospital*).

Synonymy, inclusion, and associative relations are often the basis of the structure of a **thesaurus**. While general-purpose thesauri, such as *Roget's*, leave the relationships implicit, others, especially those used in the classification of technical documents, will make them explicit with labels such as *equivalent term, broader term, narrower term*, and *related term*.

## 11.4 Lexicons are not (really) ontologies

The obvious parallel between the hypernymy relation in a lexicon and the subsumption relation in an ontology suggests that lexicons are very similar to ontologies. It even suggests that perhaps a lexicon, together with the lexical relations defined on it, *is* an ontology (or is a kind of ontology in the ontology of ontologies). In this view, we identify word senses with ontological categories and lexical relations with ontological relations. The motivation for this identification is clear from the preceding discussion (section 11.3.2).

Nonetheless, a lexicon, especially one that is not specific to a technical domain (see section 11.5.1 below), is not a very good ontology. An ontology, after all, is a set of categories of objects or ideas in the world, along with certain relationships among them; it is not a linguistic object. A lexicon, on the other hand, depends, by definition, on a natural language and the word senses in it. These give, at best, an ersatz ontology, as the following sections will show.

### 11.4.1 Overlapping word senses and near-synonymy

It is usually assumed in a genus–differentia ontology that subcategories of a category are mutually exclusive. For example, if the category domesticated-mammal subsumes the categories dog and cat, among others, then dog ∩ cat is empty: nothing is both a dog and a cat. This is not always so for the hyponymy relation in lexicons, however; rather, two words with a common hypernym will often overlap in sense—that is, they will be **near-synonyms**.

Consider, for example, the English words *error* and *mistake*, and some words that denote kinds of mistakes or errors: *blunder, slip, lapse, faux pas, bull, howler,* and *boner*. How can we arrange these in a hierarchy? First we need to know the precise meaning of each and what distinguishes one from another. Fortunately, lexicographers take on such tasks, and the data for this group of words is given in *Webster's New Dictionary of Synonyms* (Gove 1973); an excerpt appears in Fig. 11.1; it lists both denotative and connotative distinctions, but here we need consider only the former. At first, we can see some structure: *faux pas* is said to be a hyponym of *mistake*; *bull, howler,* and *boner* are apparently true synonyms—they map to the same word sense, which is a hyponym of *blunder*. However, careful consideration of the data shows that a strict hierarchy is not possible. Neither *error* nor *mistake* is the more-general term; rather, they overlap. Neither is a hypernym of the other, and both, really, are hypernyms of the more-specific terms. Similarly, *slip* and *lapse* overlap, differing only in small components of their meaning. And a *faux pas*, as a mistake in etiquette, is not really a type of mistake or error distinct from the others; a faux pas could also be a lapse, a blunder, or a howler.

---

**Error**  implies a straying from a proper course and suggests guilt as may lie in failure to take proper advantage of a guide ...

**Mistake**  implies misconception, misunderstanding, a wrong but not always blameworthy judgment, or inadvertence; it expresses less severe criticism than *error*.

**Blunder**  is harsher than *mistake* or *error*; it commonly implies ignorance or stupidity, sometimes blameworthiness.

**Slip**  carries a stronger implication of inadvertence or accident than *mistake*, and often, in addition, connotes triviality.

**Lapse**,  though sometimes used interchangeably with *slip*, stresses forgetfulness, weakness, or inattention more than accident; thus, one says a *lapse* of memory or a *slip* of the pen, but not vice versa.

**Faux pas**  is most frequently applied to a mistake in etiquette.

**Bull, howler,** and **boner**  are rather informal terms applicable to blunders that typically have an amusing aspect.

---

**Fig. 11.1.** An entry (abridged) from *Webster's New Dictionary of Synonyms* (Gove 1973).

This example is in no way unusual. On the contrary, this kind of cluster of near-synonyms is very common, as can be seen in *Webster's New Dictionary of Synonyms* and similar dictionaries in English and other languages. Moreover, the differences between the members of the near-synonym clusters for the same broad concepts are different in different languages. The members of the clusters of near-synonyms relating to errors and mistakes in English, French, German, and Japanese, for example, do not line up neatly with one another or translate directly (Edmonds and Hirst 2002); one cannot use these word senses to build an ontology of errors.

These observations have led to the proposal (Edmonds and Hirst 2000, 2002) that a fine-grained hierarchy is inappropriate as a model for the relationship between the senses of near-synonyms in a lexicon for any practical use in tasks such as machine translation and other applications involving fine-grained use of word senses. Rather, what is required is a very coarse-grained conceptual hierarchy that represents word meaning at only a very coarse-grained level, so that whole clusters of near-synonyms are mapped to a single node: their **core meaning**. Members of a cluster are then distinguished from one another by explicit differentiation of any of the **peripheral concepts** that are involved in the fine-grained aspects of their denotation (and connotation). In the example above, *blunder* might be distinguished on a dimension of severity, while *faux pas* would be distinguished by the domain in which the mistake is made.

### 11.4.2 Gaps in the lexicon

A lexicon, by definition, will omit any reference to ontological categories that are not **lexicalized** in the language—categories that would require a (possibly long) multiword description in order to be referred to in the language. That is, the words in a lexicon, even if they may be taken to represent categories, are merely a subset of the categories that would be present in an ontology covering the same domain. In fact, every language exhibits **lexical gaps** relative to other languages; that is, it simply lacks any word corresponding to a category that is lexicalized in some other language or languages. For example, Dutch has no words corresponding to the English words *container* or *coy*; Spanish has no word corresponding to the English verb *to stab* 'to injure by puncturing with a sharp weapon'; English has no single word for the German *gemütlich* or for the French *bavure* 'embarrassing bureaucratic error'. On the face of it, this seems to argue for deriving a language-independent ontology from the union of the lexicons of many languages (as attempted by Emele et al. (1992)); but this is not quite feasible.

Quite apart from lexical gaps in one language relative to another, there are many categories that are not lexicalized in *any* language. After all, it is clear that the number of categories in the world far exceeds the number of word senses in a language, and while different languages present different inventories of senses, as we have just argued, it nonetheless remains true that, by and large, all will cover more or less the same "conceptual territory", namely the concepts most salient or important to daily life, and these will be much the same across different languages, especially different languages of similar cultures. As the world changes, new concepts will arise and may be lexicalized, either as a new sense for an existing word (such as *browser* 'software tool for viewing the World Wide Web'), as a fixed phrase (*road rage*), or as a completely new word (*demutualization* 'conversion of a mutual life insurance company to a company with shareholders', *proteomics, DVD*). That large areas remain unlexicalized is clear from the popularity of games and pastimes such as Sniglets ("words that don't appear in the dictionary but should") (Hall 1987) and Wanted Words (Farrow 2000), which derive part of their humour from the identification of established concepts that had not previously been articulated and yet are immediately recognized as such when it is pointed out.

But even where natural languages "cover the same territory", each different language will often present a different and mutually incompatible set of word senses, as each language lexicalizes somewhat different categorizations or perspectives of the world. It is rare for words that are **translation equivalents** to be completely identical in sense; more usually, they are merely cross-lingual near-synonyms (see section 11.4.1 above).

An area of special ontological interest in which the vocabularies of natural languages tend to be particularly sparse is the upper ontology (see Borgo et al (2003)). Obviously, all natural languages need to be able to talk about the upper levels of the ontology. Hence, one might have thought that at this level we would find natural languages to be in essential agreement about how the world is categorized, simply because the distinctions seem to be so fundamental and so basic to our biologically based, and therefore presumably universal, cognitive processes and perception of the world. But natural languages instead prefer to concentrate the richest and most commonly used parts of their vocabulary in roughly the middle of the hierarchy, an area that has come to be known as the **basic-level categories**; categories in this area maximize both informativeness and distinctiveness (Murphy and Lassaline 1997). A standard example: one is more likely to choose the word *dog* for X in the context *Be careful not to trip over the X* than *entity, living thing, animal, mammal,* or *Beddlington terrier*, even though the alternatives are equally ontologically correct. Certainly, all languages have words similar to the English *thing, substance,* and *process*; but these words tend to be vague terms and, even here, vary conceptually from one language to another. That this is so is clear from the difficulty of devising a clear, agreed-on top-level ontology, a project that has exercised many people for many years. That is, we have found that we cannot build a satisfactory top-level ontology merely by looking at the relevant vocabulary of one or even several natural languages; see, for example, the extensive criticisms by Gangemi, Guarino, and Oltramari (2001) of the top level of WordNet as an ontology. From this, we can conclude that the upper levels of the lexical hierarchy are a poor ontology.

### 11.4.3 Linguistic categorizations that are not ontological

And yet, even though natural languages omit many distinctions that we would plausibly want in an ontology, they also make semantic distinctions—that is, distinctions that are seemingly based on the real-world properties of objects—that we probably wouldn't want to include in an ontology. An example of this is semantic categorizations that are required for "correct" word choice within the language and yet are seemingly arbitrary or unmotivated from an ontological point of view. For example, English requires the division of vehicles into categories according to whether or not the vehicle can be viewed as a container (e.g., *bus* and *canoe* versus *bicycle*), and, if a container, whether or not one can stand up in it (e.g., *bus* versus *car* and *canoe*). The verb *board* may only be used with vehicles that are containers that one can stand in; the verb *ride in* rather than *ride on* may only be used with vehicles that are containers that one cannot stand in.

Often, the linguistic categorization is not even a reliable reflection of the world. For example, many languages distinguish in their syntax between objects that are discrete and those that are not: **countable** and **mass nouns**. This is indeed an important distinction for many ontologies; but one should not look in the lexicon to find the ontological data, for in practice, the actual linguistic categorization is rather arbitrary and not a very accurate or consistent reflection of discreteness and non-discreteness in the world. For example, in English, *spaghetti* is a mass noun, but *noodle* is countable; the English word *furniture* is a mass noun, but the French *meuble* and German *Möbel* are countable.

A particularly important area in which languages make semantic distinctions that are nonetheless ontologically arbitrary is in the behaviour of verbs in their **diathesis alternations**—that is, alternations in the optionality and syntactic realization of the verb's arguments, sometimes with accompanying changes in meaning (Levin 1993). Consider, for example, the English verb *spray*:

    (1)   Nadia sprayed water on the plants.
    (2)   Nadia sprayed the plants with water.
    (3)   Water sprayed on the plants.
    (4)   *The plants sprayed with water.

(The '*' on (4) denotes syntactic ill-formedness.) These examples (from Levin 1993) show that *spray* permits the **locative alternation** (examples 1 and 2), with either the medium or the target of the spraying (*water* or *the plants*) being realized as the syntactic object of the verb, and the second case (example 2) carrying the additional implication that the entire surface of the target was affected; moreover, the agent of spraying (*Nadia*) is optional (the **causative alternation**) in the first case (example 3) but not the second (example 4).

In view of the many different possible syntactic arrangements of the arguments of a verb, and the many different possible combinations of requirement, prohibition, and optionality for each argument in each position, a large number of different kinds of alternations are possible. However, if we classify verbs by the syntactic alternations that they may and may not undergo, as Levin (1993) has for many verbs of English, we see a semantic coherence to the classes. For example, many verbs that denote the covering of a surface behave in the same manner as *spray*, including *daub, splash,* and *sprinkle.* Nonetheless, the semantic regularities in alternation behaviour often seem ontologically unmotivated, and even arbitrary. For example, verbs of destruction that include in their meaning the resulting state of an entity (*smash, crush, shatter*), fall into a completely different behaviour class from verbs that do not (*destroy, demolish, wreck*) (Levin 1993, p. 239).

Even what is perhaps the most basic and seemingly ontological distinction made by languages, the distinction between nouns, verbs, and other syntactic categories, is not as ontologically well-founded as it seems. From the viewpoint of **object-dominant** languages (Talmy 2000a) such as English (and the majority of other languages), we are used to the idea that nouns denote physical and abstract objects and events (*elephant, Abelian group, running, lunch*) and verbs denote actions, processes, and states (*run, disembark, glow*). But even within European languages, we find that occasionally what is construed as an action or state in one language is not in another; a commonly cited example is the English verb *like* translating to an adverb, a quality of an action, in German: *Nadia likes to sing: Nadia singt gern*. But there are **action-dominant** languages in which even physical objects are referred to with verbs:

> For example, in a situation in which English might say *There's a rope lying on the ground*, Atsugewi [a language of Northern California] might use the single polysynthetic verb form *ẃoswalak·a* ... [This can] be glossed as 'a-flexible-linear-object-is-located on-the-ground because-of-gravity-acting-on-it'. But to suggest its nounless flavor, the Atsugewi form can perhaps be fancifully rendered in English as: "it gravitically-linearizes-aground". In this example, then, Atsugewi refers to two physical entities, a ropelike object and the ground underfoot, without any nouns. (Talmy 2000a, p. 46)

### 11.4.4 Language, cognition, and the world

All the discussion above on the distinction between lexicon and ontology is really nothing more than a few examples of issues and problems that arise in discussions of the relationship between language, cognition, and our view of the world. This is, of course, a Big Question on which there is an enormous literature, and we cannot possibly do more than just allude to it here in order to put the preceding discussion into perspective. Issues include the degree of mutual causal influence between one's view of the world, one's culture, one's thought, one's language, and the structure of cognitive processes. The **Sapir-Whorf hypothesis** or **principle of linguistic relativity**, in its strongest form, states that language determines thought:

> We dissect nature along lines laid down by our native languages. The categories and types that we isolate from the world of phenomena we do not find there because they stare every observer in the face; on the contrary, the world is presented in a kaleidoscopic flux of impressions which has to be organized by our minds—and this means largely by the linguistic systems in our minds. We cut nature up, organize it into concepts, and ascribe significances as we do, largely because we are parties to an agreement to organize it in this way—an agreement that holds throughout our speech community and is codified in the patterns of our language. The agreement is, of course, an implicit and unstated one, *but its terms are absolutely obligatory*; we cannot talk at all except by subscribing to the organization and classification of data which the agreement decrees. (Whorf 1940/1972)

> No two languages are ever sufficiently similar to be considered as representing the same social reality. The worlds in which different societies live are distinct worlds, not merely the same world with different labels attached. (Sapir 1929/1964)

These quotations imply a pessimistic outlook for the enterprise of practical, language-independent ontology (or even of translation between two languages, which as a distinct position is often associated with Quine (1960)); but conversely, they imply a bright future for ontologies that are strongly based on a language, although such ontologies would have to be limited to use within that language community. But taken literally, linguistic relativity is certainly not tenable; clearly, we can have thoughts for which we have no words. The position is more usually advocated in a weaker form, in which language strongly influences worldview but does not wholly determine it. Even this is not broadly accepted; a recent critic, for example, is Pinker (1994), who states bluntly, "There is no scientific evidence that languages dramatically shape their speakers' ways of thinking" (p. 58). Nonetheless, we need to watch out for the un-dramatic shaping.

From a practical standpoint in ontology creation, however, while an overly language-dependent or lexicon-dependent ontology might be avoided for all the reasons discussed above, there is still much in the nature of natural languages that can help the creation of ontologies: it might be a good strategy to adopt or adapt the worldview of a language into one's ontology, or to merge the views of two different languages. For example, languages offer a rich analysis in their views of the structure of events and of space that can serve as the basis for ontologies; see, for example, the work of Talmy (2000b), in analyzing and cataloguing these different kinds of views.

## 11.5 Lexically based ontologies and ontologically based lexicons

Despite all the discussion in the previous section, it is possible that a lexicon with a semantic hierarchy might serve as the basis for a useful ontology, and an ontology may serve as a grounding for a lexicon. This may be so in particular in technical domains, in which vocabulary and ontology are more closely tied than in more-general domains. But it may also be the case for more-general vocabularies when language dependence and relative ontological simplicity are not problematic or are even desirable—for example if the ontology is to be used primarily in general-purpose, domain-independent text-processing applications in the language in question and hence inferences from the semantic properties of words have special prominence over domain-dependent or application-dependent inferences. In particular, Dahlgren (1995) has argued for the need to base an ontology for intelligent text processing on the linguistic distinctions and the word senses of the language in question.

### 11.5.1 Technical domains

In highly technical domains, it is usual for the correspondence between the vocabulary and the ontology of the domain to be closer than in the case of everyday words and concepts. This is because it is in the nature of technical or scientific work to try to identify and organize the concepts of the domain clearly and precisely and to name them unambiguously (and preferably with minimal synonymy). In some fields of study, there is a recognized authority that maintains and publishes a categorization and its associated nomenclature. For example, in psychiatry, the *Diagnostic and Statistical Manual* of the American Psychiatric Association (2000) has this role. In botanical systematics, so vital is unambiguous communication and so enormous is the pool of researchers creating new names that a complex system of rules (Greuter et al. 2000) guides the naming of genera, species, and other taxa, and the revision of names in the light of new knowledge.

Obviously, the construction of explicit, definitive ontologies, or even explicit, definitive vocabularies, does not occur in all technical domains. Nor is there always general consensus in technical domains on the nature of the concepts of the domain or uniformity in the use of its nomenclature. On the contrary, technical terms may exhibit the same vagueness, polysemy, and near-synonymy that we see exhibited in the general vocabulary. For example, in the domain of ontologies in information systems, the terms *ontology, concept*, and *category* are all quite imprecise, as may be seen throughout this volume; nonetheless, they are technical terms: the latter two are used in a more precise way than the same words are in everyday speech.

However, in technical domains where explicit vocabularies exist (including glossaries, lexicons and dictionaries of technical terms, and so on, whether backed by an authority or not), an ontology exists at least implicitly, as we will see in section 11.5.2 below. And where an explicit ontology exists, an explicit vocabulary certainly does; indeed, it is often said that the construction of any domain-specific ontology implies the parallel construction of a vocabulary for it; e.g., Gruber (1993, p. 909): "Pragmatically, a common ontology defines the vocabulary with which queries and assertions are exchanged among agents".

An example of a technical ontology with a parallel vocabulary is the Unified Medical Language System (UMLS) (e.g., Lindberg, Humphreys, and McCray 1993; *www.nlm.nih.gov/research/umls*). The concepts in the Metathesaurus component of the UMLS, along with their additional interpretation in the Semantic Net component, constitute an ontology. Each concept is annotated with a set of terms (in English and other languages) that can be used to denote it; this creates a parallel vocabulary. Additional linguistic information about many of the terms in the vocabulary is given in the separate Specialist Lexicon component. See Hahn (this volume) for more details of the UMLS.

### 11.5.2 Developing a lexically based ontology

It has long been observed that a dictionary implicitly contains an ontology, or at least a semantic hierarchy, in the genus terms in its definitions. For example, if *automobile* is defined as *a self-propelled passenger vehicle that usually has four wheels and an internal-combustion engine*, then it is implied that *automobile* is a hyponym of *vehicle* and even that automobile IS-A vehicle; semantic or ontological part–whole relations are also implied.

Experiments on automatically extracting an ontology or semantic hierarchy from a machine-readable dictionary were first carried out in the late 1970s. Amsler (1981), for example, derived a "tangled hierarchy" from *The Merriam-Webster Pocket Dictionary*; Chodorow, Byrd, and Heidorn (1985) extracted hierarchies from *Webster's Seventh New Collegiate Dictionary*. The task requires parsing the definitions and disambiguating the terms used (Byrd et al. 1987); for example *vehicle* has many senses, including *a play, role, or piece of music used to display the special talents of one performer or company*, but this is not the sense that is used in the definition of *automobile*. In the analysis of the definition, it is also necessary to recognize the semantically significant patterns that are used, and to not be misled by so-called "empty heads": apparent genus terms that in fact are not, such as *member* in the definition of *hand* as *a member of a ship's crew* (Markowitz, Ahlswede, and Evens 1986, Alshawi 1987). Perhaps the largest project of this type was MindNet (Richardson, Dolan, and Vanderwende 1998).

Often, the literature on these projects equivocates on whether the resulting hierarchies or networks should be thought of as purely linguistic objects—after all, they are built from words and word senses—or whether they have an ontological status outside language. If the source dictionary is that of a technical domain, the claim for ontological status is stronger. The claim is also strengthened if new, non–lexically derived nodes are added to the structure. For example, in The Wordtree, a complex, strictly binary ontology of transitive actions by Burger (1984), the nodes of the tree were based on the vocabulary of English (for example, to sweettalk is to flatter and coax), but names were manually coined for nodes where English fell short (to good-badman is to reverse and spiritualize; to gorilla is to strongarm and deprive).

### 11.5.3  Finding covert categories

One way that a hierarchy derived from a machine-readable dictionary might become more ontological is by the addition of categories that are unlexicalized in the language upon which it is based. Sometimes, these categories are implicitly reified by the presence of other words in the vocabulary, and, following Cruse (1986), they are therefore often referred to as **covert categories**. For example, there is no single English word for things that can be worn on the body (including clothes, jewellery, spectacles, shoes, and headwear), but the category nonetheless exists "covertly" as the set of things that can substitute for $X$ in the sentence *Nadia was wearing (an) X*. It is thus reified through the existence of the word *wear* as the category of things that can meaningfully serve as the object of this verb.

Barrière and Popowich (2000) showed that these covert categories (or some of them, at least) can be identified and added as supplementary categories to a lexically derived semantic hierarchy (such as those described in section 11.5.2 above). Their method relies on the definitions in a children's dictionary, in which the language of the definitions is simple and, unlike a regular dictionary, often emphasizes the purpose or use of the definiendum over its genus and differentia; for example, *a boat carries people and things on the water*. The central idea of Barrière and Popowich's method is to find frequently recurring patterns in the definitions that could signal the reification of a covert category. The first step is to interpret the definitions into a conceptual-graph representation (see Sowa, this volume). Then, a graph-matching algorithm looks in the conceptual-graph representations for subgraph patterns whose frequency exceeds an experimentally determined threshold. For example, one frequent subgraph is

[X]←(agent)←[carry]→(object)→(person),

which could be glossed as 'things that carry people'. This pattern occurs in the definitions of many words, including *boat, train, camel,* and *donkey*. It thus represents a covert category that can be named and added to a semantic hierarchy as a new hypernym (or subsumer, now) of the nodes that were derived from these words, in addition to any other hypernym that they already had. The name for the covert category may be derived from the subgraph, such as carry-object-person-agent for the example above. The hierarchy thus becomes more than just lexical relations, although less than a complete ontology; nonetheless, the new nodes could be helpful in text processing. The accuracy of the method is limited by the degree to which polysemy can be resolved; for example, in the category of *things that people play*, it finds, among others, *music, baseball,* and *outside,* representing different senses of *play.* Thus the output of the method must be regarded only as suggestions that require validation by a human.

Although Barrière and Popowich present their method as being for general-purpose, domain-independent hierarchies and they rely on a particular and very simple kind of dictionary, their method might also be useful in technical domains to help ensure completeness of an ontology derived from a lexicon by searching for unlexicalized concepts.

### 11.5.4 Ontologies for lexicons

As mentioned in section 11.3.1, most theories of what a word sense is relate it in some way to the world. Thus, an ontology, as a non-linguistic object that more-directly represents the world, may provide an interpretation or grounding of word senses. A simple, albeit limited, way to do this is to map between word senses and elements of or structures in the ontology. Of course, this will work only to the extent that the ontology can capture the full essence of the meanings. We noted in section 11.5.1 above that the UMLS grounds its Metathesaurus this way.

In machine translation and other multilingual applications, a mapping like this could act as an interlingua, enabling the words in one language to be interpreted in another. However, greater independence from any particular language is required; at the very least, the ontology should not favour, say, Japanese over English if it is to be used in translation between those two languages. In the twelve-language SIMPLE lexicon (Lenci et al. 2000), a hand-crafted upper ontology of semantic types serves as an anchor for lexical entries in all the languages (Lenci 2001). The semantic types are organized into four **qualia roles**, following the tenets of generative lexicon theory (see section 11.2.3 above).

Hovy and Nirenburg (1992) have argued that complete language-independence is not possible in an ontologically based interlingua for machine translation, but some degree of **language-neutrality** with respect to the relevant languages can nonetheless be achieved; and as the number of languages involved is increased, language-independence can be asymptotically approached. Hovy and Nirenburg present a procedure for merging a set of language-dependent ontologies, one at a time, to create an ontology that is neutral with respect to each. Near-synonyms across languages (section 11.4.1 above) are just one challenge for this approach. (See also Hovy (1998) and Noy (this volume).)

## 11.6 Conclusion

In this chapter, we have discussed the relationship between lexicons, which are linguistic objects, and ontologies, which are not. The relationship is muddied by the difficult and vexed relationship between language, thought, and the world: insofar as word-meanings are objects in the world, they may participate in ontologies for non-linguistic purposes, but they are inherently limited by their linguistic heritage; but non-linguistic ontologies may be equally limited when adapted to applications such as text and language processing.

## Acknowledgements

The preparation of this chapter was supported by a grant from the Natural Sciences and Engineering Research Council of Canada. I am grateful to Eduard Hovy, Jane Morris, and Nadia Talent for helpful discussions and examples.

## References

1. American Psychiatric Association (2000): *Diagnostic and Statistical Manual of Mental Disorders: DSM-IV-TR* (4th edition, text revision). American Psychiatric Association, Washington, DC.
2. Amsler, Robert A. (1981): A taxonomy for English nouns and verbs. *Proceedings of the 19th Annual Meeting of the Association for Computational Linguistics*, Stanford, 133–138.
   *www.aclweb.org/anthology/P81-1030*
3. Alshawi, Hiyan (1987): Processing dictionary definitions with phrasal pattern hierarchies. *Computational Linguistics*, 13(3/4), 195–202.
   *www.aclweb.org/anthology/J87-3001*
4. Baayen, Harald R., Piepenbrock, Richard, and van Rijn, H. (1993): *The CELEX Lexical Database. Dutch, English, German*. CD-ROM, Linguistic Data Consortium, University of Pennsylvania, Philadelphia, PA.
5. Barrière, Caroline and Popowich, Fred (2000): Expanding the type hierarchy with nonlexical concepts. In: Hamilton, Howard J. (editor), *Advances in Artificial Intelligence* (Proceedings of the 13th Biennial Conference of the Canadian Society for Computational Studies of Intelligence, Montreal, May 2000), Lecture Notes in Artificial Intelligence 1822, pages 53–68. Springer-Verlag, Berlin.
   *link.springer.de/link/service/series/0558/tocs/t1822.htm*
6. Boguraev, Branimir and Pustejovsky, James (eds.) (1996): *Corpus Processing for Lexical Acquisition*. The MIT Press, Cambridge, MA.
7. Borgo, Stefano; Gangemi, Aldo; Guarino, Nicola; Masolo, Claudio; Oltramari, Alessandro; Schneider, Luc (2003): Foundational and top-level ontologies.
8. Briscoe, Ted; de Paiva, Valeria; and Copestake, Ann (editors) (1993): *Inheritance, Defaults, and the Lexicon*. Cambridge University Press.
9. Buitelaar, Paul (1998): CORELEX: An ontology of systematic polysemous classes. In Guarino, Nicola (ed.), *Formal Ontology in Information Systems*, IOS Press, 221–235.

10. Burger, Henry G. (1984): *The Wordtree*. The Wordtree, Merriam, KS.

11. Byrd, Roy J.; Calzolari, Nicoletta; Chodorow, Martin S.; Klavans, Judith L.; Neff, Mary S.; and Rizk, Omneya A. (1987): Tools and methods for computational lexicography. *Computational Linguistics*, 13(3/4), 219–240.
    *www.aclweb.org/anthology/J87-3003*

12. Chodorow, Martin S.; Byrd, Roy J.; and Heidorn, George E. (1985): Extracting semantic hierarchies from a large on-line dictionary. *Proceedings of the 23rd Annual Meeting of the Association for Computational Linguistics*, Chicago, 299–304.
    *www.aclweb.org/anthology/P85-1034*

13. Cruse, D. Alan (1986): *Lexical Semantics*. Cambridge University Press.

14. Cruse, D. Alan (2002): Hyponymy and its varieties. In Green, Bean, and Myaeng (2002), 3–21.

15. Daelemans, Walter; De Smedt, Koenraad; and Gazdar, Gerald (1992): Inheritance in natural language processing. *Computational Linguistics*, 18(2), 205–218
    *www.aclweb.org/anthology/J92-2004*

16. Dahlgren, Kathleen (1995): A linguistic ontology. *International Journal of Human–Computer Studies*, 43(5/6), 809–818.

17. Edmonds, Philip and Hirst, Graeme (2000): Reconciling fine-grained lexical knowledge and coarse-grained ontologies in the representation of near-synonyms. *Proceedings of the Workshop on Semantic Approximation, Granularity, and Vagueness*, Breckenridge, Colorado.
    *http://www.cs.toronto.edu/compling/Publications*

18. Edmonds, Philip and Hirst, Graeme (2002): Near-synonymy and lexical choice. *Computational Linguistics*, 28(2), 105–144.
    *http://www.cs.toronto.edu/compling/Publications*

19. Emele, Martin; Heid, Ulrich; Momma, Stefan; and Zajac, Rémi (1992): Interactions between linguistic constraints: Procedural vs. declarative approaches. *Machine Translation*, 7(1/2), 61–98.

20. Evans, Roger and Gazdar, Gerald (1996): DATR: A language for lexical knowledge representation. *Computational Linguistics*, 22(2), 167–216.

21. Evens, Martha Walton (ed.) (1988): *Relational Models of the Lexicon*. Cambridge University Press.

22. Farrow, Jane (2000): *Wanted Words: From amalgamots to undercarments*. Stoddart.

23. Fellbaum, Christiane (1998): *WordNet: An electronic lexical database*. The MIT Press, Cambridge, Mass.

24. Fellbaum, Christiane (2002): On the semantics of troponymy. In Green, Bean, and Myaeng (2002), 23–34.

25. Gangemi, Aldo; Guarino, Nicola; and Oltramari, Alessandro (2001): Conceptual analysis of lexical taxonomies: The case of WordNet top-level. In Welty, Chris and Smith, Barry (eds.), *Formal Ontology in Information Systems: Collected papers from the Second International Conference*, ACM Press, 285–296.

26. Gazdar, Gerald and Daelemans, Walter (1992): Special issues on Inheritance. *Computational Linguistics*, 18(2) and 18(3).
    *acl.ldc.upenn.edu/J/J92*

27. Gove, Philip B. (editor) (1973): *Webster's New Dictionary of Synonyms*. G. & C. Merriam Company, Springfield, MA.

28. Green, Rebecca; Bean, Carol A.; and Myaeng, Sung Hyon (eds.) (2002): *The Semantics of Relationships: An interdisciplinary perspective*. Kluwer Academic Publishers, Dordrecht.

29. Greuter, W.; McNeill, J.; Barrie, F.R.; Burdet, H.M.; Demoulin, V.; Filgueiras, T.S.; Nicolson, D.H.; Silva, P.C.; Skog, J.E.; Trehane, P.; Turland, N.J.; and Hawksworth, D.L. (editors) (2000): *International Code of Botanical Nomenclature (Saint Louis Code)*. Koeltz Scientific Books, Königstein.
30. Gruber, Thomas R. (1993): Toward principles for the design of ontologies used for knowledge sharing. *International Journal of Human–Computer Studies*, 43(5/6), 907–928.
31. Hahn, Udo (2003): Ontology reuse from UMLS. This volume.
32. Hall, Rich (1984): *Sniglets (Snig'lit): Any word that doesn't appear in the dictionary, but should.* Collier Books.
33. Hovy, Eduard (1998): Combining and standardizing large-scale, practical ontologies for machine translation and other uses. *Proceedings of the 1st International Conference on Language Resources and Evaluation (LREC)*, Granada, Spain.
    *www.isi.edu/natural-language/people/hovy/publications.html*
34. Hovy, Eduard and Nirenburg, Sergei (1992): Approximating an interlingua in a principled way. *Proceedings of the DARPA Speech and Natural Language Workshop*, Hawthorne, NY.
    *www.isi.edu/natural-language/people/hovy/publications.html*
35. Iris, Madelyn Anne; Litowitz, Bonnie E.; and Evens, Martha (1988): Problems of the part–whole relation. In Evens (1988), 261–288.
36. Kilgarriff, Adam (1997): "I don't believe in word senses." *Computers and the Humanities*, 31(2), 91–113.
    *www.kluweronline.com/issn/0010-4817/*
37. Lakoff, George (1987): *Women, Fire, and Dangerous things: What categories reveal about the mind.* The University of Chicago Press, Chicago.
38. Lenci, Alessandro (2001): Building an ontology for the lexicon: Semantic types and word meaning. In Jensen, Per Anker and Skadhauge, Peter (eds.), *Ontology-based Interpretation of Noun Phrases: Proceedings of the First International OntoQuery Workshop*, University of Southern Denmark, 103–120.
    *www.ontoquery.dk/publications/*
39. Lenci, Alessandro et al. (2000). SIMPLE: A general framework for the development of multilingual lexicons. *International Journal of Lexicography*, 13(4), 249–263.
40. Levin, Beth (1993): *English Verb Classes and Alternations: A preliminary investigation.* The University of Chicago Press, Chicago.
41. Lindberg, Donald A.B.; Humphreys, Betsy L.; and McCray, Alexa T. (1993): The Unified Medical Language System. *Methods of Information in Medicine*, 32(4), 281–289.
42. Markowitz, Judith; Ahlswede, Thomas; and Evens, Martha (1986): Semantically significant patterns in dictionary definitions. *Proceedings of the 24th Annual Meeting of the Association for Computational Linguistics*, New York, 112–119.
    *www.aclweb.org/anthology/P86-1018*
43. Mel'čuk, Igor (1984): *Dictionnaire explicatif et combinatoire du français contemporain.* Les Presses de l'Université de Montréal.
44. Mel'čuk, Igor and Zholkovsky, Alexander (1988): The explanatory combinatorial dictionary. In Evens 1988, 41–74.
45. *The Merriam-Webster Pocket Dictionary.* G.&C. Merriam Company, Springfield, MA.
46. Murphy, Gregory L. and Lassaline, Mary E. (1997): Hierarchical structure in concepts and the basic level of categorization. In Lamberts, Koen and Shanks, David (eds.), *Knowledge, Concepts, and Categories*, The MIT Press, Cambridge, MA, 93–131.
47. Noy, Natalya F. (2003): Tools for mapping and merging ontologies. This volume.
48. Pinker, Steven (1994): *The Language Instinct.* William Morrow and Company, New York.

49. Pribbenow, Simone (2002): Meronymic relationships: From classical merology to complex part–whole relationships. In Green, Bean, and Myaeng (2002), 35–50.
50. Pustejovsky, James (1995): *The Generative Lexicon*. The MIT Press, Cambridge, MA.
51. Quine, Willard Van Orman (1960): *Word and Object*. The MIT Press, Cambridge, MA.
52. Richardson, Stephen D.; Dolan, William B.; and Vanderwende, Lucy (1998): MindNet: Acquiring and structuring semantic information from text. *Proceedings, 36th Annual Meeting of the Association for Computational Linguistics and the 17th International Conference on Computational Linguistics (COLING-98)*, Montreal, 1098–1104. *www.aclweb.org/anthology/P98-2180*
53. Roget, Peter Mark. *Roget's Thesaurus*. Many editions and variant titles.
54. Ruhl, Charles (1989): *On Monosemy: A study in linguistic semantics*. State University of New York Press, Albany, NY.
55. Sapir, Edward (1929/1964): The status of linguistics as a science. *Language*, 5, 207–214. Reprinted in Mandelbaum, David G. (ed.), *Culture, Language, and Personality: Selected essays of Edward Sapir*, University of California Press, Berkeley.
56. Sowa, John F. (2003): Conceptual graphs. This volume.
57. Steele, James (1990): The vocable *hope*: A family of lexical entries for an explanatory combinatorial dictionary of English. In Steele, James (ed.), *Meaning–Text Theory: Linguistics, lexicography, and implications*, University of Ottawa Press, 131–158.
58. Talmy, Leonard (2000a): The relation of grammar to cognition. In Talmy 2000b, I-21–96.
59. Talmy, Leonard (2000b): *Toward a Cognitive Semantics*, two volumes. The MIT Press, Cambridge, MA.
60. Viegas, Evelyn; Onyshkevych, Boyan; Raskin, Victor: Nirenburg, Sergei (1996): From *submit* to *submitted* via *submission*: On lexical rules in large-scale lexicon acquisition. *Proceedings, 34th Annual Meeting of the Association for Computational Linguistics,* Santa Cruz, 32–39. *www.aclweb.org/anthology/P96-1005*
61. Vossen, Piek (editor) (1998): Special issue on EuroWordNet. *Computers and the Humanities*, 32(2–3), 73–251. Reprinted as a separate volume: *EuroWordNet: A multilingual database with lexical semantic networks.* Kluwer Academic Publishers, Dordrecht. *www.kluweronline.com/issn/0010-4817/*
62. *Webster's Seventh New Collegiate Dictionary* (1963): G.&C. Merriam Company, Springfield, MA.
63. Whorf, Benjamin Lee (1940/1972): Science and linguistics. *Technology Review*, 42(6), 227–31, 247–8. Reprinted in Carroll, John B. (ed.), *Language, Thought and Reality: Selected writings of Benjamin Lee Whorf*, The MIT Press, Cambridge, MA.

# 12

# Ontology Reconciliation

Adil Hameed, Alun Preece, and Derek Sleeman

University of Aberdeen, Department of Computing Science,
Aberdeen AB24 3UE, UK
{ahameed|apreece|dsleeman}@csd.abdn.ac.uk

**Summary.** Ontologies are being applied very successfully in supporting information and knowledge exchange between people and organisations. However, for many reasons, different people and organisations will tend to use different ontologies. Therefore, in order to exchange information and knowledge, either everyone must adopt the same ontology — an unlikely scenario — or it must be possible to *reconcile* different ontologies. This chapter examines the issues and techniques in the reconciliation of ontologies. First, it examines the reasons why people and organisations will tend to use different ontologies, and why the pervasive adoption of common ontologies is unlikely. It then reviews alternative architectures for multiple-ontology systems on a large scale. A comparative analysis is provided of a number of frameworks which analyse types of mismatches between ontologies. The process of ontology reconciliation is outlined. Finally, some existing software tools that support reconciliation are surveyed, and areas are identified where further work is necessary.

## 12.1 Introduction

Ontologies are a key component of any information architecture, being an explicit specification of the conceptual model underpinning an information domain [6]. Regardless of the information architect's goal — whether it be, for example, the definition of an enterprise data model, the design of an organisation's Web site, or the creation of a corporate knowledge map — one of the first tasks is to elucidate and specify the conceptual and relational structures in the domain. For an enterprise data model, the ontology will identify aspects such as business processes, actors, and information objects [25]; for a Web site, the ontology specifies information categories, topics, labels, link types, and so on [22]; for a corporate knowledge map, the ontology defines the areas of expertise within the organisation, useful for documenting best-practices and experience, and also for "identifying who knows what" [21].

In providing a means of organising information and knowledge, ontologies also facilitate its communication and interchange. While the communication and interchange of information and knowledge is not a necessary goal of creating an ontology — an individual may choose to create a "personal ontology" to organise their own information and knowledge [9] — it is generally seen as the most valuable use of ontology techniques [3]. However, as soon as ontologies are applied in supporting information and knowledge exchange between people and organisations, a fundamental problem arises: for many reasons, different people and organisations will tend to use different ontologies. Therefore, in order to exchange information and knowledge, either everyone must adopt the same ontology — an unlikely scenario — or it must be possible to *reconcile* different ontologies.

This chapter examines the issues and techniques in the reconciliation of ontologies. The next section examines the reasons why people and organisations will tend to use different ontologies, and why the pervasive adoption of common ontologies is unlikely. Section 12.3 then compares alternative architectures for multiple-ontology systems on a large scale. Section 12.4 reviews a number of frameworks which analyse types of mismatches between ontologies. The process of ontology reconciliation is outlined in Section 12.5. Finally, some existing software tools that support reconciliation (to at least some extent) are surveyed in Section 12.6. Section 12.7 concludes, identifying some areas where further work is necessary.

## 12.2 Living in a Multiple-Ontology World

The past decade has seen many long-term, large-scale efforts to develop standard, common ontologies to support information and knowledge sharing. These include work on domain-independent so-called *upper ontologies* such as Cyc [12] and SUO[1], and domain-specific ontologies such as the Enterprise Ontology [25] and the Engineering Mathematics ontology [6]. These efforts are undoubtedly important, and have led to a substantial level of maturity and agreement in the area of ontology technology and methodology.

Nevertheless, it is unrealistic to expect that in general all people and organisations developing information and knowledge application systems will use a common, shared ontology. There are several reasons for this. Firstly, at present there is often a competing choice of "common" ontology for a particular purpose. For example, Cyc and SUO offer alternative choices of upper ontology, while the Enterprise Ontology and TOVE [4] offer alternative business models. Even if, in the long run, particular ontologies become favoured, *de facto* or *de jure* standards, by that time there will likely be many "legacy" ontologies still in existence, which use an outmoded but still valid alternative. There will then be a need to reconcile such legacy ontologies with the standard common ontology.

A second reason for expecting continuing diversity in ontologies is that an ontology is often aligned with a particular *perspective* on the world. Whether it is a "personal ontology", designed to support an individual's needs and preferences, or an ontology created by a particular company to reflect that company's view on their industry, such ontologies will have biases and necessarily subjective features. If that individual or company needs to interchange information and knowledge with other individuals or organisations, there will be a need to reconcile multiple ontologies. In

---

[1] http://suo.ieee.org/

an environment of industrial knowledge management, it is easy to envisage a scenario where:

- individual workers need to reconcile their personal ontologies with the common ontology of their department, division, or company as a whole;
- a company needs to reconcile its ontology with those of other partner companies, or the industry as a whole.

Ontology reconciliation can therefore be at several levels: inter-personal, intra-organisational, and inter-organisational.

A third reason why the need for ontology reconciliation is unlikely to be eliminated is that, even if a single common standard ontology emerged that everyone committed to, this "überontology" would still need to *evolve* over time — conceptualisations of information and knowledge domains are not static. There will then be different versions of the "standard" in existence over time, and there will be a need to reconcile these different versions, to allow migration of information and knowledge between the versions.

These arguments are underscored by recent experience of working with information architecture for the World Wide Web. The Web is the largest and most significant information system in history; part of the reason for its success is that it is extremely tolerant of diversity in information modelling. Different Web sites use different information architectures; it is easy for individual people and organisations to "do their own thing", yet the Web as a whole is still usable and useful. Recent work in the context of developing a machine-processable, Semantic Web is acknowledging this diversity. The emerging layers of the W3C's architecture are incorporating support for a multiple-ontology Semantic Web, for example:[2]

- the lowest layers are founded on distributed information architecture standards: URIs and XML namespaces for creating "object identifiers" that can be defined with respect to a local ontology, yet referenced globally;
- the higher layers are tolerant of combining information from multiple ontologies (for example, RDF descriptions that refer to more than one RDF Schema) and articulating the relationships between ontologies (for example, OWL's `sameClassAs` property).

In the context of the Web, experience suggests that ontologies will proliferate and diverge — with the appearance of many personalised small-scale local conceptualisations — rather than converging on a few, large-scale standards under central control. The Semantic Web will work as a whole only if it is possible to reconcile its diversity of ontologies.

## 12.3 Architecture

There exists a variety of alternative architectures for multiple-ontology systems, as shown in Figure 12.1. The simplest, "bottom up" approach, is merely to map between

---

[2] `http://www.w3.org/2000/Talks/1206-xml2k-tbl/slide10-0.html`

individual ontologies as needed. This architecture is shown in Figure 12.1(a). Here there is no attempt to identify common, standardised ontologies. Not all ontologies will be reconciled; only where there is a requirement to inter-relate particular individual ontologies. The advantages of this approach are its simplicity and flexibility: no overall common ontology is needed; there is great flexibility in being able to map only what's required, and mappings can be managed locally by the developers of specific individual ontologies. The most obvious disadvantage are that there will be many sets of mappings required when many ontologies need to be reconciled: $O(n^2)$ sets of (bidirectional) mappings for $n$ individual ontologies in the worst case. Another significant disadvantage is that there is no general organising principle at work here: no attempt to identify common conceptualisations across the individual ontologies in a "top-down" fashion. For both of these reasons, this approach scales very poorly for large-scale ontology systems (of which the largest is the Semantic Web).

In contrast to the "bottom-up" approach, Figure 12.1(b) illustrates the approach where a single common, standard ontology is used as a basis for reconciling the individual ontologies. To map information and knowledge from one individual ontology $O_1$ to another individual ontology $O_2$, two steps are required: first, map from $O_1$ to the common ontology, then from the common ontology to $O_2$. Avoiding the direct mappings between individual ontologies cuts the number of sets of mappings down to just $n$ (bidirectional) mappings for $n$ ontologies, a significant improvement on the "bottom-up" approach. However, there will be a major cost in developing a common ontology with sufficient power to map all the individual ontologies; in some cases, this may not even be possible, so parts of some individual ontologies may still need to be mapped directly. Moreover, some flexibility is lost, in that mappings are no longer manageable locally, but only in relation to a centralised standard.

Figure 12.1(c) shows a variant of the common ontology approach, where there are a number of common ontologies, forming *clusters* of inter-related ontologies [27]. Each individual ontology maps to the common ontology for its cluster, and the common ontologies are mapped to allow the exchange of information and knowledge between the clusters. This is the most manageable, scalable approach in practice, as it combines the advantages of both the previous approaches: there is still a reduced number of mappings, and a principled approach to identifying common conceptualisations, as in Figure 12.1(b), yet also there is greater flexibility in managing mappings in a localised context, as in Figure 12.1(a). For these reasons, this third approach appears most likely to succeed in the context of the Semantic Web.

## 12.4 Ontology Mismatches

In order to reconcile ontologies, it is necessary to analyse the *mismatches* between individual ontologies. Mismatches might be present at a conceptual level, as well as at the terminological, taxonomical, definitional, and purely syntactic levels. It is necessary to detect and resolve such discrepancies, especially among the differing semantics. Correspondences may have to be established among the source ontolo-

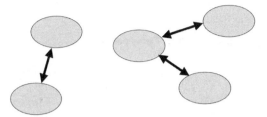

(a) Pairwise mappings between individual ontologies

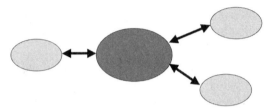

(b) Mappings to a single common ontology

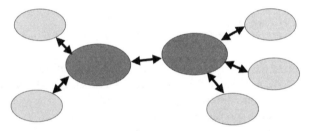

(c) Multiple ontology clusters, with inter-cluster mappings

**Fig. 12.1.** Alternative ontology reconciliation architectures: ontologies are depicted as nodes, (bidirectional) mappings as arcs; dark-shaded nodes are common ontologies; light-shaded nodes are individual ontologies.

gies, and overlapping concepts will need to be identified: concepts that are similar in meaning but have different names or structures, concepts that are unique to each of the sources [19]. This section surveys ontological mismatches from the perspective of researchers and practitioners in three areas: knowledge representation [26], databases [28], and knowledge elicitation [23]. In each case, examples of real ontological mismatches are given, drawn from an empirical study of mismatches among ontologies of four different experts in the domain of Personal Computer (PC) advising [7]. In all the examples, terms in the different experts' ontologies are differentiated by prefixing them in a similar way to XML namespace prefixes; for example, the term a:PC identifies the concept PC in the ontology of Expert A, and b:HardDisk identifies the concept HardDisk in the ontology of Expert B.

### 12.4.1 Knowledge Representation Perspective

Visser et al [26] proposed a classification of ontology mismatches to explain semantic heterogeneity in systems. They distinguish *conceptualisation mismatches* and *explication mismatches* as the two main categories, described as follows:

#### Conceptualisation mismatches

These may arise between two or more conceptualisations of a domain. The conceptualisations could differ in the ontological concepts distinguished or in the way these concepts are related, as shown below:

- *Class mismatches* are concerned with classes and their subclasses distinguished in the conceptualisation:
  - A *categorisation mismatch* occurs when two conceptualisations distinguish the same class, but divide this class into different subclasses.
    **Example:**
    c:Expert *advises* c:Staff ∪ c:Student
    b:Expert *advises* b:User ∪ b:MemberOfStaff ∪ b:Department ∪
    b:Supplier ∪ b:Expert These conceptualisations differ because the experts have partitioned the same class — as distinguished in their individual ontologies — into different aggregates of subclasses. The symbol ∪ signifies the union of the specified classes/concepts.
  - An *aggregation-level mismatch* occurs if both conceptualisations recognise the existence of a class, but define classes at different levels of abstraction.
    **Example:**
    b:PC → b:Desktop ∪ b:Laptop
    c:PC → c:Desktop ∪ c:Tower ∪ c:Portable ∪ c:Server
    The experts have identified the same (or similar) classes but defined them at dissimilar levels of abstraction. In particular, the second expert's notion of a "PC" is broader than that of the first expert — the second's includes servers, whereas the first's is restricted to users' workstations. In this example, the symbol → denotes the relation 'is defined by'.

- *Relation mismatches* are associated with the relations distinguished in the conceptualisation. They concern, for instance, the hierarchical relations between two classes or, the assignment of attributes to classes:
  - A *structure mismatch* occurs when two conceptualisations perceive the same set of classes but differ in the way these classes are structured via relations.
    **Example:**
    c:PC *isMadeOf* c:Part ∪ c:Component
    e:PC *hasComponent* e:Processor

Experts B and C have distinguished the same set of classes but differ in the way these classes are structured by means of the relations that associate their concepts. The following descriptions also reveal a difference in granularity of the domain semantics.

– An *attribute-assignment mismatch* occurs when two conceptualisations differ in the way they assign an attribute to various classes.

**Example:**

b:PC *has* b:Disk, b:PC *has* b:Space

d:PC *has* d:Disk, d:Disk *has* d:Space

The ontologies differ in the way they assign an attribute to their respective subclasses. While expert B has assigned two disjoint attributes Disk and Space to the concept PC, expert D defined a hierarchical relationship between similar concepts.

– An *attribute-type mismatch* occurs when two conceptualisations distinguish the same attribute, but differ in their assumed instantiations (range of possible value assignments).

*Explication mismatches*

These are not defined on the conceptualisation of the domain but on the way the conceptualisation is specified. They occur when two ontologies have different definitions, yet some component of the definition is identical. Visser et al distinguish three components of a definition: the *term* ($T$) used to denote a concept, the *definiens* ($D$) that comprises the body of the definition, and the underlying *concept* ($C$) being defined. Six different types have been specified, listed below. In the following examples, the $\rightarrow$ symbol denotes that the definiens which follow the arrow 'define' the term on the left-hand side of the description, and the $\wedge$ operator is used to concatenate multiple definiens.

- *Concept (C) mismatch*: the definitions have the same terms and definiens, but differ conceptually. So, while the represented definitions are apparently identical, in fact they refer to different concepts.
  **Example:** b:MinSpec ← b:Requirement ∧ b:PC ∧ b:User
  (referring to a user's hardware requirement)
  d:MinSpec ← d:Requirement ∧ d:PC ∧ d:User
  (referring to a system specification of software needed by user)
  In this case, there are identical terms and definiens but each expert is referring to a quite different concept, revealed by the context of the definition as explained in parentheses below.

- *Concept & Definiens (CD) mismatch*: the definitions share the same term, but have different concepts and definiens. Apparently, different "things" are being defined, though the terms coincide.
  **Example:** a:Spec ← a:Supplier ∧ a:StandardSpecsList
  b:Spec ← b:Specifies ∧ b:StandardSpecsList
  b:Spec ← b:Specifies ∧ b:Machine

```
b:Spec ← b:Description ∧ b:Machine ∧ b:User
c:Spec ← c:Requirement ∧ c:User
c:Spec ← c:Requirement ∧ c:Application
c:Spec ← c:Specification ∧ c:HardwareDevice
```
In these examples, an incidence of multiple descriptions for the same term implies that the expert gave distinct definitions in different contexts.

- *Definiens (D) mismatch*: the definitions have the same concept and the same term, but different definiens.
  **Example:** b:FastPC ← b:ProcessorSpeed ∧ b:MemoryAmount
  c:FastPC ← c:CPUPentium4 ∧ c:RAM64MegaBytes

- *Term (T) mismatch*: the definitions share the same concept and the same definiens, but use different terms.

- *Concept & Term (CT) mismatch*: the definitions have the same definiens, but different concepts and terms. While the actual body of the definition is the same in each case, suggesting the same "thing" is being defined, the underlying concept and the term used for that concept is different.
  **Example:** b:AdviceToUser → b:Expert *advises* b:User *about* b:Spec
  b:AdviceToSupplier → b:Expert *advises* b:Supplier *about* b:Spec
  In Expert B's ontology, the concept 'advice' refers to the provision of a 'spec' (specification) to both 'users' and 'suppliers', albeit in different contexts.
  This is an instance of a discrepancy *within* Expert B's ontology.

- *Term & Definiens (TD) mismatch*: the definitions have the same concept, but dissimilar terms and definiens. This is essentially the exact opposite to the C mismatch — the same concept is represented completely differently in the two definitions.
  **Example:**
  b:MinSpec ← b:ProcessorP3 ∧ b:Memory128MB
  c:BasicPC ← c:CPUPentium ∧ c:RAM64MegaBytes
  Although they use different terms and definiens, both experts are referring to the same concept: a specification for an entry-level PC. This interpretation might be construed as subjective, but more domain-specific knowledge would be required to explicate the subtleties in such concepts.

## 12.4.2 Database Perspective

Wiederhold [28] contends that "data obtained from remote and autonomous sources will often not match in terms of naming, scope, granularity of abstractions, temporal bases, and domain definitions." Wiederhold's perspective is especially applicable in the context of mapping between ontologies and databases. His approach proposes the following types of data resource mismatches:

- *Key difference*: different naming for the same concept, for example synonyms.
  **Example:**
  b:RMMidRangeSystemAcceleratorSpec2 (reference for customer)
  b:GCAT03234 (reference for supplier & experts)

- *Scope difference*: distinct domains, or distinct coverage of domain members.
  **Example:**
  b:Advice (advice given by expert B to users, etc)
  a:Advice (technical advice sought by expert A from expert B)
  a:Memory, d:Memory (referring to RAM)
  b:Memory, c:Memory (referring to RAM and VRAM)

- *Abstraction grain*: varied granularity of detail among the definitions.
  **Example:**
  c:FasterMachine (referring to speed of computer)
  b:FastestMachine (referring to speed of CPU)

- *Temporal basis*: mismatches concerning 'time', for example monthly versus yearly income.

- *Domain semantics* (distinct domains, and the way they are modelled) **Example:**
  b:Budget (funds/financial outlay available to user)
  b:Cost (price of machine quoted by the supplier)

- *Value semantics*: differences in the encoding of values.

Wiederhold states that in order to 'compose' large-scale software there has to be agreement about the terms, since the underlying models depend on the symbolic linkages among the components [29].

### 12.4.3 Knowledge Elicitation Perspective

Shaw and Gaines [23] identified four distinct dimensions to map knowledge elicitation problems that are likely to occur when several experts are involved during the evolution of a knowledge-based system. Because experts 'work' with knowledge entities that comprise concepts and terms, ambiguities can arise among the way concepts are agreed upon. From this perspective, there are four possible cases:

- *Conflict*: the experts use the same term for different concepts.
  **Example:** c:MinimumSpecification: requirements of a certain hardware device
  d:MinimumSpecification: minimum system requirements for satisfactorily running a software package
  a:Specifications: referring to suppliers' specification lists
  c:Specifications: referring to (i) requirements of certain applications; (ii) user requirements; (iii) certain hardware devices (video cards and monitors)

| Knowledge elicitation | Database | Knowledge representation |
|---|---|---|
| *Consensus* (same name, same concept) | No mismatch — not considered | No mismatch — not considered |
| *Conflict* (same name, different concepts) | Examples of *scope difference*, *abstract grain*, and *temporal basis* given in subsection 12.4.2 | Three cases:<br>• C mismatch<br>• CD mismatch<br>• D mismatch |
| *Correspondance* (different names, same concept) | Examples of *key difference* given in subsection 12.4.2 | Three cases:<br>• T mismatch<br>• CT mismatch<br>• TD mismatch |
| *Contrast* (different names, different concepts) | Examples of *domain semantics* given in subsection 12.4.2 | Not considered a mismatch |

**Table 12.1.** Comparisons between mismatches identified in the knowledge elicitation perspective (subsection 12.4.3), the knowledge representation perspective (subsection 12.4.1), and the database perspective (subsection 12.4.2). In column 1, we are using the word "name" to refer to what is called "term" in column 3.

- *Correspondence*: the experts use different terms for the same concept. **Example:**
  b:Memory versus c:RAM
  b:Processor versus c:CPU

- *Contrast*: the experts use different terms, and have different concepts. **Example:**
  c:Staff versus b:ApprovedSuppliers

- *Consensus*: the experts use the same term for the same concept. **Example:** a:Monitor, b:Monitor, c:Monitor — all refer to video display unit/screen

In each case with the exception of the last, *consensus*, there is a discrepancy. Shaw and Gaines developed a methodology and tools based on the repertory grid technique for eliciting, recognising and resolving such differences [23].

### 12.4.4 Comparing the Three Perspectives

Table 12.1 draws comparisons between the three perspectives in subsections 12.4.1, 12.4.2, and 12.4.3. It shows that the knowledge representation perspective (subsection 12.4.1) is essentially a finer-grained breakdown of the knowledge elicitation perspective (subsection 12.4.3), while the database perspective (subsection 12.4.2) is in some sense orthogonal to both of the others.

## 12.5 The Process of Ontology Reconciliation

Ontology reconciliation is generally a human-mediated process, although software tools can help (see Section 12.6). This is because most of the decisions on how to resolve the kinds of ontological mismatches surveyed in the previous section require a human to identify that different symbols represent the same concept, or that the same symbols represent different concepts. It is also a human's decision as to how to manage the reconciliation. There are three possibilities: *merging*, *aligning*, or *integrating*.

- *Merging* is the act of building a new ontology by unifying several ontologies into a single one [20, 24]. The ultimate goal is to create a single coherent ontology that includes all information from all the sources [19]. The new ontology is created from two or more existing ontologies with overlapping parts, and can be either virtual or physical [10].
- *Aligning* is used when sources must be made consistent and coherent with one another but kept separately [19]. It involves bringing two or more ontologies into mutual agreement, making them consistent and coherent [2, 10]. A set of alignment statements are created during this process, which collectively define the relationships between the original ontologies.
- *Integrating* entails building a new ontology by composing parts of other available ontologies [20]. Like merging, this process results in a new ontology. The difference between this approach and merging is that only parts of the original ontologies will be integrated — the goal is not to achieve a complete merger.

Once a decison has been made on how to manage the reconciliation, the next step is to identify mismatches between the candidate ontologies. As an example, Figure 12.2 shows ontology fragments from one of the examples in Section 12.4.1, together with a fragment of a common ontology. Figure 12.2(a) and Figure 12.2(b) are drawn from human experts in the PC advising domain, while Figure 12.2(c) is based on a PC technology reference textbook. In each case, a fragment of the class hierarchy of types of computer is shown; super-classes are decomposed into their sub-classes, where the super-class is defined as the union of its respective subclasses.

Figure 12.3 and Figure 12.4 give the OWL definitions corresponding to the first two ontologies in Figure 12.2 (for an introduction to OWL, see [1]. Figure 12.3 is Expert B's ontology fragment, from Figure 12.2(a), and Figure 12.4 is Expert C's ontology fragment, from Figure 12.2(b).

There are several possible reconciliations between these ontology fragments. Figure 12.5 shows one set of alignments, where classes in the two experts' ontologies are equated with classes in the common ontology. In this reconciliation, the second expert's notion of a "PC" is considered broader than that of the first expert — the second expert's notion includes servers, whereas the first expert's notion is restricted to users' workstations. If a decision had been made to align the ontologies, then these class-equivalence relationships would constitute the set of reconciliation statements.

Figure 12.6 shows some additional reconciliation statements expressed in OWL, this time directly between the two individual ontology fragments from Expert B and Expert C (the statements for the reconciliations between the experts' ontologies and

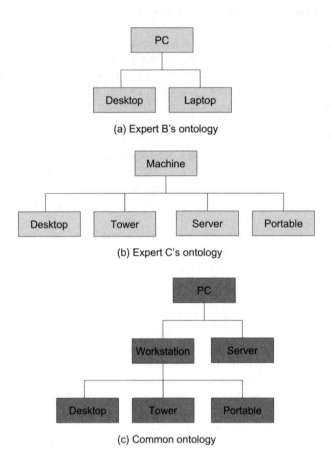

**Fig. 12.2.** Fragments of three alternative PC ontologies: those of individual experts B and C, and a common ontology for the PC domain. Each example shows super-classes decomposed into sub-classes, where the super-class is always the union of its subclasses.

the common ontology shown in Figure 12.5 would be similar). Note how OWL's `sameClassAs` property is used to express the class-equivalence.

It is worth noting that, in a process of merging the two experts' ontologies, the common ontology, in fact, can be seen as one possible result of such a merger process, as it contains all of the information from the individual experts' ontologies.

## 12.6 Ontology Reconciliation Tools

A sizeable number of software tools has been developed to assist in the process of reconciling ontologies, although few of these have moved beyond the status of

```
<!DOCTYPE rdf:RDF [
  <!ENTITY reconto
    "http://www.csd.abdn.ac.uk/research/reconto"> ]>
<rdf:RDF
  xmlns:rdf="http://www.w3.org/1999/02/22-rdf-syntax-ns#"
  xmlns:owl="http://www.w3.org/2002/07/owl#"
  xml:base="&reconto;/samples/pc/expertb">

  <owl:Class rdf:about="PC">
    <owl:unionOf rdf:parseType="Collection">
      <owl:Class rdf:about="Desktop"/>
      <owl:Class rdf:about="Laptop"/>
    </owl:unionOf>
  </owl:Class>
</rdf:RDF>
```

**Fig. 12.3.** OWL version of Expert B's ontology fragment, from Figure 12.2.

```
<!DOCTYPE rdf:RDF [
  <!ENTITY reconto
    "http://www.csd.abdn.ac.uk/research/reconto"> ]>
<rdf:RDF
  xmlns:rdf="http://www.w3.org/1999/02/22-rdf-syntax-ns#"
  xmlns:owl="http://www.w3.org/2002/07/owl#"
  xml:base="&reconto;/samples/pc/expertc">

  <owl:Class rdf:about="Machine">
    <owl:unionOf rdf:parseType="Collection">
      <owl:Class rdf:about="Desktop"/>
      <owl:Class rdf:about="Tower"/>
      <owl:Class rdf:about="Server"/>
      <owl:Class rdf:about="Portable"/>
    </owl:unionOf>
  </owl:Class>
</rdf:RDF>
```

**Fig. 12.4.** OWL version of Expert C's ontology fragment, from Figure 12.2.

research prototypes. This section provides a short survey of a number of the better-known tools, as an illustrative snapshot of this evolving activity. Other notable tools include the Methontology project's WebODE [5], Ontologging/KAON [13], and ConcepTool [15]. A survey of ontology mapping tools has been undertaken by the European OntoWeb network[3]

---

[3] See deliverables of the "Enterprise Standard Ontology Environments" SIG at: http://www.ontoweb.org

244 Adil Hameed, Alun Preece, and Derek Sleeman

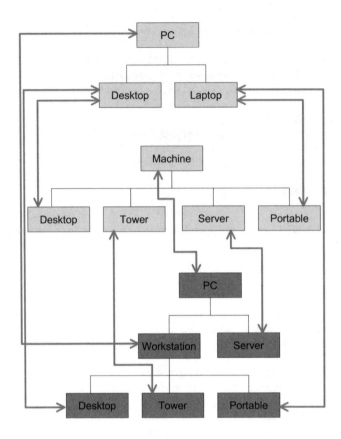

**Fig. 12.5.** Possible alignments between the three PC ontology fragments from Figure 12.2, showing classes in the two experts' ontologies equated with classes in the common ontology; the common ontology can be viewed as a merger of the two individual experts' ontologies.

### 12.6.1 Chimæra

Chimæra was developed by McGuinness et al at the Knowledge Systems Laboratory, Stanford University [14]. It is an interactive Web-based environment for merging and testing ontologies, which allows the user to bring together ontologies developed in different formalisms. The tool aims to support users in creating and maintaining distributed ontologies on the web. Chimæra uses the Ontolingua ontology editor, and is OKBC-compliant. Its Web-based user interface is simply HTML, augmented with JavaScript.

The two major functions supported by Chimæra are merging multiple ontologies, and evaluating ontologies with respect to their coverage and correctness. Chimæra

```
<!DOCTYPE rdf:RDF [
  <!ENTITY reconto
        "http://www.csd.abdn.ac.uk/research/reconto">
  <!ENTITY expertb "/samples/pc/expertb#">
  <!ENTITY expertc "/samples/pc/expertc#">
]>

<rdf:RDF
  xmlns:rdf="http://www.w3.org/1999/02/22-rdf-syntax-ns#"
  xmlns:owl="http://www.w3.org/2002/07/owl#"
  xml:base="&reconto;/samples/pc/articulation">

  <rdf:Description rdf:about="&reconto;&expertb;Desktop">
    <owl:sameClassAs
        rdf:resource="&reconto;&expertc;Desktop"/>
  </rdf:Description>

  <rdf:Description rdf:about="&reconto;&expertb;Laptop">
    <owl:sameClassAs
        rdf:resource="&reconto;&expertc;Portable"/>
  </rdf:Description>
</rdf:RDF>
```

**Fig. 12.6.** OWL version of some alignments directly between Expert B's ontology fragment, and Expert C's ontology fragment.

considers the task of merging to be one of combining two or more ontologies that may use different vocabularies and may have overlapping content. The task of evaluating single or multiple ontologies is addressed by producing a test suite that evaluates (partial) correctness and completeness of the ontologies. This involves finding and reporting provable inconsistencies, possible inconsistencies, and areas of incomplete coverage. The tool has other features like loading knowledge bases in differing formats, reorganising taxonomies, resolving name conflicts, browsing ontologies, editing terms, and so on.

Users can request analysis or guidance during the merging process. The tool will then point to the places in the ontology where attention is required. In its suggestions, Chimæra mostly relies on which ontology the concepts came from and, for classes, on their names. For example, it will point a user to a class in the merged ontology that has two slots derived from different source ontologies, or that has two sub-classes that originated in different ontologies. Help offered during the merging process includes:

- Generation of a 'name resolution' list that helps the user in the merging task by suggesting terms each of which is from a different ontology that are candidates to be merged.
- Generation of a 'taxonomy resolution' list where the tool suggests taxonomy areas that are candidates for reorganization. A number of heuristic strategies are

used for finding such points for taxonomies. Currently, the tool implements only partial support for the merging of class-subclass taxonomies.

In evaluating ontologies with respect to their coverage and correctness, Chimæra provides simple checks for incompleteness, syntactic analysis, simple taxonomic analysis, and some semantic evaluation.

Some limitations of Chimæra in its current form are that it leaves ontology reconciliation decisions entirely to the user, and does not make any suggestions itself. Also, use of Chimæra is hampered by very slow performance, a non-intuitive user interface, and a steep learning curve. Some of these weaknesses stem from the tool's Web-based architecture, which limits performance and user interface sophistication.

Ongoing work on Chimæra includes extending reasoning capabilities, providing semantic analysis in the reconciliation process, offering greater extensibility, and opening up the tool's usability to non-experts.

### 12.6.2 ONION

The ONION (ONtology CompositION) system was developed by Mitra, Wiederhold, and colleagues in the Stanford University Database Group [17]. The ONION project proposes a scalable and maintainable approach based on interoperation of ontologies. The motivation for the work is to handle distributed queries crossing the boundaries of underlying information systems. For this to be possible, the interoperation between the ontologies for the individual information systems need to be precisely defined.

The ONION approach includes an algebra for knowledge composition, featuring operators such as union, intersection, and difference. Articulation of ontology interdependencies are expressed using this algebra. The articulations essentially form a graph of ontology inter-relations, similar to the reconciliations illustrated earlier in Figure 12.5 (in the figure, the only articulation shown is class-equivalence).

To assist in creating the articulations, the ONION tool takes two sets of concepts and matches them using dictionaries (in particular, WordNet [16]) and information retrieval techniques (specifically, use of a corpus of documents). While the tool suggests possible articulations, it is left to the expert to define their chosen articulations. Input to the articulation-generation tool is in RDF, and the tool's output is plain text.

### 12.6.3 OntoView

OntoView is a tool under development by Klein et al at the Vrije University, Amsterdam, and OntoText, Sofia [11]. OntoView offers Web-based ontology versioning. In its current form, the OntoView tool is a slightly enhanced version of CVSWeb (Concurrent Versions System), an open-source network-transparent version control system. At its core, the tool identifies changes among different ontology versions. The comparison function is inspired by the UNIX *diff* (difference) file-comparison utility. However, OntoView compares ontologies at a structural level instead of line-level, showing which definitions of ontological concepts or properties have changed.

The tool is currently being re-implemented on top of a custom-designed ontology repository system. The OntoView project promises to provide a transparent interface to arbitrary versions of ontologies. It is planned that an internal specification of the relations between the different variants of ontologies will be built. This specification is based on the versions of ontologies themselves, on explicit change specifications, and on additional human input. Users will be able to differentiate between ontologies at a conceptual level and to export the differences as transformations or adaptations.

OntoView is still being developed; however, its current and proposed features include:

- read in ontologies, ontology updates, adaptations and/or mappings
- view a specific version or variant of an ontology
- provide a unique and persistent identification of versions
- allow users to assign properties to differences (type, etc)
- automatically perform inconsistency checks of version combinations
- differentiate ontologies:
  - show changed formal definitions
  - show changed comments
  - show type of change: conceptualisation or explication
- export translation/transformations/adaptations.

### 12.6.4 Prompt

The Prompt tool was developed by Noy and Musen within the Medical Informatics group at Stanford University [18]. Prompt offers a semi-automatic, interactive ontology-merging tool, which guides a user through the merging process, making suggestions, determining conflicts, and proposing resolution strategies. Prompt is implemented as a plug-in to the Protégé-2000 integrated knowledge-base editing environment. Protégé-2000 provides an extensible architecture for the creation of customised knowledge-based tools, and is compliant with the OKBC standard for frame-based KBs.[4]

The Prompt merging process aims to find 'semantically-similar' terms, although it does this through syntactic analysis. Initial suggestions are based on the lexical similarity of the frame names. The tool identifies candidates for merging as pairs of 'matching terms' — terms from different source ontologies representing similar concepts. Prompt suggests merging identical classes in two ontologies, where these classes are denoted by lexically-identical tokens. A graphical user interface helps users carry out interactive merging.

Prompt is intended to determine not only syntactic but also semantic matches based on (i) the content and structure of the source ontologies (for example, names of classes and slots, sub-classes, super-classes, domains and ranges of slot values) and (ii) the user's actions (that is, incorporating in its analysis the knowledge about the similarities and differences that the user has already identified). This algorithm relies on limited input from the user. The user does not need to analyse the structure

---

[4] http://protege.stanford.edu

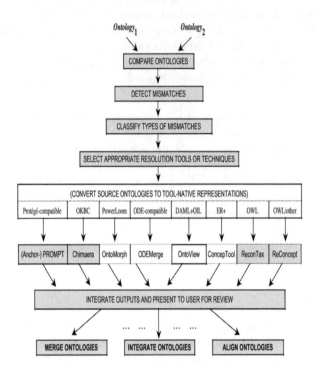

**Fig. 12.7.** Proposed workbench architecture for managing ontology reconciliations, by harnessing existing — and new — tools. The shaded components are within the scope of the current implementation; other components are planned for future expansion.

of the ontology deeply, just to determine some pairs of terms that "look similar". As such, Prompt will only be useful in cases where the candidate ontologies already have close similarities.

An enhanced version of Prompt, Anchor-Prompt, promises a number of extensions, including consideration of similarity between class hierarchies, and the use of similarity scores in determining the potential match between classes.

## 12.7 Conclusion and Way Forward

As ontology usage becomes more prevalent, the need for ontology reconciliation increases. This chapter has demonstrated that there is now a mature understanding of the kinds of mismatches that occur between different ontologies. Examining a representative sample of the software tools currently available to assist in the reconciliation process shows that, while a number of promising tools are already available, these are largely in the form of laboratory prototypes, and that more work is needed in this area. Moreover, it is unlikely that one single tool will ever emerge that satisfactorily handles all aspects of ontology reconciliation. For this reason, Hameed et al propose in [8] the creation of a *workbench* within which a variety of tools can be harnessed to assist ontology engineers in performing reconciliations. Figure 12.7 illustrates this proposed system.

The proposed workbench will guide a user in selecting appropriate tools for the kinds of mismatch identified, where a tool is selected on the basis of the kinds of mismatch it tackles, and also the knowledge representation formalisms on which it operates. Integrating the available — and newly emerging — tools in such a coherent framework, in the context of a systematic approach to identifying ontological mismatches, will be a significant step in managing the ontology reconciliation problem.

## References

1. Antoniou, G, Harmelen, Frank van. Web Ontology Language: OWL. This Book.
2. Corcho, O, Gómez-Pérez, A (2001) Solving Integration Problems of E-Commerce Standards and Initiatives through Ontological Mappings. *IJCAI-01 Workshop on Ontologies and Information Sharing*, pages 131–140
3. Fensel, D (2000) *Ontologies: Silver Bullet for Knowledge Management and Electronic Commerce*, Springer-Verlag
4. Fox, M, Gruninger, M (1998) Enterprise Modelling. *AI Magazine*, Fall, 109–121
5. Gómez-Pérez, A, Moreno, A, Pazos, J, Sierra-Alonso, A (2000) Knowledge Maps: An essential technique for conceptualisation. *Data and Knowledge Engineering*, **33**(2), 169–190
6. Gruber, T R (1993) A Translational Approach to Portable Ontology Specifications. *Knowledge Acquisition*, **5**, 199–220
7. Hameed, A, Sleeman, D H, Preece, A (2001) Detecting Mismatches in Experts' Ontologies through Knowledge Elicitation. In Bramer, M, Coenen, F, Preece, A (eds), *Research and Development in Intelligent Systems XVIII*, Springer-Verlag, pages 9–22
8. Hameed, A, Sleeman, D H, Preece, A (2002) OntoManager: A Workbench Environment to facilitate Ontology Management and Interoperability. In *EON-2002: EKAW-2002 Workshop on Evaluation of Ontology-based Tools*
9. Huhns, M N, Stephens, L M (1999) Personal Ontologies. *IEEE Internet Computing*, **3**(2) 85–87
10. Klein, M (2001) Combining and relating ontologies: an analysis of problems and solutions. *IJCAI-01 Workshop on Ontologies and Information Sharing*, pages 53–62
11. Klein, M, Kiryakov, W, Ognyanov, D, Fensel, D (2002) Ontology Versioning and Change Detection on the Web. In *13th International Conference on Knowledge Engineering and Knowledge Management (EKAW02)*, Sigüenza, Spain

12. Lenat, D, Guha, R (1990) *Building Large Knowledge-Based Systems*, Addison Wesley, Reading

13. A. Maedche, A, Motik, B, Stojanovic, L, Studer, R, Volz, R (2002) Managing Multiple Ontologies and Ontology Evolution in Ontologging. In *Proceedings Conference on Intelligent Information Processing (IIP2002)*, Kluwer

14. McGuinness, D L, Fikes, R, Rice, J, Wilder, S (2000) An Environment for Merging and Testing Large Ontologies. In Cohn, A, Giunchiglia, F, and Selman, B (eds), *KR2000: Principles of Knowledge Representation and Reasoning*, pages 483–493

15. Meisel H, Compatangelo, E (2002) EER-CONCEPTOOL: a "Reasonable" Environment for Schema and Ontology Sharing. In *Proc. of the 14th IEEE International Conference on Tools with Artificial Intelligence (ICTAI2002)*, IEEE Computer Society Press, pages 527–534

16. Miller, G A (1995) WordNet: a Lexical Database for English. *Communications of the ACM*, **38**(11), 39–41

17. Mitra, P, Kersten, M. Wiederhold, G (2000) Graph-Oriented Model for Articulation of Ontology Interdependencies. In *Proceedings of the 7th Int. Conf. on Extending Database Technology*, Springer-Verlag

18. Noy, N F, Musen, M A (2001) Anchor-PROMPT: Using Non-Local Context for Semantic Matching. In *Workshop on Ontologies and Information Sharing at the Seventeenth International Joint Conference on Artificial Intelligence (IJCAI-2001)*, Seattle, USA

19. Noy, N F, Musen, M A (2000) PROMPT: Algorithm and Tool for Automated Ontology Merging and Alignment. *IJCAI-01 Workshop on Ontologies and Information Sharing*, pages 63–70

20. Pinto, H S, Martins, J P (2001) A Methodology for Ontology Integration. In *Proceedings of the First International Conference on Knowledge Capture (K-CAP 2001)*, ACM Press

21. Preece, A, Sleeman, D H, Flett, A N, Curry, D, Meaney, N, Perry, P (2001) Better Knowledge Management through Knowledge Engineering. *IEEE Intelligent Systems*, **14**(1), 26–36

22. Rosenfeld, L, Morville, P (2002) *Information Architecture for the World Wide Web*, OReilly

23. Shaw, M L G, Gaines, B R (1989) Comparing Conceptual Structures: Consensus, Conflict, Correspondence and Contrast. *Knowledge Acquisition*, **1**(4), pp. 341–363

24. Stumme, G, Maedche, A (2001) Ontology Merging for Federated Ontologies on the Semantic Web. *IJCAI-01 Workshop on Ontologies and Information Sharing*, pages 91–99

25. Uschold, M, King, M, Moralee, S, Zorgios, Y (1998) The Enterprise Ontology. *Knowledge Engineering Review*, **13**.

26. Visser, P R S, Jones, D M, Bench-Capon, T J M, Shave, M J R (1997) An Analysis of Ontology Mismatches; Heterogeneity vs. Interoperability. In *AAAI 1997 Spring Symposium on Ontological Engineering*, Stanford, USA.

27. Visser, P R S, Tamma, V A M (1999) An Experiment with Ontology-Based Agent Clustering. In *IJCAI-99 Workshop on Ontologies and Problem-Solving Methods: Lessons Learned and Future Trends*, Stockholm, Sweden.

28. Wiederhold, G (1992) Mediators in the Architecture of Future Information Systems. *IEEE Computer*, March.

29. Wiederhold, G (1994) An Algebra for Ontology Composition. In *Proceedings of 1994 Monterey Workshop on Formal Methods*, September.

# Ontology Evaluation

Asunción Gómez-Pérez

Facultad de Informática . Universidad Politécnica de Madrid
Campus de Montegancedo, s/n. 28660 Boadilla del Monte. Madrid. Spain
asun@fi.upm.es

**Summary.** The evaluation of ontologies is an emerging field. At present, a deep core of preliminary ideas and guidelines for evaluating ontologies is missing. This paper presents a brief summary of previous works on evaluating ontologies and the criteria (consistency, completeness, conciseness, expandability and sensitiveness) used to evaluate and assess ontologies. It also addresses the possible types of errors made when domain knowledge is structured in taxonomies in an ontology: circularity errors, exhaustive and non-exhaustive class partition errors, redundancy errors, grammatical errors, semantic errors and incompleteness errors. The paper is based on the experience of evaluating ontologies in the Ontolingua Server.

## 13.1  Introduction

In recent years, considerable progress has been made in developing the conceptual bases for building technology that allows the reuse and sharing of knowledge. Right now, ontologies are widely used in Knowledge Engineering, Artificial Intelligence and Computer Science, in applications related to knowledge management, natural language processing, e-commerce, intelligent integration information, information retrieval, database design and integration, bioinformatics, education, and in new emerging fields like the Semantic Web.

As any other resources that is used in software applications, the content of ontologies should be evaluated before (re)using it in other ontologies or applications. Evaluation of the content as well as evaluation of the software environments used to build ontologies are critical before integrating them in final applications. In that sense, we could say that it is unwise to publish an ontology or to implement a software application that relies on ontologies written by others (even yourself) without first evaluating its content, that is, its concepts definitions, its taxonomy and its axioms. A well-evaluated ontology will not guarantee the absence of problems, but it will make its use safer.

Over the years, the Knowledge-Based Systems (KBS) verification and validation community developed a wide range of methods, techniques and tools for verifying and validating KBS whose KBs are formalized as rules. However, ontologies are not implemented on poduction rules, they are conceptualized with frames and first order logic as well as description logic. So, new methods and techniques are needed for their evaluation.

Although the first works on ontology content evaluation  started in 1994 [22,23], in the last two years, the interest of the Ontological Engineering community in this issue and in ontology-based technology has grown. The main efforts to evaluate the  content were made by  Gómez-Pérez on her work [19, 21, 22, 23] and the Ontoclean Method   [28]. The OntoClean method has been elaborated by the Ontology Group of the LADSEB-CNR in Padova (Italy). It is a method to clean concept taxonomies according to notions [16] such as *rigidity*, *identity* and *unity*, which are called *meta-properties*. The meta-properties are useful to remove wrong *subclass of* relations. This article summarizes the first approach.

In this paper, I will not evaluate specific ontologies implemented on a given language or during its development process, neither how well-known ontology development tools perform the evaluation.  From a KR paradigms perspective, we can say that the framework presented on this paper only covers the evaluation of taxonomic content. For evaluating other types of components (relations, attributes and axioms) frequently used when modelling with frames and first order logic new techniques are needed. In section 13.2, I present how different methodologies for building ontologies perform evaluation and how ontology evaluation is strongly related to the KR paradigm underlying the languages in which the ontology is implemented. 13.3 presents definitions of the terms "Evaluation", "Verification", "Validation" and "Assessment". 13.4 will present a few criteria (completeness, consistency and conciseness) for evaluating ontology content. Then, on section 13.5, I will focus on the evaluation of taxonomic knowledge. Section 13.6 presents tools for evaluating ontologies, and I conclude this chapter with further research topics on that field.

## 13.2   Important Dimensions on the Evaluation

Two of the main underlying ideas of this section are that the evaluation of an ontology content should be performed during the whole ontology life cycle and that ontology development tools should support the content evaluation during the ontology building process. Another important idea is that evaluation of the ontology content is strongly related to the underlying KR paradigm of the language used to implement the ontology. Along this section, these three main ideas are explained.

### 13.2.1   Methodologies and Tools

Up to now, few domain-independent methodological approaches [14, 15, 27, 40, 43] have been reported for building ontologies. A comparison study of all of them can be found in [11] and on the survey of methodologies for developing ontologies presented on the   deliverable D1.4 in ontoweb[1] [10]. What all the above approaches have in common is that they start by identifying the purpose of the ontology, the need for domain knowledge acquisition and implementation, and the need for ontology evaluation. However, the evaluation is performed differently in each one of them. Uschold and King´s  methodology [44] includes the evaluation activity but does not state how it should  be carried out. Grüninger and Fox [27] propose to evaluate the ontology by identifying a set of competency questions, which are the basis for a rigorous characterization of the knowledge that the ontology has to cover. METHONTOLOGY [14, 15, 20] proposes that evaluation be carried out throughout the entire lifetime of the ontology development process. According to METHONTOLOGY, most of the evaluation should be carried out during the conceptualization activity to prevent errors and their propagation in the implementation. On-To-Knowledge also proposes to carry out an evaluation activity during the whole ontology life-cycle [40]. There exists also a proposal for integrating the OntoClean method [28] in the conceptualisation activity of METHONTOLOGY, as presented in [13].

The work performed on the framework of the SIG3 about Enterprise Standard Ontology Environment of the ontoweb thematic network together with the comparison studies carried out by different ontology tool developers on ontoweb deliverable D1.3 [18] show that all the ontology development tools presented provided constraint checking, but only Ontoedit [41] and WebODE [2] provides advanced functionalities.

### 13.2.2   Knowledge Representation Paradigm

At the beginning of the 1990s, ontologies were mainly built using AI modeling techniques based on frames and first-order logic and description logic (DL). Ontologies are modeled in frames and first order logic using the five kinds of components presented by Gruber [26]: concepts, relations, functions, axioms and instances. Concepts are organized in taxonomies through which inheritance mechanisms can be applied. Relations represent a type of interaction between concepts of the domain and also represent attributes of concepts. Functions are special cases of relations. Axioms are used to model sentences that are always true; they are also  used to represent knowledge that cannot be formally defined by the other components. And finally, instances of concepts and instances of relations.

If the ontology is modeled using a Description Logic (DL) approach,   the ontology is then divided in two parts: the TBox and the ABox. The TBox

---

[1] http://www.ontoweb.org/

contains intensional knowledge in the form of a terminology and is built through declarations that describe general properties of concepts. The ABox contains extensional knowledge - aka assertional knowledge -, which is specific to the individuals of the discourse domain [3]. In other words, the TBox contains the definitions of concepts and roles, while the ABox contains the definitions of individuals (instances). In some DL systems, the ABox also contains rules that allow inferring information. Reasoning in DL is mostly based on the subsumption test among concepts, for which DL systems provide efficient automatic classifiers.

During these years a set of AI-based ontology implementation languages was created. Basically, the KR paradigm underlying such ontology languages was based on first order logic (i.e. KIF [17]), on frames combined with first order logic (i.e. Ontolingua [26], OCML [38], and Flogic [32] or on description logic (i.e. Loom [36]). The boom of the Internet led to the creation of ontology languages that exploited the characteristics of the Web. Such languages are usually called *web-based ontology languages* or *ontology markup languages*. Some of them are based on XML sytax, such as SHOE [35]), XOL [31], OIL [29]) and DAML+OIL [30]). The W3C (the World Wide Web Consortium) is also working to create standards and recommendations of *web languages* to be used for implementing ontologies. They proposed RDF [33] as a semantic-network based language to describe Web resources, and RDF Schema [4] as an extension to RDF with frame-based primitives. The combination of both RDF and RDF Schema is normally known as RDF(S). Right now, they are developing OWL, which is mainly based on DAML+OIL. A comparative study of the expressiveness and inference mechanisms of the above languages (except for OWL) can be found in [6] and [24].

Important connections and implications can be found between the components used to build an ontology, the knowledge representation paradigms (frames, description logic, logic) used to represent formally such components, and the languages used to implement the ontologies under a given knowledge representation paradigm. That is, an ontology built with frames or description logic can be implemented in several frames or description logic languages. This is really important from an evaluation perspective because:

1.  From subsumption tests, DL systems derive concept satisfiability and consistency in the models represented. Such classifiers are commonly built by means of tableaux calculus and constraint systems.
2.  Existing models for evaluating ontologies built using frames and first order logic must be extended with the evaluation of new ontology components (attributes, relations, axioms).
3.  Language-dependent evaluation tools able to evaluate otology content in the different traditional languages and Web-based languages are needed. Each tool will have to account the features of each language, in order to carry out the evaluation.

## 13.3  Terminology

A study of the KBS evaluation ideas served as a precedent for evaluating ontologies and also to learn from KBS successes and mistakes [23]. The main ideas taken from this study to prepare a framework for ontology evaluation are: (1) the division of evaluation into two kinds of evaluation: technical (carried out by developers) and users' evaluation; (2) the provision of a set of terms and the standard definitions of such terms; (3) the definition of a set of criteria to carry out the user's and technical evaluation processes; (4) the inclusion of evaluation activities in methodologies for building ontologies; (5) the construction of tools for evaluating existing ontologies; and (6) the inclusion of evaluation modules in tools used to build ontologies.

With regard to terminology and definitions of terms in the knowledge sharing technology field, the main terms (borrowed from the KBS evaluation field) are [25]: "evaluation", "verification", "validation" and "assessment".

**Evaluation of Knowledge Sharing Technology** means to judge technically the ontologies and Problem Solving Methods (PSMs[2]), their software environments and documentation against a reference framework during each phase and between phases of the life cycle. Examples of reference frameworks are the real world, a set of requirements or a set of competency questions. The term evaluation subsumes verification and validation.

**Verification of Knowledge Sharing Technology** refers to the technical activity that guarantees the correctness of an ontology and PSMs, their associated software environments and documentation with respect to a reference framework during each phase and between phases of the life cycle.

**Validation of Knowledge Sharing Technology** guarantees that the ontologies and PSMs, their software environments and documentation correspond with the systems that they are supposed to represent.

**Assessment of Knowledge Sharing Technology** refers to the usability and usefulness of the ontologies and PSMs, their software environments and their documentation when reused or shared in applications.

Adapting the previous definitions to the ontology field, we can say that **ontology evaluation** [21] is a technical judgment of the content of the ontology with respect to a frame of reference[3] during each phase and between phases of their lifecycle. Ontology evaluation includes ontology verification and ontology validation. Ontology evaluation should be carried out on the following elements:

- Every individual definition and axiom.
- Collections of definitions and axioms that are stated explicitly in the ontology.
- Definitions that are imported from other ontologies.
- Definitions that can be inferred from other definitions and axioms.

---

[2] A PSM is a kind of Knowledge Components that can be reused or shared.

[3] A Frame of reference can be: requirements specifications, competency questions [27] or the real-world.

**Ontology Verification** refers to building the ontology correctly, that is, ensuring that its definitions[4] implement correctly the ontology requirements and competency questions, or function correctly in the real world.

**Ontology Validation** refers to whether the meaning of the ontology definitions really model the real world for which the ontology was created. The goal is to prove that the world model (if it exists and is known) is compliant with the world modeled formally.

Finally, **ontology assessment** is focused on judging the understanding, usability, usefulness, quality and portability of the definitions from the user´s point of view. Different kind of users and different kind of applications require different means of assessing an ontology. In the ontology field, a characterization of applications that use ontologies is needed to figure out when an existing ontology is appropriate for a given application. Some work has already been done on identifying a set of features to characterize ontologies from the user´s point of view. In [1], a Reference Ontology (a domain ontology about ontologies) is presented. On the context of the ontoweb thematic network, the OntoRoadMap[5] application is an ontology-based application that allows the community to register, browse and search ontologies, methodologies, tools and languages for building ontologies and ontology-based applications in areas such as: the semantic web, e-commerce, KM, NLP, III, etc., as well as in conferences, workshops and events on this area.

## 13.4   Criteria to Evaluate Ontologies

The goal of the evaluation process is to determine what the ontology defines correctly, what it does not, and what it does incorrectly. We can say that an ontology is consistent if and only if each definition in the ontology is consistent. We have to look at the scope of the definitions and axioms by figuring out what can be inferred, cannot be inferred or can be inferred incorrectly. To evaluate a given ontology, the following criteria were identified: consistency, completeness, conciseness, expandability and sensitiveness. Formal definitions of the these criteria appear in [21].

**Consistency** refers to whether it is possible to obtain contradictory conclusions from valid input definitions. A given definition is consistent if and only if the individual definition is consistent and no contradictory sentences can be inferred from other definitions and axioms.
- A given definition is **individually consistent** if and only if it satisfies the following three conditions:

---

[4] A definition is written in natural language (informal definition) and in a formal language (formal definition).
[5] http://babage.dia.fi.upm.es/ontoweb/wp1/OntoRoadMap/index.html

o    the formal definition is metaphysically consistent, that is, if there is no contradiction in the interpretation of the formal definition with respect to the real world.

o    the informal definition is metaphysically consistent, that is, if there is no contradiction in the interpretation of the informal definition with respect to the real world.

o    the entire definition is internally consistent, that is, the formal and informal definition have the same meaning.

• A definition is **inferentially consistent** if it is impossible to obtain contradictory conclusions from  the meaning of all the definitions and axioms in the ontology, and the ontologies included by this ontology.

Let us see the previous ideas with an example. Suppose the following Ontolingua definition of the class month-name:

```
(define-class MONTH-NAME (?month)
"The months  are: house, February, March   April May
June    July      August   September   October   November
December."
   :iff-def (member ?month
           (setof house February March April May June
July  August September October November December)))
```

We can see that the definition is internally consistent (its formal and informal definitions provide the same meaning). However, both, its formal and informal definitions are not metaphysically consistent because the term house is not a month in the real world.

If we replaced the term house by the term January on the formal definition, as it is presented bellow:

```
(define-class MONTH-NAME (?month)
"The months are: House February March April May June
July  August September October November December."
   :iff-def (member ?month
           (setof January February March April May June
July  August September October November December)))
```

We could say that the definition is not internally consistent because the meaning of the formal definition is different from the meaning of the natural language definition, the informal definition is metaphysically inconsistent (the term house is not a month) and the formal definition is metaphysically consistent. And we could add that an inconsistency on the definition exists.

Finally, if we introduce the term Enero on the natural language definition, for those who are not Spanish speakers there exists still a metaphysical inconsistency in the informal definition (something other than January is written in the informal definition). However, both  for Spanish and English speakers the formal and informal definition are metaphysically consistent, although the whole definition would not be internally consistent because the term used to refer to the first month of the year in English and Spanish is different.

```
(define-class MONTH-NAME (?month)
 "The months of the year are: Enero February, March
April May June July  August September October November
December)."
    :iff-def (member ?month
             (setof January February March April May June
July  August September October November December)))
```

**Completeness.** Incompleteness is a fundamental problem in ontologies, even more when ontologies are available in such an open environment as the Semantic Web. In fact, we cannot prove either the completeness of an ontology or the completeness of its definitions, but we can prove both the incompleteness of an individual definition, and thus deduce the incompleteness of an ontology, and the incompleteness of an ontology if at least one definition is missing in  the established reference framework. So, an ontology is complete if and only if:

- All that is supposed to be in the ontology is explicitly stated in it, or can be inferred.
- Each definition is complete. This is determined by figuring out: (a) what knowledge the definition defines; and (b) for all the knowledge that is required but not explicit, it should be checked whether it can be inferred from other definitions and axioms; If it can, the definition is complete. Otherwise, it is incomplete.

**Conciseness.** An ontology is concise: (a) if it does not store any unnecessary or useless definitions, (b) if explicit redundancies between definitions of terms do not exist, and (c) if redundancies cannot be inferred from other definitions and axioms.

**Expandability** refers to the effort required to add new definitions to an ontology and more knowledge to its definitions without altering the set of well-defined properties already guaranteed.

**Sensitiveness** relates to how small changes in a definition alter the set of well-defined properties already guaranteed.

## 13.5  Method for Evaluating Taxonomic Knowledge in Ontologies

Most of the existing ontologies are built using ontology building tools whose editors allow creating taxonomies easily either from web-based forms or with graphical tools. Examples of such tools are OntoEdit [41], Protégé2000 [39],

WebODE [2, 5] and WebOnto [8]. All of them permit structuring domain concepts in taxonomies and "Ad-hoc" relationships can be created between them.

This section presents a method for evaluating consistency, completeness and conciseness on taxonomies. This method is based on the experience of evaluating ontologies implemented in Ontolingua, and it can be used with several purposes:
1.  for evaluating ontologies implemented in frame-based languages.
2.  for evaluating if ontology building tools prevent the ontologist from such kind of mistakes.
3.  for designing new ontologies.

Throughout this section, we will use the semantics of the primitives defined at the Ontolingua Server caming either from the Frame Ontology or from the OKBC ontology.

The main differences between the OntoClean method and the method presented on that serction is that the goal of the OntoClean method is to remove wrong *subclass of* relations in taxonomies according to some philosophical notions such as *rigidity*, *identity* and *unity*. The OntoClean method proposes to tag concepts on the taxonomy according to the following symbols: *is rigid* (*+R*); *is anti-rigid* (~R), *is non-rigid* (-R), *carries identity criterion* (+I), *supplies identity criterion* (+O), *carries unity* (+U), and *carries anti-unity* (~U).

## 13.5.1  Primitives for Building Taxonomies

A KR ontology [45] captures the modeling primitives used to formalize knowledge in a KR paradigm. Examples of such characteristics are classes, relations, attributes, etc. The most representative KR ontology is the Frame Ontology (FO) [26], which was built for capturing KR conventions under a frame-based approach in Ontolingua. The FO was modified and some of its primitives were moved into the OKBC ontology [7]. The reason behind this change was the creation of OKBC, a frame-based protocol for accessing knowledge bases stored in different KR systems.

When building a concept taxonomy using the FO and OKBC ontologies, the following primitives should be used:
- `Subclass-of` (`?child-class` `?parent-class`): the class `?child-class` is a subclass of the class `?parent-class`.
- `Instance-of` (`?individual` `?class`): the instance `?individual` is an instance of the class `?class`.
- `Class-Partition` (`?set-of-classes`): defines a set of disjoint classes. A partition of the class ?C into the set of classes class_p1, ..., class_pn, where class_pi $\neq$ class _pk for every i $\neq$ k is defined when any instance or subclass of any class class_pi cannot belong to any other class class-pk. When this occurs, the classes class_p1, ..., class_pn are a partition of class ?C.
- `Disjoint-Decomposition` (`?C` `?Class-partition`): defines the set of disjoint subclasses `?Class-Partition` as subclasses of the

class ?C. This classification does not necessarily have to be complete, that is, there may be instances of ?C that are not included in any of these subclasses.

- Partition(?C   ?Class-Partition): defines the set of disjoint subclasses ?Class-Partition as subclasses of the class ?C, where the class ?C can be defined as a union of all the classes that make up the partition.

Partitions can define concept classifications in a disjoint and/or complete manner. A partition is exhaustive if it adds the completeness constraint to the established subsets. If it does not, we have a non-exhaustive partition.

### 13.5.2   Evaluation of Taxonomic Knowledge in Ontologies

This section presents a set of possible errors [19] that can be made by ontologists when building taxonomic knowledge in an ontology under a frame-based approach. They are classified, as presented in Figure 1, under the criteria previously identified in section 13.4. We will not take into account expandability nor sensitiveness.

There exists an ontology implemented in Ontolingua that formalizes the knowledge that follows in this section.

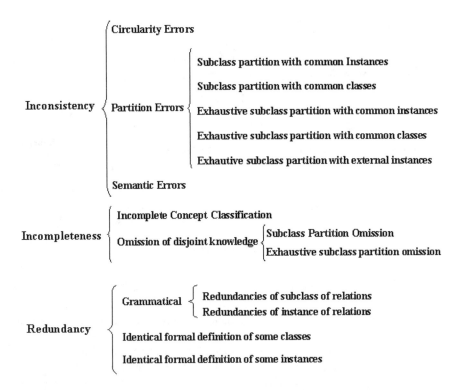

**Figure 1: Errors that might be made when developing taxonomies in frames**

### 13.5.2.1  Detecting Inconsistency Errors

**Semantic Inconsistency Errors.** They usually occur because the developer makes an incorrect semantic classification, that is, classifies a concept as a subclass of a concept to which it does not really belong; for example, classifies the concept *dog* as a subclass of the concept *house*. The same would occur with instances; for example, if the instance *Pluto* would be an instance-of of the class *house*.

**Circularity errors.** They occur when a class is defined as a specialization or generalization of itself. Depending on the number of relations involved, circularity errors can be classed as circularity errors at distance zero (a class with itself), circularity errors at distance 1, and circularity errors at distance n. Figure 2 shows them.

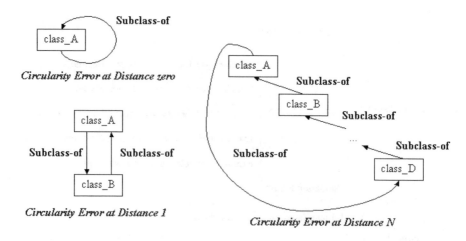

**Figure 2: Circularity errors**

**Partition Errors**. Partitions can define concept classifications in a disjoint and/or complete manner. As exhaustive subclass partitions, they merely add the completeness constraint to the established subsets. The following kinds of mistakes in partitions are identified:

- *Subclass partition with common classes*. They occur when there is a partition *class_p₁,... , class_pₙ* defined in a class *class_A* and one or more classes *class_B₁, ..., class_Bₖ* are subclasses of more than one subclass *class_pᵢ* of the partition, as presented in figure 3. For example, if *dogs* and *cats* form a subclass partition of the set of *mammals*, an error of this type would occur if we define the class *Doberman* as a subclass of both classes. The developer should remove the wrong relation to solve the problem.

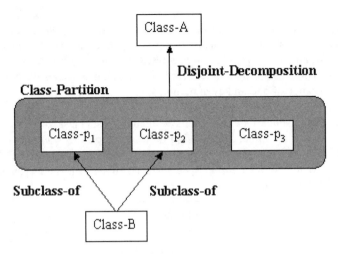

**Figure 3: Subclass partition with common classes**

- *Subclass partition with common instances.* They occur when one or several instances belong to more than one subclass of the defined partition, as shown in figure 4. For example, if *dogs* and *cats* form a subclass partition of the set of *mammals*, an error of this type would occur if we define *Pluto* as an instance of both classes. The developer should remove the wrong relation to solve this problem.

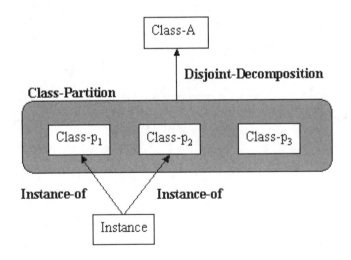

**Figure 4: Subclass partition with common instances**

- *Exhaustive subclass partition with common classes.* For example, having defined the classes *odd* and *even* as an exhaustive subclass partition of the class *number,* an error of this type appears if the class *prime* is a subclass of the *odd* and *even* numbers, as presented in figure 5. So, if we define the number *Three* as a prime number, we get the inconsistency since three would be an instance of odd and even numbers.
- *Exhaustive subclass partition with common instances.* They occur when one or several instances belong to more than one subclass of the exhaustive partition. For example, after having defined the classes *odd* and *even* as an exhaustive subclass partition of the class *number,* an error of this type appears if the number *three* is an instance of the *odd* and *even* numbers. Figure 6 shows this example.

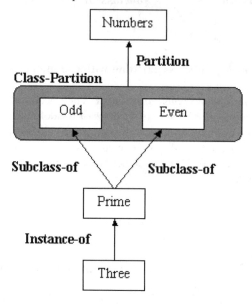

**Figure 5: Exhaustive subclass partition with common classes**

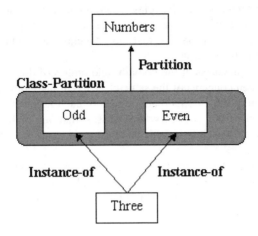

**Figure 6: Exhaustive subclass partition with common instances**

- *Exhaustive subclass partition with external instances.* They occur when having defined an exhaustive subclass partition of the base class (Class_A) into the set of classes class-$p_1$ ... class-$p_n$, there are one or more instances of the class_A that do not belong to any class class_$p_i$ of the exhaustive partition. For example, if the *numbers* classed as *odd* and *even* had been defined as forming an exhaustive subclass partition and the number *three* were defined as an instance of the class *numbers* (instead of the class *even*), we would have an error of this type, as it is presented in figure 7.

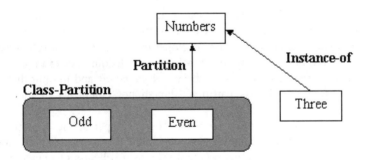

**Figure 7: Exhaustive subclass partition with external  instances**

### 13.5.2.2 Detecting Incompleteness on Taxonomies

In order to provide a mechanism for evaluating completeness in taxonomies, the following activities can be helpful to find incomplete definitions.

- Check completeness of the class hierarchy. Errors appear when the superclasses of a given class are imprecise or over-specified, and when information about subclasses that are subclass partitions or exhaustive subclass partitions is missing.
- Check the completeness of the domains and ranges of the "ad hoc" relations defined between concepts of the same or different taxonomies. The goal is to figure out whether the domain and ranges of each argument of each relation delimits exactly and precisely the classes that are appropriate for that argument. Errors appear when the domains and ranges are imprecise or over-specified.
- Check the completeness of the classes. The aim is to ascertain whether the class contains as much information as required. Errors appear when there are properties missing in the definition of a class, when different classes have the same formal definition, etc.

Most of the times, when a concept taxonomy is built, the ontologist only uses the subclass-of relationship for building the taxonomy and omits disjoint knowledge between classes. In this section, we present common omissions when building taxonomies.

**Incomplete Concept Classification**. Generally, an error of this type is made whenever concepts are classified without accounting for them all, that is, concepts existing in the domain are overlooked. An error of this type occurs if a concept classification *musical instruments* is defined considering only the classes formed by *string instruments* and *wind instruments* and overlooking, for example, the *percussion instruments*.

**Partition Errors.** They could appear when the definition of the partition between a set of classes is omitted. We have identified two types of errors:
- *Subclass partition omission.* The developer identifies the set of subclasses of a given class, but omits that the subclasses are disjoint. An example would be to define *dogs* and *cats* as a subclass of *mammals* and to omit that *dogs* and *cats* form a subclass partition (though not complete) of the set of *mammals*.
- *Exhaustive subclass partition omission.* The developer defines a partition of a class and omits the completeness constraint to the established subsets. Examples would be to define *odd* and *even* as a subclass of *numbers* or to define *odd* and *even* as a subclass partition of *numbers*. In both cases, it is omitted that the *numbers* classified as *odd* and *even* form an exhaustive subclass partition (that is, complete).

### 13.5.2.3 Detecting Redundancy

Redundancy is a type of error that occurs when we redefine expressions of the ontology that were already defined explicitly or that can be inferred from other definitions. There exist three kinds of redundancies.

**Gramatical Redundacy Errors**. They occur in taxonomies when there is more than one explicit definition of any of the hierarchical relations.

- *Redundancies of subclass-of relations* occur between classes when they have more than one subclass-of relations between them. We can distinguish direct and indirect repetition. A *Direct repetition* exists when two or more subclass-of relations between the same source and target classes are defined, that is, including the subclass of relation between the classes *dog* and *mammals* twice. An *Indirect repetition* exists, for example, if we define the class *dog* as a subclass of *pet*, and *pet* as a subclass of *animal*, when *dog* is also defined as a subclass of *animal*.
- *Redundancies of instance-of relations*. As in the above case, there are two possibilities. A *direct repetition* exists if two *instance-of* relations between the same instance and class are defined. An *indirect repetition* exists, for example, if we define the instance *Clyde* as an instance of *real elephant* and *real elephant* as a subclass of the class *elephant*. The definition of an instance of relation between *Clyde* and *elephant* would lead to a redundancy in the taxonomy.

**Identical formal definition of some classes.** It occurs when there are two or more classes in the ontology with the same formal definition, that is, the only difference between the subclasses is the name. This error type could be also be classified as an example of classes with incomplete knowledge. The developer could solve this problem by adding what distinguishes the classes of the partition or, otherwise, realizing that it does not make sense to have classes with identical formal definitions in the partition and delete one of them.

**Identical formal definition of some instances.** It occurs when there are two or more instances in the ontology with the same formal definition, that is, the only difference between them is the name. The solution is either to add more values to the attributes of the instances, so that they can be distinguished, or to remove one of the duplicated instances.

## 13.6 Tools for Evaluating Ontologies

In this section, we will see several tools that can be used to evaluate ontologies: ONE-T, OntoAnalyser and ODEClean. We have also included OntoGenerator, which can be used to evaluate a few aspects of the scalability and performance of the ontology tools.

**ONE-T** (Ontology Evaluation Tool) has been developed by the Ontology Group of the Universidad Politécnica de Madrid, UPM. ONE-T is a Java web-based application that allows verifying ontologies stored and available in any Ontolingua Server. It has been used in the verification of ontologies in the Ontolingua Server 5.0 and Ontolingua Server 6.0. As it is based on the OKBC protocol, it is easily extensible. ONE-T detects the inconsistency errors on concept taxonomies presented in section 13.4.

**OntoAnalyser** is a tool developed by the Institute AIFB and Ontoprise GmbH, and it is a pluggin of OntoEdit [41]. OntoAnalyser[6] is focused on the evaluation of ontology properties, in particular language conformity and consistency. Language conformity refers to how the syntax of the ontology representation conforms to a language. Consistency refers to what extent the tool ensures that the resulting ontologies are consistent with respect to their semantics. OntoAnalyser is a tool which uses rules, runs the Ontobroker inference engine (cf. [46]) with such rules and provides the user the results of this examination. OntoAnalyser is able to load different rule packages, each intended for a different target tool or target project.

**ODEClean** [12] is a pluggin which has been created to support the OntoClean method in WebODE. The criteria used to evaluate the ontology are expressed declaratively in WebODE conceptualisation module. It is based on Guarino and colleagues' top-level ontology of universals, enriched with metaproperties (rigidity, identity, unity, dependency) and with the evaluation rules proposed by OntoClean. The main functions provided by ODEClean are: to establish the evaluation mode, to assign meta-properties to concepts, to focus on rigid properties, and to evaluate according to the taxonomic constraints.

**OntoGenerator** is a tool developed by the Institute AIFB and Ontoprise GmbH, and it is a pluggin of OntoEdit. OntoGenerator focuses on the evaluation of ontology based tools, in particular, performance and scalability. It creates "synthetic" ontologies which are not intended to represent a domain of interest, but rather to fulfill certain technical parameters, e.g., a certain number of concepts and instances or certain kinds of rules.

## 13.7   Conclusions

The ontology evaluation field is just emerging. As we mentioned before, the ontological engineering community has just started to be interested in the evaluation issue.

From the methodological perspective, **evaluation activities should be introduced with  more detail into ontology development methodologies**. The

---

[6] http://www.aifb.uni-karlsruhe.de/WBS/ysu/publications/eon2002_whitepaper.pdf

purpose of these activities will be to raise ontologists´ awareness of the fact that evaluation should be performed throughout the entire ontology life cycle to detect errors at the earliest possible time and should not be left till the end when the ontology has been totally implemented.

There exist a lot of libraries where ontologies are published. Some of the most known are: DAML ontology library[7], Protege ontology library[8], Ontolingua ontology library[9], WebOnto ontology library[10],  SHOE ontology library[11], WebODE ontology library[12], and $(KA)^2$ ontology library[13]. Only the first one is associated to an ontology language. The others are attached to ontology tools. Right now, there are not papers describing **the process followed to evaluate ontologies before making them public in libraries**. The same occurs with very well-known and large ontologies (Cyc Ontologies [34], ontologies at the Ontoligua Server [9], SENSUS [42], etc.). It does  not exist documentation that describes how the ontologies were evaluated (if they were).

Ontologies in the Semantic Web can be developed by different groups of people or organizations, and will be available in different ontology languages. To allow a better use of ontologies in applications, and also to be reused by other ontologies, we will have to develop **language-dependent evaluation tools** capable of evaluating ontologies in the traditional (Ontolingua, OCML, Flogic, etc.) and Semantic Web (RDF, RDFS, DAML+OIL, OWL) languages. Each tool will have to take into account the features of each language to perform this evaluation.

But we need tools both for evaluating ontologies when they are already implemented and published in libraries, and for  **giving   support to the evaluation activity during the whole lifecycle of ontologies** (conceptualisation, formalization, etc.). Both kinds of tools should not only evaluate concept taxonomies, but also other ontology components, such as properties, relations, axioms, instances, etc. However, up to now, no documents exist that describe **how different ontology building tools evaluate their ontologies**  during its development.

Ontologies built with  ontology building tools are usually implemented in several ontology languages using forward translators. So we also need studies that compare the quality of the translators as well as the quality of the content generated.

---

[7] http://www.daml.org/ontologies/

[8] http://protege.stanford.edu/ontologies.html

[9] http://ontolingua.stanford.edu/

[10] http://webonto.open.ac.uk

[11] http://www.cs.umd.edu/projects/plus/SHOE/onts/index.html

[12] http://webode.dia.fi.upm.es/

[13] http://ka2portal.aifb.uni-karlsruhe.de/

When developers search for candidate ontologies for their application, they face a complex multi-criteria choice problem. Apart from the dispersion of ontologies over several servers, (a) ontology content formalization differs depending on the server in which it is stored, (b) ontologies in the same server are usually described with different detail levels, (c) there is no common format to present relevant information about the ontologies so that users can decide which ontology best suits their purpose, (d) there is no technical document describing how the ontology was evaluated. Choosing an ontology that does not match the needs of the system properly or whose usage is expensive (because it involves people, hardware and software resources, time, etc.) may force future users to stop reusing the ontology already built and force them to formalize the same knowledge again. **End-user methods to judge the usability and usefulness of an ontology** in an application are also needed.

## Acknowledgements

The first part (sections 13.3 to 13.5) of this research work has been performed at the Knowledge Systems Laboratory in Stanford University. It has been sponsored by a grant, number: PF94-9921929 of the Ministerio de Educación y Ciencia in Spain. The Ontolingua Ontology that formalized all the criteria presented in section 13.5 has been supported by the project TIC 96-1226-E funded by the Comisión Interministerial de Ciencia y Tecnología (CICYT) in Spain. Finally, section 13.6 has been sponsored by Ontoweb Thematic network IST-2000-29243. Thanks to Rosario Plaza Arteche for her help in correcting the English version.

## References

1.  Arpírez JC, Gómez-Pérez A, Lozano A, Pinto SH (2000). *Reference Ontology and (ONTO)$^2$Agent: The Ontology Yellow Pages*. Knowledge and Information System. Vol. 2. N° 4. November, 2000. Pags. 387-412.
2.  Arpírez JC, Corcho O, Fernández-López M, Gómez-Pérez A (2001) *WebODE: a scalable ontological engineering workbench*. First International Conference on Knowledge Capture (K-CAP 2001). Victoria, Canada. October, 2001.
3.  Baader F, McGuinness D, Nardi D, Patel-Schneider P (2002) *The Description Logic Handbook: Theory, implementation and applications*. Cambridge. 2002.
4.  Brickley D, Guha RV (2002) *RDF Vocabulary Description Language 1.0: RDF Schema*. W3C Working Draft, 2002. http://www.w3.org/TR/PR-rdf-schema
5.  Corcho O, Fernández-López M, Gómez-Pérez A, Vicente, A.; (2002) *WebODE: an integrated workbench for ontology representation, reasoning and exchange*. 13th International Conference on Knowledge Engineering and Knowledge Management (EKAW'02). Sigüenza. Spain. October, 2002.
6.  Corcho O, Gómez-Pérez A (2000) *A Roadmap to Ontology Specification Languages*. 12th International Conference in Knowledge Engineering and Knowledge Management, Lecture Notes in Artificial Intelligence, Springer-Verlag, Berlin, Oct. 2000, pp. 80-96.

7.  Chaudhri VK, Farquhar A, Fikes R, Karp PD, Rice JP (1998) *Open Knowledge Base Connectivity 2.0.3*. Technical Report. April, 1998. Available at http://www.ai.sri.com/~okbc/okbc-2-0-3.pdf.

8.  Domingue J (1998) *Tadzebao and WebOnto: Discussing, Browsing, and Editing Ontologies on the Web*. 11th Knowledge Acquisition for Knowledge-Based Systems Workshop. Banff, Alberta, Canada. April, 1998.

9.  Farquhar A, Fikes R, Rice J (1996) *The Ontolingua Server: A Tool for Collaborative Ontology Construction*. Proceedings of the 10th Knowledge Acquisition for Knowledge-Based Systems Workshop, (Banff, Alberta, Canada 1996) 44.1-44.19.

10. Fernández-López, M (2002). A survey on methodologies for developing, maintaining, evaluating and reengineering ontologies. D14. of the thematic network Ontoweb. 2002.

11. Fernández-López M, Gómez-Pérez A (2002a) *What methodologies can you use for building ontologies?* To appear in the International Journal of Human Computer Studies. 2002.

12. Fernández-López M, Gómez-Pérez A (2002b) *The Integration of OntoClean in WebODE*. EON2002 Evaluation of Ontology-based Tools. Proceedings of the OntoWeb-SIG3 Workshop at the 13th International Conference on Knowledge Engineering and Knowledge Management EKAW 2002 Sigüenza (Spain), 30th September 2002.

13. Fernández-López M, Gómez-Pérez A, Guarino N (2001) *The Methontology & OntoClean merge*. Technical Report, OntoWeb special interest group on Enterprise-standards Ontology Environments. Amsterdam. 2001.

14. Fernández-López M, Gómez-Pérez A, Pazos-Sierra A, Pazos-Sierra J (1999) *Building a Chemical Ontology Using METHONTOLOGY and the Ontology Design Environment*. IEEE Intelligent Systems & their applications 4(1) (1999) 37-46.

15. Fernández-López M, Gómez-Pérez A, Juristo N (1997) *METHONTOLOGY: From Ontological Art Towards Ontological Engineering*. AAAI Symposium on Ontological Engineering (Stanford, 1997).

16. Gangemi A, Guarino N, Masolo C, Oltramari, A (2001) *Understanding top-level ontological distinctions*. Proc. of IJCAI 2001 workshop on Ontologies and Information Sharing .

17. Genesereth M, Fikes E (1992) *Knowledge Interchange Format. Version 3.0. Reference Manual*. Computer Science Department. Stanford University. Report Logic-92-1. 1992.

18. Gómez-Pérez A (2002) *A Survey of Ontology Tools*. D1.3. of the thematic network Ontoweb.

19. Gómez-Pérez A (2001) *Evaluating ontologies: Cases of Study. IEEE Intelligent Systems and their Applications*. Special Issue on Verification and Validation of ontologies. Marzo 2001, Vol 16, N° 3. Pag. 391 – 409.

20. Gómez-Pérez A (1998) *Knowledge Sharing and Reuse*. The Handbook of Applied Expert Systems. Edited by J. Liebowitz. CRC. 1998.

21. Gómez-Pérez A (1996) *A Framework to Verify Knowledge Sharing Technology*. Expert Systems with Application. Vol. 11, N. 4. PP: 519-529.

22. Gómez-Pérez A (1994a) *Some ideas and Examples to Evaluate Ontologies*. Technical Report KSL-94-65. Knowledge System Laboratory. Stanford University. Also in Proceedings of the 11th Conference on Artificial Intelligence for Applications. CAIA94.

23. Gómez-Pérez A (1994b) *From Knowledge Based Systems to Knowledge Sharing Technology: Evaluation and Assessment*. Technical Report. KSL-94-73. Knowledge Systems Laboratory. Stanford University. December 1994.

24. Gómez-Pérez A, Corcho O (2002). Ontology Languages for the Semantic Web. IEEE Intelligent Systems & their applications. 17(1). January/February 2002. pp: 54-60.

25. Gómez-Pérez A, Juristo N, Pazos J (1995) *Evaluation and Assessment of the* Knowledge *Sharing Technology*. Towards Very Large Knowledge Bases. N.J.I. Mars, Ed. IOS Press, 1995.

26. Gruber TR (1993) A translation approach to portable ontology specification. Knowledge Acquisition. 5(2): 199-220.

27. Grüninger M, Fox MS (1995) *Methodology for the design and evaluation of ontologies*. In Workshop on Basic Ontological Issues in Knowledge Sharing (Montreal, 1995).

28. Guarino N, Welty C (2000) *A Formal Ontology of Properties* In R. Dieng and O. Corby (eds.), Knowledge Engineering and Knowledge Management: Methods, Models and Tools. 12th International Conference, EKAW2000, LNAI 1937. Springer Verlag: 97-112. 2000.

29. Horrocks I, Fensel D, Harmelen F, Decker S, Erdmann M, Klein M (2000) *OIL in a Nutshell*. 12th International Conference in Knowledge Engineering and Knowledge Management, Lecture Notes in Artificial Intelligence, Springer-Verlag, Berlin, Germany, Oct. 2000, pp. 1-16.

30. Horrocks I, van Harmelen F. (2001) *Reference Description of the DAML+OIL Ontology Markup Language*, Draft report, March, 2001. Available at http://www.daml.org/2000/12/reference.html (current Jan. 2002). Contributors: Tim Berners-Lee, Dan Brickley, Dan Connolly, Mike Dean, Stefan Decker, Pat Hayes, Jeff Heflin, Jim Hendler, Deb McGuinness, Lynn Andrea Stein.

31. Karp R, Chaudhri V, Thomere J (1999) *XOL: An XML-Based Ontology Exchange Language*. Version 0.3. Technical Report. July, 1999.
    http://www.ai.sri.com/~pkarp/xol/xol.html.

32. Kifer M, Lausen G, Wu J (1995) Logical Foundations of Object-Oriented and Frame-Based Languages. Journal of the ACM. Vol. 42. May, 1995.

33. Lassila O, Swick R (1999) Resource Description Framework (RDF) Model and Syntax Specification. W3C Recommendation. February, 1999.
    http://www.w3.org/TR/REC-rdf-syntax/. (current Jan 2002)

34. Lenat DB, Guha RV (1990) *Building Large Knowledge-based systems*. 12th National Conf. on Artificial Intelligence, (AAAI-94) Representation and Inference in the Cyc Project. Addison-Wesley. Reading. Massachusetts, USA. 1990.

35. Luke S, Heflin J. (2000) *SHOE 1.01. Proposed Specification*. SHOE Project.

36. MacGregor R (1991) *Inside the LOOM clasifier*. SIGART bulletin. #2(3):70-76. June, 1991.

37. Luke S, Heflin J (2000) *SHOE 1.01. Proposed Specification*. SHOE Project. February, 2000. http://www.cs.umd.edu/projects/plus/SHOE/spec1.01.htm (current Jan 2002)

38. Motta E (1999) *Reusable Components for Knowledge Modelling: Principles and Case Studies in Parametric Design*. IOS Press. Amsterdam. 1999.

39. Protégé, (2000) *Using Protégé-2000 to Edit RDF*. Technical Report. Knowledge Modelling Group. Technical report. Stanford University. February, 2000. http://www.smi.Stanford.edu/projects/protege/protege-rdf/protege-rdf.html (current Jan 2002)

40. Staab S, Schnurr HP, Studer R, Sure Y (2001) *Knowledge Processes and Ontologies*, IEEE Intelligent Systems, 16(1). 2001.

41. Sure Y, Erdmann M, Angele J, Staab S, Studer R, Wenke D (2002) OntoEdit: Collaborative Ontology Engineering for the Semantic Web. In Proceedings of the International Semantic Web Conference 2002 (ISWC 2002), June 9-12 2002, Sardinia, Italia.

42. Swartout B, Ramesh P, Knight K, Russ T (1997) *Toward Distributed Use of Large-Scale Ontologies*. Symposium on Ontological Engineering of AAAI. Stanford (California). March 1997.

43. Uschold M, Grüninger M (1996) *ONTOLOGIES: Principles, Methods and Applications*. Knowledge Engineering Review. Vol. 11; N. 2; June 1996.

44. Uschold M, King M (1995) *Towards a Methodology for Building Ontologies*. In IJCAI'95 Workshop on Basic Ontological Issues in Knowledge Sharing. Montreal, Canada. 1995.

45. Van Heist G, Schreiber ATh, Wielinga BJ (1997) *Using explicit ontologies in KBS development*. International Journal of Human-Computer Studies, 45, pp. 183-292, 1997.

46. Decker S, Erdmann M, Fensel D, Studer R (1999) *Ontobroker: Ontology Based Access to Distributed and Semi-Structured Information*. In: Meersman R et al. (eds) Semantic Issues in Multimedia Systems (DS-8). Kluwer Academic Publisher, Boston, pp 351–369.

# 14

# Ontology Engineering Environments

Riichiro Mizoguchi

The Institute of Scientific and Industrial Research, Osaka University
8-1 Mihogaoka, Ibaraki, Osaka, 567-0047 Japan

**Summary.** Ontology engineering is a successor of knowledge engineering and is expected to play a critical role in the next generation knowledge processing by contributing to knowledge sharing/reuse and semantic interoperability of metadata. Although the importance of ontology is well-understood, building a good ontology is a hard task. This paper discusses ontology engineering environments with comparison between them. Because of the space limitation, four environments are selected: OntoEdit, WebODE, Protege and Hozo each of which covers a wide rage of ontology development process rather than being a single-purpose tool which should be covered elsewhere. First, several key factors to evaluate ontology development environments are discussed. The stress is laid on development process-related aspects rather than static characteristics of an environment. According to the factors, each environment is briefly overviewed followed by comparison between them with a summary table.

## 14.1 Introduction

In order to discuss ontology engineering environments, we first need to clarify what we mean by ontology engineering. Ontology engineering is a successor of knowledge engineering which has been considered as a key technology for building knowledge-intensive systems. Although knowledge engineering has contributed to eliciting expertise, organizing it into a computational structure, and building knowledge bases, AI researchers have noticed the necessity of a more robust and theoretically sound engineering which enables knowledge sharing/reuse and formulation of the problem solving process itself. Knowledge engineering technology has thus developed into "ontology engineering" where "ontology" is the key concept to investigate.

There is another story concerning the importance of ontology engineering. It is the semantic web movement. Semantic web strongly requires semantic interoperability among metadata which are made using semantic tags defined in an ontology. The issue here is to build good ontologies to come up with meaningful sets of tags which are made interoperable by ontology alignment.

Although the importance of ontology is well-understood, it is also known that building a good ontology is a hard task. This is why there have been developed some methodologies for ontology development and have been built a number of ontology representation and editing tools. Among many tools [1,7,8,11,15,16,17,18,19], because of the space limitation, this chapter takes up OntoEdit[15,16], WebODE[1], Protégé[11] and Hozo[7,8] which cover a wide rage of ontology development process rather than being single-purpose tools which are covered elsewhere.

## 14.2    Factors of an ontology engineering environment

A comprehensive evaluation of ontology engineering tools is found in [22][23] in which the major focus is put on static characteristics of tools. The evaluation in this chapter is done focusing on dynamic aspects of the tools, that is, we here concentrate on characteristics of the ontology engineering process supported by the four environments. Let us enumerate factors by which an environment should be characterized.

- Development methodology

  The first key task of ontology engineering is ontology building which requires a sophisticated development methodology. However, a methodology itself is not sufficient. Developers need an integrated environment which helps them build an ontology in every phase of the building process. In other words, a computer system should navigate developers in the ontology building process according to a methodology.

  - Development process and its management

    Ontology building process is divided into several phases such as require-ment specification, knowledge acquisition, conceptualization, implementa-tion, evaluation, etc. An environment is required to manage these processes based on a sophisticated methodology.

  - Collaborative development

    Building an ontology is often done with collaboration of multiple developers who need help in orchestration of the collaborative activities.

  - Compliance with an ontology theory

    An ontology is not just a set of concepts but at least a "well-organized" set of concepts. An environment is expected to guide users to a well-organized ontology which largely depends on the environment's discipline of what an ontology should be rather than an ad-hoc classification of concepts or a frame representation. This is why an environment needs to be compliant with a sophisticated theory of ontology.

- Use of an ontology

  Ontology use is the other key task of ontology engineering. Users need also effective support in how to share ontology with others, how to use/reuse an ontology and how to build an instance model based on an ontology.

– Compliance with WWW standard
   There are many languages standardized by W3C: XML, RDF(S), DAML+OIL and OWL, etc. The environment is required to be compliant with these.
– Ontology/Model(instance) server
   Ontologies and instance models should be available through internet.
– Instance definition
   Instance model building is crucial to ontology applications to real-world problems.
– Inference service
   An inference engine is used to check the consistency of ontologies/models.
– Software level issue
   – Usability
      GUI as well as functionality is essential to the usability of the environment.
   – Architecture of the environment
      An environment should be designed in an advanced and sophisticated architecture to make it usable.
   – Extensibility
      It is good if users easily extend the environment.

Description of the four environments is done having these factors in mind in the following sections.

## 14.3   OntoEdit

OntoEdit[15, 16], professional version, is an ontology engineering environment to support the development and maintenance of ontologies. Ontology development process in OntoEdit is based on their own methodology, On-To-Knowledge [14][20] which is originally based on Common KADS[13] methodology and consists of major three steps such as requirement specification, refinement and evaluation processes. The requirement specification consists of description of the domain and the goal of the ontology, design guidelines, available knowledge sources, potential users and use cases, and applications supported by the ontology. The output of this phase is refined into a formal description in the next phase. Refinement is done usually collaboratively. In the evaluation phase, competency questions are used to evaluate if the ontology built can answer these questions.

### 14.3.1     Requirement specification phase

Two tools, OntoKick and Mind2Onto, are prepared for supporting this phase of ontology capture. OntoKick is designed for computer engineers who are familiar with software development process and tries to build relevant structures for building informal ontology description by obtaining competency questions proposed in [4] which the resulting ontology and ontology-based applications have to

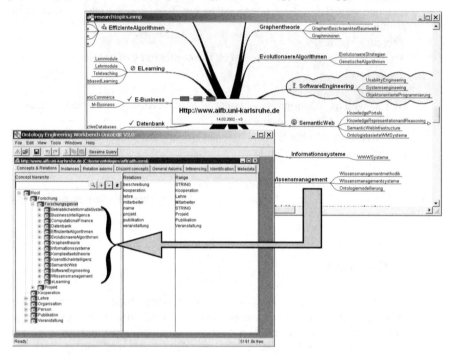

Fig. 1     Mind2Onto and translation the result to *is-a* hierarchy[16]

answer. Examples of competency questions made by OntoKick include "which research groups exist at the institute?", "which teaching courses are offered by the institute?", etc. Mind2Onto is a graphical tool for capturing informal relations between concepts. It is easy to use because it has a good visual interface and allows loose identification of relations between concepts. However, it is necessary to convert the map into a more formal organization to generate an ontology. Fig. 1 depicts the conversion process of Mind2Onto from mind maps$^{TM}$, which is a plug-in module, to an ontology.

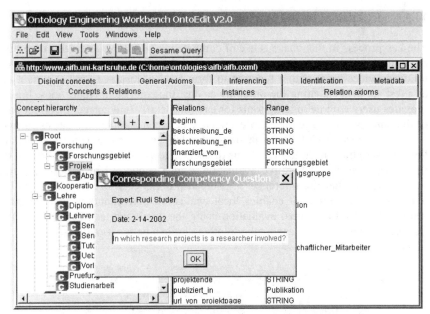

Fig.2 Dependency management between competency questions
and concepts[16]

### 14.3.2   Refinement phase[16]

This phase is for developers to use the editor to refine the ontological structure
and the definition of concepts and relations. Like most of other tools, OntoEdit
employs the client/server architecture where Ontologies are managed in a server
and multiple clients access and modify it. A sophisticated transaction control is
introduced to enable concurrent development of an ontology in a collaborative
manner. Because OntoEdit allows multiple users to edit the same class in an ontology at the same time, it needs a powerful lock mechanism of each class and
devises Strict two Phase Locking protocol: S2PL to support arbitrary nested
transactions.

### 14.3.3    Evaluation phase

The key process in this phase is use of competency questions obtained in the first phase to see if the designed ontology satisfies the requirements. To do this, OntoEdit provides users with a function to form a set of instances and axioms used as a test set for evaluating the ontology against the competency questions. It also provides users with debugging tools for ease of identify and correct incorrect part of the ontology. It maintains the dependency between competency questions and concepts derived from them to facilitate the debugging process(Fig. 2). This allows users to trace back to the origins of each concept. Another unique feature of this phase is that collaborative evaluation is also supported by introducing the name space so that the inference engine can process each of test sets given by multiple users. Further, it enables local evaluation corresponding to respective test sets followed by global evaluation using the combined test. Like WebODE, OntoEdit supports Ontoclean methodology to build a better *is-a* hierarchy.

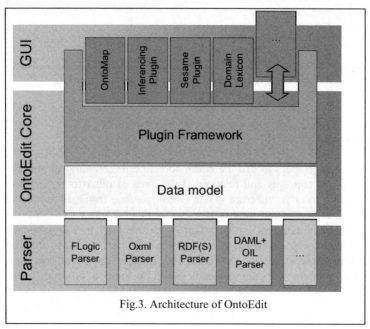

Fig.3. Architecture of OntoEdit

### 14.3.4    Inference

OntoEdit employs Ontobroker[21] and F-Logic[6] as its inference engine. It is used to process axioms in the refinement and evaluation phases. Especially, it plays an important role in the evaluation phase because it processes competency questions to the ontology to prove that it satisfies them. It exploits the strength of

F-logic in that it can express arbitrary powerful rules which quantify over the set of classes which Description logics cannot.

### 14.3.5    Architecture

Fig. 3 shows the architecture of OntoEdit consisting of three layers: GUI, On-toEdit core and Parser. Like Protégé, it employs plug-in architecture to make it easily extensible and customizable by the users. It is compliant with XML family standard in import and export the ontology.

## 14.4    Hozo

"Hozo[1]" is an integrated ontology engineering environment for building/using task ontology and domain ontology based on fundamental ontological theories[7,8]. "Hozo" is composed of "Ontology Editor", "Onto-Studio" and "Ontology Server"(Fig.4). The ontology and the resulting model are available in different formats (Lisp, Text, XML/DTD, DAML+OIL) that make it portable and reusable. One of the most remarkable features of Hozo is that it can treat the concept of *Role*. When an ontology is seriously used to model the real world by generating instances and then connecting them, users have to be careful not to confuse the *Role* such as teacher, mother, fuel, etc. with other basic concepts such as human, water, oil, etc. The former is a role played by the latter. For example, if one builds an ontology including "Mr. A is *instance-of* teacher" and "teacher *is-a* human", then when he quits the teacher job, he cannot be an instance of the class of teacher, and hence he cannot be an instance of the class human, which means he must die. This difficulty is caused by making an instance of *Role* which cannot have an instance in theory. In Hozo, three different classes are introduced to deal with the concept of role appropriately.

> *Role-concept:* A concept representing a role dependent on a context(e.g., teacher role)
> *Basic concept:* A concept which does not need other concepts for being defined(e.g., human)
> *Role holder:* An entity of a *basic concept* which is holding the role(e.g., teacher)

A basic concept is used as the *class constraint.* Then an instance that satisfies the *class constraint* plays the role and becomes a *role holder.* Hozo supports to define such a role concept as well as a basic concept.

---

[1] "Ho" is a Japanese word and means unchanged truth, laws or rules in Japanese, and we represent "ontologies" by the word. "Zo" means to build in Japanese.

### 14.4.1   Ontology development phase

**Onto-Studio** is based on a method of building task&domain ontologies, named AFM (Activity-First Method) [9]. It helps users design a domain ontology through building a task ontology from technical documents. One of the key ideas here is that task ontology provides users with the set of *Roles* played in the task

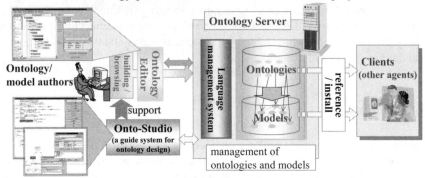

Fig.4    The architecture of Hozo

context by the domain concepts which should be organized according to the roles identified by designing task ontology. Fig. 5 shows the skeletal building process of task and domain ontologies using Onto-Studio. It consists of 4 phases and 12 steps. The following outlines these 4 phases.

1. *Extraction of task-units*: In this phase, users extract **task-units** which contain only one process(action) from the technical documents.
(1) Divide the text in the technical documents into small **blocks** to extract vocabulary easier.
(2) Extract **task-units** which contain only one process(action) from these blocks.
(3) Make a flow chart called a **concrete task-flow** by combining task-units.

2. *Organization of task-activities*: In this phase, users specify the input/output of task-activities and organize the task-activities.
(4) Conceptualize **task-activities** from verbs in the task-units.
(5) Organize the task-activities in an *is-a* hierarchy.
(6) Define role-concepts, called **task-activity roles**, which appear in the input/output of these task-activities.

3. *Analysis of task-structure*: In this phase, users analyze the flow of  the task-activities, specify the flow of the objects from input to output, and define the task-context-roles.
(7) Generalize the concrete task-flows to obtain **general task-flows**.
(8) Describe the **object-flows**, which clearly express relations between inputs and outputs of the task-activities, in the general task-flows obtained above.

(9) Define the **task-context roles** on the basis of these object-flows. By task-context roles, we mean the role-concepts dependent on the whole process of a task.

(10) Extract the **domain terms** which play a task-context role.

4. *Organization of domain concepts*: In this phase, users organize domain concepts extracted in phase 3.

(11) Discriminate between the roles dependent on the domain concepts and the basic concepts.

(12) Organize the domain concepts in an *is-a* hierarchy.

In practice, these steps are not done in a waterfall manner. Users can go back and forth during the process. In each step Onto-Studio provides users with graphical interfaces to help them perform the suggested procedures. The output of Onto-Studio is a rather informal representation of ontology which is in turn translated by the system into the Ontology editor representation to enable users to define ontology more rigorously.

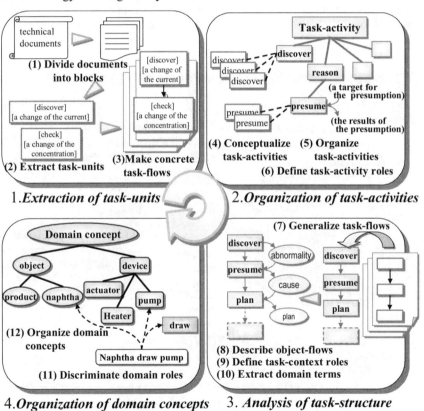

Fig. 5   The building process of ontologies using Onto-Studio

Thanks to an Onto-Studio functionality for dependency management of many of the critical decisions made during ontology building from the technical documents, it allows developers to trace back to the previous decisions down to the original words in a sentence in the document. The system provides users with a graphical interface for tracing back the dependency chain concerning the four kinds of dependencies: original text & terms extracted, verbs(task activities) & task roles, task activity roles & task-context roles and domain concepts & task/domain roles.

### 14.4.2   Ontology definition and refinement phase

Like other editors, Ontology Editor in Hozo provides users with a graphical interface through which they can browse and modify ontologies by simple mouse operations. Users do not have to worry about so-called coding to develop an ontology. The internal representation of the ontology editor, which is hidden from users, is XML and it generates DAML+OIL code to export the ontology and instance. It treats "role concept" and "relation" on the basis of fundamental consideration discussed in [7]. This interface consists of the following four parts(Fig. 6):

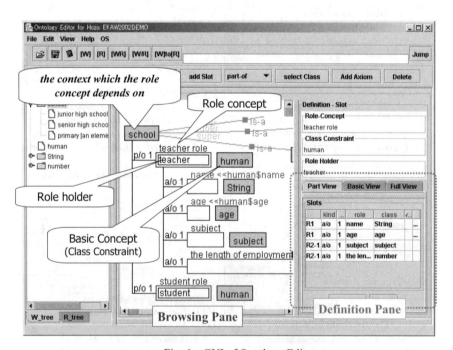

Fig. 6   GUI of Ontology Editor

1. ***Is-a* hierarchy browser** displays the ontology in a hierarchical structure according to only *is-a* relation between concepts.

2. **Edit panel** is composed of a *browsing panel* and a *definition panel*. The former displays the concept graphically, and the latter allows users to define the selected concept in the *is-a* hierarchy browser.
3. **Menu bar** is used for selecting tools
4. **Tool bar** is used for selecting commands

Collaborative development of an ontology is supported in the Ontology Editor. At the primitive level, the ontology server allows users to read and copy all the ontologies and instances, but do not allow modification of them by users other than the original developer of them. Thus, unlike OntoEdit, Hozo does not allow multiple users to edit the same concept. Instead, Ontology Editor allows users to divide an ontology into several components and manages the dependency between them to enable the concurrent development of an ontology. The dependency between the component ontologies are three fold: super-sub relation(*is-a* relation), referred-to relation(class constraint) and task-domain relation. In the current implementation, the first two are taken into account. The system observes every change in each component and notifies it to the appropriate users who are editing the ontology which might be influenced by the change. The notification is done based on the 16 patterns of influence propagation analyzed beforehand. The notified users can select a countermeasure among the three alternatives: (1)to adapt his/her ontology to the change, (2)not to adapt to the change but stay compliant with the last version of the changed ontology and (3)neglect the change by copying the last version into his/her ontology. The timing of the notification is selected by the users among the two: when the editing task has been initiated and he/she requested. Fig. 7 shows a snapshot of the collaboration window.

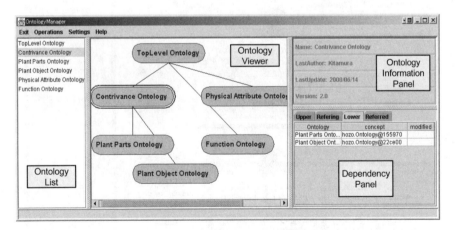

Fig. 7    Collaboration support window

### 14.4.3   Ontology use phase

Functionality and GUI of Hozo's instance editor is the same as the one for ontology. The consistency of all the instances with the ontology is automatically guaranteed, since a user is given valid classes and their slot value restrictions by the editor when he/she creates an instance. Hozo has an experience in modeling of a real-scale Oil-refinery plant with about 2000 instances including even pipes and their topological configuration which is consistent with the Oil-refinery plant ontology developed with domain experts[10]. The model as well as the ontology are served by the ontology server and can answer questions on the topological structure of the plant, the name of each device, etc. Any ontology can have multiple sets of instances which are independent of one another.

The ontology server stores ontologies and instance models in an XML format and serves them to clients through API compliant with OKBC protocol. Ontology editor is also a client of the ontology server. Inference mechanism of Hozo is not very sophisticated. Axioms are defined for each class but it works as semantic constraint checker like WebODE.

## 14.5   WebODE

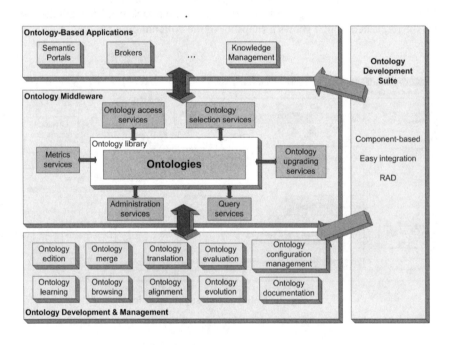

Fig. 8    Architecture of WebODE[1]

WebODE[1] is a scalable and integrated workbench for ontology engineering and is considered as a Web evolution of ODE(Ontology Development Environment[2]). It supports building an ontology at the knowledge level, and translates it into different ontology languages. WebODE is designed on the basis of a general architecture shown in Fig. 8 and to cover most of the processes appearing in the ontology lifecycle. While Protégé and OntoEdit are based on plug-in architecture, WebODE is based on a client-server architecture which provides high extensibility and usability by allowing the addition of new services and the use of existing services. Ontology is stored in an SQL database to attain high performance in the case of a large ontology.

It has export and import services from and into XML, and its translation services into and from various ontology specification languages such as RDF(S), OIL, DAML+OIL, X-CARIN, Jess and F-Logic. Like OntoEdit, WebODE's ontology editor allows the collaborative edition of ontologies. One of the most characteristic features of WebODE is that it is based on an ontology development methodology named METHONTOLOGY[2]. Although WebODE is an integrated tool sets covering most of the activities in ontology lifecycle, it has no explicit stepwise guidance function unlike Hozo.

### 14.5.1   Ontology development phase

WebODE has ontology editing service, WAB: WebODE Axiom Builder service, inference engine service, interoperability service and ontology documentation service in this phase. The ontology editor provides users with form based and graphical user interfaces, WAB provides an easy graphical interface for defining axioms. It enables users to define an axiom by using templates given by the tool with simple mouse operations. Axioms are translated into Prolog. The inference engine is based on Prolog and OKBC protocol to make it implementation independent. Interoperability services provided by WebODE are of variety. It includes ontology access API, ontology export/import in XML-family languages, translation of classes into Java beans to enable Jess system to read them and OKBC compliance.

### ODEClean[3]

Like OntoEdit, WebODE supports Ontoclean methodology to build a more convincing *is-a* hierarchy. The tool is called ODEClean whose architecture and its basic steps are shown in Fig. 9. Ontology for Ontoclean is composed of top level universal ontology developed by Guarino[5], a set of meta-properties and Ontoclean axioms which are translated into Prolog to be interpreted by WebODE inference engine. It is given to the ODEClean which works on the basis of it.

The collaborative editing of an ontology is supported by a mechanism that allows users to establish the type of access of the ontologies developed through the notion of groups of users. Synchronization mechanism is also introduced to enable several users to safely edit the same ontology. Ontologies are automatically documented in different formats such as HTML tables with Methontology's intermediate representations, HTML concept taxonomies and XML.

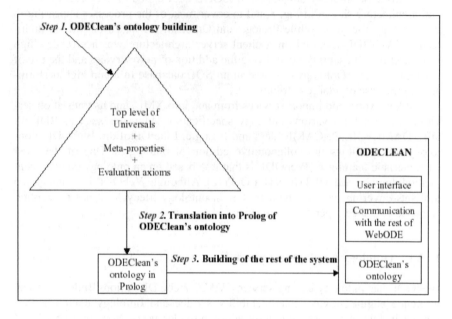

Fig. 9 Architecture of ODEClearn and its Steps[3]

### 14.5.2   Ontology use phase

To support the use process of ontology, WebODE has several functionalities. Like Hozo, it allows users to have multiple sets of instances for an ontology by introducing instance sets depending on different scenarios, and conceptual views from the same conceptual model, which allows creating and storing different parts of the ontology, highlighting and/or customizing the visualization of the ontology for each user. WebPicker is a set of wrappers to enable users to bring classification of products in the e-Commerce world into WebODE ontology. ODEMerge is a module for merging ontologies with the help of correspondence information given by the user. Methontology and ODE have been used for building many ontologies including chemical ontology[2].

## 14.6    Protégé-2000

Protégé-2000[11] whose architecture is shown in Fig. 10 is strong in the use phase of ontology: Use for knowledge acquisition, merging and alignment of existing ontologies, and plug-in new functional modules to augment its usability. It has been used for many years for knowledge acquisition of domain knowledge and for domain ontology building in recent years. Its main features include:

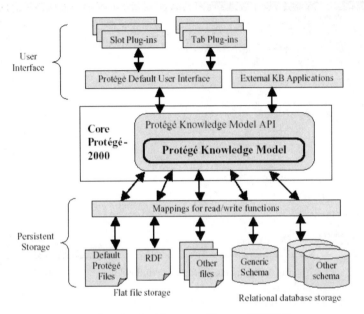

Fig. 10    Architecture of Protege2000[11]

(1)  Extensible knowledge model to enable users to redefine the representational primitives.
(2)  A customizable output file format to adapt any formal language
(3)  A customizable user interface
(4)  Powerful plug-in architecture to enable integration with other applications

These features make Protégé-2000 a meta-tool for domain model building, since a user can easily adapt it to his/her own instance acquisition tool together with the customized interface. It is highly extensible thanks to its very sophisticated plugin architecture. Unlike the other three, Protégé-2000 assumes local installation rather than use through internet using client/server architecture. Its knowledge model is based on frame similar to other environments. Especially, the fact that Protégé-2000 generates its output in many ontology languages and its powerful customizability make it easy for users to change it to an editor of a specific language. Fig. 11 shows a snapshot of the definition of a class of RDFS which is defined as a subclass of standard class of Protégé. This "meta-tuning" can be easily done thanks to Protégé's declarative definition of all the meta-classes which play a role of a template of a class.

Protégé has a semi-automatic tool for ontology merging and alignment named PROMPT[12]. It performs some tasks automatically and guides the user in performing other tasks. PROMPT also detects possible inconsistencies in the ontology, which result from the user's actions, and suggests ways to remedy them(Fig. 12).

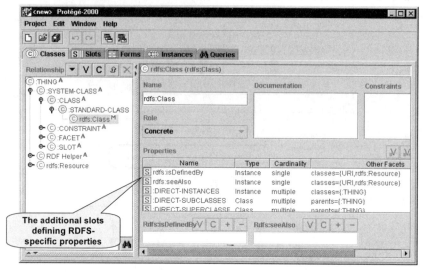

Fig.11 Metaclass definition window[11]

## 14.7    Other environments

Let us briefly discuss other environments. KAON: Karlsruhe Ontology and Semantic Web framework is a sophisticated plug-in framework with API and provides services for ontology and metadata management for E-Services[17]. Its main focus is put on the enterprise application in the semantic web age. WebOnto[18] is a support tool for ontology

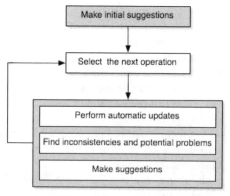

Fig. 12 Control flow of PROMPT[12]

browsing, creation and editing. When used with Tadzebao[18], a support system on discussions on ontologies, its utility is maximized because they collectively realize a collaborative development of an ontology. OilEd[19] is also an ontology editor mainly for showing how reasoning functionality is used to check the consistency of an ontology.

## 14.8    Comparison and discussion

The four environments are compared according to the factors presented above. Table 1 summarizes the comparison.

(1) **Development process management**

Philosophy of supporting ontology development is partly based on viewing an ontology as a software product. Common features of OntoEdit and WebODE include management of the well-known steps in software development process, that is, requirement specification, conceptual design, implementation and evaluation. While WebODE is mainly based on the software development process, OntoEdit on the On-To-Knowledge methodology. Protégé has no such a methodology.

The above approach is characterized as macroscopic in the sense that it manages steps of a rather large grain size in the developmental process. On the other hand, Hozo's process management is microscopic in the sense that it tries to manage finer grained activities such as what types of concepts should be focused on in a phase in the total process. It does not take care of macroscopic management of ontology development process as software development process assuming the first half of such a process has been done when a technical document has been selected. This is meaningful because Onto-Studio in Hozo supports development of task and domain ontologies from a technical document such as an operation manual of a machine and hence, in most cases, the document itself specifies the scope and goal of ontology.

The Common feature of OntoEdit and Hozo includes management of dependencies between intermediate data to enable users to retrospect the development history. This function is crucial in the case of large ontology development, since it often happens that developers need to trace back to the original data on which a resulting conceptualization, organization, or attribution depends. What OntoEdit does is to manage the dependency between competency questions and ontology. Because competency questions explicitly represent the requirement to the ontology, it can correctly navigate users back to the origin of each concept in the ontology. Especially, data-dependency management in Hozo is thorough. It allows users to trace back a long chain of dependencies between many kinds of intermediate decisions from the final ontology to the words in a sentence in the original source document following the derivation dependency chain. Onto-Studio manages four kinds of dependencies as described above.

The other two environments have no such function.

(2) **Collaboration**

Collaboration occurs in two different ways: (1)Multiple persons are involved in building a module of ontology and (2)Collaboration in building multiple modules of ontologies assuming the merge of all the modules into one ontology later on. In the case of (1), because multiple persons might modify the same class at the same time, transaction control is one of the main issues in supporting collaboration. OntoEdit and WebODE take this approach. On the other hand, Hozo takes (2) in which the system only has to take care of the dependencies between the partial ontologies because each of the modules is taken care of by one person. Transaction control is not an issue in the case of (2). When building a large ontology, (2) is very useful because it allows users the concurrent development of an ontology. To make the latter approach feasible, however, the system does need to provide developers with relevant information of changes done in other ontologies developed by others which might influence on the ontology they are developing. Hozo is designed to cope with all the possible situations developers encounter by analyzing possible patterns of influences propagated to each partial ontology in a different module according to the type of the change. Both approaches look different but they are complementary. The former can be incorporated in the latter. Protégé-2000 has no function of supporting collaboration.

(3) **Theory-awareness**

Ontology building is not easy. This is partly because a good guideline is not available which people badly need when articulating the target world and organizing a taxonomic hierarchy of concepts. An ontology engineering environment has to be helpful also in this respect. WebODE and OntoEdit support Guarino's Ontoclean method[5]. Guarino and his group have been investigating basic theories for ontology for several years and have come up with a sophisticated methodology which identifies inappropriate organization of *is-a* hierarchy of concepts. Developers who develop an ontology based on their intuition tend to misuse of *is-a* relation and to use it in more situations than are valid, which Guarino called "*is-a* overloading". Ontoclean is based on the idea of meta-property which contributes to proper categorization of concepts at the meta-level and hence to appropriate organization of *is-a* hierarchy.

OntoEdit and WebODE way of ontology cleaning can be said that post-processing way. On the contrary, Hozo tries to incorporate the fruits of ontological theories during the development process. One of the major causes of producing an inappropriate *is-a* hierarchy from Guarino's theory is lack of the concept of *Role* such as teacher, mother, food, etc. which has different characteristics from so-called basic concepts like *human, tree, fish, etc.* Ontology editor in Hozo incorporates a way of representing the concept of *Role* and Onto-Studio guides developers to identify role concepts correctly and not to confuse them with basic concepts.

Use of multiple inheritance is another source of producing inappropriate *is-a* hierarchy. It is harmful especially when a model instantiated by the ontology is seriously used. According to the proper definition of *is-a* link, it should propagate downward essential property of the thing to represent its identity which is necessarily unique. This apparently forbids any concept to have multiple inheritance paths. Ontology editor in Hozo does not allow multiple inheritance. Hozo thus realizes ontology theory- compliance during the development process. Protégé- 2000 is not ontology theory aware in this sense.

(4) **Architecture**

While WebODE and Hozo employ standardized API to the main ontology base, OntoEdit and Protégé a plug-in architecture. Both enable a module can easily added or deleted to make the environment extensible. WebODE, OntoEdit and Hozo are web-based, while Protégé is not. All the four are based on frame-like data model and have sophisticated GUI to make users free from coding using a complicated language.

(5) **Interoperability**

OntoEdit, WebODE and Protégé have import and export functionalities from and to many of the XML-family ontology languages. Hozo only can export its ontology and model in XML and DAML+ OIL.

(6) **Ontology/Model(instance) server**

Hozo has an ontology/model server which allows agents to access the ontologies and instance models through internet.

Table 1 Comparison of the four environments

| | Development process | | | | | Use of ontology/instance | | | | Software level | | |
|---|---|---|---|---|---|---|---|---|---|---|---|---|
| | Methodological support | Step-wise guidance | Collaboration support | Dependency management for editing an ontology | Ontology theory awareness | Compliance to the standard | Ontology/model server | Interoperability | Inference service | Friendly GUI | Architecture | Extensibility |
| **OntoEdit** | Yes | No | Partly. It has a sophisticated lock mechanism | Yes. | Yes. It supports Ontoclean. | High | High | High | OntoBroker | Yes | Client/server | Plugin |
| **Hozo** | Yes | Yes | Yes. Influence of each change to others are managed and suggestions for modification are provided. | Yes. Dependencies between steps down to the original document is managed. | Yes. It can deal with the role concept. Multiple inheritance is not allowed | Middle | High | Middle | Own language for constraint checking | Yes | Client/server | API |
| **WebODE** | Yes | No | Partly. Access management for each user group. | No | Yes. It supports Ontoclean. | High | Middle | High | Prolog/Jess | Yes | Client/server | API/Plugin |
| **Protégé** | No | No | No. Local installation is assumed. | No | Implicit | High | Middle | High | PAL/Jess/FaCT/F-Logic | Yes | Standalone | Plugin |

OntoEdit and Protégé have an ontology server.
(7) **Instance definition**
     Hozo and WebODE can generate multiple instance models from an ontology.
(8) **Inference**
     All the four have inference mechanisms.

## 14.9    Concluding remarks

Ontology engineering environments are still in its early phase of development. Although some are powerful as a software tool, but many are passive in the sense that few guidance or suggestion is made by the environment. Theory-awareness should be enriched further to make the environment more sophisticated. Especially, more precise guidelines for appropriate class and relationship identification are needed. Collaboration support becomes more and more important as ontology building requirements increases. Ontology alignment is also crucial for reusing the existing ontologies and for facilitating their interoperability. Combination of the strong functions of each environment of the four would realize a novel and better environment, which suggests that we are heading right directions to go.

## Literature

1.  Corcho, O., M. Fernandez-Lopez, A.Gomez-Perez and O. Vicente, WebODE: An Integrated Workbench for Ontology Representation, Reasoning and Exchange, Prof. of EKAW2002, Springer LNAI 2473 (2002) 138-153.
2.  Fernandez-Lopez, M., A.Gomez-Perez and J. Pazos Sierra, Building a Chemical Ontology Using Methontology and the Ontology Design Environment, IEEE Intelligent Systems, 14(1) (1999) 37-46.
3.  Fernandez-Lopez, M. and A.Gomez-Perez, The integration of OntoClearn in WebODE, Proceedings of the 1st Workshop on Evaluation of Ontology-based Tools (EON2002) , held at the 13th International Conference on Knowledge Engineering and Knowledge Management EKAW 2002 (2002) 38-52.
4.  Gruninger, R. and M. Fox, The design and evaluation of ontologies for enterprise engineering, Proc. of Comparison of implemented ontology, ECAI'94 Workshop, W13, pp.105-128, 1994
5.  Guarino, N. and C. Welty, Evaluating ontological decisions with OntoClean, Communications of the ACM, 2(45) (2002) 61-65.
6.  Kifer, M. G. Lausen and J.Wu, Logical foundations of object-oriented and framw-based languages, Journal of the ACM, 42 (1995) 741-843.
7.  Kouji Kozaki, Yoshinobu Kitamura, Mitsuru Ikeda, and Riichiro Mizoguchi, Development of an Environment for Building Ontologies Which Is Based on a Fundamental Consideration of "Relationship" and "Role", Proc. of the Sixth Pacific Knowledge Acquisition Workshop (PKAW2000) (2000) 205-221.
8.  Kouji Kozaki, Yoshinobu Kitamura, Mitsuru Ikeda, and Riichiro Mizoguchi, Hozo: An Environment for Building/Using Ontologies Based on a Fundamental Considera-

tion of "Role" and "Relationship" Proc. of the 13th International Conference Knowledge Engineering and Knowledge Management (EKAW2002) (2002) 213-218.

9.  Mizoguchi, R., M. Ikeda, K. Seta and J. Vanwelkenhuysen, Ontology for Modeling the World from Problem Solving Perspectives, Proc. of IJCAI-95 Workshop on Basic OntologicalIssues in Knowledge Sharing (1995) 1-12.

10. Mizoguchi, R. K. Kozaki, T. Sano and Y. Kitamura, Construction and Deployment of a Plant Ontology, Proc. of the 12th International Conference Knowledge Engineering and Knowledge Management (EKAW2000) (2000) 113-128.

11. Musen, M. A., R. W. Fergerson, W. E. Grosso, M. Crubezy, H. Eriksson, N. F. Noy and S. W. Tu, The Evolution of Protégé: An Environment for Knowledge-Based Systems Development, *International Journal of Human-Computer Interaction*(in press)

12. Noy, N. F. and M. A. Musen, PROMPT: Algorithm and Tool for Automated Ontology Merging and Alignment, *Proceedings of the Seventeenth National Conference on Artificial Intelligence (AAAI-2000.*

13. Schreiber, G. et al., Knowledge Engineering and Management: The Common KADS Methodology, MIT Press, Cambridge, Mass. (1999).

14. Staab, S. H. –P. Schunurr, R. Studer and Y. Sure, Knowledge processes and ontologies, IEEE Intelligent Systems, Special Issue on Knowledge Management, 16(1), (2001) 26-34.

15. Sure, Y., S. Staab, J. Angele. OntoEdit: Guiding Ontology Development by Methodology and Inferencing. In: R. Meersman, Z. Tari et al. (eds.). Proceedings of the Confederated International Conferences CoopIS, DOA and ODBASE (2002) Springer, LNCS 2519, 1205-1222.

16. Sure, Y., S. Staab, M. Erdmann, J. Angele, R. Studer and D. Wenke, OntoEdit: Collaborative ontology development for the semantic web, Proc. of ISWC2002, (2002) 221-235.

17. Handschuh, S. A. Maedche, l. Stojanovic and R. Volz: KAON—The KArlsruhe Ontology and Semantic Web Infrastructure, http://kaon.semanticweb.org/

18. Domingue, J.: Tadzebao and WebOnto: Discussing, browsing and editing ontologies on the web, Proc.of the 11th Knowledge Acquisition for Knowledge-Based Systems Workshop,  Banff, Canada, 1998.

19. Sean Bechhofer, Ian Horrocks, Carole Goble, Robert Stevens. OilEd: a Reason-able Ontology Editor for the Semantic Web. Proceedings of KI2001, Joint German/Austrian conference on Artificial Intelligence, September 19-21, Vienna. Springer-Verlag LNAI Vol. 2174, pp 396--408. 2001.

20. Y. Sure and R. Studer. On-To-Knowledge Methodology - Final Version. Institute AIFB, University of Karlsruhe, On-To-Knowledge Deliverable 18, 2002.

21. Decker, S., Erdmann, M., Fensel, D., & Studer, R. (1999). Ontobroker: Ontology Based Access to Distributed and Semi-Structured Information, pages 351-369. In: Meersman, R., Tari, Z., & Stevens, S. (Eds.). Database Semantics: Semantic Issues in Multimedia Systems. Kluwer Academic Publisher, 1999.

22. Gomez-Perez, A., Angele, J., Fernandez-Lopez, M., Christophides, V., Stutt, A., Sure, Y., et al. (2002). A survey on ontology tools. OntoWeb deliverable 1.3, Universidad Politecnia de Madrid.

23. Duineveld, A., Weiden, M, Kenepa, B., Benjamis, R. WonderTools? A comparative study of ontological engineering tools. Proceedings of KAW99. Banff. 1999.

# Part III

## Ontology Infrastructure

# 15

# An Extensible Ontology Software Environment

Daniel Oberle[1], Raphael Volz[1,2], Steffen Staab[1], and Boris Motik[2]

[1] University of Karlsruhe, Institute AIFB
   D-76128 Karlsruhe, Germany
   email: {lastname}@aifb.uni-karlsruhe.de
[2] FZI - Research Center for Information Technologies
   D-76131 Karlsruhe, Germany
   email: {lastname}@fzi.de

**Summary.** The growing use of ontologies in applications creates the need for an infrastructure that allows developers to more easily combine different software modules like ontology stores, editors, or inference engines towards comprehensive ontology-based solutions. We call such an infrastructure Ontology Software Environment. The article discusses requirements and design issues of such an Ontology Software Environment. In particular, we present this discussion in light of the ontology and (meta)data standards that exist in the Semantic Web and present our corresponding implementation, the KAON SERVER.

## 15.1 Introduction

Ontologies are increasingly being applied in complex applications, e.g. for Knowledge Management, E-Commerce, eLearning, or information integration. In such systems ontologies serve various needs, like storage or exchange of data corresponding to an ontology, ontology-based reasoning or ontology-based navigation. Building a complex ontology-based system, one may not rely on a single software module to deliver all these different services. The developer of such a system would rather want to easily combine different — preferably existing — software modules. So far, however, such integration of ontology-based modules had to be done ad-hoc, generating a one-off endeavour, with little possibilities for re-use and future extensibility of individual modules or the overall system.

This paper is about an infrastructure that facilitates plug'n'play engineering of ontology-based modules and, thus, the development and maintenance of comprehensive ontology-based systems, an infrastructure which we call an *Ontology Software Environment*. The Ontology Software Environment facilitates re-use of existing ontology stores, editors, and inference engines. It combines means to coordinate the information flow between such modules, to define dependencies, to broadcast events between different modules and to translate between ontology-based data formats.

Communication between modules requires ontology languages and formats. The Ontology Software Environment presented in this paper supports languages defined in the Semantic Web because they are currently becoming standards specified by the World Wide Web Consortium (W3C) and thus will be of importance in the future. We introduce the term of an *Application Server for the Semantic Web (ASSW)*, which is a particular type of Ontology Software Environment, especially designed for supporting the development of Semantic Web applications.

The article is structured as follows: First, we provide a brief overview about the Semantic Web and its languages in section 15.2 and motivate the need for an Application Server for the Semantic Web by a scenario in section 15.3. We derive requirements for such a server in section 15.4. Sections 15.5 and 15.6 describe the design decisions that immediately answer to important requirements, namely extensibility and discovery. The conceptual architecture is then provided in section 15.7. Section 15.8 presents the KAON SERVER, a particular Application Server for the Semantic Web which has been implemented. Related work and conclusions are given in sections 15.9 and 15.10, respectively.

## 15.2 The Semantic Web

In this section we want to introduce the reader to the architecture and languages of the Semantic Web that we use in our Application Server. The Semantic Web augments the current WWW by adding machine understandable content to web resources. Such added contents are called metadata whose semantics can be specified by making use of ontologies. Ontologies play a key-role in the Semantic Web as they provide consensual and formal conceptualizations of domains, enabling knowledge sharing and reuse.

The left hand side of figure 15.1 shows the static part of the Semantic Web[3], i.e. its language layers. Unicode, the URI and namespaces (NS) syntax and XML are used as a basis. XML's role is limited to that of a syntax carrier for data exchange. XML Schema defines simple data types like string, date or integer.

The Resource Description Framework (RDF) may be used to make simple assertions about web resources or any other entity that can be named. A simple assertion is a statement that an entity has a property with a particular value, for example, that this article has a title property with value "An extensible ontology software environment". RDF Schema extends RDF by class and property hierarchies that enable the creation of simple ontologies.

The Ontology layer features OWL (Web Ontology Language[4]) which is a family of richer ontology languages that augment RDF Schema. OWL Lite is the simplest of these. It is a limited version of OWL Full that enables simple and efficient implementation. OWL DL is a richer subset of OWL Full for which reasoning is known to be decidable so complete reasoners may be constructed, though they will be less efficient than an OWL Lite reasoner. OWL Full is the full ontology language which is undecidable.

---

[3] Semantic Web - XML 2000, Tim Berners-Lee,
   http://www.w3.org/2000/Talks/1206-xml2k-tbl/Overview.html
[4] W3C Working Draft, http://www.w3.org/TR/owl-ref

The Logic layer will provide an interoperable language for describing the sets of deductions one can make from a collection of data – how, given a ontology-based information base, one can derive new information from existing data[5].

The Proof language will provide a way of describing the steps taken to reach a conclusion from the facts. These proofs can then be passed around and verified, providing short cuts to new facts in the system without having each node conduct the deductions themselves.

The Semantic Web's vision is that once all these layers are in place, we will have a system in which we can place trust that the data we are seeing, the deductions we are making, and the claims we are receiving have some value. The goal is to make a user's life easier by the aggregation and creation of new, trusted information over the Web[6]. The standardization process has currently reached the Ontology layer, i.e. Logic, Proof and Trust layers aren't specified yet.

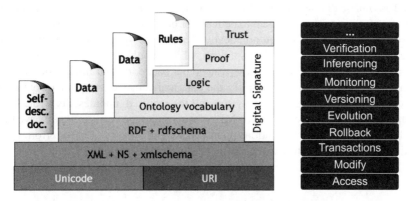

**Fig. 15.1.** Static and dynamic aspects of the Semantic Web layer cake

The right hand side of figure 15.1 depicts the Semantic Web's dynamic aspects that apply to data across all layers. Often, the dynamic aspects are neglected by the Semantic Web community, however, from our point of view, they are an inevitable part for putting the Semantic Web into practice. It is obvious that there have to be means for access and modification of Semantic Web data. According to the the well-known ACID (atomicity, consistency, independence, durability) of Database Management System (DBMS), transactions and rollbacks of Semantic Web data operations should also be possible. Evolution and versioning of ontologies are an important aspect, because ontologies usually are subject to change [23]. Like in all distributed environments, monitoring of data operations becomes necessary for security

---

[5] A better description of this layer would be "Rule layer", as the Ontology layer already features a logic calculus with reasoning capabilities. However, we want to conform to the official naming here.

[6] Building the Semantic Web, Edd Dumbill,
http://www.xml.com/pub/a/2001/03/07/buildingsw.html

reasons. Finally, reasoning engines are to be applied for the deduction of additional facts[7] as well as for semantic validation.

## 15.3 A Motivating Scenario

This section motivates the needs for the cooperation and integration of different software modules by a scenario depicted in figure 15.2. The reader may note that some real-world problems have been abstracted away for the sake of simplicity.

Assume a simple genealogy application. Apparently, the domain description, viz. the ontology, will include concepts like Person and make a distinction between Male and Female. There are several relations between Persons, e.g. hasParent or hasSister. The domain description can be easily expressed with OWL DL, e.g. Person subsumes both Male and Female concepts. However, many important facts that could be inferred automatically have to be added explicitly. E.g., information about the parents' brothers of a person are sufficient to deduce her or his uncles. A rule-based system is needed to capture such facts automatically. Persons will have properties that require structured data types, such as dates of birth, which should be syntactically validated. Such an ontology could serve as the conceptual backbone and information base of a genealogy portal. It would simplify the data maintenance and offer machine understandability. To implement the system, all the required modules, i.e. a rule-based inference engine, a DL reasoner, a XML Schema data type verifier, would have to be combined by the client applications themselves. While this is a doable effort, possibilities for re-use and future extensibility hardly exist.

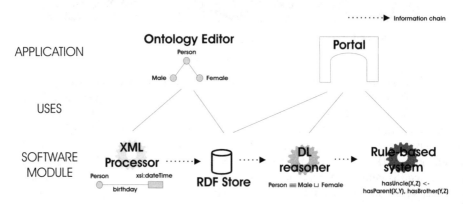

**Fig. 15.2.** Software modules in the genealogy applications

The application demands from an Application Server for the Semantic Web is to hook up to all the software modules and to offer management of data flow between them. This also involves propagation of updates and rollback behavior, if any

---

[7] E.g., if "cooperatesWith" is defined as a symmetric property in OWL DL between persons A and B, a reasoner can deduce that B cooperatesWith A, too.

module in the information chain breaks. In the following section, we will discuss requirements for an Application Server for the Semantic Web in more detail. The requirements are derived from the scenario as well as from the static and dynamic parts of the Semantic Web.

## 15.4 Requirements

Basically, the we can establish four groups of requirements. First, an Application Server for the Semantic Web should respond to the static aspects of the Semantic Web layer cake. In particular, it has to be aware of all Semantic Web languages. The need to translate between the different languages also belongs to the static aspects. Such a translation increases interoperability between existing software modules that mostly focus on one language only. Second, the dynamic aspects result in another group of requirements, viz. finding, accessing and storing of data, consistency, concurrency, durability and reasoning. Third, clients may want to connect remotely to the Application Server for the Semantic Web and must be properly authorized. Hence, a distributed system like the Semantic Web needs connectivity and security. Finally, the system is expected to facilitate a extensible and reconfigurable infrastructure. The last group of requirements therefore deals with flexible handling of modules. In the following paragraphs we will investigate on the requirements.

- **Requirements stemming from the Semantic Web's static part**
  - *Language support* One requirement is the support of all the Semantic Web's ontology and metadata standards. The Application Server for the Semantic Web has to be aware of RDF, RDFS, OWL as well as future languages that will be used to specify the logic, proof and trust layers.
  - *Semantic Interoperation* We use the term Semantic Interoperation in the sense of translating between different ontology languages with different semantics. At the moment, several ontology languages populate the Semantic Web. Besides proprietary ones, we have already mentioned RDFS, OWL Lite, OWL DL and OWL Full before. Usually, ontology editors and stores focus on one particular language and are not able to work with others. Hence, an Application Server for the Semantic Web should allow to translate between different languages and semantics.
  - *Ontology Mapping* In contrast to Semantic Interoperation, Ontology Mapping translates between different ontologies of the same language. Mapping may become necessary as web communities usually have their own ontology and could use Ontology Mapping to facilitate data exchange.
- **Requirements stemming from the Semantic Web's dynamic part**
  - *Finding, accessing and storing of ontologies* Semantic Web applications like editors or portals have to access and finally store ontological data. In addition, the development of domain ontologies often requires integration of other ontologies as starting point. Examples are Wordnet or top-level ontologies for the Semantic Web [4]. Those could be stored and offered by an Application Server for the Semantic Web to editors.

- *Consistency* Consistency of information is a requirement in any application. Each update of a consistent ontology must result in an ontology that is also consistent. In order to achieve that goal, precise rules must be defined for ontology evolution [23]. Modules updating ontologies must implement and adhere to these rules. Also, all updates to the ontology must be done within transactions assuring the properties of atomicity, consistency, isolation and durability (ACID).
- *Concurrency* It must be possible to concurrently access and modify Semantic Web data. This may be achieved using transactional processing, where objects can be modified at most by one transaction at the time.
- *Durability* Like consistency, durability is a requirement that holds in any data-intense application area. It may be accomplished by reusing existing database technology.
- *Reasoning* Reasoning engines are core components of semantics-based applications and can be used for several tasks like semantic validation and deduction. An Application Server for the Semantic Web should provide access to such engines, which can deliver the reasoning services required.
- **Connectivity and Security**
  - *Connectivity* An Application Server for the Semantic Web should enable loose coupling, allowing access through standard web protocols, as well as close coupling by embedding it into other applications. A client may want to use the system locally or connect to it remotely via web services, for instance.
  - *Security* Guaranteeing information security means protecting information against unauthorized disclosure, transfer, modification, or destruction, whether accidental or intentional. To realize it, any operation should only be accessible by properly authorized clients. Proper identity must be reliably established by employing authentication techniques. Confidential data must be encrypted for network communication and persistent storage. Finally, means for monitoring (logging) of confidential operations should be present.
- **Flexible handling of modules**
  - *Extensibility* The need for extensibility applies to most software systems. Principles of software engineering avoid system changes when additional functionality is needed in the future. Hence, extensibility is also desirable for an Application Server for the Semantic Web. In addition, such a server has to deal with the multitude of layers and data models in the Semantic Web that lead to a multitude of software modules, e.g. XML parsers or validators that support the XML Schema datatypes, RDF stores, tools that map relational databases to RDFS ontologies, ontology stores and OWL reasoners. Therefore, extensibility regarding new data APIs and corresponding software modules is an important requirement for such a system.
  - *Discovery of software modules* For a client, there should be the possibility to state precisely what it wants to work with, e.g. an RDF store that holds a certain RDF model and allows for transactions. Hence, means for intelligent discovery of software modules are required. Based on a semantic description

of the search target, the system should be able to discover what a client is
looking for.

–  *Dependencies* The system should allow to express dependencies between different software modules. For instance, that could be the setting up of event
listeners between modules. Another example would be the management of a
dependency like "module A is needed for module B".

In the following sections 15.5 to 15.7, we develop an architecture that is a result
from the requirements put forward in this section. After that we present the implementation details of our Application Server for the Semantic Web called KAON
SERVER.

## 15.5  Component Management

Due to the requirement for extensibility, we decided to use the Microkernel design
pattern. The pattern applies to software systems that must be able to adapt to changing system requirements. It separates a minimal functional core from extended functionality and application-specific parts. The Microkernel also serves as a socket for
plugging in these extensions and coordinating their collaboration [14].

In our setting, the Microkernel's minimal functionality must take the form of
simple management operations, i.e. starting, initializing, monitoring, combining and
stopping of software modules plus dispatching of messages between them. This approach requires software modules to be uniform so that they can be treated equally
by the kernel. Hence, in order to use the Microkernel, software modules that shall be
managed have to be brought into a certain form. We call this process *making existing
software deployable*, i.e. bringing existing software into the particular infrastructure
of the Application Server for the Semantic Web, that means wrapping it so that it
can be plugged into the Microkernel. Thus, a software module becomes a *deployed
component*. The word *deployment* stems service management and service oriented
architectures where it is a terminus technicus. We adopt this meaning and apply it in
our setting. We refine it as the process of registering, possibly initializing and starting
a component to the Microkernel.

Apart from the cost of making existing software deployable, the only drawback
of this approach is that performance will suffer slightly in comparison to stand alone
use, as a request has to pass through the kernel first (and possibly the network). A
client that wants to make use of a deployed component's functionality talks to the
Microkernel, which in turn dispatches requests.

But besides the drawbacks mentioned above, the Microkernel and component
approach delivers several benefits. By making existing functionality, like RDF stores,
inference engines etc., deployable, one is able to treat everything the same. As a
result, we are able to deploy and undeploy components ad hoc, reconfigure, monitor
and possibly distribute them dynamically. Proxy components can be developed for
software that cannot be made deployable for whatever reasons. Throughout the paper,
we will show further advantages, among them

•  enabling a client to discover the component it is in need of (cf. section 15.6)

- definition of dependencies between components (cf. section 15.7)
- easy realization of security, auditing, trust etc. as interceptors (further discussed in section 15.7)
- incorporation of quality criteria as attributes of a component in registry (cf. section 15.10)

Thus, we responded to the requirement of extensibility. In the following, we discuss how the discovery of software modules can be achieved.

## 15.6 Description of Components

This section responds to the requirement "discovery of software modules". As pointed out in the section 15.5, all components are equal as seen from the kernel's perspective. In order to allow a client to discover the components it is in need of, we have to make their differences explicit. Thus, there is a need of a registry that stores descriptions of all deployed components. In this section we show how a description of a component may look like. We start with the definition of a component and then specialize. The definitions result in a taxonomy that is primarily used to facilitate component discovery for the application developer.

**Component** Software module which is deployed to the kernel.

**System Component** Component providing functionality for the Application Server for the Semantic Web, e.g. a connector.

**Functional Component** Component that is of interest to the client and can be looked up. Ontology-related software modules become functional components by making them deployable, e.g. RDF stores.

**External Module** An external module cannot be deployed directly as it may be programmed in a different language, live on a different computing platform, uses interfaces unknown, etc. It equals a functional component from a client perspective. This is achieved by having a proxy component deployed relaying communication to the external module.

**Proxy Component** Special type of component that manages the communication to an external module. Examples are proxy components for inference engines, like FaCT [15].

Each component can have *attributes* like the name of the interface it implements, connection parameters or other low-level properties. Besides, we want to be able to express *associations* between components. Associations can be dependencies between components, e.g. an ontology store component can rely on an RDF store for actual storage, or event listeners etc. Associations will later be put in action by the association management component (cf. section 15.7).

We formalize taxonomy, attributes and associations in a management ontology like outlined in figure 15.3 and table 1[8]. The ontology formally defines which attributes a certain component may have and places components into a taxonomy. In

---

[8] The table shows some exemplary properties of the concept "Component". We use the term property as generalization for attribute and association. An attribute's range always is a string, whereas associations relate two concepts.

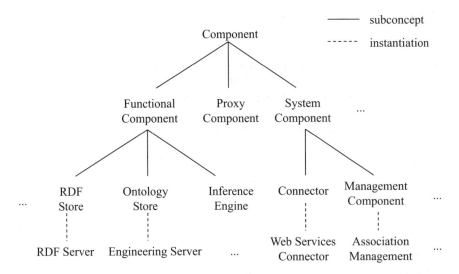

**Fig. 15.3.** Taxonomy of components

the end, actual functional components like KAON's RDF Server and the Engineering Server (cf. subsection 15.8.4) would be instantiations of RDFStore and OntologyStore, respectively.

**Table 15.1.** Attributes and associations of component

| Concept | Property | Range |
|---|---|---|
| Component | Name | String |
| | Interface | String |
| | ... | ... |
| | receivingEventsFrom | Component |
| | sendingEventsTo | Component |
| | dependsOn | Component |
| | ... | ... |

Our approach allows us to realize the registry itself as a component. As explained in section 15.5, the Microkernel manages any functionality as long as it conforms to the contract. The registry is not of direct interest to the client - it is only used to facilitate the discovery of functional and proxy components. Hence, we can declare it as an instance of system component.

So far we have discussed two requirements, viz. extensibility and discovery of software components, which led to fundamental design decisions. The next section focuses on the conceptual architecture.

## 15.7  Conceptual Architecture

When a client connects to the Application Server for the Semantic Web it discovers the functional components it is in need of. That could be an RDF store or an inference engine etc. The system tries to find a deployed functional component in the registry fulfilling the stated requirements and returns a reference.

Surrogates for the functional component on the client side can handle the communication over the network. The counterpart to the surrogate on the server side is a connector component. It maps requests to the kernel's methods. All requests finally pass the management kernel which dispatches them to the actual functional component. While dispatching, the properness of a request can be checked by interceptors that may deal with authentication, authorization or auditing. An interceptor is a software entity that looks at a request and modifies it before the request is sent the component. Finally, the response passes the kernel again and finds its way to the client through the connector.

After this brief procedural overview, the following paragraphs will explain the architecture depicted in figure 15.4. Note that in principle, there will be only three types of software entities: components, interceptors and the kernel. Components are specialized into functional, system and proxy components to facilitate the discovery for the application developer.

### Connectors

Connectors are system components. They send and receive requests and responses over the network by using some protocol. Apart from the option to connect locally, further connectors are possible for remote connection: e.g. ones that offer access per Java Remote Method Invocation (RMI), or ones that offer access per Web Service. Counterparts to a connector on the client side are surrogates for functional components that relieve the application developer of the communication details similar to stubs in CORBA.

### Management Core

The Management Core comprises the Microkernel (also called management kernel or simply kernel in the following) as well as several system components. The Management Core is required to deal with the discovery, allocation and loading of components. The registry is a system component and hierarchically orders descriptions of the components. It thus facilitates the discovery of a functional component for a client (cf. section 15.6). Another system component called association management allows to express and manage relations between components. E.g., event listeners can be put in charge so that a component A is notified when B issues an event or a component may only be undeployed if others don't rely on it. The Management Core is extensible such that additional functionality may be provided by deploying new system components.

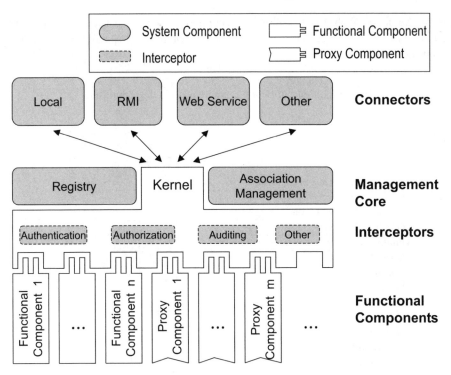

**Fig. 15.4.** Conceptual Architecture

### Interceptors

Interceptors are software entities that look at a request and modify it before the request is sent to the component. Security is realized by interceptors which guarantee that operations offered by functional components (including data update and query operations) in the server are only available to appropriately authenticated and authorized clients. A component can be registered with a stack of interceptors in the kernel. Sharing generic functionality such as security, logging, or concurrency control requires less work than developing individual component implementations.

### Functional Components

RDF stores, ontology stores etc., are deployed to the management kernel as functional components (cf. section 15.5). In combination with the registry, the kernel can start functional components dynamically on client requests.

Table 2 shows where the requirements put forward in section 15.4 are reflected in the architecture. Note that most requirements are met by functional components. That is because the conceptual architecture presented here is generic, i.e. we could make almost any existing software deployable and use the system in any domain, not just in the Semantic Web. In the following section we discuss a particular implementation, KAON SERVER, that realizes functional components specific for Semantic Web standards.

**Table 15.2.** Reflections of the requirements in the architecture

| Requirement \ Design Element | Connectors | Kernel | Registry | Interceptors | Association Management | Functional Components |
|---|---|---|---|---|---|---|
| Language Support | | | | | | × |
| Semantic Interoperation | | | | | | × |
| Ontology Mapping | | | | | | × |
| Finding, accessing, storing of ontologies | | | × | | | × |
| Consistency | | | | | | × |
| Concurrency | | × | | | | × |
| Durability | | | | | | × |
| Reasoning | | | | | | × |
| Connectivity | × | | | | | |
| Security | | | | | × | × |
| Extensibility | | × | | | | × |
| Discovery | | | × | | | |
| Dependencies | | | | | × | |

## 15.8 Implementation

This section presents our implementation of an Application Server for the Semantic Web, called KAON SERVER. KAON SERVER offers a uniform infrastructure to host functional components, in particular those provided by the KAON project.

The KAON SERVER architecture reflects the conceptual architecture presented in the previous section. In the following, an in-depth description is given. We will start with the Management Core in 15.8.1 as it is necessary to understand Connectors in 15.8.2, Interceptors in 15.8.3 and Functional Components in 15.8.5. Several of the latter are implementations of the two Data APIs defined in the KAON Tool suite which are discussed before in subsection 15.8.4.

### 15.8.1 Management Core

The Management Core of an Application Server for the Semantic Web consists of the management kernel, the registry and association management system components. We will outline all of their implementations in the subsections below.

**Kernel**

In the case of the KAON SERVER, we use the Java Management Extensions (JMX[9]) as it is an open technology and currently the state-of-the-art for component management.

Java Management Extensions represent a universal, open technology for management and monitoring. By design, it is suitable for adapting legacy systems and implementing management solutions. Basically, JMX defines interfaces of managed beans, or *MBeans* for short, which are JavaBeans[10] that represent JMX manageable resources. MBeans are hosted by an *MBeanServer* which allows their manipulation. All management operations performed on the MBeans are done through interfaces on the MBeanServer.

In our setting, the MBeanServer implements the kernel and MBeans implement the components. Speaking in terms of JMX, there is no difference between a system component and a functional component. Both are MBeans that are only distinguished by the registry.

**Registry**

We implemented the registry as MBean and re-used one of the KAON modules which have all been made deployable (cf. subsection 15.8.4). The main-memory implementation of the KAON API holds the management ontology. When a component is deployed, its description (usually stored in an XML file) is reflected by an instance of the proper concept. A client can use the KAON API's query methods to discover the component it is in need of.

**Association Management**

The management ontology allows to express associations between components. E.g., a dependency states that a given component requires the existence of another component. Therefore the server has to load all required components and be aware of the dependencies when unloading components. This essentially requires to maintain the number of clients to a component. A component can only be unloaded, if it does not have any further clients.

The JMX specification does not define any type of association management aspect for MBeans. That is the reason why we had to implement this functionality separately as another MBean. Apart from dependencies, it is able to register and manage event listeners between MBeans A and B, so that B is notified whenever A issues an event.

---

[9] http://java.sun.com/products/JavaManagement/

[10] http://java.sun.com/products/javabeans/

### 15.8.2 Connectors

The KAON SERVER comes with four system components, i.e. MBeans, that handle communication. First, there is an HTTP Adaptor from Sun that exposes all of the kernel's methods to a Web frontend. Additionally, we have developed Web Service (using the Simple Object Access Protocol) and RMI (Java Remote Method Invocation) connector MBeans. Both export the kernel's methods for remote access. Finally, we have developed a local connector that embeds the KAON SERVER into the client application.

For the client side there is a surrogate object called RemoteMBeanServer that implements the MBeanServer interface. It is the counterpart to one of the three connector MBeans mentioned above. Similar to the CORBA stubs, the application uses this object to interact with the MBeanServer and is relieved of all communication details. The developer can choose which of the three options (local, RMI, Web Service) shall be used by RemoteMBeanServer. In addition, surrogate objects may be developed that relay the communication to a specific MBean.

### 15.8.3 Interceptors

As explained in section 15.7, interceptors are software entities that look at a request and modify it before the request is sent to the component.

In the kernel, each MBean can be registered with an invoker and a stack of interceptors. A request received from the client is then delegated to the invoker first before it is relayed to the MBean. The invoker object is responsible for managing the interceptors and sending the requests down the chain of interceptors towards the MBean. For example, a logging interceptor can be activated to implement auditing of operation requests. An authorization interceptor can be used to check that the requesting client has sufficient access rights for the MBean.

Apart from security, invokers and interceptors are useful to achieve other goals. E.g., when a component is being restarted, an invoker could block and queue incoming requests until the component is once again available (or the received requests time out), or redirect the incoming requests to another MBean that is able to fulfill them.

### 15.8.4 Data APIs

The functionality described so far, i.e. the Management Core, Connectors and Interceptors could be used in any domain not just the Semantic Web. In the remaining subsections we want to highlight the specialties which make the KAON SERVER suitable for ontologies that follow Semantic Web language standards and the Semantic Web, in particular.

First, the KAON Tool suite has been made deployable. Two Semantic Web Data APIs for updates and queries are defined in the KAON framework - an RDF API and an ontology data-oriented called KAON API. Their implementations result in functional components that are discussed in subsection 15.8.5. Furthermore, we are currently developing functional components that enable the semantic interoperation of Semantic Web ontologies (cf. section 15.4) as well as an Ontology Repository. Several external modules (inference engines in particular) are also deployable, as we have developed proxy components for them. All of them are discussed in the remaining subsections. Before talking about the API implementations and other functional components, the following paragraphs describe the APIs briefly.

*RDF API*

The RDF API consists of interfaces for the transactional manipulation of RDF models with the possibility of modularization, a streaming-mode RDF parser and an RDF serializer for writing RDF models. The API features object oriented representations of entities defined in [6] as interfaces. An RDF model consists of a set of statements. In turn, each statement is represented as a triple (subject, predicate, object) with the elements either being resources or literals. The corresponding interfaces feature methods for querying and updating those entities, respectively.

*Ontology API*

Our ontology data-oriented API, also known as KAON API, currently realizes the ontology language described in [21]. We have integrated means for ontology evolution and a transaction mechanism. The interface offers access to KAON ontologies and contains classes such as Concept, Property and Instance. The API decouples a client from actual ontology storage mechanisms.

### 15.8.5  Functional Components

The KAON API is implemented in different ways like depicted in figure 15.5. All of the implementations have been made deployable and are discussed subsequently in more detail. We also included descriptions of additional functional components, i.e. Ontology Repository, OntoLift, Semantic Interoperation and finally external modules.

*RDF Mainmemory Implementation*

This implementation of the RDF API is primarily useful for accessing in-memory RDF models. That means, an RDF model is loaded into memory from an XML serialization on startup. After that, statements can be added, changed and deleted, all encapsulated in a transaction if preferred. Finally, the in-memory RDF model has to be serialized again in order to make changes persistent.

*RDF Server*

The RDF Server is an implementation of the RDF API that enables persistent storage and management of RDF models. It uses a relational database whose physical structure corresponds to the RDF model. Data is represented using four tables, one represents models and the other one represents statements contained in the model. The

RDF Server uses a relational DBMS and relies on the JBoss Application Server[11] that handles the communication between client and DBMS.

*KAON API on RDF API*

As depicted in figure 15.5, implementations of the ontological KAON API may use implementations of the RDF API. E.g., the KAON API can be realized using the mainmemory implementation of the RDF API for transient access and modification of a KAON ontology.

*Engineering Server*

A separate implementation of the KAON API can be used for ontology engineering. This implementation provides efficient implementation of operations that are common during ontology engineering, such as concept adding and removal by applying transactions. A storage structure that is based on storing information on a metamodel level is applied here. A fixed set of relations is used, which corresponds to the structure of the used ontology language. Then individual concepts and properties are represented via tuples in the appropriate relation created for the respective meta-model element. This structure is well-suited for ontology engineering, where the number of instances (all represented in one table) is rather small, but the number of classes and properties dominate. Here, creation and deletion of classes and properties can be realized within transactions.

*Integration Engine*

Another implementation of the KAON API is currently under development which lifts existing databases to the ontology level. To achieve this, one must specify a set of mappings from some relational schema to the chosen ontology, according to principles described in [22]. E.g. it is possible to say that tuples of some relation make up a set of instances of some concept, and to map foreign key relationships into instance relationships.

| KAON API | | | | | |
|---|---|---|---|---|---|
| RDF API | | | Engineering Server | Integration Engine | Other Impl |
| Mainmemory Impl | RDF Server | Other Impl | | | |

**Fig. 15.5.** KAON API Implementations

---

[11] http://www.jboss.org

*Ontology Repository*

One optional component currently developed is a Ontology Repository, allowing access and reuse of ontologies that are used throughout the Semantic Web, such as WordNet for example. Within the WonderWeb project several of them have been developed [4].

*OntoLift*

Another component realized in WonderWeb is OntoLift aiming at leveraging existing schema structures as a starting point for developing ontologies for the Semantic Web. Methods have been developed for deriving ontology structures for existing information systems, such as XML-DTD, XML-Schema, relational database schemata or UML specifications of object-oriented software systems. The Lift tool semi-automatically extracts ontologies from such legacy resources.

*Semantic Interoperation*

A functional component already developed, realizes the OWL Lite language on top of a SQL-99 compliant database system [3]. In addition, several others will later allow semantic interoperation between different types of ontology languages as a response to the requirement put forward in section 15.4. We already mentioned RDFS, OWL Lite, OWL DL and OWL Full in the introduction. Besides, there are older formats, like DAML+OIL and also proprietary ones like KAON ontologies [21]. It should be possible to load KAON ontologies into other editors, like OILEd [11], for instance. Information will be lost during ontology transformation as the semantic expressiveness of the respective ontology languages differ.

*External Modules*

External modules live outside the KAON SERVER. Proxy components are deployed and relay communication. Thus, from a client perspective, an external module cannot be distinguished from an actual functional component. At the moment we are adapting several external modules: Sesame [16], Ontobroker [6] as well as a proxy component for description logic classifiers that conform to the DIG interface[12], like FaCT [15] or Racer[7].

## 15.9 Related Work

Several systems approach some ideas relevant for an Application Server for the Semantic Web. However, all of them focus on RDF(S) or on ontology languages not specific to the Semantic Web and cannot be extended very easily.

RDFSuite [10] is provided by ICS-Forth, Greece with a suite of tools for RDF management, among those is the so-call RDF Schema specific Database (RSSDB)

---

[12] Description Logic Implementation Group, http://dl.kr.org/dig/

that allows storing and querying RDF using RQL. For the implementation of persistence an object-relational DBMS is exploited. It uses a storage scheme that has been optimized for querying instances of RDFS-based ontologies. The database structure is tuned towards a particular ontology structure.

Sesame [16] is a RDF Schema-based repository and querying facility developed by Aidministrator Nederland bv as part of the European IST project On-To-Knowledge. The system provides a repository and query engine for RDF data and RDFS-based ontologies. It uses a variant of the RDF Query Language (RQL) that captures further functionality from RDFSchema specification when compared to the RDFSuite RQL language. Sesame shares its fundamental storage design with RDF-Suite.

Stanford Research Institute's OKBC (Open Knowledge Base Connectivity) is a protocol for accessing knowledges bases (KBs) stored in Knowledge Representation Systems (KRSs) [2]. The goal of OKBC is to serve as an interface to many different KRSs, for example, an object-oriented database. OKBC provides a set of operations for a generic interface to underlying KRSs. The interface layer allows an application some independence from the idiosyncrasies of specific KRS software and enables the development of generic tools (e.g., graphical browsers and editors) that operate on many KRSs.

The Ontolingua ontology development environment [1] provides a suite of ontology authoring tools and a library of modular, reusable ontologies. The tools in Ontolingua are oriented toward the authoring of ontologies by assembling and extending ontologies obtained from a library.

Developed by the Hewlett-Packard Research, UK, Jena [18] is a collection of RDF tools including a persistent storage component and a RDF query language (RDQL). For persistence, the Berkley DB embedded database or any JDBC-compliant database may be used. Jena abstracts from storage in a similar way as the KAON APIs. However, no transactional updating facilities are provided.

Research on middleware circles around so-called service oriented architectures (SOA)[13], which are similar to our architecture, since functionality is broken into components - so-called Web Services - and their localization is realized via a centralized replicating registry (UDDI)[14]. However, here all components are stand-alone processes and are not manageable by a centralized kernel. The statements for SOAs also holds for previously proposed distributed object architectures with registries such as CORBA Trading Services [12] or JINI[15].

Several of today's application servers share our design of constructing a server instance via separately manageable components, e.g. the HP Application Server[16] or JBoss[17]. Both have the Microkernel in common but follow their own architecture which is different from the one presented in our paper. JBoss wraps services

---

[13] http://archive.devx.com/xml/articles/sm100901/sidebar1.asp
[14] http://www.uddi.org/
[15] http://www.jini.org
[16] http://www.bluestone.com
[17] http://www.jboss.org

like databases, Servlet and Enterprise JavaBeans containers or Java Messaging as components. HP applies its CSF (Core Services Framework) that provides registry, logging, security, loader, configuration facilities. However, whether JBoss nor HP AS deliver ontology-based registries, association management nor are they suitable for the Semantic Web, in particular.

## 15.10  Conclusion

This article presented the requirements and design of an Application Server for the Semantic Web as well as an implementation - the KAON SERVER. It is part of the open-source Karlsruhe Ontology and Semantic Web Tool suite (KAON). From our perspective, the KAON SERVER will be an important step in putting the Semantic Web into practice. Based on our experiences with building Semantic Web applications we conclude that such a server will be a crucial cornerstone to bring together so far disjoint components.

KAON SERVER still is work in progress. We are currently developing afore-mentioned functional components like the Ontology Repository, Semantic Interoperation, OntoLift. The Web Service connector will be enhanced by semantic descriptions whose source is the registry. In the future, we envision to integrate means for information quality - a field of research that deals with the specification and computation of quality criteria. Users will then be able to query information based on criteria like "fitness for use", "meets information consumers needs", or "previous user satisfaction" [5]. We will also support aggregated quality values, which can be composed of multiple criteria.

*Acknowledgements*

The KAON project (cf. http://kaon.semanticweb.org) is a meta-project carried out at the Institute AIFB, University of Karlsruhe and the Research Center for Information Technologies (FZI), Karlsruhe. KAON consolidates the results obtained in several government-funded projects and fulfills requirements imposed by industry projects carried out at the FZI. Individual software within KAON is developed within different projects. Development for KAON SERVER is funded by the EU-FET project WonderWeb (cf. http://www.wonderweb.org).

## References

1.  Fikes, R., Farquhar, A., Rice, J., Tools for Assembling Modular Ontologies in Ontolingua., In *Proceedings of the Fourteenth National Conference on Artificial Intelligence and Ninth Innovative Applications of Artificial Intelligence Conference, AAAI 97, IAAI 97, July 27-31, 1997, Providence, Rhode Island.*, AAAI Press / The MIT Press, 1997, pp. 436-441, ISBN 0-262-51095-2

2. Chaudhri, V., Farquhar, A., Fikes, R., Karp, P., Rice, J., OKBC: A Programmatic Foundation for Knowledge Base Interoperability.,In *Proceedings of the Fifteenth National Conference on Artificial Intelligence and Tenth Innovative Applications of Artificial Intelligence Conference, AAAI 98, IAAI 98, July 26-30, 1998, Madison, Wisconsin, USA.*, AAAI Press / The MIT Press, 1998, pp. 600-607, ISBN 0-262-51098-7

3. Grosof, B., Horrocks, I., Volz, R., Decker, S., Description Logic Programs: Combining Logic Programs with Description Logic, In *Proceedings 12th International World Wide Web Conference (WWW12), Semantic Web Track, 2003, Budapest, Hungary.*

4. Oltramari, A., Gangemi, A., Guarino, N., and Masolo, C., DOLCE: a Descriptive Ontology for Linguistic and Cognitive Engineering (preliminary report), In *Proceedings 13th International Conference on Knowledge Engineering and Knowledge Management (EKAW2002), Siguenza, Spain (in press).*

5. Felix Naumann, *Quality-driven query answering for integrated information systems*, Lecture Notes in Computer Science, vol. 2261, Springer, 02 2002.

6. Decker, S., Erdmann, M., Fensel, D., Studer, R. Ontobroker: Ontology based access to distributed and semi-structured information, In *Database Semantics - Semantic Issues in Multimedia Systems, IFIP Conference Proceedings*, Kluwer, volume 138, pages 351-369, 1998

7. Haarslev, V., Moeller, R., RACER System Description., In *Proceedings of Automated Reasoning, First International Joint Conference, IJCAR (Rajeev Goré and Alexander Leitsch and Tobias Nipkow, eds.)*, vol. 2083, Lecture Notes in Computer Science, Springer, 2001, pp. 701-706.

8. O. Lassila and R. Swick. Resource Description Framework (RDF) Model and Syntax specification. Internet: http://www.w3.org/TR/REC-rdf-syntax/, 1999.

9. Dan Brickley and R. V. Guha. Resource description framework (RDF) schema specification 1.0. Internet: http://www.w3.org/TR/2000/CR-rdf-schema-20000372/, 2000.

10. S. Alexaki, V. Christophides, G. Karvounarakis, D. Plexousakis, and K. Tolle. The ics-forth rdfsuite: Managing voluminous rdf description bases. In *2nd International Workshop on the Semantic Web (SemWeb'01), in conjunction with Tenth International World Wide Web Conference (WWW10), Hongkong, May 1, 2001*, pages 1–13, 2001.

11. S. Bechhofer, I. Horrocks, C. Goble, and R. Stevens. Oiled: a reasonable ontology editor for the semantic web. In *Proc. of the Joint German Austrian Conference on AI, number 2174 in Lecture Notes In Artificial Intelligence, pages 396-408*. Springer, 2001.

12. Juergen Boldt. Corbaservices specification, 3 1997.

13. E. Bozsak, M. Ehrig, S. Handschuh, A. Hotho, A. Maedche, B. Motik, D. Oberle, C. Schmitz, S. Staab, L. Stojanovic, N. Stojanovic, R. Studer, G. Stumme, Y. Sure, J. Tane, R. Volz, and V. Zacharias. KAON - towards a large scale semantic web. In *Proceedings of EC-Web 2002*. Springer, 2002.

14. Frank Buschmann, Regine Meunier, Hans Rohnert, Peter Sommerlad, and Michael Stal. *Pattern-Oriented Software Architecture, Volume 1: A System of Patterns*, volume 1. John Wiley and Son Ltd, 1996.

15. I. Horrocks. The fact system. In *Automated Reasoning with Analytic Tableaux and Related Methods: International Conference Tableaux'98.* Springer, 1998.

16. Frank van Harmelen Jeen Broekstra, Arjohn Kampman. Sesame: A generic architecture for storing and querying rdf and rdf schema. In *Proceedings International Semantic Web Conference 2002.* Springer, 2002.

17. Michel Klein, Atanas Kiryakov, Damyan Ognyanov, and Dieter Fensel. Ontology versioning and change detection on the web. In *13th International Conference on Knowledge Engineering and Knowledge Management (EKAW02), Sigenza, Spain, October 1-4, 2002*, 2002.

18. Brian McBride. Jena: Implementing the RDF model and syntax specification. In *Proceedings of the Second International Workshop on the Semantic Web - SemWeb'2001, Hongkong, China, May 1, 2001*, 2001.
19. Sergej Melnik. RDF API. Current revision 2001-01-19.
20. Stefan Decker Michael Sintek. Triple - an RDF query, inference, and transformation language. In *Proceedings ISWC'2002*. Springer, 2002.
21. B. Motik, A. Maedche, and R. Volz. A conceptual modeling approach for building semantics-driven enterprise applications. In *Proceedings of the First International Conference on Ontologies, Databases and Application of Semantics (ODBASE-2002)*, November 2002.
22. L. Stojanovic N. Stojanovic, R. Volz. A reverse engineering approach for migrating data-intensive web sites to the semantic web. In *IIP-2002, August 25-30, 2002, Montreal, Canada (Part of the IFIP World Computer Congress WCC2002)*, 2002.
23. L. Stojanovic, N. Stojanovic, and S. Handschuh. Evolution of metadata in ontology-based knowledge management systems. In *1st German Workshop on Experience Management: Sharing Experiences about the Sharing of Experience, Berlin, March 7-8, 2002, Proceedings*, 2002.
24. L. Stojanovic, N. Stojanovic, and R. Volz. Migrating data-intensive web sites into the semantic web. In *ACM Symposium on Applied Computing SAC 2002*, 2002.
25. Y. Sure, M. Erdmann, J. Angele, S. Staab, R. Studer, and D. Wenke. Ontoedit: Collaborative ontology development for the semantic web. In *Proceedings of the 1st International Semantic Web Conference (ISWC2002), June 9-12th, 2002, Sardinia, Italia*. Springer, 2002.
26. Raphael Volz, Daniel Oberle, and Rudi Studer. Views for light-weight web ontologies. In *Proceedings of the ACM Symposium on Applied Computing SAC 2003, March 9-12, 2003, Melbourne, Florida, USA*, 2003.

# 16

# Ontologies in Support of Problem Solving

Monica Crubézy and Mark A. Musen

Stanford Medical Informatics, Stanford University, CA 94305, USA
crubezy@smi.stanford.edu, musen@smi.stanford.edu

**Summary.** Problem-solving methods are ready-made software components that can be assembled with domain knowledge bases to create application systems. Ontologies and problem-solving methods have a long history of intricate relationships. In this chapter, we describe these relationships and how they can be used in a principled manner to construct knowledge systems. We have developed a methodology that strongly relies on ontologies: first, to describe domain knowledge bases and problem-solving methods as independent components that can be reused in different application systems; and second, to mediate knowledge between the two kinds of components when they are assembled in a specific system. We present our methodology and a set of associated tools (based on the Protégé knowledge-engineering environment) that we have created to support developers in building knowledge systems and that we have used to conduct problem-solving method reuse experiments.

## 16.1 Reusable Problem-Solving Components

Ontologies provide a structured framework for modeling the concepts and relationships of some domain of expertise. Ontologies support the creation of repositories of domain-specific reference knowledge—*domain knowledge bases*—for communication and sharing of this knowledge among people and computer applications. One step further, ontologies provide the structural and semantic ground for computer-based processing of domain knowledge to perform reasoning tasks. In other words, ontologies enable the actual use of domain knowledge in computer applications. In this section, we provide an overview of different means to specify and perform reasoning on a knowledge base. We retain one of these means, *Problem-Solving Methods*, which provide reusable reasoning components that participate in the principled construction of knowledge-based applications.

### 16.1.1 Reasoning on Domain Knowledge

There is a number of ways in which reasoning can be performed on domain knowledge. At the simplest, a set of logical axioms or rules can complement an ontology to specify the way in which new facts can be derived from existing facts. A general inference engine then can draw conclusions based on these rules or axioms to create new knowledge and eventually to solve some simple problem. Although it did not include an explicit domain ontology, a typical example of a rule-based system is the early Mycin medical-diagnosis system [4]. Mycin involved a base of rules about symptoms, medical conditions and laboratory test results and their possible association with infections by micro-organisms. Such rules are specific to a domain. More problematically, rules often embed implicit procedural knowledge (such as rule ordering and conjunct ordering) that influence the actual behavior of the inference engine. This implicit problem-solving knowledge makes the rule base unreliable and difficult to maintain as domain knowledge evolves [9].

The lessons learned from experiments with early rule-based systems were not only that domain knowledge should be represented in an explicit way (such as one supported by an ontology), but also that the problem-solving behavior of a system should be carved out in a separate component of the system. Most prominently, the KADS methodology insisted that the model of a system's components and behavior should identify three distinct, clearly interfaced layers of knowledge, namely the *domain layer*, the *task layer*, and the *inference layer* [3]. However, separating out the inferencing procedure of a knowledge system in a dedicated piece of program code is not enough. Indeed, a system developer can design a more sophisticated and custom method to reason on domain knowledge. For instance, a custom program could embed the logic extracted from the Mycin rules, and encode the order in which the rules should be fired, by grouping them and assigning them priority values depending on cases. The remaining knowledge base then would only contain factual knowledge (e.g., the possible types of laboratory tests and their results for given patients), much easier to maintain. But, like any piece of software designed specifically for an application context, such a program would be very efficient in that context, but it would be very brittle and little adaptable to any change in the domain knowledge or in the purpose of the target system.

Overcoming the limitations of both rule-based systems and custom programs, *Problem-Solving Methods (PSMs)* were introduced as a knowledge engineering paradigm to encode domain-independent, systematic and reusable sequences of inference steps involved in the process of solving certain kinds of application tasks with domain knowledge [8, 5, 22]. One of the first such strategy to have been identified, as a result of analyzing several rule-based systems such as Mycin, was `heuristic classification` [9]—the process of identifying the class of an unknown domain situation. This strategy involves three main inference steps: first, abstracting the facts about the domain situation (e.g., a patient's symptoms and condition) into higher-level features, based on domain knowledge (e.g., from the patient's white blood cell count, the patient's state can be abstracted as "immuno-suppressed"); then, matching the set of abstract features to possible explanations (e.g., "the patient has a gram-negative infection"), using a set of heuristics; and finally, refining the explanation into a more specific one (e.g., "the micro-organism responsible for the patient's infection is e. coli"). Unlike rules and axioms, PSMs abstract and isolate procedural knowledge away from domain knowledge, making both the inferencing behavior of a system and the role of domain knowledge in that system explicit and easy to adapt. Unlike custom programs, PSMs are designed to be reusable for various domains and tasks. In this chapter, we focus on this latter type of reasoning and describe the way in which it participates in the design and implementation of knowledge-based applications.

### 16.1.2  Problem-Solving Methods

PSMs became prominent as a result of: (1) observing recurring patterns of reasoning such as heuristic classification [9], as mentioned above, (2) identifying high-level *generic tasks* [5] ubiquitously performed with knowledge, such as hypothesis assessment and data abstraction, and (3) comparing different *role-limiting methods*, such as propose-and-revise and cover-and-differentiate, in the goal of characterizing a taxonomy of methods to guide system modeling [22]. PSMs were proposed as standard reasoning procedures for addressing generic tasks in a domain-independent way [8, 34, 29, 3, 11].

Over the years, the knowledge-engineering community identified and developed PSMs of general usefulness [6, 3] or for specific high-level tasks such as classification [8, 24], diagnosis [2], design [31, 23], and planning [36, 35]. A PSM that the knowledge-aquisition community studied at length is propose-and-revise [21], a method that conducts a state-based search algorithm to perform constraint-satisfaction problem solving. More specifically, propose-and-revise calculates a valid configuration of domain parameters iteratively, by assigning values to the parameters, verifying that the resulting configuration does not violate domain constraints among parameters and revising the parameter assignments according to constraint-fixing procedures. This PSM was initially developed for the benchmark task of identifying viable configurations of parts involved in the design of an elevator [31]. In this application, parameters were the dimensions and characteristics of the different parts of an elevator, including specific requirements (e.g., the height of the available doors, the desired loading capacity), and constraints and fixes were defined by a set of building codes, architectural principles and safety constraints [21]. After participating in this initial experiment [30], we studied the reuse of propose-and-revise for other types of constraint-satisfaction problems, such as predicting plausible configurations of ribosomal units from a set of experimental data [18], as we show later in this chapter.

PSMs provide a reliable form of knowledge-based reasoning: They usually are the result of both (1) a thorough analysis of the types of problems and tasks that occur in a variety of domains and (2) a good understanding of the solving of these problems at a level that entails the abstraction of the generic reasoning process involved (possibly initially written with rules or custom code). As a result, PSMs are mature algorithms, well characterized and tested, that enable system builders to abstract the procedural processing of knowledge from implementation details. When associated with a piece of program code that implements it, a PSM further becomes an operational building block that a programmer can incorporate readily in a working system [11, 20], much like an element of a mathematical subroutine library. To foster the reuse and sharing of PSMs, method providers build structured libraries [2, 29, 3, 11, 23], in which their methods are indexed for different domains and purposes.

### 16.1.3  Component-Based Knowledge Systems

A problem-solving task is one that involves reasoning on a large body of domain knowledge to reach a certain goal state or conclusion, starting from an initial set of facts. As a consequence of identifying PSMs as domain-independent reasoning components, the process of building a system to realize such a knowledge-intensive task merely involves assembling a domain knowledge component with an appropriate PSM [26]. In other words, PSMs and the ontologies that specify domain knowledge are dual building blocks of knowledge applications: PSMs provide the reasoning component of the system, which relies on the contents of the domain ontology component to solve problems in that domain. This is the first of several relationships between PSMs and ontologies, as discussed in Section 16.2.

To build the performance system of an application, a system developer first needs to select a PSM in a library, by comparing the properties and requirements of available PSMs to the characteristics of the application. An analysis of the required domain task makes those application criteria explicit [11], such as the goal of the target system, the desired performance of the application and the form and availability of domain knowledge. Second, the developer needs to configure the selected PSM for the domain at hand [11]. PSMs act as reasoning templates that need to be instantiated with domain knowledge for each new application. However, this instantiation often is not straightforward: PSMs enable domain knowledge bases to be free of procedural problem-solving knowledge, thus making them also reusable for different purposes; conversely, PSMs being reusable in different applications, they are independent of any domain. Hence, by definition, there is potentially—and in practice, invariably—a mismatch between a domain ontology and a PSM, because each is kept independent of the other. This mismatch needs to be resolved without impairing the reusability and independence of both types of components.

In the remainder of this chapter, we present a methodology for building component-based knowledge systems. At the heart of our approach, several ontologies interoperate to provide a framework for assembling independent domain and problem-solving knowledge components. We first describe our ontology-based methodology and detail the role of each type of ontology involved. We then present the tools that we have developed for supporting the activities involved in creating and managing these ontologies in the process of building a knowledge system. We illustrate the use of our tools with excerpts of experiments that we led to design and validate our approach. We finally conclude this chapter with open issues and perspectives.

## 16.2  Ontologies at the Heart of Knowledge Systems

After the introduction of PSMs, the knowledge-engineering community thought of ways to maximize the potential of ontologies as a basis for the reuse of problem-solving knowledge such as tasks and PSMs [19, 14, 7]. Among several methodologies that differ only in their nuances,[1] the Protégé methodology and associated suite of tools [17] relies on ontologies to support application developers in modeling and building knowledge-based systems.

The latest version of the Protégé tools[2] is a generic and extensible software environment which enables users to model, query and use any domain ontology. More specifically, Protégé provides an ontology-modeling editor, with which domain experts can represent their knowledge. Protégé adopts a frame-based modeling view of ontologies. Accordingly, a set of *classes* are organized in a subsumption hierarchy to represent concepts in the domain of interest, and have *slots* attached to them to represent their properties. The values that slots can take are governed by *facets*, such as cardinality, type and range. Classes are templates for individual *instances*, that have particular values for slots. From an abstract ontology model, Protégé automatically generates a set of knowledge-entry forms which end-users fill-in to populate the ontology with instances of the classes, that have specific values for slots. Domain experts can customize these forms so that the knowledge-entry activity performed by end-users is more intuitive. Although Protégé does not consider this an absolute definition anymore, we here refer to a *knowledge base* as an ontology of classes augmented with a set of individual instances of these classes.

### 16.2.1  Ontology-Based Reuse of PSMs

The use of ontologies in constructing a knowledge system is pervasive. At the very least, ontologies support the modeling of the domain-knowledge component counterpart of PSMs in knowledge applications. However, as described in Section 16.1, PSMs and domain ontologies are developed independently and therefore need to be reconciled to form a coherent knowledge system. As the basis for reconciliation, PSMs declare the format and semantics of the knowledge that they expect from the domain to perform their task [12]. In our approach, a PSM provides a *method ontology*, that elicits its input and output knowledge requirements, independently of any domain (see Section 16.2.3). For instance, the `propose-and-revise` PSM declares its input-knowledge needs in terms of state variables, constraints and fixes. This way, the method ontology assigns roles that the domain knowledge needs to fill so that the PSM can operate on that knowledge. Further, the method ontology states the assumptions that the PSM makes on domain knowledge. Besides making all domain knowledge requirements explicit, refined versions of the PSM can be modeled

---

[1] Unlike other methodologies such as CommonKADS [32] and OCML [23], Protégé does not make the task level explicit. If needed, Protégé folds task-specific knowledge into the application ontology—the domain ontology augmented with knowledge important for the specific application.

[2] `http://protege.stanford.edu`

directly by weakening or strengthening its assumptions by way of additional sets of ontological statements—or *adapter* component [13, 11].

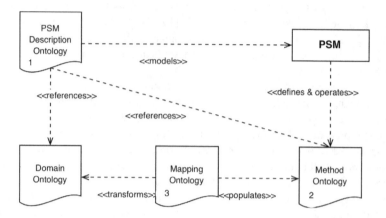

**Fig. 16.1. An ontology-based approach to developing knowledge systems.** Besides a domain ontology that states the knowledge to be processed, building a knowledge system involves using three other ontologies. (1) A *PSM-description ontology* models metadata properties and competence of the PSMs of a library, (2) a *method ontology* specifies the required inputs and expected outputs of a PSM, and (3) a *mapping ontology* structures the expression of transformation rules between the domain and method ontologies, to provide the PSM with operational knowledge.

To avoid impairing the independence of either the domain or the method ontologies, our approach includes a mediating component, as originally developed in the field of database interoperation [37]. This third, separate knowledge component holds the explicit relationships between the domain and the method ontologies assembled in a specific knowledge application [19, 28]. Underlying this mediating component is a *mapping ontology*—one of possible mapping relations that bridge the conceptual and syntactic gaps between the domain and method ontologies (see Section 16.2.4). This aspect of our approach too is in line with the notion of knowledge *adapters* [13] in the sense that our mapping relations declare and isolate the knowledge that is needed to adapt a particular PSM to work with a particular domain knowledge base.

Finally, an ontology also can provide a principled framework for modeling the important characteristics of PSMs, allowing them to be indexed and retrieved meaningfully in libraries. Our approach thus also includes a *PSM-description ontology*—an ontology of the properties and competence of PSMs, including a reference to their method ontology. Our PSM-description ontology also models the relationships of a PSM with other (refined) PSMs and with other components involved in a knowledge system—namely tasks and domain models—through the specification of adapters and task-method decomposition structures [32]. Figure 16.1 describes the many relationships that a PSM has with ontologies. In the following sections, we detail each

of the three ontologies involved in the construction of a knowledge system besides
the domain ontology, starting with the PSM-description ontology.

## 16.2.2  An Ontology for Describing PSMs

To build a knowledge system, a developer selects a PSM that suits the requirements
of the domain task and knowledge [11]. The developer thus needs to review metadata,
as well as a specification of the competence and expectations of available PSMs [12].
For instance, a developer considering the propose-and-revise PSM [21] may
want to know who implemented the PSM, what kind of constraints the PSM is capable of handling, and whether the PSM outputs an optimal solution. This information
gives the developer an indication of the degree-of-fit between the PSM and the domain at hand.

Characterizing PSMs so that they can be collected, indexed and retrieved meaningfully in libraries requires a dedicated modeling language [7, 16]. The Unified Problem-solving Method development Language[3] (UPML; [15]) is a comprehensive framework for modeling libraries of PSMs. UPML provides human-
understandable PSM descriptions, while including formal specifications that allow both PSM providers to organize their components into libraries and systems
to index and retrieve PSMs automatically. UPML takes its roots in knowledge-
engineering approaches such as *generic tasks* [5], *components of expertise* [34] and
*CommonKADS* [32], principles of software engineering and reuse, as well as recent
Semantic-Web research.

UPML covers all aspects of modeling PSMs and the way in which they are configured into running applications. Although UPML focuses on PSMs because they
are the actual performance components of a system, UPML distinguishes all three
kinds of components involved in a knowledge-based system: (1) *tasks*, which are the
functions that the system can achieve (e.g., design), (2) *PSMs*, which are the methods
that implement the reasoning process of the system to realize a task, possibly by task-
method decomposition (e.g., the propose-and-revise constraint-satisfaction
PSM), and (3) *domain models*, which are views on domain knowledge (e.g., a set
of safety rules in the elevator-configuration domain), as used by tasks and PSMs.
The connection of all three kinds of components is modeled by specific mediating
constructs: *bridges*, which express the relationship map between the ontologies of
two kinds of components, and *refiners*, which represent the stepwise adaptation of a
component to meet specific application requirements [13].

In support of this approach, UPML defines a complete (meta-)ontology of primitives for describing and publishing libraries of PSMs, tasks and domain models
(see Figure 16.2). As a first way to support the reuse of PSMs, the use of a PSM-
description ontology ensures the specification of correct, queryable models of PSMs.
Specifically, PSM attributes in UPML include a *competence*, a *method ontology*, and
an *operational description*. The competence of a PSM includes input and output role

---

[3] http://www.cs.vu.nl/~upml/

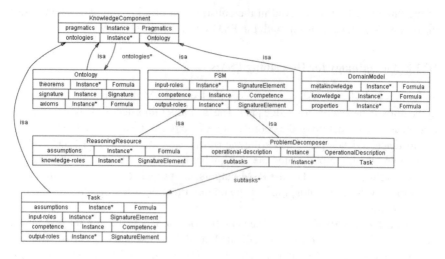

**Fig. 16.2. Part of the UPML ontology for describing libraries of PSMs.** This diagrammatic representation (derived from our Protégé model of UPML) shows a sub-hierarchy of concepts provided by UPML to specify the knowledge components involved in a system: *Tasks, domain models* and *PSMs*, each of which described in terms of its own *ontology*. In particular, the description of a PSM includes a set of *input-roles* and *output-roles*, a *competence* and, in the case of a problem decomposer, a possible *subtask* decomposition with its associated *operational description*. A parallel sub-hierarchy (not shown here) defines the UPML notions of *bridges* and *refiners*—adapter components that connect and configure the knowledge components together in a specific system.

descriptions, as well as a formalization of the preconditions and postconditions associated with that method (i.e., formulas that must hold on inputs and outputs). A separate method ontology holds definitions of the concepts and relations used by the PSM, as further explained in Section 16.2.3. The operational description of a PSM specifies the control-flow algorithm that sequences the set of subtasks that compose the method, if any. Each subtask is further realized by a particular submethod. UPML finally enables PSM providers to define pragmatics metadata about a PSM, including author information, publication references and actual location (e.g., a URL) of the PSM's code. A partial description of the `propose-and-revise` PSM in UPML follows (see also Figure 16.6):

**Pragmatics**
    title: `Propose and Revise`
**Ontology**
    element: `parameter`, as defined by class `stateVariable`
    element: `fix`, defined by class `Fix` as "A condition-expression rule associated to a constraint and a parameter"
    element: `constraint`, as defined by class `Constraint` and its subclasses
    element: `consistent`, defined as a logical predicate
    ...

**Input-roles**: `parameters, constraints, fixes`

**Output-roles**: `parameter values`
**Subtasks**: `Select next parameter, Propose next set of parameter values, Verify against constraints, Revise according to fix knowledge.`
**Competence**
 precondition:                    "`Every fix has exactly one associated constraint.`" ...
 postconditions: "`The output parameter values are consistent regarding the constraints.`" ...
**Operational Description**

 ...


### 16.2.3  An Ontology of PSM Inputs and Outputs

As mentioned in Section 16.2.2, a crucial piece of knowledge that the provider of a PSM needs to model is the ontology of concepts that represent the input and output structures on which the PSM operates [19], as well as requirements on these structures. This *method ontology* provides a signature for the PSM, that assigns roles and requirements to the domain knowledge that the PSM processes. What is more, the method ontology expresses those knowledge requirements in a way independent from any application domain. The method ontology hence is the true counterpart of a domain ontology in the construction of a knowledge-based application. By providing a domain-independent method ontology, a PSM provides a generic and explicit framework to construe the domain knowledge for its processing. Necessary reconciliation between the domain knowledge ontology and the method ontology is handled by way of a third ontology, as described in Section 16.2.4.

At the very least, a method ontology models the concepts involved in describing the inputs and outputs of the PSM, to be filled-in by domain knowledge in the appropriate format. As mentioned before, the `propose-and-revise` PSM declares an input set of `parameters` to be configured, as well as a set of condition–expression `constraints` that need to hold on the parameter values and a set of associated `fixes` to be applied when constraints are violated. The method ontology for `propose-and-revise` hence defines the classes that model these inputs, namely `StateVariable`, `Constraint` and `Fix` (see Figure 16.3). Note that an extended method ontology (as modeled in UPML) contains the entire set of primitive used to describe the behavior of the PSM, such as predicates and functions involved in expressing assumptions, preconditions and postconditions of the PSM on domain knowledge, and references to steps (i.e., subtasks) in the control structure of the PSM [14, 7]. These additional elements of the method ontology both allow a developer to make an informed selection of a PSM based on the requirements of the target application and on the knowledge that is available in the domain, and provide the basis for the refinement and specialization of a PSM to meet domain requirements by weakening or strengthening its assumptions, or by replacing some of its subcomponents by alternative, refined submethods [11, 13].

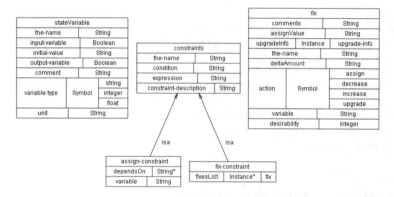

**Fig. 16.3. The method ontology of the** `propose-and-revise` **PSM.** This diagrammatic representation (derived from our model of the ontology in Protégé) shows the definition of the concepts describing inputs and outputs of `propose-and-revise`. For instance, the `fix-constraint` class of inputs requires constraint knowledge to be provided as `condition-expression` rules with associated `fixes` to apply in case that the constraint is violated.

### 16.2.4 An Ontology of Domain–PSM Mapping Relations

A method ontology and a domain ontology typically conceptualize knowledge with different perspectives, independent of one another. When we applied `propose-and-revise` to the domain of elevator configuration, we had to reconcile the state variables, constraints and fixes that the PSM expected with relevant elevator components and constraints [30]. Later, we reused `propose-and-revise` for the task of predicting plausible three-dimensional conformations of ribosomal units based on experimental data and constraints on the spatial relationships among different molecular subunits [18]. The associated ribosome-topology domain specified parameters of a configuration in terms of genomic objects such as helices and DNA strands, and constraints in terms of molecular distances and angles—a representation very different from that of `propose-and-revise`'s method ontology.

Keeping domain and method ontologies independent maximizes the possibility of reusing each of them in different knowledge systems. We therefore advocate the use of a mediating component (see Figure 16.1)—one that isolates the knowledge needed for adapting a PSM and a domain knowledge base to work together in a particular knowledge application. This middle component encodes *mapping relations* that establish the declarative connections between the concrete concepts of a domain ontology—that hence become role fillers—and the input–output templates that a PSM defines in its method ontology. More specifically, mapping relations express the transformation of domain knowledge needed so that the PSM focuses on the pieces and aspects of knowledge that it is competent to reason about. According to a set of custom mapping relations, instances of the domain concepts of interest to the PSM are transformed (by way of a mapping interpreter, see Section 16.3) into instances of corresponding method concepts, on which the PSM can operate directly.

It makes sense to categorize the types of mapping relations that can be expressed in any situation that requires domain–PSM mapping. Such categorization allows us to conceptualize the mappings in a better way and to design appropriate tool support (see Section 16.3). We hence designed a generic *mapping ontology* (shown in Figure 16.4) that provides a structured encoding of the various types of mapping relations between a source domain ontology and a target method ontology, both at the instance and at the slot levels [19, 28].

A mapping relation can be as simple as a one-to-one renaming correspondence between a domain class and its slots, and a method class and its slots. In the ribosome-conformation prediction application, `propose-and-revise` does not need to handle the whole complexity of the ribosomal objects to perform its task. Thus, it is sufficient that each (domain) ribosomal `object` and only part of its slots are renamed into a (method) `stateVariable` and associated slots. More complex instance-level mappings can express many-to-one, or many-to-many, aggregation relations between domain and method concepts, as well as one-to-many concept-decomposition relations. Slot-level mappings also can express aggregation and decomposition operations on domain slot values, and include lexical, numerical and functional transformations of slot values. For instance, in our application of the `propose-and-revise` PSM for the domain of ribosome topology, a domain constraint includes the possible definition of a range of acceptable positions of ribosomal objects. Such notion of a range has no direct equivalent in the method ontology: We thus created special mapping relations to transform each instance of the domain `constraint` class into two instances of the method `fix-constraint` class, one for each bound of the range. The relations transform constraints about lower and upper bounds of values for domain parameters into method constraints that specify a value-comparison expression and associated value-incrementing, or value-decrementing, fixes (see details in Figure 16.7).

To configure a selected PSM to operate on a given domain knowledge base, the application developer needs to instantiate our mapping ontology with the set of mapping relations that link the domain ontology to the roles defined in the method ontology. The developer thus creates a *mapping knowledge base* that contains both direct mappings—that compute the PSM's inputs out of domain instance knowledge—and reverse mappings—that translate the PSM's outputs back into domain form (see Section 16.3). It is important to note that there may be situations in which concepts expected by the method have no obvious equivalent in the domain ontology, either because the concepts do not exist at all and cannot be replaced by a constant assignment of values, or because no mapping relation would be sophisticated enough to account for the transformation of existing domain knowledge, or finally because the transformation has become mature enough in the domain to be modeled as an explicit concept. In those cases, the domain ontology needs to be extended into an *application ontology* for the purpose of building a given knowledge application. For instance, when applying the `propose-and-revise` PSM to the problem of predicting plausible ribosome conformations, we had to add the notion of a `fix` in the ribosome-topology ontology, that would map naturally to the equivalent notion in

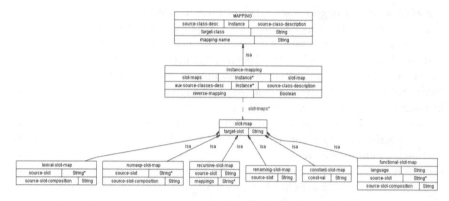

**Fig. 16.4. The generic ontology of mapping relations** (in a representation derived from our Protégé model). Each instance-level mapping relation connects one or more domain ("source") classes to one method ("target") class and defines the set of slot-level transformations that are needed to compute the values of required method slots (as attached to the method class) from the values of available domain slots. Types of slot-level mapping relations span the scope of operations that domain knowledge can undergo to fit the format and semantics specified by the method ontology.

the `propose-and-revise` method ontology, instead of creating a non-intuitive mapping out of other concepts of the domain [18].

Our mapping ontology provides the basis for expressing the adaptation knowledge needed to configure a PSM for a certain application. In that sense, our mapping ontology extends the notion of domain–PSM bridges in the UPML framework (see Section 16.2.2) by providing a structured and operational set of possible mapping axioms that bridge the ontologies of both components. It is important to note that the core knowledge that is needed to create method instances out of domain instances resides in the set of slot-level transformation operations attached to an instance-level mapping relation—operations that change the format and resolution of the domain slot values to fill-in the required values of method slots. Indeed, the piece of software that is associated to a PSM eventually needs to operate on data structures that are filled-in according to the instantiated method ontology. To this end, our mapping ontology accounts both for ontology-level alignment operations and for instance-level transformation operations. While the former is the focus of much of the current ontology-management research,[4] the latter is more traditionally found in database integration approaches.

---

[4] For space reasons, the reader is referred to other chapters of this handbook for more details on ontology management and evolution.

## 16.3  Tool Support for Reusing PSMs

Providing adequate tool support is essential in knowledge engineering. In particular, tools enable the systematic design, implementation and evaluation of methodologies. In this section, we present the kind of tools that can be developed for PSM providers and for PSM users (i.e., knowledge-system developers), to support them in using our ontology-based methodology. In particular, we describe the way in which the four ontologies of our methodology—the domain ontology, the PSM-description ontology, the method ontology and the mapping ontology—participate in the construction of running applications.

**Table 16.1.** This table presents the actors involved in the process of building a knowledge application and the tools that they use to provide expert knowledge and produce application-specific knowledge.

| Actors | Knowledge Provided | Tools | Knowledge Produced |
|---|---|---|---|
| Domain experts | domain models & facts | Protégé | domain ontology & KB |
| PSM providers | | Protégé-UPML editor | |
| | PSM models | | PSM library |
| | PSM i/o models | | method ontologies |
| | PSMs | | |
| PSM users | | PSM Librarian | |
| | domain KB | | |
| | application requirements | Selection Manager (PSM libraries) | selected PSM (ontology) |
| | application knowledge | Mapping Editor (mapping ontology) | mapping KB |
| | | Mapping Interpreter | method KB |
| | domain case inputs | execution environment (PSMs) | method case outputs |
| | | mapping interpreter (reverse) | domain case outputs |

Ontologies have been at the heart of the Protégé methodology and tools since very early versions of the system [17]; Protégé hence is suited to provide the kind of tool support that is necessary for PSM providers and users. Although we designed and improved our methodology over the years, it is not until we integrated all aspects of tool support for PSMs in Protégé that we were able to start evaluating it and extending it. Protégé supports domain experts in modeling relevant knowledge in an ontology and in customizing an associated knowledge-entry tool (see Section 16.1). In the following, we expose how we extended this native support of Protégé with tools to help PSM providers and PSM users in their respective activities. Table 16.1 summarizes the type of actors, tools and knowledge involved in the entire process of building a knowledge application.

*Tool Support for PSM Providers*

We first employed Protégé in its native form to model the UPML PSM-Description ontology (see Section 16.2.2) and to develop a dedicated knowledge-acquisition tool for PSM providers, the Protégé-UPML editor [27]. Using this tool, PSM providers model and document libraries of PSMs by entering descriptions of particular PSMs as a set of instances of the classes provided by the UPML ontology. This way, several libraries were modeled in UPML, such as our library of general-purpose search

PSMs [11, 16], as well as a library for classification problem-solving [24] and a library for information agents.[5]

In particular, PSM providers create an ontology component for each PSM in their library that lists all the terms and relations that are important to describe a PSM's competence, requirements and behavior. In addition, providers model the actual contents of the method ontologies, either directly within their UPML library (i.e., using the Protégé-UPML editor) or separately using the base Protégé system (see Figure 16.3).

## Tool Support for PSM Users

Special-purpose tools are needed for users of PSM libraries—knowledge-system developers and knowledge-system users. Typically, developers are domain experts capable of handling both the use of a system like Protégé and the principles underlying the construction of a knowledge system. The applications that they build then become templates that end-users instantiate and run with their own case data.

Support for system developers covers the range of activities involved in building a knowledge application from a domain-knowledge component and a PSM component. As an illustration, we present here the *PSM Librarian*—a tool that we have built as an extension to Protégé to provide methodological assistance to knowledge-system developers. Our PSM Librarian supports developers in the selection of an appropriate PSM for their domain problem and in the configuration of that PSM to work with the particular domain knowledge base at hand. The PSM Librarian accesses knowledge bases from Protégé and reuses user interface elements of the base environment to provide a familiar, yet customized, interaction with system developers. Figure 16.5 gives a synoptic view of the process of building an application and running it, with the support of our custom tools.[6] Underlying the tools are the four ontologies that participate in our proposed methodology for constructing knowledge systems. Subsequent figures detail the components of our PSM Librarian tool: Figure 16.6 focuses on the Selection Manager, Figure 16.7 focuses on the Mapping Editor and Figure 16.8 shows some results produced by the Mapping Interpreter.

Based on the application configured by developers with help of our tools, support for system users merely consists in providing them with case-data entry forms to populate the application knowledge base, and then in running the mapping interpreter to process these new domain instances and update the method knowledge base. Our tools only provide straightforward support for the actual execution of the configured PSM: This step usually is handled best outside of the tool, as it depends on the type of executable PSM. The PSM Librarian can interface minimally to an execution environment, and provide that environment with both the executable file of the PSM (as per the UPML specification) and the PSM's instantiated method knowledge base (including case data inputs). The result of the PSM is outputted in the

---

[5] These latter libraries were developed as part of the IBROW project—http://www.swi.psy.uva.nl/projects/ibrow/home.html

[6] When considering the activities of task selection and configuration explicitly in this process, additional steps occur before selecting a candidate PSM [10].

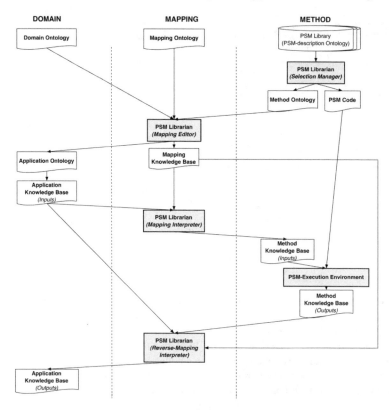

**Fig. 16.5. Building a knowledge application with our PSM Librarian.** The *Selection Manager* enables the application developer to choose a PSM from available UPML libraries, and isolates that PSM's method ontology. The *Mapping Editor* allows the developer to create a knowledge base of domain–method mapping relations, according to our mapping ontology. The *Mapping Interpreter* processes the mapping relations to transform the domain-knowledge instances (including case data) into corresponding method instances—instances of the method ontology, which the PSM can operate on directly. The mapping interpreter also processes reverse mapping relations when translating the PSM's outputs into domain-compliant instances.

method knowledge base, that the mapping interpreter translates back to the domain knowledge base, by processing the declared reverse mapping relations.

## 16.4 Conclusion

Problem-Solving Methods (PSMs) provide powerful means to model and implement the performance component of an application that solves a reasoning task on a body of domain knowledge. PSMs are naturally related to ontologies because ontologies provide the basis for modeling the domain knowledge on which PSMs operate. We argue that PSMs are related to ontologies in several additional ways that support a

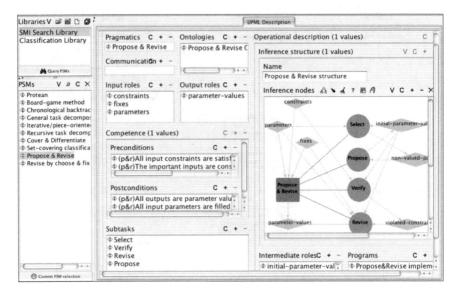

**Fig. 16.6. The PSM Librarian: Support for PSM selection with the Selection Manager.**
The left panels allow developers to load and browse libraries of PSMs. The right panel displays
the UPML-based description of the highlighted PSM—here, `propose-and-revise`—
centered around the flow-chart diagram of the PSM, that focuses on the roles and tasks defined
by the PSM. From this description, developers can inspect all characteristics of a PSM (such
as its pragmatics metadata, its ontology and its competence) and make an informed selection
of the one that meets their domain-problem requirements.

principled methodology for reusing both PSMs and domain models as components
in different applications.

Although there are nuances among modern knowledge-engineering approaches,
the Protégé methodology that we present here reflects a general consensus in the
field. A hallmark of our methodology, however, is the definition of a set of explicit
ontology-mapping relations for each new application, that mediates domain knowledge to and from the PSM's inputs and outputs. Similarly, although we presented our
Protégé-based tools here, our primary goal was to illustrate how ontologies can be
used not only as models of domains and PSMs but also as a basis for developing support tools for problem solving. Using our methodology and associated Protégé-based
tools, we led several experiments to study the reuse of PSMs in different applications [25]. Experiments reported then were initiated with earlier versions of our tools
than the ones described in Section 16.3; these experiments helped us in designing
our current tools, that now handle the past experiments in a systematic and integrated
way. In particular, our `propose-and-revise` experiments [30, 33, 18] helped us
design the mapping ontology [19, 28] and support tools for system builders, such as
the mapping interpreter.

Open perspectives of our proposed methodology and tools include integrating
the activities related to problem definition, task specification, and task configura-

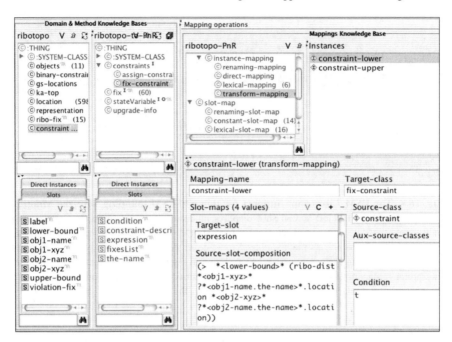

**Fig. 16.7. The PSM Librarian: Support for domain–PSM mapping with the Mapping Editor**, here used for mapping the domain of ribosome topology to the `propose-and-revise` PSM. Our Mapping Editor provides system developers with an integrated access to all elements needed to express mapping relations. The two left columns display, side-by-side, the application-domain knowledge base of ribosomal objects and the method ontology of the `propose-and-revise` PSM (classes at the top; slots below). The right panel displays the mapping knowledge base: At the top, the available classes and instances of instance-level and slot-level mapping relations; below, the contents of the selected mapping-relation instance, including the set of associated slot-level mappings for each slot of the method class (see "Slot-maps" pane at the lower left). Shown here is the transform mapping `constraint-lower`, from the domain class `constraint` to the method class `fix-constraint`. This mapping specifies how to map the lower bound value for the location of a ribosomal object into a method constraint that declares a value-comparison expression and an associated value-incrementing fix to use when the expression is violated. For instance, the lexical slot mapping for the method's `expression` slot defines a comparison predicate involving several slots of the ribosome-topology domain (using the $* < ... > *$ notation to access these slots' actual values). A similar mapping handles the upper bound value constraint (not shown). The "Mapping operations" menu above the mapping knowledge base enables the system developer to run our Mapping Interpreter, that populates the method ontology with instances created from available domain instances (see Figure 16.8), by processing the mapping relations.

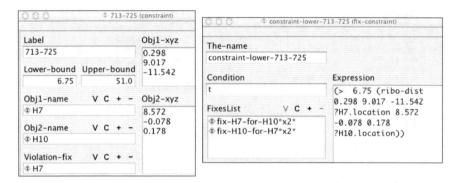

**Fig. 16.8. The PSM Librarian: Support for domain–PSM mapping with the Mapping Interpreter.** Here, the left screen shot displays an instance of the ribosome-topology domain `constraint` class, and the right screen shot displays the resulting instance of the `propose-and-revise`'s method class `fix-constraint`, as computed by the mapping interpreter according to the mapping relation shown in Figure 16.7. In particular, the mapping interpreter replaced all slot-value references by the actual value in the domain instance—for example, `6.75` replaces * `<lower-bound>` * in the `expression` slot of the method instance.

tion in the application-building process [10], as well as studying the specialization and refinement of PSMs for varying application requirements. Additional ontologies and mapping-relation types would be involved in this extended process to enable task, method and domain views on knowledge to interoperate. On another note, when reusing `propose-and-revise` for the ribosome-conformation prediction task, we realized that some mapping relations (such as the one presented in Figure 16.7) were very similar in their meaning—although specific mapping rules were different— to some mapping relations defined for the elevator-configuration application. This observation suggests that mapping relations defined for a particular application of a PSM may be reused for a different application of the same PSM. The identification of reusable mapping templates associated to a PSM might prove to reduce the amount of work involved in configuring an application. Thus the floor is open for exploring the scope, use and possible extensions of our mapping approach.

Finally, although the notion of PSM has been around for more than a decade now, we think that this approach to building knowledge systems has still long to live. In particular, the recent emergence of Web Services[7] and other distributed-reasoning resources on the World-Wide Web renew the interest and potential impact of a PSM-centered, ontology-based approach to the construction of Web-enabled applications [1, 10].

---

[7] See `http://www.daml.org/services/` and `http://www.w3.org/TR/wsdl12/`

## 16.5 Acknowledgements

This chapter includes ideas of many researchers at Stanford Medical Informatics over the past decade, including: H. Eriksson, J. H. Gennari, J. Y. Park, A. Puerta, T. E. Rothenfluh and S. W. Tu. Parts of this work were funded by the High Performance Knowledge Base Project of the Defense Advanced Research Projects Agency (contract N660001-97-C-8549), the Space and Naval Warfare Systems Center (contract N6001-94-D-6052) and the National Library of Medicine (grants LM05157 and LM05208). Figures 16.2, 16.3, and 16.4 were created with the Ontoviz plugin of Protégé, developed by M. Sintek.

## References

1. V. R. Benjamins, E. Plaza, E. Motta, D. Fensel, R. Studer, R. Wielinga, G. Schreiber, Z. Zdrahal, and S. Decker. An Intelligent Brokering Service for Knowledge-Component Reuse on the World-Wide Web. In *Workshop on Knowledge Acquisition, Modeling and Management (KAW'98)*, 1998.
2. V. Richard Benjamins. *Problem Solving Methods for Diagnosis*. PhD Thesis, University of Amsterdam, 1993.
3. J.A. Breuker and W. van de Velde, editors. *The CommonKADS Library for Expertise Modeling*. IOS Press, Amsterdam, 1994.
4. B. G Buchanan and E. H. Shortliffe. *Rule-Based Expert Systems: The MYCIN Experiments of the Stanford Heuristic Programming Project*. Addison-Wesley, 1984.
5. B. Chandrasekaran. Generic Tasks for Knowledge-Based Reasoning: High-Level Building Blocks for Expert System Design. *IEEE Expert*, 1(3):23–30, 1986.
6. B. Chandrasekaran, T. Johnson, and J.W. Smith. Task Structure Analysis for Knowledge Modeling. *Communications of the ACM*, 33(9):124–136, 1992.
7. B. Chandrasekaran, J. R. Josephson, and V. Richard Benjamins. Ontology of Tasks and Methods. In *Workshop on Knowledge Acquisition, Modeling and Management (KAW'98)*, Banff, Canada, 1998.
8. W. J. Clancey. Heuristic Classification. *Artificial Intelligence*, 27:289–350, 1985.
9. W.J. Clancey. The Epistemology of a Rule-based Expert System: A Framework for Explanation. *Artificial Intelligence*, 20:215 – 251, 1983.
10. M. Crubézy, E. Motta, W. Lu, and M. A. Musen. Configuring Online Problem-Solving Resources with the Internet Reasoning Service. *IEEE Intelligent Systems*, 18(2):34–42, 2003.
11. H. Eriksson, Y. Shahar, S. W. Tu, A. R. Puerta, and M. A. Musen. Task Modeling with Reusable Problem-Solving Methods. *Artificial Intelligence*, 79:293–326, 1995.
12. D. Fensel, H. Eriksson, M. A. Musen, and R. Studer. Conceptual and Formal Specifications of Problem-Solving Methods. *International Journal of Expert Systems*, 9(4):507–532, 1996.
13. D. Fensel and E. Motta. Structured Development of Problem Solving Methods. *IEEE Transactions on Knowledge and Data Engineering*, 13(6):913–932, 2001.
14. D. Fensel, E. Motta, S. Decker, and Z. Zdrahal. Using Ontologies For Defining Tasks, Problem-Solving Methods and Their Mappings. In E. Plaza (eds.), editor, *European Conference on Knowledge Acquisition, Modeling and Management (EKAW'97)*, volume 1319 of *Lecture Notes in Artificial Intelligence*, pages 113–128. Springer-Verlag, Berlin, 1997.

15. D. Fensel, E. Motta, F. van Harmelen, V. R. Benjamins, M. Crubézy, S. Decker, M. Gaspari, R. Groenboom, W. Grosso, M. A. Musen, E. Plaza, G. Schreiber, R. Studer, and R. Wielinga. The Unified Problem-solving Method Development Language UPML. *Knowledge and Information Systems Journal (KAIS)*, 5(1), 2003.

16. J. H. Gennari, W. E. Grosso, and M. A. Musen. A Method-Description Language: An Initial Ontology with Examples. In *Workshop on Knowledge Acquisition, Modeling and Management (KAW'98)*, Banff, Canada, 1998.

17. J. H. Gennari, M. A. Musen, R. W. Fergerson, W. E. Grosso, M. Crubézy, H. Eriksson, N. F. Noy, and S. W. Tu. The Evolution of Protégé: An Environment for Knowledge-Based Systems Development. *International Journal of Human-Computer Studies*, 58(1):89–123, 2003.

18. J.H. Gennari, R.B. Altman, and M.A. Musen. Reuse with Protégé-II: From Elevators to Ribosomes. In *ACM-SigSoft 1995 Symposium on Software Reusability*, Seattle, WA, 1995.

19. J.H. Gennari, S.W. Tu, T.E. Rothenfluh, and M.A. Musen. Mapping Domains to Methods in Support of Reuse. *International Journal of Human-Computer Studies*, 41:399–424., 1994.

20. Y. Gil and E. Melz. Explicit Representations of Problem-Solving Methods to Support Knowledge Acquisition. In *Thirteenth National Conference on Artificial Intelligence (AAAI-96)*, Portland, Oregon, 1996. AAAI Press.

21. S. Marcus, J. Stout, and J. McDermott. VT: An Expert Elevator Designer that Uses Knowledge-Directed Backtracking. *AI Magazine*, 9(1):95–112, 1988.

22. J. McDermott. Preliminary Steps Toward a Taxonomy of Problem-Solving Methods. In S. Marcus, editor, *Automatic Knowledge for Acquisition for Expert Systems*, pages 225–54. Boston: Kluwer Academic Publishers, 1988.

23. E. Motta. *Reusable Components for Knowledge Modelling: Principles and Case Studies in Parametric Design*. IOS Press, Amsterdam, 1999.

24. E. Motta and W. Lu. A Library of Components for Classification Problem Solving. Deliverable 1, IBROW Project IST-1999-19005: An Intelligent Brokering Service for Knowledge-Component Reuse on the World-Wide Web, 2000.

25. M. A. Musen. Scalable Software Architectures for Decision Support. *Methods of Information in Medicine*, 38:229–238, 1999.

26. M. A. Musen and A. T. Schreiber. Architectures for Intelligent Systems Based on Reusable Components. *Artificial Intelligence in Medicine*, 7:189–199, 1995.

27. B. Omelayenko, M. Crubézy, D. Fensel, V R. Benjamins, B. J. Wielinga, E. Motta, M. A. Musen, and Y. Ding. UPML: The Language and Tool Support for Making the Semantic Web Alive. In D. Fensel, J. Hendler, H. Liebermann, and W. Wahlster, editors, *Spinning the Semantic Web: Bringing the World Wide Web to its Full Potential*. MIT Press, 2003.

28. J.Y. Park, J.H. Gennari, and M.A. Musen. Mappings for Reuse in Knowledge-Based Systems. In *Eleventh Banff Knowledge Acquisition for Knowledge-Based Systems Workshop*, Banff, Alberta, 1998.

29. F. Puppe. *Systematic Introduction to Expert Systems, Knowledge Representations and Problem-Solving Methods*. Springer-Verlag, 1993.

30. T. R. Rothenfluh, J. H. Gennari, H. Eriksson, A. R. Puerta, S. W. Tu, and M. A. Musen. Reusable Ontologies, Knowledge-Acquisition Tools, and Performance Systems: PROTÉGÉ-II Solutions to Sisyphus-2. *International Journal of Human-Computer Studies*, 44:303–332, 1996.

31. A. Th. Schreiber and W. P. Birmingham. Editorial: the Sisyphus-VT Initiative. *International Journal of Human-Computer Studies*, 44(3/4):275–280, 1996.

32. A.T. Schreiber, J.M. Akkermans, A.A. Anjewierden, R. de Hoog, N.R. Shadbolt, W. van de Velde, and B.J. Wielinga. *Knowledge Engineering and Management: The CommonKADS Methodology*. MIT Press, Cambridge, 2000.

33. D.S. Smith, J.Y. Park, and M.A. Musen. Therapy Planning as Constraint Satisfaction: A Computer-Based Antiretroviral Therapy Advisor for the Management of HIV. In *AMIA Fall Symposium, American Medical Informatics Association*, pages 627–631, Orlando, FL, 1998.

34. L. Steels. Components of Expertise. *AI Magazine*, 11:30–49, 1990.

35. S.W. Tu, Y. Shahar, J. Dawes, J. Winkles, A.R. Puerta, and M.A. Musen. A Problem-Solving Model for Episodic Skeletal-Plan Refinement. *Knowledge Acquisition*, 4:197–216, 1992.

36. A. Valente, V. R. Benjamins, and L. Nunes de Barros. A Library of System-Derived Problem-Solving Methods for Planning. *International Journal of Human-Computer Studies*, 48(4):417–447, 1998.

37. G. Wiederhold. Mediators in the Architecture of Future Information Systems. *IEEE Computer*, 25(3):38–49, 1992.

# Ontologies in Agent Architectures

Katia Sycara and Massimo Paolucci

Carnegie Mellon University, Pittsburgh PA 15213, USA
email: katia,paolucci@cs.cmu.edu

## 17.1 Introduction

Agents display a dual behavior: on the one hand they are goal directed programs that autonomously and proactively solve problems for their users; on the other hand agents have a social dimension when they interoperate as part of Multi-Agent Systems (MAS). As autonomous problem solvers, agents need to develop a model of their environment that allows them to reason on how the actions that they perform affect their environment, and how those changes lead them to achieve their goals. Ontologies provide the conceptual framework that allows agents to construct such models: ontologies describe the type of entities that agents encounter, the properties of those entities, and the relations between them. For example, a stock reporting agent may require ontologies describing not only concepts like ticker symbol, but also the relation between stock and ticker symbol and properties of stocks such as its value expressed in some currency.

In their social dimension, agents in a MAS necessarily interact with other agents. They may compete for resources, or collaborate toward the solution of a problem or toward the achievement of a common goal. While some of these interactions are quite accidental, for example when an agent has to wait to access a resource because other agents use it, the agents' main tool for interaction and interoperations is communication. Communication allows agents to exchange information as well as requests for services. For example an agent that needs to make financial decisions may want to ask other agents for stock quotes, or it may want to subcontract parts of its financial analysis to other agents. When combining communication and problem solving, the solution of a problem is rarely restricted to the agent itself, rather it often involves other agents. Ontologies provide agents the basic representation that allows them to reason about those interactions, but also, and most importantly, ontologies provide agents with shared knowledge that they can use to communicate and work together.

In order to interact, agents must first know of each others' presence and location in the MAS. Since MAS are open systems, i.e. they are societies where agents enter or leave at unpredictable times, any attempt at programming the agents under the assumption that they know of all their peers would fail, or reduce the MAS to a closed system whose capabilities cannot be modified without re-programming all the agents and their interactions. The alternative is to introduce a *discovery* mechanism so that agents can find each other dynamically. In such a discovery scheme, agents entering the system advertise their presence, while agents in need of services, issue service requests. The objective of the discovery process is to locate those agents whose advertisement matches an issued request. Dynamic discovery removes the need for hardcoded references, while allowing agents to enter and exit the MAS and engage in flexible global interaction patterns.

The dual behavior, individual problem solving and social interactions, displayed by agents is reflected in different approaches toward ontologies. In general, we can distinguish between *private* ontologies that allow the agent to organize its own problem solving and reasoning, and *public* ontologies that the agent shares with the rest of the agents in the MAS.

Private ontologies serve the problem solving purposes of the agent. Because of this function it is often difficult to distinguish between ontologies as conceptualization of the domain of the agent, and the knowledge representation needed by the problem solving process that the agent employs. For example, an agent that uses planning technology to solve its problems may base its private ontologies on a STRIP [13, 17] like representations, with the result of representing its domain in terms of actions that the agent can perform, and plans that the agent constructs. On the other hand, an agent based on a DATALOG Data Base would instead represent its domain in terms of static facts and inference rules that allow the agent to extract the knowledge that is implicitly stored in the data base

Public ontologies are shared among multiple agents in the MAS. They are independent of the specific problem solving mechanism adopted by the agents; furthermore, ontologies need to respect the heterogeneity of the agents in the MAS. For example, while each agent in the MAS may entertain its own private knowledge representation, agents may also share knowledge using ontology languages, such as DAML+OIL [8], which provide their own formalism, and their own independent proof theory. The main role of public ontologies is to support agents in their interoperation; particularly in communication and information exchanges. Specifically, public ontologies need to provide a description of the domain of the whole MAS that is shared across all the agents, and a shared vocabulary so that agents understand the content of the messages that they exchange.

A crucial subset of the domain of an agent is the MAS the agent is part of. Other agents in the MAS affect what the agent does and how it does it. To this extent, ontologies should support the description of agents in terms of their capabilities, basic information on how to contact them, interaction protocol, reliability, reputation, security and so on. Furthermore, the social dimension of a MAS does not emerge just by developing agents and hoping that somehow they interact; rather agents need an infrastructure that provides the services such as location registries, and conventions such as standard protocols that allow agents to find each other and interact [49]. Therefore, ontologies should also support the description of the MAS infrastructure, what kind of registries it employs [54], what kind of protocols, and so on.

It is virtually impossible to find a common denominator across all possible private agent ontologies. This is because intelligent agents have been based on virtually every problem solving mechanism that has been invented in AI. Examples range from deductive agents based on ConGolog [18] that use ontologies expressed in Situation calculus [28], to agents exploiting various types of synthetic planning, as for example the RETSINA agents [46, 34] based on HTN planning [12], or BDI [36] inspired agents based on reactive planning [16, 24, 32], to agents that use decision theoretic and game theoretic approaches [26].

In this paper we concentrate on the use of public ontologies in agent discovery, interoperation and communication. The rest of the chapter is organized as follows: section 17.2 concentrates on the contribution of ontologies to agents' social activities. We will show that ontologies are essential to the description of agents' "social interfaces", and in particular the description of agents' capabilities which are needed for agent discovery in a MAS. In section 17.3 we describe ontologies for agent communication and show how ontologies contribute to mutual understanding of agent messages and interactions. Section 17.4 We will then conclude highlighting some of the open challenges.

## 17.2 Agent Discovery

Dynamic discovery mechanisms have four distinctive characteristics: the first one is a representation of the agents in the system; the second one a matching process that identifies the similarities between requests for agents, and advertisements of agents in the MAS; the third characteristic is a set of infrastructure components such as registries and protocols that support discovery; and finally, the last characteristics of discovery processes, relates to the problem solving of the agents. The different discovery schemes proposed in the literature are distinguished by the way they address the four different aspects of discovery, leading to a range of various levels of flexibility in the dynamic reconfiguration and coordination regimes of the agents in the MAS. For example, OAA [31] assumes a centralized broker which mediates all the interactions between agents; Contract Net [43] does not assume any global registry, rather agents use a bidding protocol to reply to task announcements and contract tasks.

Ontologies are an essential ingredient of discovery. They provide the means to represent the different aspects of agents and the basic mechanisms for the match between agents requests and agents advertisements. First of all, since agents are objects in the domain, any ontological representation of the domain should necessarily also represent the agents themselves. But more importantly, agents modify their environment, so any descriptions of an agent necessarily refers to the ontological description of the environment the agent lives in. In this section, we analyze the different aspects of discovery, and its relations with ontologies. Specifically we will analyze the representation of agents in advertisements and requests, and how this representation affects the matching process and the agent's problem solving.

## 17.2.1 Capability Representation

Agents can be represented at many levels of abstraction. At the physical level they are characterized by their ports and network protocols. This is essentially the representation provided by the Web services infrastructure specifications such as WSDL [6] and UDDI [51]. At a more abstract level, agents interact with other agents through a communication language, and use a set of ontologies to encode their messages and interpret the messages that they receive. From another point of view, agents are characterized by their capabilities, their interaction protocol, the problem solving procedures that they employ, the legal entity that is responsible for their correct functioning, and so on.

In this section we concentrate on the representation of capabilities which we believe is crucial for the discovery of autonomous intelligent agents in an open MAS. In such systems, agents are aware of the problem solving needs that emerges during their reasoning, but they do not know which agent in the MAS can satisfy those needs. The task of the agent is then to abstract from the specific problem to the capabilities that it expects from a provider. For example, an agent that provides financial advice may need the latest quote of the IBM stock. To this extent, the agent should transform the particular problem, i.e. get the quotes of the IBM stock, to a description of the capabilities it expects from the stock quotes provider, i.e. stock market reporting. Finally, the financial planning agent should use that capability description to locate the stock reporting agents.

A number of capability representation schemes have been proposed by the agent community and more recently by the Web Services and Semantic Web community. Each of these representation schemes makes different assumptions on the representation of the agents, and most importantly on what kind of ontologies they use in their representation. Specifically, we distinguish between two types of representation schemes: the first one assumes ontologies that provide an *explicit* representation of the tasks performed by agents. In those ontologies, each task is described by a different concept, while agents are described by enumerating the tasks that they perform. The second representation scheme describes agents by the state transformation that they produce, therefore there is no mention of the task performed by the agent; the task is *implicitly* represented by the state transformation of the agent's inputs to the outputs it produces.

The two approaches to agent representation provide two ways to use ontologies. The schemes that make an explicit use of tasks ontologies provide a straightforward way to locate agents with give capabilities. But they also require ontologies that assign a concept for each task performed by each agent in the MAS. Since agents can perform many different tasks, these ontologies can grow very large thus becoming unmanageable and may not scale up when agents with new capabilities enter the system. Another drawback of the explicit representation schemes is that they do not represent what information the provider agent needs in order to interact with a requesting agent. The implicit representation schemes require only concepts that describe the domain of the agent, and then use those concepts to describe the task computed by the agent. In addition, some implicit representation schemes provide

**Fig. 17.1.** Fragment of ontology of loan selling tasks

information (e.g. in terms of needed inputs) that a requester must provide to interact with a service provider agent. On the other hand, explicit representations facilitate the matching process since there is no need to infer the task from its implicit representation. Each capability representation scheme strikes a different balance between the two extremes depending on the ontologies that it has available, and how closely they describe the capabilities of the agents in the MAS.

### 17.2.2  Explicit Agent Capability Representations

An example of ontology which provides an explicit description of tasks and processes is the MIT Process Handbook [30]. Figure 17.1 shows a fragment of the specialization hierarchy of the ontology of tasks with the root "sell financial services" [30]. Furthermore, it shows that the concept Sell Loan is a specialization of Sell Financial Service which in turn is specialized by Sell Credit Card, Sell Mortgage and other concepts. In turn, the ontology associates to each process properties such as port that describes the I/O behavior of the process, and decomposition that describes how the process is realized by the composition of other processes described in the ontology. The MIT Process Handbook can be used to index Web services and agents for later retrieval [1]. For example, an agent that sells loans would be associated with the concept Sell Loan in the taxonomy in figure 17.1. The advantage of this approach is that it reduces the burden of modeling the agent, since it is represented by the task it performs. The disadvantage of this representation, at least in principle, is that it is impossible to distinguish between Web services or agents that sell loans whose amount is greater that $50,000 from agents that sell loans whose amount is smaller than $10,000[1]. To represent these constraints on the loan amount that the two agents offer would require, at least in principle, the definition of two subclasses of Sell Loan to describe the two different cases.

The use of explicit task ontologies for agent representation has been proposed for a number of agent representations and more recently for representation of semantic web services. InfoSleuth [33] describes different aspects of agents using con-

---

[1] We selected "amount" because it does not seem to be represented in the ontology. In general any unmodeled feature can be used here instead.

cepts drawn from different ontologies. An agent representation based on InfoSleuth is shown in figure 17.2. The representation inherits from the finance ontology the definition of stock quotes, and from the conversation ontology the specifications of the communication language that the agent uses, namely KQML. Requests for capabilities and advertisements of capabilities have the same representation; a match between an advertisement and a request is recognized when the advertised agent has all the features that are specified in the request.

```
capability example-capability
   ontology finance
     class stockQuote
       slot ticker
       slot delay in immediate
   ontology conversation
     class conversation
       slot language in kqml
```

**Fig. 17.2.** example of stock quote agent in InfoSleuth

The representation used by InfoSleuth takes advantage of the types of agents that were used in InfoSleuth applications, namely information agents. For example, from the description of the agent above there is no way of telling whether the agent provides information about conversation languages, or whether it uses a specific conversation language. In both cases the description is exactly the same. The resolution of the ambiguity is possible only with the reference to the context since no agent in InfoSleuth provides information about communication languages.

Other capability representation languages include Phosphorous [19, 45] which represents capabilities as a predicate in which the functor is the name of the task represented and the arguments are the parameters of the task. The matching process is reduced to a series of tests that analyze the subsumption relation (or the inverted subsumption) between the advertisement and the request. Another approach that makes use of the semantic web has been proposed in [50]; tasks of web services are represented by the instance of the task that they perform, and a set of properties that depend on the task. Matching of the request with the advertisement is reduced to a subsumption or inverted subsumption between the advertisements and the request.

### 17.2.3 Implicit Agent Capability Representation

LARKS [48, 47] provides an example of agent representation that uses an implicit task definition. LARKS represents the capabilities of agents as transformation from a set of inputs to a set of outputs. Consistent with this view, each LARKS advertisement and request requires the specification of seven features of the agent.

*Context* The context, or the domain, of the agent.

*InTypes* and *OutTypes*  An optional set of input and output data types.
*Inputs* and *Outputs*  The inputs that the agent expects, and the outputs that it generates.
*InConstraints* and *OutConstraints*  Sets of constraints on the inputs and outputs if the agent.
*ConcDescription*  a list of concepts used in the agent description, that do not appear in the ontologies.

Different agents are described by different settings of the parameters. For example, a stock quote reporting agent in LARKS is described in figure 17.3; the context specifies that the agent operates in the domain of Finance and that given a ticker as input, it generates a quote as output. This definition of course assumes that there exist ontologies that define the concepts of Finance, ticker, and quote and that those ontologies are shared by the agent that provides the service, all possible requesters and the infrastructure components that are responsible for the matching between the two.

```
        Context = Finance
        InTypes = String
       OutTypes = Real
         Inputs = ticker
        Outputs = quote
  InConstraints = retail ∧ banking
 OutConstraints = retail ∧ banking
ConcDescription =
```

**Fig. 17.3.** LARKS advertisement of stock reporting agent

The matching process adopted by LARKS uses a combination of information retrieval techniques such as TF/IDF [38] and logic inference to identify the relation between the advertisement and the request. The information retrieval techniques are used as heuristics that remove all the advertisements that for sure have nothing to do with the request. The logic inference is based on subsumption and on weighted relations to compute the distance between the concepts used in the advertisement and the concepts used in the request.

The LARKS matching process allows for *partial matches* to find advertisements of providers whose capabilities are *similar enough* to the capabilities requested. This is because in practice, it is unrealistic to expect that the request will match exactly one or more advertisements of agents in the MAS since the requester and provider may use local ontologies that could be different. The goal of partial matching is to maintain validity by rejecting matches of advertisements and requests that are totally unrelated, and measuring the degree of match between two capability descriptions: the more similar the services described, the higher the degree of match. LARKS deals with partial matching by measuring the conceptual distance between the advertisement and the request, and it leaves to the requester to determine a cut-off value that limits the distance between the advertisement and the request to some value acceptable to the requester. A high cut-off value would eliminate most of the providers even if their capabilities are close to the capabilities requested, a low value would include many providers whose capabilities may differ substantially from the capabilities requested.

### 17.2.4 Combining Explicit and Implicit Representation

Other approaches to capability representation use a combination of the implicit and explicit representations. These approaches combine the ease of use of ontologies of tasks, when those ontologies are present, with the ability of describing the capability of any agent provided by the implicit approach.

The most notable example of this approach is the DAML-S Service Profile[2] [2]. It provides an implicit description of agents in terms of a host of features as LARKS does. In addition profiles are concepts in a DAML ontology and therefore it is possible to organize them in a taxonomy similar to the taxonomy shown in figure 17.1.

DAML-S Profiles provide three types of agent information: the first type is a specification of an *actor* who is responsible for the advertisement or the request. The second type of information consists of a host of *Functional Attributes* such as the category of service, quality of service and additional service parameters which can be used to specify details of the service. The last type of information specifies the *Functional Specification* which defines the transformation produced by the agent in terms of the inputs, outputs, preconditions and effects. Functional Attributes and the Functional Specification describe the capability of the agent.

Functional Attributes allow to specify features of the agent that are important to decide whether the agent adequately addresses a request. For example, one of the functional attributes of a stock reporting agent may be the delay in stock reporting with respect to the market. This could be described using DAML-S by specifying a service parameter as shown in figure 17.4. In the figure, the value of the stock quoting delay is 1 minute.

```
<profile:serviceParameter>
   <profile:QuoteDelay rdf:ID="agentDelay">
     <profile:serviceParameterName rdf':value=''one minute"/>
     <profile:sParameter rdf:resource="time:#1minute"/>
   </profile:GeographicRadius>
</profile:serviceParameter>
```

**Fig. 17.4.** Example of DAML-S service parameter

---

[2] DAML-S is composed of three modules: the Service Profile that describes the agent, the Process Model that describes the workflow of the agent and the Service Grounding that describes the communication details of how to interact with the agent.

The functional representation describes the transformation computed by the agent in a way that is similar to LARKS. An example of functional representation is shown in figure 17.5. The agent requires as input a ticker symbol and it returns the quote of the stock. To execute correctly the requester will have to prove that it is a valid subscriber to the service (we assume in this example a subscription-based payment model for the stock quoting service). As a result of invoking the service, the requester's account will be charged[3]

```
     Inputs = ticker
    Outputs = quote
Preconditions = valid(membership)
    Effects = charged(account)
```

**Fig. 17.5.** DAML-S functional representation of stock agent

The matching process for DAML-S [35] recognizes a match between the advertisement and the request, in case when the advertised service could be used in place of the requested service. Specifically, the matching process uses the inputs and outputs, of the advertisement and the request to derive the different degrees of match: *exact* when the advertisement and the request are synonymous, *plugIn* when the advertisement subsumes the request, *subsumed* when the request subsumes the advertisement, and *fail* when no relation can be found. When plugIn match holds, the provider claims it provides all the requester needs, but the advertisement may be so generic that it is useless for the requester. For example, a provider may advertise that it retails all kinds of products. This advertisement partially matches a request for a book seller. When subsumed match holds, the provider provides only part of the capabilities that the requester needs, and it is up to the requester to verify if those capabilities are enough. For example, a provider may advertise that it sells Ford and Chrysler cars. This advertisement matches in a subsumed match a request for a provider of sedan cars. Presumably the provider provides Ford and Chrysler sedans, and it is up to the requester to decide whether these brands of sedans meet its needs so it would interact further with the provider.

As pointed out above the DAML-S Profile specifies a class in a DAML ontology, therefore, at least in principle it is possible to follow a different matching process that makes use of DAML classifiers to match advertisements and requests. The challenge with matchmaking of DAML-S Profiles is to combine the explicit and implicit way of matching to improve the final result.

### 17.2.5 Trade-offs

We have described how the capabilities of agents play an essential role in discovery, and we analyzed in some detail different agent and web service representation

---

[3] At the time of writing, DAML does not support a rule language, therefore, conditions like valid(membership) or charged(account) cannot be expressed.

formalisms. We classified them into two main types: explicit, when they take advantage of an extensive taxonomy of tasks, and implicit, when such an ontology is not used. There are clearly trade-offs between the two representations. Representations that use explicit representations of tasks require ontologies that are difficult to built. Furthermore, they suffer from the weakness that every time an agent with a new functionality enters the MAS, a new class must be defined in the ontology. Implicit representations do not need any explicit coding of tasks in the ontology providing a natural expression of tasks using domain ontologies already available. The tradeoff is that the use of explicit task representations makes matching of requests and advertisements much easier reducing it to test what kind of subsumption relation holds between advertisements and requests. Matching between capabilities expressed implicitly is more complex. Since there may not be an easy way to classify different tasks, matching requires a careful comparison between the input/output transformation described in the request with the transformations described in the advertisements.

## 17.3 Ontologies for Agent Communication

In a MAS, knowledge and capabilities are distributed across the agents in such a way that no single agent has a complete knowledge of the whole multiagent system and no single agent can perform all the operations that can be performed by all the other agents. Despite their limited knowledge and capabilities, agents can ask other agents to perform some action or to provide information. Ultimately, communication allows any agent to extend the set of goals that it can satisfy by asking other agents with a different set of capabilities to contribute to its plans. For example an agent in the blocks world may be able to slide boxes, but not lift them; nevertheless, it may still construct plans for stacking blocks by pushing the blocks close to each other and then asking a lifting agent to put them one on top of the other.

The ability to communicate with other agents is one of the central skills of any agent in a Multi-agent system. Furthermore, since communication extends the knowledge and the capabilities of any agent, it becomes an integral part of the problem solving of any agent. Crucially, in the example of the blocks world agent described above, the resulting plan contains both physical actions: pushing blocks together, and communicative actions: asking the lifting agent to stack blocks.

The interleaving of communication and problem solving requires the agent to decide whether to achieve its goals via direct action, or by asking other agents to achieve some of those goals. In turn, this requires communication actions to be described as any other actions: they must have preconditions and they achieve some effect. This is the approach taken by the speech act theory [3, 41, 7], which, in a nutshell, adopts the view that by saying something the speaker achieves the effect of producing either a change in its world, or a change in the beliefs and intentions of the listener. For example, some utterances have very striking effects: when a public official declares two people married, the effect is a change in their marital status. Other utterances have more subtle effects, for instance by saying "its raining" the speaker attempts to make the listener belief that indeed it is raining; similarly, by asking the listener to do something, the speaker may induce in the listener the desire to do what was asked.

### 17.3.1 Representation of Speech Acts

Speech act theory, and its predication that communicative actions are essentially equivalent to other action in the world proved to be very appealing to the agent community. First, it allows a precise definition of communication actions and of the consequences of message exchanges; second, communicative actions can be defined in terms of planning operators and they may easily inserted in the plan that the agent is developing to achieve its goals[4].

Speech act theory is the base of ontologies of communication actions such as KQML [14] and FIPA ACL[5] [15]. For example FIPA ACL specifies 22 speech acts, which are described by two properties: the first one specifies *feasibility preconditions* which are conditions that should be satisfied for the communicative action to be performed; and *rational effects* that represent the effects that the speaker hopes to achieve with the communicative action. As an example, consider the definition of the *inform* action in FIPA ACL as shown in figure 17.6. It states that it is appropriate for the speaker to inform the listener of $\phi$ when (feasibility condition: FP) the speaker believes the $\phi$ holds, and it does not believe that the listener believes that $\phi$ is true, nor the speaker is uncertain on whether the listener believes $\phi$ to be true. The result (rational effect) of the inform action is that the listener believes $\phi$.

**Inform**

$< speaker, inform(listener, \phi) >$

FP: $B_{speaker}\phi \vee \neg B_{speaker}(B_{speaker}f_{listener}\phi \wedge U_{speaker}f_{listener}\phi)$

RE: $B_{listener}\phi$

**Fig. 17.6.** FIPA definition of Inform

The use of FIPA ACL allows the speaker agent to have expectations on the behavior of the listener, but there are no guarantees that the expectation will be met by reality. The first problem is that since the listener is an autonomous agent with its own knowledge, it may already know that $\phi$ is false or it may believe that the

---

[4] The linguistic basis of the speech act theory is more complicated than described here, and cannot be represented faithfully with planning operators. Nevertheless, our description is faithful to the use that agents make of it.

[5] KQML and FIPA ACL are usually described as agent communication languages, not as ontologies. In reality they are both, they provide a syntax that can be used by agents to compile messages, and a semantics that specifies concepts like message and speech act. To this extent FIPA ACL and KQML are effectively ontologies for agent communication.

speaker is a liar and therefore it may reject the inform on those grounds. The second problem is that both FIPA ACL and the speech acts theory assume that the listener understands $\phi$, but when this assumption does not hold, the listener will fail to hold the beliefs that the speaker expects it to hold. Suppose for example that the speaker informs the listener of the IBM quotes using the message in figure 17.7. Even if we assume that both parties agree on the FIPA ACL interpretation of inform speech act, still the listener has to understand the meaning of the terms "quote", "IBM," and "$87" and the way their meanings are combined to form the meaning of the statement. Furthermore, the speaker should agree with the listener's interpretation. The failure to reach an agreement on the meaning of those terms would lead to a failure to share the same interpretation of the message and it would prevent successful communication between the speaker and the listener. This very simple example shows that in the absence of any shared ontologies that define the meaning of the terms used in the message exchange, the two parties have no way to communicate.


(inform
  :sender speaker
  :receiver listener
  :content (quote IBM $87))


**Fig. 17.7.** Example of inform message


    Ontologies provide the tools to interpret the content of the message. For example, the speaker may encode its message using the DAML+OIL ontology shown in figure 17.8. The ontology provides a description of *quote*, specify that it relates to the concept *Ticker* through the ticker relation and to a *Value* through the *hasValue* relation. Furthermore, it specifies how these concepts are related to other concepts that may be defined elsewhere. For example, the ticker symbol is related to a company description that will contain other information about that company, while the value relates to a currency and so on. In this framework, the content of the message could be expressed as an instance built on the basis of the ontology. In this case it describes a quote, using an instance of the ticker that happens to point to IBM, and the value of the quote is 89 measured in US Dollars.

    As the example shows, ontologies, by providing a shared conceptualization of the domain, effectively contribute to agent communication by providing a language and dictionary that can be used to express concepts and statements about the domain of the agents. Furthermore, those languages and dictionaries are standardized and shared by all the agents in the MAS. While each agent may have its own knowledge and its own beliefs on the value of the IBM stocks, they all share the same understanding of terms like IBM and quote so that all of them achieve the same interpretation of the statements that are communicated.

    The <u>second contribution of ontologies</u> is in the use of the knowledge that the agent receives through its communication with other agents. The rational effect of

| Message Content | Ontology |
|---|---|
| <Quote> | <class rdf:ID="**Ticker**"> |
|  <hasTicker> |  <property rdf:ID="symbol"/> |
|   <Ticker> |   <domain rdf:resource="#Ticker"/> |
|    <symbol |   <range rdf:resource="xsd#string"/> |
|     rdf:value="IBM"/> |  </property> |
|    <company |  <property rdf:ID="company"/> |
|     rdf:resource="#IBM"/> |   <domain rdf:resource="#Ticker"/> |
|   </Ticker> |   <range rdf:resource="#Company"/> |
|  </hasTicker> |  </property> |
|  <hasQuote> | < /class> |
|   <Value> | |
|    <currency | <class rdf:ID="**Value**"> |
|     rdf:resurce="#US_Dollar"/> | <property rdf:ID="currency"/> |
|    <hasValue rdf:value="89"/> |   <domain rdf:resource="#Value"/> |
|   </Value> |   <range rdf:resource="#Currency"/> |
|  </hasQuote> |  </property> |
| </Quote> |  <property rdf:ID="hasValue"/> |
| |   <domain rdf:resource="#Value"/> |
| |   <range rdf:resource="xsd#float"/> |
| |  </property> |
| | < /class> |
| | |
| | <class rdf:ID="**Quote**"> |
| |  <property rdf:ID="hasTicker"/> |
| |   <domain rdf:resurce="#Quote"/> |
| |   <range rdf:resurce="#Ticker"/> |
| |  </property> |
| |  <property rdf:ID="quote"/> |
| |   <domain rdf:resource="#Quote"/> |
| |   <range rdf:resource="#Value"/> |
| |  </property> |
| | < /class> |

**Fig. 17.8.** Description of a Quote using a DAML+OIL ontology

the inform speech act, as we defined it in figure 17.6, is that the listener believes the content of the message. This means that the content of the message has to be added to the knowledge base of the agent and used to derive new inferences. Ontologies support this integration by providing the bases for the organization of knowledge in the agents knowledge base and of a proof theory so that the agent can derive inferences from the knowledge it gathers.

## 17.3.2 Extending Communication to Conversations

The use of speech acts in communication is quite limited. It provides a framework for interpreting each message that agents exchange, but it does not provide a framework that extends to longer conversations. FIPA ACL, for example, mandates that every `query` action should be responded to with an `inform` action. But the use of FIPA ACL speech acts does not extend beyond these two message exchanges. Ideally, long conversations should be built as composition of simple atomic speech acts as human conversations are. From this point of view, agent A may ask B do X, B may query A asking for clarifications, A responds to B, and B satisfied commits to X. While humans find very easy to be part of this kind of conversations, software agents are not yet sophisticated enough to be part of the "game of language" [29].

The management of long conversations suffers from a number of serious problems. The first problem is that the compositional semantics of speech acts may result in multiple interpretations for the same sequence of speech acts. This is the so called *basic problem* [20] which may lead to ambiguity and misunderstanding between the different parties. The second problem is in the definition of speech acts in FIPA ACL: speech acts require the speaker to have a model of the private beliefs of the listener which are never available, so the very preconditions of FIPA ACL speech acts, if taken at their extreme consequences, cannot be satisfied by any agent ultimately preventing communication [42]. The last problem is that these long conversations are often constructed by agents that do not share the same goal, and that may very easily lose track of the coherence of the conversation. Furthermore, the reasoning required to maintain coherence of the conversation is extremely difficult to model, as, for example, it requires employing abductive reasoning, to construct a model of the other parties involved in the conversation to "guess" their goals [23, 27]; but abductive reasoning is rarely adopted by software agents

In addition to the problems listed above, agents often enter in very scripted interactions where the meaning of speech acts is artificially modified to fit the situation. For instance, e-commerce agents enter auctions and bid to buy widgets there. Those agents need to follow the protocol of the auction. Furthermore, e-commerce agents need to understand what counts as a valid bid, how much commitment is associated with the bid, what is the cost of retracting the bid. Much of this information cannot be represented using speech acts. While there has been a great deal of work on agents in e-commerce on exploiting game theoretic reasoning to select a winning auction strategy [40], from the communication point of view, it is always assumed that the agent is able to participate in the auction.

Agents interactions are very constrained and goal directed. Agents do not entertain each other with small talk, rather their interactions are often very well defined and constrained by the context. In the example of e-commerce agents whose interaction is constrained by the auction protocol, any communicative action that is outside what is prescribed by the auction protocol is inappropriate and potentially dangerous when interpreted as a bid. From this point of view, the power of speech acts only adds non-needed complexity to long conversations. In general, each conversation is regulated by *Conversational Policies* , or in other words "set of principles that constrains the nature and exchange of semantically coherent ACL messages" [20].

Ontologies provide a way to formalize conversational policies as objects in the domain so that they can be used by the agents to participate in long conversations. For example, an auction may be formalized as an object that has a protocol, a number of participants that should have well defined characteristics and that play well defined roles in the auction. Furthermore, an auction is characterized by negotiation rules, products to sell, and bids placed by the potential buyers. The use of ontologies to formalize conversations has two advantages: first of all it specifies in a precise and declarative way what agents should do to be part of the conversations, or as in our example of the auction, the second advantage is that the same knowledge is shared across all the agents so that they not only know what they have to do but they also have expectations on what the auctioneer and the other bidders plan to do.

A similar approach is followed by DAML-S [2] when it defines the interaction protocol with an agent[6]. Using DAML-S the agents specifies the protocol of interaction with others as a workflow that mimics its own processing workflow. Furthermore it specifies what information it needs as input what it generates as output and the format of the messages exchanged. Using DAML-S allows any agent to infer the interaction protocol and to decide what information to send at any given time.

The use of ontologies to represent conversations is producing a shift in the interpretation of agent communication languages. By representing explicitly conversations as protocols and the set of messages that have to be exchanged, the ontological representation effectively departs from the traditional representation of agent communication based on speech acts. Indeed, when the protocol is completely specified there is no need to use speech acts at all. The cost of this switch is the transition from an extremely powerful way to represent agent messages based on speech acts where agents have the ability to say all they want at any time, to a constrained way that carefully specifies the interaction protocol limiting the messages that can be exchanged with the advantage of gaining management of the conversation.

## 17.4 Social Knowledge

Communication achieves two objectives for agents. First it allows agents to work together in such a way that the work of one agent contributes to the work of other agents. For example, the performance of the requester of information, depends on the quality of the information provided and the timely answers of the provider. The second contribution of communication is to provide a coordination mechanism whereby agents negotiate how they are going to share a common resource or how they are going to collaborate toward the solution of a problem.

Agent's interaction and collaboration results in the emergence of a society of agents with its own (often implicit) social structure. As a consequence agents need

---

[6] DAML-S is designed to represent "Semantic" Web services, which are, from our prospective, indistinguishable from agents.

*social knowledge* [25] which specifies how agents work together and the *norms* of acceptable social behavior in the MAS [5, 9]. For example, asking an agent to perform an action or to provide information implies a commitment on the part of the speaker of waiting for the answer, and a commitment on the part of the listener to respond truthfully, coherently, and in a timely manner to the request [42]. When agents do not live up to their commitments, the interaction fails, therefore either the listener fails to receive an appropriate answer, or the speaker will not be able to deliver its answer to the listener. Norms provide a tool to represent explicitly what is expected by an agent in a given situation; the utility of norms is in making the MAS and the agents in it more predictable. Because of the existence of norms, agents can develop predictions on the behavior of other agents, which in turns allow higher levels of cooperation.

At the knowledge level, norms specify constraints on the behavior of the agent within what is acceptable for the rest of the agents at large. In general, it is up to the agent to decide whether to adhere or violate a norm, knowing that violations of the norm come at some cost for the agent itself, or for other agents in the MAS. Violations may result when the agent believes that the adherence to the norm is either too costly or it prevents the agent from the achievement of its goals.

While in principle, norms can be used to express any social constraint, they find their immediate application in the definition of concepts like contracts and commitments that agents develop as they work together. For example, contracts carry the obligation of the parties to perform their role in the contract, and the authorization to take some action when the contract is violated [11]. For example, the obligation of an airline to transport all passengers that have a reservation and the obligation of the passengers of paying for their ticket are shown in figure 17.9. Here the `goal` condition represents the goal that the agents have to fulfill their obligation, while the `exit` condition represents the condition that results if the agents do not fulfill their obligations.

```
obligation(airline,passenger,transport(airline,passenger)
    in:   flightReservation(passenger,airline)
    goal: transport(passenger,airline)
    exit: cancel(passenger,ticket) ⟹
    obligation(passenger,airline,payCost(passenger,airline)) ∧
    auth(airline,passenger,direct(payCost(passenger,airline)))
        cancel(airline,flight) ⟹
    obligation(airline,passenger,payCost(airline,passenger)) ∧
    auth(passenger,airline,direct(payCost(airline,passenger)))
```

**Fig. 17.9.** Example of an obligation

Authorizations provide a permission to the agent to perform an action. For instance, our example of obligation shown in figure 17.9 specifies that the passenger is authorized to ask for a reimbursement if the flight is canceled. This authorization allows the passenger to actually ask for the reimbursement. The formal definition of this authorization is shown in figure 17.10. The authorization allows the passenger to assume the goal of making the airline pay the cost of canceling the reservation.

```
auth(passenger,airline,direct(payCost(airline,passenger)))
    in:    flightReservation(passenger,airline)
    goal: payCost(airline,passenger)
```

**Fig. 17.10.** Example of an authorization

Norms provide ontologies for the specification of the expected social behavior in a given community of agents. To this extent, ontologies provide the language to express norms that are shared by every agent in the MAS; furthermore, ontologies provide the conceptual structures to represent norms as shared concepts. Despite the importance of expressing norms in the agent community, virtually no work has been done to develop an ontological representation of norms. Much of the contribution of this community has been in the study of the effects of norms on the problem solving process of the agent.

In addition to the work on norms in the agent community, there are other two sources of ontologies to represent concepts similar to norms. The first contribution is the representation of laws in legal reasoning. [53, 52]. The main task of these ontologies is indexing of laws and regulations for information retrieval and possibly for validity checking to verify that the regulations do not contradict each other. These ontologies provide a different notion of norm which is basically a description of a law, and the acts to which those norms apply, as for instance robbery or murder.

The second effort to construct ontologies for norms comes from the e-commerce community and their needs to express concepts such as contracts that regulate electronic transactions. SweetDeal [22] bases its representation on a combination of Semantic Web ontology languages such as DAML and RuleML [37] in conjunction with the MIT Process Handbook. Contracts are associated with a process such as selling, or delivery and with a set of exceptions which describe what can go wrong, such as late delivery, with the contract and the associated penalties. Furthermore, this work shows how contracts can be used in conjunction with business rules to manage risk of penalties.

## 17.5 Open Challenges

Despite the considerable effort toward the construction of ontologies that allow agents to interoperate in open MAS, very difficult and challenging problems are still open. We can divide these problems in two major sets of challenges: the first

set of challenges are related to the type of languages and logics that provide sufficient expressive power to be of use for agents in their interactions; the second set
of challenges lies in the creation of ontologies that help the agents in their everyday
interaction in MAS. We will leave the first set of challenges to other chapters of this
book, and we will concentrate on the second set of challenges.

A major challenge comes with the description of ontologies that describe concepts such as commitments, agreements and contracts. As shown in [21] these ontologies prove to be essential for a wide spread use of the Semantic Web and Semantic Web services [2] in real World e-commerce applications. Crucially, there seems to
be a schism between the use and representation of norms that comes from the agent
community which is mostly concerned with the mental attitudes that the agent adopts
as a consequences of accepting a given norm; and the Semantic Web attitude of providing a description of contracts that is consistent with the underlying semantics of
Semantic Web languages leaving to the proof theory of the language and the inference engines adopted by the agents the derivation of the appropriate consequences.

In addition to the development of ontologies for commitments, agents and Semantic Web services need ways to express and reason about the reputation and trust
of the agents that they encounter. These are fundamental evaluation criteria that we
typically use when we enter in a business relation with our partners. These concepts
need to be expanded to communities of agents so that a cheating agent is penal-
ized by its unacceptable behavior. Some seminal work in the area is represented in
[4, 55, 56].

Agents can interoperate if they adopt the same modes of communication, including agreeing on the security protocols used in their communication. Ontologies are
needed to specify the security requirements of agents [10].

Throughout the paper we referred generically to "ontologies" as if there is a consistent corpus of ontologies available to the agents. In reality many ontologies are
redundant in the sense that they present the same domain, but with little or no interoperation between the ontologies [44]. Since ontologies play a pivotal role in agent
interoperation by providing a shared representation of the domain and of the concepts that the agents need to use, agents that use different ontologies fail to interoperate. Effectively, it is as if the two agents end up speaking two different languages.
The problem of ontology interoperation is very difficult since ontologies may provide different prospective and different sets of information on the concepts that they
represent.

# References

1. Bernstein Abraham and Mark Klein. High precision service retrieval. In *ISWC 2002*,
   Sardegna, Italy, 2002.
2. The DAML Services Coalition: Anupriya Ankolekar, Mark Burstein, Jerry R. Hobbs, Ora
   Lassila, David L. Martin, Sheila A. McIlraith, Srini Narayanan, Massimo Paolucci, Terry
   Payne, Katia Sycara, and Honglei Zeng. Daml-s: Web service description for the semantic
   web. In *ISWC 2002*, Sardegna, Italy, 2002.

3. J.L. Austin. *How to Do Things with Words 2nd Edition*. Harvard University Press, Cambridge, Ma., 1962.
4. Jose Cardoso, John Miller, Amit Sheth, and Jonathan Arnold. Modeling quality of service for workflows and web service processes. *Very Large Data Bases Journal*, 2002.
5. Cristiano Castelfranchi, Frank Dignum, Catholijn M. Jonker, and Jan Treur. Deliberate normative agents: Principles and architecture. In N.R. Jennings and Y. Lespérance, editors, *Intelligent Agents VI*. Springer-Verlag, Berlin, 2000.
6. Erik Christensen, Francisco Curbera, Greg Meredith, and Sanjiva Weerawarana. Web Services Description Language (WSDL) 1.1.
http://www.w3.org/TR/2001/NOTE-wsdl-20010315, 2001.
7. Philip R. Cohen and C. Raymond Perrault. Elements of a plan-based theory of speech acts. *Cognitive Science*, 3:177–212, 1979.
8. DAML Joint Committee. DAML+OIL language, 2001.
9. Rosaria Conte, Cristiano Castelfranchi, and Frank Dignum. Autonomous norm acceptance. In Jörg Müller, Munindar P. Singh, and Anand S. Rao, editors, *Proceedings of the 5th International Workshop on Intelligent Agents V : Agent Theories, Architectures, and Languages (ATAL-98)*, volume 1555, pages 99–112. Springer-Verlag: Heidelberg, Germany, 1999.
10. Grit Denker. Towards security in daml. Technical Report 94025, SRI International, 2002.
11. Frank Dignum. Autonomous agents and social norms. In *Workshop on Norms, Obligations and Conventions (ICMAS-96)*, Kyoto, 1996.
12. Kutluhan Erol, James Hendler, and Dana S. Nau. Htn planning: Complexity and expressivity. In *AAAI94*, Seattle, 1994.
13. Richard E. Fikes and Nils J. Nilsson. STRIPS: A new approach to the application of theorem proving to problem solving. *Artificial Intelligence*, 5:189–208, 1971.
14. Tim Finin, Yannis Labrou, and James Mayfield. KQML as an agent communication language. In Jeff Bradshaw, editor, *Software Agents*. MIT Press, Cambridge, 1997.
15. FIPA. FIPA ACL message structure specification, 2002.
16. Michael P. Georgeff and Amy L. Lansky. Reactive reasoning and planning. In *AAAI87*, pages 677–682, Seattle, WA, 1987.
17. Malik Ghallab et. al. Pddl-the planning domain definition language v. 2. Technical Report, report CVC TR-98-003/DCS TR-1165, Yale Center for Computational Vision and Control, 1998.
18. Giuseppe De Giacomo, Yves Lesprance, and Hector Levesque. Congolog, a concurrent programming language based on the situation calculus. *Artificial Intelligence*, 121((1-2)):109–169, 1995.
19. Yolanda Gil and Surya Ramachandran. Phosphorus: A task-based agent matchmaker. In *Agents 2001*, Montreal, Canada, 2001.
20. Mark Greaves, Heather Holmback, and Jeffrey Bradshaw. What is a conversation policy? In Frank Dignum and Mark Greaves, editors, *Issues in Agent Communication*, pages 118–131. Springer-Verlag: Heidelberg, Germany, 2000.
21. Benjamin N. Grosof. Representing e-business rules for the semantic web: Situated courteous logic programs in ruleml. In *WITS '01*, 2001.
22. Benjamin N. Grosof and Terrence C. Poon. Representing agent contracts with exceptions using xml rules, ontologies, and process descriptions. In *International Workshop on Rule Markup Languages for Business Rules on the Semantic Web*, 2002.
23. Jerry R. Hobbs, Mark Stickel, Paul Martin, and Douglas Edwards. Interpretation as abduction. In *Proceedings of the 26th Annual Meeting of the Association for Computational Linguistics*, Buffalo, NY, 1988.

24. Marcus J. Huber. Jam: A bdi-theoretic mobile agent architecture. In *Agents'99*, Seattle, WA, 1999.
25. N. R. Jennings and J. R. Campos. Towards a social level characterisation of socially responsible agents. *IEE Proceedings on Software Engineering*, 144(1):11–25, 1997.
26. Larson K. and T Sandholm. Computationally limited agents in auctions. In *Workshop on Agent-based Approaches to B2B*, 2001.
27. Henry A. Kautz and James F. Allen. Generalized plan recognition. In *AAAI-86*, Philadelphia, Pa., 1986.
28. Y. Lespérance, H. Levesque, F. Lin, and R. Scherl. Ability and knowing how in the situation calculus. *Studia Logica*, 66(1):165–186, October 2000.
29. David Lewis. Scorekeeping in a language game. *Journal of Philosophical Logic*, 1979(8):339–359, 1979.
30. Thomas W. Malone, Kevin Crowston, Brian Pentland Jintae Lee, Chrysanthos Dellarocas, George Wyner, John Quimby, Charles S. Osborn, Abraham Bernstein, George Herman, Mark Klein, and Elissa O'Donnell. Tools for inventing organizations: Toward a handbook of organizational processes. *Management Science*, 45(3):425–443, March, 199 1997.
31. David Martin, Adam Cheyer, and Douglas Moran. The Open Agent Architecture: A Framework for Building Distributed Software Systems. *Applied Artificial Intelligence*, 13(1-2):92–128, 1999.
32. Jörg P. Müller. *The Design of Intelligent Agents*. Springer, 1996.
33. Marian Nodine, Jerry Fowler, Tomasz Ksiezyk, Brad Perry, Malcolm Taylor, and Amy Unruh. Active information gathering in infosleuth. *International Journal of Cooperative Information Systems*, 9(1/2):3–28, 2000.
34. M. Paolucci, D. Kalp, A. Pannu, O. Shehory, and K. Sycara. A planning component for RETSINA agents. In N.R. Jennings and Y. Lespérance, editors, *Intelligent Agents VI*, Lecture Notes in Artificial Intelligence. Springer-Verlag, Berlin, 2000.
35. Massimo Paolucci, Takahiro Kawamura, Terry R. Payne, and Katia Sycara. Semantic matching of web services capabilities. In *ISWC2002*, 2002.
36. Anand S. Rao and Michael P. Georgeff. Modelling rational agents within a bdi-architecture. In *Proceedings of the Second International Conference on Principles of Knowledge Representation and Reasoning*, Cambridge, MA, 1991.
37. RuleML. The RuleML Web Site. http://www.dfki.uni-kl.de/ruleml/.
38. G. Salton and A Wong. A Vector Space Model for Automatic Indexing. *Communications of ACM*, 18:613–620, 1975.
39. Tuomas Sandholm. Distributed rational decision making. In G. Wei, editor, *Multiagent Systems: A Modern Introduction to Distributed Artificial Intelligence*, pages 201–258. MIT Press, 1999.
40. Tuomas Sandholm. emediator: A next generation electronic commerce server. *Computational Intelligence*, 18(4):656–676, 2002.
41. John R. Searle. *Speech Acts*. Cambridge University Press, Cambridge, 1969.
42. Munindar P. Singh. Agent communication languages: Rethinking the principles. *IEEE Computer*, 31(12), 1998.
43. R. G. Smith. The contract net protocol: High-level communication and control in a distributed problem solver. *IEEE Transactions on Computers*, 29(12):1104–1113, 1980.
44. Gerd Stumme and Alexander Maedche. Ontology merging for federated ontologies on the semantic web using fca-merge. In *Workshop on Ontologies and Information Sharing (IJCAI '01)*, 2001.
45. Bill Swartout, Yolanda Gil, and Andre Valente. Representing capabilities of problem-solving methods. In *IJCAI 99 Workshop on Ontologies and Problem-Solving Methods.*, 1999.

46. Katia Sycara, Keith Decker, Anadeep Pannu, Mike Williamson, and Dajun Zeng. Distributed intelligent agents. *IEEE-Expert*, 11(6):36–45, 1996.

47. Katia Sycara and Mattheus Klusch. Brokering and matchmaking for coordination of agent societies: A survey. In Omicini et al, editor, *Coordination of Internet Agents*. Springer, 2001.

48. Katia Sycara, Mattheus Klusch, Seth Widoff, and Janguo Lu. Dynamic service matchmaking among agents in open information environments. *ACM SIGMOD Record (Special Issue on Semantic Interoperability in Global Information Systems)*, 28(1):47–53, 1999.

49. Katia Sycara, Massimo Paolucci, Martin van Velsen, and Joseph Giampapa. The RETSINA MAS infrastructure. *Autonomous Agents and Multiagent Systems*, 2003. forthcoming.

50. David Trastour, Claudio Bartolini, and Javier Gonzalez-Castillo. A semantic web approach to service description for matchmaking of services . In *SWWS2001*, Stanford, Ca, 2001.

51. UDDI. The UDDI Technical White Paper. http://www.uddi.org/, 2000.

52. Pepijn Visser and Trevor Bench-Capon. The formal specification of a legal ontology. In *Legal Knowledge Based Systems; foundations of legal knowledge systems. Proceedings JURIX'96*, 1996.

53. R. Winkels, A. Boer, and R. Hoekstra. Clime: Lessons learned in legal information serving. In *ECAI2002*, 2002.

54. Hao-Chi Wong and Katia Sycara. A Taxonomy of Middle-agents for the Internet. In *ICMAS'2000*, 2000.

55. Bin Yu and Munindar P. Singh. An evidential model of distributed reputation management. In *AAMAS2002*, Bologna, 2002.

56. Giorgos Zacharia, Alexandros Moukas, and Pattie Maes. Collaborative reputation mechanisms in electronic marketplaces. In *HICSS*, 1999.

# 18

# Tools for Mapping and Merging Ontologies

Natalya F. Noy

Stanford University, Stanford, CA, 94305, USA noy@smi.stanford.edu

**Summary.** Researchers in the ontology-design field have developed the content for ontologies in many domain areas. This distributed nature of ontology development has led to a large number of ontologies covering overlapping domains. In order for these ontologies to be reused, they first need to be merged or aligned to one another. We developed a set of tools to support semi-automatic ontology merging: iPrompt is an interactive ontology merging tool that guides the user through the merging process, presenting him with suggestions for next steps and identifying inconsistencies and potential problems. AnchorPrompt uses a graph structure of ontologies to find correlation between concepts and to provide additional information for iPrompt. we present the tools and results of our evaluation of the tools. We discuss other tools and approaches for mapping between ontologies, both in the field of ontology design and database-schema integration.

## 18.1 Merging And Mapping Between Ontologies

Researchers have pursued development of ontologies—explicit formal specifications of domains of discourse—on the premise that ontologies facilitate knowledge sharing and reuse [23, 14]. Today, ontology development is moving from academic knowledge representation projects to the World-Wide Web. The e-commerce companies use ontologies to share information and to guide customers through their Web sites. The ontologies on the World-Wide Web range from large taxonomies categorizing Web sites (such as on Yahoo!) to categorizations of products for sale and their features (such as on Amazon.com). Many disciplines now develop standardized ontologies that domain experts can use to share and annotate information in their fields. Medicine, for example, has produced large, standardized, structured vocabularies such as SNOMED [29] and the semantic network of the Unified Medical Language System [16]. With this widespread distributed use of ontologies, different parties inevitably develop ontologies with overlapping content. For example, both Yahoo! and the DMOZ Open Directory [24] categorize information available on the Web. The two resulting directories are similar, but also have many differences.

But what does a user do when he finds several ontologies that he would like to use but that do not conform to one another? The user must establish correspondences among the source ontologies, and determine the set of overlapping concepts, concepts that are similar in meaning but have different names or structure, concepts that are unique to each of the sources. Finding these correspondences manually is a onerous and error-prone process. A domain expert who wants to determine a correlation between two ontologies must find all the concepts in the two source ontologies that are similar to one another, determine what the similarities are, and either change the source ontologies to remove the overlaps or record a mapping between the sources for future reference. Therefore, ontology developers need automated or semi-automated help in reconciling disparate ontologies.

This reconciliation must be done regardless of whether the ultimate goal is to create a single coherent ontology that includes the information from all the sources (merging) or if the sources must be made consistent and coherent with one another but kept separately (mapping).

In this chapter, we describe two tools that we developed to aid users in ontology merging and mapping. The first tool, IPROMPT, is an interactive ontology-merging tool that guides users through the merging process and analyzes the structure of the ontologies to suggest points for further merging. The second tool, ANCHORPROMPT uses pairs of related terms from two ontologies, which it gets either from the user or from IPROMPT, and analyzes the structure of the graphs representing source ontologies to produce new pairs of related terms.

We have implemented the IPROMPT and ANCHORPROMPT tools as extensions to the Protégé-2000 ontology-editing environment.[1] Protégé-2000 is an open-source tool that allows users to create and edit ontologies and to generate knowledge-acquisition tools based on the ontologies. Protégé-2000 has a large and active user community and many of these users have asked for ability to manage multiple ontologies. The open architecture of Protégé-2000 allows developers to extend it easily with plugins for specific tasks. We implemented PROMPT as a set of such plugins.

## 18.2  The Knowledge Model

Before presenting the tools themselves, we define the frame-based knowledge model underlying PROMPT and Protégé-2000. The knowledge model, the knowledge primitives that we consider, the semantics of relations between them, inevitably affect any strategy for ontology merging and mapping. In describing the knowledge model, we will use an ontology of academic publications as an example. Our example ontology will include such notions as different types of publications, their authors and titles, dates and places of publication, and so on.

We define a **class** as a set of entities. **Instances** of a class are elements of this set (the class of an instance is called its **type**). Classes constitute a taxonomic hierarchy with multiple inheritance. For example, a class `Publication` can represent a set of all publications. Its subclass, a class `Book` represents books, all of which are also publications.

---

[1] http://protege.stanford.edu

**Slots** are also frames (i.e., slots are first-class objects in our model). When a slot is **attached** to a class (its **domain**), it defines binary relations in which instances of that class can participate in and attributes of the instances. For example, a slot `title` attached to a class `Publication` represents titles of publications.

A slot can have a **range** which restricts the values a slot can take. A slot range can be another class (e.g., a range of a slot **author** is a class `Person`), in which case a slot defines a binary relation between an instance of a class and the slot value (i.e., between an instance of `Publication` and an instance of `Person`). A slot range can also be a primitive datatype (e.g., a range of a slot `title` is a `String`). Slot values must belong to the defined range of the slot: if the range is a primitive datatype, slot values must have that datatype; if the range is a class, slot values they must be instances of that class.

The number of values a slot can have for each instance is limited by the slot's **cardinality**. Each slot has a minimum cardinality that defines the minimum number of values a slot must have and a maximum cardinality which specifies the maximum number of values for a slot. If a maximum cardinality is not defined, the slot can have any number of values.

Slot attachment is inherited from a superclass to its subclasses: a slot attached to a class is also attached to its subclasses. When we attach a slot to a class, its range and cardinality constraints are by default the same as for the frame representing the slot. However, we can further restrict the values locally. For example, suppose a slot `publishedIn`, representing a place where a publication was published, has a range `Publication` (which has such subclasses as `Journal`, `ConferenceProceedings`, and so on). When we attach the slot `publishedIn` to the class `JournalArticle`, we can restrict its range to the class `Journal` (the subclass of the global range `Publication`). Similarly, we can limit cardinality of a slot locally. Local range and cardinality restrictions are inherited to subclasses of a class. They can be further restricted in subclasses.

These definitions are the only restrictions that we impose on the input ontologies for IPROMPT and ANCHORPROMPT. Since this knowledge model is extremely general, and many existing knowledge-representation systems have knowledge models compatible with it, the solutions we developed in our framework can be applied over a variety of knowledge-representation systems. Consider, for example, such DL-based languages as the Web Ontology Language (OWL) [6] and its predecessors, OIL [11], and DAML+OIL [15]. While OWL is not a frame language itself, many of its primitives translate into a frame formalism quite naturally [1]. We can treat classes in OWL in the same way as we treat classes in our model. Properties in OWL are similar to slots: they are binary relations between instances of classes or an instance of a class and XML datatype. The notion of domain, range, and a cardinality of a property is similar to the one we use in PROMPT.

**Fig. 18.1.** Snapshots of the class hierarchies in the two source ontologies for the experiment

## 18.3 IPROMPT—An Interactive Ontology-Merging Tool

Suppose a user has two ontologies covering the same domain that were developed by different groups. Figure 18.1 presents class hierarchies from two such ontologies. These two ontologies were developed independently by two teams in the DAML project.[2] We imported two ontologies from the DAML ontology library [5]:

1. An ontology for describing individuals, computer-science academic departments, universities, and activities that occur at them developed at the University of Maryland (UMD), and
2. An ontology for describing employees in an academic institutions, publications, and relationships among research groups and projects developed at Carnegie Mellon University (CMU).

The IPROMPT algorithm takes as input two ontologies, such as these ontologies from the DAML library, and guides the user in the creation of one merged ontology as output. Figure 18.3 illustrates the IPROMPT ontology-merging algorithm. First

---

[2] http://www.daml.org

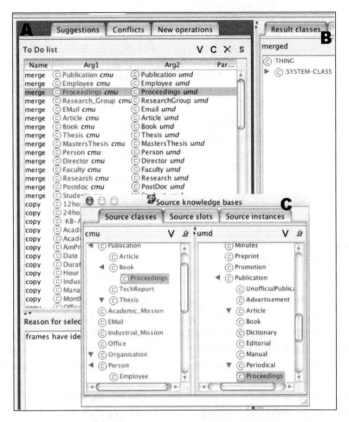

**Fig. 18.2.** A screenshot of the IPROMPT tool. Part A shows initial IPROMPT's suggestions for the ontologies in Figure 18.1. Part B displays the emerging merged ontology (which is empty at this starting point). Part C shows the two source ontologies side-by-side. The arguments to the selected operation in the suggestion list (merge two `Proceedings` classes) are selected in the *Sources* window.

IPROMPT creates an initial list of matches based on class names (Figure 18.2). Then the process goes through the following cycle: (1) the user triggers an operation by either selecting one of IPROMPT's suggestions from the list or by using an ontology-editing environment to specify the desired operation directly; and (2) IPROMPT performs the operation, automatically executes additional changes based on the type of the operation, generates a list of suggestions for the user based on the structure of the ontology around the arguments to the last operation, and determines conflicts that the last operation introduced in the ontology and finds possible solutions for those conflicts.

There are several research groups already working on methods for determining linguistic similarity among concept names (see Section 18.5). Therefore, we decided to concentrate on the steps that analyze the *structure* of the ontology. A specific im-

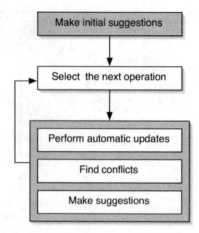

**Fig. 18.3.** The flow of IPROMPT algorithm. The user selects a new operation. The rest of the actions are performed by IPROMPT.

plementation of the IPROMPT algorithm uses whatever measure of linguistic similarity among concept names is appropriate. In our Protégé-based implementation, we use the Protégé-2000 component-based architecture to allow the user to plug in any term-matching algorithm. In IPROMPT, we start with linguistic-similarity matches for the initial comparison, but concentrate on finding clues based on the structure of the ontology and user's actions.

The following is at the heart of our approach: We identify a set of knowledge-base operations for ontology merging or alignment. For each operation in this set, we define (1) changes that IPROMPT performs automatically, (2) new suggestions that IPROMPT presents to the user, and (3) conflicts that the operation may introduce and that the user needs to resolve. When the user invokes an operation, IPROMPT creates members of these three sets based on the arguments to the specific invocation of the operation. The set of ontology-merging operations that we identified includes both the operations that are normally performed during traditional ontology editing and the operations specific to merging and alignment, such as:

- merge classes,
- merge slots,
- merge bindings between a slot and a class,
- perform a deep copy of a class from one ontology to another (includes copying all the parents of a class up to the root of the hierarchy and all the classes and slots it refers to),
- perform a shallow copy of a class (just the class itself, and not its parents or the classes and slots it refers to).

We have identified the following conflicts that may appear in the merged ontology as the result of these operations:

- name conflicts (more than one frame with the same name),

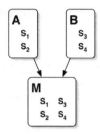

**Fig. 18.4.** Merging classes $A$ and $B$ to create a class $M$

- dangling references (a frame refers to another frame that does not exist),
- redundancy in the class hierarchy (more than one path from a class to a super-class),
- slot-value restrictions that violate class inheritance.

For example, suppose the user is merging two ontologies and he performs a `merge-classes` operation for two classes $A$ and $B$ to create a new class $M$ (Figure 18.4). IPROMPT then performs the following actions:

- For each slot $S$ that was attached to $A$ and $B$ in the original ontologies, attach the slot to $M$ with the same value type. If $S$ did not exist in the merged ontology, create $S$.
- For each superclass of $A$ and $B$ that has been previously copied into the merged ontology, make that copy a superclass of $M$ (thus restoring the original relation). Do the same for subclasses.
- For each class $C$ in the original ontologies to which $A$ and $B$ referred (that is, for each superclass, subclass, slot value, and class restricting a slot value of $A$ and $B$), if $C$ has not been copied to the merged ontology, suggest that it is copied to the merged ontology.
- For each class $C$ that was a value type for any of the slots for $A$ or $B$ and that has not been copied to the merged ontology, declare a dangling-reference conflict.
- For each pair of slots for $M$ that have linguistically similar names, suggest that the slots are merged. Later, if the user chooses to merge the slots, suggest that the classes restricting the values of these slots, are merged as well.
- For each pair of superclasses and subclasses of $M$ that have linguistically similar names, suggest that they are merged: These classes have similar names and, in addition, they were both superclasses (or subclasses) for $A$ and $B$, which the user declared to be similar.
- Check for redundancy in the parent hierarchy for $M$: If there is more than one path to any parent of $M$ (other than the root of the hierarchy), suggest that one of $M$s parents is removed.

Note, that IPROMPT bases most of the decisions in the preceding list on the internal structure of the concepts and their position in the ontology and not syntax.

## 18.4 ANCHORPROMPT—Using Non-local Context For Semantic Matching

IPROMPT analyzes only *local context* in ontology structure: Given two similar classes, the algorithms consider classes and slots that are directly related to the classes in question. The algorithm that we present now, ANCHORPROMPT uses a set of heuristics to analyze *non-local context*. The goal of ANCHORPROMPT is not to provide a complete solution to automated ontology merging but rather to augment IPROMPT by determining additional possible points of similarity between ontologies. ANCHORPROMPT also provides pairs of related terms to help users in ontology mapping and alignment. ANCHORPROMPT takes as input a set of pairs of related terms—**anchors**—from the source ontologies. Either the user identifies the anchors manually or the system generates them automatically. From this set of previously identified anchors, ANCHORPROMPT produces a set of new pairs of semantically close terms. To do that, ANCHORPROMPT traverses the paths between the anchors in the corresponding ontologies. A path follows the links between classes defined by the hierarchical relations or by slots and their domains and ranges. ANCHORPROMPT then compares the terms along these paths to find similar terms. For example, suppose we identify two pairs of anchors: classes $A$ and $B$ and classes $H$ and $G$ (Figure 18.5). That is, a class $A$ from one ontology is similar to a class $B$ in the other ontology; and a class $H$ from the first ontology is similar to a class $G$ from the second one. Figure 18.5 shows one path from $A$ to $H$ in the first ontology and one path from $B$ to $G$ in the second ontology. We traverse the two paths in parallel, incrementing the similarity score between each two classes that we reach in the same step. For example, after traversing the paths in Figure 18.5, we increment the similarity score between the classes $C$ and $D$ and between the classes $E$ and $F$. We repeat the process for all the existing paths that originate and terminate in the anchor points, cumulatively aggregating the similarity score. The central observation behind AN-CHORPROMPT is that if two pairs of terms from the source ontologies are similar and there are paths connecting the terms, then the elements in those paths are often similar as well. Therefore, from a small set of previously identified related terms, ANCHORPROMPT is able to suggest a large number of terms that are likely to be semantically similar as well.

### 18.4.1 Examples and Definitions

To illustrate how ANCHORPROMPT works, we will consider two ontologies for representing clinical trials, their protocols, applications, and results. The first ontology, the Design-a-Trial (DaT) ontology [22], underlies a knowledge-based system that helps doctors produce protocols for randomized controlled trials. The second ontology, the randomized clinical-trial (RCT) ontology [28], is used in creating electronic trial banks that store the results of clinical trials and allow researchers to find, appraise, and apply the results. Both ontologies represent clinical trials, but one of them, DaT, concentrates on defining a trial protocol itself, and the other, RCT, on

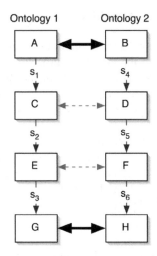

**Fig. 18.5.** Traversing the paths between anchors. The rectangles represent classes and labeled edges represent slots that relate classes to one another. The left part of the figure represents classes and slots from one ontology; the right part represents classes and slots from the other. Solid arrows connect pairs of anchors; dashed arrows connect pairs of related terms.

representing the results of the trial. The two groups developed their respective ontologies completely independent from each other. Therefore there is no intensional correlation between them. As part of the work on representing clinical guidelines in our laboratory, we needed to merge the two ontologies. In ANCHORPROMPT we represent classes, slots, and their relations in the ontologies as directed labeled graphs. Figure 18.6a, for example, shows a part of the graph representing the RCT ontology. Classes are nodes in the graph. Slots are edges in the graph. A slot $S$ connects two classes, $A$ and $B$, in the graph, if both of the following conditions are true:

1. The slot $S$ is attached to class $A$ (either as template slot or as an own slot), and
2. The class $B$ is either a value of slot $S$ for the class $A$, or $B$ is the range of allowed values for slot $S$ at class $A$.

For example, the edge representing the slot `latest-protocol` in the RCT ontology links the class TRIAL to the class PROTOCOL (Figure 18.6a). The slot `latest-protocol` at class TRIAL can have as its values instances of the class PROTOCOL. Two nodes connected by an edge in a graph are adjacent. There is a path between two nodes of a graph, $A$ and $B$, if, starting at node $A$, it is possible to follow a sequence of adjacent edges to reach node $B$. The length of the path is the number of edges in the path. The goal of the ANCHORPROMPT algorithm is to produce automatically a set of semantically related concepts from the source ontologies using a set of anchor matches identified earlier (manually or automatically) as its input.

### 18.4.2 The ANCHORPROMPT Algorithm

ANCHORPROMPT takes as input a set of **anchors**—pairs of related terms in the two ontologies. We can use any of the existing approaches to term matching to identify the anchors (Section 18.5). A user can identify the anchors manually. An automated system can identify them by comparing the names of the terms. For example, we can assume that if the source ontologies cover the same domain, the terms with the same names are likely to represent the same concepts. We can also use a combination of system-determined and user-defined anchors. We can use pairs of related terms that ANCHORPROMPT has identified in an earlier iteration after the user has validated them. For the example in this section, we will consider the following two pairs of anchors for the two clinical-trial ontologies (the first class in the pair is in the RCT ontology; the second is in the DaT ontology[3]):

> TRIAL, Trial
> PERSON, Person

Using these two pairs as input, the algorithm must determine pairs of other related terms in the RCT and DaT ontologies. It generates a set of all the paths between PERSON and TRIAL in the RCT ontology and between Person and Trial in DaT ontology (Figure 18.6 shows some of these paths[4]). It considers only the paths that are shorter than a pre-defined parameter length. Now consider a pair of paths in this set that have the same length. For example: Path 1 (in the RCT ontology):

> TRIAL → PROTOCOL → STUDY-SITE → PERSON

Path 2 (in the DaT ontology):

> Trial → Design → Blinding → Person

As it traverses the two paths, ANCHORPROMPT increases the **similarity score**—a coefficient that indicates how closely two terms are related—for the pairs of terms in the same positions in the paths. For the two paths in our example, it will increase the similarity score for the following two pairs of terms:

> PROTOCOL, Design
> STUDY-SITE, Blinding

ANCHORPROMPT repeats the process for each pair of paths of the same lengths that have one pair of anchors as their originating points (e.g., TRIAL and Trial) and another pair of anchors as terminating points (e.g., PERSON and Person). During this process it increases the similarity scores for the pairs of terms that it encounters. It aggregates the similarity score from all the traversals to generate the final similarity score. Consequently, the terms that often appear in the same positions on the paths going from one pair of anchors to another will get the highest score.

---

[3] The RCT ontology uses all UPPER-CASE letters for class names. The DaT ontology Capitalizes the class names. Therefore, it is easy to distinguish which class names come from which ontology, and we will sometimes omit the source information.

[4] We have changed the original RCT ontology slightly to simplify this example.

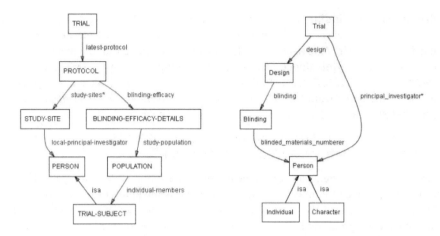

**Fig. 18.6.** (a) The paths between the classes TRIAL and PERSON in the RCT ontology; (b) the paths between the classes Trial and Person in the DaT ontology

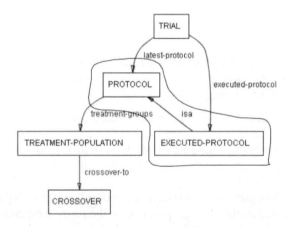

**Fig. 18.7.** A path from TRIAL to CROSSOVER: The classes EXECUTED-PROTOCOL and PROTOCOL form an equivalence group

## Equivalence Groups

In traversing the graph representing the ontology and generating the paths between classes ANCHORPROMPT treats the subclasssuperclass links differently from links representing other slots. Consider for example the path from TRIAL to CROSSOVER in Figure 18.7.

We could treat the is-a link in exactly the same way we treat other slots. However, this approach would disregard the distinct semantics associated with is-a links. Instead we can employ the difference in meaning between the is-a link and regular slots to improve the algorithm. An is-a link connects the terms that are already **similar** (e.g., PROTOCOL and EXECUTED-PROTOCOL); in fact one describes a subset of the other. Other slots link terms that are arbitrarily related to each other. ANCHORPROMPT joins the terms linked by the subclasssuperclass relation in **equivalence groups**. In the example in Figure 18.7, the classes PROTOCOL and EXECUTED-PROTOCOL constitute an equivalence group. Here is one of the paths from TRIAL to CROSSOVER in Figure 18.7 that goes through EXECUTED-PROTOCOL. We identify the equivalence group by brackets.

TRIAL → [EXECUTED-PROTOCOL, PROTOCOL] →
TREATMENT-POPULATION → CROSSOVER.

ANCHORPROMPT treats an equivalence group as a single node in the path. The set of incoming edges for an equivalence-group node is the union of the sets of incoming edges for each of the group elements. Similarly, the set of outgoing edges for an equivalence-group node is the union of the sets of outgoing edges for each of its elements. The [EXECUTED-PROTOCOL, PROTOCOL] equivalence group in Figure 18.7 has one incoming edge, executed-protocol, and one outgoing edge, treatment-groups.

### Similarity Score

We use the following process to compute the similarity score $S(C_1, C_2)$ between two terms $C_1$ and $C_2$ (where $C_1$ is a class from the source ontology $O_1$ and $C_2$ is a class from the source ontology $O_2$).

1. Generate a set of all paths of length less than a parameter $L$ that connect input anchors in $O_1$ and $O_2$.
2. From the set of paths generated in step 1, generate a set of all possible pairs of paths of equal length such that one path in the pair comes from $O_1$ and the other path comes from $O_2$.
3. For each pair of paths in the set generated in step 2 and for each pair of nodes $N_1$ and $N_2$ located in the identical positions in the paths, increment the similarity score between each pair of classes $C_1$ and $C_2$ in $N_1$ and $N_2$ respectively be a constant X. (Recall that $N_1$ and $N_2$ can be either single classes or equivalence groups that include several classes).

Therefore the similarity score $S(C_1, C_2)$ is a **cumulative** score reflecting how often $C_1$ and $C_2$ appear in identical positions along the paths considering all the possible paths between anchors (of length less than $L$).

We change the constant by which we increment the similarity score when the matching nodes along the paths include not single classes but equivalence groups. Suppose we have the following two nodes at the same position on two paths between anchors: $A_1$ and $[B_2, C_2]$, a single class $A_1$ on one side, and an equivalence group with two classes $B_2$ and $C_2$ on the other side. Do we give the same score to both pairs of classes $A_1, B_2$ and $A_1, C_2$? Is this score the same as the one we would have given the pair $A_1, B_2$ had $B_2$ been the only class at the node? Do we give the pairs

$A_1$, $B_2$ and $A_1$, $C_2$ any similarity score at all? We report on our experiments with different treatment of scores for equivalence-group members elsewhere [25].

Note that the computational complexity of the algorithm is not dependent on the size of the ontologies themselves, but rather on the number of anchors, on the maximum path length $L$, and on the fan-out factor for concepts that are within $L$ nodes from the anchors. The algorithm examines only the part of the ontology that is "circumvented" by the anchors.

**Revisiting the Example**

We provided ANCHORPROMPT with the following set of three pairs of anchors from the RCT and DaT ontologies correspondingly:

```
     TRIAL, Trial
    PERSON, Person
CROSSOVER, Crossover
```

We allowed the paths of length less than or equal to 5 and limited the equivalence-group size to 2. Here are the output results in the order of the descending similarity score.

```
            PROTOCOL, Design
      TRIAL-SUBJECT, Person
      INVESTIGATORS, Person
         POPULATION, Action_Spec
             PERSON, Character
TREATMENT-POPULATION, Crossover_arm
```

In fact, all but one of these results represents a pair of concepts that either are similar or one is a specialization (subclass) of the other. The only exception is the pair POPULATION, Action_Spec. Note that many of these pairings are specific to the domain of clinical trials (e.g., PROTOCOL, Design and TRIAL-SUBJECT, Person). The pair PERSON, Character indeed identifies the correct sense in which Character is used in the DaT ontology.

**Evaluation**

We have performed a formative evaluation of ANCHORPROMPTby comparing the two DAML+OIL ontologies described earlier in Section 18.3 [25]. Our results show that for maximum allowed paths of length 2, we achieved 100% precision. For longer paths of length 4, the precision decreases to 67%. However, note that the number of new matchers that ANCHORPROMPTproduces is usually low—10-12 matches. The user needs to sift through only these 10-12 results. 67% precision means that 7 out of 10 results are correct. Our experiments also validated the utility of equivalence groups. Without equivalence groups, 87% of the experiments produced empty result sets. If the maximum equivalence-group size is 2, only 12% of the result sets are empty. For the rest of the experiments we fix the maximum equivalence-group size at 2.

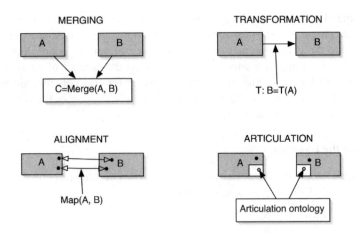

**Fig. 18.8.** Different types of tools for integrating ontologies

## 18.5 Related Work

In recent years, researchers developed a number of tools to support management of multiple ontologies. Researchers in the database field have produced a considerable body of work on automatically finding mappings between database schemas. We review these two thrusts of research in this section.

### 18.5.1 Ontology-Mapping and Merging Tools

We can classify tools that deal with finding correspondences between ontologies into four groups (Figure 18.8):

- Tools for merging two ontologies to create a new one (e.g., IPROMPT, Chimaera [18], OntoMerge [9])
- Tools for defining a transformation function that transforms one ontology into another (e.g., OntoMorph [4])
- Tools for defining a mapping between concepts in two ontologies by finding pairs of related concepts (e.g., ANCHORPROMPT, GLUE [8], OBSERVER [19], FCA-Merge [30])
- Tools for defining mapping rules to relate only relevant parts of the source ontologies (e.g., [21])

Another way to categorize the tools is by the type of input on which the tool relies in its analysis and which it requires:

- class hierarchy (e.g., Chimaera)
- class hierarchy, slots, and value restrictions (e.g., IPROMPT, ANCHORPROMPT, ONION)
- instances of classes (e.g., GLUE and FCA-Merge)

- descriptions of classes (e.g., tools based on description logic, such as OB-SERVER)

We will now describe various tools that we mentioned in more detail.

Chimaera [18] is an interactive merging tool based on Ontolingua ontology editor [10]. Chimaera allows a user to bring together ontologies developed in different formalisms. The user can request an analysis or guidance from Chimaera at any point during the merging process. The tool will then point him to the places in the ontology where his attention is required. In its suggestions, Chimaera mostly relies on which ontology the concepts came from and, for classes, on their names. For example, Chimaera will point a user to a class in the merged ontology that has two slots derived from different source ontologies, or that has two subclasses that originated in different ontologies. Chimaera leaves the decision of what to do entirely to the user and does not make any suggestions itself. The only taxonomic relation that Chimaera considers is the subclass–superclass relation. Chimaera is the tool closest to IPROMPT. However, since it uses only a class hierarchy in its analysis, it misses many of the correspondences that IPROMPT finds. These correspondences include suggestions to merge slots with similar names that are attached to merged classes, to merge domains of slots that were merged, and so on. In addition, since Chimaera relies on ontolingua user interface for class editing, the interface is quite cumbersome and hard to use for many developers.

In OntoMerge [9], a merged ontology is a union of two source ontologies and a set of **bridging axioms**. The first step in the OntoMerge merging process is to translate both ontologies to a common syntactic representation in a language developed by the authors. Then an ontology engineer defines bridging axioms, which are axioms containing terms from both ontologies. Then instance-translation process looks as following: all instances in the source ontologies are considered to be in the merged ontology. Then an inference engine draws conclusions based on the statements in source ontologies and bridging axioms, thus creating new data in the merged ontology. So, OntoMerge provides tools for instance-data translation to the merged ontology. It can probably be used in conjunction with tools such as IPROMPT or ANCHORPROMPT to help ontology engineers write bridging axioms.

Ontomorph [4] defines a set of transformation operators that can be applied to an ontology. A human expert then uses the initial list of matches and the source ontologies to define a set of operators that need to be applied to the source ontologies in order to resolve differences between them, and Ontomorph applies the operators. Therefore, aggregate operations can be performed in a single step. However, a human expert receives no guidance except for the initial list of matches.

GLUE [8] is a system that employs machine-learning techniques to find mappings. GLUE uses multiple learners exploiting information in concept instances and taxonomic structure of ontologies. GLUE uses a probabilistic model to combine results of different learners. The learners that GLUE uses currently relies on ontologies having instances and they work much better if many slot values have text in them rather than references to other instances.

The OBSERVER [19] system uses description logic to answer queries using multiple ontologies and information on mappings between them. First, users define a set of inter-ontology relations. The system helps the users with this task by looking for synonyms in the source ontologies. Having defined the mappings, users can pose queries in description-logic terms using their own ontology. OBSERVER then employs the mapping information to pose queries to source ontologies. OBSERVER relies heavily on the fact that descriptions in the ontologies and the queries are **intensional** and therefore works best in a DL setting..

FCA-Merge [30] is a method for comparing ontologies that have a set of shared instances or a shared set of documents annotated with concepts from source ontologies. Based on this information, FCA-Merge uses mathematical techniques from Formal Concept Analysis [13] to produce a lattice of concepts which relates concepts from the source ontologies. The algorithm suggest equivalence and subclass–superclass relations. An ontology engineer can then analyze the result and use it as a guidance for creating a merged ontology. However, the assumption that two ontologies to be merged share a set of instances or have a set of documents where each document is annotated with terms from both sources is a very strong one and in practice such a situation may occur only rarely. As an alternative, authors suggest the use of natural-language–processing techniques to annotate a set of documents with concepts from the two ontologies.

The ONION system [21] is based on the ontology algebra, which defines operators between ontologies. Given a set of mapping rules ("articulation rules" in ontology-algebra terms), Mitra and colleagues define intersection, union, and difference between two ontologies. Articulation rules are logical rules that express correspondences between some of the terms in the source ontologies. These rules usually include only the terms relevant to particular application—no effort to map ontologies completely is made. ONION uses both lexical and graph-based techniques to suggest articulations. The method to find lexical similarity between concept names uses dictionaries and semantic-indexing techniques based on co-occurrence of words in a text corpus. For graph-based matching, some of the techniques that ONION uses are similar to the ones we described for IPROMPT: look for nodes that have many attributes in common, look for classes with common parents, and so on.

This diversity in the types of tools makes it difficult to compare them directly. In fact, when a developer needs to choose a tool to use in management of multiple ontologies, which tool is the most appropriate will depend on the task at hand (among the tasks in Figure 18.8) and what type of input the user has. For example, if the ontologies to be merged share a set of instances, then FCA-Merge may work best. If ontologies have instances but don't share them and many slot values contain text, GLUE may be the best choice. If only parts of ontologies need to be mapped, ONION could be the tool of choice. If no instances are available and ontologies contain many relations between concepts, IPROMPT or ANCHORPROMPT may work best.

### 18.5.2 Related Work in Schema Integration

This discussion of related work would be incomplete without a brief overview of the work in schema integration. Database schemas are similar to ontologies: Both are structural representations of knowledge. The difference often lies in *scale* rather than substance: Database schemas in practice use much fewer modeling primitives than ontologies and are often smaller than ontologies. Just as with ontologies, researchers are often faced with the problem of finding correlation between different schemas. However, the more common approach in the database-schema research is to develop *mediators* rather than find point-to-point correlations. Users pose their queries in terms of the hand-made mediator schema; queries are then translated into the terms of each of the schemas.

However, in recent years there has been a significant body of work on matching database schemas directly and on doing this matching automatically. Schema matching for schema integration is similar to ontology mapping: In both cases, we need to find related concepts in two knowledge structures. At the same time, most of the schema-integration techniques consider either relational-database schemas or schemas containing trees of concepts, and perhaps, concept attributes. Rahm and Bernstein [27] survey schema-integration approaches. They define a taxonomy of these approaches and we can see many similarities to the classification of ontology-merging approaches that we discussed in Section 18.5.1. Some schema-matching techniques rely on instance data (e.g., LSD [7]) and some use only the schema itself (e.g., ARTEMIS [3], Cupid [17]). There are matchers that use linguistic information, such as synonyms, hypernyms, and homonyms (e.g., ARTEMIS, DIKE [26]), others use machine-learning techniques (e.g., LSD). Most schema machers produce one-to-one matchers, just as most ontology matchers do. A lot of power comes from hybrid approaches that integrate different techniques. There are also interactive tools for schema matching that allow users themselves to specify matching rules (e.g., Clio [20]). So, the two fields clearly can benefit from each other. The main difference between schema-matching and ontology-matching approaches (PROMPT in particular) remains the number of knowledge-modeling primitives on which the analysis relies. Schema-matching approaches do not usually consider domains and ranges of slots and complex properties. They also usually look only for matches between concepts, whereas in ontology matching finding correspondences between properties is just as important.

ICOM [12] is one example of a project that spans both the schema-integration and ontology-integration domains. It provides a conceptual model and a reasoning mechanism for schema integration, although it does not actually help designers in finding the mappings themselves. ICOM is a tool that allows users to define extended Entity-Relationship diagrams and to specify declaratively inter-schema constraints, effectively defining mappings between schema [2]. ICOM then treats the resulting system, including the different schema and the interschema relationships, as a single DL knowledge base to perform inference.

## 18.6 Concluding Remarks

In this chapter, we have introduced the tools for finding similarities between ontologies and assisting users in merging them. The PROMPT suite of tools developed in our laboratory includes not only the tools described here but also tools for other tasks in managing multiple ontologies: versioning, reorganization, factoring. The other tools leverage the algorithms for ontology merging and mapping to find differences between different versions of the same ontology and to analyze relations between ontologies when one of them includes another. Our vision is that ultimately users will be able to develop new ontologies, reuse existing ones, find mappings between them, merge ontologies, maintain different versions, separate ontologies and then bring them back together, all in one integrated framework, seamlessly switching between the tasks.

## Acknowledgments

We are very grateful to Monica Crubézy, Ray Fergerson, and Samson Tu for their many suggestions, their help with the tool, and for their comments on earlier versions of the paper. We would also like to thank everyone who participated in the evaluation experiments. Parts of this paper were published at the $17^{th}$ National Conference on Artificial Intelligence (AAAI-2000) and at the Workshop on Ontologies and Information Sharing at the $17^{th}$ International Joint Conference on Artificial Intelligence (IJCAI-2001). This work was supported in part by the grants 5T16 LM0733 and 892154 from the National Library of Medicine, by a grant from Spawar, by a grant from FastTrack Systems, Inc. and by a contract from the U.S. National Cancer Institute.

## References

1. S. Bechhofer, C. Goble, and I. Horrocks. DAML+OIL is not enough. In *The First Semantic Web Working Symposium*, Stanford, CA, 2001.
2. D. Calvanese, G. Giacomo, M. Lenzerini, D. Nardi, and R. Rosati. Information integration: Conceptual modeling and reasoning support. In *6th Int. Conference on Cooperative Information Systems (CoopIS'98)*, pages 280–291, 1998.
3. S. Castano, V. De Antonellis, and S. De Capitani di Vemercati. Global viewing of heterogeneous data sources. *IEEE Transactions on Data and Knowledge Engineering*, 13(2):277–297, 2001.
4. Hans Chalupsky. Ontomorph: A translation system for symbolic knowledge. In A. G. Cohn, F. Giunchiglia, and B. Selman, editors, *Principles of Knowledge Representation and Reasoning (KR2000)*. Morgan Kaufmann Publishers, 2000.
5. DAML. DAML ontology library, 2001.
6. Mike Dean, Dan Connolly, Frank van Harmelen, James Hendler, Ian Horrocks, Deborah L. McGuinness, Peter F. Patel-Schneider, and Lynn Andrea Stein. Web ontology language (OWL) reference version 1.0, http://www.w3.org/tr/owl-guide/, 2002.

7.  A. Doan, P. Domingos, and A. Halevy. Reconciling schemas of disparate data sources: A machine learning approach. In *ACM SIGMOD Conf. on Management of Data (SIGMOD-2001)*, 2001.
8.  A. Doan, J. Madhavan, P. Domingos, and A. Halevy. Learning to map between ontologies on the semantic web. In *The Eleventh International WWW Conference*, Hawaii, US, 2002.
9.  D. Dou, D. McDermott, and P. Qi. Ontology translation by ontology merging and automated reasoning. In *EKAW'02 workshop on Ontologies for Multi-Agent Systems*, Siguenza, Spain, 2002.
10. A. Farquhar, R. Fikes, and J. Rice. The Ontolingua server: a tool for collaborative ontology construction. In *Tenth Knowledge Acquisition for Knowledge-Based Systems Workshop*, Banff, Canada, 1996.
11. D. Fensel, I. Horrocks, F. Van Harmelen, S. Decker, M. Erdmann, and M. Klein. OIL in a nutshell. In *12th Int. Conference on Knowledge Engineering and Knowledge Management (EKAW-2000)*, Juan-les-Pins, France, 2000. Springer.
12. E. Franconi and G. Ng. The i.com tool for intelligent conceptual modelling. In *7th Intl. Workshop on Knowledge Representation meets Databases (KRDB'00)*, Berlin, Germany, 2000.
13. B. Ganter and R. Wille. *Formal Concept Analysis: Mathematical foundations*. Springer, Berlin-Heidelberg, 1999.
14. Thomas R. Gruber. Toward principles for the design of ontologies used for knowledge sharing. Technical Report KSL 93-04, Knowledge Systems Laboratory, Stanford University, August 23, 1993 1993.
15. J. Hendler and D. L. McGuinness. The DARPA agent markup language. *IEEE Intelligent Systems*, 16(6):67–73, 2000.
16. Donald A. B. Lindberg, Betsy L. Humphreys, and A.T. McCray. The unified medical language system. *Methods of Information in Medicine*, 32(4):281, 1993.
17. J. Madhavan, P. Bernstein, and E. Rahm. Generic schema matching using Cupid. In *27th Int. Conf. on Very Large Data Bases (VLDB '01)*, Italy, 2001.
18. D. L. McGuinness, R. Fikes, J. Rice, and S. Wilder. An environment for merging and testing large ontologies. In *Principles of Knowledge Representation and Reasoning (KR2000)*. Morgan Kaufmann Publishers, San Francisco, CA, 2000.
19. E. Mena, A. Illarramendi, V. Kashyap, and A. Sheth. OBSERVER: An approach for query processing in global information systems based on interoperation across pre-existing ontologies. *Distributed and Parallel Databases—An International Journal*, 8(2), 2000.
20. R. Miller, L. Haas, and M. Hernandez. Schema mapping as query discovery. In *26th International Conference On Very Large Databases (VLDB'2000)*, 2000.
21. Prasenjit Mitra, Gio Wiederhold, and Stefan Decker. A scalable framework for interoperation of information sources. In *The 1st International Semantic Web Working Symposium (SWWS'01)*, Stanford University, Stanford, CA, 2001.
22. S. Modgil, P. Hammond, J.C. Wyatt, and H. Potts. The design-a-trial project: Developing a knowledge-based tool for authoring clinical trial protocols. In *First European Workshop on Computer-based Support for Clinical Guidelines and Protocols (EWGLP 2000)*, Leipzig, Germany, 2000. IOS Press, Amsterdam.
23. M. A. Musen. Dimensions of knowledge sharing and reuse. *Computers and Biomedical Research*, 25:435–467, 1992.
24. Netscape. Dmoz open directory, 1999.

25. N. F. Noy and M. A. Musen. Anchor-PROMPT: Using non-local context for semantic matching. In *Workshop on Ontologies and Information Sharing at IJCAI-2001*, Seattle, WA, 2001.
26. L. Palopoli, D. Sacca, G. Terracina, and D. Ursino. A unified graph-based framework for deriving nominal interscheme properties, type conflicts and object cluster similarities. In *4th IFCIS International Conference On Cooperative Information Systems (CoopIS)*, pages 34–45. IEEE Computer, 1999.
27. Erhard Rahm and Philip A. Bernstein. A survey of approaches to automatic schema matching. *VLDB Journal*, 10(4), 2001.
28. I. Sim. *Trial Banks: An Informatics Foundation for Evidence-Based Medicine*. Phd dissertation, Stanford University, 1997.
29. K.A. Spackman, editor. *SMOMED RT: Systematized Nomenclature of Medicine, Reference Terminology*. College of American Pathologists, 2000.
30. G. Stumme and A. Mädche. FCA-Merge: Bottom-up merging of ontologies. In *7th Intl. Conf. on Artificial Intelligence (IJCAI '01)*, Seattle, WA, 2001.

# Ontology Matching: A Machine Learning Approach

AnHai Doan[1]*, Jayant Madhavan[2], Pedro Domingos[2], and Alon Halevy[2]

[1] Department of Computer Science
   University of Illinois, Urbana-Champaign, IL, U.S.A.
   anhai@cs.uiuc.edu
[2] Department of Computer Science and Engineering
   University of Washington, Seattle, WA, U.S.A.
   {jayant,pedrod,alon}@cs.washington.edu

**Summary.** This chapter studies *ontology matching*: the problem of finding the semantic mappings between two given ontologies. This problem lies at the heart of numerous information processing applications. Virtually any application that involves multiple ontologies must establish semantic mappings among them, to ensure interoperability. Examples of such applications arise in myriad domains, including e-commerce, knowledge management, e-learning, information extraction, bio-informatics, web services, and tourism (see Part D of this book on ontology applications).

Despite its pervasiveness, today ontology matching is still largely conducted by hand, in a labor-intensive and error-prone process. The manual matching has now become a key bottleneck in building large-scale information management systems. The advent of technologies such as the WWW, XML, and the emerging Semantic Web will further fuel information sharing applications and exacerbate the problem. Hence, the development of tools to assist in the ontology matching process has become crucial for the success of a wide variety of information management applications.

In response to the above challenge, we have developed GLUE, a system that employs learning techniques to semi-automatically create semantic mappings between ontologies. We shall begin the chapter by describing a motivating example: ontology matching on the Semantic Web. Then we present our GLUE solution. Finally, we describe a set of experiments on several real-world domains, and show that GLUE proposes highly accurate semantic mappings.

## 19.1 A Motivating Example: the Semantic Web

The current World-Wide Web has well over 1.5 billion pages [2], but the vast majority of them are in human-readable format only (e.g., HTML). As a consequence software agents (softbots) cannot understand and process this information, and much of the potential of the Web has so far remained untapped.

---

* Work done while the author was at the University of Washington, Seattle

In response, researchers have created the vision of the *Semantic Web* [5], where data has structure and *ontologies* describe the semantics of the data. When data is marked up using ontologies, softbots can better understand the semantics and therefore more intelligently locate and integrate data for a wide variety of tasks. The following example illustrates the vision of the Semantic Web.

***Example 19.1*** *Suppose you want to find out more about someone you met at a conference. You know that his last name is Cook, and that he teaches Computer Science at a nearby university, but you do not know which one. You also know that he just moved to the US from Australia, where he had been an associate professor at his alma mater.*

*On the World-Wide Web of today you will have trouble finding this person. The above information is not contained within a single Web page, thus making keyword search ineffective. On the Semantic Web, however, you should be able to quickly find the answers. A marked-up directory service makes it easy for your personal softbot to find nearby Computer Science departments. These departments have marked up data using some ontology such as the one in Figure 19.1.a. Here the data is organized into a* taxonomy *that includes courses, people, and professors. Professors have attributes such as name, degree, and degree-granting institution. Such marked-up data makes it easy for your softbot to find a professor with the last name Cook. Then by examining the attribute "granting institution", the softbot quickly finds the alma mater CS department in Australia. Here, the softbot learns that the data has been marked up using an ontology specific to Australian universities, such as the one in Figure 19.1.b, and that there are many entities named Cook. However, knowing that "associate professor" is equivalent to "senior lecturer", the bot can select the right subtree in the departmental taxonomy, and zoom in on the old homepage of your conference acquaintance.* □

The Semantic Web thus offers a compelling vision, but it also raises many difficult challenges. Researchers have been actively working on these challenges, focusing on fleshing out the basic architecture, developing expressive and efficient ontol ont

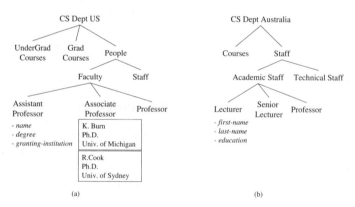

Fig. 19.1. Computer Science Department Ontologies

A key challenge in building the Semantic Web, one that has received relatively little attention, is finding *semantic mappings among the ontologies*. Given the decentralized nature of the development of the Semantic Web, there will be an explosion in the number of ontologies. Many of these ontologies will describe similar domains, but using different terminologies, and others will have overlapping domains. To integrate data from disparate ontologies, we must know the *semantic correspondences* between their elements [5, 34]. For example, in the conference-acquaintance scenario described earlier, in order to find the right person, your softbot must know that "associate professor" in the US corresponds to "senior lecturer" in Australia. Thus, the semantic correspondences are in effect the "glue" that hold the ontologies together into a "web of semantics". Without them, the Semantic Web is akin to an electronic version of the Tower of Babel. Unfortunately, manually specifying such correspondences is time-consuming, error-prone [27], and clearly not possible on the Web scale. Hence, the development of tools to assist in ontology mapping is crucial to the success of the Semantic Web [34].

## 19.2 Overview of our Solution

In response to the challenge of ontology matching on the Semantic Web and in numerous other application contexts, we have developed the GLUE system, which applies machine learning techniques to semi-automatically create semantic mappings. Since taxonomies are central components of ontologies, we focus first on finding correspondences among the taxonomies of two given ontologies: for each concept node in one taxonomy, find the *most similar* concept node in the other taxonomy.

The first issue we address is the meaning of similarity between two concepts. Clearly, many different definitions of similarity are possible, each being appropriate for certain situations. Our approach is based on the observation that many practical measures of similarity can be defined based solely on the *joint probability distribution* of the concepts involved. Hence, instead of committing to a particular definition of similarity, GLUE calculates the joint distribution of the concepts, and lets the application use the joint distribution to compute any suitable similarity measure. Specifically, for any two concepts $A$ and $B$, the joint distribution consists of $P(A, B)$, $P(A, \overline{B})$, $P(\overline{A}, B)$, and $P(\overline{A}, \overline{B})$, where a term such as $P(A, \overline{B})$ is the probability that an instance in the domain belongs to concept $A$ but not to concept $B$.

The second challenge is then computing the joint distribution of concepts $A$ and $B$. Under certain general assumptions (discussed in Section 19.5), a term such as $P(A, B)$ can be approximated as the fraction of instances that belong to both $A$ and $B$ (in the data associated with the taxonomies or, more generally, in the probability distribution that generated it). Hence, the problem reduces to deciding for each instance if it belongs to $A \cap B$. However, the input to our problem includes instances of $A$ and instances of $B$ in isolation. GLUE addresses this problem using machine learning techniques as follows: it uses the instances of $A$ to learn a classifier for $A$, and then classifies instances of $B$ according to that classifier, and vice-versa. Hence, we have a method for identifying instances of $A \cap B$.

Applying machine learning to our context raises the question of which learning algorithm to use and which types of information to use in the learning process. Many different types of information can contribute toward deciding the membership of an instance: its name, value format, the word frequencies in its value, and each of these is best utilized by a different learning algorithm. GLUE uses a *multi-strategy learning* approach [11]: we employ a set of learners, then combine their predictions using a meta-learner. In previous work [11] we have shown that multi-strategy learning is effective in the context of mapping between database schemas.

Finally, GLUE attempts to exploit available domain constraints and general heuristics in order to improve matching accuracy. An example heuristic is the observation that two nodes are likely to match if nodes in their neighborhood also match. An example of a domain constraint is "if node $X$ matches Professor and node $Y$ is an ancestor of $X$ in the taxonomy, then it is unlikely that $Y$ matches Assistant-Professor". Such constraints occur frequently in practice, and heuristics are commonly used when manually mapping between ontologies. Previous works have exploited only one form or the other of such knowledge and constraints, in restrictive settings [28, 25, 20, 24]. Here, we develop a unifying approach to incorporate all such types of information. Our approach is based on *relaxation labeling*, a powerful technique used extensively in the vision and image processing community [16], and successfully adapted to solve matching and classification problems in natural language processing [30] and hypertext classification [9].

We observe that the GLUE system is just one piece of a more complete ontology matching solution. We envisage any such tool to have a significant user-interaction component. Semantic mappings can often be highly subjective and depend on choice of target application, and can be more complex expressions than the simple correspondences produced by GLUE. User-interaction is invaluable and indispensable in such cases. We however do not address this in our solution. The automated support that GLUE will provide to a more complete tool will however very significantly reduce the effort required of any user, and in many cases reduce it to just mapping validation rather than construction.

In the rest of this chapter, we define the ontology-matching (section 19.3), discuss our approach to measuring similarity (section 19.4), and then describe the GLUE system (sections 19.5-19.6). We then present some experimental validation of our approach (section 19.7). We conclude with a review of related work (section 19.8) and avenues for future work (section 19.9).

## 19.3 Ontology Matching

For our purpose, an *ontology* specifies a conceptualization of a domain in terms of concepts, attributes, and relations [14]. The *concepts* provided model entities of interest in the domain. They are typically organized into a *taxonomy tree* where each node represents a concept and each concept is a specialization of its parent. Figure 19.1 shows two sample taxonomies for the CS department domain (which are simplifications of real ones).

Each concept in a taxonomy is associated with a set of *instances*. By the taxonomy's definition, the instances of a concept are also instances of an ancestor concept.

For example, instances of **Assistant-Professor, Associate-Professor**, and **Professor** in Figure 19.1.a are also instances of **Faculty** and **People**.

Each concept is also associated with a set of *attributes*. For example, the concept **Associate-Professor** in Figure 19.1.a has the attributes **name, degree**, and **granting-institution**. An ontology also defines a set of *relations* among its concepts. For example, a relation **AdvisedBy(Student,Professor)** might list all instance pairs of **Student** and **Professor** such that the former is advised by the latter.

Many formal languages to specify ontologies have been proposed for the Semantic Web, such as OIL, DAML+OIL, SHOE, and RDF [7, 1, 15, 6]. Though these languages differ in their terminologies and expressiveness, the ontologies that they model essentially share the same features we described above.

Given two ontologies, the *ontology-matching* problem is to find semantic mappings between them. The simplest type of mapping is a *one-to-one (1-1)* mapping between the elements, such as "**Associate-Professor** maps to **Senior-Lecturer**", and "**degree** maps to **education**". Notice that mappings between different types of elements are possible, such as "the relation **AdvisedBy(Student,Professor)** maps to the attribute **advisor** of the concept **Student**". Examples of more complex types of mapping include "**name** maps to the concatenation of **first-name** and **last-name**", and "the union of **Undergrad-Courses** and **Grad-Courses** maps to **Courses**". In general, a mapping may be specified as a query that transforms instances in one ontology into instances in the other [8].

In this chapter we focus on finding 1-1 mappings between the taxonomies. This is because taxonomies are central components of ontologies, and successfully matching them would greatly aid in matching the rest of the ontologies. Extending matching to attributes and relations and considering more complex types of matching is the subject of ongoing research.

There are many ways to formulate a matching problem for taxonomies. The specific problem that we consider is as follows: *given two taxonomies and their associated data instances, for each node (i.e., concept) in one taxonomy, find the most similar node in the other taxonomy, for a pre-defined similarity measure.* This is a very general problem setting that makes our approach applicable to a broad range of common ontology-related problems, such as ontology integration and data translation among the ontologies.

## 19.4 Similarity Measures

To match concepts between two taxonomies, we need a measure of similarity. We first identify some desiderata for any such similarity measure.

First, we would like the similarity measures to be well-defined. A well-defined measure will facilitate the evaluation of our system. It also makes clear to the users what the system means by a match, and helps them figure out whether the system is applicable to a given matching scenario. Furthermore, a well-defined similarity notion may allow us to leverage special-purpose techniques for the matching process.

Second, we want the similarity measures to correspond to our intuitive notions of similarity. In particular, they should depend only on the semantic content of the concepts involved, and not on their syntactic specification.

Finally, we note that many reasonable similarity measures exist, each being appropriate to certain situations. For example, in searching for your conference acquaintance, your softbot should use an "exact" similarity measure that maps Associate-Professor into Senior Lecturer, an equivalent concept. However, if the softbot has some postprocessing capabilities that allow it to filter data, then it may tolerate a "most-specific-parent" similarity measure that maps Associate-Professor to Academic-Staff, a more general concept. Hence, to maximize our system's applicability, we would like it to be able to handle a broad variety of similarity measures.

Most existing works in ontology (and schema) matching do not satisfy the above motivating criteria. Many works implicitly assume the existence of a similarity measure, but never define it. Others define similarity measures based on the syntactic clues of the concepts involved. For example, the similarity of two concepts might be computed as the dot product of the two TF/IDF (Term Frequency/Inverse Document Frequency) vectors representing the concepts, or a function based on the common tokens in the names of the concepts. Such similarity measures are problematic because they depend not only on the concepts involved, but also on their syntactic specifications.

### 19.4.1 Distribution-based Similarity Measures

We use joint probability distributions as a framework for multiple well-defined similarity measures. Consider modeling each concept as a *set of instances*, taken from a *universe of instances*. In the CS domain, for example, the universe consists of all entities of interest in that world: professors, assistant professors, students, courses, and so on. The concept Professor is then the set of all instances in the universe that are professors. Given this model, the notion of the *joint probability distribution* between any two concepts $A$ and $B$ is well defined. This distribution consists of the four probabilities: $P(A, B), P(A, \overline{B}), P(\overline{A}, B)$, and $P(\overline{A}, \overline{B})$. A term such as $P(A, \overline{B})$ is the probability that a randomly chosen instance from the universe belongs to $A$ but not to $B$, and is computed as the fraction of the universe that belongs to $A$ but not to $B$.

Many practical similarity measures can be defined based on the joint distribution of the concepts involved. For instance, a possible definition for the "exact" similarity measure mentioned in the previous section is

$$Jaccard\text{-}sim(A, B) = P(A \cap B)/P(A \cup B) = \frac{P(A, B)}{P(A, B) + P(A, \overline{B}) + P(\overline{A}, B)} \quad (19.1)$$

This similarity measure is known as the *Jaccard* coefficient [35]. It takes the lowest value 0 when $A$ and $B$ are disjoint, and the highest value 1 when $A$ and $B$ are the same concept. We use this measure in most of our experiments.

A definition for the "most-specific-parent" similarity measure is

$$MSP(A, B) = \begin{cases} P(A|B) & if \ P(B|A) = 1 \\ 0 & otherwise \end{cases} \quad (19.2)$$

where the probabilities $P(A|B)$ and $P(B|A)$ can be trivially expressed in terms of the four joint probabilities. This definition states that if $B$ subsumes $A$, then the more specific $B$ is, the higher $P(A|B)$, and thus the higher the similarity value

$MSP(A, B)$ is. Thus it suits the intuition that the most specific parent of $A$ in the taxonomy is the smallest set that subsumes $A$.

Instead of trying to estimate specific similarity values directly, GLUE focuses on computing the joint distributions. Then, it is possible to compute any of the above mentioned similarity measures as a function over the joint distributions.

## 19.5 The GLUE Architecture

The basic architecture of GLUE is shown in Figure 19.2. It consists of three main modules: *Distribution Estimator*, *Similarity Estimator*, and *Relaxation Labeler*.

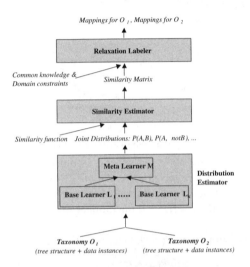

**Fig. 19.2.** The GLUE Architecture

The *Distribution Estimator* takes as input two taxonomies $O_1$ and $O_2$, together with their data instances. Then it applies machine learning techniques to compute for every pair of concepts $\langle A \in O_1, B \in O_2 \rangle$ their joint probability distribution: the four numbers $P(A, B), P(A, \overline{B}), P(\overline{A}, B)$, and $P(\overline{A}, \overline{B})$. Thus a total of $4|O_1||O_2|$ numbers will be computed, where $|O_i|$ is the number of nodes (i.e., concepts) in taxonomy $O_i$. The *Distribution Estimator* uses a set of base learners and a meta-learner. We describe the learners and the motivation behind them in Section 19.5.2.

Next, the above numbers are fed into the *Similarity Estimator*, which applies a user-supplied similarity function (such as the ones in Equations 19.1 or 19.2) to compute a similarity value for each pair of concepts $\langle A \in O_1, B \in O_2 \rangle$. The output from this module is a *similarity matrix* between the concepts in the two taxonomies.

The *Relaxation Labeler* module uses the similarity matrix and, together with domain-specific constraints and heuristic knowledge, searches for the mapping configuration that best satisfies the domain constraints and the common knowledge. This mapping configuration is the output of GLUE.

We first describe the *Distribution Estimator*. The *Similarity Estimator* is trivial because it simply applies a user-defined function to compute the similarity of two concepts from their joint distribution, and hence is not discussed further. Section 19.6 describes the *Relaxation Labeler*.

### 19.5.1 The Distribution Estimator

Consider computing the value of $P(A, B)$. This joint probability can be computed as the fraction of the instance universe that belongs to both $A$ and $B$. In general we cannot compute this fraction because we do not know every instance in the universe. Hence, we must estimate $P(A, B)$ based on the data we have, namely, the instances of the two input taxonomies. Note that the instances that we have for the taxonomies may be overlapping, but are not necessarily so.

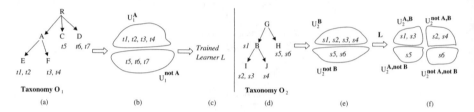

**Fig. 19.3.** Estimating the joint distribution of concepts $A$ and $B$

To estimate $P(A, B)$, we make the general assumption that the set of instances of each input taxonomy is a *representative sample* of the instance universe covered by the taxonomy.[3] We denote by $U_i$ the set of instances given for taxonomy $O_i$, by $N(U_i)$ the size of $U_i$, and by $N(U_i^{A,B})$ the number of instances in $U_i$ that belong to both $A$ and $B$.

With the above assumption, $P(A, B)$ can be estimated by the equation:

$$P(A, B) = [N(U_1^{A,B}) + N(U_2^{A,B})] \ / \ [N(U_1) + N(U_2)], \qquad (19.3)$$

Computing $P(A, B)$ then reduces to computing $N(U_1^{A,B})$ and $N(U_2^{A,B})$. Consider $N(U_2^{A,B})$. We can compute this quantity if we know for each instance $s$ in $U_2$ whether it belongs to both $A$ and $B$. One part is easy: we already know whether $s$ belongs to $B$ – if it is explicitly specified as an instance of $B$ or of any descendant node of $B$. Hence, we only need to decide whether $s$ belongs to $A$.

This is where we use machine learning. Specifically, we partition $U_1$, the set of instances of ontology $O_1$, into the set of instances that belong to $A$ and the set of instances that do not belong to $A$. Then, we use these two sets as positive and negative examples, respectively, to train a classifier for $A$. Finally, we use the classifier to predict whether instance $s$ belongs to $A$.

In summary, we estimate the joint probability distribution of $A$ and $B$ as follows (the procedure is illustrated in Figure 19.3):

1. Partition $U_1$, into $U_1^A$ and $U_1^{\overline{A}}$, the set of instances that do and do not belong to $A$, respectively (Figures 19.3.a-b).

---

[3] This is a standard assumption in machine learning and statistics, and seems appropriate here, unless the available instances were generated in some unusual way.

2. Train a learner $L$ for instances of $A$, using $U_1^A$ and $U_1^{\overline{A}}$ as the sets of positive and negative training examples, respectively.

3. Partition $U_2$, the set of instances of taxonomy $O_2$, into $U_2^B$ and $U_2^{\overline{B}}$, the set of instances that do and do not belong to $B$, respectively (Figures 19.3.d-e).

4. Apply learner $L$ to each instance in $U_2^B$ (Figure 19.3.e). This partitions $U_2^B$ into the two sets $U_2^{A,B}$ and $U_2^{\overline{A},B}$ shown in Figure 19.3.f. Similarly, applying $L$ to $U_2^{\overline{B}}$ results in the two sets $U_2^{A,\overline{B}}$ and $U_2^{\overline{A},\overline{B}}$.

5. Repeat Steps 1-4, but with the roles of taxonomies $O_1$ and $O_2$ being reversed, to obtain the sets $U_1^{A,B}$, $U_1^{\overline{A},B}$, $U_1^{A,\overline{B}}$, and $U_1^{\overline{A},\overline{B}}$.

6. Finally, compute $P(A, B)$ using Formula 19.3. The remaining three joint probabilities are computed in a similar manner, using the sets $U_2^{\overline{A},B}, \ldots, U_1^{\overline{A},\overline{B}}$ computed in Steps 4-5.

By applying the above procedure to all pairs of concepts $\langle A \in O_1, B \in O_2 \rangle$ we obtain all joint distributions of interest.

### 19.5.2 Multi-Strategy Learning

Given the diversity of machine learning methods, the next issue is deciding which one to use for the procedure we described above. A key observation in our approach is that there are *many* different types of information that a learner can glean from the training instances, in order to make predictions. It can exploit the *frequencies* of words in the text value of the instances, the instance *names*, the value *formats*, the *characteristics of value distributions*, and so on.

Since different learners are better at utilizing different types of information, GLUE follows [11] and takes a *multi-strategy learning* approach. In Step 2 of the above estimation procedure, instead of training a single learner $L$, we train a set of learners $L_1, \ldots, L_k$, called *base learners*. Each base learner exploits well a certain type of information from the training instances to build prediction hypotheses. Then, to classify an instance in Step 4, we apply the base learners to the instance and combine their predictions using a *meta-learner*. This way, we can achieve higher classification accuracy than with any single base learner alone, and therefore better approximations of the joint distributions.

The current implementation of GLUE has two base learners, *Content Learner* and *Name Learner*, and a meta-learner that is a linear combination of the base learners. We now describe these learners in detail.

**The Content Learner:** This learner exploits the frequencies of words in the *textual content* of an instance to make predictions. Recall that an instance typically has a *name* and a set of *attributes* together with their values. In the current version of GLUE, we do not handle attributes directly; rather, we treat them and their values as the *textual content* of the instance[4]. For example, the textual content of the instance

---

[4] However, more sophisticated learners can be developed that deal explicitly with the attributes, such as the XML Learner in [11].

"Professor Cook" is "R. Cook, Ph.D., University of Sidney, Australia". The textual content of the instance "CSE 342" is the text content of this course' homepage.

The Content Learner employs the Naive Bayes learning technique [13], one of the most popular and effective text classification methods. In [12] we give a detailed description of the working of this learner. In general, it applies well to long textual elements, such as course descriptions, or elements with very distinct and descriptive values, such as color (red, blue, green, etc.). It is less effective with short, numeric elements such as course numbers or credits.

**The Name Learner:**   This learner is similar to the Content Learner, but makes predictions using the *full name* of the input instance, instead of its *content*. The full name of an instance is the concatenation of concept names leading from the root of the taxonomy to that instance. For example, the full name of instance with the name $s_4$ in taxonomy $O_2$ (Figure 19.3.d) is "G B J $s_4$". This learner works best on specific and descriptive names. It does not do well with names that are too vague or vacuous.

**The Meta-Learner:**   The predictions of the base learners are combined using the meta-learner. The meta-learner assigns to each base learner a *learner weight* that indicates how much it *trusts* that learner's predictions. Then it combines the base learners' predictions via a weighted sum.

For example, suppose the weights of the Content Learner and the Name Learner are 0.6 and 0.4, respectively. Suppose further that for instance $s_4$ of taxonomy $O_2$ (Figure 19.3.d) the Content Learner predicts $A$ with probability 0.8 and $\overline{A}$ with probability 0.2, and the Name Learner predicts $A$ with probability 0.3 and $\overline{A}$ with probability 0.7. Then the Meta-Learner predicts $A$ with probability $0.8 \cdot 0.6 + 0.3 \cdot 0.4 = 0.6$ and $\overline{A}$ with probability $0.2 \cdot 0.6 + 0.7 \cdot 0.4 = 0.4$.

In the presented results (section 19.7), the learner weights are set manually based on the characteristics of the base learners and the taxonomies. However, they can also be set automatically using a machine learning approach called *stacking* [36, 33], as we have shown in [11].

## 19.6 Exploiting Constraints and Heuristic Knowledge

The *Relaxation Labeler* takes the similarity matrix from the *Similarity Estimator*, and searches for the mapping configuration that best satisfies the given domain constraints and heuristic knowledge. We first describe relaxation labeling, then discuss the domain constraints and heuristic knowledge employed in our approach.

### 19.6.1 Relaxation Labeling

Relaxation labeling is an efficient technique to solve the problem of assigning labels to nodes of a graph, given a set of constraints. The key idea behind this approach is that the label of a node is typically influenced by the *features of the node's neighborhood* in the graph. Examples of such features are the labels of the neighboring nodes, the percentage of nodes in the neighborhood that satisfy a certain criterion, and the fact that a certain constraint is satisfied or not.

This influence of a node's neighborhood on its label can be quantified using a formula for the probability of each label as a function of the neighborhood features. This is exploited in Relaxation labeling. Nodes are assigned initial labels based solely on their intrinsic properties. Then *iterative local optimization* is performed. In each iteration the formula is used to re-estimate the label of a node based on the features of its neighborhood. This continues until labels do not change from one iteration to the next, or some other convergence criterion is reached.

Relaxation labeling appears promising for our purposes because it has been applied successfully to similar matching problems in computer vision, natural language processing, and hypertext classification [16, 30, 9]. It is relatively efficient, and can handle a broad range of constraints. Even though its convergence properties are not yet well understood (except in certain cases) and it is liable to converge to a local maxima, in practice it has been found to perform quite well [30, 9].

Consider the problem of mapping from taxonomy $O_1$ to taxonomy $O_2$. We regard nodes (concepts) in $O_2$ as *labels*, and recast the problem as finding the best label assignment to nodes (concepts) in $O_1$, given all knowledge we have about the domain and the two taxonomies.

Our goal is to derive a formula for updating the probability that a node takes a label based on the features of the neighborhood. Let $X$ be a node in taxonomy $O_1$, and $L$ be a label (i.e., a node in $O_2$). Let $\Delta_K$ represent all that we know about the domain, namely, the tree structures of the two taxonomies, the sets of instances, and the set of domain constraints. Then we have the following conditional probability

$$P(X = L|\Delta_K) = \sum_{M_X} P(X = L, M_X|\Delta_K) = \sum_{M_X} P(X = L|M_X, \Delta_K)P(M_X|\Delta_K)$$

(19.4)

where the sum is over all possible label assignments $M_X$ to all nodes other than $X$ in taxonomy $O_1$. Making the simplifying assumption that the nodes' label assignments are independent of each other given $\Delta_K$, we have

$$P(M_X|\Delta_K) = \prod_{(X_i=L_i)\in M_X} P(X_i = L_i|\Delta_K) \qquad (19.5)$$

Consider $P(X = L|M_X, \Delta_K)$. $M_X$ and $\Delta_K$ constitutes all that we know about the neighborhood of $X$. Suppose now that the probability of $X$ getting label $L$ depends only on the values of $n$ features of this neighborhood, where each feature is a function $f_i(M_X, \Delta_K, X, L)$. As we explain later in this section, each such feature corresponds to one of the heuristics or domain constraints that we wish to exploit. Then

$$P(X = L|M_X, \Delta_K) = P(X = L|f_1, \ldots, f_n) \qquad (19.6)$$

If we have access to previously-computed mappings between taxonomies in the same domain, we can use them as the training data from which to estimate $P(X = L|f_1, \ldots, f_n)$ (see [9] for an example of this in the context of hypertext classification). However, here we will assume that such mappings are not available. Hence we use alternative methods to quantify the influence of the features on the label assignment. In particular, we use the sigmoid or logistic function $\sigma(x) = 1/(1 + e^{-x})$, where $x$ is a linear combination of the features $f_k$, to estimate the above probability. This function is widely used to combine multiple sources of evidence [4]. Thus:

$$P(X = L|f_1, \ldots, f_n) \propto \sigma(\alpha_1 \cdot f_1 + \cdots + \alpha_n \cdot f_n) \qquad (19.7)$$

where $\propto$ denotes "proportional to", and the weight $\alpha_k$ indicates the importance of feature $f_k$.

The sigmoid is essentially a smoothed threshold function, which makes it a good candidate for use in combining evidence from the different features. If the total evidence is below a certain value, it is unlikely that the nodes match; above this threshold, they probably do.

By substituting Equations 19.5-19.7 into Equation 19.4, we obtain

$$P(X = L|\Delta_K) \propto \sum_{M_X} \sigma\left(\sum_{k=1}^{n} \alpha_k f_k(M_X, \Delta_K, X, L)\right) \times \prod_{(X_i = L_i) \in M_X} P(X_i = L_i|\Delta_K)$$

$$(19.8)$$

The proportionality constant is found by renormalizing the probabilities of all the labels to sum to one. Notice that this equation expresses the probabilities $P(X = L|\Delta_K)$ for the various nodes in terms of each other. This is the iterative equation that we use for relaxation labeling.

In our implementation, we optimized relaxation labeling for efficiency in a number of ways that take advantage of the specific structure of the ontology matching problem. Space limitations preclude discussing these optimizations here, but see Section 19.7 for a discussion on the running time of this module.

### 19.6.2 Constraints

Table 19.1 shows examples of the constraints currently used in our approach and their characteristics. We distinguish between two types of constraints: domain-independent and -dependent constraints. *Domain-independent constraints* convey our general knowledge about the interaction between related nodes. Perhaps the most widely used such constraint is the *Neighborhood Constraint*: "two nodes match if nodes in their neighborhood also match", where the neighborhood is defined to be the children, the parents, or both [28, 20, 25] (see Table 19.1). Another example is the *Union Constraint*: "if all children of a node $A$ match node $B$, then $A$ also matches $B$". This constraint is specific to the taxonomy context. It exploits the fact that $A$ is the union of all its children. *Domain-dependent constraints* convey our knowledge about the interaction between specific nodes in the taxonomies. Table 19.1 shows examples of three types of domain-dependent constraints.

To incorporate the constraints into the relaxation labeling process, we model each constraint $c_i$ as a feature $f_i$ of the neighborhood of node $X$. For example, consider the constraint $c_1$: "two nodes are likely to match if their children match". To model this constraint, we introduce the feature $f_1(M_X, \Delta_K, X, L)$ that is the percentage of $X$'s children that match a child of $L$, under the given $M_X$ mapping. Thus $f_1$ is a numeric feature that takes values from 0 to 1. Next, we assign to $f_i$ a *positive* weight $\alpha_i$. This has the intuitive effect that, all other things being equal, the higher the value $f_i$ (i.e., the percentage of matching children), the higher the probability of $X$ matching $L$ is. In [12] we give additional examples of modeling constraints.

**Table 19.1.** Examples of constraints that can be used to improve matching accuracy

| Constraint Types | | Examples |
|---|---|---|
| *Domain-Independent* | *Neighborhood* | Two nodes match if their children also match.<br>Two nodes match if their parents match and at least x% of their children also match.<br>Two nodes match if their parents match and some of their descendants also match. |
| | *Union* | If all children of node X match node Y, then X also matches Y. |
| *Domain-Dependent* | *Subsumption* | If node Y is a descendant of node X, and Y matches PROFESSOR, then it's unlikely that X matches ASST PROFESSOR.<br>If node Y is NOT a descendant of node X, and Y matches PROFESSOR, then it is unlikely that X matches FACULTY. |
| | *Frequency* | There can be at most one node that matches DEPARTMENT CHAIR. |
| | *Nearby* | If a node in the neighborhood of node X matches ASSOC PROFESSOR, then the chance that X matches PROFESSOR is increased. |

## 19.7 Empirical Evaluation

We have evaluated GLUE on several real-world domains. Our goals were to evaluate the matching accuracy of GLUE, to measure the relative contribution of the different components of the system, and to verify that GLUE can work well with a variety of similarity measures.

**Table 19.2.** Domains and taxonomies for our experiments

| Taxonomies | | # nodes | # non-leaf nodes | depth | # instances in taxonomy | max # instances at a leaf | max # children of a node | # manual mappings created |
|---|---|---|---|---|---|---|---|---|
| Course Catalog I | *Cornell* | 34 | 6 | 4 | 1526 | 155 | 10 | 34 |
| | *Washington* | 39 | 8 | 4 | 1912 | 214 | 11 | 37 |
| Course Catalog II | *Cornell* | 176 | 27 | 4 | 4360 | 161 | 27 | 54 |
| | *Washington* | 166 | 25 | 4 | 6957 | 214 | 49 | 50 |
| Company Profiles | *Standard.com* | 333 | 30 | 3 | 13634 | 222 | 29 | 236 |
| | *Yahoo.com* | 115 | 13 | 3 | 9504 | 656 | 25 | 104 |

**Domains and Taxonomies:**  We evaluated GLUE on three domains, whose characteristics are shown in Table 19.2. The domains Course Catalog I and II describe courses at Cornell University and the University of Washington. The taxonomies of Course Catalog I have 34 - 39 nodes, and are fairly similar to each other. The taxonomies of Course Catalog II are much larger (166 - 176 nodes) and much less similar to each other. Courses are organized into schools and colleges, then into departments and centers within each college. The Company Profile domain uses taxonomies from Yahoo.com and Standard.com and describes the current business status of companies. Companies are organized into sectors, then into industries within each sector. The Standard.com taxonomy, though of same depth, has a more granular (333 nodes) organization than the Yahoo.com one(115 nodes).

For each taxonomy, we downloaded the entire set of data instances, and performed some trivial data cleaning such as removing HTML tags and phrases such as "course not offered" from the instances. We removed instances of size less than 130 bytes, because they tend to be empty or vacuous, and thus do not contribute to the matching process. We removed all nodes with fewer than 5 instances, because such nodes cannot be matched reliably due to lack of data.

**Similarity Measure & Manual Mappings:**  We chose to evaluate GLUE using the *Jaccard* similarity measure (Section 19.4), because it corresponds well to our intuitive understanding of similarity. Given the similarity measure, we manually created the correct 1-1 mappings between the taxonomies in the same domain, for evaluation purposes. The rightmost column of Table 19.2 shows the number of manual mappings created for each taxonomy. For example, we created 236 one-to-one mappings from *Standard* to *Yahoo!*, and 104 mappings in the reverse direction. Note that in some cases there were nodes in a taxonomy for which we could not find a 1-1 match. This was either because there was no equivalent node (e.g., School of Hotel Administration at Cornell has no equivalent counterpart at the University of Washington), or when it is impossible to determine an accurate match without additional domain expertise.

**Domain Constraints:**  We specified domain constraints for the relaxation labeler. For the Course Catalog I taxonomies, we specified all applicable subsumption constraints (see Table 19.1). For the other two domains, because their sheer size makes specifying all constraints difficult, we specified only the most obvious subsumption constraints (about 10 constraints for each taxonomy). For the Company Profiles taxonomies we also used frequency constraints.

**Experiments:**  For each domain, we performed two experiments. We applied GLUE to find the mappings from each taxonomy to the other. The *matching accuracy* of a taxonomy is then the percentage of the manual mappings (for that taxonomy) that GLUE predicted correctly.

### 19.7.1 Matching Accuracy

Figure 19.4 shows the matching accuracy for different domains and configurations of GLUE. In each domain, we show the matching accuracy of two scenarios: mapping from the first taxonomy to the second, and vice versa. The four bars in each scenario (from left to right) represent the accuracy produced by: (1) the name learner alone, (2) the content learner alone, (3) the meta-learner using the previous two learners, and (4) the relaxation labeler on top of the meta-learner (i.e., the complete GLUE system).

   The results show that GLUE achieves high accuracy across all three domains, ranging from 66 to 97%. In contrast, the best matching results of the base learners, achieved by the content learner, are only 52 - 83%. It is interesting that the name learner achieves very low accuracy, 12 - 15% in four out of six scenarios. This is

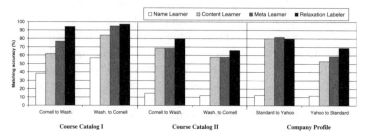

**Fig. 19.4.** Matching accuracy of GLUE

because all instances of a concept, say $B$, have very similar full names (see the description of the name learner in Section 19.5.2). Hence, when the name learner for a concept $A$ is applied to $B$, it will classify *all* instances of $B$ as $A$ or $\overline{A}$. In cases when this classfication is incorrect, which might be quite often, using the name learner alone leads to poor estimates of the joint distributions. The poor performance of the name learner underscores the importance of data instances and multi-strategy learning in ontology matching.

The results clearly show the utility of the meta-learner and relaxation labeler. Even though in half of the cases the meta-learner only minimally improves the accuracy, in the other half it makes substantial gains, between 6 and 15%. And in all but one case, the relaxation labeler further improves accuracy by 3 - 18%, confirming that it is able to exploit the domain constraints and general heuristics. In one case (from Standard to Yahoo), the relaxation labeler decreased accuracy by 2%. The performance of the relaxation labeler is discussed in more detail below. In Section 19.7.3 we identify the reasons that prevent GLUE from identifying the remaining mappings.

In the current experiments, GLUE utilized on average only 30 to 90 data instances per leaf node (see Table 19.2). The high accuracy in these experiments suggests that GLUE can work well with only a modest amount of data.

We also experimented with the *most-specific-parent* similarity measure described in Section 19.4 and found GLUE performing quite well with it. This experiment is described in more detail in [12]. The results illustrate how GLUE can be effective with more than one similarity measure.

### 19.7.2 Performance of the Relaxation Labeler

In all of our experiments, we found relaxation labeling to be very fast. The iterations were performed until the labeling converged. It took only a few seconds in Catalog I and under 20 seconds in the other two domains to finish ten iterations. This observation shows that relaxation labeling can be implemented efficiently in the ontology-matching context. It also suggests that we can efficiently incorporate user feedback into the relaxation labeling process in the form of additional domain constraints.

We also experimented with different values for the constraint weights (see Section 19.6), and found that the relaxation labeler was quite robust with respect to such parameter changes. Further details and other experiments can be found in [12].

### 19.7.3 Discussion

The accuracy of GLUE is quite impressive as is, but it is natural to ask what limits GLUE from obtaining even higher accuracy. There are several reasons that prevent GLUE from correctly matching the remaining nodes. First, some nodes cannot be matched because of insufficient training data. For example, many course descriptions in Course Catalog II contain only vacuous phrases such as "3 credits". While there is clearly no general solution to this problem, in many cases it can be mitigated by adding base learners that can exploit domain characteristics to improve matching accuracy. Second, the relaxation labeler performed local optimizations, and sometimes converged to only a local maxima, thereby not finding correct mappings for all nodes. Here, the challenge will be in developing search techniques that work better by taking a more "global perspective", but still retain the runtime efficiency of local optimization. Further, the two base learners we used in our implementation are rather simple general-purpose text classifiers. Using other leaners that perform domain-specific feature selection and comparison can also improve the accuracy. It will be interesting to consider the use of a thesaurus like WordNet to improve the performance of the Name Learner.

We note that some nodes cannot be matched automatically because they are simply ambiguous. For example, it is not clear whether "networking and communication devices" should match "communication equipment" or "computer networks". A solution to this problem is to incorporate user interaction into the matching process [27, 11, 37].

GLUE currently tries to predict the best match for *every* node in the taxonomy. However, in some cases, such a match simply does not exist (e.g., unlike Cornell, the University of Washington does not have a School of Hotel Administration). Hence, an additional extension to GLUE is to make it be aware of such cases, and not predict an incorrect match when this occurs.

## 19.8 Related Work

GLUE is related to our previous work on LSD [11], whose goal was to semi-automatically find schema mappings for data integration. There, we had a mediated schema, and our goal was to find mappings from the schemas of a multitude of data sources to the mediated schema. The observation was that we can use a set of *manually* given mappings on several sources as training examples for a learner that predicts mappings for subsequent sources. LSD illustrated the effectiveness of multistrategy learning for this problem. In GLUE since our problem is to match a pair of ontologies, there are no manual mappings for training, and we need to obtain the training examples for the learner automatically. Further, GLUE is able to exploit a much richer set of constraints using relaxation labeling than the simplistic A* search in LSD. Finally, LSD did not consider in depth the semantics of a mapping, as we do here.

We now describe other related work to GLUE from several perspectives.

**Ontology Matching:** Many works have addressed ontology matching in the context of ontology design and integration (e.g., [10, 23, 27, 26]). These works do not deal with explicit notions of similarity. They use a variety of heuristics to match ontology elements. They do not use machine learning and do not exploit information in the data instances. However, many of them [23, 27] have powerful features that allow for efficient user interaction, or expressive rule languages [10] for specifying mappings. Such features are important components of a comprehensive solution to ontology matching, and hence should be added to GLUE in the future.

Several recent works have attempted to further automate the ontology matching process. The Anchor-PROMPT system [28] exploits the general heuristic that paths (in the taxonomies or ontology graphs) between matching elements tend to contain other matching elements. The HICAL system [17] exploits the data instances in the overlap between the two taxonomies to infer mappings. [18] computes the similarity between two taxonomic nodes based on their signature TF/IDF vectors, which are computed from the data instances.

**Schema Matching:**   Schemas can be viewed as ontologies with restricted relationship types. The problem of schema matching has been studied in the context of data integration and data translation (see [32] for a survey). Several works [25, 20, 24] have exploited variations of the general heuristic "two nodes match if nodes in their neighborhood also match", but in an isolated fashion, and not in the same general framework we have in GLUE.

**Notions of Similarity:**   The similarity measure in [17] is based on $\kappa$ statistics, and can be thought of as being defined over the joint probability distribution of the concepts involved. In [19] the authors propose an information-theoretic notion of similarity that is based on the joint distribution. These works argue for a single best universal similarity measure, whereas GLUE allows for application-dependent similarity measures.

**Ontology Learning:**   Machine learning has been applied to other ontology-related tasks, most notably learning to construct ontologies from data and other ontologies, and extracting ontology instances from data [29, 22, 31]. Our work here provides techniques to help in the ontology construction process [22]. [21] gives a comprehensive summary of the role of machine learning in the Semantic Web effort.

## 19.9  Conclusion and Future Work

With the proliferation of data sharing applications that involve multiple ontologies, the development of automated techniques for ontology matching will be crucial to their success. We have described an approach that applies machine learning techniques to match ontologies. Our approach is based on well-founded notions of semantic similarity, expressed in terms of the joint probability distribution of the concepts involved. We described the use of machine learning, and in particular, of multistrategy learning, for computing concept similarities. This learning technique makes our approach easily extensible to additional learners, and hence to exploiting additional kinds of knowledge about instances. Finally, we introduced relaxation labeling to the ontology-matching context, and showed that it can be adapted to efficiently exploit a variety of heuristic knowledge and domain-specific constraints to further improve matching accuracy. Our experiments showed that we can accurately match 66 - 97% of the nodes on several real-world domains.

Aside from striving to improve the accuracy of our methods, our main line of future research involves extending our techniques to handle more sophisticated mappings between ontologies (i.e., non 1-1 mappings), and exploiting more of the constraints that are expressed in the ontologies (via attributes and relationships, and constraints expressed on them).

## Acknowledgments

We thank Phil Bernstein, Geoff Hulten, Natasha Noy, Rachel Pottinger, Matt Richardson, Pradeep Shenoy, and a host of anonymous reviewers for their invaluable comments. This work was supported by NSF Grants 9523649, 9983932, IIS-9978567, and IIS-9985114. The third author is also supported by an IBM Faculty Patnership Award. The fourth author is also supported by a Sloan Fellowship and gifts from Microsoft Research, NEC and NTT.

## References

1. www.daml.org.
2. www.google.com.
3. *IEEE Intelligent Systems*, 16(2), 2001.
4. A. Agresti. *Categorical Data Analysis*. Wiley, New York, NY, 1990.
5. T. Berners-Lee, J. Hendler, and O. Lassila. The Semantic Web. *Scientific American*, 279, 2001.
6. D. Brickley and R. Guha. Resource Description Framework Schema Specification 1.0, 2000.
7. J. Broekstra, M. Klein, S. Decker, D. Fensel, F. van Harmelen, and I. Horrocks. Enabling knowledge representation on the Web by Extending RDF Schema. In *Proceedings of the Tenth International World Wide Web Conference*, 2001.
8. D. Calvanese, D. G. Giuseppe, and M. Lenzerini. Ontology of Integration and Integration of Ontologies. In *Proceedings of the Description Logic Workshop*, 2001.
9. S. Chakrabarti, B. Dom, and P. Indyk. Enhanced Hypertext Categorization Using Hyperlinks. In *Proceedings of the ACM SIGMOD Conference*, 1998.
10. H. Chalupsky. Ontomorph: A Translation system for symbolic knowledge. In *Principles of Knowledge Representation and Reasoning*, 2000.
11. A. Doan, P. Domingos, and A. Halevy. Reconciling Schemas of Disparate Data Sources: A Machine Learning Approach. In *Proceedings of the ACM SIGMOD Conference*, 2001.
12. A. Doan, J. Madhavan, P. Domingos, and A. Y. Halevy. Learning to Map between Ontologies on the Semantic Web. In *Proceedings of the World Wide Web Confernce (WWW)*, 2002.
13. P. Domingos and M. Pazzani. On the Optimality of the Simple Bayesian Classifier under Zero-One Loss. *Machine Learning*, 29:103–130, 1997.
14. D. Fensel. *Ontologies: Silver Bullet for Knowledge Management and Electronic Commerce*. Springer-Verlag, 2001.
15. J. Heflin and J. Hendler. A Portrait of the Semantic Web in Action. *IEEE Intelligent Systems*, 16(2), 2001.
16. R. Hummel and S. Zucker. On the Foundations of Relaxation Labeling Processes. *PAMI*, 5(3):267–287, May 1983.
17. R. Ichise, H. Takeda, and S. Honiden. Rule Induction for Concept Hierarchy Alignment. In *Proceedings of the Workshop on Ontology Learning at IJCAI*, 2001.
18. M. Lacher and G. Groh. Facilitating the exchange of explixit knowledge through ontology mappings. In *Proceedings of the 14th Int. FLAIRS conference*, 2001.
19. D. Lin. An Information-Theoritic Definiton of Similarity. In *Proceedings of the International Conference on Machine Learning (ICML)*, 1998.
20. J. Madhavan, P. Bernstein, and E. Rahm. Generic Schema Matching with Cupid. In *Proceedings of the International Conference on Very Large Databases (VLDB)*, 2001.

21. A. Maedche. A Machine Learning Perspective for the Semantic Web. Semantic Web Working Symposium (SWWS) Position Paper, 2001.
22. A. Maedche and S. Saab. Ontology Learning for the Semantic Web. *IEEE Intelligent Systems*, 16(2), 2001.
23. D. McGuinness, R. Fikes, J. Rice, and S. Wilder. The Chimaera Ontology Environment. In *Proceedings of the 17th National Conference on Artificial Intelligence (AAAI)*, 2000.
24. S. Melnik, H. Molina-Garcia, and E. Rahm. Similarity Flooding: A Versatile Graph Matching Algorithm. In *Proceedings of the International Conference on Data Engineering (ICDE)*, 2002.
25. T. Milo and S. Zohar. Using Schema Matching to Simplify Heterogeneous Data Translation. In *Proceedings of the International Conference on Very Large Databases (VLDB)*, 1998.
26. P. Mitra, G. Wiederhold, and J. Jannink. Semi-automatic Integration of Knowledge Sources. In *Proceedings of Fusion'99*.
27. N. Noy and M. Musen. PROMPT: Algorithm and Tool for Automated Ontology Merging and Alignment. In *Proceedings of the National Conference on Artificial Intelligence (AAAI)*, 2000.
28. N. Noy and M. Musen. Anchor-PROMPT: Using Non-Local Context for Semantic Matching. In *Proceedings of the Workshop on Ontologies and Information Sharing at IJCAI*, 2001.
29. B. Omelayenko. Learning of Ontologies for the Web: the Analysis of Existent approaches. In *Proceedings of the International Workshop on Web Dynamics*, 2001.
30. L. Padro. A Hybrid Environment for Syntax-Semantic Tagging, 1998.
31. N. Pernelle, M.-C. Rousset, and V. Ventos. Automatic Construction and Refinement of a Class Hierarchy over Semi-Structured Data. In *Proceeding of the Workshop on Ontology Learning at IJCAI*, 2001.
32. E. Rahm and P. Bernstein. On Matching Schemas Automatically. *VLDB Journal*, 10(4), 2001.
33. K. M. Ting and I. H. Witten. Issues in stacked generalization. *Journal of Artificial Intelligence Research (JAIR)*, 10:271–289, 1999.
34. M. Uschold. Where is the semantics in the Semantic Web? In *Workshop on Ontologies in Agent Systems (OAS) at the 5th International Conference on Autonomous Agents*, 2001.
35. van Rijsbergen. *Information Retrieval*. London:Butterworths, 1979. Second Edition.
36. D. Wolpert. Stacked generalization. *Neural Networks*, 5:241–259, 1992.
37. L. Yan, R. Miller, L. Haas, and R. Fagin. Data Driven Understanding and Refinement of Schema Mappings. In *Proceedings of the ACM SIGMOD*, 2001.

# Retrieving and Exploring Ontology-based Information

Peter Eklund[1], Richard Cole[1], and Nataliya Roberts[2]

[1] School of Information Technology and Computer Science
The University of Wollongong, Wollongong NSW 2522
peklund@uow.edu.au
[2] Distributed Systems Technology Centre
The University of Queensland
St. Lucia QLD 4072, Australia nataliya@dstc.com

**Summary.** This chapter reports efforts to build an experimental platform for the retrieval and exploration of ontological data for the Semantic Web. The focus for exploring and browsing ontological data is a program called ONTORAMA, a Java client that browses ontologies in a hyperbolic-style layout. This chapter discusses some of the issues relating to visualizing ontologies, developing a peer-to-peer extension of ONTORAMA allowing cooperative ontology development and the creation of the RDF Distillery web-site as a location for the validation, collection and distribution of RDF ontologies.

## 20.1 Introduction

In order to achieve W3Cs goal of a "consistent logical web of data"[3], common standards are needed to represent knowledge. The Semantic Web will be designed to enable machine-processable information by giving it more structured meaning. Knowledge bases (including ontologies) are defined as "shared formal conceptualizations in particular domains"[1], or more commonly, a specification of a conceptualization. In other words, an ontology is a description of the concepts and relationships that can exist for an agent or a community of agents.

The aim of having one large online ontology of semantic data is realistically unachievable, so smaller (often domain specific) web-based knowledge bases will emerge (many already exist, see Ding[2]). These ontologies use metadata languages, such as RDF, DAML+OIL, CycL, F-logic, and KIF, to represent the ontological information in a form that can be communicated between both humans and computers. These formats however, are a difficult medium for human understanding. Therefore browsers are required to support human comprehension of ontological information. One such browser is ONTORAMA, a Java-based hyperbolic style browser that is able to render an ontology as a hierarchical display.

---

[3] http://www.w3.org/DesignIssues/Semantic.html

This chapter addresses issues related to browsing ontological data using a visualization metaphor. Further to this, an extension of ONTORAMA involving a peer-to-peer (P2P) based collaborative framework for constructing and editing shared ontologies is discussed. Of central interest is the way in which modifications made by different peers can be merged.

To promote ONTORAMA to a broader community, the RDF Distillery project was initiated with three main aims: (i) to make ONTORAMA widely accessible, (ii) to encourage the RDF community to submit RDF files for validation, and (iii) to become a collection and search point for sharing, indexing, merging and archiving RDF documents. The last part of this chapter will describe how the RDF distillery was constructed to fulfill these aims.

## 20.2 OntoRama

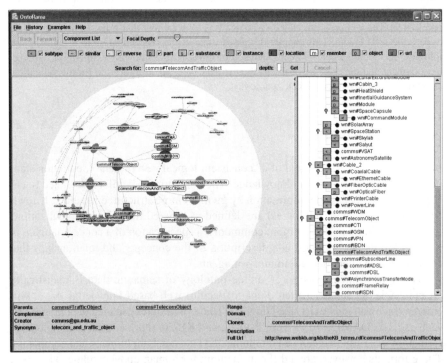

**Fig. 20.1.** ONTORAMA: ONTORAMA browsing part of an ontology relating to telecommunications

The hyperbolic tree was introduced by Lamping and Rao[3] as a mechanism for rendering large structures. The essential idea of a hyperbolic tree comes from a woodcut by M. C. Escher[4]. An element of interest is drawn in the center of the diagram, and elements further out are rendered exponentially smaller as their distance from the center of the diagram increases. See for example Figure 20.1. Since the number of elements in a balanced tree increases exponentially with tree depth, hyperbolic views are a good match, being able to display more tree levels than a conventional view. Since elements near the edge of a hyperbolic view are very small their labels commonly cannot be read. The diagram however is still able to indicate the structure and the labels can be increased in size by dragging that portion of the diagram closer to the center.

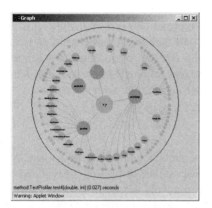 

**Fig. 20.2.** HYPERPROF (left): Hyperbolic Browser displays Java profiles. Hyperbolic Browser for INXIGHT Web-site (right).

Some examples of the hyperbolic view are INXIGHT's Star Tree[5] which uses a hyperbolic browser to view Insight trees (see Figure 20.2 (right)). More closely related to our work is HYPERPROF[6], a hyperbolic browser that creates views of a Java profile (or call graph) in a hyperbolic view (see Figure 20.2 (left)). ONTORAMA employs a spherical projection as its geometry rather than the hyperbolic projection described by Lamping and Rao. This spherical projection, while having a different theoretical basis, shares many of the properties of a hyperbolic geometry.

ONTORAMA has been used most extensively to visualize ontologies expressed in RDF but is not limited to RDF. We believe that many of the intuitions and experiences gained using ONTORAMA with RDF are applicable to a wider range of ontological languages. In order to visualize ontologies expressed in RDF, ONTORAMA defines a translation of RDF into edge labeled, vertex labeled trees. These trees are displayed simultaneously in both an explorer-style (large widget on the right of Figure 20.1 and a hyperbolic style diagram (large widget on the left of Figure 20.1). ONTORAMA is

---

[4] the Circle Limit IV woodcut
[5] http://www.inxight.com
[6] http://www.physics.orst.edu/~bulatov/HyperProf/

simply extended to visualize ontological information expressed in other languages by defining similar translations for those other languages.

ONTORAMA is designed to work as a distributed component and so operates in a query/result mode. The elements and relationships in the view are determined by the results obtained after submitting a query to a server or collection of peers (the P2P operation is detailed in the following section). Thus the ONTORAMA program downloads only the portion of the ontology needed for display. When used with a knowledge base such as WEBKB-2[4] the query contains either a keyword to be matched against terms in the ontology, or a specifier, such as a URI, for a specific term in the ontology. When used with a collection of files the query may be a filename or URL.

Since ONTORAMA renders ontological information as tree structures it is most appropriately used to visualize hierarchies. We therefore focus on the part of the ontology related to concept and relation types, and the relationships between them. Concepts and relation types are associated in some ontologies with inference reasoning rules. We have not yet attempted to visualize such rules with ONTORAMA

### 20.2.1 Translating RDF

RDF is an extensible language and is used for a number of different purposes. When applied to an RDF source, ONTORAMA focuses on the display of concept and relation types extracted from RDF documents. Commonly this information is expressed using schemes such as RDFS and DAML. Thus the translation of RDF by ONTORAMA focuses on RDFS and DAML.

RDF documents essentially consist of triples of the form *(subject, predicate, object)*. In the translation of RDF to a tree we first construct a directed graph. Each triple gives rise to a binary labeled edge. The label is set to the predicate of the triple. Both the subject and object of the triple give rise to a vertex. The two vertices are connected by the edge. Once such a graph is constructed it is converted to a tree by (i) selecting a vertex of interest, and (ii) generating a tree from the set of all paths within the graph that begin at the vertex of interest.

Since such a set of paths is closed under prefix, a tree structure results. Each vertex in the tree corresponds to a path in the graph and is labeled with the graph vertex at the end of the path. In discussing the tree displayed in a hyperbolic view it is useful to introduce the notion of a clone. One vertex in the tree is a clone of another vertex in the tree if both vertices have the same label. Clones arise when there are multiple paths in the graph from the vertex of interest to some other vertex.

Constructing a tree from a graph presents several problems. Cycles in the graph extracted from RDF lead to an infinite number of paths and so an infinite tree. This is solved limiting the depth of the tree. Even if there are no cycles the number of paths may be much larger than the number vertices. This situation is in our experience rare. Wordnet for example has an average leaf depth of 7 and over 85% of the types have a single parent. Hierarchical relations in ontologies also rarely in our experience contain cycles. If a cycle is present it generally indicates an error.

Bi-partite graphs do not allow edges to connect to other edges, however this situation can arise in RDF where the same entity can play both the role of predicate, and the role of subject. For example an RDF document may link a document to an author by the predicate s:Creator. This predicate may itself be related to other predicates by a hierarchy of relation types contained in an RDFS or DAML document. Commonly this situation is handled by making no attempt to link the edges and vertices having the same label. This is the approach taken by ONTORAMA.

Icons are used in ONTORAMA to distinguish different edge labels. A configuration file used by ONTORAMA defines the mapping from edge labels to icons. Each edge label may be assigned an icon and the user has the ability to control which edge labels are displayed. If an edge label is not selected then edges with that label are not displayed. A distinction is drawn in ONTORAMA between vertices representing relation types and vertices representing concept types. Concept types are rendered as blue circles, while relation types rendered as green triangles.

## 20.2.2 Navigation in OntoRama

A screenshot of ONTORAMA is shown in Figure 20.1. The two views dominating the screenshot are the hyperbolic view, on the left, and the tree (explorer style) view on the right. These two views both display the same ontology fragment and are linked so that selecting an object of focus in one view causes that object to receive focus in the other view. The two views are complementary in that often when one view has undesirable properties, the other view does not. For example when a vertex has many children, labels in the hyperbolic view may overlap. In this case the user can resort to the tree view in which the labels do not overlap.

ONTORAMA handles the case of multiple inheritance by creating clones. Any vertex having a clone is colored red. By selecting a vertex the clones for that vertex are marked by a line drawn from the selected vertex to each of the clones. For example consider the concept selected in Figure 20.1, namely comms#Telcom-AndTraficObject. It is connected its clone by a dotted line.

Selecting a vertex also produces information in the bottom panel. As shown in Figure 20.1, the selected vertex is comms#TelcomAndTraficObject whose creator is comms@gu.edu.au. The selected vertex doesn't have a description but does have a single clone which can be navigated using the panel. The information displayed in this panel is configurable.

Directly above the two tree views there is an entry field for entering search expressions and a row of selectable icons containing one icon for each possible edge label. These icons may be unselected thus removing all edges of that type from the two views.

Normally when an ontology fragment is returned in response to a query it has a single root vertex which acts as the default vertex of interest from which other vertices may be reached via the tree views. However it is sometimes the case that the ontology fragment returned has no root node, or indeed the fragment returned is not even connected. In this case ONTORAMA makes the different candidates for root node available in a menu item and the user may display the tree generated from each. An alternative would have been to construct an artificial root vertex and connect each of the candidate root vertices to it. ONTORAMA prefers to maintain an exact correspondence between vertices and elements in the ontology and so this was not done.

Two possibilities are provided for navigating to other concepts. Firstly the user may enter a new search expression and fetch a portion of the ontology corresponding to that search expression, or alternatively a vertex within the diagram may be selected and in doing so fetch the portion of the ontology related to that term.

It is important for the user to be able to identify clones in hyperbolic view. Any vertex that has at least one distinct clone is colored red in the diagram. When the user moves the mouse over the vertex its clones are identified by lines drawn between the selected vertex and its clones.

## 20.3 P2P OntoRama

ONTORAMA was initially designed to browse an ontology maintained on a server. The P2P extension to ONTORAMA adds two major capabilities: (i) the ability to modify the ontology, and (ii) a mechanism to mediate ontology modifications made by different peers. Peer-to-peer networks are generally seen as being more reliable, and in some cases more efficient, than centralized server approaches because of their capability to perform distributed replication and distribution of information. The peer-to-peer extension to ONTORAMA was of interest to us because of the equal standing of the peers. Each peer conforms to a required behavior, but beyond that is free to form its own idea of the ontology.

Many tools and much research effort has been devoted to the cooperative construction of ontologies. Such tools may be divided into two groups: (i) those that concentrate on building a single large general ontology, and (ii) those that focus on building small purpose built interconnected ontologies. WEBONTO[5] is an example of the former and provides a web-based interface for browsing, visualizing and editing a centralized ontology. The ONION toolkit, on the other hand, is an example of the latter approach. Recent research has focused on small purpose built ontologies arising from a belief that large general ontologies are unwieldy and difficult for humans to comprehend and lack the precise understandings required for real applications. More closely related to our work is the P2P Semantic Web (PSW).

The P2P extension to ONTORAMA defines groups of users. When a user commits changes to their ontology other members of the group are notified and they are given an opportunity to either accept, reject, or ignore the modifications. The ontology thus becomes a more complex structure as each statement within the ontology may thus be accepted, rejected or ignored by each user within the network. This raises the question of mediation between the different peers or users. We considered two approaches to this problem: that of Fridman[7] and that of Hovy[6].

According to the approach advocated by Hovy conflicts arise from different usages of the same term. The two usages of a term are either comparable, i.e. one usage is a specialization of the other, or they are incomparable. When the two term usages are comparable then the more specific usage, together with its subordinates is integrated below the more general usage. If the terms are incomparable then user intervention is required to resolve the conflict.

The approach outlined by Friedman et al. uses an automated approach to present suggested mergings of terms to the user. The user selects from a number of alternatives, and where there are conflicts introduced by the merging operations, suggestions on how to resolve the conflicts are presented to the user.

## 20.4 RDF Distillery

The RDF distillery project serves two purposes. Firstly is provides a convenient mechanism for people to download and use ONTORAMA to browse the ontological part of RDF documents. The aim here is to gain further experience of ONTORAMA with "real RDF examples".

Secondly, the RDF Distillery caches and indexes the RDF documents supplied to it thus becoming a text-searchable and knowledge-searchable repository of ontologies.

Figure 20.3 shows the home page of the RDF Distillery. It presents the user with two operations: (i) upload an RDF file for validation, or (ii) browse an existing ontology. If the user chooses the first of these options they are requested to specify a file which is uploaded using the HTTP protocol. This file is first validated using Jena, an open source API for parsing and manipulating RDF files. If the file is found to be valid RDF then the file is saved, and indexed, and the user is offered the option of starting ONTORAMA primed with the uploaded file. In this case ONTORAMA is spawned using Java's WebStart protocol. This protocol allows ONTORAMA to be passed a configuration file specifying icons to be used as edge labels and a reference to the RDF file now stored in the RDF Distillery.

If the user chooses the other main option on the home page, that of searching the repository, they are presented with a text search field. The distillery will return a list of RDF documents containing elements matching the test query and offer the ability to spawn ONTORAMA to browse each of these ontologies.

The RDF distillery is still in its early stages but provides an interesting counter point to the P2P extension to ONTORAMA. In the P2P approach peers co-operatively construct and maintain ontologies, reviewing one another's changes. In the RDF Distillery approach ontologies, expressed in RDF, are simply composed together. Two terms are the same only if their URI's are equal. A natural extension to the RDF distillery is to allow structured queries against the repository, and to browse the results using ONTORAMA.

### 20.4.1 ProntoRama

ONTORAMA when compiled and compressed is a 2 megabyte download. It is currently dependent on Java version 1.4 and so spawning ONTORAMA for the first time can result in an 80 megabyte download as both ONTORAMA and Java version 1.4 are

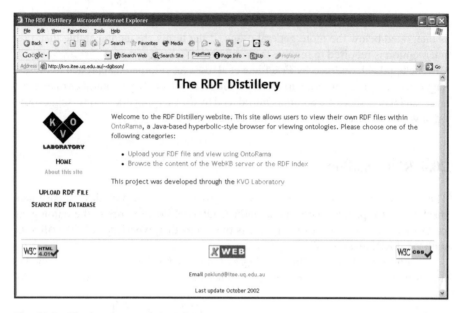

**Fig. 20.3.** The homepage of the RDF DISTILLERY project. Two functions are upload and validate an RDF file, or search and browse the repository.

downloaded and installed by Java WebStart. PRONTORAMA was an experiment to see what proportion of ONTORAMA's functionality could be achieved using a Flash Macromedia plugin and an intelligent server-side backend.

PRONTORAMA is shown in Figure 20.4. Rather than using a hyperbolic or spherical projection it performs radial layout and reduces the size of the labels as the distance from the center of the diagram increases. Since there is no projection function, elements or parts of the structure that appear small cannot be dragged into the center of the diagram. Rather as the user moves the mouse over labels they grow larger and the description of the selected term is placed in the large text area on the bottom right of the diagram. The focus of the diagram may be changed by clicking on a term which then becomes the term of interest and is promoted to the center of the diagram.

PRONTORAMA also provides an explorer-style tree view. Neither the tree view, nor the radial layout view display edge labels. The normal mode of operation of PRONTORAMA is to visualize a single relation within the ontology, for example the *subclass* relation. Clones within PRONTORAMA are indicated in response to a mouse over events by glowing halos drawn around the clones, and green lines drawn from the selected term to the clones.

PRONTORAMA employs a wrapper on the server that converts either RDF or FrameCG documents into a custom XML format specifying the tree to be displayed. This wrapper serves the same purpose as the translation layer in ONTORAMA but is located on the server rather than in the browser.

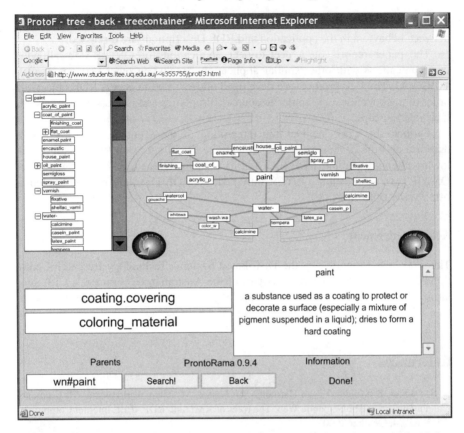

**Fig. 20.4.** PRONTORAMA: A Flash Macromedia component for browsing ontologies. It implements much of the functionality of ONTORAMA.

PRONTORAMA when compressed is a 40 kilobyte download. In terms of functionality it is close to ONTORAMA, lacking only the edge labels.

## 20.5 Conclusion

ONTORAMA has emerged as a practical tool for viewing ontologies described in RDF using Java Swing. The project has also experimented with a Macromedia Flash implementation, called PRONTORAMA, based on radial layout, that seems an ideal browsing vehicle for the RDF Distillery web-site because of its small memory footprint.

We describe a solution to hyperbolic-style layout complicated by the prevalence of multiple inheritance in most ontological structures. We further describe extensions to the usual hyperbolic-style view allowing multi-link types to be rendered and filtered. Issues of application generality, configuration files, and the correspondence between behaviors in the application and RDF Descriptions are discussed.

The paper reports on a peer-to-peer application for ONTORAMA allowing communications with other similar applications (including other versions of ONTORAMA). The P2P protocol we developed allows users to access RDF objects, in order to track identical or similar Resources, Properties and Literals by name or via their relationships.

Further, the work includes the integration of these outcomes with an RDF database and the development of a web-site that will act as an RDF Distillery allowing clients to submit RDF files and have them returned, embedded within the ONTORAMA application. ONTORAMA and the RDF Distillery can be trialled at http://www.ontorama.org

## Acknowledgement

The work was supported by the Distributed Systems Technology Research Centre (DSTC Pty Ltd) which operates as part of the Australian Government's CRC program. The authors also gratefully acknowledge the input of Peter Becker, Dion Gibson, Johan Grödahl and Henrik Åkerström and Jon Ducrou.

# References

1. S. Decker, S. Melnik, F. van Harmelen, D. Fensel, M. Klein, J. Broekstra, M. Erdmann, and I. Horrocks. The Semantic Web: The roles of XML and RDF. IEEE Internet Computing, 4(5):63-74, October 2000.
2. Ding, Y., A review of ontologies with the Semantic Web in view, Journal of Information Science 27 (6): 377-384, 2000.
3. Lamping, J. and Ramana Rao: The Hyperbolic Browser: A Focus+Context Technique for Visualizing Large Hierarchies, Proceedings of CHI'95, ACM Conference on Human Factors in Computing Systems, New York, pp. 401-408, 1995.
4. Martin, P. and P. Eklund: Knowledge Indexation and Retrieval and the Word Wide Web, *IEEE Intelligent Systems* — Special Issue on "Knowledge Management and Knowledge Distribution over the Internet, July, pp. 18-25, 2000.
5. Domingue, J. Motta, E. and Corcho Garcia, O. (1999) Knowledge Modelling in WebOnto and OCML: A User Guide. Available: http://kmi.open.ac.uk/projects/webonto/ [2002, October 3].
6. Hovy, E.H, Nirenburg, S., Approximating an Interlingua in a Principled Way, Arden House, NY USA (1992). Available: http://www.isi.edu/natural-language/people/hovy.html, [2002, October 1].
7. Fridman Noy, N, Musen, M. , An Algorithm for Merging and Aligning Ontologies: Automation and Tool Support, Stanford Medical Informatics, Stanford University, Stanford, CA USA, 1999.

# 21

## Supporting User Tasks through Visualisation of Light-weight Ontologies

Christiaan Fluit[1], Marta Sabou[2], and Frank van Harmelen[2]

[1] Aidministrator Nederland BV, Amersfoort, The Netherlands
   email: Christiaan.Fluit@aidministrator.nl
[2] Vrije Universiteit Amsterdam, The Netherlands
   email: Marta.Sabou@cs.vu.nl,
   email: Frank.van.Harmelen@cs.vu.nl

**Summary.** Since ontologies will be used to suport a variety of different tasks, and since experience from other fields has shown that visualisation techniques can be successfully used to support these tasks, this chapter investigates the use of ontology-based visualisation techniques for a variety of different tasks.

Since we expect light-weight ontologies to play a prominent role on the Semantic Web, we concentrate on visualisation for such light-weight ontologies.

We present a brief survey of visualisation techniques for the Semantic Web. Based on an analysis of the shortcomings of these techniques, we propose Cluster Maps as a novel visualisation technique, and we show how a number of user tasks can be suported with such Cluster Maps: data analysis, monitoring, querying and navigation.

Our explanations of the visualisations are backed up with illustrations from two application projects.

## 21.1 Introduction

As is abundantly clear from the other chapters in this volume, ontologies will play a central role in the development and deployment of the Semantic Web. They will be used for many different purposes, ranging across information localisation, integration, querying, presentation and navigation.

Experiences in other fields (Data Mining, Scientific Computing) have shown that visualisation techniques can be successfully employed to support many of these tasks in those areas. The question then naturally arises if visualisation techniques can also be successfully employed on the ontology-based Semantic Web.

The answer to this question of course depends strongly on the nature of the ontologies that we expect to be deployed on the Semantic Web. In our opinion, two specific features of ontologies will be important with respect to visualisation:

We expect the majority of the ontologies on the Semantic Web to be *light-weight*. Light-weight ontologies are typified by the fact that they are predominantly a taxonomy, with very few cross-taxonomical links (also known as "properties"), and with very few logical relations between the classes. Our experiences to date in a variety of Semantic Web applications (knowledge management, document retrieval, communities of practice, data integration) all point to light-weight ontologies as the most commonly occurring type [1].

We also expect that in ontologies on the Web the number of instances will typically be very large compared to the number of classes. The number of classes may be up to thousands (or even tens of thousands), while numbers of instances will easily reach millions in many applications. Two characteristics are very common for such instantiated taxonomies: incompleteness and overlap. First, the set of subclasses of a class is *incomplete* when their union does not contain all the objects of the superclass. Second, classes that share instances are *overlapping* if no specialization relationship holds between them.

Some systems already exist that exploit visualisation techniques for the Semantic Web. In this chapter, we will first survey a number of existing visualisations in the domain (section 21.2). This will lead us to identify a number of weaknesses in these existing visualisations, which can be explained by the (sometimes implicit) focus of these tools on one part of the ontology life-cycle and the tasks that take place in that part of the life-cycle. Also, these existing visualisations fall short on the scalability that we expect is required for ontologies with very large numbers of instances.

We then present the Cluster Map visualisation technique (section 21.3), and discuss a number of user tasks that it supports (section 21.5). This visualisation was developed at Aidministrator[3], a Dutch software provider, and has been used in several commercial and research projects. Our explanations of the visualisations are all backed up with illustrations from two of these projects, briefly explained in section 21.4.

## 21.2 Related Work

In this section we will review a set of relevant visualisation tools and techniques, judging them on two main criteria. For a more complete overview of the field, the interested reader is referred to [2].

The *first criterion* considers three different stages in the life cycle of an ontology. These stages require visualisations with quite different capabilities.

• Ontology development – The development stage of an ontology consists of creating its schema. At this stage a detailed visualisation of the concepts and their relationships is needed in order to enable a full understanding of the details of the ontology. The visualisation typically involves a small number of concepts and relationships. As the ontology grows, understanding and maintaining it becomes more difficult. The task of understanding it requires more coarse grained overviews with zooming facilities and the possibility to visualise different aspects of the ontology.

• Ontology instantiation – The instantiation of the ontology follows after the creation of the schema. Sometimes the process of populating ontologies is semi-automatic, performed by classifiers. The main concern of this stage is to ensure a high quality instantiation. Visualisation tools that differentiate between a schema and its instantiation are especially useful for this stage.

• Ontology deployment – Tools and methods are needed for analysing, querying and navigating ontological information spaces. These tools can target the needs of end users of the information, or the needs of developers of information systems involving the ontological information.

---

[3] http://www.aidministrator.nl

The *second criterion* for judging visualisations deals with the degree to which the ontological nature of the visualised data is exploited. The surveyed techniques range from generic data visualisers (e.g. for trees and graphs), to visualisations that strongly rely on the ontological nature of the data (i.e., that use the semantics of relations such as subclass-of, instance-of and part-of).

Two well-known systems for visualising large data structures are the Hyperbolic Tree [7] for the navigation of trees (see fig. 21.1), and The Brain[4] for navigating graphs. Applications of these visualisations typically display syntactic structures such as link structures. This of course has some semantics, but this is often very implicit and ad hoc. Additionally, the data structure used by these tools is often

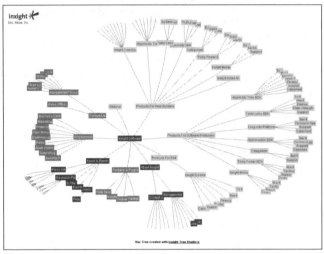

**Fig. 21.1:** A Hyperbolic Tree

a tree or at least tree-like (it is arguable whether The Brain is really suited for navigating arbitrary graphs).

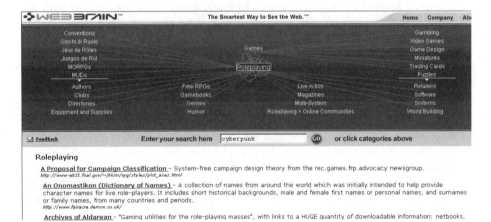

**Fig. 21.2.** Web Brain: The Brain applied to the Open Directory Project

---

[4] http://www.thebrain.com

418     Christiaan Fluit, Marta Sabou, and Frank van Harmelen

Even though developed for generic data, one can visualise semantic data with these techniques. WebBrain[5] uses the taxonomy of the Open Directory project (ODP[6]) as input for The Brain (see fig. 21.2). The AquaBrowser [14] visualises concept graphs. These systems primarily display the abstract structure. The instances are not an inherent part of the visualisation but are displayed separately (usually as a textual list).

There are visualisations that show both abstract and instance data at the same time, such as Antarcti.ca's Visual Net[7], which has also been applied to the ODP[8]. The resulting visualisation, MapNet, is shown in figure 21.3. This visualisation can also scale to large taxonomies and document sets, but has no explicit way to express overlaps (shared instances) between classes. Such overlaps typically

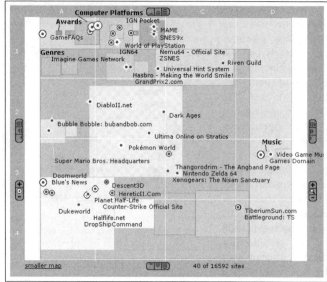

**Fig. 21.3:** MapNet

occur frequently in classification systems such as Yahoo or the ODP and may reveal additional interesting information about the classes and their instances. Unfortunately, instances that belong to several classes are simply duplicated in the visualisation, providing no indication of their multiple class memberships to the viewer.

Many ontology authoring tools [9] offer visualisation facilities that support the needs of the ontology development stage. We describe some of them.

A generic graph visualisation toolkit, which has been successfully applied to the visualisation of RDF data models, is GraphViz [5], developed at AT&T. Tools based on GraphViz, such as IsaViz[9] or RDFViz[10], are mostly employed to understand RDF data. Both schema elements and instances are shown. The visualisation allows the representation of any kind of relationship between classes and instances, being well suited for displaying complex ontologies. The scalability of the visualisation is quite poor: it is hard to understand the visualisation as soon as more relations are added.

The Protege[11] environment supports the modeling of ontologies, being used by hundreds of users world wide, in many knowledge domains. It provides some basic visualisation facil-

---

[5] http://www.webbrain.com

[6] http://www.dmoz.org

[7] http://www.antarcti.ca

[8] http://maps.map.net

[9] http://www.w3.org/2001/11/IsaViz/

[10] http://www.ilrt.bris.ac.uk/discovery/rdf-dev/rudolf/rdfviz/

[11] http://protege.stanford.edu

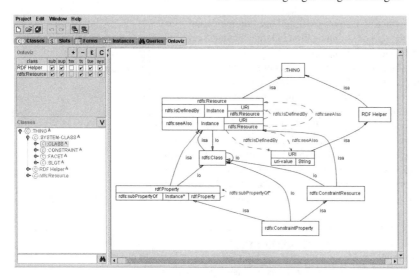

**Fig. 21.4.** Protege's OntoViz tab

ities allowing a user to gain insight in the details of the ontology so that editing it becomes easier. Many of the users of Protege felt the need for tools that provide visualisations of coarser grained structures as well as mechanisms to more easily and effectively navigate the information.

Two plugins extend Protege's basic visualisation. First, the OntoViz tab[12] uses GraphViz to visualise the ontologies (see figure 21.4). Second, the Jambalaya [13] tab allows people to browse, explore and interact with the knowledge structure. This visualisation allows a more coarse grained visualisation of the ontology class hierarchy, using two different visualisation metaphors. First, a classical tree layout can be drawn, both for the class hierarchy and for the instances. Second, a nested view visualisation allows gradual zooming from general to more specific concepts.

WebOnto [3] is a Java applet coupled with a customised web server, which allows users to browse and edit ontologies over the web. It also allows collaborative development of ontologies. The visualisation was developed for showing a fine grained view of the knowledge. Ontology classes and instances are represented with large, easy to read graphical elements, which makes scalability problematic.

The OntoEdit editor uses a visualisation similar to the GraphViz technique, but mainly focused on supporting interactive editing rather then providing a global overview of large ontologies.

---

[12] http://protege.stanford.edu/plugins/ontoviz/ontoviz.html

A number of systems exist that use ontological information for the purpose of navigation in large document repositories. We review a few of them.

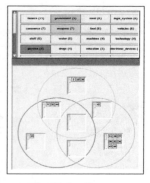

Cougar [6] is an interactive visualisation for information retrieval purposes. It assumes that each document returned by
a query has been labeled with one or more labels, indicating
the document's main topics. The user interface then allows
the user to select maximally three labels (see figure 21.5).
The three document sets associated with these labels are then
drawn as a Venn diagram, displaying if and how these document sets overlap. This method of displaying classes and their
instances is not only useful as a means to access documents in
a result set, but also as a mechanism to study how the classes
in the result set relate to each other.

**Fig. 21.5:** Cougar

InfoCrystal [12] is another visualisation technique derived from Venn diagrams that displays classes and their instances. In this visualisation (fig. 21.6), each class is represented as
a labeled node on the circumference of an imaginary circle. Icons are places inside the circle
that represent individual combinations of classes (i.e. each icon represent a segment in a Venn
diagram). The shape and position of an icon is used to indicate the set of classes it represents. Other attributes, such as size or color, can be used to indicate features such as document
density. Provisions have also been made to deal with hierarchically organized classes. Unlike
Cougar, the InfoCrystal allows the user to display more than three classes at the same time,
but at the cost of a rather cluttered display. An online Flash demo is currently available[13].

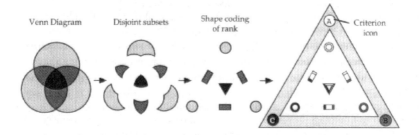

**Fig. 21.6.** The InfoCrystal technique explained visually

## Conclusions

We observe that the majority of available tools address schema level visualisations. Tools for
generic visualisation (The Brain, AquaBrowser) specialize in showing large trees and graphs,
which can be seen as very light-weight ontologies (taxonomies). They are mainly used to
facilitate navigation of large structures. At the other extreme are visualisations integrated in
ontology editing tools (Protege, OntoEdit), allowing the display of the full semantics of a
limited part of a schema in order to support the ontology development process.

---

[13] http://www.scils.rutgers.edu/~aspoerri/InfoCrystal/demo/InfoCrystal.htm

The number of tools offering instance level visualisations is small. Visualisations in ontology editors often do not make any graphical distinction at the graphical level between schema information and instances. As a result they do not scale to many instances. Also, they fail to show instance level overlaps between classes. Cougar and InfoCrystal are the only visualisations we know of that scale to large sets of instances and that show the overlaps between classes, allowing for instance level analysis of data. Unfortunately they visualise very little schema information.

These observations indicate that there is a clear lack of visualisation techniques that (a) display a simple schema with instances and (b) scale to a large number of instances. We present a visualisation that addresses these issues and that can be used for a variety of tasks.

## 21.3 Technology

We have developed the Cluster Map, for visualising populated, light-weight ontologies. It visualises the instances of a number of selected classes from a hierarchy, organized by their classifications.

Figure 21.7 shows an example Cluster Map, visualising documents from a construction-related domain, classified according to topics discussed in those documents. The big, dark gray spheres represent ontology classes (the topics), with an attached label stating their name and cardinality. When a subclass relation holds between two classes, they are

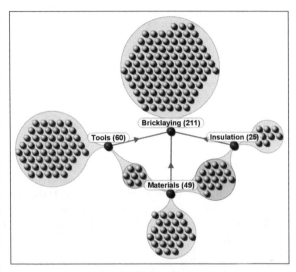

**Fig. 21.7:**  A Cluster Map example

connected by a directed edge. The smaller spheres represent instances. Balloon-shaped edges connect instances to the class(es) they belong to. Instances with the same class membership are grouped in clusters. Our example contains six clusters, two of them representing overlaps between classes.

Cluster Maps contain a lot of information about the instantiation of the classes, specifically exploiting the overlaps between them. For example, figure 21.7 shows that the *Insulation* class has a significant overlap with *Materials* (i.e. there are many documents that are both about materials and insulations) but not with *Tools*. Such observations can trigger hypotheses about the available information and the domain in general.

The graph layout algorithm used by the Cluster Map is a variant of the well-known family of spring embedder algorithms [4]. Its outcome results in the geometric closeness of objects indicating their semantic closeness: classes that share instances are located near each other, and so are instances with the same or similar class memberships.

The Cluster Map is embedded in a highly interactive GUI, shown in figure 21.8, which is designed for browsing-oriented exploration of the populated ontology. Users can subsequently

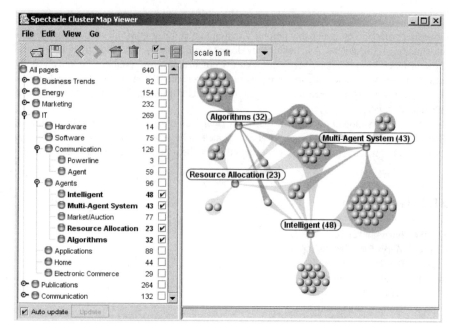

**Fig. 21.8.** The Cluster Map's graphical user interface

create visualisations of a number of classes by marking the check boxes in the class tree on the left pane. The software can animate the transition from one visualisation to the next, showing how the instances are regrouped in clusters. Through interaction a user can also retrieve information about the specific documents that are contained in a class or cluster.

The Cluster Map is available as a stand-alone viewer and as a Java library. As we will show later on, the visualisation can be fine-tuned in several ways, in order to support certain tasks, improve scalability, etc.

## 21.4 Application Scenarios

We will illustrate this chapter with examples taken from two realistic applications. One application is a portal generated for a Dutch information provider in the construction industry, Bouwradius (21.4.1). The second application is developed in the context of the SWAP European IST research project (21.4.2).

### 21.4.1 Bouwradius

Bouwradius acts as an "information broker" between a large number of producers of construction-related publications on the one hand (e.g. websites, magazines) and consumers that wish to receive a tailor-made presentation of all information relevant to them on the other hand (e.g. teachers, students, companies). Bouwradius uses Aidministrator technology to provide portals to several consumer communities. Each portal is optimized for the community's task, view on the data and vocabulary.

The content and structure of the portals depends on two kinds of knowledge structures:

- a thesaurus; a list of approximately 2000 terms, covering the whole construction domain. These terms are used to classify construction-related publications, as described below.
- various concept hierarchies, each modelling the view and vocabulary of a specific user community. Note that these view-specific concepts are not taken from the thesaurus. However there is a link between these concepts and the terms in the thesaurus: each leaf concept in a concept hierarchy is related to a set of terms from the thesaurus. These thesaurus terms define the kind of publications which are relevant for that concept. Higher nodes in the tree are implicitly defined as being the union of their children. A concept hierarchy acts as a structuring backbone for each portal as there is a page in the portal devoted to each concept. Therefore, the content of each portal page is determined by the thesaurus terms associated to the corresponding concept.

As said, the thesaurus is used for document classification. In the past this classification was performed manually by a group of domain experts within Bouwradius. This approach turned out to be very slow and expensive and also gave inconsistent results due to different interpretations of the intended meaning of terms. Recently we have started to use an automatic classification system (based on machine learning techniques) to perform the classification, resulting in cheap, timely and consistent results. However, extensive training and quality assessment of the system is still necessary to ensure good results.

We have identified several areas in which the visualisation supports management of the portals. First of all, the visualisation can help in acquiring insight into the domain, e.g. by visualising sets of related concepts, allowing the employees to construct an accurate mental model of the available information. Furthermore, they can adapt their view as the information repository changes over time. Finally, visualisation may help in the assessment of the quality of the classification system, e.g. by comparing its results to a reference set of manually classified documents.

### 21.4.2 SWAP

The goal of the IST Research Project SWAP[14] is to explore whether peer-to-peer technology can provide an alternative architecture for knowledge sharing on the Semantic Web. This combination of peer-to-peer and Semantic Web technologies promises to be mutually beneficial. On the one hand it will contribute to enrich the search facilities that are currently available for peer-to-peer systems (which are rather limited until now). On the other hand it will give knowledge repositories the capability to provide individual views in a decentralized framework with low administration overhead.

In SWAP each individual PC is treated as a peer. The information of the peer is presented to the SWAP network enriched with machine understandable semantics in terms of the concepts defined by the peer's own ontology. These semantics reflect the peer's individual view on the world. A peer can query the whole network. The peer network uses semantics to enhance query routing and answering. The answers are presented to the user in the terms of his local ontology. Peers benefit from being part of a network: by monitoring the traffic within the network they can evolve their local ontology so that it reflects the knowledge of the community.

Our visualisation technique facilitates the end user's interaction with the SWAP network. First, the user has a graphical overview of his own data, by visualising his local ontology. Second, query formulation and result interpretation are also easier with our interactive tool.

---

[14] project number IST-2001-34103, http://swap.semanticweb.org

The differences between the two application scenarios described in this section demonstrate the wide applicability of the visualisation. One of the most prominent differences between the two scenarios is the intended user. Whereas at Bouwradius the users are people managing a large information repository, in SWAP we envision end users retrieving and interpreting information for their own purposes using the visualisation. Closely related to this is the difference between supporting trained expert users vs. layman. Finally, the two scenarios differ in one having a centralized information repository whereas the other is a distributed environment in which the available information is typically only partially known.

## 21.5  Tasks

We have used Cluster Maps for supporting analysis, querying and navigation tasks in the two domains described above.

### 21.5.1  Analysis

The Cluster Map can be used for a variety of analytical tasks. We define analysis tasks as those tasks where the user's desire is to get a global insight into the information, rather than to filter and retrieve parts of it. Those tasks will be treated in the next subsections.

Most applications of the Cluster Map for analysis tasks can be characterized using the following three parameters:

- The dataset to be visualised (e.g. objects in the dataset can be documents).
- The ontology, defining the main classes of the domain.
- The classification; the assignment of objects (from the dataset) to classes (from the ontology).

We will describe a number of generic analysis tasks using different variations of these three parameters.

#### One dataset, one ontology, one classification

The simplest application is where there is one dataset, one ontology and one classification of the objects in the dataset. Visualisation of the populated classes shows how objects are distributed among classes and how classes consequently overlap. Patterns and outliers in the data are made visible, allowing for confirmation or rejection of hypotheses about the information, ultimately leading to new and confirmed insights into the information domain.

As explained before in the Cluster Map introduction, using the visualisation is typically an interactive process, where the user creates visualisations of several subsets of the complete ontology. This is necessary because visualising all classes at once will usually lead to a very cluttered and unusable visualisation. This raises the question how to select useful subsets of classes. Often, some amount of domain knowledge is necessary to do this well.

In the Bouwradius scenario, we have made visualisations of classes we knew are semantically related (e.g. because they all relate to some kind of construction work), and tried to see if the resulting visualisations could be explained or whether they produced unexpected results. Figure 21.9 shows an example of classes concerning scaffolding. Note that here we display clusters as a single visual entity rather than its individual members, in order to scale to larger document sets. One observation we can make is that the classes *Scaffolding covers*[15] (measures taken to protect construction workers against bad weather) and *Scaffolding support* (measures

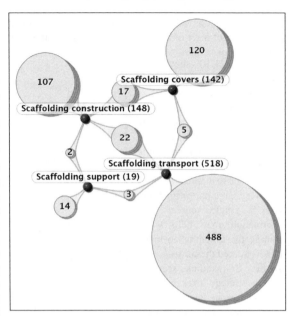

**Fig. 21.9:** Classes concerning scaffolding

taken to guarantee a stable scaffolding) do not overlap, even if the other classes overlap with each other. This can be explained because these two aspects relate to different parts of a scaffolding. One thing that could not be explained was the large amount of documents about *Scaffolding transport* that did not relate to any other scaffolding topics. This could trigger a revision of the thesaurus or of the classification system.

### One dataset, several ontologies, one classification per ontology

Another strategy for creating visualisations for analysis purposes is to apply several ontologies to the same dataset, thereby allowing for analysis of the same data from different point of views.

Within the Bouwradius scenario, this can for example be done by visualising the same data set according to different view-specific concept hierarchies. Each view will provide answers to different questions reflecting different purposes.

In the SWAP context, a peer can have multiple ontologies ("views"), classifying the same information. For example a user may want to see his files according to file-type in one view, but according to their origin in another.

### Several datasets, one ontology, one classification per dataset

One can apply the same ontology on different datasets and see whether the visualisation of a set of classes differs for each dataset. This allows comparison between datasets.

Such visualisations for dataset comparison can be achieved in two ways. One option is to create a separate visualisation for the same subset of classes for each dataset and then compare

---

[15] The presented concepts were translated from Dutch to English by non-professional translators

these visualisations. Alternatively, the datasets are merged into a single dataset and a single visualisation of a set of classes is created. The source of the objects are indicated using e.g. colors or icons.

Figure 21.10 shows the same classes as figure 21.9, but this times every cluster is displayed as a pie chart, indicating the amount of documents originating from each particular source. We see that the large cluster at the lower right that could not be explained before is for a very large part originating from a single source. This information may help when refining the thesaurus to make a finer-grained thesaurus.

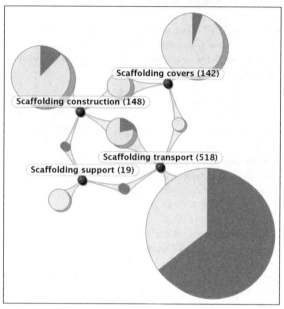

In the Bouwradius scenario such a strategy may be very beneficial, since the documents that Bouwradius distributes among their consumers originate from a variety of sources. Visualising what information comes from which source will

**Fig. 21.10:** Documents from different sources

reveal whether certain sources specialize in certain parts of the thesaurus.

A slightly different approach is to visualize the differences between the current Bouwradius document repository and all documents from a new source, in order to see whether the new source is a useful addition. For example a new source can contain many documents in scarcely populated parts of the thesaurus and therefore it is a useful addition for Bouwradius' repository.

In the SWAP scenario, peers may be interested in applying their own ontology to documents supplied by a new peer, again to investigate if the data of the new peer is a useful complement to the peer's own dataset. Sometimes a community of peers share an ontology, according to which they organise their data. For example, within a bank, a fixed ontology can exist according to which experts classify their own documents. By visualising the data of different experts according to the single ontology, one can determine how their knowledge differs according to the terms of the ontology. Certain experts will have more knowledge in certain areas. Also, they might possess documents which cannot be classified by the existing terms and therefore require an update of the knowledge model.

## One dataset, one ontology, several classifications

The parameter that has been constant up to now has been the classification: the assignment of dataset objects to ontology classes. In some scenarios there are several "classifiers" active, raising the possibility that the same object is assigned to different classes by different classifiers. We will show that visualising the differences in the classification of a dataset may be useful for a number of reasons.

Until recently, Bouwradius used a large group of domain experts to manually classify documents. When several people classify the same document, there will typically be differences in their judgment of which classes are appropriate, caused by differences in domain knowledge or even their interpretation of the precise semantics of a concept. Visualising these differences can enable management to better streamline the work of the human classifiers.

Recently, we have started applying an automatic document classification system at Bouwradius. In order to guarantee high quality output of such systems, the quality is often assessed by applying the system on a set of manually classified documents. This results in two classifications of the same dataset: the manual classification and the classification produced by the system. Visualising the differences between the two classifications can help us to gain insight in and optimize the output quality of the classifier.

Figure 21.11 shows an example visualisation of four classes taken from a test set. We use a color

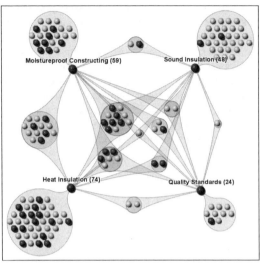

**Fig. 21.11:**  Visualising classification errors

coding to identify those documents that received a different classification from the system (the darker spheres indicate the errors). This shows a more qualitative overview of the precision of the system compared to the percentage of correct classifications, as is often used. An alternative is to visualise the classes as returned by the system and highlight those documents that have a different manual classification. This gives a qualitative overview of the recall of the system.

Of course the recall and precision per class could also be provided in a simple table, listing the two percentages for each class. However, visualising them using a Cluster Map additionally shows how these errors relate to the overlaps between classes. This is an attractive feature because a lot of errors result from the system being inable to properly differentiate between classes that are semantically close (and therefore are likely to share instances). If many errors occur in clusters connected to many classes, this may indicate problems with differentiating between classes. If on the other hand errors are more uniformly spread over the clusters of a class, this may indicate problems with the training set of that single class. In the end, this visualisation has the potential to increase the trust and understanding of the user in the system, because it sheds a light on why the system is making errors.

Still, in order to have a full overview of the quality of the system, one would like to combine the information contained in both visualisations. This visualisation would have to reveal both the produced and the ideal classification of the incorrectly classified documents. How to create such a visualisation is considered to be future work.

## Monitoring

Finally, we consider a class of analysis tasks which we call monitoring, where information is analysed as it changes over time. This task cannot really be seen as another configuration of the three parameters we used before. Rather it seems that monitoring introduces a fourth parameter, i.e. time. This means that every previous analysis task may in theory be extended with a time dimension. In the most complex case this leads to a scenario of one or more evolving datasets, one or more evolving ontologies and one or more evolving classifications. However, in practice one or two parameters are often constant, at least on the short term.

For example, in the Bouwradius scenario, it is very useful to see how the total information repository changes with respect to the thesaurus: which classes increase or decrease in size, which overlaps increase or decrease, etc. Possible outcomes are that certain parts of the ontology suddenly start to correlate because of recent events in the domain, or that certain parts of the ontology should offer a more fine-grained classification of documents because of a sudden increase of documents in certain classes.

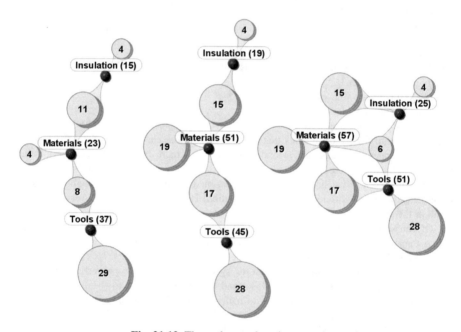

**Fig. 21.12.** Three classes changing over time

Figure 21.12 shows three Cluster Maps, each visualising the same classes at a different moment in time. Not only do we see that certain classes and clusters grow over time, but also that a new overlap of classes is introduced in the last map. This may indicate changes in what is published about these topics.

One of the novelties of SWAP is that knowledge evolves due to interaction between peers. A peer should update its ontology according to the information exchanged in the network. The way the local ontology is updated is an open issue. A completely autonomous peer would monitor the network and adapt the knowledge of the peer accordingly. This would lead to an always up-to-date knowledge. However, because of the high change rate, the user would not be able to understand the changes. To solve this, i.e. to maintain the user's understanding, the system should ask for acknowledgement for every change. This is an overload that no user would accept: continuous decisions about the knowledge structure. Therefore a balance has to be maintained between the degree of autonomy and usability of the system.

The ideal situation is that the system evolves by itself, but it is able to present the changes to the user in a way that makes them easy to understand. Using the animated transitions between different Cluster Maps one can illustrate the transition from one knowledge state to the other. This lowers the cognitive effort associated with understanding changes of knowledge structures.

## 21.5.2 Query

The goal of a query task is to find a narrow set of items in a large collection that satisfy a well-understood information need [8]. The Cluster Map viewer can be applied in the four stages of the search task [11], as described below.

*Query formulation* - the step of expressing an information need through a query is a difficult task. Users encounter difficulties when having to provide terms that best describe their information need (vocabulary problem). Furthermore, combining these terms in simple logical expressions using "AND" and "OR" is even more complicated. See [10] for a demonstration of this problem.

In the Cluster Map viewer the classes that describe the domain of a data set are explicitly shown (left pane), making the vocabulary choice much easier (see figure 21.8). To formulate a query a user only needs to select the classes of interest. There is no need to specify Boolean expressions at this stage since, as we will explain further, the visualisation of the results offers the answer to many frequent boolean queries in an intuitive manner.

Imagine that a user wants to go on holiday to the French Loire, with a group of four persons that would share two rooms in a three star accommodation. One can formulate this query in many ways, using synonyms of the most important search terms. However when using our interactive interface the user easily finds the terms that best describe his needs: "Loire", "4 persons", "2 rooms" and "3 stars".

*Initiation of action* - After a set of classes are selected in the left panel, the search is launched at a mouse-click.

*Review of results* - the results of the query are graphically presented to the user. For a set of selected classes the following is shown:

- (1) the union of the classes (disjunction of all query terms)
- (2) all possible intersections of the selected classes (conjunction of some query terms)
- (3) the intersection of all classes (different conjunctions of all query terms) - if it exists. This is a particular case of (2).

Note that the results of simple Boolean expressions are intuitively shown in the map. If the user wants a disjunction of the query terms (1) he will analyse all the presented objects. Indeed, Fig. 21.13 shows all available holiday destinations which are in Loire, all destinations for groups of four persons, all destinations with two rooms and all offers with three stars. As an added value the user sees how the corresponding classes overlap (2). Fig. 21.13 reveals sets of items that satisfy certain query terms only, for example all destinations with two rooms in Loire. A more interesting (and probably more frequent) case is when users want the conjunction of the terms. This is also the case in our example. In that scenario, two extreme situations can happen:

- the result set is too large (under-specification)
- the result set is empty (over-specification)

If the result set is empty, the user can at least find objects that partially satisfy the query. The degree of relevance of certain clusters is suggested by their color: the more relevant the darker the shade of the color. We refer to the phenomena of dropping some of the requirements as query relaxation. For our example query, the result returned by the system shows that there are no items that satisfy all criteria. However, the user can relax his query. Two destinations are still interesting if the customer dropped one requirement (either quality of accommodation or location).

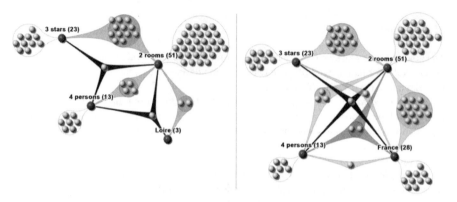

**Fig. 21.13.** Using Cluster Map for query relaxation(left) and broadening(right)

*Refinement* - according to the conclusions of the result interpretation step, the user can narrow or broaden the scope of his search by refining the query.

If the result set is too large, the user can replace some classes with more specific subclasses. Therefore his query is narrowed. At the other extreme, in case of an empty set, some classes can be replaced by their superclass, broadening the scope of the query. Note that both narrowing and broadening the scope of the query are possible due to the ontological nature of the domain description. The Cluster Map viewer facilitates choosing more specific or more general classes.

In the depicted scenario, the user can broaden his search by replacing Loire with its superclass, France (right of Fig. 21.13). Now there is a single holiday destination that matches all criteria. At the other extreme imagine that the customer would like to go to France and that the system returns a huge cluster that satisfies all the criteria. Instead of looking at each returned object, the customer can refine his query with a more specific class, for example Loire. This would narrow the scope of the query and return a smaller set of options.

Support for the query task is valuable in the context of SWAP. The Cluster Map viewer fulfils the functionality of a query interface between the user and the peer-to-peer system. First, such an interface eases the task of query formulation. Second, graphically presenting the results facilitates a better review of the results. Finally, it allows further actions in case that the user is not satisfied (relaxation/refinement).

### 21.5.3 Navigation

Finally, Cluster Maps can be used for graphical navigation of information spaces. We have employed them as image maps in web sites based on ontological data. Two navigation scenarios have been implemented, as described below.

In the first scenario, the Cluster Map is used in addition to another, more traditional navigational structure (a textual tree). It plays the role of a site map that is invoked by the user when needed. It presents an overview of the whole data set: it shows the most important classes, their relations and instances. An interesting aspect is the way the data is accessed: one can access a whole class (click on a class) or an overlap of interest (click on a cluster). The result is a representation of the contents of the selected entity in the form of a textual list. Entries in this list present extra information about the instances as well as a link to the actual data. The role of the map is to facilitate a quick understanding of the available content and to provide quick access to individual items.

In the second scenario, the Cluster Map is always present as the only navigation facility. Maps gradually present deeper levels of the ontology: the user starts at the top of the ontology and can navigate towards more specific topics by clicking the classes of interest (drilling down into the information). At any point, the map shows the current class, its parent and its subclasses. For the current class, its elements are also presented in a textual list. This semantical zooming facilitates a leveled understanding of the data.

## 21.6 Summary

We expect the Semantic Web to be no different from other fields of Computer Science: visualisation of data and data-structures can be an important tool. For the Semantic Web, this will mean the visualisation of ontologies and meta-data.

The type of visualisation that must be employed depends strongly on the nature of the data to be displayed, and on the task that is to be supported with the visualisation.

Concerning the nature of the data to be displayed, we expect that many of the ontologies on the Semantic Web will be so-called "lightweight" ontologies: simple hierarchies of partially overlapping classes, with little or no cross-taxonomical properties. Furthermore, we expect the number of instances will outweigh by far the number of classes in such an ontology.

It is therefore surprising that most of the visualisation tools in the literature focus mostly on the visualisation of complex ontology schema's without showing the related instances, or vice versa, if they are capable of showing large numbers of instances, then they tend to ignore ontological information.

Having identified this gap in available ontology-based visualisation tools, we have presented a visualisation technique that is specially tailored to visualising light-weight ontologies with large numbers of instances, exploiting both the hierarchical and the overlapping nature of the class hierarchy. After having presented the generic technology for this visualisation, we have shown how this visualisation technology can be employed to support a variety of users in a variety of tasks (data analysis, querying and navigation).

## References

1. J. Davies, D. Fensel, and F. van Harmelen, editors. *Towards the Semantic Web: Ontology-driven Knowledge Management*. Wiley, 2002.

2. M. Dodge and R. Kitchin. *Atlas of Cyberspace*. Addison-Wesley, London, 2001.

3. J. Domingue. Tadzebao and WebOnto: Discussing, browsing, and editing ontologies on the web. In *Proceedings of the 11th Knowledge Acquisition for Knowledge-Based Systems Workshop*, Banff, Canada, 1998, April 1998.

4. P. Eades. A heuristic for graph drawing. *Congressus Numerantium*, 42:149–160, 1984.

5. E. Gansner and S.C. North. An open graph visualization system and its applications to software engineering. *Software Practice and Experience*, 1999.

6. M. Hearst. Using categories to provide context for full-text retrieval results. In *Proceedings of the RIAO '94*, Rockefeller, New York, 1994.

7. J. Lamping, R. Rao, and P. Pirolli. A focus+context technique based on hyperbolic geometry for visualising large hierarchies. In *ACM conference on human factors in Software*, pages 401–408, 1995.

8. G. Marchionini. *Information seeking in electronic environments*. Cambridge University Press, Cambrigde, UK, 1995.

9. OntoWeb. Deliverable 1.3: A survey on ontology tools, May 2002.

10. B. Shneiderman. The eyes have it: a task by data type taxonomy for information visualizations. In *Proceedings of the 1996 IEEE symposium on visual languages (VL '96)*, pages 336–343, 1996.

11. B. Shneiderman. *Designing the user interface*, pages 509–551. Addison-Wesley, Menlo Park, 1998.

12. A. Spoerri. InfoCrystal: a visual tool for information retrieval and management. In *Proceedings of the second international conference on Information and knowledge management*, Washington, D.C., United States, 1993.

13. M.A. Storey, M. Musen, J. Silva, C. Best, N. Ernst, R. Fergerson, and N. Noy. Jambalaya: Interactive visualization to enhance ontology authoring and knowledge acquisition in Protege. In *In Workshop on Interactive Tools for Knowledge Capture*, Victoria, B.C. Canada, October 2001.

14. A. Veling. The Aqua Browser: visualisation or large information spaces in context. *Journal of AGSI*, 3:136–142, 1997.

# Part IV

Ontology Applications

# Ontologies for Knowledge Management

Andreas Abecker and Ludger van Elst

German Research Center for Artificial Intelligence
– Knowledge Management Department –
67655 Kaiserslautern, Germany
(aabecker,elst)@dfki.uni-kl.de

> 'People can't share knowledge, if they don't speak a common language.' (Tom Davenport)

**Summary.** Since the term *ontologies* in AI was coined within the *Knowledge Sharing and Reuse Effort* [68] for engineering of knowledge–based systems ([40, 41]), it is not surprising that it heavily entered Knowledge Management ([21, 25], KM) research: *Sharing* and *reuse*—in this case of organizational knowledge—are among the core knowledge processes tackled within every KM endeavor.

In this chapter we briefly introduce the main ideas of KM and the role and requirements for information technology (IT) in KM. We then discuss the potential of ontologies as main elements in IT solutions for KM. We characterize their current role in research and practice, derive a working focus for the near future, and conclude with an outlook on possible future trends in KM software and their implications on ontologies.

## 22.1 Information Technology for Knowledge Management

Knowledge Management (KM) is a young interdisciplinary science with roots in Business Sciences, Information Technology, Pedagogics, Psychology, and Organizational Theory (cp. [21, 47]). According to Eppler [32] we can define **Knowledge Management** as a:

- *systematic approach* (with a background in information technology, human resources, strategy, and organizational behavior)
- that views *implicit and explicit knowledge* as a key strategic resource, and
- aims at improving the handling of knowledge *at the individual, team, organization, and inter-organizational level*
- *in order to improve* innovation, quality, cost-effectiveness and time-to-market.

From the very beginning of the KM endeavor two streams of research and applications could be identified which we called the *Process-centered* and the *Product-centered view on KM* (see [54]), which was called the *Personalization versus Codification Strategy* by [45], *the Organic versus the Mechanistic* approach by [99], or the *Community Model versus Cognitive Model* view by [97], and which could be identified as two basic dimensions of KM activities in consulting practice as well (cp. [63]):

1. The *process-centered view* mainly understands KM as a social communication process. It is based on the observations that the most important knowledge source in an organization are its employees, and that solving *wicked problems* [20] is merely a process of achieving social commitment than one of problem solving. Hence knowledge exists, is created, and is further developed in the interaction among people and tasks such that the focus of IT should be to enable, facilitate, and support communication and collaboration.

   Technical solutions in this area comprise, e.g., yellow page and expert finder systems for determining the right communication partner, Computer-Supported Collaborative Work (CSCW) systems for effective collaboration between geographically separated people, or Skill Management systems for the systematic and planned acquisition and development of human skills and competencies, etc.

   In this view, organizational measures such as installation of expert networks, training courses, virtual teams, and all kinds of cultural KM support play a particularly important role.

2. The *product-centered view* focuses on knowledge documents, their creation, storage, and reuse in computer-based *organizational memories* (OMs). It is based on the idea of explicating, documenting, and formalizing knowledge to have it as a tangible resource, and on the idea of supporting the user's individual knowledge development and usage by presenting the right information sources at the appropriate time. Hence the main assumption is that knowledge can exist outside of people and can be treated as an object dealt with in IT systems.

   Of course, the transition from intangible (implicit and tacit) to tangible (explicit) knowledge in the form of standardized processes and templates, FAQs, lessons learned and best practices, etc., allows a company to enhance its structural capital, maybe at the price of loosing creativity and flexibility. Basic techniques for this approach come from Document Management Systems, Knowledge-Based Systems and Information Systems.

   In this view, organizational measures aim at fostering the use and improving the value of information systems by bonus systems, or by installing organizational roles and editing processes for high-quality knowledge content management.

Figure 22.1 gives an idea of typical software support for both dimensions. Analyzing the history of IT support for KM one may identify the following types of KM applications:

## Type 1 Applications: Conventional Software Basis.

*Type 1a Applications: Standard Software Applications.* As, e.g., [24] show, especially the early success stories of KM were—although IT-enabled and heavily IT-dependent—not building upon any new IT solutions, but used conventional technology like databases or discussion boards. This area should not be underestimated in practice. However, it is not interesting in the context of this book.

*Type 1b Applications: Integrated Standard Software.* The first specific KM solutions are characterized by the explicit approach to combine manifold aspects of KM support in one integrated software suite, hence incorporating both the product and the process aspects of KM. Typical representatives are the big KM tool suites still successful in the market, like, e.g.:

- Coming from the knowledge process side, e.g., Livelink or Lotus Notes-based solutions, which combine comprehensive groupware and process management support, many types of synchronous and asynchronous communication, with standard document management functionalities.

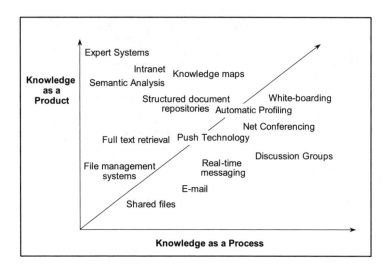

**Fig. 22.1.** Software support for the product and the process approach to KM

- Coming from the knowledge product side, e.g., Verity's or Inxight's product suites which attach many individual and organization-wide information management functions (push and pull services, content management support, Intranet portal functionalities etc.) around advanced information classification and retrieval technology.

Figure 22.2 gives an idea of the elements of a somehow ideal KM toolbox which incorporates data and information from manifold sources, organizes them according to a common corporate knowledge map, provides collaboration and discovery services working upon these organizational knowledge sources (such reflecting the process and the product view, respectively), and finally feeds these services via a common knowledge portal into operational and knowledge-level meta business processes. Although Type 1 applications normally do not maintain a knowledge-rich, explicit ontological basis, nevertheless indicates the box 'Knowledge Map' in the middle of the picture the central role of a shared language to connect people to people, people to information, and information to information in the company. This is the target for more 'heavy-weight' knowledge-based approaches for improving KM systems and services by ontological power.

## Type 2 Applications: Intelligent Software Basis.

*Type 2a Applications: Intelligence-Enhanced Solutions.*  While Type 1 applications are based on 'traditional' IT approaches, we here subsume applications based on Artificial Intelligence (AI) methods, including ontologies as a core enabler. Figure 22.3—adapted from [110]—gives some examples arranged according to their role in different KM core processes. While Type 1 Applications represent the current state of practice in industry and administrations, Type 2 applications represent mostly the status of mature prototypes with some in-

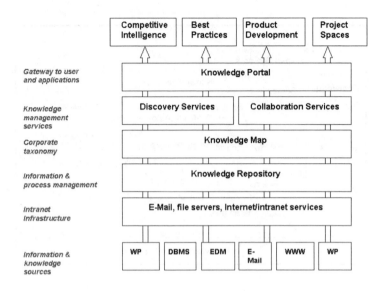

**Fig. 22.2.** Abstract KM System architecture, adapted from OVUM

dustrial showcases.[1] Type 2a applications are today's most important field of application for ontologies in KM, in particular for creating Semantic Community Web Portals, for supporting Intelligent Search and Retrieval algorithms in Intranet and Internet, and for providing a target data structure for Information Gathering, Information Extraction and Information Integration techniques. We will discuss these fields in more detail below in Section 22.3.

*Type 2b Applications: Enhanced Solutions Integrated.* It is both a challenge and a chance of well-understood approaches to KM software design that they always should try to capture 'the whole picture', i.e. integrate the product and the process view and cover the whole architecture sketched in Fig. 22.2. Certainly, Type 1b applications are the first software artifacts which deserve to bear the dedicated name 'KM software'. Since KM is by definition *boundary spanning*, bridging the gaps between departments and organizations, between people and information, and between different kind of software services, the interesting question for Type 2 applications is the hardly ever posed question how different knowledge-based functions in a comprehensive KM application can exploit synergies. We will sketch some ideas in a section below in Section 22.4.

While the first generation KM success stories were typical type 1a, or, seldom type 2a applications—like a Lessons Learned database, an Expert System, or a Yellow Page system—the big commercial KM toolboxes are comprehensive type 1b approaches trying to integrate manifold complementary functionalities. Seen from the IT—or, AI point of view, the interesting questions are to which extent 1a services can be improved towards ontology-based 2a approaches, and what possibilities arise when thinking about integrated type 2b applications.

---

[1] Of course, for concrete software products it is sometimes difficult to make a clear distinction between Type 1 and Type 2 applications. However, for the purpose of this book it is sufficient to clarify whether an application is based on explicit, formal ontologies, or not.

| | Share knowledge | Distribute knowledge | Capture & codify knowledge | Create knowledge |
|---|---|---|---|---|
| Traditional systems | E-Mail, Group Collaboration, Discussion Groups, P2P technology, Intranet Portals | Word processing, DTP, Document Management | *All systems that codify knowledge are knowledge-based* | Brainstorming software, mindmapping, statistical analysis |
| Knowledge-based systems | Ontology-based portals | Expert Systems, Lessons-Learned + Best Practice Systems | Knowledge acquisition and coding tools | Knowledge discovery and data mining systems, Creativity systems |

**Fig. 22.3.** Traditional vs. Knowledge-Based KM Technology (i.e. Type 1 vs. Type 2 Applications), from [110]

Before we come to these questions, we will shortly discuss some general requirements for KM software and their implications for the use of ontologies.

## 22.2 Requirements for KM Software and Ontologies

Several authors analyzed barriers for the introduction of KM solutions as well as success criteria and requirements for IT-enabled KM (see, e.g., [54]). We discuss three major requirements and their implications for the ontology topic:

**R1: Minimalization of upfront knowledge engineering**    Since KM is considered an additional organizational task orthogonal to the 'productive' work, expensive start-up activities may be a big barrier for a successful KM introduction. On the other hand, it seems clear that no ontology-based approach can be introduced without an explicit commitment of all people involved and without their contributions to creating the shared ontological space. Hence, all topics dealing with a smooth and cost-efficient introduction of ontology-based applications turned out to be particularly important for ontology-based KM solutions:

- **Ontology Learning.** At least the 'first cut' ontologies to start ontology engineering in an organization should avoid the typical 'cold start' problems by building as much as possible upon structures already explicit in the organization (e.g. Intranet organization, DB schemata [84], department structures, etc.) or hidden in organizational text documents (technical reports and documentation, web pages, etc). The use of machine learning and text analysis algorithms for ontology structuring and population is discussed in this book in [59] and [69].

- **Ontology Reuse.** Though having been a main motivation for introducing ontologies in the area of Knowledge-Based Systems, it is still more research and development than daily practice that companies reuse substantial parts of externally created ontologies for their internal use. Besides technical and methodological provisions to be made to this end (cp. [91] and [70] in this book), it is mainly a 'political' challenge to bring together a significant number of companies—naturally being competitors—to invest in a joint effort for creating a shareable ontology of their application domain. So, the major areas where such endeavors were already successful are driven by public efforts and research scientists; here, the most important example are medicine and—to some extent—biology and genetics [38]. Other areas with good reuse chances concern broadly shared concepts in product and business modelling required for e-commerce and product data sharing [33]. Other promising areas for the future are dominated by few global players which are powerful enough to push broad standardization efforts which may lead to shared ontologies in the future; an example might be the insurance sector (see http://www.acord.org). In such sectors, ontologies are already useful for data exchange and resource integration, but all of them can profit even more from comprehensive KM approaches.

- **Methodology-Embedded Ontology Engineering.** There are several far-developed ontology modelling and management tools like Protégé (http://protege.stanford.edu), KAON (http://kaon.semanticweb.org), WebODE (http://delicias.dia.fi.upm.es/webODE/) and others [28]. In the KM environment we identify the highest demands on such a framework. The ontology shall often be built and maintained for a community-spanning use, seen from different perspectives, in an evolving domain, by non-Knowledge Engineers. Hence we expect in the ideal case not only incorporation of legacy structures and text analysis results, as mentioned above, plus technical solutions for the distributed creation and use of an ontology, but also a convincing methodological approach built into the ontology tool suite to guide and support the user. This concerns community concepts like distributed discussion support, versioning concepts etc. (see Tadzebao [31] and WebODE [11]), help for managing the informal-formal transition in a group discussion process for ontology building (cp. [62]), and, in the ultimate solution, an integrated support for all steps of a business-oriented KM methodology—which is not necessarily the same as a research-oriented KM methodology. For instance, in the DECOR project about Business-Process Oriented Knowledge Management (BPOKM, [7]), an amalgamation of the CommonKADS approach for top-level business-process analysis and the IDEF5 for ontology creation is proposed [75]; in the PROMOTE project, the Business Process Management Systems (BPMS) Paradigm is extended by Knowledge Management Process and Organizational Memory Modelling which includes the description of ontological structures with Topic Maps [52]; in the SPEDE project, Business Process Improvement is supported by knowledge captured with traditional knowledge acquisition (KA) tools in a KA process guided and assisted in a business-process oriented manner with the help of: a representation ontology for process knowledge; a high level process ontology; and process modules for modularization of complex processes [22, 23].

**R2: Integration of KM support with everyday work procedures**
In order to achieve a good user acceptance and to realize a maximum effect on knowledge workers' task performance, it is useful to integrate KM software as seamlessly as possible with the tools already in use for daily work. Several research prototypes [3, 6, 89] as well as industrial case studies [76, 52] can be found which address this goal by coupling knowledge storage and retrieval processes with workflow enactment which controls the operational business process. Here, the ontology is the 'glue' between operative and KM tasks on one hand, describing task-specific knowledge needs expressed in terms of an application domain ontology, and the Organizational Memory archive system on the other hand, providing ontology-based annotated knowledge resources.

[49] go a step further: they propose an ontological foundation of all business modelling based upon (i) a static ontology (the things in the world their attributes and relationships); (ii) a dynamic ontology (states, state transitions, and processes); (iii) a social ontology (agents, positions, roles, organization forms); and (iv) an intentional ontology (believes, goals, etc. of

agents). Such a comprehensive semantics-based business model could be the basis for powerful KM services and systems.

The EULE system presented by [80] formally represents and enacts even more task knowledge: process aspects (temporal and causal relationships), normative aspects (deontic knowledge), and terminological aspects (concepts and their relationships) are modelled in an insurance application, in order to realize partially automatic problem-solving and far-reaching inferences for information retrieval. Of course, from an ontological point of view, such 'heavyweight' approaches are much more interesting than simple IR applications. However, they have still to demonstrate their feasibility in practice. Maybe, domains which are heavily regulated by law, norms, and regulations, are well-suited for such an approach since, there, a deep level of formalization can be achieved, as well as deep inferences, and capture of legal regulations can be done economically, since bigger parts of the relevant ontologies can be reused in a wide range of applications (cp. [16, 105]). An application field with similar characteristics, not only regulated by law, but nevertheless highly controlled, is the area of medical guidelines and standards: there, ontological foundations for KM are (i) useful because of their high importance, and (ii) possible because of the broad range of potential applicants (cp., e.g., [78]).

**R3: Integration of heterogeneous information**

If one tries to find a *practical* definition of 'knowledge' (in contrast to data and information), it seems important that knowledge is always somehow oriented towards *action*—this aspect is already treated with the paragraph above; other aspects concern the fact that knowledge is normally strongly related to *context* and that it has a *network* character—showing how pieces belong together. Technically, this leads to the requirement that KM applications often have to process data, information, and information sources created to capture knowledge (like lessons learned entries or best practice documents) in a highly integrated manner (cp. [54]). As a solution approach, such knowledge documents are annotated with metadata which can be processed automatically and set into relation with application data. Hence, a KM application should be built upon an ***Information Ontology*** [3] which defines:

- which types of documents occur;
- what metadata attributes they have and which ontologies determine the value ranges of these attributes, where:
  - this may differ from document type to document type: a lesson learned may have a pointer to the project it was created in and the question how successful this project was, whereas a technical report may have an attribute for the location of the hardcopy of the document in the library, or links to experts for the technology described)
  - this can also be application specific; e.g. in an *e-Learning* application (which can be seen as a specific KM task) it might be important to specify how difficult to understand a document is and which prior knowledge is required, while in a *Knowledge Trading* scenario [10] attributes for pricing models, IPR issues and contract models might be required
- what relationships between documents are represented; linking logically related documents is a powerful mechanism for representing context; for example, in the EULE system knowledge with different degree of formalization is linked together (e.g. formal inference rules and textual explanations) [79]; discourse representation and group decision support systems implement in a somehow 'hardwired' manner an information ontology by providing different kinds of message types (e.g., issues, arguments, questions) and relationships (e.g., explains, corroborates, contradicts) for documenting argumentation structures in meetings or discussion processes (see [67] for some applications); in an e-learning sys-

tem specific relations may describe that some lessons require other lessons as (mandatory or useful) prior knowledge, or that an example illustrates some definition.

Although the issue of Information Ontology is not yet tackled very deeply, we consider this an interesting point of application for putting more semantics into KM applications.

One area where this happened already is *Experience Management for software development* processes, where sophisticated domain-specific information ontologies have been developed in order to identify the facets of a development experience, which are important to assess its later reusability in another situation [108, 98]. Other areas which employ case-based reasoning approaches for reuse of, e.g, technical designs, go into similar directions (cp. [82]).

Of course, real-world KM applications (and their ontology aspects) must not only meet the requirements described above, but also hold a *rigorous cost-benefit analysis*. A detailed analysis of an expected ontology life cycle can be a powerful guide to achieve an optimal level of formalization in terms of costs and benefits. Likewise an explicit handling of an ontology's sharing scope helps minimizing negotiation costs as well as the complexity of revision processes in case of ontology evolution (cf. [103]).

After these fundamental design considerations, we show some practical examples in the following sections.

## 22.3 Ontologies in Intelligence-Enhanced Applications

O'Leary characterizes the role of IT in KM—and in particular the role of Artificial Intelligence (AI) technology in KM—as 'converting and connecting' [72]. In detail, he lists the following KM functions to be supported by IT (cp. [74]): conversion of data and text into knowledge, conversion of individual and group's knowledge into accessible knowledge, connection of people and knowledge to other people and other knowledge, communication of information between users, collaboration between different groups, and creation of new knowledge that would be useful to the organization. Typical ontology-based KM applications to support these functions are:

*(1) Knowledge Portals for Communities of Practice.* Following [8, 71], a *Community of Practice* (CoP) is a, typically, informal, self-organizing group of individuals with an interest in a particular practice, for example the group of people in a company who do the same (or partially overlapping) jobs. The CoP might be contained within an organization, or spread across several. The CoP members have in common a desire to develop their competence, either for pleasure or pride in their ability, or for improving their work efficiency. CoP members typically exchange 'war stories', insights or advice on specific problems, or tasks connected with their common practice. A CoP can act as a part of the organizational memory, transfer best practice, provide mechanisms for situated learning, and act as a focus for innovation.

*Knowledge Portals*, or, Community Portals act as an information intermediary who structures all aspects relevant to a given, specific topic, in order to allow a community of users to flexibly and easily access a huge amount of information in different formats (today, usually text documents) related to this topic, to exchange information and communicate about the topic in quest, and to maintain and extend the content base accessed via this Internet (or, Intranet) portal (cp., e.g. [88, 87]). Normally, such a portal comprises browsing and searching mechanisms for documents, as well as community services such as online forums, mailing lists and news articles. Examples comprise the OntoWeb Semantic Web community portal [86], the KM portal http://www.brint.com, or the RiboWeb portal for molecular biology [9].

*(2) Organizational Memories.* An Organizational Memory Information System OMIS, or, for short, Organizational Memory OM [3, 29]—or, as a specialization, a Project Memory [35, 39]—is a computer system within an organization which continuously gathers and actualizes knowledge and information (from within and from outside the organization) and provides it to the end user in a context-dependent and task-specific, manner, thus giving proactive assistance to a knowledge worker working on knowledge-intensive tasks. It integrates manifold types of information, such as, e.g., best practice and lessons learned documents, continuous news articles, document templates, company regulations and manuals, CAD drawings, minutes of meetings, etc. Typical functionalities comprise integration of knowledge with different degree of formalization [79], intelligent problem-solving assistance by automatic generation of partial problem solutions [80, 54], and context-aware, task-specific retrieval of information [6, 89].

*(3) Lessons Learned Archives.* A Lesson Learned is a piece of knowledge gained through experience, which if shared, would benefit the work of others.[2]. It is typically generated from a customer project in a debriefing step, or created by an innovation or adverse experience which lead to some shareable insight to promote repeated application, or avoid reoccurrence, respectively.

Lessons Learned (LL) systems are typically used in Consulting firms [73], large technology companies, or in big government institutions, like military. Technologically, the challenge in LL systems lies in finding (and filling) an appropriate metadata schema (or, information ontology) which allows to precisely assess the potential value of a given LL as a reuse candidate in a new situation [106, 109]. As a related problem, the question of matchmaking arises (compare stored LL metadata with characteristics of the current situation to estimate whether the application of the LL will be useful) which is today often addressed by methods from the CBR (Case-Based Reasoning) and textual CBR area. [106] distinguishes four types of LL systems according to the way the systems capture their input *(passive versus (semi-)automatic)* and according to the way the Lessons Learned are published to the users *(push versus pull).*

*(4) Expert Finder and Skill Management Systems.* Since it is generally agreed upon that tacit and not (yet) explicated knowledge is at least as important in KM as explicit, documented knowledge, the 'classical' means for connecting people to people—yellow page systems, simple expert directories, and personal web pages—belong to the typical 'quick win' applications for KM (cp. [12, 13]).

More advanced approaches for expert finders (e.g. for project team configuration, specific technical questions, or strategic knowledge development plans in the organization) try to avoid the manual creation and continuous maintenance of skill profiles by exploiting and analyzing existing explicit information like documents created by a person, documented trainings and formal qualifications, project membership, collaboration or co-authorship relations, information flows, etc., in order to acquire and evolve such competency maps automatically [112, 111]. Further improvements comprise sophisticated faceted descriptions of competencies and elaborated matching functions for retrieval purposes [14, 94]. In the ideal case such functionalities are combined with and integrated into the personal and organizational skill and Human Resource management functions for planning, monitoring, staffing, etc. Further extensions comprise additional value-adding services like automatic scheduling of appointments for knowledge exchange between users, provision of extra information during interactions, negotiation support for knowledge exchange planning etc. [107].

Ontologies are normally used to structure the area of competencies, sometimes also to structure the environemnt in which competencies were acquired, used and further developed, i.e.

---

[2] See http://www.aic.nrl.navy.mil/ aha/lessons/, cp. [109]

projects, publications etc. (in order to allow for further inferences for skill assessment and re-trieval). Requirements for comfortable expert finder systems include (cp. [111]): (i) incremen-tal and interactive visualization / browsing and query mechanisms; (ii) support for expertise analysis (e.g. seeing different relationships between experts, having dynamic ranking mech-anisms etc); (iii) more intelligent concept-expert relationships taking into account in which document context (CV paragraph, self-assessment, title of Ph.D. thesis, footnote in workshop paper, ...) a keyword indicating a concept occurs.

Examples for ontology-based skill management include the SwissLife case study from a big insurance company [57], and the OntoProper case deployed in a large IT department [94].

## Use of Ontologies

In the above mentioned, major knowledge-based KM applications, ontologies are typically used for the following three general purposes:

### O1: Ontologies support knowledge visualization

Different aspects of visualization for information search have been discussed in the liter-ature on Human-Computer Interaction (HCI) and in the Digital Library community (see, e.g., [55]). With the advent of the Internet society, such methods gain growing interest (cp. [19]) for surveying and analyzing big amounts of information and complex interconnections. Recently, [46] gave a survey about applicable visualization methods, such as (i) basic *graph layout ap-proaches* (like H-tree layouts, balloon views, radial views, tree-maps, cone trees, hyperbolic views, etc.); (ii) *navigation and interaction* techniques (such as zoom-and-pan, focus+context techniques like fisheye distortion, and approaches to incremental exploration); and (iii) *clus-tering* for grouping data based on a chosen semantics and reducing the number of shown nodes or the complexity of the created view by methods like ghosting, hiding, or grouping.

Such methods can be used for inspecting the metadata and content descriptions of knowl-edge stocks in order to create new knowledge by analysis and recombination of existing knowledge. In such cases visualization may help to illustrate structure (e.g. content density) and distribution of content in a document corpus, as well as relationships between specific metadata attributes (like time or geographic relationships regarding document content or doc-ument creation, or co-authorship relations between people). Visualization of content structures in order to get a rough overview of topics discussed, their textual manifestation, and their in-terrelationships, or in order to have a quick topics-based access to document parts can even be used for intra-document analysis when dealing with long documents (like government re-ports, classical literature, socio-economic almanacs, etc). Visualization is also valuable for finding useful knowledge items in very vaguely specified search situations where (partially) exploring the information space is a part of problem-solving and helps clarifying the problem specification and/or its solution space.

With the success of the IEEE Topic Map standard, visualization for topic-oriented docu-ment access went into commercial practice. For instance, USU AG (http://www.usu.de) pro-vides knowledge networks as an interface to document corpora (see Fig. 22.4); other inter-esting visualization tools are offered, e.g., by AIdministrator [93] or intelligent views GmbH (http://www.i-views.de/).

Independent from the question which visualization is used for knowledge access (even in the case of a simple tree-structured browsing interface), the fact that KM usually deals with sharing complex knowledge content between people with quite different background and in-terests normally leads to the requirement that *multiple views* onto the same knowledge base should be provided. Although this is to some extent contradicting to the goal of creating a

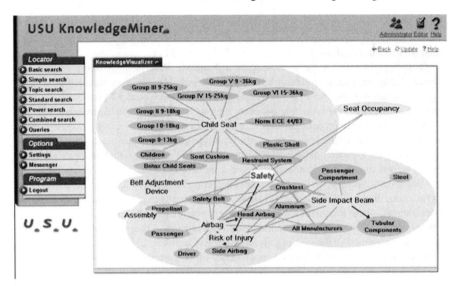

**Fig. 22.4.** Knowledge visualization in the USU knowledge miner

widely shared ontology to enable real communication between people, this requirement cannot be neglected in practice, in particular regarding the future trends of even more distributed KM scenarios introduced in Section 22.5. In [84] we made some preliminary considerations about the technical support for such scenarios, based upon the idea that specific, user-oriented GUI views can be created from special presentation ontologies created by selection and transformation operations from one (or more) core ontologies.

**O2: Ontologies support knowledge search, retrieval, and personalization**

The most important application of ontologies in KM—besides organization of browsing interfaces (with or without sophisticated visualization methods) in Knowledge Portals—is certainly to improve search and retrieval of documents by exploitation of ontological background knowledge about the application domain.

In [60] the basic ideas of using taxonomic relationships for increasing information retrieval (IR) recall for browsing and querying are described. Normally, in the case of an empty or small answer set, taxonomic knowledge is used for extending the query by subconcepts or superconcepts. The more specific a domain is modelled and the better understood typical queries and query situations are, the better can similar ideas be applied to other, non-taxonomic relationships. For instance, in the Electronic Fault Recording system for structured documentation and retrieval of maintenance experiences (fault events, maintenance measures, repair actions, etc.) for a complex and large mechanical device [15], the retrieval of potentially useful documented experience is not only supported by a detailed machine model in terms of is-a and has-part relations; similarity of potentially useful situations can also be assessed using modelled links describing hydraulic and electrical connections between machine parts, as well as analogy relationships because of similar construction plans. [58] propose an easy, declarative specification formalism for search heuristics for an ontology-based skill management approach: potentially useful information is inferred via graph-traversal activities following domain-specific links in the knowledge-base, e.g. about project team membership etc. A similar idea is realized in [94] using declarative rules about relationship instantiations for skill inferencing ('If a programmer X worked in a software project P which used the programming language L, then we can assume the X is knowledgeable in L').

Of course, in general, the more specific a domain is described, the more powerful inferences for query expansion and reformulation are possible; however, detailed models are expensive to acquire and maintain, such that here we have the typical KM trade-off asking for economic rationality when deciding between 'high-tech' and 'low-tech' approaches.

While the above approaches usually increase recall of IR, precision is not so often treated very explicitly. One example is the KonArc prototype [84] for sophisticated storage and retrieval of experiences in a database for software solution designs, which used also domain-specific information about incompatibilities of search constraints (e.g. between operating systems and specific software packages) for early detecting empty answers sets (and also explaining the contradictions to the user). [43] show for the example case of yellow pages and product catalogues—both important application areas in enterprise KM—that an ontology coupled with a linguistic knowledge-base can increase both recall and precision because it supports query disambiguation in the case of polysemous query terms.

Compared to the already discussed approaches which describe information *pull* situations, ontologies are, of course, often used to provide the vocabulary for expressing personal interest profiles for information *push services* which automatically deliver knowledge and information for categories a user is interested in. For instance, the myPlanet system realizes a personalized news service with the help of an ontology-based user profile [50].

**O3: Ontologies serve as the basis for information gathering and integration**

As mentioned above, KM deals with knowledge resources of different degree of formality, often informal text documents. On the other hand, the more formally represented information we have, the more formal inferences for query answering and passage retrieval, for derivation of new knowledge, and for comparing and integrating facts and documents from different sources, are possible. This allows, e.g., to partially automate problem solving and to integrate information retrieval results into operative business applications. The basis for such inferences are the information ontology structuring the metadata of informal knowledge sources, and domain ontologies structuring the content area of documents and providing background knowledge for inferences. This background knowledge may comprise information *search knowledge* as well as domain-specific *application knowledge*. *Information Extraction* (IE) algorithms [69] for (semi-)automatically annotating metadata to documents and *Text Categorization* techniques [83] for finding semantic content indexes map informal sources to formal metadata attribute values.

For realizing Business Intelligence applications in a KM context, domain ontologies provide the target data structures for gathering information from different sources in the Internet or a corporate Intranet. For example, [72] describes a Price Waterhouse Coopers application filling information frames about management changes in companies by analyzing a stream of business news articles. Similar applications are reported for filtering specific events out of news articles about economy or politics, for analyses in the military sector, and for fact extraction from personal web pages or publication web pages (see [56] for a technology survey). [53] describe an ontology-based application which creates narrative biographical sketches of artists based upon information automatically gathered, extracted and integrated from Web pages.

The Ontobroker project [27] showed how formal inferences can support information retrieval and analysis in the WWW in the case of a-priori ontologically annotated web pages. The CREAM suite represents a comprehensive set of software tools for starting and using such a solution [44].

Since Type 2A applications more or less represent the state-of-the-art in using ontologies for KM, we summarize here some challenges which we see for the near future of research and technology transfer in this area:

**Evaluation:** It is already an indispensable need for KM applications to show their economic benefits to the project sponsors—which is not easy. In order to be successful, we should define *success criteria* and develop *metrics* to assess success with respect to these criteria, to demonstrate that ontology-based applications are more useful than solutions with 'low tech' approaches. Although there exist already first comprehensive methodologies for ontology-based KM projects [95], the aspect of benchmarking or quantitative performance metrics is rarely tackled.

**Evolution:** Since we are talking about long-living systems in dynamic environments, also ontological structures must be evolved cost-effectively to avoid decreasing system performance. Recently a maintenance methodology for Case-Based Reasoning systems has been proposed [81] which could probably be transferred to the KM case. What would be required are *quantitative quality and performance indicators* for the KM system. [92] gave a well-structured analysis of the field of change discovery for ontologies distinguishing between structure-driven (obvious structural deficiencies of the ontology), data (instance) driven, and usage-driven change indications.

**Inference:** As already argued, exploiting the power of inferences would show the usefulness of knowledge-rich ontological system approaches in contrast to, e.g., taxonomy-based ones. We should search for domains requiring powerful reasoning mechanisms and expressive domain descriptions in KM. This may include aspects not yet fully adopted in ontology-based KM systems, such as the use of manifold link types [101], the representation of uncertainty and vagueness in domain modelling, and the definition of similarity on top of ontologies as required in CBR systems.

## 22.4 Ontologies Towards Enhanced Integrated Solutions

We mentioned already that exploitation of synergy effects between different applications in the complex KM scenario are an interesting source of innovation for both new services and improved effectiveness of existing services. Although this area—especially with respect to ontologies—is not yet explored very well, we give some examples for work into this direction:

- [4] report on performance improvements for document analysis (DA) and information extraction from paper documents by using expectations generated taking into account open workflow instances. The link between workflow system and DA is established by process, domain and DA ontologies and their mutual mappings. Similarly, task-specific IR is realized by coupling IR needs to workflow tasks.

- The ONTOCOPI system [8] is a tool for identifying potential members of a (hidden) Community of Practice by uncovering informal relationships between people trough traversal of instantiations of ontologically described formal relationships, like *is-coauthor-of*. Recommender systems learn about user preferences over time for realizing precise information push [66]. [65] describe how both systems can mutually benefit using the same ontological basis as the link between them.

- Typical software systems for supporting the process-view on KM comprise groupware (CSCW) and workflow systems. If, on the other hand, personal interest and skills are described formally on an ontological basis, groupware and CSCW support can be improved using this information. Examples for more intelligent CSCW support are more knowledgeable task assignment to employees in a workflow application, more knowledgeable project staffing when configuring a new team, or better informed briefing of participants before a virtual meeting.

## 22.5 Future Trends

Though the sections above show that ontologies in KM applications still provide chances and challenges enough, we would nevertheless like to give an idea of possible future trends. Comprehensive KM frameworks emphasize that Knowledge Management can take place at the individual, the group, organizational, and interorganizational level (e.g., [63]). The software functionalities discussed in Sections 22.3 and 22.4 are mostly used to support effectivity at the group and organizational level. Focussing on at the personal and the interorganizational level are logical next steps (cp. [100]). Economically, the transition to interorganizational KM is driven by the movements towards the *Extended Enterprise* which tries to integrate logistics and production processes along the whole production chain (cp. [77]), and towards the *Virtual Enterprise* which is configured ad-hoc for specific projects from normally independent small units, in order to dynamically establish a temporary value-creation chain. One can easily see that suitable KM approaches are even more important in such scenarios than in traditional enterprises, and that such scenarios also provide big chances to enhance effectiveness by appropriate KM measures.

Technically, the concepts of *Distributed Organizational Memory* (DOM) [103] and *Agent-Mediated Knowledge Management* [30, 104] have been introduced recently in order to deal with such highly dynamic and highly distributed environments. Projects dealing with aspects of this area comprise:

- The NAUTICUS system [85] envisions a collaboration between role agents and knowledge agents for achieving both just-in-time knowledge support (put task-specific best practice at empolyees' fingertips) and just-in-place knowledge management (ensure that shared knowledge is deployed and changed locally by its stakeholders).
- Jasper II [64] shall provide collaborating agents for knowledge capture, retrieval, summarization, and user profile refinement in a virtual community of users.
- The COMMA project [37, 36] identified the following sub-societies for an agent-based OM systen and demonstrated its feasibility using existing RDF and Semantic Web technologies: (i) the annotation-dedicated sub-society; (ii) the ontology and model sub-society; (iii) the user-dedicated sub-society; and (iv) the matchmaker sub-society.
- The FRODO project [5] added workflow task and role agents to this list and thus improved the notion of task-specific context-sensitivity.
- The KDE project [48] used already a CommonKADS extension for analyzing task specific knowledge needs in a knowledge-intensive workflow and realizing a knowledge-worker desktop using ontologies and agent technology.
- The EDAMOK project also elaborated on the notion of context in OM systems [17].

Today it is nearby to think about Peer-to-Peer technology as an appropriate means for realizing such functionalities as mentioned above (cp. [34, 96, 100]). From the projects above, only few address this technology explicitly, and even fewer tackle the problem of ontologies in DOM and P2P-KM scenarios in detail. Among those are **EDAMOK** [17] which explicitly suggests to engineer social order into P2P-KM agent systems for coordinating agents' activities related to contextualized knowledge search and retrieval as well as meaning negotiation [2, 102, 51] and **FRODO** which proposed to manage ontological issues in a DOM scenario by installing a society of ontology management and usage agents which are structured by social mechanisms (rights and obligations, [103]). In general, the basic problem to be dealt with is how to balance efficiently private issues and organizational issues in a complex and dynamic scenario. This area provides manifold challenging technical questions and is nevertheless highly relevant for industrial practice.

# References

1. *13th International Workshop on Database and Expert Systems Applications (DEXA 2002), 2-6 September 2002, Aix-en-Provence, France*. IEEE Computer Society, 2002.
2. Bouquet P (2002) Meaning Negotiation – Papers from the AAAI Workshop. Technical Report WS-02-09. AAAI Press
3. Abecker A, Bernardi A, Hinkelmann K, Kühn O, Sintek M (1998) Toward a technology for organizational memories. IEEE Intelligent Systems 13(3):40–48
4. Abecker A, Bernardi A, Maus H, Sintek M, Wenzel C (2000) Information supply for business processes – coupling workflow with document analysis and information retrieval. Knowledge-Based Systems 13(5):271–284
5. Abecker A, Bernardi A, van Elst L (2003) Agent technology for distributed organizational memories. In: Proceedings ICEIS-03, 5th International Conference on Enterprise Information Systems
6. Abecker A, Decker S, Maurer F (2000) Special Issue on Knowledge Management and Organizational Memory. Int Journal on Information Systems Frontiers (ISF) 2(3/4)
7. Abecker A, Hinkelmann K, Maus H, Müller H-J (eds) (2002) Geschäftsprozessorientiertes Wissensmanagement. xpert Press Springer, Berlin Heidelberg
8. Alani H, O'Hara K, Shadbolt N (2002) ONTOCOPI: methods and tools for identifying communities of practice. In: Intelligent Information Processing Conference, IFIP World Computer Congress (WCC), Montreal Canada
9. Altmann R, Bada M, Chai X, Carillo MW, Chen R, Abernethy N (1999) RiboWeb: an ontology-based system for collaborative molecular biology. IEEE Intelligent Systems 14(5):68–76
10. Apostolou D, Mentzas G, Abecker A, Eickhoff W-C, Georgolios P, Kafentzis K (2002) Challenges and directions in knowledge asset trading. In: Karagiannis D, Reimer U (eds) PAKM2002 - Fourth Int Conf on Practical Aspects of Knowledge Management. Springer, Berlin Heidelberg
11. Arpírez JC, Corcho O, Fernández-López M, Gómez-Pérez A (2001) WebODE: a workbench for ontological engineering. In: First Int Conference on Knowledge Capture (K-CAP 2001)
12. Becerra-Fernandez (2000) The role of artificial intelligence technologies in the implementation of people-finder knowledge management systems. In: Staab S, Tsui E, Garner B (eds) Proc AAAI Spring Symposium Bringing Knowledge to Business Processes
13. Becerra-Fernandez I (2001) Locating expertise at NASA. Knowledge Management Review 4(4):33–37
14. Benjamins VR, Cobo JML, Contreras J, Casillas J, Blasco J, de Otto B, García J, Blázquez M, Dodero JM (2002) Skills management in knowledge-intensive organizations. In: Gómez-Pérez A, Benjamins VR (eds) Knowledge Engineering and Knowledge Management. Ontologies and the Semantic Web – 13th Int Conf (EKAW 2002). Springer, Berlin Heidelberg

15. Bernardi A (1997) Electronic fault recording: A corporate memory for maintenance support of complex machines. In: Barthès JP (ed) Proc Int Symposium on the Management of Industrial and Corporate Knowledge

16. Boer A, Hoekstra R, Winkels R (2001) The CLIME ontology. In: Proc Second Int Workshop on Legal Ontologies, University of Amsterdam

17. Bonifacio M, Bouquet P, Mameli G, Nori M (2002) KEx: A peer-to-peer solution for distributed knowledge management. In: Karagiannis D, Reimer U (eds) PAKM2002 - Fourth Int Conference on Practical Aspects of Knowledge Management, Springer, Berlin Heidelberg

18. Borghoff UM, Pareschi R (1998) Information Technology for Knowledge Management. Springer, Berlin Heidelberg

19. Börner K, Chen C (eds) (2001) Visual Interfaces to Digital Libraries - Its Past, Present, and Future / Workshop at the The First ACM+IEEE Joint Conference on Digital Libraries JCDL-2001, URL http://vw.indiana.edu/visual01/

20. Conklin E, Weil W (1997) Wicked problems: Naming the pain in organizations. White Paper of Group Decision Support Systems Inc

21. Cortada JW, Woods JA (eds) (2000) The Knowledge Management Yearbook (1999-2000). Butterworth-Heinemann

22. Cottam H (1999) Ontologies to assist process oriented knowledge acquisition. Technical Report SP142, SPEDE Project, University of Nottingham

23. Cottam H (1999) Process knowledge editor – user guide. Technical Report SP143, SPEDE Project, University of Nottingham

24. Davenport T, Jarvenpaa S, Beers M (1996) Improving knowledge work processes. Sloan Management Review 37(4):53–65

25. Davenport T, Prusak L (1997) Working Knowledge: How Organizations Manage What They Know. Harvard Business School Press

26. Davies J, Fensel D, van Harmelen F (eds) (2002) Towards the Semantic Web: Ontology-Driven Knowledge Management. John Wiley and Sons, London

27. Decker S, Erdmann M, Fensel D, Studer R (1999) Ontobroker: Ontology based access to distributed and semi-structured information. In: [61]

28. Denny M (2002) Ontology building: A survey of editing tools. URL: http://xml.coverpages.org/Denny-OntologyEditorSurveyText20021111.html

29. Dieng-Kuntz R, Matta N (eds) (2002) Knowledge Management and Organizational Memories. Kluwer Academic Publishers, Dordrecht

30. Dignum V (2002) An overview of agents in knowledge management. URL: http://www.cs.uu.nl/people/virginia/amkm.pdf

31. Domingue J (1998) Tadzebao and webonto: Discussing, browsing, and editing ontologies on the web. In: 11th Knowledge Acquisition for Knowledge-Based Systems Workshop

32. Eppler M (2002) Definition of knowledge management in the NetAcademy glossary. Available via URL: http://www.knowledgemedia.org

33. Fensel D (2003) Ontologies and e-business. In: [90]

34. Fensel D, Staab S, Studer R, van Harmelen F (2002) Peer-2-peer enabled semantic web for modern knowledge management. In: [26]

35. Frank U, Fraunholz B, Schauer H (2001) A multi layer architecture for integrated project memory and management systems. In: Khoshrow-Pour M (ed) Managing Information Technology in a Global Economy: Proc of the 2001 Information Resources Management Association Int Conf. Idea Group Publishing.

36. Gandon F (2002) Distributed Artificial Intelligence and Knowledge Management: ontologies and multi-agent systems for a corporate semantic web. PhD thesis, INRIA and University of Nice - Sophia Antipolis

37. Gandon F, Poggi A, Rimassa G, Turci P (2002) Multi-agent corporate memory management system. Journal of Appl Artificial Intelligence 16(9–10):699–720

38. Goble C, Stevens R, Ng G, Bechhofer S, Paton N, Baker P, Peim M, Brass A (2001) Transparent Access to Multiple Bioinformatics Information Sources. IBM Systems Journal Special issue on deep computing for the life sciences, 40(2):532 – 552

39. Golebiowska J, Dieng-Kuntz R, Corby O, Mousseau D (2001) Building and exploiting ontologies for an automobile project memory. In: Gómez-Pérez A, Gruninger M, Stuckenschmidt H, Uschold M (eds) IJCAI-01 Workshop on Ontologies and Information Sharing, CEUR-Proceedings 47, URL: http://sunsite.informatik.rwth-aachen.de/Publications/CEUR-WS/Vol-47/

40. Gruber T (1991) The role of common ontology in achieving sharable, reusable knowledge bases. In: Allen J, Fikes R, Sandewall E (eds) Proc of the 2nd Int Conf on Principles of Knowledge Representation and Reasoning, Morgan Kaufmann Publishers

41. Gruber T (1995) Toward principles for the design of ontologies used for knowledge sharing. Int Journal of Human-Computer Studies, 43(5,6):907–928

42. Guarino N (ed) (1998) Formal Ontology in Information Systems – Proceedings of FOIS'98. IOS Press

43. Guarino N, Masolo C, Vetere G (1999) Ontoseek: Content-based access to the web. IEEE Intelligent Systems, 14(3):70–80

44. Handschuh S, Staab S, Maedche A (2001). CREAM - Creating relational metadata with a componentbased, ontology driven annotation framework. In: First Int Conf on Knowledge Capture (K-CAP 2001)

45. Hansen M, Nohria N, Tierney T (1999) What's your strategy for managing knowledge? Harvard Business Review, reprint 990206

46. Herman I, Melancon G, Marshal MS (2000) Graph visualization and navigation in information visualization: A survey. IEEE Transactions on Visualization and Computer Graphics 6(1):24–43

47. Holsapple C (ed) (2002) Handbook on Knowledge Management. International Handbooks on Information Systems. Springer, Berlin Heidelberg

48. Jansweijer W, van de Stadt E, van Lieshout J, Breuker J (2000) Knowledgeable information brokering. In: Stanford-Smith B, Kidd P (eds) E-business: Key Issues, Applications and Technologies. IOS Press

49. Jurisica I, Mylopoulos J, Yu E (1999) Using ontologies for knowledge management: An information systems perspective. In: Proc 62nd Annual Meeting of the American Society for Information Science (ASIS99)

50. Kalfoglou Y, Domingue J, Motta E, Vargas-Vera M, Buckingham-Shum S (2001) MyPlanet: an ontology-driven web-based personalised news service. In: Gmez-Prez A, Gruninger M, Stuckenschmidt H, Uschold M (eds) IJCAI-01 Workshop on Ontologies and Information Sharing. CEUR-Proceedings 47 URL: http://sunsite.informatik.rwth-aachen.de/Publications/CEUR-WS/Vol-47/

51. Kalfoglou Y, Schorlemmer M (2002) Information-flow-based ontology mapping. Informatics Research Report EDI-INF-RR-0135 University of Edinburgh

52. Karagiannis D, Woitsch R (2002) The PROMOTE Prototype: A Meta2Model Based Process Oriented KMS. In: [1]

53. Kim S, Alani H, Hall W, Lewis P, Millard D, Shadbolt N, Weal M (2002) Artequakt: Generating tailored biographies from automatically annotated fragments from the web.

In: Workshop on Semantic Authoring, Annotation & Knowledge Markup (SAAKM02) at the 15th European Conf on Artificial Intelligence, (ECAI02)

54. Kühn O, Abecker A (1998) Corporate memories for knowledge management in industrial practice: Prospects and challenges. In: [18]

55. Kumar V, Furuta R, Allen RB (1997) Metadata visualization for digital libraries: interactive timeline editing and review. In: Proc Third ACM Conf on Digital Libraries

56. Laender A, Ribeiro-Neto B, da Silva A, Teixeira J (2002) A brief survey of web data extraction tools. ACM SIGMOD Record 31(2)

57. Lau T, Sure Y (2002) Introducing ontology-based skills management at a large insurance company. In: Modellierung 2002, Modellierung in der Praxis - Modellierung für die Praxis

58. Liao M, Hinkelmann K, Abecker A, Sintek M (1999) A competence knowledge base system for the organizational memory. In: Puppe F (ed) XPS-99 / 5. Deutsche Tagung Wissensbasierte Systeme. Springer, Berlin Heidelberg

59. Maedche A, Staab S (2003) Ontology learning. In: [90]

60. McGuiness D (1998) Ontological issues for knowledge-enhanced search. In: [42]

61. Meersman R, Tari Z, Stevens SM (eds) Database Semantics - Semantic Issues in Multimedia Systems, IFIP TC2/WG2.6 Eighth Working Conference on Database Semantics (DS-8). IFIP Conference Proceedings 138. Kluwer

62. Meier D, Tautz C, Traphöner R, Wissen M, Ziegler J (2001) Building ontologies for knowledge management applications in group sessions. In: K-CAP 2001 Workshop on Interactive Tools for Knowledge Capture

63. Mentzas G, Apostolou D, Young R, Abecker A (2002) Knowledge Asset Networking. Advanced Information and Knowledge Processing. Springer London

64. Merali Y, Davies J (2001) Knowledge capture and utilization in virtual communities. In: First Int Conf on Knowledge Capture (K-CAP 2001)

65. Middleton S, Alani H, Shadbolt N, Roure DD (2002) Exploiting synergy between ontologies and recommender systems. In: Eleventh Int World Wide Web Conference (WWW2002), Semantic Web Workshop

66. Middleton S, Roure DD, Shadbolt N (2003) Ontology-based recommender systems. In: [90]

67. Mulholland P, Zdrahal Z, Domingue J, Hatala M (2000) Integrating working and learning: a document enrichment approach. Journal of Behaviour and Information Technology 19(3):171–180

68. Neches R, Fikes R, Finin T, Gruber T, Patil R, Senator T, Swartout W (1991) Enabling technology for knowledge sharing. AI Magazine, 12(3):36–56

69. Nedellec C, Nazarenko A (2003) Ontologies and information extraction. In: [90]

70. Noy N (2003) Tools for mapping and merging ontologies. In: [90]

71. O'Hara K, Alani H, Shadbolt N (2002) Identifying communities of practice – analysing ontologies as networks to support community recognition. In: Intelligent Information Processing Conference, IFIP World Computer Congress (WCC)

72. O'Leary D (1998) Knowledge management systems: Converting and connecting. IEEE Intelligent Systems 13(3)

73. O'Leary D (1998) Using AI in knowledge management: Knowledge bases and ontologies. IEEE Intelligent Systems 13(3)

74. O'Leary D (1999) Reengineering and knowledge management. In: Fensel D, Studer R (eds) Knowledge Acquisition, Modeling and Management – 11th European Workshop, EKAW '99. Springer, Berlin Heidelberg

75. Papavassiliou G, Mentzas G, Abecker A (2002) Integrating knowledge modelling in business process management. In: The Xth European Conference on Information Systems (ECIS-2002)
76. Papavassiliou G, Ntioudis S, Mentzas G, Abecker A (2002) Managing knowledge in weakly-structured administrative processes. In: Online Proceedings Third European Conference on Organizational Knowledge, Learning, and Capabilities (OKLC-2002)
77. Pedersen MK, Larsen MH (2000) Inter-organizational systems and distributed knowledge management in electronic commerce. In: Svensson L, Snis U, Sorensen C, Fägerlind H, Lindroth T, Magnusson M, Östlund C (eds) Proceedings IRIS 23 URL: http://iris23.htu.se/proceedings/
78. Pisanelli DM, Gangemi A, Steve G (2000) The role of ontologies for an effective and unambiguous dissemination of clinical guidelines. In: Dieng R, Corby O (eds) Knowledge Engineering and Knowledge Management. Methods, Models, and Tools – 12th International Conference (EKAW 2000). Springer, Berlin Heidelberg
79. Reimer U (1999) Knowledge integration for building organisational memories. In: 11th Banff Knowledge Acquisition for Knowledge-Based Systems Workshop
80. Reimer U, Margelisch A, Staudt M (2000) EULE: A Knowledge-Based System to Support Business Processes. Knowledge Based Systems, 13(5):261–269
81. Roth-Berghofer T (2002) Knowledge maintenance of case-based reasoning systems. The SIAM methodology. PhD thesis, University of Kaiserslautern
82. Schaaf M, Maximini R, Bergmann R, Tautz C, Traphöner R (2002) Supporting Electronic Design Reuse by Integrating Quality-Criteria into CBR-Based IP Selection. In: Proc 6th European Conf on Case Based Reasoning
83. Sebastiani F (2002) Machine learning in automated text categorization. ACM Computing Surveys, 34(1):1–47
84. Sintek M, Tschaitschian B, Abecker A, Bernardi A, Müller H-J (2000) Using ontologies for advanced information access. In: Domingue J (ed) PAKeM 2000, The Third Int Conf and Exhibition on The Practical Application of Knowledge Management
85. Sorli A, Coll GJ, Dehli E, Tangen K (2002) Knowledge sharing in distributed organizations. In: [29]
86. Spyns P, Oberle D, Volz R, Zheng J, Jarra M, Sure Y, Studer R, Meersman R (2002) Ontoweb - a semantic web community portal. In: Fourth Int Conf on Practical Aspects of Knowledge Management (PAKM-2002)
87. Staab S, Angele J, Decker S, Erdmann M, Hotho A, Mdche A, Schnurr H-P, Studer R, Sure Y (2000) Semantic community web portals. WWW9 / Computer Networks (Special Issue: WWW9 - Proc 9th Int World Wide Web Conference), 33(1–6):473–491
88. Staab S, Maedche A (2000) Knowledge portals: Ontologies at work. The AI Magazine, 22(2):63–75
89. Staab S, Schnurr H-P (2000) Smart task support through proactive access to organizational memory. Knowledge-based Systems 13(5):251–260
90. Staab S, Studer R (eds) (2003) Handbook on Ontologies in Information Systems. International Handbooks on Information Systems, Springer
91. Staab S, Studer R, Sure Y (2003) Ontology engineering methodology. In: [90]
92. Stojanovic L, Stojanovic N, Maedche A (2002) Change discovery in ontology-based knowledge management systems. In: Second Int Workshop on Evolution and Change in Data Management (ECDM 2002)
93. Stuckenschmidt H, van Harmelen F (2001) Knowledge-based validation, aggregation and visualization of meta data: Analyzing a web-based information system. In: Zhong N, Yao Y, Ohsuga S (eds) Web Intelligence: Research and Development – Proc First Asia-Pacific Conference on Web Intelligence (WI'2001). Springer, Berlin Heidelberg

94. Sure Y, Maedche A, Staab S (2000) Leveraging Corporate Skill Knowledge - From ProPer to OntoProPer. In: Mahling D, Reimer U (eds) Proc Third Int Conference on Practical Aspects of Knowledge Management (PAKM-2000)
95. Sure Y, Staab S, Studer R (2002) Methodology for development and employment of ontology based knowledge management applications. ACM SIGMOD Record 31(4)
96. Susarla A, Liu D, Whinston A (2002) Peer-to-peer knowledge management. In: [47]
97. Swan J, Newell S, Scarbrough H, Hislop D (1999) Knowledge management and innovation: Networks and networking. Journal of Knowledge Management 3(3):262–275
98. Tautz C (2000) Customizing Software Engineering Experience Management Systems to Organizational Needs. PhD thesis, Universität Kaiserslautern
99. Trittmann R (2001) The organic and the mechanistic form of managing knowledge in software development. In: Althoff K-D, Feldmann R, Müller W (eds) Advances in Learning Software Organizations. Springer, Berlin Heidelberg
100. Tsui E (2001) Technologies for personal and peer-to-peer knowledge management.
101. Tudhope D, Alani H, Jones C (2001) Augmenting thesaurus relationships: possibilities for retrieval. The Journal of Digital Information 1(8)
102. van Elst L, Abecker A (2002) Negotiating domain ontologies in distributed organizational memories. In: [2]
103. van Elst L, Abecker A (2002) Ontologies for information management: Balancing formality, stability, and sharing scope. Expert Systems with Applications 23(4):357–366
104. van Elst L, Dignum V, Abecker A (eds) (2003) Agent-Mediated Knowledge Management - Papers from 2003 AAAI Spring Symposium. Technical Report SS-03-01, AAAI Press.
105. van Engers TM, Kordelaar PJ, den Hartog J, Glassée E (2002) POWER: Programme for an ontology based working environment for modelling and use of regulations and legislation. In: DEXA-2002 Electronic Government Workshop
106. van Heijst G, van der Spek R, Kruizinga E (1998) lessons learned cycle. In: [18]
107. Vivacqua A (1999) Agents for expertise location. In: Proc 1999 AAAI Spring Symposium Workshop on Intelligent Agents in Cyberspace
108. Gresse von Wangenheim C (2002) Operationalizing Reuse of Software Measurement Planning Knowledge. infix, Berlin
109. Weber R, Aha D, Becerra-Fernandez I (2001) Intelligent lessons learned systems. International Journal of Expert Systems Research & Applications 20(1):17–34
110. Weber R, Kaplan R (2002) Knowledge-based knowledge management. In: Faucher C, Jain L, Ichalkaranje N (eds) Innovations in Knowledge Engineering. Physica, Heidelberg
111. Yimam D (2000) Expert finding systems for organizations: Domain analysis and the DEMOIR approach. In: Ackerman M, Cohen A, Pipek V, Wulf V (eds) Beyond Knowledge Management: Sharing Expertise. MIT Press
112. Yimam D, Kobsa A (2000) DEMOIR: a hybrid architecture for expertise modeling and recommender systems. In: Proc 9th IEEE Workshops on Enabling Technologies: Infrastructure for Collaborative Enterprises

# 23

# Ontology-based Content Management in a Virtual Organization

Peter Mika[1], Victor Iosif[2,3], York Sure[4], and Hans Akkermans[1]

[1] Vrije Universiteit Amsterdam, The Netherlands
   pmika@cs.vu.nl, hansa@cs.vu.nl
[2] EnerSearch AB, Malmö, Sweden
   victor@enersearch.se
[3] Lund University, Sweden
   School of Economics and Management
   Department of Business Administration and Management
[4] Institute AIFB, University of Karlsruhe, Germany
   sure@aifb.uni-karlsruhe.de

**Summary.** In this paper we describe an ontology-based content management and re- trieval system, a kind of Document-based Corporate Memory. This system has been realized in the setting of a virtual organization, a new kind of business partnership at the forefront of ontology-based Knowledge Management due to the special needs for organizing corporate knowledge using flexible, but well-understood and machine processable structures. The goal of our development was to improve on the traditional ways of managing both information items (documents, in our case) and domain knowledge used to organize information, while minimizing the additional effort required from content managers and knowledge workers. In order to evaluate our methods, we designed and carried out a field experiment that compared the effectiveness of the ontology-based search and browse methods to the traditional way of information seeking. Our results show that with appropriate interfaces it is possible to out-perform keyword-based search methods even by using less formal, lightweight ontologies obtained through automated extraction.

## 23.1 Introduction

Ontologies discussed in Artificial Intelligence are formal models of a shared understanding within a domain. Ontologies are considered as a key technology for Knowledge Management largely for their promise of bringing a consensus in the way a particular area of expertise is described. This consensus extends not only to terminology, but also the way concepts and objects may be organized and structured in the domain. Due to the formality of ontologies they also have the advantage to be processable by information systems.

The consensual nature and machine processibility of descriptions opens up new possi- bilities in the area of Corporate Memories [4]. A Corporate Memory is a collection of the knowledge assets of the enterprise, which may include knowledge on products, clients, tasks and processes, human resources etc. The purpose of such a knowledge store is to locate and make visible enterprise knowledge, to retain, access and maintain it, diffuse it and leverage it, put it in synergy and ultimately derive a value of this synergy.

In practice, it is often the case the information to be integrated comes from a number of sources and in a variety of formats and in such cases it's often unclear what should be the basis for normalization. Ontologies come to the rescue by serving as the basis for domain standard descriptions. These descriptions (markup or metadata) are expressed in terms of the ontology that members of the domain are committed to. In case users trying to retrieve information from such Corporate Memory are also committed to the same ontology and formulate their queries accordingly, ambiguities can be avoided in interpreting both queries and replies. (As we will see later, commitment to the ontology can also be built through the use of this method.) Ultimately, such normalization and retrieval promises precision in search beyond what is possible with current keyword-based methods, which are unaware of the semantics of terms.

In this paper we describe an ontology-based content management and retrieval system, a kind of Document-based Corporate Memory (see [4]). This system has been realized in the setting of a virtual organization, a new kind of business partnership at the forefront of ontology-based Knowledge Management due to the special needs for organizing corporate knowledge using flexible, but well-understood and machine processable structures.

The goal of our development was to improve on the traditional ways of managing both information items (documents, in our case) and domain knowledge used to organize information, while minimizing the additional effort required from content managers and knowledge workers. This meant the application of automated methods for creating ontologies, even if such methods produce a quality that falls short of the results attainable by manual methods. Our approach also required us to put an emphasis on intelligent interfaces that help the user to effectively discover and query the domain while hiding the complexity of ontologies and ontology-based queries.

In order to evaluate our methods, we designed and carried out a field experiment that compared the effectiveness of the ontology-based search and browse methods to the traditional way of information seeking. Our results show that with appropriate interfaces it is possible to outperform keyword-based search methods even by using less formal, lightweight ontologies obtained through automated extraction.

The rest of the paper is organized as follows. In Sect. 23.2 we describe the context of our case study, the EnerSearch virtual organization and the On-To-Knowledge project. Next, we turn to the ontology-based content management use case and the building of a supporting system for EnerSearch. In Sect. 23.4, we discuss the field experiment we carried out for evaluation. Lastly, we draw conclusions from the experiences described before.

## 23.2 Context of the Case Study

A well-adapted knowledge management has been increasingly identified as a key asset in maintaining the competitiveness of companies. This holds particularly true for knowledge-oriented virtual organizations such as EnerSearch. EnerSearch and the context in which the company operates are to be introduced in this Section.

EnerSearch turned to novel ontology-based Knowledge Management methods to improve the dissemination of scientific knowledge to both its members, shareholders and industry specialists. Research and development on an ontology-based solution was carried in the framework of the European On-To-Knowledge project. This project aimed at developing an ontology language, tools, and a correspond methodology for ontology-based Knowledge Management in the small- and medium enterprise. The main contributions of the project are also described in this Section.

## 23.2.1 Knowledge Management at EnerSearch

EnerSearch AB is an industrial research consortium investigating new IT based business strategies and customer services in deregulated energy markets. Its aim is to create and disseminate knowledge on how the use of advanced IT will impact the energy utility sector, particularly in view of the fact that this industry branch is being liberalized across Europe. This liberalization is leading to strong market competition, supplier choice for customers, and major changes in industry structure such as mergers and acquisitions that cut across the traditional regional-national monopolistic borderlines. Thus, a key issue for energy utilities is how they should strategically position themselves in a new deregulated market environment.

Apart from these market forces, new developments in both IT and energy technology are also an important factor in this strategic positioning. Innovations in energy technology increase the importance of decentralized local production and storage (e.g. "green" renewable energy, CHP) leading to the concept of a "distributed utility". Advances in networked IT strengthen this trend, because they make it much easier to manage distributed utility operations at lower cost, but also open up the possibility of delivering novel energy e-services, and thus getting closer to the customer, for example via the Internet and the Web.

These fundamental changes in the business environment are reflected by the structure of EnerSearch. Unlike traditional research institutes, EnerSearch operates as a *virtual organization* from the knowledge creation perspective. While employing a minimal number of permanent staff, projects are mainly carried out by a network of researchers spread across the continent. Many of them, although funded for their work, are not even employees of EnerSearch.

The insights derived from the conducted research are aimed at both industry experts and members of the consortium. Here, EnerSearch has the structure of a limited company, which is owned by a number of companies in the industry sector that have an express interest in the research carried out. Shareholding companies include large European utilities as well as worldwide IT suppliers to this sector.

Distributing the produced knowledge on IT and energy is a key function of EnerSearch. Due to the wide geographical spread of its audience, the organization has the character of a virtual organization also from the knowledge distribution point of view. With an eye on digital publishing to conserve resources, EnerSearch maintains a website[5] where it presents its research results in the form of papers, reports and books. This portal is crucial to EnerSearch as it is the primary means to connect its audience with the latest developments in the field of IT and energy. (In fact, one of the present shareholding companies joined EnerSearch directly as a result of getting to know it from the web.)

The EnerSearch website in its previous form offered the facilities most commonly found on corporate sites. Visitors could browse the domain by using a topic hierarchy. Publications on the site were presented in table that could be sorted by various criteria. Further, a search engine, known as the EnerSearcher, was provided to perform keyword-based search on the entire publication set.

Interviews conducted with shareholders and outsiders indicated dissatisfaction with this arrangement. The perceived problems centered around the task of finding information efficiently and effectively. The conclusion was that users wanted a system that leads to the de-

---

[5] http://www.enersearch.se

sired information in fewer clicks then currently possible, sorts out irrelevant information and suggests related topics, i.e. guides the user in the task.

The fixed browsing hierarchy was perceived as a hurdle because it constrained navigation to the paths predefined by the creators of the website. This is the result of a supply-side (or inside-out) rather than demand-side (or outside-in) style of information provisioning. By coming to the portal, the user finds some central "about us" information, an overview of what projects have been done and what researchers are involved. From there one finds the many electronic papers, reports and books that contain the EnerSearch research results in various knowledge areas. So, the real entry to what constitutes the heart of the EnerSearch - insights on how advanced IT may impact the energy business in a deregulated market environment - is along the lines of projects and authors. Clearly, this is very much a website organization driven by the information suppliers - projects and authors.

Consequently, the site did not adequately cater for the demand-side needs of information seekers - for example users from interested utility companies. These visitors are generally not at all interested in knowing what the projects or who the authors are, but rather in finding answers to questions that are important in this industry domain. For example: Does load management lead to cost savings; if so, how big are they, and what are the upfront investments needed? Can powerline communication be technically competitive to cable modems or ADSL? Is there an interest in the residential market in new energy services? Et cetera.

While browsing was monolithic and lead to too few results, searches using keywords were prone to spelling mistakes and ambiguities. Useful hits were lost in the sea of irrelevant information (high recall, low precision). Support for generalization and refinement based on the context of the query was lacking. As with browsing, users also missed structure in the responses, i.e. the ability to organize or cluster the results in meaningful ways.

While neither the task of information-seeking, nor the solutions or problems presented here are specific to EnerSearch, the company attributed particularly high value to finding the right information due to its position as a virtual knowledge organization. This warranted an interest in novel semantic technologies, which promised to alleviate, if not eliminate, some of these complaints.

### 23.2.2  The On-To-Knowledge Project

The recently concluded On-To-Knowledge research project is a joint European research effort that aims to improve on the state-of-the-art of knowledge management solutions for small- and medium-size organizations (SMEs) by leveraging ontologies [1, 2]. More specifically, the project aims to improve access to existing unstructured or semi-structured information sources and corporate knowledge (commonly referred to as a Corporate Memory), while reducing the costs in acquiring and maintaining this knowledge. Ontologies drive the acquire-preserve-use chain by providing a shared description of the domain that both human and machine agents involved in the process can rely on.

While the goal of the project was to create a framework for ontology-based solutions in the context of single enterprises, many of the tools and technologies developed in the project are now considered as part of Semantic Web applications. The contributions of the project are the following:

- The OIL ontology language which significantly extends the expressiveness of the RDF standard, while firmly grounded in the formal rigor of Description Logics. OIL is predecessor to the DAML+OIL and OWL languages discussed in a separate chapter of this book and is therefore not covered here in more detail.

- A set of tools for acquiring, engineering, storing and reasoning with ontologies, plus application components for ontology-based information retrieval and visualization. Important to note that the project did not result in a single, out-of-the-box solution for Knowledge Management, but rather provided for the interoperability between these components so that they can be used to create custom tailored solutions.
- A methodology on ontology-based Knowledge Management based on the experience from a number of case studies, where domain specific ontologies were developed and integrated with other On-To-Knowledge components into comprehensive solutions. This methodology is also discussed in a separate chapter of this book.

In the following we briefly introduce the On-To-Knowledge tools used in the case study. Tools that were not used in the case study are the OMM ontology middleware for versioning and security, the BOR DAML+OIL reasoner, the OntoShare knowledge sharing environment and the OntoWrapper tool used for extracting specific information from weakly structured documents. For more information on these tools, we refer the reader to the appropriate deliverables of the project.

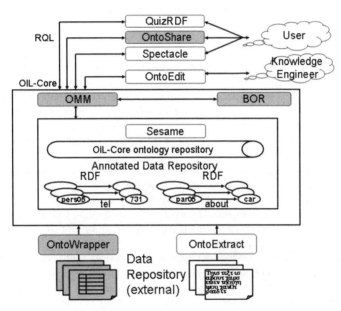

**Fig. 23.1.** A generic architecture of On-To-Knowledge tools and components. Tools not used in the EnerSeach system are colored grey

On-To-Knowledge tools are based on a three-layered architecture of information access, information storage, and information access shown in Fig. 23.1.

Information extraction and ontology generation from natural texts and semi-structured information sources is performed by tools situated in the extraction layer. In case of large volumes of unstructured or weakly structured information sources, this process requires an automated approach.

The OntoExtract tool supports the acquisition of lightweight ontologies through Natural Language Processing (NLP) techniques. OntoExtract works in three steps. First, a web handler component gathers input for the analysis by crawling the web. In a second step, the proprietary NLP engine performs lexical, morphological and semantic analysis on the corpus. The result of the analysis is then augmented with ontological metainformation (such as keywords and a short summary) using the Dublin Core standard [6]. The ontology is subsequently stored in a Sesame repository.

The Sesame server is the central component of the On-To-Knowledge architecture. Sesame allows persistent storage of RDF data and schema information and subsequent on-line querying of that information. In this system, the RDF data is stored within repositories, an abstract concept for an RDF model that hides the actual nature of physical storage. (In fact, any kind of persistent storage can be employed from files to relational databases and peer-to-peer networks.) Users of the server can have multiple repositories and repositories can be shared among users as well. Sesame allows a number of operations on repositories:

- Data Manipulation. This includes the upload and extraction of data in RDF(S), the removal of statements or the clearing of the entire repository. During upload, the RDF model of the document is merged with the model of the repository and extended by computing the closure described in the RDF Model Theory [9]. Removal of statements is facilitated by a Truth Maintenance System, which helps to identify inferred statements that are no longer supported after the transaction.
- Semantic Query. Sesame currently provides implementations of the RQL [11] and RDQL [16] languages. RQL supports querying of both RDF data (e.g. instances) and schema information (e.g. class hierarchies, domains and ranges of properties). RQL also supports path-expressions through RDF graphs, and can combine data and schema information in one query. RDQL is a simpler, SQL-like query language for RDF only. In both cases, the query results are returned either in an HTML table for human readers or in RDF-XML format for machine processing.
- Administration. This includes configuration of the server such as the management of access control, logging etc.

All of these operations may be carried out through the web interface of Sesame, which also serves as a simple browsing interface for quick exploration of the content of a repository. With the exception of administration, functionality is also available for remote applications. For convenience, application programmers are provided with a Java Client API, which hides communication with the server behind simple method calls. Implementations are provided for HTTP, RMI and SOAP based access.

The OntoEdit ontology development environment provides well-known features of ontology editors with the option to extend its functionality through various plug-ins. Modelling ontologies using OntoEdit involves (1) modelling at a conceptual level, i.e. independently of a concrete representation language as possible, and (2) using multiple graphical views on conceptual structures (concepts, concept hierarchy, relations, axioms) rather than codifying knowledge in ASCII. Ontologies can be imported and exported in an expressive internal XML representation, RDF(S) or F-Logic. Plugins have been developed for inference support, ontology evolution, ontology evaluation etc. Support for integrating with Sesame is also provided as a plugin.

Besides the OntoEdit tool, which is intended for the knowledge engineer, the information access layer also provides user interface components to be adapted and reused in comprehensive ontology-based solutions. Common to all these components is that they take an ontology from a Sesame repository as input.

QuizRDF is a generic search engine that combines traditional keyword-based queries with searching metadata describing web pages. In QuizRDF [3] the classifications of pages and attached attribute values are used as metadata. This information is stored in a complex index structure along the results of a full text indexing of the documents. Based on this information, the interface allows to query for specific classes of documents and for specific values for the properties of a given class. These criteria may be combined with each other (i.e. return instances of the Art class where the property Painter has the value of Picasso and the property Style has the value Cubist). Criteria on metadata may also be combined with traditional keyword based search at will. The method falls back gracefully on keyword based search whenever there is no ontological information present about a document. This property will be important in the first stages of Semantic Web, when annotations will be scarce.

Spectacle is a platform for creating web portals that separate navigation from the content and design of the web site. Spectacle allows building presentations with highly flexible navigation structures. In sites created with Spectacle, (1) items can appear under multiple categories, (2) there can be multiple paths to the same item, (3) different views can be defined for specific target groups. Spectacle achieves this flexibility by focusing on the various classifications that can be defined over the data items, instead of fixing the navigation structure. During navigation, the user is always offered the full set of classifications pertinent to the remaining set of items, i.e. the items not excluded by previous choices. This way the user is free to decide on the order of specifying his search criteria, as opposed to having to make selections in a pre-defined order. Instead of prescribing the navigation, the task of the designer is to specify the navigation paths that are excluded, e.g. to rule out inconsistent selections.

We will return to our experiences with these technologies in Sect. 23.3.2, where we discuss the development of the EnerSearch system that integrates the components described above.

## 23.3  Ontology-based Content Management

Given a predisposition for innovation and the availability of ontology-driven technology through the On-To-Knowledge project, EnerSearch decided to investigate how its content management and retrieval methods could benefit from the use of novel technology. This Section starts with the outcome of this analysis, the use case for ontologies in content management.

In the remainder of this Section, we describe the most significant experiences that resulted from the realization of an ontology-based system based on this use case. This system was to replace the website and the traditional search method described previously and was implemented in three phases. The first phase consisted of the acquisition of an ontology, the second concerned storage, query and transformations of the ontology, while the third required the creation of ontology-based interfaces for information retrieval. We share the most valuable lessons from our work with respect to all three phases.

Besides this technology-oriented analysis, the system was also tested through the field experiment described in Sect. 23.4.

### 23.3.1  The Potential for Ontologies

EnerSearch joined the On-To-Knowledge project largely for what ontologies promise with respect to improving on the state-of-the-art of information retrieval and presentation: greater user satisfaction through more effective searching and browsing. How ontologies may fulfill this promise is the topic of this section.

By their most common definition, ontologies represent a shared and formal understanding of a domain [8]. In this definition, the term *shared* refers to the fact that ontologies embody a consensus among members of a given community. The term *formal* indicates the grounding of representation in some sort of well understood logic, i.e. ontologies go beyond simple vocabularies (terminologies) by providing definitions of concepts based on how they relate to other concepts and relationships. Lastly, formal also refers to the fact that ontologies may be expressed in machine processable formats, which makes them applicable in information systems.

All of these properties of ontologies are crucial in enabling more focused information retrieval and presentation. This application scenario for ontologies is generalized by Uschold under the title "Indexing" [17]. Building on his diagram, the ontology-based content management use case can be visualized as shown in Fig. 23.2.

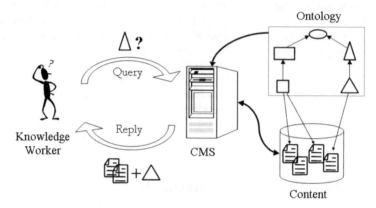

**Fig. 23.2.** The content management use case for ontologies

In this scenario, first an ontology is used to annotate the content that is of interest to the user, which might either mean that ontology-based descriptions are embedded in the documents themselves or references to the documents are added to the ontology.

Subsequently, a Knowledge Worker (KW) trying to find some information forms a semantic query in terms of the *same* ontology and submits it to the application for processing. In its reply, the system returns (references to) resources and helps the KW to refine his query, e.g. by suggesting generalizations, more specialized terms or related terms. If the reply is not satisfactory, i.e. it doesn't contain an answer or the reply is too large to handle, the KW can use this information to refine his query in an iterative fashion until an answer is found. This can also be negative, for example when no answer is found within a certain time frame or the system does not know the answer.

In this use case the ontology is used to mediate the communication between the creators of content (with markup) and the knowledge worker trying to access the information. Both of these actors use the same ontology in forming their messages to one another, in this case queries and replies. Without the consensus embodied in the ontology, this communication would be filled with ambiguities and misunderstandings, as it is the case with syntactical, keyword-based searches on the internet. The fact that ontologies are machine storable is also a crucial element, as the communication we encounter here is typically asynchronous.

It's also worth noting that even if the ontology is not known in advance to the KW, the KW can discover and *learn* the ontology by interacting with the system. With each reply the context is also returned, which greatly facilitates the interpretation of the answer and the adaptation of the query. Even formulating an initial query can be made easier by offering a select number of entry points based on the ontology.

There are two distinct advantages of this technology that made it particularly appealing for EnerSearch.

First, the mixed audience of the portal meant that it was important that the new interfaces did not require significantly more human effort to master. Advances in creating ontology-based search and browse interfaces meant that much of the technology could be made transparent for the knowledge worker.

In fact, ontology-based web interfaces operate with the usual elements of web pages (links, tables, forms etc.) The difference to a traditional website is that users experience an interface that is more "knowledgeable" with respect to the domain. When searching, the interface helps the user to formulate complex ontology-based queries by providing customized forms for entering values for class membership, attributes, relations etc. When browsing, the interface helps the user to keep in focus by showing the context of the concept that he is currently exploring. The interface also creates a presentation from the items resulting from browsing or search. This presentation provides context information and helps to organize the returned instances in meaningful ways.

Secondly, EnerSearch was attracted by the advances in natural language technologies that made it possible to automate ontology extraction. EnerSearch possesses a large content base that reached the proportions where manual methods to annotation were not scalable any more. Furthermore, it was important to minimize the tasks of content providers. As mentioned before, members of the virtual organization are loosely affiliated to EnerSearch (typically hold other affiliations) and tolerate little extra burden with respect to their membership in EnerSearch.

## 23.3.2 Development of the EnerSearch System

The role of EnerSearch in On-To-Knowledge was to integrate ontology-based tools and components into a complete solution that would enact the use case described in the previous section. From the perspective of the project, EnerSearch served to evaluate the On-To-Knowledge approach both from a technical perspective and from an end-user point of view. The highlights of our experience with the technology are described in this section, while the field experiments with the final system is treated in Sec. 23.4.

Since the EnerSearch system was built using tools and technologies developed within On-To-Knowledge, it follows many of the design decisions taken within the project. We spell out some of the most important choices and the rationale below.

- A centralized approach to Knowledge Management. On-To-Knowledge targeted the business context of SMEs. In particular, requirements were set for addressing the needs of typical corporate intranets of $O(10^4)$ pages and domain ontologies of $O(10^3)$ concepts. It was expected and verified that it is indeed possible to retain the advantages of central management and still being able to scale up to this size. In particular, it was proven that a central Sesame storage facility was well able to handle the size of ontologies generated by automated extraction from intranets of this size [7].
- A loose coupling of tools through web-based protocols. On-To-Knowledge tools that took part in the case study were installed on various web servers of the tool providers and communicated using HTTP. The choice for web technologies and a loose coupling were suggested by the widely accepted notion of the Semantic Web as an extension to the current web. Web technologies provide interoperability with legacy web-based systems,

while ensure that On-To-Knowledge components could be used in realizing the vision of the Semantic Web.

We note that standardization beyond an agreement on interfaces was not considered at the time. In particular, the use of Web Services were out of the scope of the project.

- The choice of RDF(S) as a knowledge interchange format. The choice for RDF(S) was dictated by the finding that neither of the case studies in the project required the expressivity of Full OIL. This does not mean that expressivity of Full OIL (now: OWL) may not be a requirement for other domains such as medical science and technical engineering. It seems to be the case that the circumstances for those communities are substantially different from a business Knowledge Management environment where domain experts are often unskilled in modelling ontologies and work in an environment were business pressure means that little time and effort can be devoted to modelling rich ontologies [7] In the EnerSearch case, the heavy use of automated methods also degraded the quality of ontologies. See Sect. 23.3.3.

- Conformance to a commonly agreed upon data model. On-To-Knowledge tools conformed to the shared data model shown in Fig. 23.3. This data model has been created within the project as a modelling template for metadata about internet pages. The model was determined by the capabilities of the extraction tools and the information needs of the ontology-based application components.

  In general, an agreement on a data model is crucial when multiple agents are involved, because the same knowledge may be modelled in very different ways. We may note that the On-To-Knowledge architecture did not include provisions for ontology mapping. The use of such technique may have relaxed the need for an ontological commitment.

The implementation of the EnerSearch system took six person-months. The development of the ontology-based application was divided in three phases of (1) developing an ontology, (2) storing, querying and transforming the ontology and (3) creating the ontology-based browsing and search interfaces. These three phases are to be described next.

### 23.3.3 Ontology Engineering

The process of setting up the system began with acquiring a base ontology by configuring and running the OntoExtract tool on the website of EnerSearch.

The ontology that resulted in this process was extremely lightweight, i.e. weak in formality (see also [12]). While the ontology contained a large number of concepts, the distribution of these concepts reflected some of the weakness of automated extraction.

For example, initially a large number of the concepts where such that they occurred in too few publications to be relevant enough. On the other hand, concepts ranked higher by OntoExtract occurred in too many of the documents, which made them less useful for retrieval, because they did not narrow down the queries well enough.

However, cutting out a large number of the concepts that were deemed too specific or overly generic meant that we would loose coverage of the domain. In short, it took a lot of experimentation with the parameters of extraction (1) to find the right balance between specific and generic concepts, and (2) preserving coverage of the domain while having an ontology that is as compact as possible.

The ontology that resulted was also lightweight in terms of relationships. As it can be seen from the data model shown in Fig. 23.3, there are only generic properties at the class level that express various strength of relatedness. Furthermore, the overwhelming majority of concepts extracted turned out to be direct subclasses of the top level class. So even though the

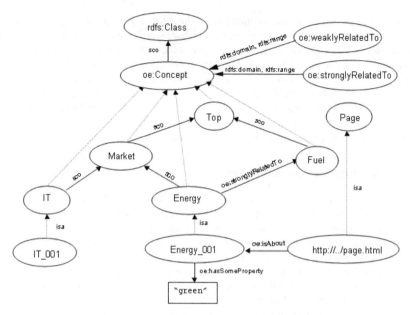

**Fig. 23.3.** Example ontology formatted according to the On-To-Knowledge data model

data model allowed to define concept hierarchies using the RDF(S) subClassOf relationship, the extracted ontology contained very few such statements.

Moreover, the extraction results in a single generic property for instances called oe:hasSomeProperty. (The oe:isAbout relationship is used to connect concept occurrences to the pages where they can be found.) In theory, assigning names to these generic properties could significantly enrich the ontology. In practice, however, finding names turns out to be too much of a challenge: the values are, in many cases, only distantly related to the concept. Therefore, if one would like to find out what is the nature of the relationship, he would need to revisit the original document.

We believe that the difficulty of extracting subclass relationships and naming properties in an automated way is due to fundamental reasons rather than technological shortcomings. Our own modelling experience shows that finding consensus on the key concepts in a domain is significantly easier than arranging the concepts in a subclass (or even subtopic) hierarchy in a mutually agreeable way or finding shared names for the relations between concepts. In short, modelling relations seems to present a stronger need for consensus and involve more modelling *choices*, which cannot be expected to be made by a computer. Unless this consensus is explicitly spelled out in the natural text (which is often not the case), improvements may only come from the application of domain-specific background knowledge, i.e. a combination of manual and automated approaches to ontology engineering.

Nevertheless, in our work we decided not to manually re-engineer the extracted ontology as we were specifically interested in the reach of purely automated methods. We were motivated in this choice by the vision of a Semantic Web. Similarly to users in our business scenario, we expect that the typical web user will prefer to work with simple taxonomies or would not want to construct an ontology at all, which makes automated extraction indispensable.

As a last step in this phase, we transformed the schema and instance base from the pre-existing publication database into a ontology. The EnerSearch publication database contained metadata about the publications, namely the name of the author(s), the title of the publication, the date of the publication, the project that the publication belongs to and the URL of the abstract and the full publication. This database is stored in Microsoft Access format and was used to generate a table of publications that appears on the website of the company. As the database was in a highly structured, relational format, this step presented no difficulties from the knowledge point of view. Merging this ontology with the extracted domain ontology was equally straightforward, as both ontologies referenced the location of publications.

### 23.3.4 Ontology Storage and Query

In a second step, the resulting ontology was stored in the central repository and queried to extract the semantics necessary for ontology-based information retrieval. As it turned out, some small transformations were also necessary on the ontology.

Here our greatest challenge turned out to be finding the right balance in the workload between Sesame and its clients, the Spectacle portal generator and the QuizRDF search engine. Note that both queries and transformations can be described as inference tasks over an ontology. Where the bulk of this inference was performed had serious consequences on the performance of the entire system.

For example, we quickly observed that small, frequent queries to Sesame were quite inefficient. We also noted in some cases that complex queries required by the applications took considerable time to evaluate. Query evaluation performance was improved through a close collaboration with the developers of Sesame. Nevertheless, their feedback indicates that it is close to impossible to optimize every possible query with such an expressive language as RQL; the goal is to optimize those queries that are most required by application developers. (Unfortunately, there are very few real applications to provide a feedback to this work.) Nevertheless, both deficiencies meant that it often made more sense to perform simpler, wider queries on the server and then store and further process the results on the client side.

We also discovered tell-tale patterns in the time needed to perform the same inference tasks as the size of the repository grows and new data is added. To illustrate this, it's instructive to look at the inference task Sesame performs when data is uploaded. This task consists of computing the closure of the RDF model as described in [9].

Figure 23.4 shows the processing speed for a series of 17 consecutive uploads to an originally empty repository using an older and an improved implementation of the Sesame inference routine. The logarithmic trend line fitted on the graph reveals that the time needed for the inference is proportional to the number of statements already in the repository. Even more interesting is the cause for jumps in the upload speed, i.e. the noise that seems to be superposed over the general declining trend.

The sharp dips correspond to comparatively small uploads on the order of a few hundred statements compared to several thousand statements for the other uploads. The difference in the time needed for the uploads to complete was not nearly as big as the difference in sizes. In other words, the speed of processing smaller uploads is significantly lower then for processing larger ones. The explanation concerns the fixed administration costs of carrying out an upload. We concluded that similarly to frequent queries, frequent manipulation of smaller parts of the dataset caused again a performance bottleneck.

As an initial solution to these problems, we moved part of the inference work (queries, rules and transformations) to the client-side to ease the burden on the central Sesame repository. This choice seemed also appropriate because some of our transformations required data

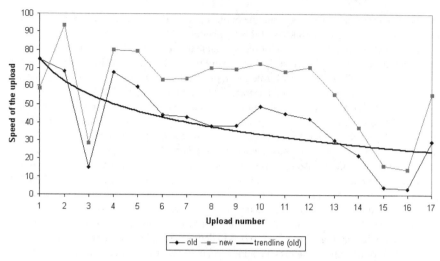

**Fig. 23.4.** Number of statements processed per second over a series of 17 uploads for the old and new implementation of the inference engine, with a logarithmic trend line for the former

manipulation using data types not supported by rule languages. In the future, however, we envision the use of Portable Inference Modules (PIM) as a solution [13]. PIMs are a sharable, reusable form of inference knowledge captured in a procedural form. The portability of these modules means that they can be executed at any node of the network to balance the load.

### 23.3.5 Ontology-based Information Retrieval

In a third and last phase, two separate presentations for search and navigation were generated from the ontological data using QuizRDF and Spectacle, respectively.

For QuizRDF, this is theoretically a one-step operation, in which the engineer has to select the Sesame server and repository where the annotations are located. The combined metadata and keyword-based index mentioned previously is automatically created based on the metadata stored in Sesame and the text of the documents referenced therein. Similarly, the web interface used to compose queries is also automatically generated based on the ontology.

The disadvantage of such automation is the limited room for customization. In our case, the initial number of concepts in the ontology resulted in an overcrowded drop-down box for concept selection. Only after the reduction of the number of concepts (by filtering out lower ranked concepts) did we arrive to a satisfactory arrangement. Had there been a possibility to customize the interface, we would have also chosen a different presentation. Similarly, the interface did not make it possible to show class-level relationships, which are a significant aspect in our ontology. (These are the relations between classes such as the oe:stronglyRelatedTo.)

In general, we also note that search using QuizRDF is geared toward retrieving instances based on known values for the superclass, attributes and relations to other instances. Thus QuizRDF performs best on rich ontologies, which typically feature a well defined class hierarchy with distinguishing attributes and relations. This limited the usefullness of the tool in the EnerSearch case, where the extracted domain ontology contains only a single attribute on the instance level and the subclass hierarchy is also particularly shallow. The part of the ontology that has been reverse engineered from the publication database contains a richer set of facets and therefore shows the capabilities of this tool better.

In contrast to QuizRDF, the use of the Spectacle tool is a considerable programming task. Spectacle in turn provides a great deal of flexibility in the transformation from ontology to a navigational structure. The transformational, programmatic approach of Spectacle makes it possible to create web portals using cheaper, lightweight ontologies.

The first major design decision that needs to be taken when programming with Spectacle is the definition of classifications over the data items, in our case the documents of parts thereof[6] The flexibility of the Spectacle approach is shown by the multitude of classification features that can be used. Classification may mean clustering items by classes, relations, attribute values or ranges thereof. In case of pages, we chose to classify by concepts, authors, projects and the year of publication. Concepts are classes in the ontology, while authors and projects are attribute values. (See Fig. 23.3) Classification by year is an example of classification by a range of attribute values, since a year is defined as a range of date values.

When the classifications are defined, the next task was to determine on the navigation paths through the ontology. Instead of having to define the navigation tree explicitly, however, it is enough to determines the classifications to be offered to the user at each level of navigation. Based on the definition of the navigation levels, Spectacle can render the navigation tree by determining the paths that may lead from a node at a higher level to nodes at the level below.

The most straightforward option here is to establish a direct mapping between the class hierarchy in the ontology and the navigation tree of the website. The EnerSearch ontology, however, lacked a firm class hierarchy, which meant that we had to look for alternate ways of navigation.

As an alternative to direct mapping, we implemented the inclusive variation of the hierarchical access method described by Sabou [15, 14]. With this method each node of the navigation tree represents an intersection of the classes selected by the user up to that point. For example, if the navigation has proceeded through the classes A, B and C in any particular order (e.g A/B/C, A/C/B etc.) than the node will map the intersection $A \cap B \cap C$. Put it differently, when the navigation reaches that particular node, the selection of entities will be restricted to those that are classified as both A, B and C. (If there are no other constraints there are n! such navigation paths for n classes. Spectacle can be made aware of such permutations.)

The hierarchical access method is a powerful way to imitate a topic hierarchy even if the ontology is too lightweight to contain a well-defined topic structure. We strengthened the feeling of a topic hierarchy by showing only the highest ranked (most prominent) concepts at the top level of navigation.

On the other hand, we encountered difficulties with the hierarchical access method due to the unusual characteristics of our ontology. In a direct mapping from class hierarchy to navigation hierarchy the number of nodes of the navigation tree equals the number of classes in the ontology. With the hierarchical access method, however, the number of nodes is largely a function of the overlap between classes. As the size of the EnerSearch domain ontology grown, the number of pages that were needed to be rendered increased dramatically due to the overlaps between classes. At the time this presented a problem, because navigation was pre-rendered for a faster response to clients. The remedy to this problem came in the form of a new version of Spectacle that allows just-in-time page rendering. With this method the portal generator application is embedded within the content server and called on-demand whenever a

---

[6] Where it was possible, we used anchors in the original documents to break them into sections.

node needs to be rendered, i.e. whenever a user tries to visit a node that has not been rendered before.

Besides programmer convenience, the machine processibility of navigation trees makes it possible to define rules and heuristics of navigation. Spectacle itself contains several predefined, configurable heuristics to identify navigation steps that are unlikely to be useful and to spot branches of the tree that need not be extended further.

For example, those navigation options that would not cut back on the selection of items significantly enough are not shown. The rationale behind is that these choices lengthen the navigation path without adding much to the definition of the user's query. (This also filters out odd navigation paths such as A/A or A/B where A is a subclass of B). Also, nodes that contain less than a minimum number of entities are not extended any further, as its expected that the user can handle a small selection without further help from the system.

These heuristics can be extended with domain specific logic, such as restrictions on the order of certain selections. In more complex cases, for example in the example of a travel agency, such a rule may prohibit a visitor from selecting a mode of transport before specifying the intended destination.

The application of built-in heuristics and custom rules determines the final shape of the navigation tree. Once the shape of the tree is determined by these mechanisms, the programmer can decide on what to show in the pages corresponding to nodes of the tree. This concerns only content and design, navigation elements are rendered by Spectacle.

As a further option with Spectacle, a number of views may be defined on the navigation tree. Views restrict the set of entities to some useful subset determined by a number of classification terms. Views may be used for user profiling, but also to offer specialized versions of the navigation. The advantage of views in that case is that the navigation need not be computed and rendered again. In the EnerSearch case, for example, a view is used to restrict the navigation to key concepts. Moreover, a separate view is created for every author, project and year of publication.

For example, the section 'By Author/Ygge, Fredrik' contains the view that restricts the set of pages to those written by the author Fredrik Ygge. Navigation going through this section follows the same structure as navigating over all concepts, except that the selection of pages is immediately limited to those written by the author. The navigation options are cut back as well: the concepts that do not occur in the documents written by the author are not shown any more.

In summary, Spectacle provided large flexibility in creating a presentation from our ontology at the cost of high programming complexity. QuizRDF takes a different tradeoff in generating an interface automatically that cannot be customized by the system developer.

## 23.4  End-user Evaluation

At the current state-of-the-art few applications are known to exist that could provide a cogent demonstration with respect to the potential of ontologies in an industrial setting. Even fewer are the cases where the benefit of using ontologies was scientifically measured and contrasted to more conventional, but also more mature and readily available technologies.

In the following we describe the field experiment carried out by EnerSearch to evaluate the effectiveness of the ontology-based search and browsing interfaces we built against traditional keyword-based searching. We put a special emphasis on the discussion of considerations regarding the design of such an experiment. Those planning to set up and carry out an evaluation with Semantic Web tools might find this especially valuable for their work. Lastly, we turn to the setup of the experiment and summarize the findings.

### 23.4.1 Design Considerations

The goal of our field experiment was measuring the success of information retrieval in the context of the EnerSearch publication base. Upon determining the quality to measure, the first step in the design of our experiment was the identification of the dimensions to be explored. These dimensions would then provide the variables of our measurements.

These dimensions should be chosen to cover significant aspects of the information retrieval task, i.e. aspects that are expected to have a large influence on the effectiveness of information seeking. Also, the dimensions should be preferably orthogonal or at least provide interesting combinations of settings.

For our purposes, we have chosen the dimensions of information modes, user groups and cognitive styles:

1. **Information Modes.** As mentioned before, it is important to establish a clear reference point for comparison. In our case, the reference point was the usual way of gathering information on the web: keyword-based search and simple, taxonomy-based browsing. This provides the yardstick with which we can measure how good alternative semantic approaches are. Here, we consider two different semantic web-style information modes: (i) ontology-based search; (ii) ontology-based browsing. In particular, we measured the conventional keyword-based search tool of EnerSearch (the so called EnerSearcher) against the ontology-based search and browsing interfaces developed using QuizRDF[7] and Spectacle[8].

2. **User groups.** In general it is very important to carry out a proper segmentation of target users in cases where there are significant differences in their relation to the information seeking task.

   In the case of EnerSearch, target user groups and their differentiators are fairly easy to identify. Externally we find interested staff and management in utility companies, while internally researchers involved in IT and energy projects. These two groups are very different. Utility staff is generally more interested in business issues. Even when it concerns new technology, the interest will not first of all be with the technicalities, but more with envisioning the potential applications (what can we do with it?) and establishing the business case for it (what are the benefits?). For researchers, it is more or less the other way around. Refereed publications containing a strong and technically detailed, usually formal, line of argument are key to academics.

   Last but not least, there seems to be (as measured by hits and downloads on the website) a third user group of the EnerSearch website that is much more diffuse, viz. the more general public that is unknown but interested in various bits and pieces of the research results and trends.

3. **Cognitive Style.** Yet another dimension that will influence the outcome of Semantic Web tests and experiments lies in the fact that people differ in the personal style with which they handle information and make corresponding decisions.

   We investigated the workings of Michael Drivers theory on decision styles [5]. According to Drivers work, people differ markedly in how much information they use in decisions (maximizing vs. satisficing personality) and whether they aim at a single definite course

---

[7] Available online at http://i97.labs.bt.com/rdfferret-bin/rdfsearch/pmika2.89

[8] Available online at http://otkdemo.cognit.no

of action or tend to view information as leading to a variety of different possible solutions (unifocus vs. multifocus personality). Here our intention was to find out the possible correlations between the various styles of decision making and the way our users carry out the information retrieval task.

In sum, when it comes to designing Semantic Web experiments, its important to consider a number of different dimensions, including variations in information modes, in target user groups, and in individual information-processing styles. Finally, an experiment must be based on one or more clearly formulated hypotheses that can be verified or falsified, for example by empirical-statistical methods. Based on the above dimensions, a possible list of testable hypotheses regarding Semantic Web-based information seeking is:

1. Users will make fewer mistakes during a search task using the ontology-based semantic access tools than with the current mainstream keyword-based free text search.
2. Users will be able to complete information-finding tasks in less time using the ontology-based semantic access tools than with the current mainstream keyword-based free text search.
3. The reduction in completion and number of mistakes will be more noticeable for less experienced users.
4. The reduction in time will also be more noticeable for users lacking a detailed knowledge of the underlying technical system implementation.
5. The ontology-based semantic access tools will be perceived as more useful than free text search by different types of persons for a broad range of domains and knowledge-acquisition scenarios.
6. The effort for developing and maintaining the ontology and information structure will not significantly exceed the effort to develop and maintaining the free text approach.

In a field experiment, hypotheses such as these are tested for their significance, and it is investigated how their validity varies with different information modes, target user groups, and individual information-processing styles.

## 23.4.2  Setting up the Experiment

A careful analysis of the test environment in terms of the persons involved, the tasks to be performed and methods of measurement is important to identify and neutralize external factors that may influence the results.

In terms of users, a key aspect is to consider previous knowledge (or the lack thereof) with respect to the content (the energy market) and methods (internet search) of the experiment. In our case, we identified three clusters of users through a set of pretrial interviews. As a result, the evaluation experiment includes three different types of interest groups. One group consists of staff members from four different shareholder companies. A second group consists of researchers from different scientific fields, several having at some time participated in EnerSearch projects. The third and final group is intended to represent a general outside audience and consists of students studying at the department of software engineering and computer science at the Blekinge Institute of Technology in Sweden. All of these test users were instructed in the use of all three retrieval tools (EnerSEARCHer, Spectacle, QuizRDF). Those who have not been familiar with EnerSearch (mostly those in the third group) were also introduced to the organization and the current website.

With respect to the task to be performed, all users were presented with a questionnaire of 30 questions over the energy industry. We were aware of the possibility of a transfer error, which means that users will be unlikely to repeat errors the second time they do the task, that they will remember how they did something and will not need to figure it out the second time around. Therefore we mixed up the order of the questions as well as the tools that each test group had to use for answering the questions. In practice, this meant that each group had three sections of the test, with 10 questions each. The order of questions, however, were mixed for each group. Moreover, all groups used different tools to answer different sections of the test.

The method we used to collect the results was designed to be minimally intrusive, yet enforcing the rules of testing. As mentioned before, we designed an online questionnaire for convenience. The layout was such that the questionnaire was showed next to the search tool the participant was using to answer a given question. The questions were showed one by one so the questionnaire occupied only a small segment of the screen. Users were allowed to stop and continue testing at a later time. The system, however, made sure that the participants could not "cheat" by skipping questions, moving backwards or forwards etc.

### 23.4.3  Results of the Experiment

We carried out the evaluation with 45 test persons, which we believe is enough to do statistical comparative studies. The data from the experiment was gathered in a log file maintained by the evaluation server. Each log entry contains the following items: question number, answer (text), name of the user who gave the answer, time duration for answering the question, the group to which the user belongs, the tool used for getting the answer and how easy the user found to answer this question with the particular tool (on a scale from 1-"easy" to 5-"hard" plus 6-"I give up"). Due to a lack of space, we only provide an analysis here with respect to the first two hypotheses we put forward in Sect. 23.4.1. For more information, we refer the reader to [10].

Figure 23.5 shows the calculated results for answering the question: "How relatively often did users give (W)rong, (R)ight or (N)o answers with each tool?". The figure shows the following preliminary results: For EnerSEARCHER, 23,19% of the questions answered in total (with EnerSEARCHer) were wrongly answered, 37,68% were answered right and in 39,13% of the cases the user gave up, thus resulting in having no answer at all for the question. For QuizRDF, 10,20% of the questions were answered wrong, 57,14% were answered right and in 32,65% the user gave up. For Spectacle, 23,73% of the questions were answered wrong, 40,68% were answered right and in 35,59% of the cases the user gave up.

Thus, as a first result, our hypothesis 2, "Users will make fewer mistakes during a search task using the ontology-based semantic access tools than with the current mainstream keyword-based free text search", is supported by this result.

Figure 23.6 shows the calculated results for answering the question: "What was the relative average time our users needed for (W)rong, (R)ight or (N)o answer of one single question?". We highlight the most relevant detail of this figure (the reader might use the figure for further interpretations): To answer a question right, users needed in average the shortest amount of time with QuizRDF (25,77%), followed by EnerSEARCHer (34,71%) and Spectacle (39,52%).

Thus, as a second result, our hypothesis 1, "Users will be able to complete information-finding tasks in less time using the ontology-based semantic access tools than with the current mainstream keyword-based free text search", is partially supported by this result.

Note that due to the method of evaluation and the use of an online questionnaire in specific, participants of our evaluation were not constrained by time in providing answers. As a result, for some of the answers we measured answer times beyond the typical time. We detected such outliers and excluded them from the sample.

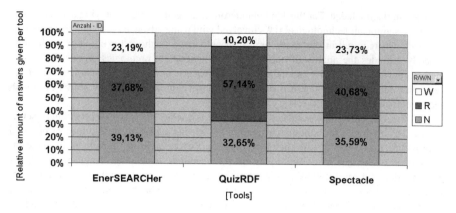

**Fig. 23.5.** How relatively often did users give (W)rong, (R)ight or (N)o answers with each tool?

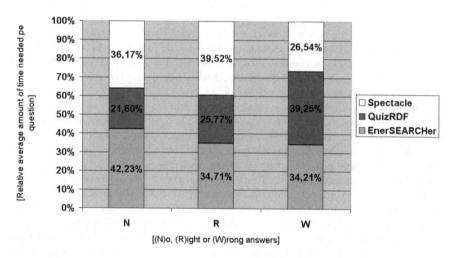

**Fig. 23.6.** What relative average amount of time needed users for (W)rong, (R)ight or (N)o answer to a single question?

## 23.5 Conclusions

In this paper we have demonstrated the building of a practical ontology-based application, starting from an analysis of the context and use case to the evaluation of the final system by the end users. Although industrial applications such as the one demonstrated are closely fitted for a particular setting, several conclusions may be drawn from our experience with the technology. Those planning to engage in constructing an ontology-based system for Knowledge Management may find the following points worth considering.

The business case for ontology-based search and navigation is particularly strong for virtual enterprises, such as EnerSearch, whose main value driver is the creation and dissemination of (scientific) knowledge. For this kind of enterprise, the gains from employing ontologies can offset the significant technological risks involved with using advanced semantic technologies.

Although required in our case, the use of automated methods for ontology acquisition severely degrades the quality of ontologies. The lightweight ontologies produced by these methods are low in formality and indiscriminate in the use of modelling constructs. Nevertheless, our evaluation shows that it is possible to improve on keyword-based search even with such ontologies.

Further, our case study validated the On-To-Knowledge approach of providing a set of tools and technologies for building customized knowledge management solutions, as opposed to providing a one-size-fits-all knowledge system. Beyond a strong agreement over the interpretation of the data model (which is not fully captured in ontology languages) such approach requires a careful consideration with regard to the overall architecture. In our case, we identified a bottleneck in integrating the ontology storage facility and the ontology-based applications: the division of query and transformation work between client and server inhibited creating applications that would have scaled up to industrial standards. The fact that such bottlenecks show up only as a result of integration suggests that more effort is needed to investigate scalable, modular frameworks (architectures) of ontology-based applications.

When working with automatically generated lightweight ontologies special attention needs to be paid to the design of interfaces. Interfaces for retrieval should hide the weaknesses of the ontology while still make use of the available semantics. As we learned, such adaptation or customization requires a complex transformation from an ontology to the search or browsing interface. Due to their complexity, these transformations need to be described in a programmatic way, as with the Spectacle tool.

The evaluation of ontology-based systems in the field require a very careful experiment design. In most cases evaluation on a solely technical basis is not enough; most semantics-based systems by their very nature rely on the human to interpret and rate the outcome. Therefore prospective test user groups and test tasks must be carefully balanced with respect to the dimensions to be measured. Hypotheses or expectations must be explicitly formulated in advance. Empirical data gathering in such experiments must be rich, including various qualitative methods - such as pre- and post-trial semi-open interviews, collecting verbal protocols during the experiment, onsite observation - as well as quantitative methods - for example electronic logging of actions and execution times, and statistical processing of resulting data.

Lastly, we may note that the proof of the Semantic Web pudding is in the eating: additional industrial cases and long term experience with the use and maintenance of ontology-based systems would be necessary to ascertain the scope of the results with regard to ontology-based methods.

# References

1. The On-To-Knowledge project (EU-IST-1999-10132).
   http://www.ontoknowledge.org.
2. John Davies, Dieter Fensel, and Frank van Harmelen, editors. *Towards the Semantic Web: Ontology-Driven Knowledge Management*. John Wiley & Sons, 2003.
3. John Davies, Richard Weeks, and Uwe Krohn. QuizRDF: Search Technology for the Semantic Web. In *Real World RDF and Semantic Web Applications Workshop, colocated with WWW2002*, 2002.

4. Rose Dieng, Olivier Corby, Alain Giboin, and Myriam Ribiere. Methods and Tools for Corporate Knowledge Management. *International Journal of Human-Computer Studies (IJHCS)*, 51:567–598, 1999.
5. Michael J. Driver, Kenneth R. Brousseau, and Phillip L. Hunsaker. *The Dynamic Decision Maker*. Jossey-Bass, San Francisco, CA, 1993.
6. Dublin Core Metadata Element Set, Version 1.1: Reference Description. http://dublincore.org/documents/dces/, July 1999.
7. Dieter Fensel, Frank van Harmelen, Ying Ding, Michel Klein, Peter Mika, Hans Akkermans, Jeen Broekstra, Arjohn Kampman, Jos van der Meer, Rudi Studer, York Sure, John Davies, Alistair Duke, Robert Engels, Victor Iosif, Atanas Kiryakov, Thorsten Lau, Ulrich Reimer, and Ian Horrocks. Final Report. On-To-Knowledge Deliverable 43, 2002.
8. Tom R. Gruber. Towards Principles for the Design of Ontologies Used for Knowledge Sharing. In N. Guarino and R. Poli, editors, *Formal Ontology in Conceptual Analysis and Knowledge Representation*, Deventer, The Netherlands, 1993. Kluwer Academic Publishers.
9. Patrick Hayes. RDF Model Theory. Technical report, World Wide Web Consortium (W3C), November 2002.
10. Victor Iosif and Peter Mika. EnerSearch Virtual Organization Case Study: Evaluation Document. On-To-Knowledge Deliverable 29, 2002.
11. Gregory Karvounarakis, Sofia Alexaki, Vassilis Christophides, Dimitris Plexousakis, and Michel Scholl. RQL: A Declarative Query Language for RDF. In *Proceedings of the 11th International Conference on the WWW (WWW2002)*, Hawaii, 2002.
12. Peter Mika. Applied Ontology-based Knowledge Management: A Report on the State-of-the-Art. Master's thesis, Vrije Universiteit, Amsterdam, Amsterdam, August 2002.
13. Peter Mika. Integrating Ontology Storage and Ontology-based Applications Through Client-side Query and Transformations. In *Proceedings of Evaluation of Ontology-based Tools (EON2002) workshop at EKAW2002, Sigüenza, Spain*, 2002.
14. Marta Sabou. Employing Ontological Metadata in Information Presentation. Master's thesis, Vrije Universiteit, Amsterdam, August 2001.
15. Marta Sabou. Creating portals using light-weight ontologies: a transformational approach. Submitted for STAIRS'2002 and accepted as poster, 2002.
16. Andrew Seaborne. RDQL: A Data Oriented Query Language for RDF Models. Technical report, Hewlett-Packard, 2001.
17. Mike Uschold and Robert Jasper. A Framework for Understanding and Classifying Ontology Applications. In *Proceedings of the IJCAI99 Workshop on Ontologies and Problem-Solving Methods(KRR5), Stockholm, Sweden*, 1999.

# 24

# Ontology-based Recommender Systems

Stuart E. Middleton, David De Roure and Nigel R. Shadbolt

Intelligence, Agents, Multimedia Group,
Department of Electronics and Computer Science, University of Southampton,
Southampton, SO17 1BJ, UK
{sem99r,dder,nrs}@ecs.soton.ac.uk

**Summary.** We explore a novel ontological approach to user profiling within recommender systems, working on the problem of recommending on-line academic
research papers. Our two experimental systems, Quickstep and Foxtrot, create user
profiles from unobtrusively monitored behaviour and relevance feedback, representing the profiles in terms of a research paper topic ontology. A novel profile
visualization approach is taken to acquire profile feedback. Research papers are
classified using ontological classes and collaborative recommendation algorithms
used to recommend papers seen by similar people on their current topics of interest. Ontological inference is shown to improve user profiling, external ontological
knowledge used to successfully bootstrap a recommender system and profile visualization employed to improve profiling accuracy.
Two small-scale experiments, with 24 subjects over 3 months, and a large-scale
experiment, with 260 subjects over an academic year, are conducted to evaluate
different aspects of our approach. The overall performance of our ontological recommender systems are also presented and favourably compared to other systems
in the literature.

## 24.1 Introduction

The mass of content available on the World-Wide Web raises important questions
over its effective use. Information on the web is largely unstructured, with web
pages authored by many people on a diverse range of topics. This makes simple
browsing too time consuming to be practical. Web page filtering has thus become
necessary for most web users in order to find the things they need.

Search engines are effective at filtering pages that match explicit queries. Unfortunately, most people find articulating a search query to specify what they need
difficult, especially if forced to use a limited vocabulary such as keywords. As

such search queries are often poorly formulated, resulting in long lists of search results that contain only a few useful pages.

The Semantic Web offers some potential for help, allowing more intelligent search of web pages by utilizing semantic metadata. Semantic Web technology is, however, very dependant on the degree to which web pages are annotated by their authors. Annotation requires a degree of selflessness in authors because the annotations provided do not directly help the authors themselves. Because of this, the vast majority of web pages are not annotated, and in the foreseeable future will not become so. This lack of annotation will compromise the ability of the semantic web to enhance effective search and retrieval.

### 24.1.1 Recommender systems

People find articulating exactly what they want difficult, but they are good at recognizing it when they see it. This insight has led to the utilization of relevance feedback, where people rate items as interesting or not interesting and the system tries to find items that match the "interesting", positive examples and do not match the "not interesting", negative examples. With sufficient positive and negative examples, modern machine learning techniques can classify new pages with impressive accuracy.

Obtaining sufficient examples is difficult however, especially when trying to obtain negative examples. The problem with asking people for examples is that the cost, in terms of time and effort, of providing the examples generally outweighs the reward people will eventually receive. Negative examples are particularly unrewarding, since there could be many irrelevant items to any typical query.

Unobtrusive monitoring provides positive examples of what the user is looking for, without interfering with the user's normal work activity. Heuristics can also be applied to infer negative examples from observed behaviour, although generally with less confidence. This idea has led to content-based recommender systems, which unobtrusively watch user behaviour and recommend new items that correlate with a user's profile.

Another way to recommend items is based on the ratings provided by other people who have liked the item before. Collaborative recommender systems do this by asking people to rate items explicitly and then recommend new items that similar users have rated highly. An issue with collaborative filtering is that there is no direct reward for providing examples since they only help other people. This leads to initial difficulties in obtaining a sufficient number of ratings for the system to be useful, a problem known as the cold-start problem [15].

Hybrid systems, attempting to combine the advantages of content-based and collaborative recommender systems, have also proved popular to-date. The feedback required for content-based recommendation is shared, allowing collaborative recommendation as well.

Recommender systems can recommend many types of item, including web pages, new articles, music CDs and books. Normally a database of some sort exists in a recommender system, containing a set of items that can be recommended. If enough feature information is available about items then a content-based approach can be employed, using machine-learning techniques to find content-based patterns. If many users require the same type of items then a collaborative approach can be employed, sharing the likes and dislikes of previous users.

### 24.1.2 User profiling

User profiling is typically either knowledge-based or behaviour-based. Knowledge-based approaches use static models of users and dynamically match users to the closest model. Questionnaires and interviews are often employed to obtain this user knowledge. Once a model is selected for a user, specialist domain knowledge for that user type can be applied to help the user. Behaviour-based approaches use the user's behaviour as a model, commonly using machine-learning techniques to discover useful patterns in the behaviour. Behavioural logging is employed to obtain the data necessary from which to extract patterns. [11] provides a good survey of user modelling techniques.

The user profiling approach used by most recommender systems is behavioural-based, commonly using a binary class model to represent what users find interesting and not interesting. Machine-learning techniques are then used to find potential items of interest in respect to the binary model, recommending items that match the positive examples and do not match the negative examples. There are a lot of effective machine learning algorithms based on two classes. A binary profile does not, however, lend itself to sharing examples of interest or integrating any domain knowledge that might be available. [19] provides a good survey of current machine learning techniques.

In our recommender systems we employ a multi-class user profile representation, using classes that represent each topic of interest. Each class has a set of examples. This allows us to map classes of interest to classes within an ontology. The example ontology we use is a simple is-a taxonomy where classes are connected using generalization relationships. We can then use the relationships within the ontology to assist the profiling process, inferring interest in classes not directly observed through the monitoring of behaviour. This however comes at the price of a lower classification accuracy, due to splitting examples between many classes, from the machine learning technique employed.

### 24.1.3 Ontologies

An ontology is a conceptualisation of a domain into a human-understandable, but machine-readable format consisting of entities, attributes, relationships, and axioms [9]. Ontologies can provide a rich conceptualisation of the working domain of an organisation, representing the main concepts and relationships of the work activities. These relationships could represent isolated information such as an employee's home phone number, or they could represent an activity such as authoring a document, or attending a conference.

Ontologies can assist recommender systems in a variety of ways, which we demonstrate by way of three experiments conducted on a couple of recommender systems. The problem domain in which we base our experimental recommender systems is described next.

### 24.1.4 Problem domain

The Web is increasingly becoming the primary source of research papers to the modern researcher. With millions of research papers available over the web from thousands of web sites, finding the right papers and being informed of newly available papers is a problematic task. Browsing this many web sites is too time consuming and search queries are only fully effective if an explicit search query can be formulated for what you need. All too often papers are missed.

We address the problem of recommending on-line research papers to the academic staff and students at the University of Southampton. Academics need to search for explicit research papers and be kept up-to-date on their own research areas when new papers are published. We examine an ontological recommender system approach to support these two activities. Unobtrusive monitoring methods are preferred because researchers have their normal work to perform and would not welcome interruptions from a new system. Very high accuracy on individual recommendations is not critical since recommendations are presented in manageable sets, allowing users to ignore poor recommendations and choose the good ones. What is important that there is at least one good recommendation each visit.

Real world knowledge acquisition systems [20] are both tricky and complex to evaluate. A lot of evaluations are performed with user log data, simulating real user activity, or with standard benchmark collections, such as newspaper articles over a period of one year, that provide a basis for comparison with other systems. Although these evaluations are useful, especially for technique comparison, it is important to back them up with real world studies so we can see how the benchmark tests generalize to the real world setting. Similar problems are seen in the agent domain where, as Nwana [18] describes, it is difficult to extrapolate from benchmark tests to real world usefulness without substantial experimentation. This is why a real problem has been chosen upon which to evaluate our work.

### 24.1.5 Evaluation overview

Three experiments are described later that were performed on our two recommender systems. The first experiment used the Quickstep recommender system [16] to measure the effectiveness of using ontological inference in user profiling. Two 1.5 month trials were run using 24 members from the IAM research laboratory, comparing use of ontological profiles and inference to that of using unstructured profiles.

The second experiment integrated the Quickstep system with a personnel and publication ontology. This experiment measured how effectively an external ontology can bootstrap a recommender system to reduce the recommender system cold-start problem [15]. Behaviour logs from the previous experiment were used as the basis for this evaluation.

The third experiment took the Foxtrot recommender system and measured its overall effectiveness and the performance increase obtained when profiles are visualized and profile feedback acquired. The trial was run using 260 staff and students from the computer science department of the University of Southampton for an academic year, comparing performance of those subjects who provided profile feedback to those who did not.

## 24.2 Key aspects of a recommender system

There are several key aspects a recommender system must provide in order to be successful. There must be a database of items from which recommendations can be formulated, and for content-based recommendation a classifier must be able to match items in the database to positive and negative examples of user interest. Examples of interest are normally obtained via interface feedback or behaviour monitoring, and a profiler used to create individual user profiles. A recommender algorithm is then used to correlate the user profiles with appropriate items in the database, formulating a set of recommendations for each user. Recommender systems work with a set of users, all sharing in some way behavioural information for the common good. The term 'recommender' is used since system suggestions derive from other people's experience. Figure 1 describes a generic recommender system approach.

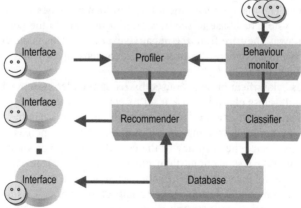

Fig. 1. Generic recommender system

## 24.2.1 Database

Recommender system databases come in a variety of forms. Many systems do not use a formal database package, instead opting for a simple list if items held in a useful representation. Information held within the database will depend on the problem domain. For music CD recommendation, each CD's artist, publisher, set of tracks etc. may be stored, where as for book recommendation the author, title, genre and reviews may be stored. What matters is that each item in the database has a set of features associated with it, so that the profiler can create a profile of the domain features a user prefers.

Our two experimental recommender systems use a simple flat database of research papers, containing a term vector of normalized word frequencies for each paper along with date, title, classification, links and source URL feature information. The classifier then uses these features to categorize new research papers based on a set of training examples. The labels for the training examples are taken from a research paper topic ontology.

Of related interest to our academic problem domain are digital library systems. Specifically, systems such as CiteSeer [4] and CORA [14] maintain large digital libraries of research papers using a manual categorization according to a manually created ontology of computer science topics. Where our recommender systems differ is that our database of research papers is automatically updated by the browsing of the users, as opposed to growing via manual additions to the library.

## 24.2.2 Classification

Content-based recommender systems require some form of classification algorithm in order to perform similarity matching, allowing items of interest to be identified. Recommender systems typically hold a set of positive and negative examples of interest, using these example items as a training set for a machine learning algorithm. The machine learning algorithm then classifies new items in the recommender system database to see how similar they are to the positive examples, and how far away they are from the negative examples. This is the common binary classification model, where the user profile consists of two classes of example, positive and negative.

Multi-class classification is also used by recommender systems, but is not very common. Multi-class classifiers use a set of classes to categorize items, and use a separate training set of example items for each class. This has the advantage that users can use a common training set, sharing examples to increase the size of the training set and hence the accuracy of the classifier. However, multi-class classification is inherently less accurate than binary class classification, since the more classes there are the lower the classification accuracy will be.

Both our recommender systems take a multi-class approach, using a set of ontological classes to represent research paper topics. We use a k-Nearest Neighbour variant IBk classifier [1], which we boost using an AdaBoostM1 [7] algorithm.

Each class within our research paper topic ontology has a manually created set of example papers, used by the classifier for a training set. This is a new approach in the field of recommender systems.

A classic example of a content-based recommender system is Fab [2], which uses a binary class k-Nearest Neighbour classifier. Other binary class examples include personal assistant agents such as NewsDude [3], using a naive Bayes classifier, and NewsWeeder [13], using a TF-IDF based classifier, which profile individual user interests and try to find items of interest. An example of multi-class recommendation is RAAP [6], which uses a simple set of categories to represent individual user profiles. Many machine learning techniques are utilized outside the field of recommender systems, but we have constrained ourselves to look only at the recommender system domain.

### 24.2.3 Behaviour monitoring

Behaviour monitoring is needed in some form to obtain the behavioural information required by the profiler. While it is possible to ask users for information about what they are doing in an intrusive way, this would continually interrupt normal workflow and hence severely limit the usefulness the system. Unobtrusive monitoring methods are thus used by recommender systems.

One common method of obtaining behaviour is to record all user interaction with the recommender system itself. This works best when the system allows browsing of items, such as books or music, since items the user looks at can be used as examples of positive interest. Negative examples of interest are difficult to infer, however, since it is difficult to discriminate between items avoided because they are not interesting and items as yet unseen because the user is unaware of them.

Monitoring browsing behaviour can be achieved by using a web proxy, which acts as a middleman between the web browser and final connection. A web proxy can thus log all browsed URLs, along with who is browsing and when.

One other common technique is to use existing logged information such as newsgroup postings. Such information is generated by users and can hold rich information about user preferences.

Our two recommender systems use a web proxy to monitor user browsing, and also log all interactions with the system and any feedback provided by users. In the Foxtrot recommender system profiles are visualized and profile feedback acquired. This gives the profiler several rich sources of information with which to build user profiles.

Logging of user interaction is employed by many systems such Fab [2], which records user feedback on recommendations, and NewsDude [3], which logs voice feedback on news stories. An example of the web proxy approach is Personal WebWatcher [17] and the GroupLens [12] project is an example of a system using existing newsgroup articles to provide a recommendation service.

## 24.2.4 Interface

Interfaces used by recommender systems vary widely, with web-based interfaces being the most common. Web pages lend themselves well to serving the needs of the multiple users. Relevance feedback is often elicited by offering a 5 or 7-point scale so users can comment on items, and the recommendations themselves are often displayed as a side bar to a web page or in a search engine style list.

Both of our recommender systems use a web interface, exploiting the search engine metaphor to display recommendation results. The Foxtrot system visualizes user profiles via a time/interest graph, allowing users to draw their own interests on the visualizations via a drawing package style interface. This provides profile feedback for the profiler. Email notification is also supported by Foxtrot, notifying users each week of the top three recommended research papers.

## 24.2.5 Profiling

User profiling in most recommender systems is closely linked to the classification process. The user profile structure consists of a set of positive and negative examples of interest, which are used by the classifier to identify items of likely interest. The number of examples in a user profile increases as a result of observing user behaviour. This approach only models the users overall interests, taking no account of the interests that are most current to a user or interests associated with a transient task.

Multi-class recommender systems represent user profiles in terms of the categories users are interested in, rather than a raw set of examples. Profiles thus hold the topics of interest to a user; no account is made of current interests.

A few recommender systems support two user models, one for short-term interests and one for longer-term interests. The short-term interest profile holds a set of recent examples of interest while the long-term interest profile holds the set of all examples of interest. With a long and short term profile recommendations are often split into two sets, each based on one type of user profile.

Both our recommender systems use a multi-class ontological representation of user profiles, storing the ontological classes of interest to each user. Ontological inference is then used to infer other general interests, beyond that which can be directly observed. A time-decay function is applied to the profile's interest values to ensure that current interests dominate historical interests. In the Foxtrot recommender system direct profile feedback is acquired and used to explicitly set interest values. It should be noted that we model the topics of interests of a user, and not the direct relevance of individual papers to that user in the way a binary profile would model. The granularity of our profiles is thus at the topic level not the specific paper level.

The vast majority of recommender systems use a single historical profile, such as Fab [2] or RAAP [6]. NewsDude [3] supports the idea of a long and short term model.

**24.2.6 Recommendation**

Content-based recommender systems recommend items with the highest similarity to the positive examples; the classifier performs this similarity measurement. If other information, such as a quality rating, is available then the list of potential items can be sorted into a ranked order and the top few items chosen for recommendation.

Collaborative recommendation aims to find similar people whose profiles closely match the profile of a target user, for which recommendations are being formulated. This correlation is often performed by a statistical function, with the Pearson r correlation being the most popular in the literature today. A good overview of statistical correlation techniques is provided by [10]. Having obtained a list of similar users, the top few are selected upon which to base recommendations. The similar user's behaviour can then be examined to identify interesting items that are new to the target user. The top few items found form the basis for the target users recommendations.

Our Quickstep recommender system uses a simple content-based approach to recommendation, taking items that match a current user's profile and recommending the closest matches. Our Foxtrot recommender system expends on this method and adds a collaborative method, based on a Pearson r correlation of user profiles.

GroupLens [12] is an early example of the popular Pearson r correlation technique, while Fab [2] is an example of a simple content-based recommendation algorithm.

## 24.3 Ontological recommender systems

Our two experimental recommender systems, Quickstep and Foxtrot, explore the novel idea of using an ontological approach to user profiling in the context of recommender systems. Representing user interests in ontological terms involves losing some of the fine grained information held in the raw examples of interest, but in turn allows inference to assist user profiling, communication with other external ontologies and visualization of the profiles using ontological terms understandable to users. Figure 2 shows the general approach taken by both our recommender systems. Quickstep implements only the basic recommendation interface, while Foxtrot implements all the shown features.

A research paper topic ontology is shared between all system processes, allowing both classifications and user profiles to use a common terminology. The ontology itself contains is-a relationships between appropriate topic classes; a section from the topic ontology is shown in figure 3. The Quickstep ontology was based on the open directory project's [8] computer science topic classification, while the Foxtrot ontology was based on the CORA [14] digital library paper classification; manual enhancements were made to each ontology to better reflect some of the more specialist sub-topics researchers required. Re-using existing classifications saves time and provides a source for training examples, especially with the CORA digital library, which contained many pre-classified research papers.

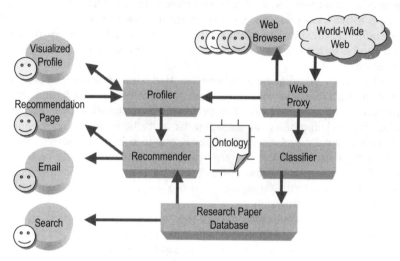

Fig. 2. Our ontological approach to recommender systems

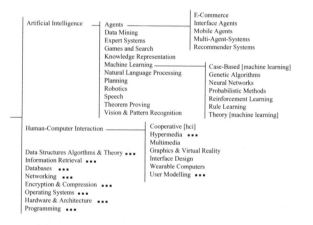

Fig. 3. Section from the Foxtrot research paper topic ontology

### 24.3.1 Classification using a research paper topic ontology

Sharing training examples, within the structure of an ontology, allows for much larger training sets than would be possible if a single user just provided examples of personal interest. Larger training sets improve classifier accuracy. However, multi-class classification is inherently less accurate than binary class classification, so the increased training set size has to be weighed along with the reduction in accuracy that occurs with every extra class the system supports.

Both the Quickstep and Foxtrot recommender systems use the research paper topic ontology to base paper classifications upon. A set of labelled example papers is manually provided for each class within the ontology, and then used by the classifier as a labelled training set. In the Quickstep system users can add new examples of papers as time goes by, allowing the training set to reflect the continually changing needs of the users.

In addition to larger training sets, having users share a common ontology enforces a consistent conceptual model, which removes some of the subjective nature of selecting categories for research papers. A common conceptual model also helps users to understand how the recommender system works, which helps form reasonable user expectations and assists in building trust and a feeling of control over what the system is doing.

### 24.3.2 Ontological inference to assist user profiling

Ontological inference is a powerful tool to assist user profiling. An ontology could contain all sorts of useful knowledge about users and their interests, such as related research subjects, technologies behind each subject area, projects people are working on, etc. This knowledge can be used to infer more interests than can be seen by just observation.

Our two experimental recommender systems both use ontological inference to enhance user profiles. Is-a relationships within the research paper topic ontology are used to infer interest in more general, super-class topics. We add 50% of the interest in a specific class to the super-class. This inference has the effect of rounding out profiles, making them more inclusive and attuning them to the broad interests of a user.

The profiling algorithm used is shown in figure 4. A time-decay function is applied to the observed behaviour events to form the basic profile. Inference is then used to enhance the interest profile, with the 50% inference rule applied to all ontological is-a relationships, up to the root class, for each observed event.

$$\text{Topic interest} = \sum_{1..\text{no of instances}}^{n} \text{Interest value}(n) / \text{days old}(n)$$

Event
interest values
Paper browsed = 1
Recommendation followed = 2
Topic rated interesting = 10
Topic rated not interesting = -10

Interest value for
super-class per instance = 50% of sub-class

Fig. 4. Profiling algorithm

The event interest values were chosen to balance the feedback in favour of explicitly provided feedback, which is likely to be the most reliable. The 50% inference value was chosen to reflect the reduction in certainty you get the further away from the observed behaviour you move. Determining optimal values for these parameters would require further empirical evaluation.

### 24.3.3 Bootstrapping with an external ontology

Recommender systems suffer from the cold-start problem [15], where the lack of initial behavioural information significantly reduces the accuracy of user profiles, and hence recommendations. This poor performance can deter users from adopting the system, which of course prevents the system from acquiring more behaviour data; it is possible that a recommender system will never be used enough to overcome its cold-start.

In one of our experiments we take an external ontology containing publication and personnel data about academic researchers and integrate it with the Quickstep recommender system. The knowledge held within the external ontology is used to bootstrap initial user profiles, with the aim of reducing the cold-start effect. The external ontology uses the same research topic ontology as the Quickstep system, providing a firm basis for communication. The external ontology contains publications and authorship relationships, projects and project membership, staff and their roles and other such knowledge. Knowledge of publications held within the external ontology is used to infer historical interests for new users, and network analysis of ontological relationships is used to discover similar users whose own interests might be used to bootstrap a new user's profile.

The two bootstrapping algorithms used in our experiment are shown in figures 5 and 6. The new-system initial profile algorithm takes all the publications of a user and creates a profile of historical interests. The assumption is that a user's previous publications indicate that user's interests. The new-user initial profile algorithm takes a set of similar users, obtained via network analysis of the external ontologies project membership and inter-staff relationships, and includes these users interests into the bootstrap profile. Historical publication interests from the new user are also added as before.

$$\text{topic interest}(t) = \sum_{\substack{1..\text{ publications} \\ \text{belonging to class } t}}^{n} 1 \,/\, \text{publication age}(n)$$

new-system initial profile = (t, topic interest(t))*

t = <research paper topic>

$$\begin{array}{l}\text{Interest value for} \\ \text{super-class per topic}\end{array} = 50\% \text{ of sub-class}$$

Fig. 5. New-system initial profile algorithm

$$\text{topic interest}(t) = \frac{\gamma}{N_{\text{similar}}} \sum_{1..\,N_{\text{similar}}}^{u} \text{profile interest}(u,t)$$

$$+ \sum_{1..\,N_{\text{pubs } t}}^{n} 1 \,/\, \text{publication age}(n)$$

profile interest(u,t) = interest of user u in topic t * confidence
new-user initial profile = (t, topic interest(t))*

t = research paper topic
u = user
$\gamma$ = weighting constant >= 0
$N_{\text{similar}}$ = number of similar users
$N_{\text{pubs } t}$ = number of publications belonging to class t
confidence = confidence in similarity of user

$$\begin{array}{l}\text{Interest value for} \\ \text{super-class per topic}\end{array} = 50\% \text{ of sub-class}$$

Fig. 6. New-user initial profile algorithm

In addition to using the ontology to bootstrap the recommender system, our experiment uses the interest profiles held within the recommender system to continually update the external ontology. Interest acquisition is a problematic task for ontologies that are based on static knowledge sources, and this synergistic relationship provides a useful source of personal knowledge about individual researchers.

### 24.3.4 Profile visualization using ontological concepts

Since users can understand the topics held within the ontology, the user profiles can be visualized. These visualizations allow users to see what the system thinks they are interested in and hence allow them to gain an insight into how the system works. Profile visualization thus provides users with a conceptual model of how the profiling algorithm works, allowing users to gain trust in the system and providing users with a feeling of control over what's going on. With a better conceptual model user expectations should be more realistic.

The Foxtrot recommender system visualizes profiles using a time/interest graph. In addition to simply visualizing profiles, a drawing package metaphor is used to allow users to draw interest bars directly onto the time/interest graph. This allows the system to acquire direct profile feedback, which can be used by the profiler to improve profile accuracy and hence recommendation accuracy. Figure 7 shows the profile visualization interface.

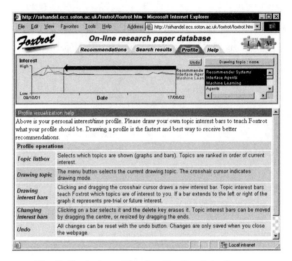

Fig. 7. Foxtrot profile visualization interface

## 24.4 Experimentation

We have conducted three experiments with our two recommender systems. The Quickstep recommender system is used to measure the performance gain seen when using profile inference, and the reduction in the cold-start seen when an external ontology is used for bootstrapping. The Foxtrot recommender system is used to measure the effect profile visualization has on profile accuracy, and to perform a large-scale assessment of our overall ontological approach to recommender systems.

### 24.4.1 Using ontological inference to improve recommendation accuracy

Our first experiment used the Quickstep recommender system to compare subjects whose profiles were computed using ontological inference with subjects whose profiles did not use ontological inference. Two identical trials were conducted, the first with 14 subjects and the second with 24 subjects, both over 1.5 months; some interface improvements were made for the second trial. Subjects were taken from researchers in a computer science laboratory and split into two groups; one group used a topic ontology and profile inference while the other group used an unstructured flat list of topics with no profile inference. An overall evaluation of the Quickstep recommender system was also performed. This experiment is published in more detail in [16].

This experiment found that ontological profile users provided more favourable feedback and had superior recommendation accuracy. Figures 8 and 9 shows these results. Users provide feedback on their individual recommendations, rating them as 'interesting', 'uninteresting' or 'no comment'. Good topics are those not rated as 'uninteresting' by users. A jump is where the user jumps to a recommended paper by opening it via the web browser. Jumps are correlated with topic interest feedback, so a good jump is a jump to a paper on a good topic. Recommendation accuracy is the ratio of good jumps to recommendations, and is an indication of the quality of the recommendations being made as well as the accuracy of the profile.

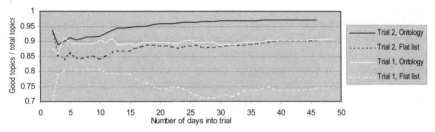

Fig. 8. Good topics to total topics ratio

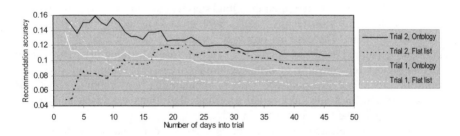

Fig. 9. Recommendation accuracy

The ontology groups from the two trials have a 7% and 15% higher topic acceptance. In addition to this trend, the first trial ratios are about 10% lower than the second trial ratios, probably as a result of the interface improvements that made the feedback options less confusing. There is a small 1% improvement in recommendation accuracy by the ontology group. Both trials show between 7-11% recommendation accuracy.

Since 10 recommendations were provided at a time, a recommendation accuracy of 10% means that on average there was one good recommendation in each set presented to the user. We regard providing one good recommendation upon each visit to the recommendation web site as demonstrating significant utility.

Direct comparison of these results with other recommender systems in the literature is difficult due to the lack of published trials with real users. Entrée [5] is a restaurant recommender system that uses a knowledge-base, reporting a recommendation accuracy of 65-70% based on analysis of historically logged user activity of a web site; however, a random choice algorithm obtained 57-60% accuracy so the Entrée system makes just a 5-13% improvement on random guessing. NewsWeeder [13] is a personal assistant agent that uses a content-based user profile, reporting 40-60% classifier accuracy in a 2 user trial. In cross-validation tests Quickstep has reports 45-50% classifier accuracy, but this does not take into account the power inference brings to the final recommendation accuracy. When the difficulty of our problem domain with real users is taken into account, Quickstep compares favourably with other systems in the literature with 7-11% recommendation accuracy.

While not statistically significant due to sample size, the results suggest how using ontological inference in the profiling process results in superior performance over using a flat list of unstructured topics. The ontology users tended to have more "rounder" profiles, including topics of interest that were not directly browsed. This increased the accuracy of the profiles, and hence usefulness of the recommendations.

### 24.4.2 Ontological bootstrapping to reduce the cold-start problem

Our second experiment integrated the Quickstep recommender system with an external ontology to evaluate how using ontological knowledge could reduce the cold-start problem. The external ontology used was based on a publication database and personnel database, coupled with a tool for performing network analysis of ontological relationships to discover similar users. The behavioural log data from the previous experiment was used to simulate the bootstrapping effect both the new-system and new-user initial profiling algorithms would have. This experiment is published in more detail in [15].

Subjects were selected from those in the previous experiment who had entries within the external ontology. We selected nine subjects in total and their URL browsing logs were broken up into weekly log entries. Seven weeks of browsing behaviour were taken from the start of the Quickstep trials, and an empty log created to simulate the very start of the trial where no behaviour has yet been recorded.

Two bootstrapping algorithms were tested, the new-system and new-user initial profile algorithms describes earlier. The new-system algorithm bootstraps a completely cold-start, so we tested from week 0 to 7. The new-user algorithm requires the system to have been running for a while, so we added the new user on week 7, after the new-system cold-start was over.

Two measurements were made to measure the reduction in the cold-start. The first, profile precision, measures how many topics were mentioned in both the bootstrapped profile and benchmark profile. Profile precision is an indication of how quickly the profile is converging to the final state, and thus how quickly the effects of the cold-start are overcome. The second, profile error rate, measures how many topics appeared in the bootstrapped profile that did not appear within the benchmark profile. Profile error rate is an indication of the errors introduced by the two bootstrapping algorithms. Figure 10 shows the precision results. The new-user result appears on week 0 to indicate the first week for the new-user, even though the system itself had been running for 7 weeks.

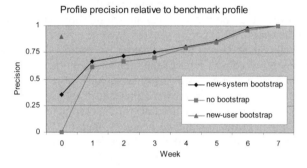

Fig. 10. Bootstrapping algorithm performance

The new-system algorithm produced profiles with a low error rate of 0.06 and a reasonable precision of 0.35. This reflects that previous publications are a good indication of users current interests, and so can produce a good starting point for a bootstrap profile. The new-user algorithm achieved good precision of 0.84 at the expense of a significant 0.55 error rate.

This experiment suggests that using an ontology to bootstrap user profiles can significantly reduce the impact of the recommender system cold-start problem. It is particularly useful for the new-system cold-start problem, where the alternative is to start with no information at all and hence a profile precision of zero.

### 24.4.3 Visualizing profiles to improve profile accuracy

Our third experiment used the Foxtrot recommender system to compare subjects who could visualize their profiles and provide profile feedback with subjects who could only use traditional relevance feedback. An overall evaluation of the Foxtrot recommender system was also performed.

This experimental trial took place over the academic year 2002, starting in November and ending in July. Of the 260 subjects registered to use the system, 103 used the web page, and of these 37 subjects used the system 3 or more times. All 260 subjects used the web proxy and hence their browsing was recorded and daily profiles built. By the end of the trial the research paper database had grown from 6,000 to 15,792 documents as a result of subject web browsing.

Subjects were divided into two groups. The first 'profile feedback' group had full access to the system and its profile visualization and profile feedback options; the second 'relevance feedback' group were denied access to the profile interface. It was found that many in the 'profile feedback' group did not provide any profile feedback at all, so in the later analysis these subjects are moved into the 'relevance feedback' group. A total of 9 subjects provided profile feedback

Towards the end of the trial an additional email feature was added to the recommender system. This email feature sent out weekly emails to all users who had used the system at least once, detailing the top three papers in their current recommendation set. Email notification was started in May and ran for the remaining 3 months of the trial.

Recommendation accuracy was measured, recording the number of recommended papers browsed as a ratio of the number recommended. Profile accuracy and profile predictive accuracy was also measured. Profile accuracy measures the number of papers jumped to or browsed that match the top 3 profile topics each day. This is a good measure of the accuracy of the current interests within a profile at any given time. Profile predictive accuracy measures the number of papers jumped to or browsed that match the top 3 profile topics in a 4 week period after the day the profile was created. This measures the ability of a profile to predict subject interests. Figures 11 and 12 show these results.

The 'profile feedback' group outperformed the 'relevance feedback' group for most of the metrics, and the experimental data revealed several trends.

Web page recommendations were better for the 'profile feedback' group, especially early on in the first few weeks after registering. Email recommendation appeared to be preferred by the 'relevance feedback' group, and especially by those users who did not regularly check their web page recommendations. A reason for this could be that since the 'profile feedback' group used the web page recommendations more, they needed to use the email recommendations less. There is certainly a limit to how many recommendations any user needs over a given time period; in our case nobody regularly checked for recommendations more than once a week. The overall recommendation accuracy was about 1%, or 2-5% for the profile feedback group.

The profile accuracy of both groups was similar, but there was a significant difference between the accuracy of profile predictions. This reflects the different types of interests held in the profiles of the two groups. The 'profile feedback' group's profiles appeared to be longer term, based on knowledge of the users general research interests provided via the profile interface. The 'relevance feedback' profiles were based solely on the browsing behaviour of the users current task, hence contained shorter-term interests. A combination of profile feedback-based longer-term profiles and behaviour-based short-term profiles would probably be most successful.

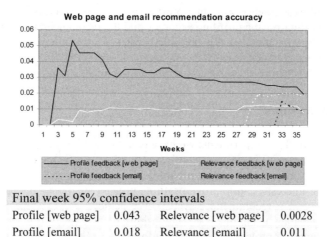

Fig. 11. Recommendation accuracy

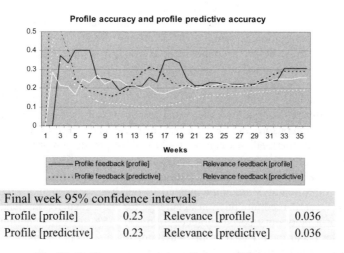

Fig. 12. Profile accuracy and predictive profile accuracy

As with the Quickstep system, direct comparison of these results with other recommender systems is difficult. The Quickstep system is the best system with which to compare Foxtrot, reporting a 7-11% recommendation accuracy. Foxtrot has a 2-5% recommendation accuracy, but this lower value reflects the increased size of the user group and the less friendly audience. In the Quickstep trials volunteers were taken from our research lab who tended to be enthusiastic to try the system. In Foxtrot a department of people were targeted, hence subjects only used the system if it offered significant benefit to their everyday work.

This third experiment shows that profile visualization and profile feedback can significantly improve the profiling accuracy and the recommendation process. Our ontological approach makes this possible because user profiles are represented in terms the users can understand.

## 24.5 Conclusions

Through our three experiments we have demonstrated that using an ontological approach to user profiling offers significant benefits to recommender systems.

Ontological inference, even simple inference such as using is-a relationships to infer general interests, can improve profiling process and hence the recommendation accuracy of a recommender system. We achieve a 7-15% increase recommendation accuracy using just is-a relationships, and we feel it is clear that a more complete domain ontology, with more informative relationships, could perform significantly better.

External ontologies can be used to reduce significantly the cold-start problem recommender systems face. We have shown that a bootstrap profile precision of 35% is achievable given the right ontological knowledge to drawn upon. While further experimentation is required to determine exactly how good a bootstrap profile needs to be before a cold-start is avoided, it is clear that external knowledge sources offer a practical way to achieve this.

Most recommender systems hold user profiles in cryptic formats generated by techniques such as neural networks or Bayesian learners. Using an ontological approach to user profiling allows the visualization of user profiles using ontological terms users understand, and hence a way to elicit feedback on the profiles themselves. This profile feedback can be used to adjust profiles, improving their accuracy significantly. We have demonstrated increases in profiling accuracy of up to 50% of that which is achievable by traditional relevance feedback.

These three features are implemented in our two experimental recommender systems. Overall recommendation accuracy, for individual recommendations, of 7-11% for a laboratory based subject group and 2-5% recommendation accuracy for a larger department based group is demonstrated. This gives an average of one good recommendation per set of recommendations provided for the small group of about 20 users, and one every other set for the larger group of about 200 users. Both these systems compare favourably with other systems in the literature when the problem domains are taken into account.

# Acknowledgements

This work was funded by EPSRC studentship award number 99308831 and the Interdisciplinary Research Collaboration In Advanced Knowledge Technologies (AKT) project GR/N15764/01.

# References

1.  Aha D, Kibler D, Albert M (1991) Instance-based learning algorithms, Machine Learning 6, 37-66.
2.  Balabanović M, Shoham Y (1997) Fab: Content-Based, Collaborative Recommendation, Communications of the ACM 40,3, 67-72.
3.  Billsus D, Pazzani M J (1998) A Personal News Agent that Talks, Learns and Explains, In Autonomous Agents 98, Minneapolis MN USA.
4.  Bollacker K D, Lawrence S, Giles C L (1998) CiteSeer: An Autonomous Web Agent for Automatic Retrieval and Identification of Interesting Publications, In Autonomous Agents 98, Minneapolis MN USA.
5.  Burke R (2000) Knowledge-based Recommender Systems, In: A. KENT (Ed.) Encyclopedia of Library and Information Systems, Vol. 69, Supplement 32.
6.  Delgado J, Ishii N, Ura T (1998) Intelligent collaborative information retrieval, Proceedings of Artificial Intelligence-IBERAMIA'98, Lecture Notes in Artificial Intelligence Series No. 1484.
7.  Freund Y, Schapire R E (1996) Experiments with a New Boosting Algorithm, Proceedings of the Thirteenth International Conference on Machine Learning.
8.  Gerhart A (2002) Open Directory Project Search Results and ODP Status. Search Engine Guide.
9.  Guarino N, Giaretta P (1995) Ontologies and Knowledge bases: towards a terminological clarification, Towards Very Large Knowledge Bases: Knowledge Building and Knowledge Sharing. N. Mars, IOS Press, 25-32.
10. Kachigan S K (1986) Statistical Analysis: An Interdisciplinary Introduction to Univariate & Multivariate Methods, Radius Press
11. Kobsa A (1993) User Modeling: Recent work, prospects and Hazards. In Adaptive User Interfaces: Principles and Practice SCHNEIDER-HUFSCHMIDT, M. KÜHME, T. MALINOWSKI, U. (Ed.) North-Holland.
12. Konstan J A, Miller B N, Maltz D, Herlocker J L, Gordon L R, Riedl J (1997) GroupLens: Applying Collaborative Filtering to Usenet News, Communications of the ACM 40,3, 77-87.
13. Lang K (1995) NewsWeeder: Learning to Filter NetNews, In ICML95 Conference Proceedings, 331-339.
14. Mccallum A K, Nigam K, Rennie J, Seymore K (2000) Automating the Construction of Internet Portals with Machine Learning, Information Retrieval 3,2, 127-163.
15. Middleton S E, Alani H, Shadbolt N R, De Roure D C  (2002) Exploiting Synergy Between Ontologies and Recommender Systems, International Workshop on the Se-

mantic Web, Proceedings of the 11th International World Wide Web Conference WWW-2002, Hawaii, USA.

16. Middleton S E, De Roure D C, Shadbolt N R (2001) Capturing Knowledge of User Preferences: ontologies on recommender systems, In Proceedings of the First International Conference on Knowledge Capture K-CAP 2001, Victoria, B.C. Canada.

17. Mladenić D (1996) Personal WebWatcher: design and implementation, Technical Report IJS-DP-7472, Department for Intelligent Systems, J. Stefan Institute.

18. Nwana H (1996) Software agents: an overview, In The Knowledge Engineering Review, Vol 11:3, 205-244.

19. Sebastiani F (2002) Machine learning in automated text categorization, ACM Computing Surveys.

20. Shadbolt N, O'Hara K, Crow L (1999) The experimental evaluation of knowledge acquisition techniques and methods: history, problems and new directions, International Journal of Human-Computer Studies 51, 729-755.

# The Knowledge Portal "OntoWeb"

Daniel Oberle[1] and Peter Spyns[2]

[1] Institute AIFB, University of Karlsruhe
   76128 Karlsruhe, Germany
   email: {lastname}@aifb.uni-karlsruhe.de
[2] STAR Lab, Vrije Universiteit Brussels,
   B-1050 Brussels, Belgium
   email: {first.lastname}@vub.ac.be

**Summary.** The recent years have seen a tremendous progress in managing semantically heterogeneous data sources. Core to this semantic reconciliation between the different sources is a rich conceptual model that the various stake-holders agree on, an *ontology*. Similarly, in recent years the information system community has successfully strived to reduce the effort for managing complex web sites. The core to these different web site management approaches also is a rich conceptual model that allows for accurate and flexible access to data. SEAL (SEmantic PortAL), a framework for building community web sites, has been developed to use ontologies as key elements for managing community web sites and web portals. In addition, semantic data stores underpinning (community) web sites have to be scalable, re-usable and interoperable. DOGMA (Developing Ontology Guided Mediation for Agents) provides a robust framework making use of database technology that copes with these issues. This chapter presents a combination of the SEAL and DOGMA frameworks and elaborately illustrates our approach with examples from the OntoWeb community portal of the EU thematic network with the same name.

## 25.1 Introduction

Supporting communities in sharing and exchanging knowledge is an important aspect of Knowledge Management. This holds e.g. for communities of practice being organized within enterprizes or by a collection of cooperating enterprizes or for scientific communities that are spread all over the world and thus urgently need support in sharing knowledge tailored for their particular and local purposes. In that context, knowledge portals [31] play a part in offering means for providing and accessing globally on a unified and semantic level knowledge that is stored in a heterogeneous and distributed manner. In essence, knowledge portals exploit an ontology for achieving a conceptual foundation for all their functionalities: i.e., information integration as well as information selection and presentation are glued together by a conceptual model. The SEAL framework for developing and managing knowledge portals exploits Semantic Web technologies to offer mechanisms for acquiring, structuring, integrating, sharing and accessing distributed knowledge between human and/or machine agents [21, 17]. The DOGMA framework for ontology engineering takes agreed semantical knowledge out of an

IT application that makes use of an external ontology. This is done in much the same way that "classical" databases take data structures out of these applications.

The topic of this chapter is the application and extension of SEAL and the combination with DOGMA for realizing the OntoWeb community portal (http://www.ontoweb.org). OntoWeb is a EU IST thematic network that propagates ontologies in the context of eBusiness and Knowledge Management and that currently has more than one hundred members from research and industry. The knowledge portal that will be used as a case study throughout the chapter is a joint effort between the Free University of Brussels - STAR Lab - and the University of Karlsruhe - Institute AIFB. Each lab has its particular contribution to the realization of this knowledge portal. On the one hand, the process of knowledge provisioning and publishing has to be supported by an appropriate workflow. Therefore, the AIFB SEAL framework has been extended by methods and tools for defining and handling a publishing workflow, realized by a comprehensive content management system (CMS). On the other hand, access to the knowledge is equally important, and the information extraction technology of the portal has to take advantage of the underlying ontology to come up with (more) relevant answers than traditional search or query mechanisms. Therefore, for the purposes of the OntoWeb portal, the STAR Lab ontology server (called DOGMA server see [18]) has been modified and extended with a query facility that processes user information requests via a graphical interface that exploits the underlying ontology [29].

The chapter is structured as follows. In section 25.2 we first talk about the OntoWeb project and the aims of its portal in general. We then briefly introduce the DOGMA initiative (section 25.3), followed by a description of the main components and functionalities of the SEAL framework in section 25.4. Section 25.5 outlines the scenario that is set up for the OntoWeb portal. The following sections elaborate more on the specialties of the OntoWeb portal. We focus on how content can be provided in section 25.6 (via content management facilities and by the syndication of metadata). Section 25.7 talks about how the content (or community knowledge) can be accessed, viz. by browsing, template-based querying and their combination. Finally, section 25.8 briefly sketches the graphical presentation of the data. We conclude with a discussion of related work (section 9.5) and an outline of open research problems (section 15.10).

## 25.2  The OntoWeb Project

The EU thematic network "OntoWeb – Ontology-based information exchange for knowledge management and electronic commerce" aims at bringing together researchers and industrials to "enable the full power of ontologies". The project aims at improving information exchange in areas such as: information retrieval, knowledge management, electronic commerce, and bio-informatics. It will also strengthen the European influence on standardization efforts in areas such as web languages (RDF, XML), upper-layer ontologies, and content standards such as catalogues in electronic commerce (cf. [1]).

One of the tasks was to create a portal serving as a platform for internal communication and also with other members of the Word Wide Web. Through this portal, knowledge can be gathered, stored, secured and accessed by the OntoWeb community. It is an open community, i.e. new members can join at any time. The positive effects of such a portal are multiple. Only the most important ones will be mentioned. The portal serves as an inventory of knowledge available in the community. In the case of an Internet portal, knowledge has been made available outside of the organization of the original producer or owner. E.g., members of the community get a good overview of the skills and profiles of the various community members.

In the case of an intranet, it may stimulate the communication between departments of a same company and support the local (technology) innovation management process.

Turning information into knowledge that suits the situation mentioned above, requires a shared conceptualization of the domain in question. In the present case, the domain spans a conceptualization of the OntoWeb organization (e.g., companies, research institutions, special interest groups etc.), of various kinds of documents (e.g., meeting minutes, deliverables, papers etc.), of events and their organizations (e.g., conferences, workshops, internal meetings etc.), of scientific results and material (e.g., cases, programs, etc.), and so forth. A formal version of such a shared conceptualization is commonly called an ontology [24]. When relating specific terms to concepts, a controlled vocabulary or some other common terminological framework can be created.

## 25.3 DOGMA – The Core Idea

In this section, we shortly present the DOGMA initiative for a formal ontology engineering framework - for more details, see [18, 28]. The initiative is based on the double articulation of an ontology: we decompose an ontology into an ontology base, which holds (multiple) intuitive conceptualisation(s) of a domain, and a layer of ontological commitments, where each commitment holds a set of domain rules (see Figure 25.1). We adopt a classical database model-theoretic view in which conceptual relationships are separated from domain rules. They are moved - conceptually - to the application "realm". This distinction may be exploited effectively by allowing the explicit and formal semantical interpretation of the domain rules in terms of the ontology. Experience shows that agreement on the domain rules is much harder to reach than one on the conceptualisation [23].

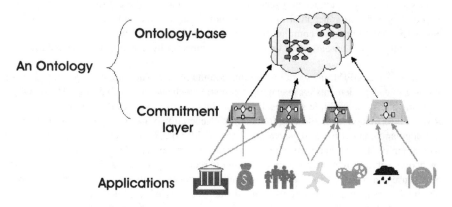

**Fig. 25.1.** The double articulation of a DOGMA ontology

The ontology base consists of sets of intuitively "plausible" domain fact types, represented and organised as sets of context-specific binary conceptual relations, called lexons. The layer of ontological commitments mediates between the ontology base and its applications. Each ontological commitment corresponds to an explicit instance of an (intensional) first order interpretation of a task in terms of the ontology base. Each commitment consists of rules that specify which lexons from the ontology base are visible for usage in this commitment and the rules that constrain this view (= commits it ontologically). As a result, (re-)usability, shareability, interoperability and reliability of the knowledge will be enhanced. As a result, ontologies built in accordance with the principle of the double articulation achieve a form of semantical independence for IT applications. A modified version (closer to RDF) of the DOGMA server functions as the central knowledge repository of the OntoWeb portal. The ontology server layer has been extended with a specific query facility on top of which a graphical interface has been implemented (see Figure 25.3) .

## 25.4 SEAL – The Core Approach

The recent decade has seen a tremendous progress in managing semantically heterogeneous data sources. Core to the semantic reconciliation between the different sources is a rich conceptual model that the various stake-holders agree on, an *ontology* [11]. The conceptual architecture developed for this purpose now generally consists of a three layer architecture comprising (cf. [34]) (i) heterogeneous **data sources** (e.g., databases, XML, but also data found in HTML tables), (ii) **wrappers** that lift these data sources onto a common data model (e.g. OEM [25] or RDF [19]), (iii) integration modules (**mediators** in the dynamic case) that reconcile the varying semantics of the different data sources. Thus, the complexity of the integration/mediation task could be greatly reduced.

Similarly, in recent years the information system community has successfully strived to reduce the effort for managing complex web sites [2, 5, 12, 22]). Previously ill-structured web site management has been structured with process models, redundancy of data has been avoided by generating it from database systems and web site generation (including management, authoring, business logic and design) has profited from recent, also commercially viable, successes [2]. Again we may recognize that core to these different web site management approaches is a rich conceptual model that allows for accurate and flexible access to data. Similarly, in the hypertext community conceptual models have been explored that implicitly or explicitly exploit ontologies as underlying structures for hypertext generation and use (e.g. [6]).

SEAL[3], the AIFB framework for building community web sites, has been developed to use ontologies as key elements for managing community web sites and web portals. The ontology supports queries to multiple sources, but beyond that it also includes the intensive use of the schema information itself allowing for automatic generation of navigational views[4] and mixed ontology and content-based presentation. The core idea of SEAL is that Semantic Portals for a community of users that contribute *and* consume information [30] require web site management *and* web information integration. In order to reduce engineering and maintenance efforts SEAL uses an ontology for semantic integration of existing data sources as well as for web site management and presentation to the outside world. SEAL exploits the ontology to offer mechanisms for acquiring, structuring and sharing information by means of semantic annotations [16] between human and/or machine agents. Thus, SEAL combines the advantages of the two worlds briefly sketched above.

---

[3] Cf. [21] on the history of SEAL.

[4] Examples are navigation hierarchies that appear as `has-part`-trees or `has-subtopic` trees in the ontology.

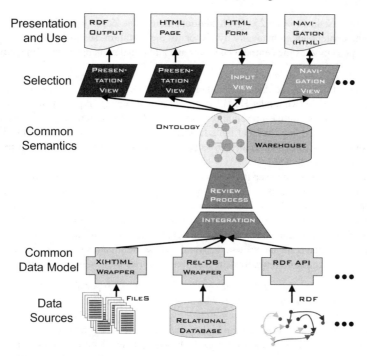

**Fig. 25.2.** Extended conceptual SEAL architecture

## 25.5 Applying SEAL to OntoWeb

The OntoWeb portal is structured according to an ontology that serves as a shared basis for supporting communication between humans and machines. The general goal of our approach is the semi-automatical construction of a community portal using the community's metadata to enable information provision, querying and browsing of the portal. For this purpose we could reuse the framework as explained in Section 25.4, but we also had to provide new modules for content management resulting in the extended architecture depicted in Figures 25.2 and 25.3. In the following, we explain how SEAL is applied to OntoWeb (paragraphs *Integration* and *Presentation*) and talk about the specific extension of the portal by a content management system.

**Integration**  One of the core challenges when building a data-intensive web site is the integration of heterogeneous information on the WWW. The recent decade has seen a tremendous progress in managing semantically heterogeneous data sources [34, 12]. The general approach SEAL pursues is to "lift" all the different input sources onto a common data model, in our case RDF. Additionally, the ontology acts as a semantic model for the heterogeneous input sources. As mentioned earlier and visualized in our conceptual architecture in Figure 25.2, we consider different kinds of **Web data sources** as input. However, to a large part the Web consists of static HTML pages, often semi-structured, including tables, lists, etc. In our case, we had to integrate the DOGMA Server that serves as a knowledge base for syndicated metadata as further discussed in section 25.6.1. In addition, there is the Zope Object Database (ZODB[5]), containing content added manually by visitors of the portal (cf. section 25.6.2). The object oriented Zope is used as the central web server and additional content server of the portal (cf. section 25.6).

**Presentation**   Based on the integrated data in the warehouse we define user-dependent **presentation views**. First, we render HTML pages for human agents. Typically *queries for content* of the warehouse define presentation views by selecting content, but also *queries for schema* might be used, e.g. to label table headers. Second, as a contribution to the Semantic Web, our architecture is dedicated to satisfy the needs of software agents and produces machine understandable RDF.

To maintain a portal and keep it alive its content needs to be updated frequently not only by information integration of different sources but also by additional inputs from human experts. The **input view** is defined by *queries to the schema*, i.e. queries to the ontology itself. Similar to [13] we support the knowledge acquisition task by generating forms out of the ontology. The forms capture data according to the ontology in a consistent way which are stored afterwards in the warehouse. To navigate and browse the warehouse we automatically generate navigational structures, i.e. **navigation views**, by using *combined queries for schema and content*.

**Extensions to SEAL**   During the development of the OntoWeb portal we recognized rather soon that the process of knowledge provisioning and publishing has to be supported by an appropriate content management system in order to be able to control what content is put into the portal by whom. Only then can the high quality of content be guaranteed. Therefore, the SEAL framework has been extended by methods and tools for defining and handling a publishing workflow. Such a workflow represents an important constituent of the overall approach for managing a running knowledge portal to make user focussed access to the OntoWeb portal maintainable. In Figure 25.2 this is depicted as "Review Process", further discussed in section 25.6.2.

In addition to content management, ontology-based annotation of the community information is a prerequisite in order to offer the possibility of knowledge retrieval and extraction (also known as conceptual or intelligent search — cf. [20] as an example). The usage of well-defined semantics allows for the knowledge exchange between different OntoWeb community members. Members are encouraged to publish annotated information on the web, which is then crawled by a syndicator and stored in the portal knowledge base. This mechanism can be considered as another extension to SEAL and is discussed in section 25.6.1.

## 25.6  Content Provision

Basically, there are two ways of providing content to the OntoWeb portal. First, there is the syndication mechanism, i.e., automatically gathering metadata from participating sites. Second, the portal allows for content provision itself. Both possibilities are discussed in subsections 25.6.1 and 25.6.2, respectively.

### 25.6.1  Content Syndication

The portal allows centralized access to distributed information that has been provided by participants on their own sites. To facilitate this, participants can enrich resources located outside

---

[5] cf. http://www.zope.org

of the portal with metadata according to the shared OntoWeb ontology. This annotation process can be supported semi-automatically by the Ontomat Annotizer tool [16] for instance.

As depicted in Figure 25.3, syndicating information from participants is done by replicating their metadata. The information finds its way in the DOGMA Server [18] that exploits a relational DBMS for storing and can be queried by users via a specific GUI (cf. section 25.7 for a detailed discussion). Within the portal, authenticated users may generate content objects on their behalf (cf. subsection 25.6.2). As we use Zope as underlying technology, such objects are stored in its respective database (called ZODB). Additionally, metadata, both conforming to Dublin Core [32] as well as to the Ontoweb ontology, are generated for all the portal's objects. This can be achieved easily as all metadata are stored within Zope's own database. When adding new content to the portal, users have the possibility to supply metadata accordingly. In order to maintain consistency, the syndicator also crawls Zope's pages and thus stores the metadata in the DOGMA server. Comparing this technical architecture to the conceptual one depicted in Figure 25.2, we find that Zope is used for presentation as well as for storage. In addition, the DOGMA Server provides the main storage capabilities in our case. The ontology forms the central part for the structuring of knowledge.

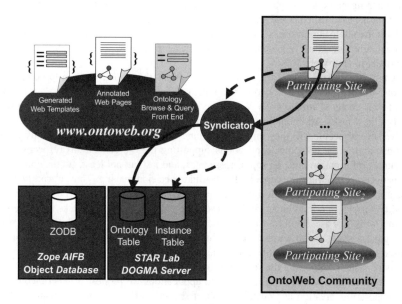

**Fig. 25.3.** Content Syndication

## 25.6.2  Content Objects

We acknowledge the fact that some members might not be able to publish data on the web on their own due to corporate restrictions or other reasons. Therefore OntoWeb participants staff members are provided with a personal space to create and manage content for the portal. To facilitate this, the portal includes a fully-fledged content management system. Additionally, all content created within the portal is automatically associated with the predefined OntoWeb design to achieve an integrated visual experience with a consistent appearance. In the personal space people can provide the following types of content: HTML-documents, arbitrary files and folders, and selected predefined content types based on ontological concepts: Publications, News, Events, Scientific Events, Jobs, etc. When searching for content, both the ZODB and the DOGMA Server is queried. The user can seamlessly browse the results and is not aware that there are two databases.

If a member chooses to create new content based on the predefined content types, appropriate metadata is automatically generated. Second, all content is associated with standard Dublin Core metadata to keep track of publishing information such as date of creation, last modification, authorship and subject classification.

## Process Model for Publishing Workflows

As mentioned in section 25.2, OntoWeb is an open community posing additional constraints since data that is (re)published through the portal could be provided by arbitrary people. In order to guarantee quality of data in such an environment, an additional model regulating the publishing process is required, which prevents foreseeable misuses. To support this requirement the established portal architecture was extended with a workflow component which regulates the publishing process. In the following we will begin with introducing the concept of a publishing workflow in general. Afterwards we explain how we instantiated this generic component in OntoWeb.

A publishing workflow is the series of interactions that should happen to complete the task of publishing data. Business organizations have many kinds of workflow. Our notion of workflow is centered around tasks. Workflows consist of several tasks and several transitions between these tasks. Additionally, workflows have the following characteristics: (i) they might involve several people, (ii) they might take a long time, (iii) they vary significantly in organizations and in the computer applications supporting these organizations respectively, (iv) sometimes information must be kept across states, and last but not least, (v) the communication between people must be supported to facilitate decision making. Thus, a workflow component must be customizable. It must support the assignment of tasks to (possibly multiple) individual users. In our architecture these users are grouped into roles. Tasks are represented within a workflow as a set of transitions which cause state changes. Each object in the system is assigned a state, which corresponds to the current position within the workflow and can be used to determine the possible transitions that can validly be applied to the object. This state is persistent supporting the second characteristic mentioned above. Due to the individuality of workflows within organizations and applications we propose a generic component that supports the creation and customization of several workflows. In fact, each concept in the ontology, which is used to capture structured data within a portal, can be assigned a different workflow with different states, transitions and task assignments. As mentioned above, sometimes data is required to be kept across states[6]. To model this behavior, the state machine underlying our workflow model needs to keep information that "remembers" the past veto. Thus, variables are attached to objects and used to provide persistent information that transcends states. Within our approach, variables also serve the purpose of establishing a simple form of communication between the involved parties. Thus, each transition can attach com-

---

[6] For example, envision the process of passing bills in legislature, a bill might be allowed to be revised and resubmitted once it is vetoed, but only if it has been vetoed once. If it is vetoed a second time, it is rejected forever.

ments to support the decision made by future actors. Also metadata like the time and initiator of a transition is kept within the system.

## Workflows in OntoWeb

Figure 25.4 depicts the default workflow within OntoWeb. There are three states: private, pending, and published. In the private state the respective object is only visible to the user himself, the pending state makes it visible to reviewers. In the published state, a given object is visible to all (possibly anonymous) users of the portal. If a user creates a new object[7], it is in private state. If the user has either a reviewer or a manager role the published state is immediately available through the publish transition. For normal users such a transition is not available. Instead, the object can only be sent for a review leading to the pending state. In the pending state either managers or reviewers can force the transition into the published state (by applying the transition "publish") or retract the object leading back to the private state. The reject transition deletes the object completely. When an object is in the private state, only the user who created it and users with manager roles can view and change it. Once an object is in published state, the modification by the user who created it resets the object into pending state, thus the modification must be reviewed again. This does not apply to modifications by site managers. The workflow is realized by Zope's Content Management System (CMF). States and transitions in Figure 25.4 are the defaults in CMF and they suit our process model. However, one can flexibly introduce new states and transitions anytime without effort.

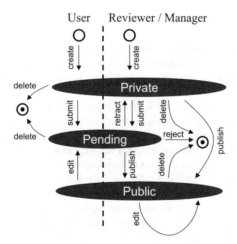

**Fig. 25.4.** OntoWeb Publishing workflow

---

[7] Currently only within the portal, the content syndicated from other OntoWeb member web sites and within the databases is "trusted". We assume that this kind of data already went through some kind of review.

## 25.7 Content Access

As has already been mentioned in section 25.2, the OntoWeb semantic portal offers an ontology-based browse and query facility. It has been developed as a highly generic system that allows to explore the available information at a conceptual level. Stated otherwise, the searches are performed on meta-data and not actual data. Currently, a (human) user can access information in the OntoWeb semantic portal in three different ways (see also [[30]:p.476]):

- *browsing*: a user doesn't know the vocabulary (s)he needs to search with and/or is rather unfamiliar with the domain [8]
- *querying*: a user is quite familiar with the domain and its vocabulary
- a *combination* of the above: a user has some insights in the structure of the domain and is vaguely aware of the vocabulary (s)he needs to access the information (s)he needs

Any attempt to access information necessarily starts with an initial selection of a concept from the IsA hierarchy (displayed at the left hand side of Figure 25.5). As a result, a reduction of the search space is achieved. The system performs queries for content and schema in order to generate navigation views (see section 25.2). The main distinctions to keep in mind are the ones between sub- and superconcepts and between literal and non-literal properties of the various concepts or instances. Note that the user interface is still work in progress. E.g., a hyperbolic view [[30]:p.482] or a landscape view [27] would be an alternative way of displaying search results for subsequent selection. Also note that clicking the OntoWeb symbol (root of the IsA hierarchy) restarts the search process from scratch.

### 25.7.1 Browsing

An ontology, as it is by definition a shared agreement on an intended conceptualization of a domain [14], represents how a (majority of members of a) user community "sees" the structure of an application domain [9]. Therefore, a visualization of the domain model can be considered as a shared "mental roadmap" that helps users in locating and finding the desired information more rapidly. An expandable tree representation of the IsA hierarchy (see Figure 25.5), combined with an overview of semantic relationships and properties for a selected concept instance, provides a local and partial view on the domain conceptualization. Note that the hierarchy supports multiple inheritance (nodes can have more than one parent in the "tree").

A user can view instances associated to a concept of the IsA hierarchy (= the tree in the left pane) by expanding its nodes and selecting the concept of interest. The instances of this concept will then be displayed (in the middle part of the right pane). Moving up or down the concept hierarchy corresponds to performing a generalized or specialized look-up of corresponding instances. By selecting a subtype of the current concept, the look-up precision should improve since the instances of the supertype (i.e. the concept originally selected), including all the instances of its subtypes that do not belong to the subtype newly selected, are excluded from the search space. An independent (but partial) validation of this hypothesis can be found in [15]. Also the recall should improve since the conceptual hierarchical relation between a type and its subtypes (specialisation) is taken into account, in opposition to many regular search engines that do not semantically relate tokens. Of course, recall and precision results crucially depend on the quality of the semantic annotation process. Generalization (i.e.

---

[8] See section 25.2 for a description of the OntoWeb domain.

[9] Note that an application domain transcends a data model for a single application - see [28] for more details

moving up one level in the hierarchy or clicking on the supertype displayed) on the other hand broadens the scope of the query, exploiting the concept hierarchy to expand the query to all instances of the siblings (and their subtypes) of the concept originally of interest to a user (cf. also [3]).

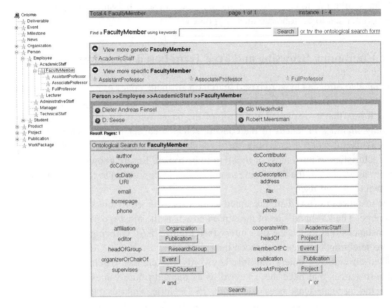

**Fig. 25.5.** Ontology-based searching for information

## 25.7.2  Typed Term-based Querying

A user is presented with a search form (see the lower part of Figure 25.5), containing text boxes in which attribute values (literals) can be specified. In addition, additional buttons labelled with a concept name allow to refine the query by imposing restrictions on related concept instances. Clicking on a such "concept button" leads to another form that allows to specify related instances (= entering new attribute values) of the concept newly selected (i.e. the one now shown in bold on the titlebar of the form). There are as many buttons as there are relationships associated with the concept originally selected. This means that the forms are generated dynamically on basis of the underlying ontology. The terms are typed - but no explicit type-checking is done yet - since each attribute has a meaningful range (e.g., it doesn't make sense to enter a date in the address attribute field). The range for the associated relationships is restricted to a single concept, namely the one of which the label is displayed on the corresponding button. One can enter attribute values for several cascaded forms.

The form-based specifies a query path across the ontology (displayed in the titlebar of the form). For each node in the path, a user can add restrictions on the attribute values. All the attributes values filled in in the various forms constitute a complex query on the instance base. This can be considered as a form of interactive query refinement. However, this kind of query refinement is guided by the ontology before the actual look-up process is activated and not on basis of (intermediary) search results as it is usually the case. The hypothesis is that recall should improve since underlying semantic properties are taken into account instead of only the formal appearance of a character string. Also the precision should improve as the semantic properties have a higher discriminative power (compared to pattern matching that is the basic traditional search mechanism) to rule out non relevant search results. However, experimental data is still needed to corroborate these hypotheses.

### 25.7.3  Combining Browsing and Free Term-based Querying

The portal also offers a keyword based search on attribute values of instances without the need to specify the attribute. A user may opt at any moment to enter one or more search terms in the search box that is displayed at the top of the page. When a query is executed, the search space only includes instances of the concept selected earlier (and its subtypes). This search strategy is useful when a user only has a rough idea of what (s)he is looking for. Some of the characteristics (= attributes) of the item to be looked for are known but exactly how these characteristics relate to the item being searched for (in opposition to form based querying) are not known to an end-user.

The instances retrieved are presented to the user grouped by links pointing to the instance details page. The left hand side of the screen now lists the most specific concepts corresponding to instances that match the user query (see Figure 25.6). Clicking on a concept in the list equals to selecting a particular view on the results [10].

When an end-user enters multiple keywords, the engine searches for conceptual paths between instances that have these keywords as their attribute values and, if found, displays paths including related instances (see Figure 25.7). Notice that this particular feature enables a user to discriminate between meaningful and meaningless combinations, and in addition, helps him/her to select these meaningful combinations that are relevant for him/her. The strength of a semantically-based search engine is fully exploited and valorized in this situation. Traditional search engines, lacking underlying semantics, simply cannot offer a similar powerful feature.

## 25.8  Content Presentation

What strategy (as has been described in the previous section) a user has applied to specify his/her search request, eventually (s)he selects a particular instance. When displaying the detailed information for that instance, a distinction is made between the attributes and relationships. Attribute values - modelled in the ontology as literal properties - provide a user with specific instance information, while "relationship values" are shown as hyperlinks, enabling a user to jump to instances of related concepts. The distinction between attributes and relationships is decided by the ontology modeler [11].

Attributes are displayed at the upper part of the page. These concern e.g., in the case of a person, the name, telephone number and email... An overview of the relevant conceptual relationships is displayed in the middle part of the page. The "relationship values" are presented at

---

[10] Of course, "ALL" is not a concept, but merely represents a exhaustive view of the result list.

[11] The range of an attribute is "STRING", while the range of a relationship is a concept of the domain ontology.

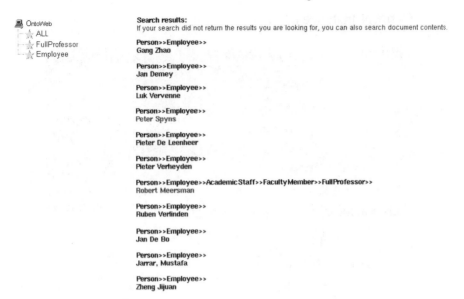

**Fig. 25.6.** Search results for "STARLab" combined with the "Person" concept

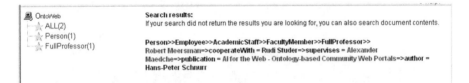

**Fig. 25.7.** Search results for "Robert Peter" combined with the "Person" concept

the lower part of the page grouped by relationship. They point to instances of related concepts (cf. Figure 25.8). Again, the screen is dynamically generated: only those attributes and relationships are shown for which instance data is stored in the instance base. Whenever relevant (depending on the ontology) and/or applicable (depending on the instance data), also a URL is displayed that brings the user to the web site that stores the original data. Remember that the portal basically contains meta-data (except for the content objects as described in section 25.6.2) crawled by the syndicator (see section 25.6.1).

## 25.9 Related Work

The ontological foundation of the OntoWeb portal is the main distinctive feature when comparing it to approaches of the information systems area.

Using an ontology to support the access of content has been discussed before. E.g., the Yahoo-a-lizer [9] transforms a knowledge base into a set of XML pages that are structured like the term hierarchy of Yahoo. These XML-files are translated via an XSL-stylesheet into ordinary HTML. Within Ontobroker-based web portals [7], a Hyperbolic View Applet allows

## Concept Instance label
FullProfessor : Robert Meersman

**Attributes**

| address | Department of Computer Science, Vrije Universiteit Brussel Bldg. G-10, Pleinlaan 2, B-1050 Brussels Belgium |
|---|---|
| email | robert.meersman@vub.ac.be |
| fax | ++32-(0)2-629-3525 |
| name | Robert Meersman |
| phone | ++32-(0)2-629-3308 |
| photo | http://www.starlab.vub.ac.be/images/robert.gif |

**Attribute values (literals)**

| affiliation | cooperateWith | headOf | headOfGroup | organizerOrChairOf |
|---|---|---|---|---|
| rksAtProject | | | | |

**Relationships**          **Relationships (overview)**

| affiliation | Systems Technology and Applications Research Laboratory |
|---|---|
| cooperateWith | Rudi Studer |
| headOf | DOGMA |
| headOfGroup | Systems Technology and Applications Research Laboratory |
| organizerOrChairOf | ▶ DOA<br>▶ IFCIS |
| supervises | ▶ Ben Majer<br>▶ Jarrar Mustafa<br>▶ Zheng Jijuan |

**Instances (hyperlinks)**

| worksAtProject | DOGMA |
|---|---|

**Instance URI**

| URI-reference : | http://starpc14.vub.ac.be:8000/OntoWeb/Browse/allInstances#RM |
|---|---|

**Fig. 25.8.** Content presentation

for graphical access to an ontology and its knowledge base. Other related work is the KAON Portal[12] that takes an ontology and creates a standard Web interface out of it. A similar system is the Open Learning Repository that is a metadata-based portal for e-learning courses [8], but it lacks the query facilities. The OntoSeek prototype uses a linguistic ontology and structured content representations to search yellow pages and product catalogs [15]. The importance of conceptual indexing for information retrieval has been acknowledged since quite some time in the medical information processing field [10, 26, 35].

Given the difficulties with managing complex Web content, several papers tried to facilitate database technology to simplify the creation and maintenance of data-intensive web-sites. Systems such as Araneus [22] and AutoWeb [5], take a declarative approach, i.e. they introduce their own data models and query languages, although all approaches share the idea to provide high-level descriptions of web-sites by distinct orthogonal dimensions. The idea of leveraging mediation technologies for the acquisition of data is also found in approaches like Strudel [12] and Tiramisu [2], they propose a separation according to the aforementioned task profiles as well. Strudel does not concern the aspects of site maintenance and personalization. It is actually only an implementation tool, not a management system. Basically, Strudel relies

---

[12] cf. http://kaon.semanticweb.org/Portal

on a mediator architecture where the semi-structured OEM data model is used at the mediation level to provide a homogeneous view on the underlying data sources. Strudel then uses 'site definition queries' to specify the structure and content of a Web site. When compared to our approach Strudel lacks the semantic level that is defined by the ontology. An ontology offers a rich conceptual view on the distributed and hetereogeneous underlying sources that is shared by the Web site users and that is made accessible at the user interface for e.g. browsing and querying.

The Web Modelling Language WebML [5] provides means for specifying complex Web sites on a conceptual level. Aspects that are covered by WebML are a.o. descriptions of the site content, the layout and navigation structure as well as personalization features.Thus, WebML addresses functionalities that are offered by the presentation and selection layer of the SEAL conceptual architecture. Whereas WebML provides more sophisticated means for e.g. specifying the navigation structure, our approach offers more powerful means for accessing the content of the Web site, e.g. by semantic querying.

Other related work is situated in the area of federated databases and database mediation in general ([33] and see e.g. [4]). Issues as data heterogeneity, schema integration, database interoperability etc. that are also encountered in the ontology research domain should be coped with in a more flexible way by the DOGMA approach thanks to its double articulation.

In short, from our point of view the OntoWeb portal is quite unique with respect to the collection of methods used and the functionalities provided.

## 25.10  Future Work and Conclusion

For the future, we see some new important topics appearing on the horizon. For instance, we consider approaches for ontology learning in order to semi-automatically adapt to changes in the world and to facilitate the engineering of ontologies. Currently, we work on providing intelligent means for providing semantic information, *i.e.* we elaborate on a semantic annotation framework that balances between manual provisioning from legacy texts (*e.g.* web pages) and information extraction. Finally, we envision that once semantic web sites are widely available, their automatic exploitation may be brought to new levels. Semantic web mining considers the level of mining web site structures, web site content, and web site usage on a semantic rather than at a syntactic level yielding new possibilities, *e.g.* for intelligent navigation, personalization, or summarization, to name but a few objectives for semantic web sites.

A next important step to take is to enter a significantly large amount of real life data in the instance base so that a truly useful knowledge base is created. Before doing that, an update of the ontology is foreseen as well. As a general consideration, the user interface will be refined as well. After these steps, a large-scale assessment on the strengths and flaws (also as perceived by end-users) of the OntoWeb portal becomes possible.

In this chapter, we have shown the combination of two frameworks (SEAL and DOGMA) for building a knowledge portal. In particular, we have focused on four issues. First, we have described the general architecture of both frameworks. Second, we have presented our real world case study, the OntoWeb portal. Third, to meet the requirements of the OntoWeb portal, we extended our initial conceptual architecture by publishing workflows to make user focussed access to the portal maintainable. Finally, we created a specific semantically driven user interface on top of a semantic query facility to improve the information retrieval process.

# Acknowledgements

We want to thank several colleagues at the Free University of Brussels - STAR Lab, headed by Robert Meersman, and at the University of Karlsruhe - Institute AIFB, headed by Rudi Studer, for their contribution to this work. This includes York Sure, Raphael Volz, Jens Hartmann and Steffen Staab at AIFB as well as Jijuan Zheng, Mustafa Jarrar and Ben Majer for STAR Lab. This work has been funded under the EU IST-2001-29243 project "OntoWeb". P. Spyns has been funded by the Flemisch IWT-GBOU 2001 010069 project "OntoBasis".

# References

1. OntoWeb Consortium. Ontology-based information exchange for knowledge manage-ment and electronic commerce - IST-2000-25056.
   http://www.ontoweb.org, 2001.
2. C. R. Anderson, A. Y. Levy, and D. S. Weld. Declarative web site management with Tiramisu. In *ACM SIGMOD Workshop on the Web and Databases - WebDB99*, pages 19–24, 1999.
3. A. Aronson and T. Rindflesch. Query expansion using the UMLS. In R. Masys, edi-tor, *Proceedings of the AMIA Annual Fall Symposium 97, JAMIA Suppl*, pages 485–489. AMIA, 1997.
4. S. Bergamaschi, S. Castano, M. Vincini and B. Beneventano D. Semantic integration of heterogeneous information sources. Data &amp; Knowlegde Engineering 36 (3): 215-249, 2001.
5. S. Ceri, P. Fraternali, and A. Bongio. Web modeling language (WebML): a modeling language for designing web sites. In *WWW9 Conference, Amsterdam, May 2000*, 2000.
6. M. Crampes and S. Ranwez. Ontology-supported and ontology-driven conceptual navi-gation on the world wide web. In *Proceedings of the 11th ACM Conference on Hypertext and Hypermedia, May 30 - June 3, 2000, San Antonio, TX, USA*, pages 191–199. ACM Press, 2000.
7. S. Decker, M. Erdmann, D. Fensel, and R. Studer. Ontobroker: Ontology Based Access to Distributed and Semi-Structured Information. In R. Meersman et al., editors, *Database Semantics: Semantic Issues in Multimedia Systems*, pages 351–369. Kluwer Academic Publisher, 1999.
8. H. Dhraief, W. Nejdl, B. Wolf, M. Wolpers. Open Learning Repositories and Metadata Modeling. In *Proceedings of the First International Semantic Web Working Symposium (SWWS01)*, pages 495–514, 2001
9. M. Erdmann. *Ontologien zur konzeptuellen Modellierung der Semantik von XML*. Isbn: 3831126356, University of Karlsruhe, 10 2001.
10. D. Evans, D. Rothwell, I. Monarch, R. Lefferts, and R. Côté. Towards representations for medical concepts. *Medical Decision Making*, 11 (supplement):S102–S108, 1991.
11. D. Fensel, J. Angele, S. Decker, M. Erdmann, H.-P. Schnurr, R. Studer, and A. Witt. Lessons learned from applying AI to the web. *International Journal of Cooperative In-formation Systems*, 9(4):361–382, 2000.
12. M. F. Fernandez, D. Florescu, A. Y. Levy, and D. Suciu. Declarative specification of web sites with Strudel. *VLDB Journal*, 9(1):38–55, 2000.
13. E. Grosso, H. Eriksson, R. W. Fergerson, S. W. Tu, and M. M. Musen. Knowledge mod-eling at the millennium: the design and evolution of PROTEGE-2000. In *Proceedings of the 12th International Workshop on Knowledge Acquisition, Modeling and Mangement (KAW-99)*, Banff, Canada, October 1999.

14. N. Guarino, and P. Giaretta, (1995). Ontologies and Knowledge Bases: Towards a Termi-nological Clarification. N. Mars (editor), *Towards Very Large Knowledge Bases: Knowledge Building and Knowledge Sharing*, pages 25–32. IOS Press, Amsterdam, 1995.

15. N. Guarino, C. Masolo, and G. Vetere. Ontoseek: Content-based access to the web. *IEEE Intelligent Systems*, May-June4-5:70–80, 1999.

16. S. Handschuh and S. Staab. Authoring and annotation of web pages in CREAM. In *The Eleventh International World Wide Web Conference (WWW2002), Honolulu, Hawaii, USA 7-11 May*, 2002. To appear.

17. A. Hotho, A. Maedche, S. Staab, and R. Studer. SEAL-II - The soft spot between richly structured and unstructured knowledge. *Universal Computer Science (J.UCS)*, 7(7):566–590, 2001.

18. M. Jarrar and R. Meersman. Formal Ontology Engineering in the DOGMA Approach. In R. Meersman, Z. Tari and al., editors, *On the Move to Meaningful Internet Systems 2002: CoopIS, DOA, and ODBASE; Confederated International Conferences CoopIS, DOA, and ODBASE 2002 Proceedings*, pages 1238–1254. LNCS 2519, Springer Verlag, 2002.

19. O. Lassila and R. Swick. Resource Description Framework (RDF). Model and syntax specification. Technical report, W3C, 1999.
http://www.w3.org/TR/REC-rdf-syntax.

20. H. Lowe, I. Antipov, W. Hersh, and C. Arnott Smith. Towards knowledge-based re-trieval of medical images. the role of semantic indexing, image content representation and knowledge-based retrieval. In C. Chute, editor, *Proceedings of the 1998 AMIA Annual Fall Symposium*, pages 882–886. AMIA, Henley & Belfus, Philadelphia, 1998.

21. A. Maedche, S. Staab, R. Studer, Y. Sure, and R. Volz. Seal — tying up information integration and web site management by ontologies. *IEEE Data Engineering Bulletin*, 25(1):10–17, March 2002.

22. G. Mecca, P. Merialdo, P. Atzeni, and V. Crescenzi. The (short) Araneus guide to web-site development. In *Second Intern. Workshop on the Web and Databases (WebDB'99) in conjunction with SIGMOD'99*, May 1999.

23. R. Meersman. Semantic Web and Ontologies: Playtime or Business at the Last Frontier in Computing ? NSF-EU Workshop on Database and Information Systems Research for Semantic Web and Enterprises. pages 61–67, 2002.

24. R. Meersman and M. Jarrar. Scalability and reusable in ontology modeling. In *Proceedings of the International conference on Infrastructure for e-Business, e-Education, e-Science, and e-Medicine (SSGRR2002s)*, 2002. (only available on CD-ROM).

25. Y. Papakonstantinou, H. Garcia-Molina, and J. Widom. Object exchange across hetero-geneous information sources. In *Proceedings of the IEEE International Conference on Data Engineering, Taipei, Taiwan, March 1995*, pages 251–260, 1995.

26. T. Rindflesch and A. Aronson. Semantic processing in information retrieval. In C. Safran, editor, *Seventeenth Annual Symposium on Computer Applications in Medical Care (SCAMC 93)*, pages 611–615. McGraw-Hill Inc., New York, 1993.

27. V. Sabol, W. Kienreich, M. Granitzer, J. Becker, K. Tochtermann, K. Andrews. Applica-tions of a Lightweight, Web-based Retrieval, Clustering, and Visualisation Framework. In D. Karagiannis and U. Reimer (editors), *Proceedings of the Fourth International Conference on Practical Aspects of Knowledge Management (PAKM02)*. pages 359–369. LNAI 2569, Springer Verlag, 2002

28. P. Spyns, R. Meersman and J. Jarrar. Data modelling versus Ontology engineering. *SIGMOD Record Special Issue on Semantic Web, Database Management and Information Systems*, 31 (4).

29. P. Spyns, D. Oberle, R. Volz, J. Zheng, M. Jarrar, Y. Sure, R. Studer, R. Meersman. On-toWeb - A Semantic Web Community Portal. In D. Karagiannis and U. Reimer (editors),

*Proceedings of the Fourth International Conference on Practical Aspects of Knowledge Management (PAKM02).* pages 189–200. LNAI 2569, Springer Verlag, 2002

30. S. Staab, J. Angele, S. Decker, M. Erdmann, A. Hotho, A. Maedche, H.-P. Schnurr, R. Studer, and Y. Sure. Semantic community web portals. In *WWW9 / Computer Networks (Special Issue: WWW9 - Proceedings of the 9th International World Wide Web Conference, Amsterdam, The Netherlands, May, 15-19, 2000)*, volume 33, pages 473–491. Elsevier, 2000.

31. S. Staab and A. Maedche. Knowledge portals - ontologies at work. *AI Magazine*, 21(2), 2001.

32. S. Weibel, J. Kunze, C. Lagoze, and M. Wolf. *Dublin Core Metadata for Resource Discovery.* Number 2413 in IETF. The Internet Society, September 1998.

33. G. Wiederhold. An algebra for ontology composition. In Proceedings of the 1994 Monterey Workshop on Formal Methods, Monterey CA, pp. 56–61, 1994.

34. G. Wiederhold and M. Genesereth. The conceptual basis for mediation services. *IEEE Expert*, 12(5):38–47, Sep.-Oct. 1997.

35. P. Zweigenbaum, J. Bouaud, B. Bachimont, J. Charlet, B. Séroussi, and J.-F. Boisvieux. From text to knowledge: a unifying document-oriented view of analyzed medical language. *Methods of Information in Medicine*, 37(4-5):384–393, 1998.

# Ontologies and Hypertext

Leslie Carr[1], Simon Kampa[1], Wendy Hall[1], Sean Bechhofer[2], and Carole Goble[2]

[1] Intelligence, Agents, Multimedia Group
   Department of Electronics & Computer Science
   University of Southampton
   Highfield
   Southampton SO17 1BJ
   http://www.iam.ecs.soton.ac.uk/
   {lac,srk,wh}@ecs.soton.ac.uk
[2] Information Management Group
   Department of Computer Science
   Kilburn Building
   University of Manchester
   Oxford Road
   Manchester M13 9PL
   http://img.cs.man.ac.uk/
   {seanb,carole}@cs.man.ac.uk

**Summary.** Hypertext is a discipline which deals with the composition and arrangement of documents. Common hypertext preoccupations are the ways in which web pages can be linked together and the types of navigation pathways that provide users with convenient access to relevant information. Until now, the linking task has been left to the intelligence of the document author or the web site designer because the rationale for linking is inevitably based upon human understanding of the document contents.

Previous attempts to automate the linking process have often yielded disappointing results. Now, the ability to model a domain of discourse with an ontology holds out the promise of computationally reasoned and reasonable linking services. This chapter describes some attempts to augment hypermedia systems with ontologies in order to provide, or improve, hypertext.

## 26.1 Hypertext: Knowing What we are Talking About

Thanks to the World Wide Web, hundreds of millions of people now think of hypertext in terms of pages of information that are connected by clickable blue links. In fact, the Web's *simple navigational hypertext* is just one example of the use of a family of techniques that are intended to transcend the limitations of static, sequential presentations of text [25]. Hypertext[3] uses computer effects to improve familiar textual communication — not only links

---

[3] The term *hypermedia* can be used to emphasise the multimedia applications of the same techniques.

for making connections, but also summarisation, visualization, comparison, clustering, structuring and active indexing. In other words, hypertext adds computer-mediated extensions to familiar forms of textual communication and is the practice of "things that can be said" using computer-manipulated media, databases and links.

Ontology is the study of "things that exist"; within the domain of computer science an ontology is a formal model that allow reasoning about concepts and objects that appear in the real world and (crucially) about the complex relationships between them [16]. It seems reasonable to imagine that some kinds of complex structures may be required for expressing and exploring objects' inter-relationships when we make hypertext statements about them. Normal hypertext design practice would be to analyse the texts themselves in order to devise a suitable hypertext infrastructure [8]. By contrast, *ontological hypertext* derives the structuring of its component texts from the relationships between objects in the real world.

## 26.1.1 Hypertext: Links or Knowledge

An influential early analysis of hypertext [12] noted that links were either *extensional* (explicitly authored and stored e.g. to implement an intended navigational ordering) or *intensional* (not explicitly stored as links but derived in some manner from the content). The study recommended an increase in the support for intensional linking, based on the requirements for managing the complex interconnectedness of a scholarly literature (particularly for biblical or literary studies).

Subsequent systems (e.g. Hyperbase [27], Hyper-G [1], Devise Hypermedia [17], Microcosm [10], the World Wide Web [4]) and standards (Dexter [18], HyTime [21], HTML [26], XLink [13]) which addressed the concept of linked documents focused on links which were explicitly authored and stored (either as part of, or separately from the documents). In fact, a significant amount of effort over the subsequent years has been directed in the standards committees at the thorny issues of *how* to model and express extensional links in a reasonably robust and universal fashion. Even the ability to 'point at' or address the appropriate part of a document's content is complex and difficult to implement, let alone the ability to describe the semantics for a collection of pointers that form a link. A well-rehearsed problem with extensional links in the context of the Web is how to store and manipulate links as first-class objects, independently of documents, while maintaining referential integrity in an uncontrolled authoring environment [11].

Although intensional links avoid these problems, they crucially depend on an understanding of the document content. If this is not achieved by an author's intelligence, then there must be some computational entity capable of (i) recognising a potential link anchor and (ii) working out what to link it to. This recognition software can be a part of the system (and configured to 'know' the appropriate requirements of the application) or independent of the system which must perform a retro-fit of the suggested links. In the Web, an example of the former case is a script on a company's Web server which links the names of that company's products to their Web pages. An example of the latter case is a general language service which annotates technical terms with explanatory notes; only those explanations relevant to the specific user should be maintained ([12] suggests a dictionary or part-of speech linker that would affect every word in the document).

The Microcosm system [10] and its Web-based successor DLS [5] implemented linking semantics which were a combination of extensional and intensional linking. An entry in a linkbase (extensional) declared that occurrences of a particular term may be linked to a particular destination but devolved the responsibility of recognising where the term occurred and under what circumstances the link should be activated to the runtime browsing environment (intensional). This split paradigm relied on both a skilled link author (to make appropriate generic links to lead into their documents and out to other resources) and on a skilled hypertext integrator (to partition the various links appropriately between modular sets of linkbases which can be automatically activated for the right users when they visit the right pages). Experience shows that failure in the authoring task results in a familiar paucity of links whereas failure in the system administrator's task results in users being overwhelmed by inappropriate selections of links (see figure 26.1). We refer to this second case as the *prolific but ignorant linker*.

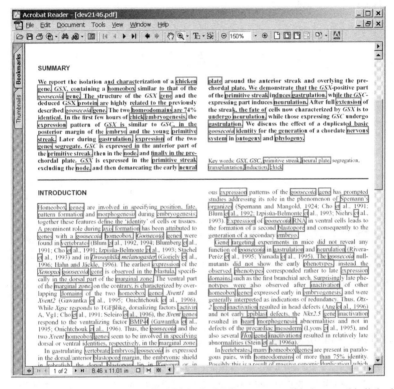

**Fig. 26.1.** Example of Uncontrolled Links in DLS  every possible keyword is linked

The problems of extensional linking are well-known and widely experienced: the significant authoring effort required to create and maintain links may not be forthcoming, even in an environment such as scientific research where longevity of access to publications is a key requirement [24]. An intensional approach to bibliographic linking [19] uses linking software adapted to understand the formats of bibliographies and to look up the results in a database of digital library holdings (see Figure 26.2). Even so, both the roles of authorship (writing the bibliography) and hypertext integration (collecting a suitable database of articles to act as link destinations) are still apparent.

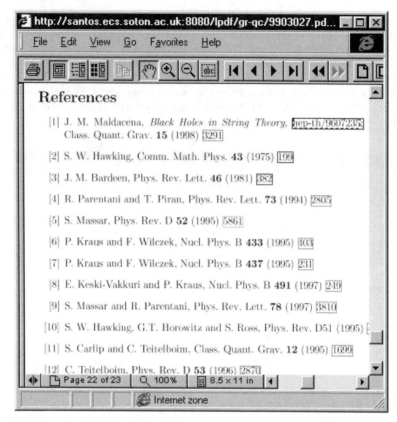

**Fig. 26.2.** Intensional Bibliographic Linking (coloured links represent different classes of linked articles)

### 26.1.2 The Need for Ontologies

In order to decrease the reliance on authoring effort in a linking environment, we need to employ more sophisticated content recognition software. We want to be able to recognise the kinds of things that are mentioned in the text, and understand the relationship between those things and other things which we may have links to, which may feature in glossaries, dictionaries or subject-specific portals.

The promise of ontology-driven linking then, is the potential to use an agreed common collection of significant concepts, expressed as an agreed vocabulary in a given natural language, modelled together with agreed inter-relationships. In fact, the key objective is to *reuse* a model which has already been constructed for other knowledge management purposes (in other words, to get improved linking functionality "for free"). Not only can the lexicons of the ontology identify the natural language terms which signify a significant concept, but the explicit relationships (and carefully quantified semantics) can help to overcome the problem of 'prolific linking' by providing an understanding of *what can be linked* which dovetails with the linking application's in-built knowledge of *what kinds of things should be linked* (subject key terms, foreign terms, named entities, general concepts) in order to achieve a particular goal (glossary explanation, tutorial support, related information).

## 26.2  Building Ontological Hypertexts

If ontologies are used to define the entities of interest that are to feature in a computing application, then different perspectives on those entities will result in different ontologies, and even different applications. When creating a hypertext, for example, one can create a subject ontology which reflects the topics under discussion in the documents, an argumentation ontology that represents the rhetorical structures used to communicate the ideas in the documents or a community ontology that exposes the authors, projects and institutions that are responsible for producing the documents. Each of these approaches will result in very different linked structure in the hypertext, and probably web sites that are suitable for entirely different purposes. This section describes some of the various kinds of hypertexts that result from each of these approaches; the main emphasis is placed on the author's experience of hypertext with ontologies that model the subject domain.

### 26.2.1  Ontology of the Subject Domain

The COHSE project [7] produced an experimental ontological hypermedia system from an ontological reasoning service and an open hypermedia link service to enable documents to be linked via the concepts referred to in their contents. COHSE was particularly concerned with the authoring process: it is well-known that the manual construction of hypertexts for non-trivial Web applications (where documents need to be linked in many dimensions based on their content) is often inconsistent and error-prone [14]. Attempts to improve the linking through simple lexical matching (using the DLS as described above) had serious limitations due to the uncontrolled method of adding links. The aim of the COHSE project therefore was to combine the DLS architecture with an ontological model to provide linking on the concepts that appear in Web pages, as opposed to linking on simple text fragments.

An ontological hypertext environment needs to have some mechanism for interpreting the ontology and exposing the concepts and relationships in the real world as links (or other artefacts) in the hypertext. COHSE used a standard Web browser controlled by a *Dynamic Link Resolution Service* (DLRS, a variation of the existing DLS described above) which used three independent services to manipulate the exposed DOM, resulting in the effect of ontologically-controlled hypertext.

Ontology Service  The ontology service manages ontologies (sets of concepts related according to some schema) and answers specific queries about them. The ontologies are internally represented using DAML+OIL [2] and queries are satisfied using the FACT reasoner [20]. The purpose of the service is to answer fundamental questions about the concepts in an ontology, for example:

- What is the parent of this concept?
- How is this concept represented in a natural language?
- What concept does this string describe?
- Are these two concepts similar or the same?

The ontology server does not use the ontologies' *specific relationships* to answer ontology- (and hence domain-) specific questions (*e.g.* who wrote this paper, what kind of person manages an academic project or who can be a chartered engineer?) nor does it export such ontological information using a knowledge model like OKBC [9].

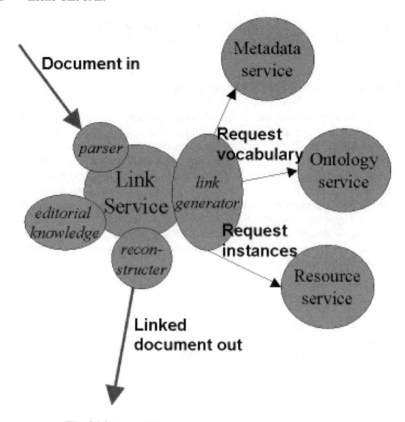

**Fig. 26.3.** An architecture to provide ontological hypertext.

Metadata Service  The metadata service is a simple annotation engine, similar in principle to
   Annotea [23], except that it annotates regions of a document with a concept, rather that
   a simple piece of text. An XPointer is used to identify each region in the document; a
   fragment of RDF which corresponds to a DAML+OIL statement identifies the concept.

Resource Service  The resource service is a simple librarian which is used to lookup Web
   pages which are *examples of* a particular concept (*i.e.* which can be used to *illustrate* a
   concept).

   In this architecture, the DLRS first contacts the ontology service to obtain a complete listing of all the language terms that are used to represent the concepts in the ontology. When a
new document is loaded into the browser, the DLRS searches for each language term and, if
found, requests its associated concept. The metadata service is also used to determine whether
any regions in the document have been annotated by authors with concept descriptors (allowing concepts to be recognised even if the document does not use the 'approved' language
terms). Having identified the significant concepts in the document, the DLRS contacts the
resource service to obtain a list of documents that are about instances of this concept.

   At this point, a number of potential link anchors and destinations have been identified for
the page. If the number of links is not consistent with the formation of a well-linked document,
the DLRS may choose to request broader or narrower concepts from the ontology service in
order to expand or cull the set of anchor destinations. When the whole document has been

considered, the DLRS can augment the DOM with links and annotations. The decisions about link culling and presentation are controlled by behaviour modules which define the navigation and interaction semantics of the resulting ontological hypertext.

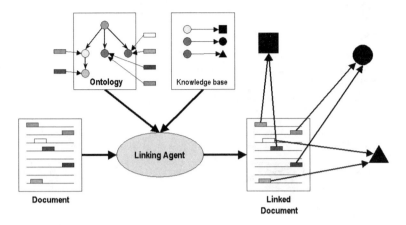

**Fig. 26.4.** Concept Links Augment Textual Links. The coloured blocks represent lexical terms, coloured circles represent concepts in an ontology, and black shapes represent Web pages.

### 26.2.2  Example: The Java Tutorial

As an example we demonstrate the application of COHSE to the *Java Tutorial*[4], a site whose educational objectives provides many possibilities to increase the breadth and accuracy of the linking in order to help students learn about the Java language.

At the very least, an ontology represents a community-agreed vocabulary that describes a collection of concepts significant to that community [30]. The first stage in applying the ontological hypertext techniques (described in the opening section) is to use the lexical representations of the ontology's concepts as search terms within the document. Any matches in the text indicate a site where a link to the matching concept could be attached (*i.e.* a potential ontological link anchor).

Beyond the programming language issues, the Java ontology contains some concepts relevant to the software development cycle and business environment as well as the history of the Java phenomenon. These concepts are required to model something about the contents of the non-technical areas of the Java Tutorial Web site. For example, these concepts could offer 'further information' about people or companies who are mentioned within the page. Of course, the nature of the further information offered depends on the 'application'. In the *Industry Connection* section of the wider Java site for example, some company names are linked to their entries under the *Solutions Marketplace* whereas some technical publications choose to link company names to a stock ticker. We choose to link to the company homepage. For links on named people, we link to their home page and to any significant documents they have written. (These choices were made by hand as a part of populating the Resource Service, and not by inference based on the information in the ontology or knowledge base.)

---

[4] http://java.sun.com/docs/books/tutorial/

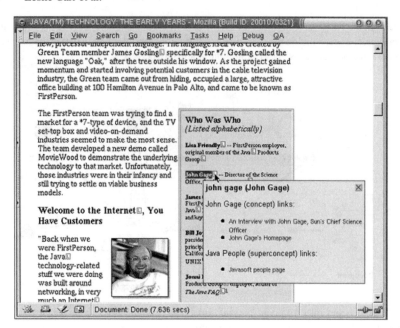

**Fig. 26.5.** Adding links on named entities

The example shown in figure 26.5 shows various name links added to the "Who Was Who" of Java community (the square boxes containing an 'L' indicate an added link). The individual chosen has resources listed about him and about the more general concept of *Javasoft people*.

This simple example illustrates a philosophical and practical problem engaging in *named entity recognition*. Specific (named) people, places or companies should be modelled as individuals in a knowledge-base, rather than concepts in an ontology. "Sun Microsystems" is not a class of things, but a individual that is a member of a class (*i.e.* Computer Companies). In the system under discussion we do not use an explicit knowledge-base, and so these entities are modelled as singleton classes within the ontology. This is also particularly applicable to our current evaluation as the Java Tutorial pages make several references to actual class names, such as a `java.io.BufferedInputStream`, which should also modelled as individuals.

The aim of ontological linking is to improve the understanding of what is being linked (and why) so our system can exert greater control over the linking process. A frequent problem with naive link-matching techniques is the tendency for over-linking, when too many words are recognised as key terms. This is particularly true in tutorial material, where many concepts are being explained. Previous attempts to control this problem in the DLS have been indiscriminate thresholding systems, which simply delete links without reference to their utility [6].

The ontology provides a better way to manage this situation: we can examine each potential link and reject it if it is 'uninteresting', for example, any link to the same kind of material as the current page. Figure 26.6a shows a tutorial page about "Working with Filter Streams", including links that explain the terms *stream* and *filter streams*. Since these types are explained on the current page, the links are redundant. In this case the author may decide to annotate the page to declare that it is about the concept *Stream*. Our conceptual model has represented this

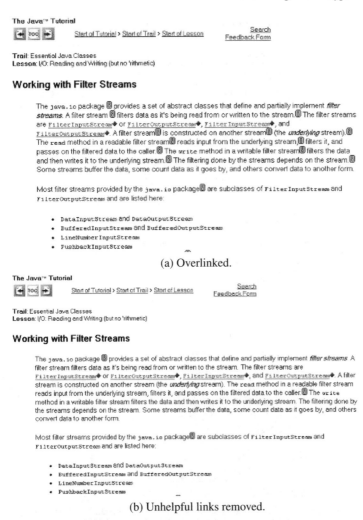

(a) Overlinked.

(b) Unhelpful links removed.

**Fig. 26.6.** Removing links based on similarity of concept

term as a concept. It has subconcepts, such as *Filter Stream*, *File Stream* and *Object Stream*. The linker can now determine that terms such as *Filter Stream* are *subconcepts* of the page's main topic. It does this by querying the ontology service for its subconcepts. It can then decide which concepts that appear in the text are unhelpful (see figure 26.6b) and it culls these while retaining links on unrelated terms such as *package* and *caller*.

Figure 26.7 illustrates some examples of how ontological linking improves the breadth and quality of linking available to users of the Java Tutorial. In Figure 26.7a the concept *Input and Output* has been linked to the relevant tutorial. The service delivers a description for the meaning of the phrase together with the most appropriate link to it. The link is structural as it actually points to the start of the current lesson. Links are also offered to two similar concepts, as determined by querying the ontology service. Figure 26.7b illustrates how the *Stream* con-

**Random Access⊠ Files**

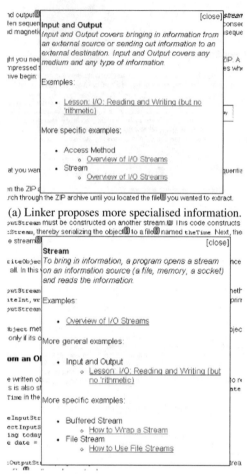

(a) Linker proposes more specialised information.

(b) Linker proposes both more specialised, as well as broader, information.

(c) Linker proposes broader information.

**Fig. 26.7.** Example linking

cept has had links provided. This time a more generalised concept is offered, in addition to more specific ones. Figure 26.7c demonstrates how the specialised concept, *Filter Stream*, has been linked. The ontology service proposes a link to the broader concept of *Stream*.

### 26.2.3 Ontologies of Argumentation

Instead of building an ontology to model the topics under discussion in the content of the documents, it can be useful to consider the structure (or rhetoric) of the discussion itself. The ScholOnto project [28] highlights the advantage of exploring the rhetorical claims that exist in scholarly and technical literature in order to build networks of knowledge. The project allows claims made inside papers to be annotated against an ontology to assert relationships between the papers. This is possible because authors make claims about their work and back these up through citations to other literature. ScholOnto captures these claims and categorises them into relationships such as *addresses*, *analyses*, *modifies*, *predicts*, and *uses*, and so an intricate network of claims is established. Figure 26.8 illustrates the claims ontology used by ScholOnto to capture the relationships between papers.

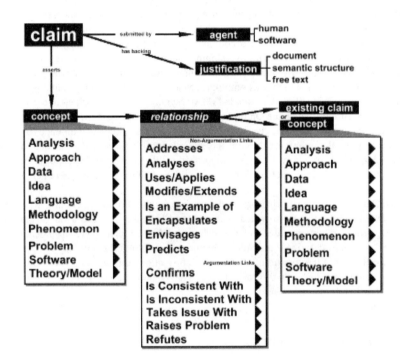

**Fig. 26.8.** A claim in the ScholOnto ontology

These broad claim types are able to capture most relationships evident in scholarly works. Analysing ScholOnto claims enables sociological queries to be answered, such as "What motivated the Dexter Hypertext Reference Model" and "What impact did Einstein's theory of relativity have?" To answer the former query, all claims in the ScholOnto knowledge base where the 'Dexter Reference Model' concept (a concept of type 'Theory/Model') has a claim relationship with another 'Theory/Model' concept are retrieved. A simple solution is then to return those claims with a relationship type of 'Modifies/Extends', 'Uses/Applies', 'Takes Issues With', 'Raises Problem', and 'Refutes'.

In theory, ScholOnto provides an elegant solution to answering otherwise complex questions, although the editorial overhead in identifying claims in source documents is likely to be large. The payoff for this overhead is a better information discovery environment, where researchers can quickly track an emerging argument or consensus across many papers in a wide-ranging digital library.

### 26.2.4 Ontologies of the Community

Instead of building ontologies to model what documents say, an alternative approach to building a hypertext environment is to model the context in which the documents are produced. A *community ontology* can be used to make explicit the network of authors, projects and affiliations whose work resulted in the production of a report or article.

The Knowledge Acquisition Community Ontology ($KA^2$) has been deployed in a community-based distributed authoring effort to make the process of annotating Web resources a joint activity between all the members of an esoteric community and provides the resulting knowledge in the form of a community portal [29]. This scenario is particularly suitable for any group of users with overlapping interests who wish to create a community-oriented research service. The technical underpinning for producing these web portals is the Ontobroker project [15], which uses ontologies to annotate Web documents and provides an ontology-based query facility. An extended HTML syntax is used to mark up documents with ontological constructs, which the Ontobroker crawler then processes. The annotated pages are parsed and the extracted knowledge represented internally as F-Logic, a language for reasoning about objects. By combining the concepts and relationships specified in the ontology with the facts collected from the Web pages, Ontobroker enables users of the web portals to pose a variety of complex queries, such as: What are the titles of all the projects where person X is a member?

The OntoPortal project [22] also provides a framework for producing community-oriented portals based on the structure provided in an ontology. Here the emphasis is not on harvesting knowledge from author-annotated web pages, but providing a principled environment to allow an editorial team to describe a research community. The role of the ontology is to guide the authors of the portal into providing the correct information; a graphical visualization of the chosen ontology (see figure 26.9) is also used as a navigation interface to help the users of the portal to locate relevant information.

## 26.3 Concluding Remarks

The objective of an ontological hypertext system must be to allow a structured knowledge model to affect a user's interaction collection of documents *in some manner*. This may be evidenced in the links placed in the documents while the user is browsing, or in the searching environment that is used to navigate to a particular document.

For a hypertext system, a significant issue may be the degree to which the knowledge (processing, inference, querying) can be integrated with the document handling environment and with the presentation of the documents themselves. This kind of system integration problem is

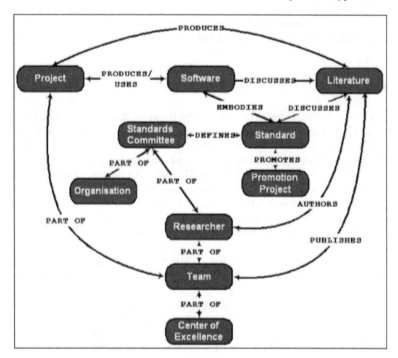

**Fig. 26.9.** A representation of an OntoPortal Community Ontology which is used as a web navigation interface

a familiar one to the open hypermedia research community; the COHSE system described in this chapter uses one typical solution. The contribution of its ontological linking service is the ability to recognise linking opportunities in the contents of the Web site by using a pre-existing terminological model of its domain of discourse and to further take advantage of this model to make simple editorial decisions on the *quality* of the links.

Although ontologies do provide a way to build *intensional* linking processes, they are not a silver bullet for hypertext designers. The effort required to author links has not been eliminated. It has rather been moved from the activity of creating explicit connections between parts of a document into creating an ontology and possibly annotating parts of a document. At first sight, this leaves a hypertext designer worse off. Creating an ontology is a substantial piece of work, and is not yet well-supported by software tools. However, many communities are in the process of defining their own ontologies for other knowledge management purposes. The expectation is that we will be able to apply these models for linking application.

Beyond investing in an ontology, the process of annotating a document with its concepts is an task shared by all the systems described in this chapter. Although it bears similarities with the activity of annotating a document with a textual comment or a link, its results can be used in a number of different applications: knowledge inferencing, intelligent querying as well as document linking.

Without the knowledge that ontologies embody, the linking of hypertext materials is either constrained by simple database design schemas or left open to the intelligence (and whim) of the author/editor. With that knowledge, ontological hypertext has the opportunity to provide a rich and principled mechanism for creating effective hypertexts.

# References

1. Andrews K., Kappe, F. and Maurer, H. (1995) Hyper-G: Towards the Next Generation of Network Information Technology. Journal of Universal Computer Science, April 1995.
2. Bechhofer, S. and Goble, C. (2001) Towards Annotation using DAML+OIL. K-Cap Workshop on Knowledge Markup and Semantic Annotation, Victoria, B.C., Canada.
3. Benjamins, V., Fensel, D. and Pérez, A. G. (1998) Knowledge Management through Ontologies. Proceedings of the 2nd International Conference on Practical Aspects of Knowledge Management (PAKM98), Basel, Switzerland.
4. Berners-Lee, T., Cailliau, J., Groff, R. and Pollermann, B. (1992) World-Wide Web: The information universe. Electronic Networking: Research, Applications and Policy, Vol. 2, No. 1, 52-58.
5. Carr L., De Roure, D., Hall, W. and Hill, G. (1995) The Distributed Link Service: A Tool for Publishers, Authors and Readers. World Wide Web Journal 1(1), 647-656, O'Reilly & Associates
6. Carr, L., De Roure, D., Davis, H. and Hall, W. (1998) Implementing an Open Link Service for the World Wide Web, World Wide Web Journal. Vol. 1, No. 2, 61-71.
7. Carr, L., Bechhofer, S., Goble, C., and Hall, W. (2001) Conceptual Linking: Ontology-based Open Hypermedia. In WWW10, Tenth World Wide Web Conference, Hong Kong.
8. Ceri S, Fraternali P, Bongio A. (2000) Web Modelling Language (WebML): a modelling language for designing Web sites. In Proceedings of the 9th International WWW Conference, Amsterdam, May 2000
9. Chaudhri, V., Farquhar, A., Fikes, R., Karp, P. and Rice, W (1998) OKBC: A Programmatic Foundation for Knowledge Base Interoperability. In AAAI-98, Madison, WI, 600-607.
10. Davis, H., W. Hall, I. Heath, G. Hill, R. Wilkins (1992) Towards an Integrated Information Environment with Open Hypermedia Systems, in ECHT '92, Proceedings of the Fourth ACM Conference on Hypertext, Milan, Italy, ACM Press, 181-190.
11. Davis, H. (1998) Referential Integrity of Links in Open Hypermedia Systems. In Proceedings of the Ninth ACM Conference on Hypertext and Hypermedia, Hypertext '98, Pittsugh, Pennsylvania, 207-216.
12. DeRose, S. (1989) Expanding the Notion of Links. In Proceedings of the Second Annual ACM Conference on Hypertext, 249-257.
13. DeRose, S., Maler, E. and Orchard, D. (eds.) (2001) XML Linking Language (XLink) Version 1.0, W3C Recommendation 27 June 2001.
14. Ellis, D., Furner, J., and Willett, P. (1996) On the creation of hypertext links in full-text documents - measurement of retrieval effectiveness. Journal of the American Society for Information Science, Vol. 47, No. 4, 287-300.
15. Fensel, D., Decker, S., Erdmann, M. and Studer, R. (1998) Ontobroker in a Nutshell. European Conference on Digital Libraries, Crete, Greece, 663-664.
16. Fensel D., van Harmelen, F., Horrocks, I., McGuinness, D.L., Patel-Schneider, P.F. (2001) OIL: An Ontology Infrastructure for the Semantic Web, IEEE INTELLIGENT SYSTEMS, Vol. 16, No. 2, 38-45.
17. Grønbæk, K., Hem, J. A., Madsen, O. L. and Sloth, L. (1993) Designing Dexter-based cooperative hypermedia systems. In Proceedings of ACM Hypertext 93, 25-38.

18. Halasz, F. and Schwartz, M. (1990) The Dexter Hypertext Reference Model, Proceedings of the Hypertext Standardization Workshop by National Institute of Science and Technology (NIST). reprinted Communications of ACM, Vol. 37, No. 2, 30-39, February 1994.

19. Hitchcock, S., Carr, L., Jiao, Z., Bergmark, D., Hall, W., Lagoze, C. and Harnad S. (2001) Developing services for open eprint archives: globalisation, integration and the impact of links. In Proceedings of 5th ACM Conference on Digital Libraries, 143-151.

20. Horrocks, I. (2000) Benchmark analysis with fact. In Proceedings of TABLEAUX 2000, 62-66.

21. International Standards Organisation. (1992) Hypermedia/Time-based Structuring Language (HyTime), ISO/IEC Standard 10744.

22. Kampa, S. (2002) Who Are The Experts? E-Scholars In The Semantic Web. PhD Thesis, University of Southampton, UK.

23. Koivunen, M. and Swick, R. (2001) Metadata Based Annotation Infrastructure offers Flexibility and Extensibility for Collaborative Applications and Beyond. K-Cap Workshop on Knowledge Markup and Semantic Annotation, Victoria, B.C., Canada.

24. Lawrence, S., David, M., Pennock, G., Flake, R., Krovetz, F., Coetzee, E., Finn, A., Kruger, A. and Giles, C. (2001) Persistence of Web References in Scientific Research, IEE Computer, Vol. 34, No. 2, 26-31.

25. Nelson, T. 1987. Literary Machines. 87.1 edn. Computer Books.

26. Ragget, D., Le Hors, A. and Jacobs, I. (eds.) (1999) HTML 4.01 Specification, W3C Recommendation 24 December 1999.

27. Schnase, J., Leggett, J., Hicks, D., Nürnberg, P., and Sanchez, J. A. (1993) Design and implementation of the HB1 hyperbase management system.

28. Shum, S. Buckingham, Motta, E., & Domingue, J. 1999. Representing Scholarly Claims in Internet Digital Libraries: A Knowledge Modeling Approach. Pages 423-442 of: Proceedings of 3rd European Conference on Research and Advanced Technology for Digital Libraries. Edusite.

29. Staab, S., Angele, J., Decker, S., Erdmann, M., Hotho, A., Maedche, A., Schnurr, H., Studer, R., & Sure, Y. 2000 (May). Semantic Community Web portals. In: Proceedings of the Tenth World Wide Web Conference, Hong Kong, China. Available from: http://www9.org/w9cdrom/index.html.

30. Uschold, M. and Gruniger, M. (1996) Ontologies: principles, methods and applications. The Knowledge Engineering Review, Vol. 11, No. 2, 93-136.

# Semantic Layering with Magpie

John Domingue, Martin Dzbor, and Enrico Motta

Knowledge Media Institute, The Open University, Milton Keynes, UK
{J.B.Domingue, M.Dzbor, E.Motta} @open.ac.uk

**Summary.** Web browsing involves two tasks: finding the right web page and then *making sense* of its content. So far, research has focused on supporting the task of finding web resources through 'standard' information retrieval mechanisms, or semantics-enhanced search. Much less attention has been paid to the second problem. In this paper we describe Magpie, a tool which supports the interpretation of web pages. Magpie offers complementary knowledge sources, which a reader can call upon to quickly gain access to any background knowledge relevant to a web resource. Magpie automatically associates an ontology-based semantic layer to web resources, allowing relevant services to be invoked within a standard web browser. From this perspective, Magpie may be seen as a step towards a *semantic web browser*. The functionality of Magpie is illustrated using examples of how it has been integrated with our lab's web resources.

## 27.1 Introduction

Browsing the web involves two main tasks: finding the right resource and making sense of its content. A significant amount of research has gone into supporting the task of finding web resources, either by means of 'standard' information retrieval mechanisms, or by means of semantics-enhanced search [11, 17]. Less attention has been paid to the second problem, supporting the interpretation of web pages. Annotation technology [15, 21, 25] allows users to associate meta-information with web resources, which can then be used to facilitate their interpretation. While this technology provides a useful way to support group discussion and shared interpretation, it is nevertheless very limited. Annotation is normally carried out manually, which means that the quality of the sensemaking support is dependent on the willingness of stakeholders to provide annotation and their ability to provide valuable information. This is of course even more of a problem, if a formal approach to annotation is assumed, based on semantic web technology [1].

This chapter describes Magpie, a technology supporting the interpretation of web pages. Magpie acts as a complementary knowledge source, which a reader can call upon to quickly gain access to any background knowledge relevant to a web resource. Magpie follows a different approach from that used by the afore-mentioned annotation technology: it automatically associates a semantic layer to a web resource, rather than relying on manual annotations. This process relies on the availability of an ontology [10], an explicit, declaratively specified representation of a domain of discourse. Ontologies are the cornerstone of the emerging semantic web: they provide the conceptual interoperability needed to allow semantic agents to make sense of information on the web and to collaborate with other semantically aware agents. Magpie uses ontologies in a similar way: to make it possible for Magpie to associate meaning with the items of information found on a web page and then, on the basis of the identified meaning, to invoke the relevant services, or offer the user the appropriate functionalities.

The Magpie-mediated association between an ontology and a web resource essentially provides an interpretative viewpoint or context over the resource in question. Indeed the overwhelming majority of web pages are created within a specific context. For example, the personal home page of a member of the Knowledge Media Institute would have normally been created within the context of that person's affiliation and organizational role. Of course, some readers would be very familiar with such context, while others would not. In the latter scenario the use of Magpie is especially advantageous, given that the context would be made explicit to the reader and context-specific functionalities will be provided. Because different readers have differing levels of familiarity with the information shown in a web page and with the relevant background domain, they require different levels of sensemaking support. A semantic layer in Magpie is consequently designed with a specific type of user in mind.

In a seminal study of how users browse the web, Tauscher and Greenberg [24] found the following statistics on the types of actions users typically carry out:

- 58% of pages visited are revisits,
- 90% of all user actions are related to navigation,
- 30% of navigation actions are through the 'Back' button,
- less than 1% of browsing actions use a history mechanism

A fairly obvious conclusion of these statistics is that web users need support in capturing what they have seen previously. Current history mechanisms, 'Back' button aside, are of little help. Magpie, automatically tracks interesting items found in a browsing session within a *semantic log*. The semantic log allows trigger services to be created, which are activated when a specific pattern of items has been found. One type of trigger service offered in Magpie is a *collector*, which collects items from a browsing session using an ontology-based filter; e.g. displaying all instance of a particular class satisfying a given condition. The following sections present several examples of the collectors as well as the illustration of sensemaking support through semantic services.

## 27.2  A Magpie Usage Scenario

Imagine a journalist is writing an article on the Knowledge Media Institute (KMi) for a magazine. One of her tasks is to collect information about the important projects led by senior KMi staff. Using a web browser with a Magpie extension, she starts with a visit to the home page of the lab's director, Enrico Motta. After loading the page, she wants to highlight interesting concepts denoting researchers, collaborating organizations, projects and research areas in the page. These concepts draw upon an existing ontology of academic and research organizations that has been populated with automatically mined instances representing the people, projects and research areas of KMi and the collaborating organizations. Fig. 1 shows the journalist's browser with the concepts of interest highlighted using the Magpie toolbar. A key requirement for the design of Magpie was that a web page viewed through the system should look the same as when viewed in a standard web browser. This constraint reduces the confusion that can occur when the content and/or appearance of a web page are altered. The Magpie toolbar (see close-up in Fig. 2) allows users to toggle highlighting for the specified types of entities (these are ontology dependent), which were annotated in the page using an *ontology-based lexicon* (gazetteer) approach. The 'Services' button in the toolbar activates a context dependent Semantic Services menu, which replaces the standard web browser's right-click menu.

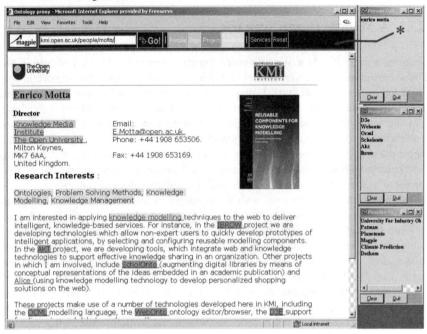

**Fig. 1.** Enrico Motta's home page viewed through Magpie. Known *people*, *organizations*, *projects* and *research areas* are highlighted using the Magpie toolbar (marked by '*'). On the right-hand side are three Magpie collectors – the top two log the people and projects found in the browsing session. The bottom one shows the projects associated with the people found in the page, which were not explicitly mentioned anywhere on that page.

On the right-hand side of Fig. 1 are three Magpie collectors. These are automatically filled by Magpie trigger services as the user browses. During a browsing session, all entities found on accessed web pages are asserted into a semantic log knowledge base (KB). Collectors are set up to show a particular, semantically filtered view of the semantic log. For instance, the top two collectors in Fig. 1 show the people and projects that have been recognized. So far, only one person

**Fig. 2.** Details of the Magpie toolbar after selecting '*People*' and '*Project*' entity types (classes)[1]. The button labeled '*Services*' (marked by '♠') toggles a right-click 'Semantic services' menu in the browser.

---

[1] Toolbar buttons come from the ontology selected by the user. In our scenario, the journalist uses AKT reference ontology; hence, the labels represent top-level AKT classes.

and six projects have been explicitly mentioned.

The bottom collector shows the projects associated with any people recognized during the session. Note that these projects have not been mentioned explicitly on any page; rather, they originate from the populated domain ontology. As we can see from Fig. 1, Enrico Motta is associated with six additional projects not mentioned explicitly in his web page.

From the content of the web page our journalist can see that the ScholOnto project might be one of the sought-after projects for her report. Hence she wonders if any related projects could be included in the same section. She right-clicks the 'ScholOnto' term, and the semantic services menu shown in Fig. 3 appears.

The choices in the menu depend on the class of the selected entity within the se-

**Fig. 3.** Specific 'semantic services' menu associated with the selected concept *'ScholOnto'*. Choices displayed depend on the class of the item selected – in this case a *'Project'*[2].

lected ontology. In our case, 'ScholOnto' is classified as a project, so project-related options are displayed. The journalist selects an option labeled 'Shares Research Areas With' to get an answer to her question. Magpie responds by

---

[2] The same caveat applies as earlier, the services are associated with the classes, classes depend on the selected ontology; hence, the semantic services are in principle user-customizable (via ontology selection/subscription).

**Fig. 4.** Results of the '*Shares Research Areas With*' semantic query for the '*ScholOnto*' project shows a list of similar projects ordered by the number of shared areas and then alphabetically.

displaying projects that share one or more research areas with ScholOnto. The results are ordered by the number of common research areas and alphabetically (see Fig. , foreground window). The journalist notices that two of the projects related hence, are related to Enrico. She decides to view the Climate Prediction project's details by selecting 'Climate Prediction' in the collector, and then the 'Web Page' option in the displayed menu. Selecting items in collectors brings up the same semantic services menu as when items are selected on a web page.

## 27.3  Magpie Design Principles

The overall goal in designing Magpie is to support the interpretation of arbitrary web documents through the addition of an ontology-derived semantic layer. Let us now unpack this overall goal into a set of design principles. These principles may be treated as high-level functional requirements for a tool providing ontology-based sensemaking support for navigating the web. The implementation of the individual principles is detailed further. Each principle is listed below together with an applicable part of the scenario that provides a justification for it:

- Magpie should run in and extend a *standard web browser* – we want to minimize the steps that users go through to use our tool (also many large organizations mandate a specific web browser).

- Magpie should *preserve the appearance* of a web page – users would quickly get confused if web pages browsed through a semantic browser did not look the same as when browsed traditionally or changed their appearance.
- Magpie should *separate the mark-up* (the populated ontology) from the documents – this enables different viewpoints (from different communities) to be layered on top of the same web resources.
- Magpie should let the users select their particular *viewpoint* – i.e. the ontology used for mark-up and annotation should be customizable by the user. (Note that our scenario uses a single ontology but the mechanism for ontology selection is built into other applications of Magpie).
- Consequently, Magpie should allow the user to choose a sub-set of *interesting concepts* from a particular ontology, which would be used for the entity annotation, highlighting and association of the semantic services (not in the scenario described earlier).
- Magpie should work with *any web page* – this means that it should work without the aid of manual pre-processing or relying on a richly marked-up content (e.g. XML or RDF). We assume the documents are not 'pre-marked-up' manually by an author or librarian[3].
- Magpie users should not incur any significant time penalty. This means that in contrast with most approaches to Named Entities Recognition (NER), Magpie must always provide *fast, real-time mark-up* mechanisms. More precise mark-up can still carried out in the background by an independent NER semantic service, while the user browses a page. Such additional mark-up may then be delivered to the user's browser in an *incremental* (progressive) fashion, thus refining and complementing the fast mechanisms.

## 27.4  Magpie Architecture

The architecture of Magpie is shown in Fig. . Magpie acts as a bridge – a mediator between formally structured ontological descriptions and semantically unstructured HTML documents. The Magpie server provides HTTP access to a library of knowledge models containing domain ontologies, populated KBs, semantic services and a semantic log KB. HTTP access is handled by a customized web server [23], which offers a library of methods to dynamically generate the appropriate content and reason about it. Magpie accepts ontologies represented in RDF(S) [2], DAML+OIL [5], Ontolingua [8] and OCML [18]. The latter is the internal representation for the reasoning. Shortly, we shall include ontologies represented in OWL [22]. The services (as those in Fig. and Fig. ), are defined in a 'Services' module of the Magpie server, and detailed in section '*On-*

---

[3] However, although Magpie does not require any explicit mark-up in the documents, it is also able to exploit the existing mark-up if this is available for the web page being loaded.

*demand Semantic Services'*. The semantic log KB – the last component of the server, is used by the Magpie trigger services, which are described in section '*Trigger Semantic Services*' further in this chapter.

A set of techniques ('populators') is used to populate the ontology from heterogeneous data stored in web accessible RDF documents, and mined from ODBC compliant databases or standard web pages. The ontology population process is briefly mentioned in section '*Before Deploying Magpie*' further in this chapter, and a separate paper shall devote more space to the issue of ontology population and usage of ontology-based lexicons. Here, we present a broad overview of the Magpie technology and they main benefits it may bring to the users.

### 27.4.1  Magpie Plug-In

We will now describe the Magpie plug-in in detail. As can be seen in Fig. 6, the architecture of the Magpie plug-in is broadly composed of three main parts:
- The *Magpie Proxy* – this component is responsible for parsing HTML-based web pages and annotating them according to an ontology-derived lexicon. All

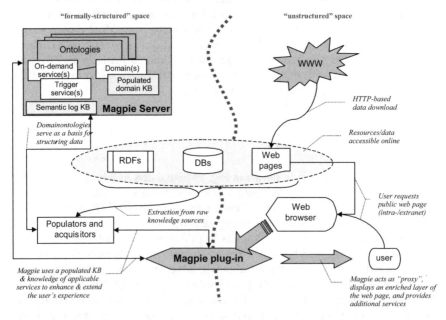

**Fig. 5.** Overall architecture of the Magpie framework for semantic browsing

this takes place on the fly, before a document is displayed in a user's browser.
- The *Magpie Browser Extension* – this part of the plug-in sits in the browser and controls all the interactions with Magpie. Specifically, it contains the user

interface components which visualize entities found in a web page and enables users to interact with the semantic services

- The *Magpie Browser/Server Interface* – this component mediates between the Magpie Browser Extension and the Magpie Server. It handles both user-requested (from a right mouse click) and trigger semantic services.

The Magpie proxy has two parts. The HTML parser parses incoming web pages and applies pre-defined parsing rules to each HTML tag type. The content of the web page is matched against an ontology-derived lexicon residing on the Magpie server. Lexicon entries are generated overnight from the instances within the populated ontological knowledge base. We use several simple linguistic rules, such as recognition of abbreviations or people's names. Also, ontology specific transformation rules can be defined. For example, the classes in our ontology have `pretty-name` and `variant-names` slots, which are used to generate the lexicon, and consequently, to recognize the concepts of interest on a web page. In addition to these, common-sense variants to peoples' names are derived by rules, for example "E. Motta" or "Motta, E." from a `pretty-name` "Enrico Motta". These simple rules assume uniqueness of the instance in the ontology. The scenario shown earlier uses the AKT reference ontology, which satisfies this rather hard constraint[4].

We are currently investigating how other named entity extraction mechanisms can be incorporated into the document parser to enhance its precision and recall. Simultaneously, we explore another path to improve the capabilities of the parser, namely through providing the parsing through a set of independent *semantic web services*. The user would be able to choose which of several implementations of parser/NER algorithms to use based on his or her specific time and precision constraints. These 'parsing services' may run in parallel and may each focus on a slightly different aspect of the web page.

Once an entity from the lexicon has been recognized in the web page, the second component of the Magpie proxy – the HTML annotator, annotates it using <SPAN...> tags and links it with a relevant ontological instance/class within the chosen ontology. Following the principle of not altering the appearance of web pages the new tags are initially not visible. If the user moves the mouse over a semantically layered tag, or if the class of entities is selected in the Magpie toolbar (see Fig. 2), the corresponding text on the page is highlighted. Our approach to visualizing the semantic layers means that users remain in control of what type of entities is visible at any time. We argue that this improves navigation through the content. Recognized entities are then passed to a Semantic Log Updater (a component from the Magpie browser/server interface), where, through the KB Assert Interface, they are asserted into the Semantic Log KB that resides on the Magpie server. The purpose of semantic logging is addressed later.

---

[4] The ontology is available for inspection on http://www.aktors.org.

The Magpie Browser Extensions incorporate user interface components, which allow users to interact with the semantic services. First, the Visual Highlighter highlights the matched entities found in the page. Second, the semantic services menu (shown in Fig. ) is generated by the 'Context' component that co-operates with the 'Services' module of the Magpie server. Finally, the Magpie trigger services are provided by the Collector, Summarizer and Visualizer components of

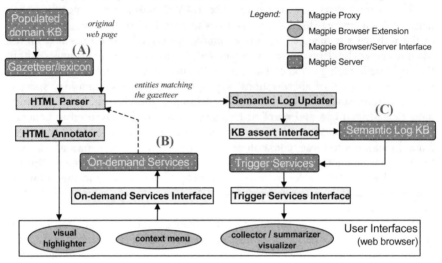

**Fig. 6.** Interaction model of the Magpie plug-in architecture with three basic 'threads'

the browser extension. Trigger services and the components are described later. The Magpie Browser Extension also includes the graphical user interface (GUI) for the main Magpie toolbar shown in Fig. 2. The Magpie Browser/Server interfaces handle all interactions between the Magpie server, and the user interfaces in the Magpie Browser extension (including HTTP requests).

We should emphasize (again) that within Magpie the ontology provides a specific viewpoint onto the web. We envisage that users can select a particular ontology depending on their current task from a set of 'subscribed' ontologies. In this way, the same web resources may cater for the very different interests of different communities. These communities may have different viewpoints onto the 'shared' web resources. Hence, the content may need to be re-interpreted in the light of a new ontology (i.e. re-parsed and re-annotated). Our assumption is that at any time, only one ontology is actively used for the annotation, which avoids most of the consistency issues between multiple knowledge sources.

### 27.4.2 Annotation and Lexical Clashes

As we mentioned earlier the lexicon used for matching against items in a web page is generated from an ontology during a setup phase. The issue of ontological and lexical clashes is one of the biggest obstacles in the practical deployment of gazetteer or lexicon-based entity recognition methodologies. We shall discuss these issues more thoroughly in future papers, so let us only mention a few types of clashes our Magpie is able to deal with – for example, when two distinct entities within an ontology generate the same lexical term. Two types of lexical clashes can occur; possible ways how they could be treated are listed below a particular clash type:

1. An entity is an instance of different top-level classes; for example, 'Magpie' may be a 'Project' or a 'Developed Technology'. These classes lead to slightly different semantic services, so an appropriate disambiguation is needed:
   - one entity/class may take precedence over the other by virtue of a rule, or
   - the user is asked to indicate, which class should be used for the interpretation.

2. The clashing entities are instances of the same top level class. For example, using our trivial rules for generating the lexicon from the ontology the instances of `enrico-motta` and `emanuela-motta` could derive the same lexical term "Motta, E.". In such case:
   - one entity takes precedence over the other by virtue of some rule, or
   - semantic services carried out on the term return the combined results for both instances, and let the user to choose.

## 27.5  Semantic Services

In the previous section, we presented the conceptual architecture of Magpie, and showed how a semantic layer is created, displayed and activated. The main benefits of using Magpie however are generated from the ability to deploy semantic services on top of the semantic layer. These services are provided to the user as a physically independent layer over a particular HTML document. Magpie distinguishes between two types of semantic services, each having a specific user interaction model – in Fig. 6 depicted as interaction threads (B) and (C).

According to the process model in Fig. 6, the parser identifies entities from a chosen ontological lexicon in the raw web page (thread A). Each discovered entity is annotated and recorded in a semantic log, and the annotated document is displayed in the user's web browser. This process was described in section '*Magpie Plug-in*' above. Thread (B) represents services activated on a user's request; i.e. a reader explicitly selects an entity s/he is interested in, and using a right mouse click invokes a contextual *Services menu*. The *on-demand* semantic services are described in the next sub-section. Alternatively, semantic services may be based on certain patterns or *footprints* of the entities that co-occur in a particular document or during a particular browsing session (thread C). In this chapter, we refer to this log-based functionality as *trigger services*.

### 27.5.1 On-Demand Semantic Services

As already mentioned, semantic services are enabled by clicking on the 'Services' button in the Magpie toolbar (see the marker '♠' in Fig. 2). When the semantic services are activated, the contextual (right-click) menu of a web browser is over-ridden by an *on-demand services menu*. The 'on-demand services' menu is also context-dependent as could be expected; however, in this case, we are dealing with a semantic context defined by the membership of a particular entity to a particular ontological class. The information on these memberships is contained in the lexicon generated from the ontology in a setup phase (see previous section).

In addition to domain ontologies, Magpie uses a Services module (see boxes labeled 'Services' in the top-left corner of Fig. ). This module formally defines what operations can be performed on particular class(es) of entities, and the semantics of each operation. Generally, the semantic services can be defined and published in line with standards of the emerging web services technology. Thus, different groups of users may see different services to suit their knowledge and expertise. We have tools to tackle service publication, and we are currently working on the full integration of the publishing process with Magpie. In the scenario of using Magpie as a semantic portal for organizational research, we assumed that the services were defined by the knowledge engineer and associated with the appropriate ontological classes. For instance, class Project included the following operations (see menu displayed in Fig. 3):

- Show a project's details, members, website;
- Show the research areas tackled by a particular project;
- Show the project publications and bibliographic data;
- Show the technologies resulting from a project; and
- Show projects tackling similar issues (share research scope).

Similarly to parsing and annotation, the 'on-demand services' menu is also generated on the fly. When a right click occurs, it is handled by the Magpie browser extension, and through the Magpie browser/server interface the Magpie server is asked for the services that are available for a particular entity. The request uses the information about class membership of a particular entity that was created while annotating the content. If there are any applicable semantic services available, Magpie displays them in a menu, and lets the user choose what s/he is interested in. A selection of an option leads to another request to the 'Services' module of the Magpie server to perform the requested reasoning and/or execute the applicable method. The knowledge-level reasoning provides the requested context for a particular entity. This is delivered to the web browser, annotated by the Magpie proxy (as any other web page), and finally, displayed in a dedicated browser window on a user's computer.

Thus, Magpie provides two complementary methods for web browsing. First, it implements *syntactic browsing* through the <A HREF=...> anchors inserted into a document by its author. A document accessed via usual anchors is treated as described in the previous section; i.e. it is parsed, annotated, and displayed with a Magpie toolbar to facilitate semantically enriched user interaction. The second browsing method in Magpie follows the customized *semantic anchors* created by the Magpie proxy, and the applicable, dynamically generated semantic services. While the first method gives access to the *statically linked content*, the second method makes available the *semantic context* of a particular entity. The two methods are visually differentiated to minimize any confusion, and provide complementary functionality. Fig. shows a sample semantic services menu for term 'ScholOnto' (which belongs to the 'Project' class). The semantic context corresponding to the user's request for similar projects, is displayed in Fig. , and in this case contains a list of ontologically related projects that are displayed in a new browser window.

```
(def-watcher collect-peoples-projects  peoples-projects
   (found-item ?time ?address ?page-url ?person)
   (person ?person)
   (has-project-member ?project ?person)
   (not (found-item ?time2 ?address ?page-url2 ?project))
   :action (collect ?project ?page-url)))
```

**Fig. 7.** Watcher definition for trigger service "People's Projects" written in OCML. The results of using this method with the semantic log KB are displayed in the bottom right-hand collector in Fig. 1.

### 27.5.2  Trigger Semantic Services

User-requested (or on-demand) semantic services are not the only means for interacting with the relevant background knowledge. A number of researchers stress the importance of active or push services. Active services take different forms; e.g., activity critics in domain dependent design environments [9], or content guides in an online shopping context [6]. The main feature distinguishing the active services from the user-requested ones is that they tend to "look over the user's shoulder", gather useful facts, and present appropriate conclusions.

Such services are depicted in Fig. 6 by the interaction thread (C) on the right hand side. As can be seen, a pre-condition for having active services is to keep *history logs* of browsing, particularly a log of the recognized entities. The label 'browsing history' is more than appropriate because a log accumulates findings not only from the current web page, but also from previously visited pages in the same browsing session.

The process of semantic logging runs in parallel with the web page annotation (see Fig. 6). While an annotated web page is displayed in a browser, the data from the log are sent to the Magpie server component responsible for semantic log maintenance. The data from the logs are asserted as facts into a 'working' KB. Several *watchers* monitor and respond to patterns in the asserted *facts*. When the relevant assertions have been made for a particular watcher, a semantic service response is *triggered*, and applicable information delivered to the dedicated window in the user's web browser. A few examples of the results of a trigger service firing are shown on the right-hand side of Fig. 1 ('People', 'Projects' and 'People's Projects' collector windows).

Fig. 7 shows the definition for the `collect-peoples-projects` watcher that is a part of the trigger service `peoples-projects`, shown at the bottom right of Fig. 1. When a web page is viewed in Magpie the Semantic Log Updater (see Fig. 6) asserts `found-item` facts, for each of the lexical entities found, into the Semantic Log KB. The watcher from Fig. 7 triggers if a person is found in the log, and s/he is a member of a project, which is not yet present in the log. After triggered, the project and the URL of the page where the person was found on are collected. Future work will enable Magpie users to create watchers using a direct publication interface.

The information deliverable in this way may range from a simple collection of relevant items to sophisticated guidance on browsing or browsing history visualization. Since the reasoning server component taps into a knowledge base constructed potentially from the logs of community members, the guidance or history visualization may draw on community knowledge and behaviors. A community for these purposes can be understood both narrowly and broadly. Narrowly, it can be a possibly formal group of individuals who work together or are members of the same organization. Broadly, a community can be more dynamic, and can consist of the individuals subscribing to the same viewpoint (ontology) when browsing web. Such a broader sense would be clearly relevant in our scenario, where a journalist was not a formal member of KMi, nonetheless, s/he could share the same reference ontology to interpret KMi web pages.

Such a management of browsing history is clearly beneficial, especially if we follow the argument mentioned in the introduction that 58% of all visits to web documents are to sites visited previously [24], but that history mechanisms are used infrequently. This large number of re-occurring visits calls for a more sophisticated approach to the management of browsing histories. Indeed, one of design recommendations from their study was that bookmarks should have a meaningful representation. History management based on the semantics of the visited pages, and implemented by a *triggered semantic layer* may help to alleviate issues with current, syntactic and linear (access time ordered) methods.

Although the design goal for our two types of services is the same – to provide users with additional knowledge to support the interpretation of web pages and to assist in information gathering – the underlying frameworks are different. The 'on-demand' services are invoked by a specific user request. Backward chaining (goal-driven) reasoning from the user's query gives a response, which is typically presented as a new web page. The trigger service is invoked when a watcher matches a pattern within the semantic log. The pattern causes forward chaining (data-driven) reasoning, results of which are displayed by a change in the interface. In Fig. 1, trigger services amend one of the three collectors. The two types of services are briefly summarized in Table 1.

**Table 1.** Magpie on-demand and trigger services comparison

| Feature | On-demand | Trigger |
|---|---|---|
| Source of service | User's request | Pattern in semantic log |
| Reasoning method | Backward chaining | Forward chaining |
| Delivery form | 'Pull' (on-demand) | 'Push' (triggered) |

Note that the Magpie trigger services are different from the growing number of existing web logging tools [26]. The goal of these web-logging tools is to monitor user's activity with the intention to measure the usability of a particular web site. In the Magpie architecture, the semantic logs are kept to provide trigger services that could support the interpretation of a web document and/or information gathering.

## 27.6  Before Deploying Magpie

Deploying Magpie within a particular domain involves the following two steps, which can be understood as *pre-conditions* of a meaningful user's interaction with the Magpie tool:

1. Choosing or developing an ontology – within the Magpie context it is important that the ontology represents the intended viewpoint (with respect to the web resources, and it is able to support the desired semantic services.
2. Population of the ontology – the ontology itself is a skeleton for clarifying the domain structure; it should be populated with specific entities, which represent items of interest to the intended users. For scalability, the ontology population should be automated, and (possibly) integrated with working practices. We briefly discuss some techniques for population below.

A lot of publications have been written about ontology design whether from a perspective of knowledge acquisition or knowledge representation. The theory of ontology construction and/or implementation is beyond the scope of this chapter. Some examples from our earlier work showing how we have constructed and implemented ontologies for a variety of domains are given in [6, 7, 19].

In addition to the ontologies Magpie takes advantage of populated knowledge bases, which are the primary source of knowledge for the process of parsing and annotation. We currently use three techniques for ontology population, each of them suitable for different types of domain and content:

- Importing from *online semantic resources* – as mentioned earlier, Magpie takes ontologies represented in RDF(S), DAML+OIL and Ontolingua.
- Importing from an *ODBC compliant database* – the Magpie server includes tools for mining data from a database and converting them into OCML instances of a chosen ontology.

- By *information extraction* – we have used a dedicated tool – MnM [25] developed in-house, which enables information extraction engines, such as Amilcare [4], to be integrated with the Magpie knowledge model component.

Techniques corresponding to the first bullet point assume an existing repository of structured knowledge. For example, screen scraping is a technique that can gather a lot of data that can in turn be used to populate ontologies. Screen scraping techniques (i.e. various scripts accessing the content of web pages) have led to the construction of RDF resources by encoding data from all UK computer science departments. These repositories are available from Hyphen.info, and were used in the AKT project[5]. Techniques from the category under second and third bullet points are more knowledge-intensive and focus on extracting knowledge from the raw texts or databases.

## 27.7  Related Work

One of the inspirations for Magpie was the COHSE system [3]. COHSE combines an Open Hypermedia System with an ontology server into a framework for ontological linking – an ontology-derived lexicon is used to add links to arbitrary web pages. The links are added either by proxy server or by an augmented Mozilla™ browser. The distinctions between Magpie and COHSE are due to their differing design goals. The design goals for COHSE were to a) separate web links from the web pages and b) to make these links conceptual (i.e. potentially generated from ontology). The goal for Magpie is to support interpretation and information gathering. Magpie's interface enables ontological differences to be highlighted, and the services provided are dependent on the class of entity found. While services can be used for 'semantically browsing' the context of the recognized entities, the main purpose of the services is to give users the access to richer information, embed a particular web resource into its context, and eventually facilitate semantics-oriented browsing history management. Magpie also offers trigger services using the semantic log. Neither type of Magpie service is meant to replace the static web links; they act as an auxiliary knowledge source available at the user's fingertips. The COHSE framework is described by Les Carr *et al.* in this book.

In the last few years, a number of tools have emerged that support the annotation of web pages. A classic example is the Amaya HTML editor, which implements the Annotea infrastructure [15]. Annotea facilitates the RDF-based markup of documents as they are created. The authors or viewers may add various meta-statements to a document, which are separate from the document itself and are accessible to collaborating teams via a centralized annotation server. The annotation in this sense centers on attaching additional information to a chunk of content on an arbitrary web page. This feature of Annotea makes it a powerful

---

[5] For details see URLs http://www.hyphen.info and http://www.aktors.org.

tool for the joint authoring of documents where a small group of collaborating agents share a common goal. However, the same feature may make it more difficult to facilitate a similar form of annotation sharing in 'open' user communities. In these cases, there is no guarantee that a freely articulated annotation would convey the same meaning to the different users.

Another difference of the Annotea framework as compared to Magpie is the source of annotations. Annotea assumes that at least one author (human) is willing to invest additional effort into making a page semantically richer. Magpie is more liberal and assumes a reader subscribes to a particular domain ontology, which is then used to provide relevant background knowledge. It may be argued that ontology creation takes even more effort than manual document mark-up. This is true; however, ontology is a domain model, a shared viewpoint that can be re-used for different purposes, not solely for the annotation of a single document. Thus, the effort spent on designing a shared ontology is greater in the short term but in the longer term, it is a more cost-effective way of recording a shared point of view.

A similar approach to annotating documents can be found in other research projects. Within the Enrich project [20], organizational learning was facilitated by enriching web pages with discussion pages and shared ontologies. Ontological enrichment has been carried out at the page level of granularity. The CREAM-based Ont-O-Mat/Annotizer [12] is a tool similar to our MnM [25], which integrates ontologies and information extraction tools. As with MnM, Amilcare [4] provides information extraction support, and ontologies are represented in DAML+OIL. Annotations in this framework are very close to those advocated in this paper. Any ontological instance, attribute or relation known in a particular ontology may be utilized as an annotation. A key feature of the Ont-O-Mat tool is its use of discourse representations to structure the relatively flat output of Amilcare according to the chosen ontology, thus facilitating the ontology population.

The CREAM research project demonstrates an important feature of ontology-based annotation and document enrichment. Namely, any annotating tool must be aware of already recognized entities and their relationships to the ontological instances. This is important to bear in mind especially if one wants to include newly recognized entities into the ontology; the issues of redundancy and multiple definitions of an entity may occur rather frequently. CREAM's annotation inference resembles our trigger services produced by a data-driven reasoning. On the other hand, our 'on-demand' services smoothly and seamlessly address the issue identified above – the awareness of the existing relationships and the actual context of ontological instances.

The SHOE project [14] proposed an extension to HTML to allow the specification of ontological information within HTML-based documents. In addition to the inclusion of a semantically rich, ontological knowledge, SHOE attempted to make these inclusions re-usable and understandable 'throughout the web'. An editor was developed to support web page annotation. As with the tools mentioned above, and unlike our Magpie framework, SHOE relies on the offline mark-up of web documents. Once that is accomplished, the enriched documents are published, and dedicated tools may use the contextual knowledge (e.g. Exposé web crawler [13]).

## 27.8 Conclusions

Reducing the information overload caused by the growing web is often cited as the premise for work on supporting the retrieval of relevant documents. But finding relevant documents is only half of the story. Their interpretation involves a reader in understanding the surrounding context, in which the document was created. In order to gain the full understanding a reader will require knowledge of the specific terms mentioned and the implicit relationships contained both within the document and between the document and other external knowledge sources. Magpie addresses this issue by capturing context within an ontology, which then is used to enrich web documents with a semantic layer. Semantic services expose relevant segments of the background context according to the user's needs.

As we described above, certain design criteria are critical if semantic layering is to be both useful and usable. If desired Magpie users are able to browse the web in a standard way with negligible differences in the user experience. Magpie can achieve this because it works in standard web browsers with standard markup languages, presents web pages without altering their layout or appearance, and involves only a small time overhead – it takes less than 1 second to parse even relatively large web pages.

The key principle underlying the design of Magpie is that the user is able to control to what extent semantic browsing comes to the fore. The Magpie toolbar enables terms to be made visible according to their ontological category. The Magpie framework enables arbitrary semantic actions to be triggered on patterns of items found within a semantic log. Trigger services allow certain types of tasks to be delegated. The simple examples from the scenario enable semantically designated types of entities to be collected for later inspection. However, more complex trigger services can be implemented. For example, the Magpie proxy has an option to automatically parse web pages linked to the current page. This allows *reconnaissance services* [16] to be set up, which would alert the user when an interesting neighbouring page is identified.

Magpie tackles some of the issues found by Tauscher and Greenberg in their study [24] of browsing behavior. They concluded that users need better support in managing the histories of visited web pages. The semantic log in Magpie can help with this as it forms the basis for semantic bookmarks. Previously accessed pages can be found by a semantic query on the entities found in the page; as e.g. "find a page seen early last week mentioning semantic web research funded by a large Petroleum Company". Among other issues mentioned earlier, our future work will investigate how can a query answering system using visual and natural languages be integrated with the Magpie framework.

Another topic of interest for the Magpie effort in specific, as well as semantic web research in general, is the issue of *disambiguation*. In other words, how can the existing linguistic techniques be employed for the exploration of a concept neighbourhood? How can the sliding windows over such a neighbourhood be used to pull out the meaning and the context of a particular concept? One research strand of our future works aims to investigate the interplay between various similarity-based techniques, 'brute-force' key term extraction techniques and methods taking in the account the 'ontological' rather than syntactic neighbourhood.

Attention as opposed to information is now widely acknowledged to be the scarce resource in the Internet age. Consequently, tools that can leverage semantic resources to take some of the burden of the interpretation task from the human reader are going to be of enormous use. Magpie – the technology as well as the tool, is one of the steps towards achieving this goal.

## Acknowledgements

The Magpie effort is supported by the climate*prediction*.net and the Advanced Knowledge Technologies (AKT) projects. Climate*prediction*.net is sponsored by the UK Natural Environment Research Council and UK Department of Trade and Industry's eScience Initiative, and involves Oxford University, CLRC Rutherford Appleton Labs and The Open University. AKT is an Interdisciplinary Research Collaboration (IRC) sponsored by the UK Engineering and Physical Sciences Research Council by grant GR/N15764/01. The AKT IRC comprises the Universities of Aberdeen, Edinburgh, Sheffield, Southampton and The Open University.

This paper has benefited from the conversations with Marc Eisenstadt, Nigel Shadbolt, Maria Vargas-Vera, and other colleagues from KMi and the University of Southampton. The Magpie graphics are work of Harriett Cornish from KMi.

## References

1.    Berners-Lee, T., Hendler, J., and Lassila, O., *The Semantic Web*. Scientific American, 2001. **279**.

2.    Brickley, D. and Guha, R., *Resource Description Framework (RDF) Schema Specification*, 2000, World Wide Web Consortium. (URL: http://www.w3.org/TR/2000/CR-rdf-schema-20000327).

3.    Carr, L., Bechhofer, S., Goble, C., *et al. Conceptual Linking: Ontology-based Open Hypermedia*. In *Proc. of the 10th International WWW Conference*. 2001. Hong Kong.

4.    Ciravegna, F. *Adaptive Information Extraction from Text by Rule Induction and Generalisation*. In *Proc. of the 17th International Joint Conference on AI*. 2001. Washington, USA.

5.  DAML.org, *Reference description of the DAML+OIL ontology mark-up language.* 2001, http://www.DAML.org/2001/03/reference.html.

6.  Domingue, J., Martins, M., Tan, J., *et al. Alice: Assisting Online Shoppers Through Ontologies and Novel Interface Metaphors.* In *Proc. of the 13th European Knowledge Acquisition Workshop (EKAW).* 2002. Spain.

7.  Dzbor, M., Paralic, J., and Paralic, M. *Knowledge Management in a Distributed Organisation.* In *Proc. of the 4th IEEE/IFIP Conference on IT for Balanced Systems (BASYS'2000).* 2000. Berlin, Germany.

8.  Farquhar, A., Fikes, R., and Rice, J. *The Ontolingua Server: a Tool for Collaborative Ontology Construction.* In *Proc. of the Knowledge Acquisition Workshop.* 1996. Banff, Canada.

9.  Fischer, G. *Domain-Oriented Design Environments.* In *Proc. of the 7th Knowledge-Based Software Engineering Conference (KBSE'92).* 1992: IEEE Computer Society.

10. Gruber, T.R., *A Translation approach to Portable Ontology Specifications.* Knowledge Acquisition, 1993. **5**(2): p.199-221.

11. Guarino, N., Masolo, C., and Vetere, G., *OntoSeek: Content-Based Access to the Web.* IEEE Intelligent Systems, 1999. **14**(3): p.70-80.

12. Handschuh, S., Staab, S., and Maedche, A. *CREAM - Creating relational metadata with a component-based, ontology driven annotation framework.* In *Proc. of the International Semantic Web Working Symposium (SWWS).* 2001. California, USA.

13. Heflin, J. and Hendler, J., *A Portrait of the Semantic Web in Action.* IEEE Intelligent Systems, 2001. **16**(2): p.54-59.

14. Heflin, J., Hendler, J., and Luke, S. *Reading Between the Lines: Using SHOE to Discover Implicit Knowledge from the Web.* In *Proc. of the AAAI-98 Workshop on AI and Information Integration.* 1998.

15. Kahan, J., Koivunen, M.-R., Prud'Hommeaux, E., *et al. Annotea: An Open RDF Infrastructure for Shared Web Annotations.* In *Proc. of the 10th International WWW Conference.* 2001. Hong-Kong.

16. Lieberman, H., Fry, C., and Weitzman, L., *Exploring the web with reconnaissance agents.* Communications of the ACM, 2001. **44**(8): p.69-75.

17. McGuinness, D.L. *Ontological Issues for Knowledge-Enhanced Search.* In *Proc. of the Formal Ontology in Information Systems.* 1998.

18. Motta, E., *Reusable Components for Knowledge Modelling.* Frontiers in AI and Applications. 1997, The Netherlands: IOS Press.

19. Motta, E., Buckingham Shum, S., and Domingue, J., *Ontology-Driven Document Enrichment: Principles, Tools and Applications.* International Journal of Human-Computer Studies, 2000. **52**(5): p.1071-1109.

20. Mulholland, P., Zdrahal, Z., Domingue, J., *et al., Integrating working and learning: a document enrichment approach.* Journal of Behaviour and Information Technology, 2000. **19**(3): p.171-180.

21. Ovsiannikov, I.A., Arbib, M.A., and Mcneill, T.H., *Annotation Technology.* International Journal of Human-Computer Studies, 1999. **50**: p.329-362.

22. Patel-Schneider, P.F., Horrocks, I., and van Harmelen, F., *OWL Web Ontology Language 1.0 Abstract Syntax.* 2002, (URL http://www.w3.org/TR/owl-absyn/).

23. Riva, A. and Ramoni, M., *LispWeb: A Specialised HTTP Server for Distributed AI Applications.* Computer Networks and ISDN Systems, 1996. **28**(7-11): p.953-961.

24. Tauscher, L. and Greenberg, S., *How People Revisit Web Pages: Empirical Findings and Implications for the Design of History Systems.* International Journal of Human Computer Studies, 2001. **47**(1): p.97-138.

25. Vargas-Vera, M., Motta, E., Domingue, J., *et al. MnM: Ontology Driven Semi-automatic and Automatic Support for Semantic Markup.* In *Proc. of the 13th European Knowledge Acquisition Workshop (EKAW).* 2002. Spain.

26. Zaiane, O.R., Xin, M., and Han, J. *Discovering Web Access Patterns and Trends by Applying OLAP and Data Mining Technology on Web Logs.* In *Proc. of the Advances in Digital Libraries (ADL).* 1998. California, USA.

# Ontologies and Metadata for eLearning

Jan Brase[1] and Wolfgang Nejdl[2]

[1]  Information System Institute, University of Hannover
[2]  Learning Lab Lower Saxony, Hannover

**Summary.** This chapter gives an overview over the use of **Ontologies and Metadata for eLearning** as well as about innovative approaches and techniques we developed for enhanced eLearning scenarios. After a brief introduction to the field of metadata, metadata bindings and metadata annotations in the context of a large computer science testbed we will introduce different ontologies we used for metadata classifications to describe content /topic of a resource. Finally we will discuss the usage of these ontologies in the context of the Edutella project, which represents the first RDF-based peer-to-peer network for digital resources and for the exchange of learning objects and services.

## 28.1  Using Metadata for eLearning

ELearning, or online learning, stands for all forms of Internet-enabled and/or computer supported learning. It refers to the use of computer and computer network technologies to create, deliver, manage and support learning, usually independent of specific locations or times. eLearning can involve complete online courses, where all aspects of learning, from learner enrollment to tuition and support take place online. At the other end of the eLearning spectrum, these elements may well take place in a face to face situation, with only the learning resources available on the internet. Accessibility of learning resources is accompanied by the need to annotate the resources with rich, standardized and widely used metadata.

This chapter gives an overview over the use of metadata in eLearning as well as about innovative approaches and techniques we developed for enhanced eLearning scenarios. The first section will give a brief introduction to the field of metadata and metadata bindings. In section 28.2 we will discuss our experiences with these metadata, metadata schemas and metadata annotations in the context of a large computer science testbed. In section 28.3 we will discuss the need for metadata classifications to describe content / topic of a resource. We will introduce different ontologies we used and discuss their use and how they and other kinds of metadata are used to query the for specific resources in more detail. Section 28.4 generalizes the setting from a server based to a peer-to-peer scenario and discusses the Edutella project in more detail, which represents the first RDF-based peer-to-peer network for digital resources and for the exchange of learning objects and services.

## 28.1.1 Relevant metadata standards

Metadata is data about data that helps us to achieve better search results. Instead of hoping that a full text search through a learning resource will find the author's name nejdl for example, we can annotate the resource with a metadata description "author is nejdl". While this seems plausible, we also easily realize the two major difficulties this method holds: the technical realisation of "attaching metadata at a resource, and the standardisation of descriptions in order to avoid misunderstanding by using different attributes for the same purpose like "author is nejdl", "creator is nejdl" or "written by nejdl".

Let us first take a look on the idea of using specific vocabularies or schemas for metadata to describe digital resources.

One of the most common metadata schemes on the web today is the "Dublin Core Schema" (DC) by the DCMI. The Dublin Core Metadata Initiative (DCMI) [9] is an organization dedicated to promoting the widespread adoption of interoperable metadata standards and developing specialized metadata vocabularies for describing resources, that enable more intelligent information discovery for digital resources.

Each Dublin Core element is defined using a set of 15 attributes from the ISO/IEC 11179 standard for the description of data elements, including for example: Title, Identifier, Language, Comment. To annotate the author of a learning resource DC suggests to use the element creator, and thus we write dc:creator = nejdl

Whereas "Simple Dublin Core" uses only the elements from the Dublin Core metadata set as attribute-value-pairs, "Qualified Dublin Core" employs additional qualifiers to further refine the meaning of a resource. The DCMI recommends a set of qualifiers called "Dublin Core Qualifiers" (DCQ), which include for example Name, Label, Definition or Comment as alternative qualifiers to refine the Title element. For a complete description, we refer the reader to [9]. Since Dublin Core is designed for metadata for any kind of (digital) resource, it pays no heed to the specific needs we encounter in describing learning resources. The "Learning Objects Metadata Standard" (LOM) [18] by the Learnig Technology Standards Committee (LTSC) of the IEEE was therefore established as an extension of Dublin Core. Each learning object can now be described using a set of more than 70 attributes divided into these nine categories:

- 1. General
- 2. Lifecycle
- 3. Meta-Metadata
- 4. Technical
- 5. Educational
- 6. Rights
- 7. Relation
- 8. Annotation
- 9. Classification

Work on the LOM schema has started in 1998, the current version is 6.4. Once the standard has been accepted, which hopefully will happen 2003, it will be LOM 1.0. Since LOM was developed to be used for any kind of learning resource, LOM users soon find out that they do not really need to use all 70 attributes. On the other hand, regardless of the very useful work that has been done in developing the LOM standard, the standard still fails to specify important educational aspects of learning resources, which lead us to investigate ways to extend LOM with additional attributes depending on which educational setting learning objects are used in (see [3] for more details). However, in the following chapter we will concentrate on a minimal set of metadata attributes we have used in a larger computer science testbed and focus on the use of different topic ontologies useful for this context.

## 28.1.2 Metadata bindings

The second issue to investigate is the technical realisation of how to "bind" metadata to a resource? For this purpose, two possible approaches have been developed in the context of the World Wide Web, based on the XML and RDF formalisms. XML stands for Extensible markup language and was derived from a document description language called SGML (an international standard for structured documents). RDF stands for Resource Description Framework, and was explicitly developed to annotate resources referenced by URIs in the context of the World Wide Web. For learning metadata, bindings have been developed for both formalisms, lately in the context of the IMS Global Learning Consortium. The RDF binding of LOM has been developed by a group led by Michael Nilsson from SweLL (Swedish Learning Lab) [22], with input from our own group and input from the Viennese colleagues from the UNIVERSAL project [12]. We will not discuss the details of these types of binding, but shortly describe, why we chose the RDF-binding to annotate our resources.

XML Bindings define an exchange format for metadata. The metadata might be contained in a database and an XML representation is usually generated on demand, for export to other tools and environments. Thus, an XML metadata record is a self-contained entity with a well-defined hierarchical structure, and there is seldom a natural way to reuse other metadata standards (or specific fields from other standards).

On the other hand, RDF statements are just triples consisting of a subject, a predicate and an object, where the subject is referenced by an URL/URI. So we can annotate resources on the Internet, e.g. a resource at http://www.xyz.com/resource.html, with its author's name using RDF as follows:

Subject: http://www.xyz.com/resource.html
Predicate: dc:creator
Object:"nejdl"

Using the XML syntax proposed by the W3C this statement can be written as:

```
<rdf:RDF
xmlns:rdfs="http://www.w3.org/2000/01/rdf-schema#"
xmlns:dc="http://purl.org/dc/elements/1.1#">
<rdf:Description about=http://www.xyz.com/resource.html>
<dc:creator>nejdl</dc :creator>
</rdf:Description>
</rdf:RDF>
```

The namespace "dc:" refers to an URL containing an RDF schema that describes the structure of the metadata attributes of dublin core, dc:creator in this case. This schema is called the RDF-binding for DC. If we want to describe a resource with rdf and use LOM, we write triples like the one above in a rdf-file and refer to the RDF binding of the LOM attributes we use. A final metadata description is just a set of these triples. The use of namespaces makes it a part of a global network of information, where anyone has the capability of adding metadata to any resource, using standardized or specialized schemas describing these metadata. This modularity of the architecture leads to naturally reusable constructs. The LOM RDF binding is directly compatible with Dublin Core RDF binding, and therefore Dublin Core elements are used directly instead of defining new LOM elements for these DC properties. This of course helps a lot to enhance the interoperability between resources that are annotated with DC and others that are annotated with LOM. In the latest draft for the RDF binding of LOM ([22]) for example, about 80 percent of the LOM elements are defined using DC and DCQ.

## 28.2 General Metadata Elements

### 28.2.1 Elements for distributed computer science education

The ULI project (University teaching network for computer science) is funded by the german government, and tries to establish an exchange of course material, courses and certificates in the area of computer science. 11 german universities with 18 different professors have agreed to exchange their courses and to allow students from one university to attend courses at another university, using advanced eLearning technologies. For more information about the project, we refer to ([27]). We have used this testbed to experiment with different kinds of annotations for the learning materials in these courses, this chapter describes our current setup.

Though the courses usually differ in the kind and amount of learning materials they use, their use of learning resources is surprisingly homogeneous. The average course is divided in 6 to 7 units or knowledge modules which themselve can be split into 3 to 7 learning resources. This leads to an average number of about 35 learning resources per course, with a learning resource being the slides of the lecture, a video or any other set of pages dealing with one subject.

For annotating these resource, we defined a best-practice subset of 15 elements which is summarized in the following table, using the categories defined in LOM:

It turned out that these 15 attributes are enough to annotate and query our resources, and represent a compromise between more abstract and more detailed annotation sets. The annotations of one whole course can be included in a single rdf-file. All RDF-triples are then imported into a relational database, to customize the display of the resources described and to query for specific learning resources. Let us take a closer look at the attributes and their use. Our examples contain metadata descriptions of 6 diffferent courses, 5 of them are part of the ULI project:

1. ULI_Algorithmentheorie.rdf : Description of the ULI lecture "Theory of Algorithms" held in winter 2001 in Freiburg by Prof. Ottman.
2. ULI_Datenbanken.rdf : Description of the ULI lecture "Databases" held in winter 2001 in Freiburg by Prof. Lausen.
3. ULI_InternetApplications.rdf : Description of the ULI lecture "Algorithms for Internet Applications" held in winter 2001 in Karlsruhe by Prof. Schmeck.
4. ULI_Multimediatechnik.rdf : Description of the ULI lecture "Techniques for Multimedia" held in winter 2001 in Mannheim by Prof. Effelsberg.

**Table 28.1.** Best-practice subset of elements

| 1. General | 1.2 Title | **dc:title** |
|---|---|---|
| | 1.3 Language | **dc:language** |
| | 1.4 Description | **dc:description** |
| 2.Lifecycle | 2.3 Contribute | **dc:creator** with a **lom:entity** and the author in vCard format "name surname" dcq:created with the date in W3C format |
| 6.Rights | 6.3 Description | **dc:rights** |
| 7. Relation | | **dcq:hasFormat** **dcq:isFormatOf** **dcq:hasPart** **dcq:isPartOf** **dcq:hasVersion** **dcq:isVersionOf** **dcq:requires** **dcq:isRequiredBy** |
| 9.Classification | | **dc:subject** for content classification. This attribute links to an entry in a hierarchical ontology, that is an instance of **lom_cls:Taxonomy** (see next section) |

5. ULI_Ki.rdf : Description of the lecture "Artificial Intelligence" held in winter 2002 in Hannover by Prof. Nejdl.
6. Softwaretechnik.rdf : Description of the lecture "Software engineering" held in winter 2001 in Hannover by Priv. Doz. Steimann.

   The complete RDF-files can be found at http://www.kbs.uni-hannover.de/Uli

### 28.2.2 Details

#### dc:title

The title of a learning resource or a construct. As the title is usually the first thing to be displayed as a result of a query, it should be as explicit as possible.

<dc:title >Techniques for Multimedia WS 2001 (Mannheim) Part 2a from 17.10.2001:
Compression1</dc:title>
*(Example from course 4.)*

**dc:description**

Further description of the learning resource, either as a list of keywords as in our example, or as a full text.

<dc:description >Internet history, internet technology, IP, DNS, Routing, TCP, IP and ATM1</dc:description>
*(Example from course 3.)*

**dc:creator**

The creator of the resource will be displayed as a part of a lom:entity in the vCard Format "name surname". Usually the author will appear once in the definition of the course, and is inherited to all parts of the course. If the course contains resources from other authors, these resources will have a new dc:creator annotation.

```
<dc:creator>
      <lom:entity>
          <vCard:FN>Wolfgang Nejdl</vCard:FN>
      </lom:entity>
</dc:creator>
```
*(Example from course 5.)*

**dcq:created**

The time, when the course was created, formated in W3C format. Usually only one appearance in the definition of the course.

```
<dcq:created>
      <dcq:W3CDTF>
          <rdf:value>2001-09-15</rdf:value>
      </dcq:W3CDTF>
</dcq:created>
```
*(Example from course 4.)*

**dcq:hasPart, dcq:isPartOf**

The structure of a course is described using these attributes. A unit for example links with dcq:hasPart to its chapters which link with dcq:isPartOf back to the unit they belong to (dcq:isPartOf could be inferred automatically as inverse property of dcq:hasPart).

**dc:language**

The language of the learning resource. An important search criterium to ensure that you receive only results you can understand.

**dcq:hasVersion, dcq:isVersionOf, dcq:hasFormat, dcq:isFormatOf**

Two resources are versions of the same content. If a resource has two equivalent versions, e.g. one german, one english, both versions are connected via dcq:isVersionOf. If a resource is divided up into smaller versions, we display this hierarchy by annotating the "bigger" resource with dcq:hasVersion and the parts with dcq:isVersionOf, in order to know in which direction we can inherit properties. In the special case of two resources with identical content, but different technical versions, e.g. slides and videos, we use dcq:isFormatOf and dcq:hasFormat. The resource that is easier to display is annotated with the "higher-rated" dcq:hasFormat.

**dcq:requires, dcq:isRequiredBy**

We use these attributes, if the content from one resource cannot be understood without knowledge of another resource. The resource receives an dcq:requires entry, while the resources with the background information receives a dcq:isRequiredBy.

## 28.3  Content Classification with dc:subject

General metadata annotation as discussed in the last section is useful, but not enough for finding specific resources. Another important metadata description is classifying the content of a learning resource. It is obvious that self-defined keywords can only be a first solution to this problem. To provide for better search results, keywords used should be part of an ontology, in order to specify both sub- and super-topics. Defining a private ontology for a specific field unfortunately works only in the closed micro world of a single university. To be more general, we therefore decided to use ontologies which are already part of internationally accepted classification systems. In this section we will introduce the three different solutions we came up with.

### 28.3.1  One complete ontology - the ACM CCS

The ACM Computer Classification system ([1]) has been used by the Association for Computer Machinery since several decades to classify scientific publications in the field of computer science. On the basic level, we find 11 nodes that split up in two more levels. Part of the classification hierarchy is reproduced inthe following.

- A. General Literature
- B. Hardware
- C. Computer Systems Organization
- D. Software
  - D.0 GENERAL
  - D.1 PROGRAMMING TECHNIQUES
  - D.2 SOFTWARE ENGINEERING
  - D.3 PROGRAMMING LANGUAGES

- – D.4 OPERATING SYSTEMS
- – D.m MISCELLANEOUS
- E. Data
- F. Theory of Computation
- G. Mathematics of Computing
- H. Information Systems
- I. Computing Methodologies
  - – I.0 GENERAL
  - – I.1 SYMBOLIC AND ALGEBRAIC MANIPULATION
  - – I.2 ARTIFICIAL INTELLIGENCE
    - · I.2.0 General
    - · I.2.1 Applications and Expert Systems
    - · I.2.2 Automatic Programming
    - · I.2.3 Deduction and Theorem Proving
    - · I.2.4 Knowledge Representation Formalisms and Methods
    - · I.2.5 Programming Languages and Software
    - · I.2.6 Learning
    - · I.2.7 Natural Language Processing
    - · I.2.8 Problem Solving, Control Methods, and Search
    - · I.2.9 Robotics
    - · I.2.10 Vision and Scene Understanding
    - · I.2.11 Distributed Artificial Intelligence
    - · I.2.m Miscellaneous
  - – I.3 COMPUTER GRAPHICS
  - – I.4 IMAGE PROCESSING AND COMPUTER VISION
  - – I.5 PATTERN RECOGNITION
  - – I.6 SIMULATION AND MODELING
  - – I.7 DOCUMENT AND TEXT PROCESSING
  - – I.m MISCELLANEOUS
- J. Computer Applications
- K. Computing Milieux

The classification has a fourth level containing unordered keywords, thus including about 1600 entries on all four levels. For our use of the ACM CCS as a classification, we also numbered the keyword lists in the fourth level to receive unique ids like: B.1.1.2 for the keyword "Microprogrammed logic arrays" that is accessible via the taxon path: Hardware(B)/CONTROL STRUCTURES AND MICROPRO-GRAMMING(B.1)/Control Design Styles(B.1.1)

In the context of the ULI project this classification turned out to fit very well, because it covers the whole field of computer science, just as the different ULI courses cover the whole discipline. Typically a course received approximately 5 classification entries from the ACM CCS, and one entry per chapter was a typical distribution. Therefore classification with ACM CCS is excellent for the exchange of complete knowledge modules. If we look for a taxonomy that allows us to annotate different submodules and small, single learning resources, we have two other possibilities: extending the ACM CCS, or looking for another classification system.

### 28.3.2  More details - extending ACM CCS

In an article for the AI magazine in the mid 80's D. Waltz suggested an extension of the node I.2 Artificial Intelligence of the ACM CCS [28]. He refined the keywords in the fourth level as nodes for two more levels, gaining about 100 more entries focussing on the field of artificial intelligence. As an example, the keyword entry "games" in the node I.2.1 Applications and Expert Systems was extended to:

- I.2.1 Applications and Expert Systems
  - I.2.1.0 Cartography
  - I.2.1.1 Games
    - · I.2.1.1.0 Chess
    - · I.2.1.1.1 Checkers
    - · I.2.1.1.2 Backgammon
    - · I.2.1.1.3 Biding Games
    - · I.2.1.1.4 Wagering Games
    - · I.2.1.1.5 War Games
    - · I.2.1.1.6 Games, Other
  - I.2.1.2 Industrial automation
  - I.2.1.3 Law
  - I.2.1.4 Medicine and science
  - I.2.1.5 Natural language interfaces
  - I.2.1.6 Office automation

As we had labelled the keywords of the fourth level for the use of the classical ACM CCS as well, it was easy for us to adapt his suggestions to the modern (1998) version of the ACM CCS, leading to a quite detailed ontology to classify our learning resources in the discipline of Artificial Intelligence.

### 28.3.3  An ontology for a specific sub-discipline - the SWEBOK

For our course in software engineering we found a different solution by using the SWEBOK ontology. The SWEBOK has been developed as a Guide to the Software Engineering Body of Knowledge in context of an IEEE/ACM working group. On their webpage [26] the working group states their goal as follows: "The purpose of this guide is to provide a consensually-validated characterization of the bounds of the software engineering discipline and to provide a topical access to the Body of Knowledge supporting that discipline." Almost 500 software engineering professionals from 41 countries have hierarchically structured the field of software engineering in 10 Knowledge Areas and almost 300 topics, based on their number of publications. This therefore represents a very nice example for a consensually derived ontology in a specific community. The main knowledge areas are:

- Software requirements
- Software design
- Software construction
- Software testing

- Software maintenance
- Software configuration management
- Software engineering management
- Software engineering process
- Software engineering tools and methods
- Software quality

To use the SWEBOK for our courses in the context of exchanging learning resources with other peers, it was important to define mapppings between these knowledge areas and the ACM CCS. These mappings were for example:

**D.2.1 Requirements/Specifications** maps with *Software requirements*

**D.2.2 Design Tools and Techniques** maps with *Software engineering tools and methods / Software tools / Software design tools* and of course the whole *Software design* (since **D.2.10 Design** no longer used as of January 1998)

**D.2.9 Management** maps to *Software configuration management* and *Software engineering management*, same as **K.6.3 Software Management**

So we finally had what we needed: One ontology to use in a world wide context of exchanging learning resources in the field of computer science, plus two specialized ontologies to classify the content of our own lectures, detailed enough to differentiate between the content of single learning resources, but mapping perfectly to the global ontology, if other peers want to access the resources.

### 28.3.4 How to use dc:subject

To classify a resource, the IEEE Learning Object RDF Binding Guide (Draft Version) [22] suggests the use of dc:subject with elements of a taxonomy that must be found on the Internet. Such a taxonomy hierarchy is an instance of lom-cls:Taxonomy and must be formated in a rdf-file where the topics and subtopics are separated using lom_cls:Taxon and lom_cls:rootTaxon.

The RDF-files of our three ontologies can be found at [5], [4] and [6]. The main structure is always as in this example from the SWEBOK ontology:

```
<dcq:SubjectScheme rdf:ID="mySWEBOK">
<rdfs:label>Software Engineering Book of Knowledge Field Classification </rdfs:label>
</dcq:SubjectScheme>

<lom_cls:Taxonomy>
        <lom_cls:rootTtaxon>
        <swtOnt:mySWEBOKrdf:about="http://www.kbs.uni-hannover.de/Uli/
        SWT_Ontologie.rdf#SWEnginManagement">
        <rdf:value>Software engineering management</rdf:value>
                <lom_cls:taxon>
                <swtOnt:mySWEBOK rdf:about="http://www.kbs.uni-
                hannover.de/Uli/SWT_Ontologie.rdf#SWEnginMeasurement">
                <rdf:value>Software engineering measurement</rdf:value>
```

```
            <lom_cls:taxon>
             <swtOnt:mySWEBOK rdf:about="http://www.kbs.uni-
             hannover.de/Uli/SWT_Ontologie.rdf#MeasSWDevelopment">
             <rdf:value>Measuring software and its development
             </rdf:value>
             </lom_cls:taxon>
          </lom_cls:taxon>
       </lom_cls:rootTaxon>
</lom_cls:Taxonomy>
```

This extract from the ontology shows the definition of one knowledge area (Software engineering management), refined in this example into one subtopic (Software engineering measurement), which is itself refined into a subtopic (Measuring software and its development).

To annotate our learning resources, we link dc:subject to the entry in the ontology:

```
<rdf:Description rdf:about="http://www.kbs.uni-hannover.de/Lehre/SE/OLR/S1T1.pdf">
<dc:subject rdf:resource="http://www.kbs.uni-hannover.de/Uli/
SWT_Ontologie.rdf#MeasSWDevelopment"/ >
</rdf:Description>
```

All RDF-triples representing the ontology are stored in the database as well. Let us now have a look on how we use the content classification for our own learning resources.

### 28.3.5  Querying our learning resources

We have been using a metadata driven system designed and implemented at our institute to display our courses, the open learning repository (OLR). The examples and figures in this case study come from the OLR2. Our open learning repositories, versions 1 to 3, are connected to an Oracle database, which stores the metadata of a course, but not the content. Therefore, it is easy to include material from different sources throughout the internet in the context of a course, if the copyright is granted. If copyright was restricted for certain resources, we have used dc:rights, and an appropriate algorithm to hide these resources from general access. For further information about the OLR we refer to [29]. We will now have a closer look on how the metadata are queried.

Parts of our little example and of the SWEBOK Taxonomy can be found in the database as (in Datalog notation):

```
...
'dc:title'('http://www.kbs.uni-hannover.de/Lehre/SE/OLR/S1T1.pdf',
    "Software engineering course, Hannover WS2001 - slide1")
'dc:language'('http://www.kbs.uni-hannover.de/Lehre/KI/OLR/S1T1.pdf',
    'http://www.kbs.uni-hannover.de/Uli/lang.rdf#en')
'dc:subject'('http://www.kbs.uni-hannover.de/Lehre/KI/OLR/S1T1.pdf',
```

'http://www.kbs.uni-hannover.de/Uli/SWT_Ontologie.rdf#MeasSWDevelopment')
...
'lom_cls:taxon'
   ('http://www.kbs.uni-hannover.de/Uli/SWT_Ontologie.rdf#SWEnginMeasurement',
    'http://www.kbs.uni-hannover.de/Uli/SWT_Ontologie.rdf#MeasSWDevelopment')
'rdf:value'('http://www.kbs.uni-hannover.de/Uli/SWT_Ontologie.rdf#MeasSWDevelopment',
    "Measuring software and its development"
...

When we display a learning resource in the OLR, one can decide between looking at the content, by choosing a layer labelled "content" or looking at their classification-entries, by choosing the layer labelled "taxon".

If you choose "taxon" the system will query the database for dc:subject entries via the (simple) Datalog query:


?- 'dc:subject'('http://www.kbs.uni-hannover.de/Lehre/KI/OLR/S1T1.pdf',X)

The Taxon entry is displayed not with its original entry but the system retrieve the 'rdf:value' of this entry from the taxonomy as the title, and also the taxon-structure identified by "taxon"-attribute. Remember that the complete taxonomy is also stored as triples in the database.In our example the entry 'MeasSWDevelopment' will be displayed as:

Software engineering management / Software engineering measurement / Measuring software and its development

We decided to display the entry as a hyperlink, leading to a brief description of the subject.

### 28.3.6  Related resources

Furthermore, the related resources (Resources with the same classification-entry "MeasSWDevelopment" from the same Taxonomy mySWEBOK) are retrieved from the database via:


?- 'dc:subject'(X,'http://www.kbs.uni-hannover.de/Uli/
SWT_Ontologie.rdf#MeasSWDevelopment

And displayed as a hyperlink to the resource.

### 28.3.7  Annotating chapters

Since a course is only represented by an RDF-Schema, only single learning resource are usually annotated via their RDF-description. A whole course or a single lecture is defined by additional relationships between these learning resources (often hier-archic). Therefore, lectures and courses usually inherit their taxon-entries from their child-units. If the user chooses the layer "taxon" while he is not in a learning re-source, but looks at the structure of a unit, the sub-units of this unit and their taxon entries are displayed together with the learning resource they come from. Displaying the taxon entries of a whole course works in the same way, it only takes one iteration more to receive the taxon entries from the "grandchildren".

## 28.4 Exchanging Learning Resources World Wide - Edutella

### 28.4.1 Decentralized P2P networks

As discussed before, exchanging learning resources is one of the greatest advantages in eLearning and eTeaching. A system for the exchange of learning resources how-ever has to build on the fact that most universities or departments have already estab-lished their own way of storing their learning resources and do so locally in almost all cases. Since all these institutions are not interested in losing this independence by giving their learning resources away to central "knowledge pools" the best way to establish such an exchange system is by building up a peer-to-peer (P2P) network. These P2P networks have already been successful for special cases like exchanging music files, which is encouraging. However, retrieving a song like "Material Girl from Madonna" does not need complex query languages nor complex metadata, so special purpose formats for these P2P applications have been sufficient. In other sce-narios, like exchanging educational resources, queries are more complex, and have to build upon standards like IEEE-LOM/IMS [18, 15] as discussed before, which might even be complemented by domain specific extensions.

Furthermore, by concentrating on domain specific formats, current P2P imple-mentations appear to be fragmenting into niche markets instead of developing uni-fying mechanisms for future P2P applications. There is indeed a great danger (as already discussed in [10]), that unifying interfaces and protocols introduced by the World Wide Web get lost in the forthcoming P2P arena.

### 28.4.2 Edutella infrastructure

The Edutella project [11, 21, 20] addresses these shortcomings by building on the W3C metadata standard RDF [17, 7] as the basis for a so-called schema-based P2P network. The project is a multi-staged effort to scope, specify, architect and imple-ment an RDF-based metadata infrastructure for P2P-networks based on the recently announced JXTA framework [13]. The initial Edutella services are *Query Service* (standardized query and retrieval of RDF metadata), *Replication Service* (provid-ing data persistence / availability and workload balancing while maintaining data integrity and consistency), *Mapping Service* (translating between different metadata vocabularies to enable interoperability between different peers), *Mediation Service*

(define views that join data from different metadata sources and reconcile conflicting and overlapping information) and *Annotation Service* (annotate materials stored
anywhere within the Edutella Network).

The Edutella infrastructure aims to provide the metadata services needed to enable interoperability between heterogeneous JXTA applications. The main application area we have been focussing on is the P2P exchange of educational resources
(using schemas like IEEE LOM, IMS, and ADL SCORM [2] to describe course materials), but other application areas are possible as well.

### 28.4.3 Edutella query service

Having agreed on the basic infrastructure and the use of RDF and LOM metadata for
annotating our resources, we still need a standardized query language to cope with
the different solutions each peer may have found to structure and store its learning
resources. The Edutella Query Service is a standardized query exchange mechanism
for RDF metadata stored in distributed RDF repositories and serves both as query
interface for individual RDF repositories located at single Edutella peers as well as
query interface for distributed queries spanning multiple RDF repositories (storing
RDF statements based on arbitrary RDFS schemata).

One of the main purposes is to abstract from various possible RDF storage layer
query languages (e.g., SQL) and from different user level query languages (e.g.,
RQL, TRIPLE): The Edutella Query Exchange Language and the Edutella Common
Data Model provide the syntax and semantics for an overall standard query interface
across heterogeneous peer repositories for any kind of RDF metadata. The Edutella
network uses the query exchange language family RDF-QEL-i (based on Datalog semantics and subsets thereof) as standardized query exchange language format which
is transmitted in an RDF/XML-format.

We will start with a simple RDF knowledge base and a simple query with the
following RDF XML Serialization:

```
<lib:Book about='http://www.xyz.com/sw.html'>
    <dc:title>Software Engineering</dc:title>
</lib:Book>

<lib:Book about='http://www.xyz.com/ia.html'>
    <dc:title>Intelligent Agents</dc:title>
    <dc:subject
        rdf:resource='http://www.kbs.uni-hannover.de/Uli/ACM_CCS#I.2' />
</lib:Book>

<lib:Book about='http://www.xyz.com/ai.html'>
    <dc:title>Artificial Intelligence</dc:title>
</lib:Book>

<lib:AI-Book about='http://www.xyz.com/pl.html'>
    <dc:title>Prolog</dc:title>
</lib:AI-Book>
```

To simplify the query, we assume that the book on intelligent agents is annotated with the ACM CCS node I.2 ARTIFICIAL INTELLIGENCE. Otherwise, we could easily query for supertopics of the entry by using the lom_cls:taxon attribute and the fact that the ontology is also part of the knowledge base. We will show you a small example of this handling of subtopics later.

Edutella peers can be highly heterogeneous in terms of the functionality (i.e., services) they offer. A simple peer has RDF storage capability only. The peer has some kind of local storage for RDF triples (e.g., a relational database) as well as some kind of local query language (e.g., SQL). In addition the peer might offer more complex services such as annotation, mediation or mapping.

To enable the peer to participate in the Edutella network, Edutella wrappers are used to translate queries and results from the Edutella query and result exchange format to the local format of the peer and vice versa, and to connect the peer to the Edutella network by a JXTA-based P2P library. To handle queries, the wrapper uses the common Edutella query exchange format and data model for query and result representation. For communication with the Edutella network, the wrapper translates the local data model into the Edutella Common Data Model ECDM and vice versa, and connects to the Edutella Network using the JXTA P2P primitives, transmitting the queries based on ECDM in RDF/XML form.

In order to handle different query capabilities, Edutella defines several RDF-QEL-i exchange language levels, describing which kind of queries a peer can handle (conjunctive queries, relational algebra, transitive closure, etc.) The same internal data model is used for all levels.

**Edutella Common Data Model (ECDM)**   The ECDM is based on Datalog, which is a well-known non-procedural query language based on Horn clauses without function symbols. A Datalog program can be expressed as a set of rules/implications (where each rule consists of one positive literal in the consequent of the rule (the head), and one or more negative literals in the antecedent of the rule (the body)), a set of facts (single positive literals) and the actual query literals (a rule without head, i.e., one or more negative literals). Literals are predicates expressions describing relations between any combination of variables and constants such as title(http://www.xyz.com/book.html, 'Artificial Intelligence'). Disjunction is expressed as a set of rules with identical head. Additionally, we can use negation as failure in the antecedent of a rule, with the semantics that such a literal cannot be proved from the knowledge base. A Datalog query then is a conjunction of query literals plus a possibly empty set of rules [25].

Datalog queries easily map to relations and relational query languages like relational algebra or SQL. In terms of relational algebra, Datalog is capable of expressing selection, union, join and projection and hence is a relationally complete query language. Additional features include transitive closure and other recursive definitions.

The example knowledge base in Datalog reads

title('http://www.xyz.com/ai.html','Artificial Intelligence').
type('http://www.xyz.com/ai.html',Book).

title('http://www.xyz.com/ia.html','Intelligent Agents')
subject('http://www.xyz.com/ia.html','http://www.kbs.uni-hannover.de/Uli/ACM_CCS#I.2').
type('http://www.xyz.com/ia.html,Book').
title('http://www.xyz.com/sw.html','Software Engineering').
type('http://www.xyz.com/sw.html',Book).
title('http://www.xyz.com/pl.html','Prolog').
type('http://www.xyz.com/pl.html',AI-Book).


Each RDF repository can be viewed as a set of ground assertions either using binary predicates as shown above, or as ternary statements "s(S,P,O)", if we include the predicate as an additional argument. In the following examples, we use the binary surface representation.

We will have a closer look on the evaluating of the following query (plain English)

"Return all resources that are a book having the title "Artificial Intelligence" or have content, that is a subtopic of "Artificial Intelligence" or that are an AI book."

### Example Query in (binary) Datalog notation.

aibook(X) :- title(X, 'Artificial Intelligence'),
                      type(X, Book).
aibook(X) :- type(X, AI-Book).
aibook(X) :- subject(X,'http://www.kbs.uni-hannover.de/Uli/ACM_CCS#I.2').

?- aibook(X).


Since our query is a disjunction of three (purely conjunctive) subqueries, its Datalog representation is composed of three rules with identical heads. The literals in the rules' bodies directly reflect RDF statements with their subjects being the variable X and their objects being bound to constant values such as 'Artificial Intelligence'. Literals used in the head of rules denote derived predicates (not necessarily binary ones). The query expression "aibook(X)" asks for all bindings of X, which conform to the given Datalog rules and our knowledge base, with the results:

aibook('http://www.xyz.com/ai.html')
aibook('http://www.xyz.com/ia.html')
aibook('http://www.xyz.com/pl.html')


It is of course easy to extend the examples to subtopics of 'Artificial Intelligence', if our ontology is also a part of the knowledge base. We would then extend our query with the search for supertopics, by defining the new concept 'content' and then replacing the last subquery with:

aibook(X):- content(X,"http://www.kbs.uni-hannover.de/Uli/ACM_CCS#I.2").

content(X,Y):- subject(X,Y).

content(X,Y):- subject(X,Z),
                  subtopic(Z,Y).
suptopic(Z,Y):- taxon(Y,Z).
suptopic(Z,Y):- taxon(Y,W),
                  taxon(W,Z).

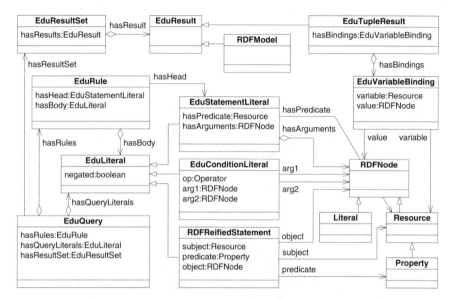

**Fig. 28.1.** Edutella Common Data Model (ECDM)

Internally Edutella Peers use a Datalog based model to represent queries and their results. Figure 28.1 visualizes this data model as UML class diagram. The Edutella Wrapper API includes the ECDM as well as wrappers for different query languages, and is available as source code from the Edutella Project Page: http://edutella.jxta.org/.

Our current prototype environment features a set of different peers to demonstrate various aspects of the translation from ECDM to local query languages. It contains the QEL query exchange mechanism, a simple mediator and the wrapping of different repository peer types, including an OLR (Open Learning Repository) based peer [8] using a subset of IMS/LOM RDF metadata stored in a relational database, a DbXML-based peer [23] as a prototype for an XML repository using a simple mapping service to translate from RDF-QEL-1 queries (conjunctive queries) to Xpath queries over the appropriate XML-LOM schema, AMOS-II-based peers [24] with local repositories, KAON-based peers [19] allowing remote annotation [14] using an RDF-based ontology format, and an O-Telos-Peer [16] and [30].

## 28.5 Acknowledgements

The basic versions of the OLR were created and implemented by Boris Wolf. We also gratefully acknowledge important input and discussion on the design and use of the OLR from Hadhami Dhraief. The Edutella project has had numerous contributors, too many to mention here, but we refer to the various Edutella publications written together with them. We gratefully acknowledge all their input and work on these topics. We want to especially thank Wolf Siberski, Martin Wolpers, Changtao Qu, Steffen Staab, Christoph Schmitz and Bernd Simon for recent input to our work.

# References

1. *The ACM Computing Classification System–1998 Version*     valid in 2002, http://www.acm.org/class/1998/
2. Technical Team ADLSCORM *Specification V1.2* http://www.adlnet.org/Scorm/scorm.cfm
3. H. Allert, H. Dhraief, W. Nejdl. *How are Learning Objects Used in earning Process?* ED-MEDIA 2002, World Conference on Educational Multimedia, Hypermedia & Telecommunications, Denver Colorado, United States, June 24-29, 2002
4. J. Brase *AIOnt – An extension of the ACM CCS for the field of Artificail Intelligence, based on a paper by D.L. Waltz* http://www.kbs.uni-hannover.de/Uli/AI_Ontologie.rdf
5. J. Brase *mySWEBOK – A classification for Software enginering, based on the SWEBOK* http://www.kbs.uni-hannover.de/Uli/SWT_Ontologie.rdf
6. J. Brase *ACMCCS – The ACM Classification for Computer Science as a rdf-file* http://www.kbs.uni-hannover.de/Uli/SWT_Ontologie.rdf
7. D. Brickley and R. V. Guha *W3C Resource Description Framework (RDF) Schema Specification* http://www.w3.org/TR/1998/WD-rdf-schema
8. H. Dhraief, W. Nejdl, B. Wolf and M. Wolpers *Open Learning Repositories and Metadata Modeling* International Semantic Web Working Symposium (SWWS), jul 2001, Stanford, CA
9. The Dublin Core Metadata Initiative http://dublincore.org/
10. R. Dornfest and D. Brickley *The Power of Metadata* excerpted from the book "Peer-to-Peer: Harnessing the Power of Disruptive Technologies, 2001 http://www.openp2p.com/pub/a/p2p/2001/01/18/metadata.html
11. *The Edutella Project* http://edutella.jxta.org
12. S. Guth, G. Neumann, B. Simon *UNIVERSAL - Design Spaces of Learning Media* Proceedings of the 34th Hawaii International Conference on System Sciences, Maui (USA), January, 2001
13. L. Gong *Project JXTA: A Technology Overview* http://www.jxta.org/project/www/docs/TechOverview.pdf
14. S. Handschuh, S. Staab and A. Maedche *CREAM - Creating relational metadata with a component-based, ontology-driven annotation framework* First International Conference on Knowledge Capture (K-CAP'2001), Victoria, BC, Canada
15. *IMS Learning Resource Metadata Specification V1.2.1* http://www.imsproject.org/metadata/index.html
16. M. Jarke, R. Gallersdörfer, M. Jeusfeld, M. Staudt and S. Eherer "ConceptBase - a deductive object base for meta data management Journal on Intelligent Information Systems 1995, 4(2): 167 -192

17. O. Lassila and R. R. Swick *W3C Resource Description Framework (RDF) Model and Syntax Specification* http://www.w3.org/TR/REC-rdf-syntax

18. Learning Technology Standards Comittee of the IEEE: *Draft Standard for Learning Objects Metadata IEEE P1484.12.1/D6.4*12. June 2002). http://ltsc.ieee.org/doc/wg12/LOM_1484_12_1_v1_Final_Draft.pdf/

19. A. Mädche, S. Staab, R. Studer, Y. Sure and R. Volz *SEAL — Tying Up Information Integration and Web Site Management by Ontologies* IEEE Data Engineering Bulletin Mar 2002 http://www.research.microsoft.com/research/db/debull

20. W. Nejdl, B. Wolf, C. Qu, S. Decker, M. Sintek, A. Naeve, M. Nilsson, M. Palmr and T. Risch *EDUTELLA: a P2P Networking Infrastructure based on RDF* 11th International World Wide Web Conference Hawaii, USA, May 2002 http://edutella.jxta.org/reports/edutella-whitepaper.pdf

21. W. Nejdl, B. Wolf, S. Staab and J. Tane *EDUTELLA: Searching and Annotating Resources within an RDF-based P2P Network* Semantic Web Workshop, 11th International World Wide Web Conference, may 2002, Honolulu, Hawaii, USA

22. M. Nilsson. *IMS Metadata RDF binding guide*, May 2001 http://kmr.nada.kth.se/el/ims/metadata.html

23. C. Qu and W. Nejdl *Towards Interoperability and Reusability of Learning Resources: A SCORM-conformant Courseware for Computer Science Education* Proc. of 2nd IEEE International Conference on Advanced Learning Technologies (IEEE ICALT 2002), Kaza, Russia, September 2002.

24. T. Risch and V. Josifovski *Distributed Data Integration by Object-Oriented Mediator Servers* Concurrency and Computation: Practice and Experience 2001 13(11):933 - 953

25. A. Silberschatz, H. F. Korth and S. Sudarshan *Database Systems Concepts* McGraw-Hill Higher Education 2001 4

26. *The guide to the Software engeneering body of Knowledge* http://www.swebok.org

27. *The ULI-project homepage* http://www.uli-campus.de

28. D. Waltz *Scientific datalink's artificial intelligence classification scheme* The AI Magazine 1985, 6(1):58-63.

29. B. Wolf, H. Dhraief, M. Wolpers, W. Nejdl. *Open Learning Repositories and Metadata Modeling* International Semantic Web Working Symposium (SWWS) Stanford University, California, USA, July 30 - August 1, 2001

30. M. Wolpers, W. Nejdl and I. Brunkhorst *Using an O-Telos Peer to Provide Reasoning Capabilities in an RDF-based P2P-Environment* Proceedings of the International Workshop on Agents and Peer-to-Peer Computing, Bologna, Italy, July, 2002

# Ontology of the Process Specification Language

Michael Grüninger

Institute for Systems Research, University of Maryland, College Park, MD 20742
gruning@cme.nist.gov

**Summary.** The Process Specification Language (PSL) has been designed to facilitate correct and complete exchange of process information among manufacturing systems. We give an overview of the PSL Ontology, including its formal characterization as a set of theories in first-order logic and the concepts that are axiomatized in these theories.

## 29.1 Motivation

Representing activities and the constraints on their occurrences is an integral aspect of commonsense reasoning, particularly in manufacturing, enterprise modelling, and autonomous agents or robots. In addition to the traditional concerns of knowledge representation and reasoning, the need to integrate software applications in these areas has become increasingly important. However, interoperability is hindered because the applications use different terminology and representations of the domain. These problems arise most acutely for systems that must manage the heterogeneity inherent in various domains and integrate models of different domains into coherent frameworks. For example, such integration occurs in business process reengineering, where enterprise models integrate processes, organizations, goals and customers. Even when applications use the same terminology, they often associate different semantics with the terms. This clash over the meaning of the terms prevents the seamless exchange of information among the applications. Typically, point-to-point translation programs are written to enable communication from one specific application to another. However, as the number of applications has increased and the information has become more complex, it has been more difficult for software developers to provide translators between every pair of applications that must cooperate. What is needed is some way of explicitly specifying the terminology of the applications in an unambiguous fashion.

The Process Specification Language (PSL) ([13], [8]) has been designed to facilitate correct and complete exchange of process information among manufacturing system [1]. Included in these applications are scheduling, process modeling, process planning, production planning, simulation, project management, workflow, and business process reengineering. This chapter will give an overview of the PSL Ontology, including its formal characterization as a set of theories in first-order logic and the range of concepts that are axiomatized in these theories.

## 29.2 Formal Properties of the PSL Ontology

We will begin by considering the distinguishing formal characteristics of the PSL Ontology, independently from its content.

### 29.2.1 Semantics and Axiomatization

The PSL Ontology is a set of theories in the language of first-order logic, and the semantics of a first-order theory are based on the notion of an interpretation that specifies a meaning for each symbol in a sentence of the language. In practice, interpretations are typically specified by identifying each symbol in the language with an element of some algebraic or combinatorial structure, such as graphs, linear orderings, partial orderings, groups, fields, or vector spaces; the underlying theory of the structure then becomes available as a basis for reasoning about the concepts and their relationships.

We can evaluate the adequacy of the application's ontology with respect to some class of structures that capture the intended meanings of the ontology's terms by proving that the ontology has the following two fundamental properties:

- Satisfiability: every structure in the class is a model of the ontology.
- Axiomatizability: every model of the ontology is isomorphic to some structure in the class.

The purpose of the Axiomatizability Theorem is to demonstrate that there do not exist any unintended models of the theory, that is, any models that are not specified in the class of structures. In general, this would require second-order logic, but the design of PSL makes the following assumption (hereafter referred to as the Interoperability Hypothesis): *The ontology supports interoperability among first-order inference engines that exchange first-order sentences.* By this hypothesis, we do not need to restrict ourselves to elementary classes of structures when we are axiomatizing an ontology. Since the applications are equivalent to first-order inference engines, they cannot distinguish between structures that are elementarily equivalent. Thus, the unintended models are only those that are not elementary equivalent to any model in the class of structures.

Classes of structures for theories within the PSL Ontology are therefore axiomatized up to elementary equivalence – the theories are satisfied by any model in the

---

[1] PSL has been accepted as project ISO 18629 within the International Organisation of Standardisation, and as of October 2002, part of the work is under review as a Draft International Standard.

class, and any model of the core theories is elementarily equivalent to a model in the class. Further, each class of structures is characterized up to isomorphism.

### 29.2.2 Invariants and Classification

Many ontologies are specified as taxonomies or class hierarchies, yet few ever give any justification for the classification. If we consider ontologies of mathematical structures, we see that logicians classify models by using properties of models, known as invariants, that are preserved by isomorphism. For some classes of structures, such as vector spaces, invariants can be used to classify the structures up to isomorphism; for example, vector spaces can be classified up to isomorphism by their dimension. For other classes of structures, such as graphs, it is not possible to formulate a complete set of invariants. However, even without a complete set, invariants can still be used to provide a classification of the models of a theory.

Following this methodology, the set of models for the core theories of PSL are partitioned into equivalence classes defined with respect to the set of invariants of the models. Each equivalence class in the classification of PSL models is axiomatized using a definitional extension of PSL. In particular, each definitional extension in the PSL Ontology is associated with a unique invariant; the different classes of activities or objects that are defined in an extension correspond to different properties of the invariant. In this way, the terminology of the PSL Ontology arises from the classification of the models of the core theories with respect to sets of invariants. The terminology within the definitional extensions intuitively corresponds to classes of activities and objects.

This approach can also be justified by the original motivation for PSL. If the ontologies of two software applications have the same language, then the applications will be interoperable if they share the semantics of the terminology in their corresponding theories. Sharing semantics between applications is equivalent to sharing models of their theories, that is, the theories have isomorphic sets of models. We therefore need to determine whether or not two models are isomorphic, and in doing so, we can use invariants of the models.

### 29.2.3 Types and Process Descriptions

If two software applications both used an ontology for algebraic fields, they would not exchange new definitions, but rather they would exchange sentences that expressed properties of elements in their models. For algebraic fields, such sentences are equivalent to polynomials. Similarly, the software applications that use PSL do not exchange arbitrary sentence, such as new axioms or even conservative definitions, in the language of their ontology. Instead, they exchange process descriptions, which are sentences that are satisfied by particular activities, occurrences, states, or other objects (see Figures 29.4 and 29.5).

Within PSL, we formally characterize a process description as a boolean combination of n-types [2] for the PSL Ontology that are realized by some model of the ontology. In the algebra example, polynomials are n-types for elements in an algebraic field. In the PSL core theory $T_{complex}$, formulae that specify the constraints under which subactivities of an activity occur are types for complex activities. In the axiomatization of situation calculus in [11], precondition and effect axioms are types for actions.

For general theories, there may exist elements whose types cannot be defined by a sentence in the language. For example, although polynomials are types for elements in an algebraic field, there exist real numbers that are not definable using polynomials, namely transcendental numbers such as $\pi$ and $e$. Within PSL, the definable types for elements in each class of models are specified as classes of sentences using a BNF grammar. If an activity does not have a definable type, then the process description cannot be axiomatized, just as transcendental numbers cannot be specified by polynomials.

### 29.2.4 Relationship to Other Process Ontologies

There have been a variety of process ontologies developed within the artificial intelligence community, particularly in the context of robotics and planning systems.

One family of projects has attempted to provide a sharable ontology of planning information for use by disparate and communicating systems. The Sharable Plan and Activity Representation (SPAR) [16] specified an abstract ontology setting out major categories (such as space, time, agents, actions, reasoning, and plans), and a set of modular specialised ontologies which augment the general categories with sets of concepts and alternative theories of more detailed notions commonly used by planning systems, such as specific ontologies and theories of time points, temporal relations, and complex actions. SPAR evolved out of earlier work with the Common Plan Representation [9] and the O-Plan project [15] at the University of Edinburgh.

Another plan-oriented process ontology is the Planning Domain Definition Language (PDDL) [1], which is used extensively in the AIPS planning competition. PDDL is intended to express the particular domain used in a planning system, including a specification of states, the set of possible activities, the structure of complex activities, and the effects of activities.

The Cognitive Robotics Group at the University of Toronto has proposed the language GOLOG [6] as a high-level robotics programming language. GOLOG provides mechanisms for specifying complex activities as programs in a second-order language that extends the axiomatization of situation calculus found in [11].

[2] An n-type for a first-order theory $T$ is a set of formulae $\Phi(x_1, ..., x_n)$, such that for some model $\mathcal{M}$ of $T$, and some n-tuple $\bar{a}$ of elements of $\mathcal{M}$, we have $\mathcal{M} \models \phi(\bar{a})$ for all $\phi$ in $\Phi$. If $t$ is an n-type, then a model $\mathcal{M}$ realizes $t$ if and only if there are $a_1, ..., a_n \in M$ such that $\mathcal{M} \models \phi(a_1, ..., a_n)$ for each $\phi \in t$. An n-type for a theory is a therefore consistent set of formulae (each of which has $n$ free variables) which is satisfied by a model of the theory.

The Workflow Management Coalition has been developing a standard terminology which can serve as a common framework for different workflow management system vendors. The ontology for this effort is the Workflow Process Definition Language (WPDL) [17].

In the context of the Semantic Web, much work has been done using the DARPA Agent Markup Language (DAML) [4]. In particular, the DAML-S ontology [7] provides a set of process classes that can be specialized to describe a variety of Web services.

These approaches to process representation lack one or more of the formal properties of the PSL Ontology. Ontologies such as SPAR, CPR, INOVA, WPDL, and DAML-S do not provide a model theory. The ontologies for WPDL, PDDL, and those found in [12] specify a formal semantics, but they do not provide any axiomatization of this semantics. Finally, ontologies such as Golog and PDDL only specify syntactic classes of process descriptions without any underlying theory for complex activities.

## 29.3 Overview of PSL Core Theories

Within the set of first-order theories that comprise the PSL Ontology, there is a distinction between core theories and definitional extensions [3]. Core theories introduce new primitive concepts, while all terms introduced in a definitional extension that are conservatively defined using the terminology of the core theories.

All core theories within the ontology are consistent extensions of PSL-Core ($T_{psl\_core}$), although not all extensions need be mutually consistent. Also, the core theories need not be conservative extensions of other core theories. The relationships among the core theories in the PSL Ontology are depicted in Figure 29.1. The lexicon of the core theories can be found in Table 29.1.

In the remainder of this section, we will consider the intuitions for each of the core theories in Figure 29.1. The definitional extensions in the PSL Ontology will be discussed in the next section.

### 29.3.1 PSL-Core

The purpose of PSL-Core is to axiomatize a set of intuitive semantic primitives that is adequate for describing the fundamental concepts of manufacturing processes [4]. Consequently, this characterization of basic processes makes few assumptions about their nature beyond what is needed for describing those processes, and the Core is therefore rather weak in terms of logical expressiveness.

---

[3] The complete set of axioms for the PSL Ontology can be found at http://www.mel.nist.gov/psl/psl-ontology/. Core theories are indicated by a .th suffix and definitional extensions are indicated by a .def suffix

[4] The axiomatization of PSL-Core is based on the results of the earlier Process Interchange Format project [5].

**Table 29.1.** Lexicon for core theories in the PSL Ontology

| $T_{pslcore}$ | $activity(a)$ | $a$ is an activity |
|---|---|---|
| | $activity\_occurrence(o)$ | $o$ is an activity occurrence |
| | $timepoint(t)$ | $t$ is a timepoint |
| | $object(x)$ | $x$ is an object |
| | $occurrence\_of(o, a)$ | $o$ is an occurrence of $a$ |
| | $beginof(o)$ | the beginning timepoint of $o$ |
| | $endof(o)$ | the ending timepoint of $o$ |
| | $before(t_1, t_2)$ | timepoint $t_1$ precedes timepoint $t_2$ on the timeline |
| $T_{subactivity}$ | $subactivity(a_1, a_2)$ | $a_1$ is a subactivity of $a_2$ |
| | $primitive(a)$ | $a$ is a minimal element of the $subactivity$ ordering |
| $T_{atomic}$ | $atomic(a)$ | $a$ is either primitive or a concurrent activity |
| | $conc(a_1, a_2)$ | the activity that the concurrent composition of $a_1$ and $a_2$ |
| $T_{occtree}$ | $successor(a, s)$ | the element of an occurrence tree that is the next occurrence of $a$ after the activity occurrence $s$ |
| | $legal(s)$ | $s$ is an element of a legal occurrence tree |
| | $initial(s)$ | $s$ is the root of an occurrence tree |
| | $earlier(s_1, s_2)$ | $s_1$ precedes $s_2$ in an occurrence tree |
| | $poss(a, s)$ | there exists a legal occurrence of $a$ that is a successor of $s$ |
| $T_{disc\_state}$ | $holds(f, s)$ | the fluent $f$ is true immediately after the activity occurrence $s$ |
| | $prior(f, s)$ | the fluent $f$ is true immediately before the activity occurrence $s$ |
| $T_{complex}$ | $min\_precedes(s_1, s_2, a)$ | the atomic subactivity occurrence $s_1$ precedes the atomic subactivity occurrence $s_2$ in an activity tree for $a$ |
| | $root(s, a)$ | the atomic subactivity occurrence $s$ is the root of an activity tree for $a$ |
| $T_{actocc}$ | $subactivity\_occurrence(o_1, o_2)$ | $o_1$ is a subactivity occurrence of $o_2$ |
| | $root\_occ(o)$ | the initial atomic subactivity occurrence of $o$ |
| | $leaf\_occ(s, o)$ | $s$ is the final atomic subactivity occurrence of $o$ |
| $T_{duration}$ | $timeduration(d)$ | $d$ is a timeduration |
| | $duration(t_1, t_2)$ | the timeduration whose value is the "distance" from timepoint $t_1$ to timepoint $t_2$ |
| | $lesser(d_1, d_2)$ | the linear ordering relation over timedurations |

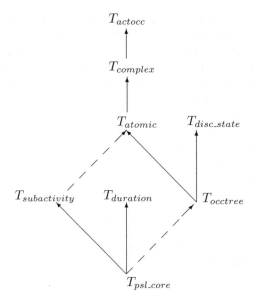

**Fig. 29.1.** The core theories of the PSL Ontology. Solid lines indicate conservative extension, while dashed lines indicate an extension that is not conservative.

The basic ontological commitments of PSL-Core are based on the following intuitions:

**Intuition 1:** *There are four kinds of entities required for reasoning about processes – activities, activity occurrences, timepoints, and objects.*

There are some approaches (e.g. [3]) that do not distinguish between timepoints and activity occurrences, so that activity occurrences form a subclass of timepoints. However, activity occurrences have preconditions and effects, whereas timepoints do not. Other approaches hold that timepoints are primitives but activity occurrences are not; for example, [14] claims that one can derive timepoints as "ticks" of a clock activity; however, such an approach ties the temporal ontology too closely to the process ontology.

**Intuition 2:** *Activities may have multiple occurrences, or there may exist activities which do not occur at all.*

In contrast to many object-oriented approaches, activity occurrences cannot considered to be instances of activities, since activities are not classes within the PSL Ontology. [5]

---

[5] One can of course specify classes of activities in a process description. For example the term $pickup(x, y)$ can denote the class of activities for picking up some object $x$ with manipulator $y$, and the term $move(x, y, z)$ can denote the class of activities for moving object $x$ from location $y$ to location $z$. Ground terms such as $pickup(Block1, LeftHand)$ and $move(Shipment1, Seattle, Chicago)$ are instances of these classes of activities, and each instance can have different occurrences.

There are also some historical reasons for making activity occurrences distinct from the notion of instances. The core theory $T_{occtree}$ introduces the notion of occurrence trees, which are isomorphic to situation trees without the initial situation $S_0$ (i.e. situations are identified as being occurrences of activities), and the situation calculus treats both activities and situations as first-order elements – situations are not instances of activities.

**Intuition 3:** *Timepoints are linearly ordered, forwards into the future, and backwards into the past.*

There are several options that may be taken to formalize this intuition. Within PSL-Core, an additional ontological commitment was made so that the timeline is infinite, with two endpoints, $inf-$ and $inf+$. This was done in order to capture the intuition that some objects exist only for a finite period of time, while other objects always exist, that is, there is no timepoint at which they are created or destroyed.

There are also different ontological commitments about time that are not made within the PSL Ontology, such as the denseness of the timeline. Any such commitments must be axiomatized within a core theory extension to PSL-Core.

**Intuition 4:** *Activity occurrences and objects are associated with unique timepoints that mark the begin and end of the occurrence or object.*

Note that the ontology allows for the existence of infinite activity occurrences; in these cases, $beginof$ or $endof$ will take on the values of $-inf$ or $+inf$.

### 29.3.2 Occurrence Trees

Models for the core theory $T_{occtree}$ are extensions of models of $T_{pslcore}$ by adding occurrence trees.

**Intuition 5:** *An occurrence tree is a partially ordered set of activity occurrences, such that for a given set of activities, all discrete sequences of their occurrences are branches of the tree.*

An occurrence tree contains all occurrences of *all* activities; it is not simply the set of occurrences of a particular (possibly complex) activity. Because the tree is discrete, each activity occurrence in the tree has a unique successor occurrence of each activity.

Occurrence trees are closely related to the situation trees that are models of Reiter's axiomatization of situation calculus ([11], [10]) if we interpret situations to be activity occurrences. However, there are some differences between $T_{occtree}$ and situation calculus. One interpretation of situation calculus is that the situations are sequences of actions, with the initial situation $S_0$ being the null sequence; since $S_0$ is not the occurrence of any activity, it has no corresponding object within PSL. Also, Reiter employs a second-order axiom to eliminate trees whose branches are isomorphic to nonstandard models of the natural numbers. However, such nonstandard trees are elementarily equivalent to standard trees, so that by the Interoperability Hypothesis, there is no need to invoke a second-order axiom.

**Intuition 6:** *There are constraints on which activities can possibly occur in some domain.*

This intuition is the cornerstone for characterizing the semantics of classes of activities and process descriptions. Although occurrence trees characterize all sequences of activity occurrences, not all of these sequences will intuitively be physically possible within the domain. We will therefore want to consider the subtree of the occurrence tree that consists only of *possible* sequences of activity occurrences; this subtree is referred to as the legal occurrence tree. For example, in Figure 29.2, there is no legal successor occurrence of *make_frame* after $o_{16}^4$, and there is no legal successor occurrence of *assemble* after $o_1^1$. We will later discuss how the definitional extensions of the PSL Ontology use different constraints on possible activity occurrences as a way of classifying activities.

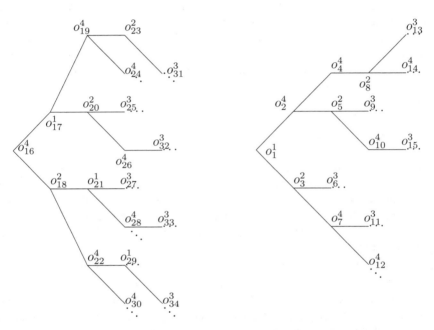

**Fig. 29.2.** Example of legal occurrence trees. The activities in the domain are *make_body*, *make_frame*, *paint*, and *polish*. The elements $o_i^1$ denote occurrences of the activity *make_body*, $o_i^2$ denote occurrences of the activity *make_frame*, $o_i^3$ denote occurrences of the activity *paint*, and $o_i^4$ denote occurrences of the activity *polish*; for example, $o_4^4 = successor(make\_frame, o_1^1)$. The activity occurrences $o_1^1$ and $o_{16}^4$ are the initial occurrences in their respective occurrence trees.

**Intuition 7:** *Every sequence of activity occurrences has an initial occurrence (which is the root of an occurrence tree).*

This intuition is closely related to the properties of occurrence trees. For example, one could consider occurrences to form a semilinear ordering (which need not have a root element) rather than a tree (which must have a root element). However, we are using occurrence trees to characterize the semantics of different classes of activities, rather than using the occurrence tree to represent history (which may not have an explicit initial event). In our case, it is sufficient to consider all possible interactions between the set of activities in the domain, and we lose nothing by restricting our attention to initial occurrences of the activities. For example, given the query "Can the factory produce 1000 widgets by Friday?", one can take the initial state to be the current state, and the initial activity occurrences being the activities that could be performed at the current time.

**Intuition 8:** *The ordering of activity occurrences in a branch of an occurrence tree respects the temporal ordering.*

Several approaches to temporal ontologies ([3]) conflate the ordering over activity occurrences with the ordering over timepoints. Within the theory of occurrence trees, these are distinct ordering relations. The set of activity occurrences is partially ordered (hence the intuition about occurrence *trees*), but timepoints are linearly ordered (since this theory is an extension of PSL-Core). However, every branch of an occurrence tree is totally ordered, and the intuition requires that the $beginof$ timepoint for an activity occurrence along a branch is $before$ the $beginof$ timepoints of all following activity occurrences on that branch.

### 29.3.3 Discrete States

Most applications of process ontologies are used to represent dynamic behaviour in the world so that intelligent agents may make predictions about the future and explanations about the past. In particular, these predictions and explanations are often concerned with the state of the world and how that state changes. The PSL core theory $T_{disc\_state}$ is intended to capture the basic intuitions about states and their relationship to activities.

**Intuition 9:** *State is changed by the occurrence of activities.*

Intuitively, a change in state is captured by a state that is either achieved or falsified by an activity occurrence. We therefore need a relation that specifies the state that is intuitively true prior to an activity occurrence and also a relation that specifies the state that is intuitively true after an activity occurrence.

This illustrates another difference between PSL and versions of the situation calculus that use only the *holds* relation for reified fluents [6]. Since the situation $S_0$ does not correspond to an activity occurrence, the state prior to an initial activity occurrence is the same as the state that holds for $S_0$. However, since PSL refers only to initial activity occurrences, it requires an additional relation for the prior state such that all initial activity occurrences agree on the states prior to their occurrence; that is, if a fluent $f$ holds prior to the initial activity occurrence of one occurrence tree, then it holds prior to the initial activity occurrence of all occurrence trees in the model. For example, in Figure 29.2, the same fluents hold prior to both initial activity occurrences $o_1^1$ and $o_{16}^4$.

---

[6] Within situation calculus, fluents are situation dependent properties. In a nonreified approach, these properties are represented by predicates, whereas in the reified approach (adopted by the PSL Ontology), fluents are elements of the domain.

**Intuition 10:** *State can only be changed by the occurrence of activities.*

Thus, if some state holds after an activity occurrence, but after an activity occurrence later along the branch it is false, then an activity must occur at some point between that changes the state. This also leads to the requirement that the state holding after an activity occurrence will be the same state holding prior to any immediately succeeding occurrence, since there cannot be an activity occurring between the two by definition.

**Intuition 11:** *State does not change during the occurrence of an activity in the occurrence tree.*

$T_{disc\_state}$ cannot represent phenomena in which some feature of the world is changing as some continuous function of time (hence the name "Discrete State" for the extension). State can change only during the occurrence of complex activities.

### 29.3.4 Subactivities

The PSL Ontology uses the *subactivity* relation to capture the basic intuitions for the composition of activities. This relation is a discrete partial ordering, in which primitive activities are the minimal elements.

The core theory $T_{subactivity}$ alone does not specify any relationship between the occurrence of an activity and occurrences of its subactivities. For example, consider the activities used in Figure 29.2. We can compose *paint* and *polish* as subactivities of some other activity, say *surfacing*, and we can compose *make_body* and *make_frame* into another activity, say *fabricate*. However, this specification of subactivities alone does not allow us to say that *surfacing* is a nondeterministic activity, or that *fabricate* is a deterministic activity.

### 29.3.5 Atomic Activities

The primary motivation driving the axiomatization of $T_{atomic}$ is to capture intuitions about the occurrence of concurrent activities. Since concurrent activities may have preconditions and effects that are not the conjunction of the preconditions and effects of their activities, $T_{atomic}$ takes the following approach:

**Intuition 12:** *Concurrency is represented by the occurrence of one concurrent activity rather than multiple concurrent occurrences.*

Atomic activities are either primitive or concurrent (in which case they have proper subactivities). The core theory $T_{atomic}$ introduces the function *conc* that maps any two atomic activities to the activity that is their concurrent composition. Essentially, what we call an atomic activity corresponds to some set of primitive activities, leading to the following intuition for this theory:

**Intuition 13:** *every concurrent activity is equivalent to the composition of a set of primitive activities.*

Although $T_{subactivity}$ can represent arbitrary composition of activities, the composition of atomic activities is restricted to concurrency; to represent complex, or nonatomic, activities requires the next core theory.

### 29.3.6 Complex Activities

The core theory $T_{complex}$ characterizes the relationship between the occurrence of a complex activity and occurrences of its subactivities. Occurrences of complex activities correspond to sets of occurrences of subactivities; in particular, these sets are subtrees of the occurrence tree.

> **Intuition 14:** *An activity tree consists of all possible sequences of atomic subactivity occurrences beginning from a root subactivity occurrence.*

In a sense, activity trees are a microcosm of the occurrence tree, in which we consider all of the ways in which the world unfolds *in the context of an occurrence of the complex activity.* For example, if occurrence of the complex activity $fabricate$ consists of an occurrence of $make\_frame$ followed by an occurrence of $make\_body$, then $\{o_1^1, o_{20}^2, o_{23}^2\}$ and $\{o_1^1, o_5^2, o_8^2\}$ can be two activity trees for $fabricate$. If an occurrence of the complex activity $surfacing$ consists of either an occurrence of $polish$ or an occurrence of $paint$, then $\{o_9^3, o_{10}^2\}$ and $\{o_{13}^3, o_{14}^4\}$ can be two activity trees for $surfacing$.

Any activity tree is actually isomorphic to multiple copies of a minimal activity tree arising from the fact that other external activities may be occurring during the complex activity. For example, $\{o_1^1, o_5^2\}$ and $\{o_1^1, o_8^2\}$ are two isomorphic copies of the tree that captures the intuition "make the frame and then make the body". In the first case, $o_2^4$ and $o_4^4$ are occurrences of the activity $polish$ during the occurrence of $fabricate$.

> **Intuition 15:** *Different subactivities may occur on different branches of the activity tree i.e. different occurrences of an activity may have different subactivity occurrences or different orderings on the same subactivity occurrences.*

In this sense, branches of the activity tree characterize the nondeterminism that arises from different ordering constraints or iteration. For example, the $surfacing$ activity is intuitively nondeterministic; the activity trees for $surfacing$ contain two branches, one branch consisting of an occurrence of $polish$ and one branch consisting of an occurrence of $paint$.

Finally, there may be branches of a subtree of the occurrence tree that are isomorphic to branches of an activity tree, yet they do not correspond to occurrences of the activity. For example, in Figure 29.2, $\{o_{17}^1, o_{23}^2\}$ need not be an activity tree for $fabricate$, even though it is isomorphic to a branch of an activity tree.

> **Intuition 16:** *An activity will in general have multiple activity trees within an occurrence tree, and not all activity trees for an activity need be isomorphic. Different activity trees for the same activity can have different subactivity occurrences.*

Following this intuition, the core theory $T_{complex}$ does not constrain which subactivities occur. For example, conditional activities are characterized by cases in which the state that holds prior to the activity occurrence determines which subactivities occur. In fact, an activity may have subactivities that do not occur; the only constraint is that any subactivity occurrence must correspond to a subtree of the activity tree that characterizes the occurrence of the activity.

**Intuition 17:** *Not every occurrence of a subactivity is a subactivity occurrence. There may be other external activities that occur during an occurrence of an activity.*

This theory does not force the existence of complex activities; there may be subtrees of the occurrence tree that contain occurrences of subactivities, yet not be activity trees. This allows for the existence of activity attempts, intended effects, and temporal constraints; subtrees that do not satisfy the desired constraints will simply not correspond to activity trees for the activity.

### 29.3.7 Complex Activity Occurrences

Within $T_{complex}$, complex activity occurrences correspond to activity trees, and consequently occurrences of complex activities are not elements of the legal occurrence tree. The axioms of the core theory $T_{actocc}$ ensure complex activity occurrences correspond to branches of activity trees. Each complex activity occurrence has a unique atomic root occurrence and each finite complex activity occurrence has a unique atomic leaf occurrence. A subactivity occurrence corresponds to a sub-branch of the branch corresponding to the complex activity occurrence.

### 29.3.8 Duration

The core theory for duration essentially adds a metric to the timeline by mapping every pair of timepoints to a new sort called *timeduration* that satisfy the axioms of algebraic fields. All models of this theory are isomorphic to a projective vector space (since timedurations must also be values for durations with the timeline's endpoints at infinity). Of course, the duration of an activity occurrence is of most interest, and is equal to the duration between the endof and beginof timepoints of the activity occurrence.

## 29.4 Definitional Extensions

As discussed earlier, the set of models for the core theories of PSL are partitioned into equivalence classes defined with respect to the set of invariants of the models. Each equivalence class in the classification of PSL models is axiomatized within a definitional extension of the PSL Ontology. In this section, we will highlight the classes of activities in some of the definitional extensions of the PSL Ontology; in each case we will consider the invariants associated with the concepts and give examples of process descriptions for activities that are members of these classes.

Many of the invariants with definitional extensions in the PSL Ontology are related to the automorphism groups [7] for different substructures of the models. We will

---

[7] An automorphism is a bijection from a structure to itself that preserves the extensions of the relations and functions in the structure. Intuitively, automorphisms are the symmetries of a structure.

use the following notation for the relevant substructures: $\mathcal{T}$ is the timeline and $\mathcal{F}$ is the structure isomorphic to the extension of the *prior* relation. $Aut(\mathcal{F})$ is the group of permutations that map activity occurrences only to other activity occurrences that agree on the set of fluents that hold prior to them. $Aut(\mathcal{T})$ is the group of permutations that map activity occurrences only to other activity occurrences that agree on their *beginof* timepoints.

### 29.4.1 Occurrence Constraints

We first consider permutations of activity occurrences that map the predecessor of a legal occurrence of an activity **a** to other predecessors of legal occurrences of **a** in the occurrence tree. This set of permutations forms a group, which we will refer to as $OP(\mathbf{a})$. Each invariant related to occurrence constraints is based on subgroups of this group. For example, if we consider the activity *paint* and the occurrence trees in Figure 29.2, $OP(paint)$ is the group of permutations on the set that includes the activity occurrences $o_1^1, o_3^2, o_5^2, o_7^4, o_8^2, o_{10}^4$.

The most prevalent class of occurrence constraints is the case of Markovian activities, that is, activities whose preconditions depend only on the state prior to the occurrences (e.g. see Equation 29.6). The class of Markovian activities is defined in the definitional extension *state_precond.def* (see Figure 29.3). The invariant associated with this extension is the group $\mathcal{P}^{\mathcal{F}}(\mathbf{a})$, which is the maximal normal subgroup of $Aut(\mathcal{F})$ that is also a subgroup of $OP(\mathbf{a})$. If $\mathcal{P}^{\mathcal{F}}(\mathbf{a}) = Aut(\mathcal{F})$, then these permutations preserve the legal occurrences of an activity, and the activity's preconditions are strictly Markovian; this is axiomatized by the *markov_precond* class in Figure 29.3. If $\mathcal{P}^{\mathcal{F}}(\mathbf{a})$ is only a subgroup of $Aut(\mathcal{F})$, then there exist additional non-markovian constraints on the legal occurrences of the activity; this is axiomatized by the *partial_state* class in Figure 29.3. If $\mathcal{P}^{\mathcal{F}}(\mathbf{a})$ is the trivial identity group, then there are no Markovian constraints on the legal occurrences of the activity; this is axiomatized by the *rigid_state* class in Figure 29.3.

Additional relations are defined to capture the action of the automorphism groups on the models. Two activity occurrences $o_1, o_2$ are *state_equiv* iff there exists a permutation in $Aut(\mathcal{F})$ that maps $o_1$ to $o_2$; the two activity occurrences are *poss_equiv* iff there exists a permutation in $OP(\mathbf{a})$ that maps $o_1$ to $o_2$.

There are other kinds of preconditions that are independent of state. For example, there may be temporal preconditions, in which the legal occurrences of the activity depend only on the time at which the activity is to occur (e.g. Equation 29.7). The invariant for this extension (*time_precond.def*) in the PSL Ontology is the group $\mathcal{P}^{\mathcal{T}}(\mathbf{a})$, which is the maximal normal subgroup of $Aut(\mathcal{T})$ that is also a subgroup of $OP(\mathbf{a})$. If $\mathcal{P}^{\mathcal{T}}(\mathbf{a}) = Aut(\mathcal{T})$, then all legal occurrences of the activity are preserved by the permutations in $Aut(\mathcal{T})$, which is the case with temporal preconditions.

### 29.4.2 Effects

Effects characterize the ways in which activity occurrences change the state of the world. Such effects may be context-free, so that all occurrences of the activity change

$$(\forall o_1, o_2)\, state\_equiv(o_1, o_2) \equiv (\forall f)\, (prior(f, o_1) \equiv prior(f, o_2)) \tag{29.1}$$

$$(\forall a, o_1, o_2)\, poss\_equiv(a, o_1, o_2) \equiv (poss(a, o_1) \equiv poss(a, o_2)) \tag{29.2}$$

$$(\forall a)\, markov\_precond(a) \equiv$$
$$((\forall o_1, o_2)\, state\_equiv(o_1, o_2) \supset poss\_equiv(a, o_1, o_2)) \tag{29.3}$$

$$(\forall a)\, partial\_state(a) \equiv$$
$$(\exists o_1)\, ((\forall o_2)\, state\_equiv(o_1, o_2) \supset poss\_equiv(a, o_1, o_2))$$
$$\wedge (\exists o_3, o_4)\, state\_equiv(o_3, o_4) \wedge \neg poss\_equiv(a, o_3, o_4) \tag{29.4}$$

$$(\forall a)\, rigid\_state(a) \equiv$$
$$(\forall o_1)(\exists o_2)\, state\_equiv(o_1, o_2) \wedge \neg poss\_equiv(a, o_1, o_2) \tag{29.5}$$

**Fig. 29.3.** Classes of activities with state-based preconditions (from the definitional extension $state\_precond.def$).

the same states, or they may be constrained by other conditions. The most common constraints are state-based effects that depend on the context (e.g. Equation 29.8). However, other kinds of constraints also arise in practice, such as time-based effects (e.g. Equation 29.9) and duration-based effects (e.g. Equation 29.10).

With respect to effects, activities are classified by the automorphism group of the structure that specifies which activity occurrences achieve or falsify a fluent. For example, if permutations of activity occurrences that preserve state are also automorphisms of this structure, then the effects of the activity depend only on the state; the associated classes of activities are found in the definitional extension $state\_effects.def$.

### 29.4.3 Conditional and Triggered Activities

There are several distinct classes in the PSL Ontology that are based on the relationship between fluents and activity occurrences. For conditional activities, fluents determine which subactivities occur (e.g. Equation 29.11). For triggered activities, fluents determine determine the conditions under which an activity must occur (e.g. Equation 29.12). Triggered activities differ from preconditions, which only specify the conditions under which an activity may possibly occur.

The automorphism groups for conditional activities consist of permutations of root occurrences of an activity tree that also preserve the structure of the minimal activity tree. In particular, if two activity occurrences are $state\_equiv$, then they are the roots of isomorphic minimal activity trees.

*Mixing is not performed unless the moulding machine is clean.*

$$(\forall o, x)\; occurrence\_of(o, mixing(x)) \wedge legal(o) \supset prior(clean(x), o) \qquad (29.6)$$

*The pre-heating operation can only be performed on Tuesday or Thursday.*

$$(\forall o, x)\; occurrence\_of(o, preheat(x)) \wedge legal(o) \supset$$

$$(beginof(o) = Tuesday) \vee (beginof(o) = Thursday) \qquad (29.7)$$

*If the object is fragile, then it will break when dropped.*

$$(\forall o, x)\; occurrence\_of(o, drop(x) \wedge prior(fragile(x), o)$$

$$\supset holds(broken(x), o) \qquad (29.8)$$

*If we remove the coffee pot before the brewing activity completes, then the burner will be wet.*

$$(\forall o_1, o_2, x, y)\; occurrence\_of(o_1, brew(x, y)) \wedge occurrence\_of(o_2, remove(x, y))$$

$$\wedge before(beginof(o_2), beginof(o_1)) \supset holds(wet(y), o_1) \qquad (29.9)$$

*The time on the clock display will change after pressing the button for three seconds.*

$$(\forall o, x)\; occurrence\_of(o, press(x)) \wedge duration(endof(o), beginof(o)) = 3$$

$$\supset holds(display(x), o) \qquad (29.10)$$

*Within the painting activity, if the surface of the product is rough, then sand the product.*

$$(\forall s, o_1, x)\; occurrence\_of(o_1, paint(x)) \wedge root_o cc(o_1) = s \wedge (prior(rough(x), s)$$

$$\supset (\exists o_2)\; occurrence\_of(a_2, sand(x)) \wedge root\_occ(o_2) = s) \qquad (29.11)$$

*Deliver the product when we have received three orders.*

$$(\forall s, x)\; prior(order\_quantity(x, 3), s) \supset$$

$$(\exists o)\; occurrence\_of(o, deliver(x)) \wedge s = root\_occ(o) \qquad (29.12)$$

**Fig. 29.4.** Examples of process descriptions in PSL associated with occurrence constraints, effects, conditional activities, and triggered activities.

The invariant for a triggered activity characterizes which subtrees are activity trees by looking at the automorphism groups that preserve occurrences of the activity. In this way, triggered activities are characterized by mappings in which permutations that preserve fluents also preserve the existence of activity trees for the activity.

### 29.4.4 Ordering Constraints

One of the most common intuitions about processes is the notion of process flow, or the specification of some ordering over the subactivities of an activity (e.g. Equation 29.13). The orderings themselves may also be nondeterministic. For example,

*Making the frame involves the cutting and punching in parallel, followed by painting.*

$$(\forall o, x)\ occurrence\_of(o, make(x)) \supset (\exists o_1, o_2, o_3)\ occurrence\_of(o_1, cut(x))$$

$$\land occurrence\_of(o_2, punch(x)) \land \land occurrence\_of(o_3, paint(x))$$

$$\land min\_precedes(root\_occ(o_1), root\_occ(o_3))$$

$$\land min\_precedes(root\_occ(o_2), root\_occ(o_3)) \tag{29.13}$$

*Final assembly of the car consists of installation of either the manual or automatic transmission.*

$$(\forall o, x)\ occurrence\_of(o, final(x)) \supset (\exists o_1)\ subactivity\_occurrence(o_1, o)$$

$$\land (occurrence\_of(o_1, manual(x)) \lor occurrence\_of(o_1, automatic(x))) \tag{29.14}$$

*If the machine is not ready, then perform the painting before final assembly.*

$$(\forall o, o_1, o_2, x, y)\ occurrence\_of(o, assembly(x, y))$$

$$\land occurrence\_of(o_1, paint(x)) \land occurrence\_of(o_1, final(x))$$

$$\land \neg prior(ready(y), root\_occ(o)) \supset min\_precedes(root\_occ(o_1), root\_occ(o_2)) \tag{29.15}$$

**Fig. 29.5.** Examples of process descriptions in PSL associated with ordering constraints.

there could be alternative process plans to produce the same product depending on the customer, (such as the process description in Equation 29.14) or the ordering may depend on state (as in the process description in Equation 29.15) Note that this latter constraint is distinct from conditional activities, since both painting and final assembly will occur; the nondeterminism in this case arises from the ordering of the occurrences of these activities.

The automorphism groups in this case consist of permutations of subactivity occurrences that are also automorphisms of the activity trees considered as graphs; the corresponding classes of activities are found in the definitional extension *ordering.def*.

## 29.5 Summary

Within the increasingly complex environments of enterprise integration, electronic commerce, and the Semantic Web, where process models are maintained in different software applications, standards for the exchange of this information must address not only the syntax but also the semantics of process concepts. PSL draws upon well-known mathematical tools and techniques to provide a robust semantic foundation for the representation of process information. This foundation includes first-order theories for concepts together with complete characterizations of the satisfiability and axiomatizability of the models of these theories. The PSL Ontology also provides a justification of the taxonomy of activities by classifying the models with respect to invariants. Finally, process descriptions are formally characterized as syntactic classes of sentences that are satisfied elements of the models.

# References

1. Ghallab, M. et al. (1998) *PDDL: The Planning Domain Definition Language v.2.* Technical Report CVC TR-98-003, Yale Center for Computational Vision and Control.
2. Gruninger, M., and Fox, M.S., (1995), The Role of Competency Questions in Enterprise Engineering, *Benchmarking: Theory and Practice*, Rolstadas, A. (ed). Kluwer Academic Publishers, Boston.
3. Hayes, P. (1996) *A Catalog of Temporal Theories.* Artificial Intelligence Technical Report UIUC-BI-AI-96-01, University of Illinois at Urbana-Champaign.
4. Hendler, J. amd McGuinness, D.L. (2001): DARPA Agent Markup Language. *IEEE Intelligent Systems*, 15:72-73.
5. Lee, J., Gruninger, M., Jin, Y., Malone, T., Tate, A., Yost, G. (1998) The PIF Process Interchange Format and Framework, *Knowledge Engineering Review*, 2:1-30.
6. Levesque, H., Reiter, R., Lesperance, Y., Lin, F., and Scherl, R. (1997): GOLOG: A logic programming language for dynamic domains. *Journal of Logic Programming*, 31:92-128.
7. McIlraith, S., Son, T.C. and Zeng, H. (2001) Semantic Web Services, *IEEE Intelligent Systems*, Special Issue on the Semantic Web. 16:46–53, March/April, 2001.
8. Menzel, C. and Gruninger, M. (2001) A formal foundation for process modeling, *Second International Conference on Formal Ontologies in Information Systems*, Welty and Smith (eds), 256-269.
9. Pease, A. and Carrico, T.D. *Core Plan Representation.* Armstrong Lab Report AL/HR-TP-96-9631, Armstrong Laboratory, US Air Force, January 1997. Object Modeling Working Group.
10. Pinto, J. and Reiter, R. (1993) Temporal reasoning in logic programming: A case for the situation calculus. *Proceedings of the 10th International Conference on Logic Programming*, Budapest, Hungary, June 1993.
11. Reiter, R. (2001) *Knowledge in Action : Logical Foundations for Specifying and Implementing Dynamical Systems.* MIT Press.
12. Sandewall, E. (1994) *Features and Fluents.* Oxford Science Publications.
13. Schlenoff, C., Gruninger, M., Ciocoiu, M., (1999) The Essence of the Process Specification Language, *Transactions of the Society for Computer Simulation* vol.16 no.4 (December 1999) pages 204-216.
14. Sowa, J. (2000) *Knowledge Representation: Logical, Philosophical, and Computational Foundations.* Brooks/Cole Publishing.
15. Tate, A., Drabble, B., Kirby, R. (1994) O-Plan: An open architecture for command, planning, and control. In M. Fox and M. Zweben (eds.) *Intelligent Scheduling.* Morgan Kaufmann, 1994.
16. Tate, A. (1998), "Roots of SPAR - Shared Planning and Activity Representation", *The Knowledge Engineering Review*, Vol 13(1), pp. 121-128, Special Issue on Putting Ontologies to Use (eds. Uschold. M. and Tate, A.), Cambridge University Press, March 1998.
17. Workflow Management Coalition (1999) *Process Definition Meta-Model and WPDL*, WfMC-TC-1016-P v1.1.

# The Role of Ontologies in eCommerce

Y. Ding[2], D. Fensel[2], M. Klein[1], B. Omelayenko[1], and E. Schulten[1]

[1] Vrije Universiteit Amsterdam VUA, Division of Mathematics and Informatics, De Boelelaan 1081a, NL-1081 HV Amsterdam, The Netherlands

[2] Leopold-Franzens Universität Innsbruck, Institut für Informatik, Technikerstrasse 25, A-6020 Innsbruck, Austria

**Summary.** Web technology is starting to penetrate many aspects of our daily life and its importance as a medium for business transactions will grow significantly during the next few years. In terms of market volume, B2B will be the most interesting area where new technology will lead to drastic changes in established customer relationships and business models. Simple and established one2one trading relationships will be replaced by open and flexible n2m relationships between customers and vendors. However, this new flexibility in electronic trading also creates serious challenges for the parties who want to realize it. The main problem is the heterogeneity of information descriptions used by vendors and customers. Product descriptions, catalog formats, and business documents are often unstructured and non-standardized. Intelligent solutions that help to mechanize the process of structuring, standardizing, aligning and personalizing are key requisites to successfully overcoming the current bottlenecks of eCommerce and enabling its further growth. This paper discusses the main problems of information integration in this area and describes how ontology technology can help solve many of them.

## 30.1  Introduction

eCommerce in business-to-business (B2B) is not a new phenomenon. Initiatives to support electronic data exchange in the business processes between different companies already existed in the 1960s. In order to exchange business transactions the sender and receiver have to agree on a common standard (a protocol for transmitting the content and a language for describing the content). In general, the automation of business transactions has not reached the expectations of its propagandists. Establishing an eCommerce relationship requires a serious investment and it is limited to a predefined number of trading partners. It also is limited to a specific type of extranet that needs to be set up for mechanizing the business relationships.

Web-enabled eCommerce helps users contact a large number of potential clients without running into the problems associated with implementing numerous communication channels. However, enabling flexible and open eCommerce requires contending with other serious problems. One has to deal with the question of heterogeneity in the product, catalogue, and document description standards of the trading partner. The effective and efficient management of different styles of description becomes a key obstacle for this approach.

Web-enabled eCommerce needs to be open to a large numbers of suppliers and buyers. Its success is closely related to its ability to mediate a large number of business transactions. Web-enabled eCommerce provides its users with one key advantage - they can communicate with many customers through a single communication channel. This open, flexible, and dynamic channel reduces the number of special-purpose communication links for its user community. However, in order to provide this service, there must be solutions that solve the significant normalization, mapping, and updating problems for the clients. A successful approach has to deal with numerous aspects. It has to integrate various hardware and software platforms and provide a common protocol for information exchange. However, the real problem is the openness, heterogeneity and dynamic nature of the exchanged content. There are at least three levels at which this heterogeneity arises: the content level, the level of product catalogs structures, and the level of document structures.

- The actual content of the exchanged information needs to be modelled. Many different ways to categorize and describe products have evolved over time. Vendors often have their own way of describing their products. Structuring and standardizing the product descriptions, ensuring the different players can actually communicate with each other, and allowing customers to find the products they are looking for are significant tasks in B2B eCommerce. Ontologies define real-world semantics that make it possible to link machine-processable content with meaning for humans based on consensual terminologies.
- eCommerce is about the electronic exchange of business information. Product descriptions are just one element, but they are the building blocks of an electronic catalog, together with information about the vendor, the manufacturer, the lead- time etc. Furthermore, a catalog provider needs to include quality control information, such as the version, date, and identification number of the catalog. If two electronic catalogs are involved, the structure of these catalogs must be aligned as well.
- The next step in the process is the actual use of the catalog. A buyer may want to send a purchase order, after retrieving the necessary information from a catalog. The vendor has to reply with a confirmation, and then the

actual buying process begins. A common language is needed in order for the buyer and the vendor to read and process each other's business documents. Marketplace software designers like Commerce One developed their structures based on xCBL[1]. This provides a large collection of document structures reflecting different aspects of a trading process. Aligning these document structures with other document definitions from, for example, Ariba (cXML)[2], is not certainly a trivial task.

The first type of mismatch that arises primarily concerns with the real-world semantics of the exchanged information. People describe the same products in different ways. The second and third types arise in relation to the syntactical structure of the exchanged information. These problems are more serious, reflecting the dynamic nature of eCommerce. New players arise, new standards are proposed, and new products and services enter the marketplace. No static solution can deal with this constantly changing and evolving situation. Given the requirements there is only one IT technology available that can provide at least a partial solution - ontology. This technology and its promises for eCommerce are examined in the reminder of this paper.

*Ontology-based solution paths.* Ontologies (cf. [Fensel, 2001]) are a key enabling technology for the semantic web. They interweave human understanding of symbols with machine-processability. Ontologies were developed in Artificial Intelligence to facilitate knowledge sharing and reuse. Since the early nineties, ontologies have become a popular research topic and a subject of study by several Artificial Intelligence research communities, including Knowledge Engineering, Natural Language Processing and Knowledge Representation. More recently, the concept of ontology has spread to other fields, such as intelligent information integration, cooperative information systems, information retrieval, electronic commerce, and knowledge management. The reason ontologies are becoming so popular is primarily due to what they promise: a shared and common understanding of a domain that can be communicated between people and application systems. In essence, Ontologies are formal and consensual specifications of conceptualizations that provide a shared and common understanding of a domain, an understanding that can be communicated across people and application systems. Ontologies glue together two essential factors that help to bring the Web to its full potential:

- Ontologies define formal semantics for information that allows information processing by a computer.
- Ontologies define real-world semantics that make it possible to link machine-processable content with meaning for humans based on consensual terminologies.

---

[1] http://www.xcbl.org
[2] http://www.cxml.org

The latter aspect makes ontology technology especially interesting. Ontologies must have a network architecture and be dynamic. Ontologies deal with heterogeneity in space and development in time. Ontology is networks of meaning where, from the very beginning, heterogeneity is an essential requirement. Tools for dealing with conflicting definitions and strong support in interweaving local theories are essential in order to make this technology workable and scalable. Ontologies are used as a method of exchanging meaning between different agents. They can only provide this if they reflect an inter-subjectual consensus. By definition, ontologies can only be the result of a social process. For this reason, ontologies cannot be understood as a static model. An ontology is as much required for the exchange of meaning as the exchange of meaning may influence and modify an ontology. Consequently, evolving ontologies describe a process rather than a static model. Indeed, evolving over time is an essential requirement for useful ontologies. As daily practice constantly changes, ontologies that mediate the information needs of these processes must have strong support in versioning and must be accompanied by process models that help to organize consensus.

*Contents of the paper.* The structure of this paper reflects the issues discussed above. In Section 2, we explore the role of standardization in eCommerce, as openness cannot be achieved without agreements. In Section 3 and 4, we explain the need for heterogeneity in these descriptions. Section 3 focuses on heterogeneity in space (i.e. on aligning standards), and Section 4 focuses on heterogeneity in time (i.e. on evolving these standards). Section 5 covers an aspect we have not yet mentioned - that Ontologies are structures for describing actual content. This section also describes methods and tools to allow this in a scalable and economic fashion. Finally, conclusions are provided in Section 6.

## 30.2     Openness: Harmonization and Standardization in eCommerce

A fundamental premise - and the major economic drive - behind eCommerce is that labor intensive and time consuming human interactions can be replaced with (semi-) automated internet-enabled processes. Looking at actual eCommerce solutions, we see rather simple applications for the final customers, such as product search and selection without the help of a sales representative. There are slightly more sophisticated solutions between enterprises, such as server-to-server communication for enterprise inventory management. Despite these solutions, the slower-than-expected adoption of electronic buying and the bankruptcy of many dotcoms point to the complexity of replacing the human element. Of course, this is not difficult to understand. In the human world, dialog is structured by grammatical, semantic, and syntactic rules that are expressed in a shared context of social and cultural conventions. The young eCommerce world is lacking this rich consensual background, and we are still far from achieving the vision of a Universe of Network-Accessible Information - as the W3C defines the Web. The need for consensus in a trading community arises on many different levels, which is reflected in the different areas of focus of these harmonization initiatives. Figure 1 illustrates the basic processes and documents exchanged through an e-marketplace based on SAP technology. Depending on the level of sophistication, the Business Connector allows integration with the back-end system of the business partners and the billing process is automated through the marketplace. Looking from a business perspective, we first encounter the level of the basic building blocks of any commercial transaction; the descriptions of the products and services themselves. Clearly, without agreement on the name of an item to be bought or sold, any degree of transaction automation becomes quite complex. We then arrive at the level where these descriptions are represented in an electronic catalogue. The catalogue requires specific content and an agreed format because the many-to-many communication in an electronic marketplace presupposes a shared catalogue. Finally, there is the level where the electronic catalogue is actually used. Here the business processes and the business documents involved have to be aligned. Consider the straightforward example of purchasing a non-stock item, such as writing paper, through an electronic marketplace. The business partners at a minimum need to be able to exchange a Purchase Order and a Purchase Order Confirmation and in a more sophisticated application. the Billing process, Order Status Tracking, and the Goods Receipt Process are included as well. Hence, business processes and documents throughout the supply chain are involved in this alignment process.

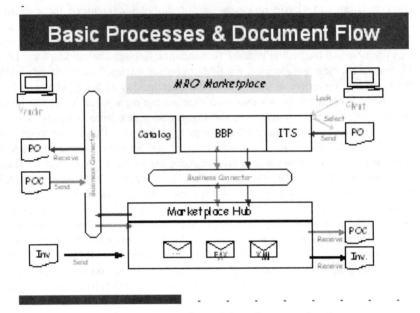

**Fig. 1.** Basis processes and documents exchanged through an e-marketplace

We will now discuss standardization and harmonization initiatives that have a significant impact on the development of electronic business. First, Table 1. provides a summary and classification of the product and service standards.

**Table 1.** Survey of product and service standards

| Name | Design perspective | Main classification concept | Major use | Domain |
|---|---|---|---|---|
| ecl@ss, www.eCl@ss.de | Supply side | Material of construction. | Building blocks for electronic catalogues in B2B marketplaces. | Intending to cover services and products, but current focus on products. The automotive and the electrical industry are strongly represented. |
| HS: Harmonised System, www.wcoomd.org | Supply side | Material of construction. | Collection of customs duties and international trade statistics. | Intending to cover services and products, but strong focus on products. |
| NAICS/NAPCS: North American Industry Classification System/ North American Product Classification System, www.census.gov | NAICS: supply side NAPCS: demand side | NAICS: Production process. NAPCS: not yet decided | NAICS & NAPCS: Statistics on a.o. productivity, unit labor. | NAICS: intending to cover services and products, but strong focus on products. NAPCS: intending to cover services and products, first focus will be on services because they have in the past been neglected by classification systems. |
| RosettaNet, www.rosettanet.org | Supply side | Product category | Building blocks for electronic catalogues in B2B marketplaces | Products in IT industry, automotive industry, consumer electronics and telecommunications industries. |
| SYMAP/CVP: Système d'Information pour les Marchés Publics / Common Procurement Vocabulary, www. simap.eu.int | Supply side | Industry of origin | Purchasing in public sector. | Intended to cover services and products, but focus on products. |
| UNSPSC: United Nations Standard Products and Services Codes, www.un-spsc.net | Supply side | Product category | Building blocks for electronic catalogues. | Intending to cover services and products, but currently very shallow. |

These content standards are complemented by proposals for the alignment of business processes. Examples are: BizTalk, www.biztalk.org and www.microsoft.com/biztalk/; Commerce XML: cXML, www.cxml.org; Electronic Business XML: ebXML, www.ebxml.org; Open Buying on the Internet Consortium OBI, www.openbuy.org; Open Applications Group Integration Specification: OAGIS, www.openapplications.org; Organization for the Advancement of Structured Information Standards: OASIS, www.oasis-open.org; Rosettanet, www.rosettanet.org; UN/CEFACT, www.unece.org/cefact; and XML Common Business Library: xCBL, www.xcbl.org.

In order to elevate electronic business beyond the buying and selling of mere commodities such as a desktop computer or a CD, customers need a generic classification system with a high level of detail. It is clear that the current classification systems are built for different purposes, with different classification concepts and structures, and cover different domains. Some do not provide the level of detail required for an electronic catalogue, others neglect the important area of services, and most are developed from a supply instead of a demand perspective. In short, a universal product and service classification system that is useful for a customer dealing with an electronic catalog does not exist. Therefore, the question of the compatibility between these classification systems is a crucial one. This will be addressed in the following section.

Sophisticated electronic commerce also presupposes that the business processes of the engaged partners are aligned and that the related business documents and catalogues are standardized. We can see the major industry players in this field recognize the importance of consensus and harmonization, and they increasingly ensure compliance with international independent bodies such as the W3C and ebXML.

In an ideal world, all electronic commerce between businesses would utilize one universal standard covering the issues on all the levels that we have discussed in this chapter. Nevertheless, for at least two reasons, this does not look feasible in the real world. First, because business requirements and technology possibilities alter at a rapid rate, and therefore, standards will always be in development. Second, businesses will not wait decades for a global standard to 'arise'. Indeed, notwithstanding the lack of proper standards, many enterprises already engage in electronic business in different ways, utilizing different languages. Multilinguality is not a problem itself; instead, it often allows creativity and refreshing diversity. However, things get trickier when lacking the means for translation. This is exactly the case in many parts of B2B electronic commerce and brings to mind the biblical building of the Tower of Babel.

## 30.3   Flexibility: Alignment of Standards

The heterogeneity of eCommerce cannot be captured by one standard and personalization is needed anyway. Therefore, scalable mediation service between different standards is essential. We will now describe how Ontology mapping methods can contribute a solution to this problem, focusing on the alignment of business documents and product classifications.

### 30.3.1  The Domain Ontology

The B2B area operates with substantial number of different business documents. There are several non-XML plain text document standards already accepted and widely used by the industry. The first is the well-known EDIFACT format approved by the United Nations Economic Commission for Europe.[3] An EDIFACT document is presented with complicated formatted text not understandable by a non-specialist. Several text wrappers able to translate an EDIFACT catalog into XML are now available. For example, the XML-EDIFACT[4] wrapper transfers EDIFACT documents into their XML representation and vice versa. Another non-XML standard is ISO 10303 [ISO, 2000] (also known as STEP) that is an International Standard for the computer-interoperable representation and exchange of product data. It contains a rich set of modeling primitives that allow building hierarchical product specifications. ISO has developed an XML syntax for STEP that is now being standardized as part 28 of the ISO 10303 specification.

**Table 2.** A fragment of the xCBL and cXML formats

| | |
|---|---|
| CatalogSchema | PunchOutOrderMessage |
| SchemaVersion> 1.0 | BuyerCookie> 342342ADF |
| SchemaStandard> UNSPSC | ItemIn |
| SchemaCategory | quantity> 1 |
| CategoryID> C43171801 | ItemID |
| ParentCategoryRef> C43170000 | SupplierPartID> 1234 |
| CategoryName> Computers | ItemDetail |
| CategoryAttribut | UnitPrice |
| AttributeName> Processor Speed | Money |
| CatalogData | currency> USD |
| Product | Money> 1250 |
| SchemaCategoryRef> C43171801 | Description> Armada M700 PIII 700 |
| ProductID> 140141-002 | UnitOfMeasure> EA |
| Manufacturer> Compaq | Classification |
| CountryOfOrigin> US | domain> SPSC |
| ShortDescription> COMPAQ Armada | Classification> 43171801 |
| AM700PIII 700 | ManufacturerPartID> 140141-002 |
| LongDescription> This light,... | ManufacturerName> Compaq |
| ObjectAttribute | |
| AttributeID> Warranty, years | |
| AttributeValue> 1 | |
| ProductVendorData | |
| PartnerRef> Acme_Laptops | |

---

[3] http://www.unece.org/trade/untdid/welcome.htm
[4] http://www.xml-edifact.org

| | |
|---|---|
| VendorPartNumber> 12345 ProductPrice   Amount> 1250   Currency> USD | |
| (a) xCBL | (b) cXML |

In addition to legacy standards, there exist a number of recently processed XML standards. Besides the common serialization language of XML, they significantly differ from the underlying document models.

One typical example of these differences is the diverse ways to represent a list of products in a purchase order when the products are grouped per transaction or in delivery order where the products are grouped per container. Document integration requires regrouping of the records.

Conceptually equivalent properties can be named and re-grouped in different ways. For example, consider the fragments of the document structures represented in Table 2. for (a) xCBL[5] and (b) cXML[6] standards. The tags in the figure represent the elements of the structure and roughly correspond to the XML tags, which describe the instance documents. The values of the tags are displayed in the italics to illustrate the intended meaning of the tags. Graphical tags nesting represent the part-of relation. We see the structures provide slightly different representations for very similar content. Both standards introduce internal product IDs and import the manufacturer's product IDs and names. They also contain pricing information, product descriptions, and a reference to a certain content standard.

Finally, the documents tend to be substantially different in capturing and representing is-a relations. For example, the fact that an address is either a physical address or a legal address (both are subclasses from a generic address) can be represented as tag nesting (making a tag sequence <! ELEMENT Address (PhysicalAddress | LegalAddress)>) explicitly capturing the is-a relationship at the schema level or with a certain attribute value assigned to element (<!ATTLIST Address type (Physical | Legal) #REQUIRED>) where value "Physical" being assigned to attribute type would specify that the address is a physical one. The second way encodes the is-a relation with attribute values at the level of values. The Ontology-mediated business integration framework [Omelayenko, 2002(b)] specifically addresses these issues by performing three steps of document integration.

*First*, document conceptual models are extracted from document DTDs, explicitly representing objects with string (#PCDATA) properties. This can be done automatically following existing work [Mello and Heuser, 2001]. It is important to mention that element and attribute names tend to be reused in DTDs with different associated meaning. For example, tag value may represent several completely different values if assigned to different elements (price value and docu-

---

[5] http://www.commerceone.com/solutions/business/content.html
[6] http://www.ariba.com/

ment revision value). These specific cases should be separated during the model extraction.

*Second*, these document models are mapped to a mediating unified conceptual model. This is done by means of RDFT mapping meta-ontology that specifies maps between conceptual models in RDF Schema consisting of bridges. Each bridge represents a certain relation between the concepts being mapped and this relation is then interpreted by inference engine that uses these bridges. The bridges link (several) source and (several) target roles, where each role stands for either a class, a property being attached to a specific class, or property value. Such bridge structure allows dealing with the heterogeneity in the modeling described above.

*Third*, the conceptual models and RDFT maps can then be easily converted to Prolog (See Figure 2 for a sample) to perform different reasoning tasks like validation checking for the maps.

To summarize, the document needs to be integrated stepwise via a mediating conceptual model to overcome the tremendous heterogeneity in underlying document models. The maps linking these models need to be capable of dealing with these differences and inference can be used to analyze the maps.

```
:- export([ l_triple/3, o_triple/3, namespace_def/2 ]).
namespace_def('rdf','http://www.w3.org/1999/02/22-rdf-syntax-ns#').
namespace_def('rdfs','http://www.w3.org/TR/1999/PR-rdf-schema-19990303#').
namespace_def('rdft','http://www.cs.vu.nl/~borys/RDFT#').
namespace_def('myns','http://cs.vu.nl/~borys/mediator#').
o_triple('Bridge_001','http://www.cs.vu.nl/~borys/RDFT#SourceClass','Role_002').
o_triple('Bridge_001','http://www.cs.vu.nl/~borys/RDFT#SourceClass','Role_003').
o_triple('Bridge_001','http://www.cs.vu.nl/~borys/RDFT#TargetClass','Role_001').
o_triple('Bridge_001','http://www.w3.org/1999/02/22-rdf-syntax-ns#type',
    'http://www.cs.vu.nl/~borys/RDFT#Class2Class').
o_triple('Role_001','http://www.cs.vu.nl/~borys/RDFT#Class','http://cs.vu.nl/~borys/mediator#Requestor').
o_triple('Role_001','http://www.w3.org/1999/02/22-rdf-syntax-ns#type','http://www.cs.vu.nl/~borys/RDFT#Roles').
o_triple('Role_002','http://www.cs.vu.nl/~borys/RDFT#Class','ext:').
o_triple('Role_002','http://www.cs.vu.nl/~borys/RDFT#Property','OAGI004#at_000_value').
o_triple('Role_002','http://www.w3.org/1999/02/22-rdf-syntax-ns#type','http://www.cs.vu.nl/~borys/RDFT#Roles').
o_triple('Role_003','http://www.cs.vu.nl/~borys/RDFT#Class','ext:').
o_triple('Role_003','http://www.cs.vu.nl/~borys/RDFT#Property','OAGI004#at_001_value').
o_triple('Role_003','http://www.w3.org/1999/02/22-rdf-syntax-ns#type','http://www.cs.vu.nl/~borys/RDFT#Roles').
```

**Fig. 2.** RDFT Map in Prolog

### 30.3.2    Alignment of Content Standards

Different eCommerce applications naturally use different content standards. For example, the UNSPSC standard mentioned earlier is primarily targeted at vendor's needs, while the eCl@ss standard largely represents buyer's needs. Therefore, different content standards need to be aligned and mapped in a scalable and efficient way [Fensel, 2001].

Mapping the content standards by specifying pairs of equivalent categories is not always possible due to different principles used to aggregate the products into categories of the same abstraction level. For this reason, for example, mapping UNSPSC to ecl@ss includes creating many-to-many bridges regrouping the products to categories. There are also prominent examples of aligning specific content standards to more generic ones. These mappings are manually created and verified, and sometimes have normative status. We can point to the UNSPSC crosswalk files linking it to NAICS and several other standards used for reporting and statistical purposes. Another example is mapping RosettaNet standard that specifies 445 categories and 2660 attributes for the electronic components to UNSPSC. Rosetta Net is specific in describing these components, but it does not cover concepts left beyond the primary focus. The mapping links only 136

UNSPSC elements out of more than 17,000 - most of which belong to the bottom level in the UNSPSC hierarchy - and thus expanding these 136 categories with all the Rosetta Net classes and attributes. The specific standards are very precise in describing the items on which they are focused. At the same time, they are even shallower than the generic standards in describing the things that lay beyond their focus.

Essentially, the content standards can be seen as lightweight ontologies containing hierarchies of classes with (possibly) several attributes attached to each class. They still have quite limited expressiveness to be regarded as logical theories, and thus form a simple playground for Ontology mapping and integration techniques. There exist several approaches for representing the maps between different ontologies ranging from UML-based representations like CWM [CWM, 2001] to those based on mapping ontologies represented in RDF Schema like RDFT [Omelayenko, 2002(b)] or MAFRA [Maedche et al., 2002]. However, the standards represent little formal semantics with no explicitly represented axioms or formal relations. As a result, it is difficult to perform inference over the standard and maps between them, as well as to specify formal interpretation of the maps. The categories are mainly interpreted in terms of product descriptions classified to each specific category. The categories possess mostly extensional information and they are interpreted in terms of instance data. Hence, any formal way of mapping the standards should be augmented with instance processing techniques linking the maps to actual product descriptions. A case study described in [Omelayenko, 2002(a)] presents the use of two Naïve-Bayes classifiers trained on two datasets that employ instance information for this problem.

To summarize, manual mapping of content standards is possible in some cases leaving quite a demand for automated mapping techniques. The categories are primarily interpreted in terms of instance product descriptions; the standards are lacking formal relations and axioms and as a result ontology-based mapping approaches should be improved by machine learning algorithms.

## 30.4   Dynamics: Versioning of Standards

The dynamic and open character of eCommerce requires that classification standards, as described in Section 2, are extended or adapted when new products or services arise. However, this presents new problems such as how to manage classification hierarchies that change over time, in such a way that the old and new versions can be used intermixed. If no special arrangements are taken, the evolution of standards might cause operability problems that will seriously hamper eCommerce applications. Solutions are required to allow changes to classification standards without making their present use invalid. In this section, we will first look at what typical changes in the UNSPSC classification system. We will then describe the requirements for a change management system, and explain some methods and tools for the versioning of ontologies.

### 30.4.1   Changes in UNSPSC

The high change rate of the classification hierarchies and the way in which those changes are handled is a serious threat for electronic commerce. For example, an examination of UNSPSC reveals:

- There were 16 updates between 31 January 2001 and 14 September 2001;
- Each update contained between 50 and 600 changes;
- In 7.5 month, more than 20% of the current standard is changed!

Although some parts of the UNSPSC schema might be more stable than other parts, it is clear this number of changes cannot be ignored. Such a high change rate can quickly invalidate many of the actual classifications of products. For example, the product "Binding elements" in version 8.0 is removed from the standard and three new products are added in version 8.1 ("Binding spines or snaps", "Binding coils or wire loops", and "Binding combs or strips"). This means that all products that were classified as "Binding elements" are unclassified under the new version. This is a serious problem because of the high costs for producing the right classifications for products. Moreover, if companies use local extensions of the standard they have to adapt these extensions to new versions as well. A versioning mechanism that allows partly automatic transformation of data between content standard versions is essential.

An effective versioning methodology should take care of the different types of changes in ontologies, as those might have different effects on the compatibility of data that is described by them [Klein & Fensel, 2001]. An analysis of differences between several versions of content standards yielded the following typical changes: class-title changes, additions of classes, relocations of classes in the hierarchy (by moving them up or down in the hierarchy or horizontally), relocations of a whole subtree in the hierarchy, merges of two classes (in two variants: two classes become one new class, or one class is appended to the other class), splits of classes, and pure deletions. However, current versioning techniques for content standards are often quite simple. In UNSPSC, for example, all changes are encoded as additions deletions, or edits (title changes). This means the relocation of a subtree is specified as a sequence of "delete a list of classes" and "add a list of classes".

### 30.4.2   Requirements for Content Standard Versioning

The need to cope with changing data structures is not new in computer science. Much of the research in database technology has focused on the topic of database schema evolution. However, while there are quite a few similarities between Ontology versioning and database schema evolution, there are also many differences (For a detailed discussion, see [Noy & Klein, 2002]). An important difference is that with ontologies the distinction between data and schema is not as clear as it is in databases. Ontologies themselves - and not just the data - are often used in applications, (i.e. as controlled vocabularies, or navigation structures). The UNSPSC standard, for example, might be used in an application to structure the website of sales company. In addition, ontologies are even more distributed by nature than are databases. We often have a clear picture of the locations where changes might have an impact on distributed databases. However, with content standards like UNSPSC the author of the Ontology has absolutely no clue as to which applications use the Ontology. It is not possible to synchronize changes with all users.

Due to these differences, the traditional distinctions [Roddick, 1995] between evolution (new schemas that are backward compatible) and versioning (multiple views of the data via different versions) and between reading and updating compatibility are not very relevant to ontology versioning. Changes to ontologies will occur and some are likely to cause incompatibilities. Therefore, versioning methodologies for ontologies cannot guarantee prevention of any information loss. However, it should make the effects of changes explicit. The management of changes is the key issue in support for evolving ontologies.

The mechanisms and techniques to manage those changes to ontologies should aim at achieving maximal interoperability with existing data and applications. This means that it should retain as much information and knowledge as possible without deriving incorrect information. This methodology should feature the following:

- *Identification mechanism:* for every use of a concept or a relation, a versioning framework should provide an unambiguous reference to the intended definition
- *Change specification mechanism:* the relation of one version of a concept or relation to other versions of that construct should be made explicit, both by specifying the ontological relation (i.e. subclass of) and the intention of the change (i.e. replacement)
- Transparent access: methods for rendering a valid interpretation to as much data as possible (i.e. automatically translating and relating the versions and data sources to the maximum possible extent).

Ontology comparison techniques can help companies find and describe the differences between the new versions of the standards and the old versions that were used to classify data. Descriptions of the semantics of the discovered changes can facilitate the transformation of data classification. For example, in the most trivial case, it can specify that a new version is a combination of two other classes; all products that were classified under the old classes can then be classified under the new class. Complicated specifications of the logical consequences, possibly with approximations, will further decrease the negative effects of the evolution of content standards.

**30.4.3  Tools for Ontology Versioning**

OntoView [Klein et al., 2002] is a change management tool for ontologies. The main function of OntoView is to provide a transparent interface to arbitrary versions of ontologies. To achieve this it maintains an internal specification of the relation between the different variants of ontologies. This specification consists of three aspects: the meta-data about changes (author, date, time etc.), the conceptual relations between versions of definitions in the ontologies, and the transformations between them. This specification is partly derived from the versions of ontologies themselves, but it also uses additional human input about the meta-data and the conceptual effects of changes.

To help the user to specify this information, OntoView provides the utility to compare versions of ontologies and highlight the differences. This helps in finding changes in ontologies, even if those have occurred in an uncontrolled way (i.e., possibly by different people in an unknown order). The comparison function is inspired by UNIX diff, but the implementation is quite different. Standard diff compares file version at line-level, highlighting the lines that textually differ in two versions. OntoView, in contrast, compares version of ontologies at a structural level, showing which definitions of ontological concepts or properties are changed.

The comparison function distinguishes between the following types of change:
- Non-logical change (i.e. in a natural language description). These are changes in the label of a concept or property, or in comments inside definitions.
- Logical definition change. These changes in the definition of a concept affects its formal semantics. Examples of such changes are alterations of subclass statements or changes in the domain or range of properties. Additions or deletions of local property restrictions in a class are also logical changes.
- Identifier change. This is when a concept or property is given a new identifier (i.e. a renaming).
- Addition of definitions
- Deletion of definitions

Each type of change is highlighted in a different color, and the altered lines are printed in boldface. An example of the visual representation of the result of a comparison is shown in Figure 3. For this picture, a subset of the two versions of the UNSPSC classification was used (i.e. segment 40 till 49 of UNSPSC version 8.0 and 8.4). The figure shows two classes that are added to the new version, two that are moved in the hierarchy (with another superclass and a different code), and one in which the superclass has changed.

The comparison function also allows the user to characterize the conceptual implication of the changes. For the first three types of changes, the user is given the option to label them either as "identical" (i.e., the change is an explication change) or as "conceptual change". In the latter case, the user can specify the conceptual relation between the two versions of the concept, for example, by stating the property "Stamp_pads" in version 8.4 is a subset of "Ink_or_stamp_pads" in version 8.0.

Another function is the possibility to analyze the effect of changes. Changes in ontologies do not only affect the data and applications that use them, but they can also have unintended, unexpected, and unforeseeable consequences in the ontology itself. The system provides some basic support for the analysis of these effects. First, on request it can highlight the places in the ontology where changed concepts or properties are used. For example, if a property "hasChild" is changed, it will highlight the definition of the class "Mother", which uses the property "hasChild". This function can also exploit the transitivity of properties to show the propagation of possible changes through the ontology. A foreseen second effect analysis feature is the connection to FaCT, which allows checking the formal consistency of the suggested conceptual relations between different versions of definitions.

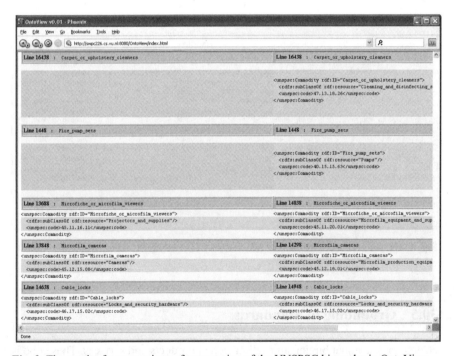

**Fig. 3.** The result of a comparison of two version of the UNSPSC hierarchy in OntoView

610    Ying Ding et al.

When an ontology does not have persistent identifiers for concepts, there is another task involved in comparing the two versions - finding the mappings between concepts in the two versions. This task is closely related to the task of ontology alignment in general. PromptDiff [Noy & Musen, 2002] is a tool that integrates different heuristics for comparing ontology versions. PromptDiff uses heuristics similar to those that are used to provide suggestions for ontology merging in Prompt [Noy & Musen, 2000]. Figure 4 shows the differences that are detected between version 8.0 and 8.4 of the UNSPSC classification (ignoring the persistent EGCI code). The tool lists the concept names in the two versions, whether their name is changed (and the reason behind this conclusion), and whether the structure is changed.

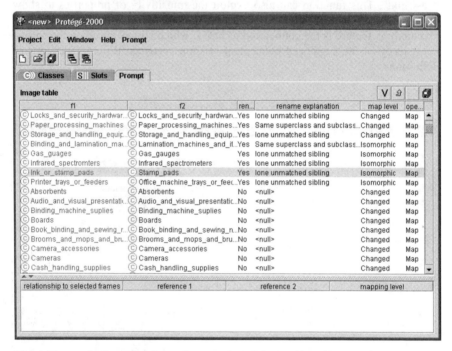

**Fig. 4.** The result of a comparison of two version of the UNSPSC hierarchy in promptDiff

## 30.5    Grounding of Standards

eCommerce is about buying and selling actual products and services. These goods need to be classified and described in terms of standardized categorizations for reasons of reporting and searching. In this section, we portray the prototype of automatic classification of product description in the B2B marketplace (called

GoldenBullet) to realize a semi-automatic way to populate ontologies in eCommerce.

### 30.5.1   GoldenBullet: Automatic Classification of Product Description

Finding the right place for a product description in a standard classification system such as UNSPSC is not a trivial task. Each product must be mapped to corresponding product category in UNSPSC to create the product catalog. Product classification schemes contain huge number of categories with far from sufficient definitions (i.e. over 15,000 classes for UNSPSC), and millions of products must be classified according to them. This requires tremendous effort and the product classification stage takes altogether up to 25 percent of the time spent for content management [Fensel et al., 2002(a)].

GoldenBullet is a software environment targeted to support product classification according to certain content standards. It is currently designed to automatically classify the products based on their original descriptions and existing classification standards (such as UNSPSC). It integrates different classification algorithms from the information retrieval and machine learning, and some natural language processing techniques to pre-process data and index UNSPSC to improve classification accuracy. The system helps to mechanize an important and labor-intensive task of content management for B2B eCommerce.

We will first describe the main components. A wrapper factory gathers various wrappers to convert the raw data description from external formats (Database, Excel, XML-like, formatted plain text,...) into internal formats, and subsequently convert the final results to preferable output formats (Database, Excel, XML-like, plain text,...) or user-designed formats. No matter how the data are imported manually or automatically, before they are passed to be pre-processed, they are validated by the GoldenBullet data validator. Basic validation is checked. For instance, to see if a description is too long or too short, or the Product ID is missing or incorrect. The validated product data will be pre-processed before the automatic classification has been performed. Some of the Natural Language Processing algorithms have been implemented into GoldenBullet. The product data will be stemmed (grouping different words with the same stems) and tagged (extracting noun-phrases). Furthermore, UNSPSC is also being pre-processed (stemmed and tagged) to make sure that noisy words or information have been screened out. A stop word list has been generated, updated and extended during the whole process. The learning algorithm has been embedded in GoldenBullet; the classification rules and instances learned during the online or offline learning procedure are stored in the system to enrich UNSPSC and the classification rule base. Thus, the loop of the entire system has been formed and the system can be self-improved. The more data it processes, the more intelligence it gains. Currently, GoldenBullet can handle English and French product data.

The essence of GoldenBullet is its ability to automatically classify product descriptions. This requires two important properties: (1) Intelligence in classification: We implemented and evaluated various classification strategies; (2) Knowledge in the domain: We acquired and used ten thousands of manually classified product data to learn from it. To satisfy the above two requirements, the following algorithms have been implemented in GoldenBullet:

- The standard Vector space model (VSM, [Salton et al., 1975]) has been applied to represent document (in our case product description) and existing categories (in our case UNSPSC). The category (UNSPSC) can then be assigned to a document (product) when the cosine similarity between them exceeds a certain threshold.
- Another algorithm implemented here is based on the k-Nearest Neighbor method (KNN). The algorithm uses the set of pre-classified examples directly to classify an example, passes the whole set of training examples, searches for the most similar one, and then assigns the class to the new example that equals to the class of the most similar one.
- The Naïve-Bayes classifier (NB, [Mitchell, 1997]) was also employed to learn and train our pre-classified data and ten thousands of manually classified product data from the vendors

VSM was adopted to find the match between UNSPSC commodities and product descriptions. We implemented two strategies. Both treat an unclassified product description as a query; however, they differ in what they use as a document collection:

- The first takes each commodity as a document. The examples are used to enrich the commodity description. Essentially, we extract words from pre-classified product data and add them to the word list describing the commodity.
- The second takes each pre-classified product description as a document. We use VSM to retrieve the instance that best fits to a new product description and infer the UNSPSC code of the latter from the known UNSPSC code of the former.

Content management has to structure, classify, re-classify, and personalize large volumes of data to make product descriptions automatically accessible via B2B market places. GoldenBullet applies the information retrieval and machine learning metaphor to the problem of automatically classifying product descriptions according to the existent product classification standards. Furthermore, GoldenBullet will challenge other existing problems in the B2B marketplace, such as mapping and reclassifying product descriptions according to different product classification standards, personalizing the marketplace view to divergent customers, and offering flexible input and output services.

## 30.6   Conclusions

No technology can survive without convincing application areas. However, the reader should also be aware about the time span of innovation. For example, it took the Internet 30 years before it was hidden by its killer application, the World Wide Web. Lets hope we need less than a generation for the next killer. Ontology technology certainly has promising potential in areas such as knowledge management, Enterprise-Application Integration, and eCommerce.

*eCommerce* in business to business (B2B) is not a new phenomenon. However, Internet-based electronic commerce provides a much higher level of openness, flexibility, and dynamics that will help to optimize business relationships. This type of eCommerce technology may change the way business relationships are established and performed. In a nutshell, web-enabled eCommerce helps its users to contact a large number of potential clients without running into problems associated with implementing numerous communication channels. This enables virtual enterprises that are form in reaction to demands from the market and vica versa it enables to brake large enterprises up into smaller pieces that mediate their eWork relationship based on eCommerce relationships. In consequence, flexible and open eCommerce has to deal with serious problems (cf. [Fensel et al., 2002(a)]).

- *Openness* of eCommerce cannot be achieved without standardization. Such a lesson can be learned from the success of the web; however, the requirements on standardization are much higher here. We also require standardization of the actual content exchanged, which goes far beyond the requirements of standardizing protocols and document layouts (i.e., we require ontologies).
- *Flexibility* of eCommerce cannot be achieved without multi-standard approaches. It is unlikely that a standard will arise that covers all aspects of eCommerce that is acceptable for all vertical markets and cultural contexts. Nor would such a standard free us from the need to provide user-specific views on it and the content it represents.
- *Dynamic* of eCommerce requires standards that act as living entities. Products, services, and trading modes are subject of high change rates. An electronic trading device must reflect the dynamic nature of the process it is supposed to support.

Given these requirements only ontology technology can promise to provide at least a partial solution.

## 30.7    References

[CWM, 2001]
CWM, "Common Warehouse Model Specification", Object Management Group, 2001. http://www.omg.org/cwm/.

[Davis et al., 2002]
J. Davis, D. Fensel, and F. van Harmelen (eds.): *Towards the Semantic Web: Ontology-Driven Knowledge Management*, Wiley, 2002.

[Ding et al., 2002]
Y. Ding, M. Korotkiy, B. Omelayenko, V. Kartseva, V. Zykov, M Klein, E. Schulten, and D. Fensel: GoldenBullet in a nutshell. In *Proceedings of the 15th International FLAIRS Conference*, AAAI Press, May 16-18, 2002 (in press).

[Fensel, 2001]
D. Fensel: *Ontologies: Silver Bullet for Knowledge Management and Electronic Commerce*, Springer-Verlag, Berlin, 2001.

[Fensel et al., 2001]
D. Fensel, Y. Ding, B. Omelayenko, E. Schulten, G. Botquin, M. Brown, and A. Flett: Product Data Integration for B2B E-Commerce, *IEEE Intelligent Systems*, 16(4), 2001.

[Fensel et al., 2002(a)]
D. Fensel, B. Omelayenko, Y. Ding, M. Klein, A. Flett, E. Schulten, G. Botquin, M. Brown, and G. Dabiri: *Intelligent Information Integration in B2B Electronic Commerce*, Kluwer Academics Publishers, Boston/Dordrecht/London, 2002.

[Fensel et al., 2002(b)]
D. Fensel, J. Hendler, H. Lieberman, and W. Wahlster (eds.): *Spinning the Semantic Web: Bringing the World Wide Web to its full Potential*, MIT Press, Boston, 2002.

[ISO, 2000]
Standard, I. S. O., "Integrated generic resource: Fundamentals of product description and support", International Standard ISO 10303-41, Second Edition, 2000.

[Klein et al., 2002]
M. Klein, A. Kiryakov, D. Ognyanov, and D. Fensel: Ontology versioning and change detection on the web. In *Proceedings of the 13th International Conference on Knowledge Engineering and Knowledge Management (EKAW02)*, Siguenza, Spain, October 2002.

[Klein & Fensel, 2001]
M. Klein and D. Fensel: Ontology versioning on the Semantic Web. In *Proceedings of the First Semantic Web Working Symposium*, Stanford, July 2001.

[Maedche et al., 2002]
A. Maedche, B. Motik, N. Silva, R. and Volz: MAFRA - A MApping FRAmework for Distributed Ontologies. In A. Gomez-Perez and R. Benjamins (eds.), *Proceedings of the 13th International Conference on Knowledge Engineering and Knowledge Management (EKAW-2002)*, Springer-Verlag, LNCS 2473, Siguenza, Spain, October 2002.

[Mello and Heuser, 2001]
R. Mello and C. Heuser: A Rule-Based Conversion of a DTD to a Conceptual Schema. In H. Kunii et al. (eds.), *Conceptual Modeling - ER'2001*, Springer, LNCS 2224,

November 27-30, 2001, pp. 133-148.

[Mitchell, 1997]

T. Mitchell, *Machine Learning*, McGraw Hill, 1997.

[Noy & Klein, 2002]

N. F. Noy and M. Klein: Ontology Evolution: Not the Same as Schema Evolution. SMI technical report SMI-2002-0926, 2002.

[Noy & Musen, 2000]

N. F. Noy and M. Musen: PROMPT: Algorithm and tool for automated ontology merging and alignment. In Proceedings of the 17th Nat.Conf. on Artificial Intelligence (AAAI-2000), 2000.

[Noy & Musen, 2002]

N. F. Noy and M. Musen: PromptDiff: A Fixed-Point Algorithm for Comparing Ontology Versions. In *Proceedings of the Eighteenth National Conference Artificial Intelligence (AAAI-02)*, Edmonton, Alberta. AAAI Press. 2002.

[Omelayenko, 2002(a)]

B. Omelayenko: Integrating Vocabularies: Discovering and Representing Vocabulary Maps. In *Proceedings of the First International Semantic Web Conference (ISWC-2002)*, Springer, LNCS (in press), June 2002.

[Omelayenko, 2002(b)]

B. Omelayenko: RDFT: A Mapping Meta-Ontology for Business Integration. In *Proceedings of the Workshop on Knowledge Transformation for the Semantic for the Semantic Web* at the 15th European Conference on Artificial Intelligence (KTSW-2002), July 2002.

[Roddick, 1995]

J. F. Roddick: A survey of schema versioning issues for database systems, *Information and Software Technology*, 37(7):383–393, 1995.

[Salton et al., 1975]

G. Salton, A. Wong, and C. S. Yang: A vector space model for automatic indexing, *Communications of the ACM*, 18(7): 613-620, 1975.

# An Ontology-based Platform for Semantic Interoperability

Michele Missikoff, Francesco Taglino

LEKS, IASI-CNR, Viale Manzoni 30, 00185 Rome, Italy

email:{missikoff, taglino}@iasi.rm.cnr.it

**Summary.** In this chapter the main issues of an Ontology-based platform for semantic interoperability, with particular attention to the underlying methodology, are illustrated. The solutions presented here have been developed in the context of Harmonise, an IST project aimed at developing an interoperability platform for SMEs in the tourism sector. The illustrated platform is an advanced software solution, based on the use of computational ontologies, aiming at the reconciliation of conceptual, structural, and formatting differences that hamper information exchange. The proposed approach relies on the availability of a domain ontology, used as a semantic reference for cooperating systems. Then we elaborate on semantic clashes, arising when a conceptual local schema is contrasted with the ontology. Semantic clashes are taken into account when the elements of a conceptual local schema are semantically annotated. Semantic annotation is requested to reconcile existing differences of cooperating information systems. Having illustrated the underlying approach, we briefly report on the main phases required to an information system to enter in the Harmonise space (i.e., to acquire interoperability capability) and, finally, on the overall Harmonise platform.

## 31.1 Semantic Interoperability

### 31.1.1 Goal

The goal of semantic interoperability is to allow the (seamless) cooperation of two software applications (SAs) that were not initially developed for this purpose.

The cooperation will be possible without requiring the SAs to modify their software or their data organization. Semantic interoperability, in a broad vision, concerns process and information interoperability. Information interoperability is surely a precondition for process interoperability: in this chapter the former will be addressed.

The approach to information interoperability described in this chapter can be classified as "Local As View" (LAV) [1]. This approach has been initially proposed in the area of heterogeneous information sources integration. The LAV approach (for information interoperability) implies that each application system interacts with any other system as if its own data organisation was the only existing solution, i.e., as if all the other SAs were organised in the same way. Since, indeed, this is not the case, such a LAV approach requires a set of intermediary processing solutions aimed at reconciling the different information organisations. The LAV approach is based on the possibility of building a common view of the business scenario where the cooperation takes place. This common view (that should not be confused with an integrated super-schema required by the "Global As View" approach [2]) is implemented by a shared ontology. By using the shared ontology, the information elements that a system needs to exchange can be annotated, aiming at representing their intended meaning. In such a case we will say that an information element is "semantically annotated". In essence, a semantic annotation is an expression built upon the concepts represented in the ontology.

In this chapter we describe the method and the software architecture developed within the IST European Project *Harmonise*, aimed at implementing a semantic interoperability platform for European SMEs (Small and Medium Enterprises) operating in the tourism domain.

### 31.1.2 The Complexity of the Interoperability

The incredible flexibility and openness provided by the Internet to connect computer systems does not correspond to a similar possibility for software applications that need to interoperate. In particular, applications that are built independently (typically, at different moments, by different teams, possibly using different technologies), even within the same enterprise, have problems in exchanging data, not to mention the possibility of integrating their specific services (i.e., to achieve process interoperability), to produce a set of more comprehensive enterprise applications. The problem is of the same nature, although significantly scaled up, if interoperability is sought for activities that cross the enterprise boundaries, involving several different enterprises.

In the past a large amount of technical and scientific work has been devoted to solve the information interoperability problem. In the area of databases, a significant corpus of interesting results have been produced aiming at the integration of heterogeneous data sources [3]. Important results have been achieved in the field of Data Warehousing [4]. A second important area is represented by Enterprise Application Integration (EAI). In this area the solutions are essentially based on the presence of a middleware layer on top of which customised "ad hoc" solutions are built. EAI is successful inasmuch that programming effort is spent to build specific *"adapters"*, while automatic solutions are still to come. Another area that addresses similar problems requiring an advanced level of interoperability, but at a different level of abstraction, is that of multi-ontology environment and ontology mapping [5] [6]. This is a very important and challenging research area, but still to be developed.

In principle, given two applications, A1 and A2, that need to exchange information, it is possible to build an adapter that, knowing the respective data organisations, is able to transform a data packet produced by, say, A1 in the format required by A2. The inverse adapter is required when the data flow from A2 to A1.

An adapter is a complicated piece of software, that requires a complete understanding of the data organisation of the two SAs. Often, the knowledge on data organisation is not sufficient, since the data, to be correctly transformed, must be "interpreted", i.e., it is necessary to know the semantics of data. Intuitively a data structure pertains to a business entity that represents its *structural semantics* (on a formal level, a denotational semantics) and to its intended use that represents its *functional semantics* (the operational semantics).

Besides the technical difficulty of building adapters, the second problem is the inherent complexity of this approach, that is quadratic in the number of cooperating applications. In fact, given $n$ applications that need to cooperate, we need to develop $O(n^2)$ adapters (more precisely: $(n^2-n)$).

The third problem is represented by the time needed to implement the new adapters required at the start of a new cooperation. Today, with the advent of the e-Business, partnerships and cooperation are created (and dissoluted) at an incredible speed. In setting up a consortium of several enterprises (say $k$) wanting to cooperate, it is not possible to wait that the programmers of the different enterprises start a project to develop $(k^2-k)$ adapters, necessary for the respective SAs to interoperate. Furthermore, when all the adapters have been developed and the cooperation starts, if one partner modifies his application there is the need to propagate this modification to the $(k-1)$ adapters interfacing the modified SA.

For the above reasons, a procedure that eases the development of adapters is highly sought of. One radical solution is represented by the definition of a unique standard, to be imposed to everybody, in order to eliminate the problem of adapters development. In this case, everyone conforming to the standard is automatically able to exchange information with anyone else, adhering to the standard. Standards have been developed and widely adopted at a lower level, e.g., with TCP/IP and packets exchange. It is evident (from a logical and an empirical point of view) that standards are winning solutions at a more technical level. In fact when we take into consideration higher levels, closer to human beings (with their peculiarities in communicating and carrying on business), software solutions get more complicated and less prone to be solved with standards (in essence, using a metaphor, we may say that we need to "standardise the bricks, not the houses"). Indeed, for specific sectors, or for specific activities (such as tax-related processes and information, highly regulated by laws), a certain level of standardisation is achievable.

However, proposed standards are always partial and, furthermore, not widely accepted. One technique often proposed to avoid quadratic complexity consists in adopting a common interchange format. But in general the existing proposals, from EDI (Electronic Data Interchange [7]) to Step/Express [8], to KIF (Knowledge Interchange Format [9]), are not particularly successful in supporting runtime applications interoperability mainly because they address the syntactic level. Format standardisation does not appear today as the winning solution to solve the interoperability problem in the B2B scenario of the next decade.

We believe that major interoperability problems will be solved with the use of a reference ontology: such an approach represents one of the key aspect of the emerging Semantic Web [10]. This is also the core of our proposal, that will be elaborated in the rest of this chapter. It is centrally based on a domain ontology, that allows for a semantic-based approach, highly automated, to the construction of customised adapters. We refer to this as *semantic reconciliation*.

In conclusion, it is evident that standards, although important, will not solve the interoperability problem. Similarly, solutions based on adapters are too expensive and inflexible to be used on a large scale. We need to find different solutions, based on an extensive use of semantic technologies.

## 31.2 A Semantic Approach to Interoperability

A reconciliation process is based on the idea that there is a common view of the world (more precisely, of the business domain) that can be used as a reference point. If a common understanding is missing at "human level", application interoperability will necessarily fail, no matter what technology will be used. This common view is represented by a domain ontology.

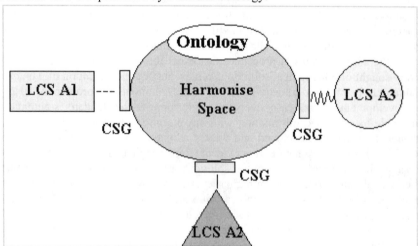

**Fig. 1.** The harmonise cooperation space

In our proposal, interoperability takes place within a common, "harmonised" co-operation space (Fig. 1), accessible through a Custom Semantic Gateway (CSG, one for each partner). A CSG is developed starting from the local data organisation (Local Conceptual Schema: LCS) and a common, shared ontology.

The Harmonise solution is based on the results produced by the Harmonise project in three research areas: (i) the ontology, that represents a common, shareable view of the application domain; (ii) the analysis of interoperability clashes, caused by the differences in the conceptual schemas that can be found in two co-operating applications; (iii) the semantic annotation, achieved to represent the meaning of a local conceptual schema, expressed by using the concepts available in the above mentioned ontology. These three areas are further elaborated below.

### 31.2.1 The Domain Ontology

The approach to semantic clashes analysis represents a key element of the proposed solution.

The first key element of the proposed approach is the common ontology. The ontology is used to give meaning to the information structures that an application wishes to exchange with other applications. According to the most popular proposals[11], in Harmonise, the ontology is based on the definition of entities and relationships. The representation method, referred to as OPAL (Object, Process, Actor modelling Language [12]) follows the Frame-Slot-Facet paradigm [13].

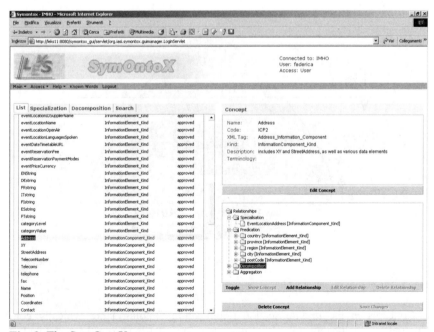

**Fig. 2.** The SymOntoX system

It includes constructs such as: ISA (with multiple inheritance) and aggregation (partOf) hierarchies, similarity, and various kinds of built-in constraints (such as cardinality constraints, enumeration). Based on OPAL, we developed the ontology management system *SymOntoX* [14] (Fig. 2). A complete treatment of SymOntoX, and the related ontology model, is outside the scope of the chapter.

The concepts in a domain ontology can be organised according to a (complex) hierarchical structure, where the most general (and comprehensive) concepts are located at the top; moving downward we meet more specific, but also more (structurally) complex concepts. At the lowest level we find elementary concepts, that cannot be further decomposed nor refined. This organisation gives rise to a shape that resembles a chestnut, as reported in Fig. 3. In the top part (Upper Domain Ontology) we have generic concepts, such as *process, actor, event, goal*. In the bottom part (Lower Domain Ontology: LDO) we have elementary concepts, such as: *price, streetNumber, cost, internetAddress*. Generally, it is relatively easy to reach a consensus on these two parts. The difficult section is the middle part: the Application Ontology. Here concepts and definitions heavily depend on a specific application, the kind of problems addressed, the method used to solve them, not to mention the underlying technology (that often contaminates the conceptual model) and the cultural aspects. Typical concepts of this layer are: *invoice, customer, discount, reliableCustomer, approval*, or more sector-dependent notions, such as: *hotelReception, confirmedReservation, advancePayment, lightMeal, gymTrainer* (in the tourism sector).

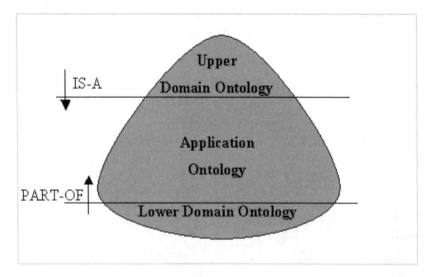

**Fig. 3.** The ontology "chestnut"

Concepts in the middle section (Application Ontology) are typically constructed by composing non elementary concepts, starting from those defined in the LDO. Then, application-specific concepts are classified according to the more general concepts that are located in the UDO.

In the construction of the domain ontology, our methodology requires that the modelled concepts be particularly rich in the section of the basic information elements (LDO). More structured information elements are assembled in a bottom-up fashion. For example, *phoneNumber* is a composition of *countryCode, areaCode, localNumber*.

As anticipated, continuing, in a bottom-up fashion, more specific (and application dependent) concepts will be defined by composition of simpler concepts, to form the Application Ontology. Finally, once an application concept has been defined in terms of (more elementary) ontology concepts, its definition is completed by categorising it according to the structure given in the Upper Domain Ontology. This operation can be achieved with a top-down process, based on the refinement (ISA) relation. The constructive, bottom-up approach is used also to annotate (define) the information elements of the Local Conceptual Schema, as illustrated in section 31.2.3.

### 31.2.2 Interoperability Clashes

In designing the Harmonise platform, one of the first activities was the careful analysis and the identification of possible interoperability clashes that may arise in an unanticipated cooperation between two applications. As said before, such an interoperability is generally hampered by the different data organisation of the two applications. In the Harmonise approach, this difference is reconciled by using a reference ontology. Therefore, our analysis of interoperability clashes is performed by contrasting the Local Conceptual Schemas with the reference ontology. This represents a weak approach to interoperability clashes (a strong approach would be to directly contrast the LCSs of the two cooperating parties, but this is ineffective in an large open scenario, such as the Internet). In our approach, the possible clashes have been classified in two main groups:

> **Lossless clash** – This group includes all the clashes that can be solved without loss of information. This means that there exists a transformation that, given an input information packet (infopack), produces an output infopack with a different representation but the same information content. These clashes are quite intuitive and essentially of a syntactic nature. Among the most usual there are: *naming* clashes, when the same information is represented by different labels; *structural* clashes, when information elements are grouped in a different way; *encoding* clashes, when a scalar value (typically an amount of money, or a distance) is represented with different units of measure.

> **Lossy clash** – This group includes all the clashes for which any conceivable transformation (in one direction or the other) will cause a loss of information.

Typical cases are when a Local Conceptual Schema organizes information at different levels of granularity, of refinement, or of precision with respect to the ontology. For example, in expressing the distance of a hotel from the airport, a local schema simply reports: e.g., "*near airport*", while the ontology requests this information to be expressed in terms of "miles from the airport": e.g., "*5 miles from airport*". Another example is when a local schema just specifies the presence of a "*swimming pool*", while the ontology holds more accurate information, e.g., "*indoor swimming pool*" or "*outdoor swimming pool*". Another case of information loss is the presence, locally, of information that is not represented at all in the ontology. For instance, a hotel provides information on the average seasonal temperatures, but this concept was not considered in the ontology.

Table 1 reports the lossless and lossy clashes that have been founded out.

**Table 1.** Clashes list

| Lossless clashes | Lossy clashes |
|---|---|
| Encoding: different formats of data or units of measure | Content: different content denoted by the same concept (typically expressed by enumeration) |
| Typing: different data types to represent information | Coverage: differ the presence/absence of information |
| Path-Naming: different names for the same content | Precision: the accuracy of information |
| Structuring: different structures about the same content | Abstraction: level of specialisation refinement of the information |
| | Granularity: level of decomposition refinement of the information |
| | Field length: number of bytes of the attribute field |

It is important to note that there are situations where it is not possible to tell in advance if a transformation will give rise to a loss or not and consequently if a communication between two SAs will be successful or not. Only for two SAs that have both lossless clashes a safe communication is fully guaranteed. Indeed, also an exchange of information between two "lossy" sites may result in a lossless exchange. In fact, if the two LCSs have the same lossy clash with respect to the ontology, the information coming from the sender and lost during the transformation, could not be used by the receiver. Then, the loss of information will not affect the communication between the two SAs.

Another example is the transmission of an information structure that is richer (and matching the ontology) on the sender side than on the receiver side. In sending, the information is fully encoded and transferred, but the loss takes place at the destination (however, the information actually received is "complete" with respect to the receiver).

The identification of the above classes of interoperability clashes required a careful study, mainly carried out analysing a significant number of proposed standards. Having considered published standards, we were guaranteed to avoid peculiar interoperability problems caused by (marginal) applications solutions, with unusual design characteristics.

Below in Table 2 an example is reported, where we have a fragment of a LCS, and in particular the information concerning a hotel, and the corresponding fragment of the reference ontology.

Following the two concepts specifications, here is an analysis of the interoperability clashes emerging from the comparison of the two structures.

**Table 2.** Example of Local Conceptual Schema vs Ontology

| Local Hotel Schema (LHS) | Ontology Hotel Schema (OHS) |
|---|---|
| Denomination: String<br>Address: String | Name: String<br>Address [<br>   Street: String<br>   City: String<br>] |
| Telephone1: String<br>Telephone2: String<br>Fax: String | Contact_Info [<br>   Phone: String<br>   Fax: String<br>   Email: String<br>] |
| Distance_from_airport: enum('at airport', 'next to', 'near') | Location [<br>   Distance_from_airport(km): Integer<br>   Distance_from_cityCentre(km): Integer<br>] |
| Category: enum('*', '**', '***', '****')<br>Prices [<br>   Min: Integer<br>   Max : Integer<br>] | Category: enum('&', '&&', '&&&')<br>Rates [<br>   Single [<br>      Min: Integer<br>      Max: Integer<br>   ]<br>   Double [<br>      Min: Integer<br>      Max: Integer<br>   ]<br>] |
| Hotel_Services: enum('shuttle', 'security box', 'disco') | Services: enum('pool', 'parking', 'gym', 'safe', 'discotheque') |

Fig. 4 shows the interoperability clashes that can be identified analyzing the two schemas in Table 2.

Path-Naming Clashes (lossless clashes)

- **LHS**.Denomination vs **OHS**.Name

- **LHS**.Prices vs **OHS**.Rates

- **LHS**.Telephone vs **OHS**.Contact_Info.Phone

- **LHS**.Hotel_Services vs **OHS**.Services

- **LHS**.Distance_from_airport vs **OHS**.Location.Distance_from_airport


Structural Clashes (lossless clashes)

- (**LHS**.Telephone1 & Telephone2) vs **OHS**.Contact_Info.Phone

- **LHS**.Address vs (**OHS**.Address.Street &.City)

- **LHS**.Prices vs **OHS**.Rates

- **OHS**.Email vs **LHS**.???


Content Clashes (lossy clashes)

- **LHS**.Hotel_Services vs **OHS**.Services


Precision Clashes (lossy clashes)

- **LHS**.Distance_from_airport vs **OHS**.Location.Distance_from_airport

- **LHS**.Prices vs **OHS**.Rates

**Fig. 4.** A clashes analysis

Note that different kinds of clashes may appear on the same information item; *prices* and *rates* exhibit 3 different conflicts on the same information.


### 31.2.3 The Semantic Annotation

In the proposed approach to interoperability, the primary goal of the ontology is to provide a unique semantic reference for each application that wishes to expose a given interface (referred to as Local Conceptual Schema: LCS), both for exporting and importing information. In essence, every piece of information in the LCS will be annotated by using the ontology content and the Semantic Mediation and Application Interoperability Language (SMAIL) illustrated below. For a given application entity (represented as a data structure in the LCS), the annotation process consists in identifying the Lower Domain Ontology elements present in the reference ontology; then the meaning of the LCS data structure is defined by composing a SMAIL expression that uses these elements of the ontology. These SMAIL expressions are used to generate reconciliation rules, at extensional level, that essentially represent a mapping between the local conceptual structures and the interchange representation. Therefore we will have one custom reconciliation rules set for each application entering in the Harmonise space.

---

sa:= *lcs_elem* con se

con::= **<:** | **=:**

se:= **to**(oe, *cond*) | **to**(oe, *cond*) , se | **to**(oe, *cond*) ; se

where:

- *sa* = Semantic annotation expression: a SLAM sentence that expresses the meaning of an element in local conceptual schema, according to the reference ontology;
- *lcs_elem* = the information element in the LCS to be semantically annotated;
- *con* = connectors; they represent the fact that the annotation fully captures the intended meaning (=:) or not (<:);
- *se* = semantic expression built by using elements of the reference ontology;
- *to* = Transformation Operator, operator that transforms semantic elements to solve clashes between a LCS and the ontology. Table 3 reports the list of the identified transformation operators. For each operator the type of clash the operator aims to solve is specified;
- *oe* = ontology expression, expression involving ontology element;
- *cond* = conditions under which semantic transformation takes place.

Two separators are available: "," (commas, as AND), ";" (semicolon, as OR). Note that terminals symbols are in bold.

---

**Fig. 5.** The Semantic Mediation and Application Interoperability Language (SMAIL) syntax

Semantic annotation is obtained by writing a set of expressions that have a head on the left, represented by the label (name or path) of a local information item from a LCS and a body, on the right, representing the meaning expressed in terms of ontology concepts. The semantic annotation is performed in accordance with the syntax in Fig. 5.

**Table 3.** Transformation operators

| Operator | Description | Solved clashes |
|---|---|---|
| assoc (associate) | Maps a lcs_elem with a concept in the ontology (1 to 1) | Naming |
| pack | Maps a lcs_elem with several concepts in the ontology (1 to m) | Structuring |
| extract | Maps a lcs_elem with a fragment of a concept instance in the ontology | Structuring |
| a_val (associate value) | Maps a possible value of a lcs_elem with a possible value of an ontology concept (especially for enumerated) | Content |
| c_val (compute value) | Computes the value of a lcs_elem by using operators (i.e. +, -, …) | Encoding |
| cast | Converts from a basic data type of a lcs_elem into that of a ontology concept | Typing Precision |

In Fig. 6 we illustrate a few instances of SMAIL expressions that solve the clashes illustrated in Fig. 4.

Annotation expressions at an intentional level (i.e., involving LCS elements and ontology concepts) correspond to the transformation rules at extensional level, to be applied to exchanged data packets. Transformations are applied to local data to code them according to the Harmonise Interoperability Representation (HIR). Note that this approach is inherently different from the approaches that propose an interchange format, such as KIF (Knowledge Interchange Format) [9], which are "neutral" with respect to the application domain. In the HIR, the information to be exchanged is represented by using ontology terms only (coded in the reference ontology). Another approach in line with our proposal is PIF (Process Interchange Format) [15]. However, the main difference is that PIF proposes a format which relies on a predefined (limited) process ontology, which is given with the standard. Conversely, HIR is based on a rich domain ontology, whose content is not provided by the OPAL method. The domain ontology is initially built by domain experts, and continuously evolves to remain aligned with the evolving reality. Accordingly, the HIR evolves, since its vocabulary is (a subset of) the ontology.

In essence, semantic annotation and transformation rules represent a correspondence between the local view and the ontology view of the application domain, at a conceptual and data level, respectively. The transformation rules are used to build the *reconciliation* rules that allow for semantic operability between any two applications. A reconciliation rule is obtained by juxtaposition of two symmetric transformations rules having a common ontology. Intuitively, we have:

$$rec(A1,A2) = trans(A1,HIR) + trans(HIR,A2)$$

A specific set of transformation rules, with the reconciliation engine necessary to process it, implementing the transformation functions, is referred to as the *Cus-*

*tom Semantic Gateway* (see Fig. 1). In the Harmonise Project we are experimenting a modified version of *Xalan* [16] as reconciliation engine. Another solution is based on the KAON system [17].

---

Naming Clash

LHS.Denomination =: **assoc**(OHS.Name)

LHS.Price =: **assoc**(OHS.Rates)

LHS.Telephone =: **assoc**(OHS.Contact_Info.Phone)

LHS.Hotel_Services =: **assoc**(OHS.Services)


Structural Clash

LHS.Address =: **pack**(OHS.Address.Street,',', OHS.Address.City)


In the pack transformation, a separator between the concepts to be concatenated can be specified (e.g. ','').


Content Clash

LHS.Hotel_Services =: **assoc**(OHS.Services),

  **a_val**(LHS.Hotel_Services('security box'), OHS.Services('safe')),

  **a_val**(LHS.Hotel_Services('disco'), OHS.Services('discotheque'))


In the Content reconciliation rule, first the label names are associated, then the indicated values are pairwise matched.

---

**Fig. 6.** Example of SMAIL expressions

## 31.3 A Phased Approach to Achieve Interoperability

The operations required by the Harmonise solution can be organised into three main phases. The first phase concerns ontology building (and management in general, to keep it always aligned with the ever-changing reality). The second is the Customisation phase, that is required for each application site to enter in the Harmonise cooperation space. The third is the Cooperation phase, which concerns the actual run-time business activity and the corresponding information exchange.

Each phase is supported by a dedicated system, and all together, they compose the Harmonise Suite.

### 31.3.1 The Ontology Management Phase

As mentioned before, the Harmonise solution is centrally based on the availability of a reference (domain) ontology (Interoperable Minimum Harmonise Ontology: IMHO), primarily used to annotate the Local Conceptual Schema of the application that intends to enter the Harmonise space. Due to its central role, the ontology construction requires a careful and reliable methodology: it must be widely agreed and shared with minor problems. To this end, in the Harmonise Project we developed a dedicated groupware, the consensus system HarmoConsys [18], to support a group of domain experts in building and maintaining the ontology. We expect that the domain experts activities will continue then after the completion of the first release of the ontology, to maintain it in the future, keeping it aligned with the evolution of business reality.

### 31.3.2 The Customisation Phase

This is the phase where the Local Conceptual Schema is analysed and annotated by using the reference ontology. Semantic annotation is typically performed by the local IS manager, who is supposed to know the actual meaning of the local schema elements. Therefore he is responsible of the semantic annotation of the information resources that need to be exchanged, giving them a "universally" understood meaning. The corresponding subsystem is based on a graphical interface that shows in the left pane the LCS, in the right pane the reference ontology, and in the central part a space to draw correspondence relations, associating to them specific functions (if necessary, e.g., currency transformation).

The customisation phase then requires that the semantic annotation expression, defined at an intentional level, be transformed into reconciliation rules, aimed at operating on actual data. This is mainly performed automatically, requiring, only in special cases, a minimum human intervention. The output of this phase is a set of semantic annotations of the LCS, and a set of custom transformation rules to be applied in the next phase. The latter, jointly with the necessary engine, forms the Custom Semantic Gateway (CSG), necessary to actually perform the data exchange.

### 31.3.3 The Co-operation Phase

This is the operational phase that takes place every time an application needs to exchange information with other "harmonised" partners. There are two sets or rules, depending on the exchange direction, referred to as Forward Harmonisation

Rules, when a data packet is sent out, and Backward Harmonisation Rules, when it is received.

Fig. 7 presents the global architecture of the Harmonise Suite. Note that we assume that local data are organised and stored in any possible format. Conversely, the Local Normalized Data are represented in XML. Similarly for what concerns the Local Conceptual Schema that, in order to be correctly annotated, needs to be coded in RDFS. To this end two additional transformation engines are required: C-Normalisation and D-Normalisation, at the intentional and the extensional level, respectively.

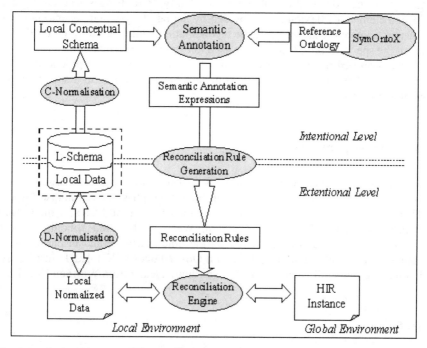

**Fig. 7.** Logical architecture of harmonise

## 31.4 Conclusion

In this chapter the main lines of the Harmonise Suite have been presented. This presentation intended to give an overview of the semantic interoperability developed in the Harmonise Project (and their related issues), necessarily leaving out many technical details. The goal of the Harmonise Project is to provide a comprehensive suite of software systems to support semantic interoperability at the information level. This represents the possibility for any pair of application systems to interact and exchange information, within unanticipated cooperation activities, without the need to change their data organisation. By using the Harmonise Suite, every application exchanges information with other applications as if its own data organisation was universally adopted. This is possible since exchanged data elements have been semantically annotated by using a common reference ontology.

The proposed solution is based on an innovative approach to mediators (i.e., the CSG), introducing significant elements of flexibility for information interoperability among applications. The flexibility is obtained by using an interchange representation, HIR, which is based on a shared domain ontology. When the ontology changes, due to the evolution of the reality, HIR changes accordingly. The second element of flexibility is provided by the ontology-based generation of the Custom Semantic Gateway, i.e., the reconciliation engine, customised on the basis of the specific application, that is used to exchange information.

The proposed method is at the basis of the main deliverable produced by the Harmonise Project: the Harmonise Suite, available according to a specific Open Source protocol.

## Acknowledgements

We wish to acknowledge that the work described in this chapter is largely due to an intense team work, carried on within the design phase of Harmonise Project. Therefore credits are due primarily to the colleagues at the LEKS, namely Anna Formica, Giorgio Callegari and Xiao Feng Wang. Within the Harmonise Project, a fundamental role has been played by the other partners, and in particular by Hannes Werthner, Mirella Dell'Erba and Oliver Fodor at ICT-IRST. In identifying the interoperability clashes, a key contribution came from Wolfram Hoepken.

## Reference

[1] Levy, A.Y.: Logic-Based Techniques in Data Integration. In Logic Based Artificial Intelligence, Jack Minker (ed.). Kluwer, 2000.

[2] Lenzerini, M.: Data Integration: A Theoretical Perspective, Proceedings. of PODS Conference, 2002.

[3] Naumann, F., Leser, U., Freytag, J. C.: Quality-driven integration of heterogenous information systems. In Proceedings. of the 25th Int. Conf. on Very Large DataBases (VLDB'99), pages 447–458, 1999.

[4] Calvanese, D., De Giacomo, G., Lenzerini, M., Nardi, D., Rosati, R.: Source Integration in Data Warehouse, Proc. of IEEE Workshop on Data Warehouse Design and OLAP Technology, p.192-197, Wien, 1998.

[5] Maedche, A., Motik, B., Silva, N., Volz, R.: MAFRA - A MApping FRAmework for Distributed Ontologies. Proceedings. of  EKAW 2002, pages 235-250, Siguenza (Spain), October 2002.

[6] Doan, A., Madhavan, J., Domingos, P., Halevy, A.: Learning to Map between Ontologies on the Semantic Web. Proceedings of the World-Wide Web Conference (WWW-2002). ACM Press.

[7] Osório, A.L., Gibon, P., Barata, M.M.: Electronic commerce with XML/EDI, in Proceedings of IFIP Working Conference E-Business and Virtual Enterprises: Managing Business-to-Business Cooperation, Brazil, Dec. 2000.

[8] Schenck, D.A., Wilson, P.R.: Information Modeling: The EXPRESS Way, Oxford University Press, 1994.

[9] The KIF Specification. http://logic.stanford.edu/kif/dpans.html.

[10] Berners-Lee, T., Hendler, J., Lassila, O.: The Semantic Web, The Scientific American, May 2001.

[11] Uschold, M., Gruninger, M.: Ontologies: Principles, Methods and Applications; The Knowledge  Engineering Review, V.11, N.2, 1996.

[12] Formica, A., Missikoff, M.: An extended XML approach to ontology engineering; 6th World Multiconference on Systemics, Cybernetics and Informatics (SCI'02), Orlando, USA, pp. 69-71, July 14-18 2002.

[13] Reimer, U., Hahn, U.: A formal approach to the semantics of a frame data model, in Proceedings of the Eighth IJCAI, Karlsruhe, Germany, 337-339, 1983.

[14] Missikoff, M., Taglino, F.: Business and Enterprise Ontology Management with SymOntoX, in Proceedings of the International Semantic Web Conference (ISWC-2002), Sardinia, June 2002, Springer Verlag.

[15] Lee, J., Grunninger, M., Jin, Y., Malone, T., Tate, A., Yost, G., and other members of the PIF Working Group: The PIF Process Interchange Format and Framework Version 1.2,.The Knowledge Engineering Review, Vol. 13, No. 1, pp. 91-120, March 1998, Cambridge University Press.

[16] http://xml.apache.org/xalan-j/overview.html.

[17] Bozsak. E., at Al: KAON - Towards a Large Scale Semantic Web. EC-Web, 2002 pages 304-313.

[18] M.Missikoff, XF Wang: "A group decision system for collaborative ontology building", Proc. Of Int'l Conference on Group Decision and Negociation 2001, pp. 153-160, La Rochelle, 4-7 June 2001.

# 32

# Ontologies in Bioinformatics

Robert Stevens, Chris Wroe, Phillip Lord and Carole Goble

Department of Computer Science, University of Manchester, Oxford Road, Manchester UK, M13 9PL. email: `robert.stevens|cwroe|carole@cs.man.ac.uk`

**Summary.** Molecular biology offers a large, complex and volatile domain that tests knowledge representation techniques to the limit of their fidelity, precision, expressivity and adaptability. The discipline of molecular biology and bioinformatics relies greatly on the use of community knowledge, rather than laws and axioms, to further understanding, and knowledge generation. This knowledge has traditionally been kept as natural language. Given the exponential growth of already large quantities of data and associated knowledge, this is an unsustainable form of representation. This knowledge needs to be stored in a computationally amenable form and ontologies offer a mechanism for creating a shared understanding of a community for both humans and computers. Ontologies have been built and used for many domains and this chapter explores their role within bioinformatics. Structured classifications have a long history in biology; not least in the Linnean description of species. The explicit use of ontologies, however, is more recent. This chapter provides a survey of the need for ontologies; the nature of the domain and the knowledge tasks involved; and then an overview of ontology work in the discipline. The widest use of ontologies within biology is for conceptual annotation – a representation of stored knowledge more computationally amenable than natural language. An ontology also offers a means to create the illusion of a common query interface over diverse, distributed information sources – here an ontology creates a shared understanding for the user and also a means to computationally reconcile heterogeneities between the resources. Ontologies also provide a means for a schema definition suitable for the complexity and precision required for biology's knowledge bases. Coming right up to date, bioinformatics is well set as an exemplar of the Semantic Web, offering both web accessible content and services conceptually marked up as a means for computational exploitation of its resources – this theme is explored through the <sup>my</sup>GRID services ontology. Ontologies in bioinformatics cover a wide range of usages and representation styles. Bioinformatics offers an exciting application area in which the community can see a real need for ontology based technology to work and deliver its promise.

## 32.1 Introduction

This chapter gives an overview of the application of ontologies within bioinformatics. Bioinformatics is a discipline that uses computational and mathematical techniques to store, manage and analyse biological data, in order to answer and explore biological questions. Bioinformatics has received a great deal of attention in the past few years from the computer science community. This is largely due to the complexity, time and expense of performing bench experiments to discover new biological knowledge. In conjunction with traditional experimental procedures, a biologist will use computer based information repositories and computational analysis for investigating and testing a hypothesis. These have become known as *in silico* experiments.

Laboratory bench and *in silico* experiments form a symbiosis. The *in silico* representation of the knowledge that forms a core component of bioinformatics is the subject of this chapter.

The biological sciences, especially molecular biology, currently lack the laws and mathematical support of sciences such as physics and chemistry. This is not to say that the biological sciences lack principles and understanding that, for instance, in physics allows us to predict planetary orbits, behaviour of waves and particles etc. We cannot, however, yet take a protein sequence and from the amino acid residues present deduce the structure, molecular function, biological role or location of that protein. The biologist has two options: First, to perform many laboratory experiments, *in vitro* and *in vivo* to acquire knowledge about the protein; second, the biologist takes advantage of one of the principles of molecular biology, which is that sequence is related to molecular function and structure. Therefore, a biologist can compare the protein sequence to others that are already well characterised. If the uncharacterised sequence is sufficiently similar to a characterised sequence, then it is inferred that the characteristics of one can be transferred to the other. So a key tool of bioinformatics is the sequence similarity search [4]; the characterisation of single sequences lies at the heart of most bioinformatics, even the new high-throughput techniques that investigate the modes of action of thousands of proteins per experiment. As the first method is expensive, both in terms of time and money, the latter can reduce the time to characterise unknown biological entities. Thus, we often see a cycle between laboratory bench and the computer.

### 32.1.1  Describing and Using Biological Data

It has been said that biology is a knowledge based discipline [7]. Much of the community's knowledge is contained within the community's data resources. A typical resource is the SWISS-PROT protein database [6]. The protein sequence data itself is a relatively small part of the entry. Most of the entry is taken up by what the bioinformatics community refers to as 'annotation' which describe: physico-chemical features of the protein; comments on the whole sequence, such as function, disease, regulation, expression; species; names and so on. All this can be considered as the knowledge component of the database. Figure 32.1 shows a typical annotation from SWISS-PROT; note that the knowledge is captured as textual terms describing the findings, not numeric data, making use of shared keywords and controlled vocabularies. Whilst this style of representation is suitable for human readers, the current representation of the knowledge component is difficult to process by machine. SWISS-PROT itself now has over 100 000 entries (and growing exponentially), so

# NiceProt View of SWISS-PROT: P08100

### General information about the entry

| | |
|---|---|
| Entry name | **OPSD_HUMAN** |
| Primary accession number | **P08100** |
| Secondary accession number | Q16414 |
| Entered in SWISS-PROT in | Release 08, August 1988 |
| Sequence was last modified in | Release 08, August 1988 |
| Annotations were last modified in | Release 40, October 2001 |

### Name and origin of the protein

| | |
|---|---|
| Protein name | **Rhodopsin** |
| Synonym | **Opsin 2** |
| Gene name | **RHO** or **OPN2** |
| From | Homo sapiens (Human) [TaxID: 9606] |
| Taxonomy | Eukaryota; Metazoa; Chordata; Craniata; Vertebrata; Euteleostomi; Mammalia; Eutheria; Primates; Catarrhini; Hominidae; Homo. |

### Comments

- *FUNCTION:* VISUAL PIGMENTS ARE THE LIGHT-ABSORBING MOLECULES THAT MEDIATE VISION. THEY CONSIST OF AN APOPROTEIN, OPSIN, COVALENTLY LINKED TO CIS-RETINAL.
- *SUBCELLULAR LOCATION:* Integral membrane protein.
- *TISSUE SPECIFICITY:* ROD SHAPED PHOTORECEPTOR CELLS WHICH MEDIATES VISION IN DIM LIGHT.
- *PTM:* SOME OR ALL OF THE CARBOXYL-TERMINAL SER OR THR RESIDUES MAY BE PHOSPHORYLATED.
- *DISEASE:* DEFECTS IN RHO ARE ONE OF THE CAUSES OF AUTOSOMAL DOMINANT RETINITIS PIGMENTOSA (ADRP). PATIENTS TYPICALLY HAVE NIGHT VISION BLINDNESS AND LOSS OF MIDPERIPHERAL VISUAL FIELD; AS THEIR CONDITION PROGRESSES, THEY LOSE THEIR FAR PERIPHERAL VISUAL FIELD AND EVENTUALLY CENTRAL VISION AS WELL.
- *DISEASE:* DEFECTS IN RHO ARE ONE OF THE CAUSES OF AUTOSOMAL RECESSIVE RETINITIS PIGMENTOSA (ARRP).

**Fig. 32.1.** An extract of the SWISS-PROT entry for Human Rhodopsin. Much of the information is held in the comment field.

its size makes it no longer suitable for human analysis and computational support is needed.

As well as this knowledge component, biological data is characterised in the following ways:

- Large quantity of data – The genome sequencing projects now mean that data is being produced at increasing rates; a new sequence is deposited in the public genome database EMBL every 10 seconds[1]. Microarray experiments measuring gene expression and other high-through-put techniques now mean that other data are also being produced in vast quantity at petabytes per year [40].
- Complexity of data – It is difficult to represent most biological data directly in numeric form. Bioinformatics resources need non-scalar data types such as collections and records [10, 22]. Bioinformatics does not have a convenient data model; much bioinformatics data is kept in a natural language text-based form, in either

---

[1] http://www.ebi.ac.uk/

annotations or bibliographic databases. As well as the basic data-representation, a characteristic of biology's data are the many relationships held by each entity. For instance, any one protein has a sequence, function, a process in which it acts, a location, a structure, physical interactions it makes, diseases in which it may be implicated, and many more. Capturing this knowledge makes biological data an extreme example of complexity in representation.

- Volatility of data – Once gathered, biological data is not static. As knowledge about biological entities changes and increases, so the annotations within data resources change.
- Heterogeneity of data – Much biological data is both syntactically and semantically heterogeneous [12]. Individual concepts, such as that of a gene, have many different, but equally valid, interpretations. There is a widespread and deep issue of synomyny and homonymy in the labels used for concepts within biology and as well as those used for the names of individuals.
- Distribution of data – Bioinformatics uses over 500 data resources and analysis tools [13] found all over the Internet. They often have Web interfaces and biologists enter data for analysis; cut-and-paste results to new Web resources or explore results through rich annotation with cross-links [23].

As well as the large number of data resources there are many analytical tools that work over these data resources to generate new data and knowledge. These tools suffer from the problems of distribution, heterogeneity, discovery, choice of suitable tool, etc. Some investigations can be carried out in one resource, but increasingly, many resources have to be orchestrated in order to accomplish an investigation. Often data resources lack query facilities usual in DBMS. The semantic heterogeneity between the resources exists both in schema and the values held within those schema. The vocabulary used by biologists to name entities, functions, processes, species, etc. can vary widely.

This scene leaves both the curators of bioinformatics resources and their users with great difficulties. A typical user, as well as a bioinformatics tool builder, is left trying to deal with the following problems in order to attempt tasks:

- Knowing which resources to use in a task;
- Discovering instances of those resources;
- Knowing how to use each of those resources, and how to link their content;
- Understanding the content of the resources and interpreting results;
- Transferring data between resources and reconciling values;
- Recording all that occurred during the *in silico* experiment.

All these steps require knowledge on the part of the biologists. It is no longer tenable for an individual biologist to acquire and retain this range and complexity of knowledge. This means bioinformatics needs computational support for storing, exploring, representing and exploiting this knowledge. Buttler [11] gives a description of a bioinformatics task workflow.

Ontologies describe and classify knowledge. Though biologists may not have used the term 'ontology', the use of classification and description as a technique for collecting, representing and using biological knowledge has a long history in the field. For example, the Linnaean classification of species is ubiquitous[2] and the Enzyme Commission has a classification of enzymes by the reaction that they catalyse [18]. Families of proteins are also classified along axes such as function and structural architecture [16]. Over the past five years there has been a surge of interest in using ontologies to describe and share biological data reflecting the surge in size, range and diversity of data and the need to assemble it from a broad constituency of sources. The Gene Ontology Consortium has launched OBO (Open Biological Ontologies)[3] which offers an umbrella to facilitate collaboration and dissemination of bio-ontologies.

### 32.1.2  The Uses of Ontologies in Biology

Ontologies are used in a wide range of biology application scenarios [38]:

- A defining database schema or knowledge bases. Public examples include RiboWeb, EcoCyc and PharmGKB [2, 25, 36]. Commercial knowledge bases include Ingenuity[4].

- A common vocabulary for describing, sharing, linking, classifying querying and indexing database annotation. This is currently the most popular use of ontologies in bioinformatics, and among many examples we can count The Gene Ontology, MGED[5], as well as those originating from the medical community such as UMLS[6].

- A means of inter-operating between multiple resources. A number of forms appear, for example: indexing across databases by shared vocabularies of their content (domain maps in BIRN [9]), inter-database navigation in Amigo using the Gene Ontology[7]; a global ontology as a virtual schema over a federation of databases and application (TAMBIS [15]); and a description of bioinformatics services inputs, outputs and purpose used to classify and find appropriate resources, and control the workflows linking them together. ( $^{my}$GRID [42]).

- A scaffold for intelligent search over databases (e.g. TAMBIS) or classifying results. For example, when searching databases for 'mitochondrial double stranded DNA binding proteins', all and only those proteins, as well as those kind of proteins, will be found, as the exact terms for searching can be used. Queries can be refined by following relationships within the ontologies, in particular the taxonomic relationships. Similarly, Fridman Noy and Hafner [28] use an ontology of experimental design in molecular biology to describe and generate forms to query a repository of papers containing experimental methods. The extensions to

---

[2] http://www.ncbi.nlm.nih.gov/Taxonomy/
[3] http://obo.sourceforge.net
[4] http://www.ingenuity.com
[5] http://www.mged.org
[6] http://www.nlm.nih.gov/research/umls/
[7] http://www.godatabase.org

a typical frame based representation allow them to describe accurately the trans-formations that take place, the complexes that form within an experiment and then make queries about those features.

- Understanding database annotation and technical literature. The ontologies are designed to support natural language processing that link domain knowledge and linguistic structures.
- A community reference, where the ontology is neutrally authored in a single language and converted into different forms for use in multiple target systems. Generally, ontologies have been developed to serve one of the previous categories of use, and then adopted by others for new uses. For example, the Gene Ontology, which will be the first of our detailed case studies, was developed solely for database annotation but is now used for all the purposes outlined above. As we will discuss, this has had an impact on its form, representational language and content.

Not only do ontologies offer a means for biologists to improve representation of knowledge in their resources, but the very size, volitility and complexity of the domain has potential benefit for computer scientists involved in ontology research. If the technologies proposed by ontology researchers can deal with the biological domain, then it is most likely that it can cope with a wide range of other domains, both natural and human-made. Before we explore some these uses in more detail through a number of case studies, we should point out some of the difficulties in modelling biological knowledge.

### 32.1.3  The Complexity of Biological Knowledge

One of the interesting aspects of the use of ontologies within bioinformatics is the complexity and difficulty of the modelling entailed. Compared to the modelling of man-made artefacts such as aeroplanes, some argue that natural systems are difficult to describe [19]. Biology is riddled with exceptions and it is often difficult to find the *necessary* conditions for class membership, let alone the *sufficiency* conditions. Often, biologists will 'know' that x is a member of y, despite it not having some of the same characteristics as all the other members of y. There are several potential reasons for this, including:

- Membership claims are in fact incorrect;
- Current biological knowledge is not rich enough to have found the appropriate necessary and sufficiency conditions;
- In the natural world, the boundaries between classes may be blurred. Evolution is often gradual and the properties that distinguish one class from another may be only partially represented in some individuals.

Jones et al. [19] gives the following examples and reasons for how difficult modelling biology can be:

1. **Atypical examples** – Where an example of the class differs from one of the defining features. For example, all eukaryote cells contain a nucleus, but red blood cells do not [1, p18].

2. **Multiple sibling instantiation** – Where a class instance is a member of multiple children of that class. For example, neuroendocrine cells behave like both endocrine and nerve cells (both kinds of remote signaling cells) [1, p26], but do not satisfy all the characteristics of either cell type.

3. **Context sensitive membership** – Some classes only exist in certain contexts. Chemists talk about a defined set of chemical bonds, but biochemists sometimes also include certain 'weak bonds', such as hydrophobic bonds, when talking about molecules [1, p88].

4. **Excluded instances** – 'Small organic molecules' are divided into four kinds, 'simple sugars', 'amino acids', 'fatty acids' and 'nucleotides' [1, p84]. The same source, however, then defines other kinds of molecules that do not fall into these classes.

5. **Non-instance similarity** – where individuals exhibit similar features to those defining a class, but are not close enough to be a member of that class. For instance, mitochondria and chloroplasts, parts of eukaryotic cells, are very similar to prokaryotic cells. These entities are thought to have arisen from prokaryotes, but have become symbiotic and divergent from their ancestors.

Jones *et al* give several such examples of the difficulties in modelling biology. It is not necessarily that modelling is more difficult in biology than other domains, but several of the commonly occurring factors come together in modelling biology. The sample of 'atypical examples' given above, bears some investigation. Jones *et al*'s examples are taken from an undergraduate text book; such books often give 'simplified truth' or 'staged revelation', thus it is dangerous to take defining criteria from such resources. Like all modelling, the conceptualisation has to come from many sources and depends upon the task to which the ontology is to be used.

In the rest of this chapter the use, nature and representation of some exemplar bio-ontologies will be described. In Section 32.2 the need for a shared vocabulary for the annotation of database entries is described. The Gene Ontology is used as the exemplar for this topic – it can be seen as the driving force behind much of the ontology activity in bioinformatics. Section 32.3 continues the theme of *ontology as specification* when the knowledge bases RiboWeb and EcoCyc are explored. In Section 32.4 we move to the use of ontology for *query management across multiple databases* with TAMBIS. Finally, in Section 32.5 several of these uses come together in an ontology of bioinformatics services used for discovery in the ^my GRID project.

The ontologies we describe come in three representational forms:

- Structured hierarchies of concept names;
- Frames defining concepts asserted into an isa hierarchy. Slots on frames carry the properties of each concept and constrain their fillers. Both the structured hierarchies of terms and frames require all concepts to be comprehensively pre-enumerated;
- Description Logics (DL) whose concepts can be combined dynamically via relationships to form new, compositional concepts. These compositional concepts are automatically classified, using reasoning. Compositional concepts can be made in a post co-ordinated manner: That is, the ontology is not a static artefact, users

can interact with the ontology to build new concepts, composed of those already in the ontology, and have them checked for consistency and placed at the correct position in the ontology's lattice of concepts.

Biology is naturally compositional and hard to pre-enumerate; however even simple hand-crafted hierarchies are extremely useful.

## 32.2 Annotation: the Gene Ontology

The need for annotation is the driving force behind much of the ontology activity within bioinformatics. Information about *model organisms* has grown at a tremendous rate, leading to the development of model organism databases. Each has been built by an independent community of scientists, but the driving aim is to unify the results to synthesize an overall understanding of biological processes. Their effective use therefore demands a shared understanding in order to combine results. The Gene Ontology Consortium[8] set out to provide 'a structured precisely defined common controlled vocabulary for describing the roles of genes and gene products in any organism' [40].

### 32.2.1  Features of the Gene Ontology

The GO is really a handcrafted ontology in which phrases are placed in a structure of only is-a and part-of relationships. For example 'GO:0019466 ornithine catabolism, via proline' is a phrase which informs the biologist that the term represents the concept of catabolism of the chemical ornithine with a particular intermediate chemical form proline. These phrases form the controlled vocabulary with which to annotate three specific aspects of a gene product:- its functions; its role in a biological process; and its localization within a cell. Instead of using scientific English, annotation can now take place with terms taken from GO. This leads to better precision and recall of information within one database and more effective integration of information *across* databases.

   **Concept Definitions**- Appropriate and consistent use of GO concepts requires all annotators to have a common understanding of what each concept represents. Therefore the GO consortium (GOC) places a great deal of effort in providing a definition for each concept. Currently over 60% of GO concepts have a textual definition. The concepts are represented as strings descriptions of increasing detail coupled with a unique identifier that carries no semantics. This separates the labels as they are used in the databases from the current definition of the term.

   **Hierarchial organisation**- It is impractical to deliver such a large vocabulary as a simple list. Therefore the concepts are organized into hierarchies. The semantics of the parent child link is stated explicitly as either subsumption or partomomy. Each concept can have any number of parents and so its place in the hierarchy is represented as a directed acyclic graph (DAG).

---

[8] http://www.geneontology.org

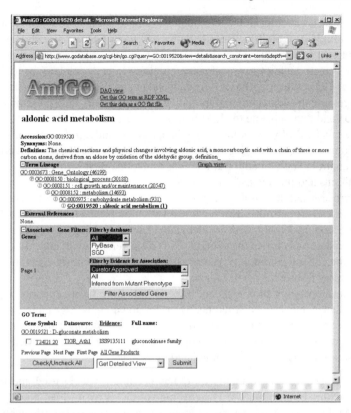

**Fig. 32.2.** Screenshot of the Amigo browser showing how a Gene Ontology concept 'aldonic acid metabolism' has been used to annotate a Gene product entry in the TIGR database.

The hierarchical structure is used by users for a number of purposes:

- **Internal Navigation**. The hierarchy acts as a way of grouping similar concepts and so allowing annotators to find the concept they require quickly;
- **Database content browsing**. The hierarchy acts as a index into each database. GO Browsers, e.g. AmiGO[9] allow users to link directly from the hierarchical view of the ontology to database entries annotated with those concepts (see Figure 32.2).
- **Aggregate information**. A GO Slim is a non-overlapping subset of high-level GO concepts. Aggregating all entries annotated with hierarchical descendants of each GO Slim term can produce useful summary statistics. The 'GO summary' feature of the AmiGO browser demonstrates how this information is used to provide a high level view of GO annotation statistics.

At the time of writing the Gene Ontology stands at some 15,000 concepts and continues to rapidly expand. Its success is attributed to many factors, including:

---

[9] http://www.godatabase.org

- There was no attempt to try to model everything but instead to chose a narrow, but useful part of biology. Despite its narrow focus GO has already gained wide acceptance and it is already being used for purposes outside annotation;
- There was no attempt to wait for the ontology to be 'complete' or 'correct'; as soon as GO was useful, the GOC used it and put in place mechanisms to deal with changes and the deprecation of terms. The GO identifiers hold no semantic information and thus separate the labelling of database entries from the interpretation of the labels. Biological knowledge changes constantly as do ways of modelling that knowledge. As development is continuous they use CVS[10] to manage version control. The GO editorial team also annotate their terms with author date, definitions and provenance argumentation.
- The process and the ontology is open and involves the community. The development of GO is controlled by a small team of curators who manage the publication and versioning activity, with a wider team of active ontology developers who provide, update and correct the content. The GO developers will take all suggestions from the general community, process them and incorporate or reject with reasons in a timely fashion.
- The developers are biologists and experts who have been supported by knowledge management tools. Attempts by professional knowledge engineers to elicit knowledge from experts and do the modelling are doomed to failure: the GO curators are all post-doctoral biologists and the GO represents their and their communities distilled and accumulated knowledge.

By these procedures and principles GO has become a widely used and respected ontology within bioinformatics. The coverage of GO is narrow, but nonetheless important. Molecular biology is a vast domain and an attempt to cover the whole would have undoubtedly failed. GO was also created for a specific purpose, namely that of annotation – there are many task that GO does not support in its current representation, such as mappings to linguistic forms that would make generation of natural language annotations of databases easier. GO has, however, demonstrated to the community that even with a simple representation, a shared view on the three major attributes of gene products may be achieved.

### 32.2.2  Computationally Amenable Forms of GO

All the uses of GO described above revolve around human interpretation of the phrase's meaning. However, there is a growing need for applications to have access to a more explicit machine interpretable description of each phrase. For example, instead of relying on similarities of proteins by the similarity of their sequences, they could be clustered on the similarity of their function by grouping their Gene Ontology terms. This requires several measures of 'semantic similarity', for example those of [29, 30] which exploit both the DAG structure of GO, and the usage of GO terms within the various databases now annotated with GO. This uses the notion of

---

[10] http://www.cvshome.org/

'information content', which says commonly occurring terms, like 'receptor' are not likely to be very discriminatory [32].

The definition of a metric for 'semantic similarity' between GO terms, allows us to exploit the machine interpretable semantics of GO for large datasets. By comparing these metrics to sequence similarity measures we managed to isolate a number of errors in either GO, or the use of GO within the annotated databases [29]. We have also investigated the use of these metrics as the basis for a search tool, to allow querying within a database[11].

Perhaps the most pressing need is that of maintaining the structure of the Gene Ontology itself. The growing size and complexity of GO is forcing its curators to spend more and more time on the mundane task of maintaining the logical consistency and completeness of its internal structure. Within GO many concepts have multiple parents. The maintenance of these links is a manual process. Experience from the medical domain has shown that numerous parent-child links are omitted in such hand crafted controlled vocabularies [35]. While of less importance to manual interpretation, machine interpretation will falter in the face of such inconsistencies.

The Gene Ontology Next Generation project (GONG)[12] aims to demonstrate that, in principle, migrating to a finer grained formal conceptualization in DAML+OIL [17] will allow computation techniques, such as description logics, to ensure logical consistency freeing the highly trained curators to focus on capturing biological knowledge [43]. GO is large so GONG takes a staged approach in which progressively more semantic information is added *insitu*. Description logic reasoning is used early and often, and suggested amendments sent to the GO editorial team.

To use the description logic to maintain the links automatically, the concepts are dissected, explicitly stating the concepts definition in a formal representation. This provides the substrate for description logic reasoners to infer new is-a links and remove redundant links.

Within a large phrased based ontology such as GO, which contains many concepts within a narrow semantic range, it is possible to use automated techniques to construct candidate dissections by simply parsing the term name. For example many metabolism terms in GO follow the pattern 'chemical name' followed by either 'metabolism','catabolism' or 'biosynthesis'. If a term name fits this pattern a dissection can be created from the relevant phrase constituents as shown in Figure 32.3. These patterns have to be spotted by a developer and the scripts that generate the DL representation targeted at the appropriate regions of the GO. This provides a semi-automated, targeted approach, which avoids patterns being too general: For example, confusing 'Protein Expression' and 'Gene Expression', which may fit a general pattern, but where the former describes a 'target' and the latter a 'source'.

The process of dissection breaks down the existing concept into more elemental concepts related together in a formal semantic manner. These elemental concepts are then placed in orthogonal taxonomies. Taxonomic information such as the classification of chemical substances which was previously implicit and repeated in many

---

[11] http://gosst.man.ac.uk
[12] http://gong.man.ac.uk

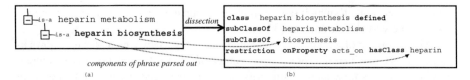

**Fig. 32.3.** Diagram showing the dissection of (a) the GO concept heparin biosynthesis in its original DAG into (b) a DAML+OIL like definition with additional semantic information.

sections of the GO ontology is now made explicit in an independent chemical on-tology. The reasoner combines the information in these independent taxonomies to produce a complete and consistent multi-axial classification. The changes reported by the DL reasoner represent mostly additional relationships hard to spot by human eye, and not errors in biological knowledge. The effect of adding descriptions and using the reasoner can be seen in Figure 32.4.

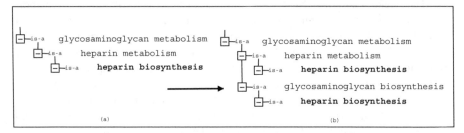

**Fig. 32.4.** Directed acyclic graph showing additional parent for heparin biosynthesis found using the reasoner.

For example, the reasoner reported that 'heparin biosynthesis' has a new is-a par-ent 'glycosaminoglycan biosynthesis'. These reports can then be sent to the editorial team for comment and action if necessary. Even at this early stage of the GONG project, the utility of the approach can be recognised. Many missing and redundant is-a relationships have been spotted, making GO more complete and robust. Mem-bers of the GO editorial team have recognised the potential of using such a logic based approach to automatically place concepts in the correct location – a task seen as difficult by the team in GO's current hand-crafted form.

## 32.3 Schema Definition: EcoCyc

The complexity of biological systems means that relational databases do not make good management systems for biological data and their associated knowledge [22]. It is possible to develop relational schemata for such complex material, but it is hard work. Major sequence repositories are stored in relational form, but using highly complex, less than intuitive schema. Such repositories are managed by skilled bioin-formaticians and database administrators. For biologists investigating the data differ-ent presentations are required. An object style approach, with its complex data types (especially collections and user defined classes as domains for attributes) makes on-tological modelling of the data much easier. Object databases have not reached the same level of technical reliability as the relational form, but frame based knowl-edge bases provide an object like view of the world, but can store and retrieve large amounts of data efficiently. While many bioinformatics resources have simply used a flat-file system to hold these data, others have explored the use of ontologies to describe the data contained within that resource.

The elements within the ontology describe the data held in the resource and these descriptions are used to gather and represent the facts described by the ontology. These knowledge bases form one of the earlier uses of ontology within bioinformat-ics. Indeed, the development of the EcoCyc [25] KB necessitated the description of a classification of the function of gene products [34]; an early forerunner of GO. Eco-Cyc uses frames as a knowledge representation formalism; using slots to gather all the attributes that describe, for instance, a protein.

### 32.3.1 EcoCyc: Encyclopaedia of E.coli

EcoCyc uses an ontology to describe the richness and complexity of a domain and the constraints acting within that domain, to specify a database schema [24]. Classes within the ontology form a schema; instances of classes, with values for the at-tributes, form the facts that with the ontology form the knowledge base. EcoCyc is presented to biologists using an encyclopaedia metaphor. It covers *E. coli.* genes, metabolism, regulation and signal transduction, which a biologist can explore and use to visualise information [26].

The instances in the knowledge base currently include 165 Pathways, involv-ing 2604 Reactions, catalysed by 905 Enzymes and supported by 162 Transporters and other proteins expressed by 4393 Genes [26]. EcoCyc uses the classification of gene product function from Riley [34] as part of this description. Scientists can visualise the layout of genes within the *E. coli.* chromosome, or of an individual bio-chemical reaction, or of a complete biochemical pathway (with compound structures displayed).

EcoCyc uses the frame-based language Ocelot, whose capabilities are similar to those of HyperTHEO [24], to describe its ontology. The core classes that describe the *E. coli* genome, metabolism, etc. include a simple taxonomy of chemicals, so that DNA, RNA, polypeptides and proteins may be described. Chromosomes are made of DNA and Genes are segments of DNA, located on a Chromosome. Pathways are collections of Reactions, that act upon Chemicals. All *E. coli* genes are instances of the class gene and consequently share the properties or attributes of that class. Each EcoCyc frame or class contains slots that describe either attributes of the biological object that the frame represents, or that encode a relationship between that object and other objects. For example, the slots of a polypeptide frame encode the molecular weight of the polypeptide, the gene that encodes it, and its cellular location.

EcoCyc's use of an ontology to define a database schema has the advantages of its expressivity and ability to evolve quickly to account for the rapid schema changes needed for biological information [24]. The user is not aware of this use of an ontology, except that the constraints expressed in the knowledge captured mean that the complexity of the data held is captured precisely. In EcoCyc, for example, the concept of Gene is represented by a concept or class with various attributes, that link through to other concepts: Polypeptide product, Gene name, synonyms and identifiers used in other databases etc. The representation system can be used to impose constraints on those concepts and instances which may appear in the places described within the system. EcoCyc's ontology has now been used to form a generic schema MetaCyc, that is used to form the basis for a host of genomic knowledge bases [27]. These ontologies are used to drive pathway prediction tools based upon the genomic information stored in the knowledge base. From the presence of genes and knowledge of their function, knowledge can be inferred about the metabolomes of the species in question [21]. Such computations are not only possible with the use of ontology, but EcoCyc's developers would argue that their ontology based system and the software it supports makes such a complex task easier.

The rich, structured and constrained nature of these knowledge bases mean that they form a better founded platform for bioinformatics software than would be usual with, for instance, the community's reliance upon flat-file storage. Ecocyc uses the knowledge base to generate pathways, perform cross-genome comparisons and generate sophisticated visualisations. Similarly, RiboWeb [2] uses the constraints in its ontological model to guide a user through the analysis of structural data: it captures knowledge of which methods are appropriate for which data and can use knowledge to perform validations of results. Ontologies as bioinformatics database schema prove their worth in capturing knowledge with high fidelity and managing the modelling of complex and volatile data and associated knowledge.

## 32.4 Query Formulation: TAMBIS

This section presents an approach to solving the problems of querying distributed bioinformatics resources called TAMBIS (Transparent Access to Multiple Bioinformatics Information Sources) [15]. The TAMBIS approach attempts to avoid the problems of using multiple resources by using an ontology of molecular biology and bioinformatics to manage the presentation and usage of the sources. The ontology allows TAMBIS: to provide a homogenising layer over the numerous databases and analysis tools; to manage the heterogeneities between the data sources; and to provide a common, consistent query-forming user interface that allows queries across sources to be precisely expressed and progressively refined.

A concept is a description of a set of instances, so a concept can also be viewed as a query. The TAMBIS system is used for retrieving instances described by concepts in the model. This contrasts with queries phrased in terms of the structures used to store the data, as in conventional database query environments. This approach allows a biologist to ask complex questions that access and combine data from different sources. However, in TAMBIS, the user does not have to choose the sources, identify the location of the sources, express requests in the language of the source, or transfer data items between sources.

The steps in the processing of a TAMBIS query are as follows:

1. A query is formulated in terms of the concepts and relationships in the ontology using the visual *Conceptual Query Formulation Interface*. This interface allows the ontology to be browsed by users, and supports the construction of complex concept descriptions that serve as queries. The output of the query formulation process is a *source independent conceptual query*. The query formulation interface makes extensive use of the TAMBIS *Ontology Server* which supports various reasoning services over the ontology, to ensure that the queries constructed are biologically meaningful.

2. Given a query, TAMBIS must identify the sources that can be used to answer the query, and construct valid and efficient source independent query plans for evaluating the query given the facilities provided by the relevant sources. Concepts and relationships from the Ontology are associated with the services provided by the sources.

3. The *Query Plan Execution* process takes the plan provided by the planner and executes that plan over the *Wrapped Sources* to yield an answer to the query. Sources are wrapped so that they can be accessed in a syntactically consistent manner.

The TAMBIS ontology describes both molecular biology and bioinformatics tasks. Concepts such as `Protein` and `Nucleic acid` are part of the world of molecular biology. An `Accession number`, which acts as a unique identifier for an entry in an information source, lies outside this domain, but is essential for describing bioinformatics tasks in molecular biology. The TAMBIS ontology has been designed to cover the standard range of bioinformatics retrieval and analysis tasks [39]. This means that a broad range of biology has been described. The model is quite shallow, although the detail present is sufficient to allow most retrieval tasks supportable using the integrated bioinformatics sources to be described. In addition, precision can arise from the ability to combine concepts to create more specialised concepts. The model is described in more detail in [7] and can be browsed via an applet on the TAMBIS Web site[13].

The TAMBIS ontology is described using an early Description Logic called GRAIL [31]. The GRAIL representation has a useful extra property in its ability to describe constraints about when relationships are allowed to be formed. For example, it is true that a `Motif` is a component of a `Biopolymer`, but not all motifs are components of all biopolymers. For example, a `PhosphorylationSite` can be a component of a `Protein`, but not a component of a `Nucleic acid`, both of which are `Biopolymers`. The constraint mechanism allows the TAMBIS model to capture this distinction, and thus only allow the description of concepts that are

---

[13] http://img.cs.man.ac.uk/tambis

described as being biologically meaningful, in terms of the model from which they are built.

The task of query formulation involves the user in constructing a concept that describes the information of interest. By using a post-co-ordinated ontology, TAMBIS is able to provide a variety of complex queries over a range of diverse bioinformatics resources. Mappings from concepts to resource specific calls or values allows TAMBIS to deal with the heterogeneity present in the resources and give the illusion of a common query interface. A small sample of such queries are: *'Find the active sites of hydrolase enzymes, with protein substrates and metal cofactors'* and *'Find all chimpanze proteins similar to human apoptosis proteins'*.

## 32.5 Service Discovery: the $^{my}$GRID Service Ontology

Both data and analytical resources provide services to bioinformaticians. A characteristic of bioinformatics is the *discovery* of suitable resources and the marshalling of those resources to work together to perform a task. However, the 'craft-based' practice of a biologist undertaking the discovery, interoperation and management of the resources by hand is unsupportable, as described in Section 32.1. These difficulties mean that the discovery and assembly of resources or services on those resources must be at least semi-automated.

Users will typically have in mind a task they want to perform on a particular kind of data. They must match this task against available services taking into account the function of the service, the data it accepts and produces and the resources it uses to accomplish its goal. In addition, they must select, from the candidates that can fulfill their task, the one that is best able to achieve the result within the required constraints. This choice depends on metadata concerning function, cost, quality of service, geographical location, and who published it. The discovery process as a whole requires a much more conceptual description of a service than the metadata usually associated with a web service which focuses on its low level syntactic interface.

The process of narrowing down a selection into the appropriate set is currently supported by simple conceptual classifications rather than sets of individual conceptual descriptions, in a manner analogous to using the Yellow Pages$^{TM}$. This classification of services based on the functionality they provide has been widely adopted by diverse communities as an efficient way of finding suitable services. For example, the EMBOSS suite [33] of bioinformatics applications and repositories has a coarse classification of the 200 or so tools it contains, and free text documentation for each tool. The bioinformatics integration platforms ISYS [37] and BioMOBY (http://www.biomoby.org) use taxonomies for classifying services. The Universal Description, Discovery, and Integration specification (UDDI) [41] supports web service discovery by using a service classification such as UNSPSC [14] or RosettaNet [20].

The advent of the Semantic Web has meant that there is increasing interest not only in the semantic description of content, but in the semantic description of the services provided through the Web [8]. As with EcoCyc described earlier, ontologies have been used as a schema for the description of web services. DAML-S [3] offers an upper level ontology for the description of Web Services. Within ᵐʸGRID (see below) ontologies can also provide the vocabulary of concepts with which to compose these descriptions. Working with a formal representation such as DAML+OIL also allows classifications to be validated/ constructed from these description as has been described with the GONG project.

ᵐʸGRID [14] is a UK e-Science pilot project specifically targeted at developing open source high-level middleware to support personalised semantics-rich *in-silico* experiments in biology. The emphasis is on database integration, workflow, personalisation and provenance, with a primary focus on the use of rich ontology based semantics to aid in the discovery and orchestration of services. ᵐʸGRID uses a suite of ontologies expressed in DAML+OIL [5], to provide: (a) a schema for describing services based on DAML-S; (b) a vocabulary for expressing service descriptions and (c) a reasoning process to both manage the coherency of the classifications and the descriptions when they are *created*, and the service discovery, matching and composition when they are *deployed*.

### 32.5.1 Extending DAML-S in Terms of Properties

A key bottleneck in the utilisation of services is the discovery from the myriad available those that will fulfil the requirements of the task at hand. This discovery involves matching the users requirements against functional descriptions of the available services.

DAML-S provides a high level schema in DAML+OIL with which to capture some of these functional attributes together with additional attributes describing authorship, cost etc. From our experience in writing over 100 descriptions, during the development of ᵐʸGRID, for preexisting bioinformatics services we have found DAML-S defined attributes describing the inputs and outputs to the service the most discriminatory. In addition, we felt it necessary to add a set of attributes to the service profile to capture common ways of describing bioinformatics service. These include a generic description of the overall *task*; associated *resources* used to fulfil the task; software *tools* and *algorithms* with which the task is performed.

ᵐʸGRID has additionally built a suite of DAML+OIL ontologies specific to bioinformatics and molecular biology which provides the vocabulary for the services to be described. Figure 32.5 shows how these ontologies are interrelated.

A *standard upper level ontology* forms the foundation for the suite of ontologies. An *informatics ontology* captures the key concepts of data, data structures, databases, metadata and so forth. As the DAML-S service ontology is designed specifically to support web services it becomes an extension of the informatics ontology. A **bioinformatics ontology** builds on the informatics ontology adding specific types of bioinformatics resource such as SWISS-PROT database, BLAST application, and specific bioinformatics data such as protein sequence. By explicitly separating general informatics concepts from more specific concepts

---

[14] http://www.mygrid.org.uk

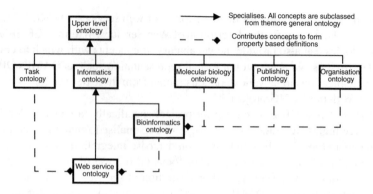

**Fig. 32.5.** Suite of ontologies used in <sup>my</sup>GRID and their inter-relationships.

applicable only to bioinformatics, we hope to reuse as much as possible of the ontology suite for other domains. A *molecular biology* ontology with which to describe the content of data passed into and out of bioinformatics services. Examples of concepts include protein, nucleic acid, and sequence. These concepts tend to be much more general than found in existing ontologies such as the Gene Ontology. Small *publishing*, *organisation* and *task* ontologies have also been constructed to provide the necessary vocabulary for service descriptions.

Figure 32.6 gives an example of the formal definitions for one of the operation BLAST-n which compares a nucleotide sequence against a nucleotide sequence database using alignment.

```
class   BLAST-n service operation defined
    subClassOf atomic service operation
    restriction onProperty performs_task    hasClass
        aligning  restriction onProperty has_feature    hasClass local
                  restriction onProperty has_feature    hasClass pairwise
    restriction onProperty produces_result hasClass
        report    restriction onProperty is_report_of  hasClass sequence alignment
    restriction onProperty uses_resource   hasClass
        database restriction onProperty contains        hasClass
            data  restriction   onProperty  encodes    hasClass
                sequence   restriction onProperty is_sequence_of hasClass
                    nucleic acid molecule
```

**Fig. 32.6.** Fully expanded formal description of the BLAST-n service operation written in a human-readable pseudo version of DAML+OIL.

Within <sup>my</sup>GRID, this ontology of services and its contributory ontologies have provided the vocabulary for about a hundred bioinformatics service descriptions. These descriptions have been linked to entries within a UDDI service registry allowing users to search and find appropriate registered services via a <sup>my</sup>GRID 'web portal'. The use of a reasoner and the consequent post co-ordinated nature of the ontology means that a flexible variety of views or queries by the user can be provided.

As well as searching for services by the descriptions already asserted in the ontology, new 'partial descriptions' can be created, that provide more general descriptions of classes. It is easy for instance, to create a new class 'all services provided by the European Bioinformatics Institute' or 'all services that take a protein sequence as input'.

Concepts from the bioinformatics ontology can be used to give semantic descriptions of data, both inputs and outputs, stored in a bioinformatician's personal storage. This annotation would allow services to be sought by the kind of data in hand. Such an activity could also work backwards. Given a particular 'analytical goal', workflows could be composed backwards to suggest protocols to users. A bioinformatician could ask the question 'how do I generate a phylogenetic tree?'. Starting with the concept 'Phylogenetic tree', an inverse of the 'output' relation would be followed to find the service that generates such a tree. Continuing this process would generate a range of possible paths by which that output could be derived. Similarly, decoration of all these data with semantic annotations allows a variety of views to be taken of those data. They can be organised along multiple axes, including experiment, experimenter, genes, proteins, species, etc. Such flexible semantic views allow a personalisation of science that is traditionally difficult to achieve.

In the $^{my}$GRID service ontology many themes of this chapter come together. The integrated ontology itself, provides a global schema, giving a common view over all the services it includes. Like TAMBIS, it allows 'query concepts' to be built to retrieve services suited to the query. Heterogeneity in the services are reconciled to the $^{my}$GRID ontology to give a common view. Fragments of the ontology are also used for annotation of data and results (that may also form data for input in their own turn) can be queried and assembled using those semantic descriptions. Here, annotation, schema definition and query formulation can be seen at one time in a bioinformatics ontology.

## 32.6 Discussion

Ontologies have become increasingly widely used in biology because of need. Science is all about increase in the understanding of the world about us; so, the communities within a scientific discipline need to have a shared understanding. The Gene Ontology's principle purpose is to provide a shared understanding between different model organism communities. The use of ontologies to deliver terminologies for annotation of data is undoubtedly the area of greatest use of ontologies within biology. The need for confidence in the use of terms when curating and querying resources is a strong driving force behind this effort. The GO is without doubt the largest of these efforts, but many others exist within the domain. To accommodate these efforts, the Gene Ontology Consortium has launched OBO (Open Biological Ontologies)[15], which offers an umbrella to facilitate collaboration and dissemination of bio-ontologies and offers a set of rules for inclusion. One ontology will not cover

---

[15] http://obo.sourceforge.net

654    Robert Stevens, Chris Wroe, Phillip Lord, Carole Goble

the whole of biology, so a range of ontologies will have to work together; moreover, ontologies need to be exchanged and preferably represented using the same formalism. The community originated the XOL exchange markup language, that was one of the influences on the OIL ontology language, later to become DAML+OIL. OBO has enthusiastically embraced DAML+OIL as a common language.

The original need to provide a shared understanding mainly for humans, is now leading towards an increased emphasis on shared understanding within and between humans and computers. The GONG project (Section 32.2) shows how modern Description Logic representation in the form of DAML+OIL can be used to manage GO to give a more complete and robust GO. This is a good demonstration of the computer science ontology community aiding domain experts in building an ontology and a domain offering a superb test bed for a new language and technology. Bioinformaticians have a role to act as intermediaries between biologists and the knowledge engineering community.

Knowledge models are not simply created as instances of truth and beauty – they need to work and be useful. Knowledge bases such as EcoCyc provide complex visualisation and prediction systems based upon their knowledge and the representations have to work in order for this to happen.

Biology provides real world examples of interesting, useful problems for computer scientists to explore and solve. Technology should be able to free the scientists to do his or her science. If knowledge engineers believe ontologies to be useful, then they should be able to be useful in biology. Are we able to express the range and complexity of the biological world with high-fidelity in our knowledge representation languages? Are our technologies, such as reasoning services, scalable to the size and complexity of the domain? Are we able to cope with the volatility of scientific knowledge? Trying to cope with all these aspects will push at the boundaries of our technologies.

This interplay can be seen within the ontologies discussed in this chapter: The GO is relatively simple, but very widely used, with a huge community. It is also an on-going effort, being updated and released continually, as the domain knowledge itself grows. EcoCyc uses an ontology in a standard knowledge representation language to create a large knowledge base of instances that can drive sophisticated visualisation and querying tasks. Again, this ontology evolves with the community knowledge and has a large user base. The other ontologies described lie more within the computer science research comunity and use bioinformatics as a rigorous test domain. GONG demonstrates that description logics can aid such a community in building and maintaining large, complex ontologies. TAMBIS and <sup>my</sup>GRID again show that complex domains can be represented and managed with modern DL technology. These projects currently lie within the research domain and will become more widely used as the bioinformatics community itself starts enlarging and using the ontologies.

Classification is an old, tried and tested scientific tool. The computer scientists' understanding of the meaning of ontology is often wider than just classification, but it is no surprise that biologists take to the technology. Classification has formed an underpinning of science from the periodic table of elements to the linnaean taxonomy of species. From organising data and classes of data, new scientific insights may arise – the most prominent example of this is the periodic table of elements; the taxonomy of species also reflects evolutionary change. New fields of scientific investigation, like genomics and the wider field of bioinformatics, mean vast new fields of data now need to be organised. Ontologies offer a good, flexible way of organising these data and what we know about these data. The ultimate dream of those who model knowledge is that their modelling will lead to new scientific insights. Maybe this will happen with bio-ontologies.

**Acknowledgements:** Chris Wroe and Phillip Lord are funded by EPSRC GR/R67743 eScience project <sup>my</sup>GRID and the GONG DARPA DAML Stanford sub-contract PY-1149.

# References

1. B. Alberts, D. Bray, J. Lewis, M. Raff, K. Roberts, and J.D. Watson. *Molecular Biology of the Cell*. Garland, New York, 1989.
2. R. Altman, M. Bada, X.J. Chai, M. Whirl Carillo, R.O. Chen, and N.F. Abernethy. RiboWeb: An Ontology-Based System for Collaborative Molecular Biology. *IEEE Intelligent Systems*, 14(5):68–76, 1999.
3. A. Ankolekar, M. Burstein, J. Hobbs, O. Lassila, D. Martin, S. McIlraith, S. Narayanan, M. Paolucci, T. Payne, K. Sycara, and H. Zeng. DAML-S: Semantic Markup for Web Services. In *Proceedings of the International Semantic Web Working Symposium (SWWS)*, 2001.
4. T.K. Attwood and D.J. Parry-Smith. *Introduction to bioinformatics*. Addison Wesley Longman, 1999.
5. F. Baader, D. McGuinness, D. Nardi, and P. P. Schneider, editors. *The Description Logic Handbook Theory, Implementation and Applications* . Cambridge University Press, 2003.
6. A. Bairoch and R. Apweiler. The SWISS-PROT Protein Sequence Data Bank and its Supplement TrEMBL in 1999. *Nucleic Acids Research*, 27:49–5, 1999.
7. P.G. Baker, C.A. Goble, S. Bechhofer, N.W. Paton, R. Stevens, and A Brass. An Ontology for Bioinformatics Applications. *Bioinformatics*, 15(6):510–520, 1999.
8. T. Berners-Lee, J. Hendler, and O. Lassila. The Semantic Web. *Scientific American*, pages 28–37, May 2001.
9. Maryann E. Martone Bertram Ludscher, Amarnath Gupta. Model-based mediation with domain maps. In *Conference on Data Engineering (ICDE), Heidelberg, Germany*. IEEE Computer Society, 2001.
10. P. Buneman, S.B. Davidson, K. Hart, C. Overton, and L. Wong. A Data Transformation System for Biological Data Sources. In *Proceedings of VLDB*, pages 158–169. Morgan Kaufmann, 1995.
11. David Buttler, Matthew Coleman1, Terence Critchlow1, Renato Fileto, Wei Han, Ling Liu, Calton Pu, Daniel Rocco, and Li Xiong. Querying multiple bioinformatics data sources: Can semantic web research help? *SIGMOD Record*, 2002. Special Issue.
12. I.A. Chen and V.M. Markowitz. An Overview of the Object-Protocol Model (OPM) and the OPM Data Management Tools. *Information Systems*, 20(5):393–418, 1995.
13. C. Discala, X. Benigni, E. Barillot, and G. Vaysseix. DBcat: A Catalog of 500 Biological Databases. *Nucleic Acids Research*, 28(1):8–9, 2000.

14. Electronic Commerce Code Management Association Technical Secretariat. Universal Products and Services Classification Implementation Guide , June 2001. Available: `http://eccma.org/unspsc`.

15. C.A. Goble, R. Stevens, G. Ng, S. Bechhofer, N.W. Paton, P.G. Baker, M. Peim, and A. Brass. Transparent Access to Multiple Bioinformatics Information Sources. *IBM Systems Journal Special issue on deep computing for the life sciences*, 40(2):532 – 552, 2001.

16. Caroline Hadley and David T. Jones. A Systematic Comparison of Protein Structure Classifications: SCOP, CATH and FSSP. *Structure*, 7(9):1099– 1112, 1999.

17. I. Horrocks. DAML+OIL: a reason-able web ontology language. In *Proc. of EDBT 2002*, pages 2–13. Lecture Notes in Computer Science, 2002.

18. International Union of Biochemistry . *Enzyme Nomenclature 1984 : Recommendations of the Nomenclature Committee of the International Union of Biochemistry on the Nomenclature and Classification of Enzyme-Catalyzed Reactions*. Academic Press (for The International Union of Biochemistry by), Orlando, FL, 1984.

19. D.M. Jones, P.R.S. Visser, and R.C. Paton. Addressing Biological Complexity to Enable Knowledge Sharing. In *AAAI'98 Workshop on Knowledge Sharing Across Biological and Medical Knowledge-based Systems*, 1998.

20. R. Kak and D. Sotero. Implementing RosettaNet E-Business Standards for Greater Supply Chain Collaboration and Efficiency, 2002. RosettaNet White Paper Available: `http://www.rosettanet.org`.

21. M. Karp, P. amd Krummenacker, S. Paley, and J. Wagg. Integrated pathway/genome databases and their role in drug discovery. *Trends in Biotechnology*, 17:275–281, 1999.

22. P. Karp. Frame representation and relational data bases: Alternative information management technologies for systematics. In R. Fortuner, editor, *Advanced Computer Methods for Systematic Biology: Artificial Intelligence, Database Systems, Computer Vision*. The Johns Hopkins University Press, 1993.

23. P. Karp. A Strategy for Database Interoperation. *Journal of Computational Biology*, 2(4):573–586, 1995.

24. P. Karp and S. Paley. Integrated Access to Metabolic and Genomic Data. *Journal of Computational Biology*, 3(1):191–212, 1996.

25. P.D. Karp, M. Riley, M. Saier, I.T. Paulsen, S.M. Paley, and A. Pellegrini-Toole. The EcoCyc and MetaCyc Databases. *Nucleic Acids Research*, 28:56–59, 2000.

26. Peter D. Karp, Monica Riley, Milton Saier amd Ian T. Paulsen amd Julio Collado-Vides, Suzanne M. Paley, Alida Pellegrini-Toole, and esar Bonavides amd Socorro Gama-Castro. The EcoCyc Database. *Nucleic Acids Research*, 30(1):56–58, 2002.

27. Peter D. Karp, Monica Riley, Suzanne M. Paley, and Alida Pellegrini-Toole. The MetaCyc Database. *Nucleic Acids Research*, 30(1):59–61, 2002.

28. Natalya Fridman Noy and Carole D. Hafner. Representing scientific experiments: Implications for ontology design and knowledge sharing. In *AAAI/IAAI*, pages 615–622, 1998.

29. P.W.Lord, R.D. Stevens, A. Brass, and C.A.Goble. Investigating semantic similarity measures across the Gene Ontology: the relationship between sequence and annotation. *Bioinformatics*, 19(10):1275–83, 2003.

30. P.W.Lord, R.D. Stevens, A. Brass, and C.A.Goble. Semantic similarity measures as tools for exploring the Gene Ontology. In *Pacific Symposium on Biocomputing*, pages 601–612, 2003.

31. A.L. Rector, S.K. Bechhofer, C.A. Goble, I. Horrocks, W.A. Nowlan, and W.D. Solomon. The GRAIL Concept Modelling Language for Medical Terminology. *Artificial Intelligence in Medicine*, 9:139–171, 1997.

32. P. Resnik. Semantic similarity in a taxonomy: An information-based measure and its application to problems of ambiguity in natural language. *Journal of Artificial Intelligence Research*, 11:95–130, 1999.

33. P. Rice, I. Longde, and A. Bleasby. EMBOSS: The European Molecular Biology Open Software Suite . *Trends in Genetics*, 16(6):276–277, 2000.

34. M. Riley. Functions of the gene products of Escherichia coli. *Microbiological Reviews*, 57:862–952, 1993.

35. J.E. Rogers, C. Price, A.L. Rector, W.D. Solomon, and N. Smejko. Validating Clinical Terminology Structures: Integration and Cross-Validation of Read Thesaurus and GALEN. In *AMIA Fall Symposium*, 1998.

36. Daniel L. Rubin, Farhad Shafa, Diane E. Oliver, Micheal Hewett, and Russ B. Altman. Representing genetic sequence data for pharmacogenomics: an evolutionary approach using ontological and relational models. In Chris Sander, editor, *Proceedings of Tenth International Conference on Intelligent Systems for Molecular Biology*, volume 18 Supplement 1, pages 207–215, 2002.

37. A.C. Siepel, A.N. Tolopko, A.D. Farmer, P.A. Steadman, F.D. Schilkey, B.D. Perry, and W.D. Beavis. An integration platform for heterogenous bioinformatics software components. *IBM Systems Journal*, 40(2):570–591, 2001.

38. R. Stevens, C.A. Goble, and S. Bechhofer. Ontology-based Knowledge Representation for Bioinformatics. *Briefings in Bioinformatics*, 1(4):398–416, November 2000.

39. R.D. Stevens, C.A. Goble, P. Baker, and A. Brass. A Classification of Tasks in Bioinformatics. *Bioinformatics*, 17(2):180–188, 2001.

40. The Gene Ontology Consortium. Gene Ontology: Tool for the Unification of Biology. *Nature Genetics*, 25:25–29, 2000.

41. UDDI. UDDI Technical White Paper, September 2000. Available: http://www.uddi.org.

42. Chris Wroe, Robert Stevens, Carole Goble, Angus Roberts, and Mark Greenwood. A Suite of DAML+OIL Ontologies to Describe Bioinformatics Web Services and Data. Accepted for publication in the International Journal of Cooperative Information Systems, 2003.

43. C.J. Wroe, R.D. Stevens, C.A. Goble, and M. Ashburner. A Methodology to Migrate the Gene Ontology to a Description Logic Environment Using DAML+OIL. 8th Pacific Symposium on biocomputing (PSB), 2003.

# Author Index